Fodor's

CANCÚN AND THE RIVIERA MAYA

D0440972

WELCOME TO CANCÚN AND THE RIVIERA MAYA

Mexico's Yucatán Peninsula remains enduringly popular with travelers, and there's little wonder why. Stellar attractions include the region's magnificent beaches and the extensive reefs off Cozumel and the southern Yucatán coast, as well as myriad Mayan ruins, the remains of a vast empire that ruled here long before the Spanish. Limestone pools called *cenotes,* great for a swim or dive, dot the countryside, even in Playa del Carmen. All-inclusive resorts predominate in Cancún, but luxurious retreats and simple guest-houses also offer different kinds of hospitality.

TOP REASONS TO GO

★ **Coral Reefs:** Cozumel's are among the best, drawing both divers and snorkelers.

★ **Beaches:** Cancún's are busy and beautiful; the Riviera Maya's are sugary soft and quieter.

★ **Mayan Ruins:** The pyramids of Chichén Itzá soar; Tulum overlooks a perfect beach.

★ **Nightlife:** Cancún and Playa del Carmen range from raucous to sophisticated.

★ **Spas:** Almost every big resort has a spa, and many are notable for their pampering.

★ **Nature:** Pockets of pristine beauty remain, despite widespread development.

Fodor's CANCÚN AND THE RIVIERA MAYA

Publisher: Amanda D'Acierno, *Senior Vice President*

Editorial: Arabella Bowen, *Editor in Chief*; Linda Cabasin, *Editorial Director*

Design: Tina Malaney, *Associate Art Director*; Chie Ushio, *Senior Designer*; Ann McBride, *Production Designer*

Photography: Jennifer Arnow, *Senior Photo Editor*; Jennifer Romains, *Photo Researcher*

Production: Linda Schmidt, *Managing Editor*; Evangelos Vasilakis, *Associate Managing Editor*; Angela L. McLean, *Senior Production Manager*

Maps: Rebecca Baer, *Senior Map Editor*; David Lindroth, *Cartographers*

Sales: Jacqueline Lebow, *Sales Director*

Marketing & Publicity: Heather Dalton, *Marketing Director*; Katherine Punia, *Publicity Director*

Business & Operations: Susan Livingston, *Vice President, Strategic Business Planning*; Sue Daulton, *Vice President, Operations*

Fodors.com: Megan Bell, *Executive Director, Revenue & Business Development*; Yasmin Marinaro, *Senior Director, Marketing & Partnerships*

Copyright © 2016 by Fodor's Travel, a division of Random House LLC

Editors: Sue MacCallum Whitcomb, Douglas Stallings

Writers: Marlise Kast-Myers, Mark S. Lindsey, Jeffrey Van Fleet
Production Editor: Jennifer DePrima

4th Edition

ISBN 978-1-101-87837-8

ISSN 2166-6253

SPECIAL SALES

This book is available at special discounts for bulk purchases for sales promotions or premiums. For more information, e-mail specialmarkets@penguinrandomhouse.com

PRINTED IN THE UNITED STATES OF AMERICA

10 9 8 7 6 5 4 3 2 1

CONTENTS

CONTENTS

ABOUT THIS GUIDE

Fodor's Recommendations

Everything in this guide is worth doing—we don't cover what isn't—but exceptional sights, hotels, and restaurants are recognized with additional accolades. **Fodor's Choice★** indicates our top recommendations. Care to nominate a new place? Visit Fodors.com/contact-us.

Trip Costs

We list prices wherever possible to help you budget well. Hotel and restaurant price categories from $ to $$$$ are noted alongside each recommendation. For hotels, we include the lowest cost of a standard double room in high season. For restaurants, we cite the average price of a main course at dinner or, if dinner isn't served, at lunch. For attractions, we always list adult admission fees; discounts are usually available for children, students, and senior citizens.

Hotels

Our local writers vet every hotel to recommend the best overnights in each price category, from budget to expensive. Unless otherwise specified, you can expect private bath, phone, and TV in your room. For expanded hotel reviews, facilities, and deals visit Fodors.com.

Top Picks	Hotels &
★ **Fodor's**Choice	**Restaurants**
	⌂ Hotel
Listings	⌖ Number of
✉ Address	rooms
✉ Branch address	⦿ Meal plans
☎ Telephone	✕ Restaurant
🖷 Fax	⬘ Reservations
⊕ Website	⯅ Dress code
✉ E-mail	⊟ No credit cards
🎫 Admission fee	$ Price
⊙ Open/closed	
times	**Other**
Ⓜ Subway	⇨ See also
⊹ Directions or	☞ Take note
Map coordinates	🏌 Golf facilities

Restaurants

Unless we state otherwise, restaurants are open for lunch and dinner daily. We mention dress code only when there's a specific requirement and reservations only when they're essential or not accepted. To make restaurant reservations, visit Fodors.com.

Credit Cards

The hotels and restaurants in this guide typically accept credit cards. If not, we'll say so.

EUGENE FODOR

Hungarian-born Eugene Fodor (1905–91) began his travel career as an interpreter on a French cruise ship. The experience inspired him to write *On the Continent* (1936), the first guidebook to receive annual updates and discuss a country's way of life as well as its sights. Fodor later joined the U.S. Army and worked for the OSS in World War II. After the war, he kept up his intelligence work while expanding his guidebook series. During the Cold War, many guides were written by fellow agents who understood the value of insider information. Today's guides continue Fodor's legacy by providing travelers with timely coverage, insider tips, and cultural context.

1

EXPERIENCE CANCÚN & THE RIVIERA MAYA

WHAT'S WHERE

2 Cancún. This thriving coastal city (otherwise known as the "Spring Break Capital of the World") is Mexico's most popular beach destination and the gateway to the Riviera Maya. In the waterfront area known as the Zona Hotelera, high-rise resorts offer creature comforts; inland at Cancún's downtown El Centro, accommodations are reasonably priced and offer a more authentic Mexican experience.

3 Isla Mujeres. A quick jaunt across the water from Cancún, Isla Mujeres is light years away in temperament. This quaint fishing village is made up of dirt roads generally traveled by golf cart, moped, or bike. It's more laid-back, less crowded, and cheaper than almost anywhere on the mainland.

4 The Riviera Maya. The dazzling white sands and glittering blue waters here beckon everyone from snorkelers and sunbathers to spa goers. Most travelers come for the sugary beaches, but the seaside ruins of Tulum, the jungle-clad pyramids of Cobá, and the sidewalk cafés of Playa del Carmen are also enticing. Numerous theme parks, dolphin programs, and hidden cenotes cater to families. Farther south, the Costa Maya offers the ultimate in isolation.

5 Cozumel. The island is hugely popular with scuba divers and cruise-ship passengers. Ever since Jacques Cousteau first made Cozumel's interconnected series of coral reefs famous in the 1960s, divers and snorkelers have flocked here. Giant ships ferry day-trippers to Cozumel. Avoid the crowds by visiting the island's windward side in search of crumbled monuments to the goddess Ixchel.

6 Yucatán and Campeche States. Mérida, the capital city of Yucatán, is the cultural hub of the entire peninsula. Known for its weekend festivals, Mérida's restaurants, hotels, shops, and museums bring visitors back year after year. Near the remote north coast, you'll find shell-strewn beaches and charming villages. The area's major claim to fame, however, is its spectacular Mayan architecture, including sites at Chichén Itzá and Uxmal.

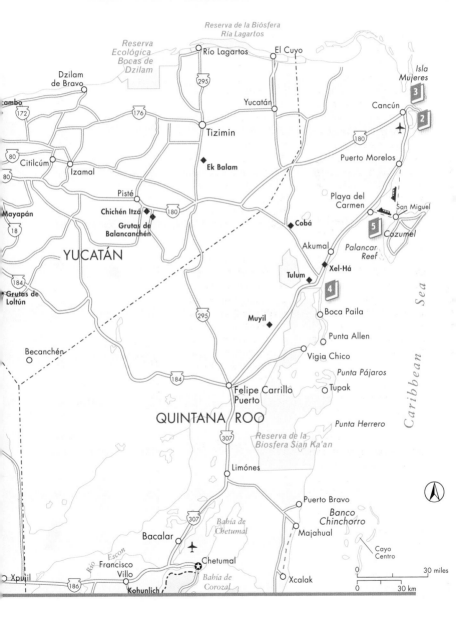

THE YUCATÁN PENINSULA PLANNER

When to Go

High season lasts from late November through the first week in April, with Christmas holiday prices being up to 50% above regular rates. Beach resorts—particularly in Cancún—tend to fill up with college students during summer months and Spring Break (primarily February and March). You can save 20% to 50% during low season (the day after Easter to mid-December). The closing months of spring break and summer (May and October) still offer plenty of sunshine.

Climate

November through March, winter temperatures hover around 27°C (80°F). Occasional winter storms called *nortes* can bring blustery skies and sharp winds that make air temperatures drop and swimming unappealing. During the spring (especially April and May), there's a period of intense heat that tapers off in June. The hottest months, with temperatures reaching up to 43°C (110°F), are May, June, and July. The busiest part of Hurricane season—July through the end of September—is also hot and humid.

Getting Here

The Yucatán Peninsula has international airports in Cancún, Mérida, and Cozumel. Domestic airports are in Playa del Carmen, Chichén Itzá, Isla Holbox, Isla Mujeres, and Mahahual.

Few people travel to the Yucatán Peninsula by car, especially with the risks involved just south of the U.S. border. Those who do so will need a valid driver's license, a temporary car-importation permit, a car registration, a copy of the car title, and an FM-T form.

The most practical way to explore the Yucatán Peninsula is to fly to your region and rent a car for the duration of your stay. The best flight deals, however, are usually arriving and departing from the Cancún airport. Auto insurance is mandatory in Mexico, regardless of what travel-insurance package you have back home.

Getting Around

Compared to other parts of Mexico, the roads in the Yucatán Peninsula are nicely paved. Carretera 307 serves as the coastal route between Cancún and the Belize border, but this stretch of highway is known for its speed traps and large *topes* (speed bumps). Toll road 180, the four-lane highway from Cancún to Mérida, is nicely paved and has exits at major towns along the way. From Cancún, you can reach Mérida in about five hours, but you will pay close to $40 in tolls, an excellent investment in terms of time and ease of driving. (Tolls must be paid in cash in pesos.) Regardless of where you drive, be sure to arrive by sunset.

If you are nervous about driving, take a domestic flight to your ultimate destination; Aeroméxico and Mexicana travel to most places in Mexico. The cheapest way to get around is by bus. Luxury liners like ADO (⊕ www.ado.com.mx), Omnibuses de Mexico (⊕ www.odm.com.mx), and Primera Plus (⊕ www.primeraplus.com.mx) travel throughout the Yucatán Peninsula. *Colectivos* (mini-buses) run along Carretera 307 from Cancún to Tulum. Although affordable, traveling by bus means you'll have to either walk or organize additional transportation from the bus stop. Taxis will cost you about $20 per hour.

Festivals and Celebrations

Among the many Navidad (Christmas) events are *posadas*, during which families gather to eat and sing, and lively parades with colorful floats and brass bands, culminating December 24, on **Nochebuena** (Holy Night).

Carnaval festivities take place in February the week before Lent, with parades, floats, outdoor dancing, music, and fireworks; they're especially spirited in Mérida, Cozumel, Isla Mujeres, Campeche, and Chetumal.

Semana Santa is the most important holiday in Mexico. Reenactments of the Passion, family parties and meals, and religious services are held during this week leading up to Easter Sunday.

Since 1991, the **Cancún Jazz Festival,** held the last weekend in May at Oasis Resort, has featured such top musicians as Wynton Marsalis and Gato Barbieri.

Founder's Day, August 17, celebrates the founding of Isla Mujeres with six days of races, folk dances, music, and regional cuisine.

Día de Independencia (Independence Day) is celebrated throughout Mexico with fireworks and parties beginning at 11 pm on September 15, and continuing on the 16th.

Fiesta del Cristo de las Ampollas (Feast of the Christ of the Blisters) is an important religious event that takes place late September or early October, with daily mass and processions during which people dress in traditional clothing; dances, bullfights, and fireworks take place in Ticul and other small villages.

Ten days of festivities and a solemn parade mark the **Fiesta del Cristo de Sitilpech,** during which the Christ image of Sitilpech village is carried to Izamal. The biggest dances (with fireworks) are toward the culmination of the festivities on October 28.

Día de los Muertos (Day of the Dead), called Hanal Pixan in Mayan, is a joyful holiday during which graves are refurbished and symbolic meals are prepared to lure the spirits of family members back to earth for the day. Deceased children are associated with All Saints Day, November 1, while adults are fêted on All Souls Day, November 2.

Money Matters

Mexican currency is the *peso*. When you arrive, it's a good idea to have smaller bills and some *centavos* (change) to pay for tips, bus fare, or taxis. Avoid having anything larger than a MX$50, since change is sometimes difficult to find. Do not accept damaged pesos, which are of no value to merchants or banks.

Traveler's checks can be changed at some banks for a processing fee. A passport is required when exchanging U.S. dollars or traveler's checks; foreign travelers may not exchange more than $1,500 U.S. dollars (cash) per person per month into Mexican pesos. However, credit card transactions, traveler's checks, and non-U.S. foreign currencies are not affected by this law.

ATMs are the most convenient ways to get cash, are readily available, and charge the official exchange rate. Make sure your PIN has only four numbers, and inquire about foreign transaction fees processed by your U.S. bank. Larger resorts have ATMs on the premises, and most hotels will exchange dollars for pesos.

Most businesses accept major credit cards but may add a surcharge to compensate for their own hefty processing fee. In Mexico, American Express, Discover, and Diner's Club are not as readily accepted as Visa or MasterCard.

IF YOU LIKE

Spas

There are dozens of spa resorts scattered throughout the Yucatán Peninsula, primarily along the coast. Here decadent treatments are offered in luxurious seaside settings. Some incorporate indigenous healing techniques into their services, including *temazcal* (an ancient Mayan sweat-lodge ritual). Many spas use native plant extracts in aromatherapy treatments; others feature seawater and marine algae in mineral-rich thalassotherapy treatments; still others go the high-tech route with cutting-edge flotarium tanks, seven-jet Vichy massage tables, and Kinesis fitness machines. You won't have any trouble getting your pampering fix here—especially in the areas around Playa del Carmen and the rest of the Riviera Maya—but you'll likely pay top dollar for it.

The spas that get the most consistent raves include Bahia Petempich's **Zoëtry Paraíso de la Bonita,** where you can soak away stress in specially built saltwater pools. The **Wayak Spa at Viceroy** in Punta Bete offers lava treatments and seaweed body wraps in jungle palapas; and **Banyan Tree,** in Mayakoba, has a 12-step Rainforest Experience that combines hydrotherapy with infrared light to revitalize the body. Cancún's **JW Marriott Spa** is justifiably famous for Mayan-inspired treatments like the chocolate massage, ground-corn exfoliation, and chaya detoxification. At Fiesta Americana Grand Coral Beach Cancún Resort, the 40,000-square-foot **Gem Spa** promises innovative treatments inspired by gemstone therapy.

Diving and Snorkeling

Mexico's Caribbean Coast is lined by stunning coral reefs, underwater canyons, and sunken shipwrecks—all teeming with marine life. Visibility can reach 100 feet, so even on the surface you'll be amazed by what you can see.

The **Mesoamerican Barrier Reef System** (also known as the Great Mayan Reef), stretches some 1,000 km (621 miles)—and more than 100 dive operators on the island offer deep dives, drift dives, wall dives, night dives, wreck dives, and underwater photography dives.

Farther south, the town of Tankah is known for its **Gorgonian Gardens,** a profusion of soft corals and sponges that has created an underwater Eden. Near the Belize border, Mexico's largest coral atoll, **Banco Chinchorro,** is a graveyard of vessels that have foundered on the corals over the centuries. Experienced divers won't want to miss Isla Contoy's **Cave of the Sleeping Sharks.** Here, at 150 feet, you can see the otherwise dangerous creatures "dozing" in a state of relaxed nonaggression. From June to mid-September, divers and snorkelers can swim with whale sharks, which can grow up to 50 feet in length. These docile creatures migrate near the tropical waters of Isla Holbox and Isla Contoy.

The freshwater cenotes that punctuate the Quintana Roo, Yucatán, and Campeche states are also favorites with divers and snorkelers. Many of these are private and secluded, even though they lie right off the highways; others are so popular that they've become tourist destinations. At Xenotes Oasis Maya, near Puerto Morelos, for example, you can visit four cavernous sinkholes filled with stalactites, stalagmites, and rock formations.

Mayan Ruins

The ruins of ancient Mayan cities are magical, and they're scattered all across the Yucatán. Although **Chichén Itzá,** featuring the enormous and oft-photographed Castillo pyramid, is the most famous of the region's sites, **Uxmal** is the most graceful. Here the perfectly proportioned buildings of the Cuadrángulo de las Monjas (Nun's Quadrangle) make a beautiful "canvas" for facades carved with snakes and the fierce visages of Mayan gods. At the more easterly **Ek Balam,** huge monster masks protect the mausoleum of a Mayan ruler. On the amazing friezes, winged figures dressed in full royal regalia gaze down.

At **Cobá,** the impressive temples and palaces—including a 79-foot-high pyramid—are surrounded by thick jungle, and only sparsely visited by tourists. In contrast, nearby **Tulum** is the peninsula's most visited archaeological site. Although the ruins here aren't as architecturally arresting, their location—on a cliff overlooking the blue-green Caribbean—makes Tulum unique among major Mayan sites.

Farther afield, in Campeche State, thousands of structures lie buried under the profuse greenery of Mexico's largest ecocorridor at the **Reserva de la Biósfera Calakmul,** where songbirds trill and curious monkeys hang from trees. These and other intriguing cities have been extensively excavated for your viewing pleasure.

Exotic Cuisine

Pickled onions tinged a luminous pink, blackened habanero chiles floating seductively in vinaigrette, lemonade spiked with a local plant called *chaya*—Yucatecan cuisine is different from that of any other region in Mexico. In recent years, traditional dishes made with local fruits, chiles, and spices have also embraced the influence of immigrants from Lebanon, France, Cuba, and New Orleans. The results are deliciously sublime.

Among the best-known regional specialties are *cochinita pibil* and *pollo pibil* (pork or chicken pit-baked in banana leaves). Both are done beautifully at **Hacienda Teya,** an elegant restaurant outside Mérida that was once a henequen hacienda. The *poc chuc* (pork in a sour orange sauce served with pickled onions and a plateful of other condiments) is delicious at **El Príncipe Tutul-Xiu,** an off-the-beaten-path eatery in the ancient Yucatán town of Maní. *Papadzules*—crumbled hard-boiled eggs rolled inside tortillas and drenched in a sauce of pumpkin seed and fried tomatoes—are a specialty at **Labná,** in Cancún's El Centro district.

In Campeche, a signature dish is *pan de cazón,* a casserole of shredded shark meat layered with tortillas, black beans, and tomato sauce; the best place to order it is at **La Pigua,** in Campeche City. Some of the Yucatán's tastiest treats come in liquid form. Xtabentún, a thick liqueur of fermented honey and anise, can be sipped at room temperature, poured over ice, or mixed with a splash of sparkling water.

CANCÚN AND THE RIVIERA MAYA TOP ATTRACTIONS

Cenotes

(**A**) For an underwater adventure, plunge into one of Mexico's *cenotes*—limestone pools fed by the subterranean springs that flow throughout the Yucatán. Swimmers can take a refreshing dip in the sacred sinkholes, accompanied by tiny fish that dart between the crevices; experienced divers can explore the underwater tunnels that connect these hidden gems.

Tulum

(**B**) Although the Yucatán has plenty of ruins to choose from, none are quite as spectacular as those in Tulum. Skirting the ancient architecture is a powdery stretch of coastline that fades into four shades of turquoise water. South of the ruins are dozens of eco-lodges that operate on solar power, wind turbines, and recycled rainwater.

Isla Mujeres

(**C**) Find a shady spot under the arching palms of Playa Norte, a blissful beach on Isla Mujeres where time is nonexistent. Those who come here fall victim to the *mañana* mentality, spending days admiring tangerine sunsets while island life sweeps them away. Calm, warm waters make this aquatic paradise ideal for swimming, snorkeling, diving, or fishing.

Reserva de la Biósfera Ría Celestún

(**D**) On a pristine beach west of Mérida, this 146,000-acre wildlife reserve has one of the largest colonies of flamingoes in North America, and more than 365 other species of birds. Flat-bottom boats float through the mangroves in search of turtles, crocodiles, cormorants, egrets, and herons. Nature lovers can take a break from bird-watching to enjoy the area's beaches, cenotes, or sweet water springs.

Chichén Itzá

(E) Considered one of the New Seven Wonders of the World, this archaeological city is best known for its ancient Temple of Kukulcán. Also referred to as "El Castillo," the Mayan ruin stands a staggering 78 feet high and features a towering pyramid with four stairways. This surrounding area has dozens of other archaeological sites, as well as the famed Cenote Sagrado (Sacred Cenote).

Grutas de Loltun

(F) Roughly one hour southeast of Uxmal, these natural caverns show signs of man dating back to 800 BC. Illuminated pathways meander past stalactites, stalagmites, and limestone formations. Here you can admire the spectacular rays of light shining down on "musical" columns that are formed by the union of stalactites and stalagmites.

Playa del Carmen

(G) Located in the heart of the Riviera Maya, Playa del Carmen has all the makings of a great vacation destination. Once a quiet fishing village, the town is booming with hotels and restaurants, and now ranks among the world's fastest-growing communities. For a day of pampering, relax at one of the nearby luxury spas, or try zip-lining at Xcaret, a 250-acre ecological theme park.

Mahahual and Xcalak

(H) Although it's a bit of a haul to get here, Mahahual and Xcalak—a pair of colorful Costa Maya towns—are perfect places to unplug. Incredible offshore diving awaits at Banco Chinchorro and the Mesoamerican Barrier Reef, the second longest in the world. Serious anglers will enjoy flyfishing in the nearby saltwater flats of the peninsula.

FAQS

Do I need any special documents to get into Mexico?

You must have a valid passport to enter Mexico and to reenter the United States. Before landing in Mexico, you'll be given an FMM (tourist permit) to be stamped at immigration. This allows you to stay in the country for 180 days. Keep this card safe, because you'll need to present it on departure. If you lose your FMM card (or overstay your time), you will need to visit an immigration office and pay heavy fines before leaving the country.

How difficult is it to travel around the Yucatán?

It's relatively easy, thanks to improved roadways and amped-up airline schedules. Mexico's bus system is an excellent way to travel around the country. Deluxe buses are more expensive, but have air-conditioning, reclining seats, movies, and fewer stops. Intercity transportation (used mainly by locals) is extremely reliable, and a great way to experience Mexican culture.

Are the roads as bad as they say?

Compared to other parts of Mexico, the roads in the Yucatán Peninsula are safe, flat, and well maintained. The main highway between Cancún and Belize, known as Carretera 307, is clearly marked and well paved. Even most secondary roads are in decent shape, but tend to get pitted with potholes during and after the rainy season. Only in remote areas like Punta Allen will you find major potholes. Toll road 180D runs between Cancún and Mérida and is by far your safest option. Throughout the peninsula, beware of unmarked *topes* (speed bumps) that can leave you airborne. Although road conditions have improved tremendously, avoid driving at night, since most areas lack street lighting.

What should I do when a police officer pulls me over?

It's not common, but there are some police officers who expect bribes from drivers. When renting a car, ask the agency if they offer a "Tourist Traffic Card," which can be handed to police upon receiving a traffic violation. Although some police may refuse to honor it, the card allows you to pay the ticket at the rental agency when you return your vehicle rather than spending several hours at the police station. It also helps eliminate corruption. At all costs, avoid the occasional scenario of a police officer demanding you follow him to an ATM to withdraw cash.

Should I get insurance on the rental car?

Yes! Regardless of what coverage you have from your credit card or travel insurance, you must (by law) have additional Mexican auto insurance to rent a car. Average daily insurance rates start around $45, which is often more than the daily rental fee if you happened to find a good deal online. When renting a car, make sure that your insurance coverage includes an attorney and claims adjusters who will come to the scene of an accident.

Should I consider a package?

Yes, packages that combine airfare, your hotel, and usually your airport transfers can be a good value in the Yucatán Peninsula. While guided tours aren't necessary, they are a good option if you prefer to travel with a group, and they can be arranged quite easily at your hotel's tour desk after your arrival. There's no need to book these in advance unless you are planning a particularly special trip.

Do I need a local guide?

Guides are helpful if you're visiting a wildlife area or an archaeological site

where local knowledge or history is needed. Most wildlife guides will bring a telescope or binoculars and can locate hidden animals and identify various species that the average traveler might overlook. If you do hire a guide, be sure to tip accordingly, since some (especially in rural areas) depend on tips as their main source of income.

Will I have trouble if I don't speak Spanish?

Sí y no. If you stay within the main tourist areas, nearly everyone will speak English, and if they don't, someone nearby certainly will. In remote towns and areas less visited by travelers, you'll have to speak "Spanglish" or rely on a dictionary or phrase book.

Can I drink the water?

Better not. Tap water in Mexico is not potable. Most resorts and restaurants have purified water, but if you are concerned about contaminated water (or ice) ruining your vacation, then opt for bottled water.

Are there any worries about the food?

Most restaurants are clean and cater to fussy travelers. If you are sensitive to spicy food, you may have a difficult time at some of the more genuine Mexican eateries. High-trafficked tourist areas will always have plenty of dining options, and coastal towns serve fresh-caught fish. If you visit a roadside market, unpeeled fruit or crunchy pork rinds are safe road-trip snacks. Unless you are in a nice restaurant, it's best to avoid uncooked vegetables, salads, rare meat, and milk products. Make sure that food is thoroughly cooked and hasn't been sitting under a heat lamp.

Do I need to get any shots?

Travelers visiting the Yucatán Peninsula do not need to get vaccinations or take any special medications. According to the U.S. Centers for Disease Control and Prevention, there's some concern about malaria along the Guatemala and Belize borders in the state of Quintana Roo.

Should I bring any medications?

To prevent bug bites, use insect repellent containing at least 10% DEET. If you can bear the heat, wear long pants when you go out at night. It's a good idea to bring along antihistamine cream to keep you from scratching. Mild cases of diarrhea respond best to Imodium (known generically as loperamide or lomotil) or Pepto-Bismol, both of which you can buy over the counter. To avoid problems at customs, any prescription drugs you bring with you should be in their original pill bottle. Over-the-counter medications are very expensive at resort gift shops, but in town you can find what you need at any local pharmacy.

Can I use my ATM card?

Yes. Most ATMs in Mexico accept U.S. credit and debit cards. Before your trip, make sure your PIN has only four numbers, since ATMs in Mexico do not recognize more digits. Foreign transaction fees can be high, as much as M$135 per withdrawal.

Do most places take credit cards?

Outside of remote areas like Xcalak and Mahahual, most tourist-oriented businesses accept Visa and MasterCard, but some places charge 5% to 10% more for credit-card payments to help offset high processing fees. It's always a good idea to have at least some cash on hand.

YUCATÁN PENINSULA TODAY

Government

Quintana Roo, Yucatán, and Campeche are three of the 31 states (plus one federal district) that make up Mexico's federal republic. The government consists of three branches: the executive, the legislative, and the judicial. The president of Mexico is elected to a one-time, six-year term by popular vote, and holds such extensive control that the position has been coined "the six-year monarchy." Enrique Peña Nieto, a member of the Institutional Revolutionary Party, took office as Mexico's president in 2012.

Each of Mexico's states is headed by a governor who also serves a single term that cannot exceed six years. Elected in 2012, Rolando Zapata Bello now fills that position in the state of Yucatán. Roberto Borge Angulo is the governor of Quintana Roo, and Fernando Ortega Bernés holds the title in Campeche; their terms end in 2016 and 2015 respectively. Though elected by a simple majority of the populace, the actual selection of state governors has historically been largely controlled by Mexico's presidents.

Much of Yucatán's revenue (like those of the other states) comes from the federal government. Such funding is then channeled to the mayors for distribution to their respective municipalities.

Economy

Before 1970, the Yucatán Peninsula relied on agriculture, fishing, and forestry to support its economy, but in the 1980s, the region was successfully marketed as a travel destination, especially Cancún and the Riviera Maya. As a result tiny fishing villages were transformed into bustling beach towns. Each year millions of tourists are drawn to the area's waterfront resorts and archaeological sites; these attractions inject a steady cash flow into the economy. This influx of mass tourism created more jobs and a higher standard of living. Travelers have also shown more interest in local culture. This has spurred the development of historical museums, including the state-of-the-art Gran Museo del Mundo Maya in Mérida, and reawakened interest in exquisite Yucatán crafts, which have long been known for the quality of workmanship. The Yucatán's economy is also helped by exports of henequen products such as twine, rugs, and wall hangings.

Tourism

In the late 1960s, the Mexican government created a strategy to increase tourism in the Yucatán Peninsula, with Cancún selected as the primary destination. As a result, the city's population increased from 18,000 in 1976 to more than 800,000 in 2014. Growth has since expanded to neighboring regions, creating a solid infrastructure that has made the Yucatán Peninsula one of the most visited destinations in Mexico.

Today the country faces the challenge of protecting its natural resources while allowing development to continue. Cancún's beaches alone are lined with more than 150 towering hotels, many of which have contributed to coastal erosion. Fortunately, building restrictions are now in place in neighboring communities such as Puerto Morelos. Ecotourism in Tulum and most of Costa Maya has helped protect area wildlife and the natural surroundings, although Tulum is currently developing at a rapid pace.

Hurricane Gilbert in 1988, Hurricane Wilma in 2005, the Swine Flu in 2009, and the state of the U.S. economy in 2010 all had a negative impact on tourism here;

however, these setbacks have not permanently affected tourism as the peninsula's driving force of economic development.

Religion

Although Mexico has no official religion, 89% of the population consider themselves Roman Catholic. Second only to Brazil, Mexico has more Catholics than anywhere else in the world, even though less than half attend church. Only 7% of the population consider themselves Protestant, followed by Eastern Orthodox, Seventh-Day Adventists, Jehovah's Witnesses, and Mormons. Very few Maya people in the Yucatán Peninsula still practice traditional rituals of offerings and sacrifices of small animals. Central to the Maya religion is the idea of the duality of the soul, one part eternal, and the other supernatural.

Sports

Soccer (or *fútbol*) is the most popular sport in Mexico. Locals have taken the game very seriously ever since it became professional in 1900. The country's most successful teams are Club Deportivo Guadalajara, Club América, Toluca, Cruz Azul, and Chivas. Second to soccer is boxing, with Mexico's biggest knockout rival being Puerto Rico. After the United States, Mexico has produced the most boxing world champions. For more than 100 years, baseball has been popular in Mexico. There are 16 teams competing in the Liga Mexicana de Béisbol (Mexican Baseball League). With more than 150 fairways dotting the country, golfing has gained notoriety among the locals, and has helped promote tourism with five professional tournaments, including the Mayakoba Golf Classic. More traditional sports include bullfighting, Mexican wrestling (also known as *lucha libre*), and *charrería*, based on a series of Mexican equestrian events.

Cash Crops

Although tourism is the Yucatán Peninsula's main source of income, both agriculture and fishing are also great economic contributors. Until 1960 the main crop was *henequen*, an indigenous plant that produces sisal fiber used to make rope. The henequen here once had a global reputation of being "green gold." The advent of similar man-made fibers destroyed the international market, but henequen is still manufactured in the north-central region. The peninsula's eastern area raises 65% of the state's livestock, while the southern region, near Peto and Tzucacab, is known for corn, citrus, sugarcane, and cattle. Today the Yucatán Peninsula exports more than 1,500 products, ranging from sponges and oranges to furniture and chocolates.

WEDDINGS AND HONEYMOONS

Imagine exchanging vows on a white sandy beach against a backdrop of swaying palms and the turquoise waters of the Caribbean. Your dream wedding can become a reality as long as you know the necessary steps to take when saying "I do" in Mexico.

Unfortunately, you'll need a lot more than just the wedding rings when organizing your tropical nuptials. Couples will need to bring passports, original birth certificates, tourist cards, and results of blood tests taken in Mexico 14 days before the wedding. Most clinics charge MX$2703 per couple for the required RPR, HIV, and blood-type tests. A judge's fee of MX$8787 must be paid in advance, and, if all documents are not presented, the judge will not perform the ceremony.

You also must have four witnesses at the ceremony, all of whom must be over 18 and have passports. If either the bride or groom was previously married, it's mandatory to wait a full year from the date that the divorce was final. Divorce papers must be translated into Spanish and notarized. In the case of a deceased spouse, you have to present a certified copy of the death certificate.

In Mexico the only marriages that are legally recognized are those that are conducted at the Oficina del Registro Civil (Civil Registers Office). The fee can be as much as MX$3379, and you'll find that most people there don't speak English, so plan accordingly. Regulations vary from state to state in Mexico, so contact the Mexican Tourism Board for specifics about your desired wedding location.

Beautiful Backdrops

The Yucatán Peninsula is one of the most sought-after spots for destination weddings. In fact, this growing trend in beachside nuptials has increased by 200% in the last decade. It's no wonder: the Caribbean coast not only makes for an incredible backdrop, but it's also a great way to combine a wedding and honeymoon.

Surprisingly, exchanging vows in Mexico can be much cheaper than a traditional wedding back home. Some smaller hotels can organize beautiful ceremonies, including food and music, for under $5,000. If you book your entire wedding party at the hotel, special rates and upgrades are generally available, and you can have the entire place to yourselves. Between May and November, rates are at their lowest, but you might end up with a soggy ceremony, especially during prime hurricane period—July through September.

There are dozens of wedding planners and professional photographers in Cancún, Cozumel, Isla Mujeres, Mérida, and Playa del Carmen. Whether you choose a white sandy beach in Cozumel or a colorful hacienda in Mérida, there's no shortage of ceremony settings for your big day.

Honeymoons

The peninsula's countless treasures, ranging from Mayan ruins to fishing villages, make it a haven for honeymooners. Beach-bound newlyweds have plenty of resort options along the Riviera Maya, many of which have luxury spas with treatments for two. Ideal for both weddings and honeymoons, Tulum offers ancient ruins, beautiful beaches, and dozens of eco-lodges willing to host simple weddings with vegetarian buffets and yoga classes between events. Other popular honeymoon spots are Isla Mujeres, where you can swim with nurse sharks, and Cozumel, with its excellent snorkeling and diving.

KIDS AND FAMILIES

Riddled with natural wonders, the Yucatán Peninsula has plenty of activities that the whole family can enjoy. The warm Caribbean waters are ideal for water sports such as swimming, snorkeling, and kayaking, and some areas even have roped-off sections designated for children. If you're vacationing in Cancún, beaches facing Bahía de Mujeres tend to have calmer waters and softer sand than those facing the Caribbean. Farther out, there may be undertows or riptides, so take note of warning signs and colored flags posted daily.

Kid-Friendly Activities

For teens, there are adrenaline-pumping water activities like Jet Skiing, banana boat rides, parasailing, and diving. Smaller children may prefer interactive programs like those available at Dolphin Discovery, which has locations in Isla Mujeres, Cozumel, and Puerto Aventuras; the tour includes encounters with manatees and sea lions, plus a chance to swim with the dolphins.

For parents wanting to introduce their children to history, combine a tour of the Tulum ruins with a day at the beach, or opt for the Cobá ruins, where your entire family can explore jungle trails by mountain bike. Cancún's all-inclusive resorts have plenty to keep the kids busy, including swimming pools, children's programs, and on-site water sports. The nearby Isla Shopping Village has an interactive aquarium. Also located in Zona Hotelera is Plaza Kukulcán, an upscale mall with a food court and play area on the second floor. In the Riviera Maya, JOYÀ by Cirque du Soleil is a whimsical show filled with entertainment and acrobatics for the entire family.

Isla Mujeres is home to El Garrafón National Park, where you can go snorkeling, swimming, hiking, or biking. To blend nature and education, visit the island's turtle farm, where you can see rescued turtle hatchlings.

Choosing a Destination

Just 16 km (10 miles) south of Tulum, the Reserva de la Biósfera Sian Ka'an has hundreds of species of wildlife in their freshwater lagoons, mangrove swamps, and tropical forests. The beaches here are excellent for swimming, snorkeling, and camping.

The colorful city of Mérida has folkloric shows, free concerts, and open-air markets where local crafts are sold. South of Mérida are the impressive Grutas de Loltún, one of the largest cave systems on the Yucatán Peninsula.

The quaint fishing villages of Puerto Morelos and Puerto Aventuras are excellent for families and close to the 250-acre ecological theme park, Xcaret. Here families can experience a butterfly pavilion, aviary, bat cave, and dozens of water activities. Catering to adventure-seekers, the neighboring Xplor lets you swim in a stalactite river, ride in an amphibious vehicle, or soar across the park on the longest zip-line in Mexico. At the entrance to Puerto Morelos is Croco-Cun, an animal farm where you can feed monkeys and hold baby crocodiles.

To escape the heat, families can visit the natural aquarium park, Xel-Há or take a dip in one of the hundreds of cenotes that dot the peninsula. These freshwater pools are ideal for snorkeling and swimming.

GREAT ITINERARIES

CANCÚN AND DAY TRIPS

Cancún is the place where you'll likely start your visit. If sunbathing, water sports, and parties that last until the wee hours of the morn are what you're after, you won't need to set foot outside the Zona Hotelera (or even your resort). If you're staying for a week or so, though, you should definitely check out some of the attractions that are an easy day-tripping distance from Cancún.

■**TIP**➜ Driving is the best way to see the peninsula, especially if your time is limited. However, there's nothing in this itinerary that can't be accessed by either bus or taxi.

Days 1 and 2: Arrival and Cancún

After arriving at your hotel, spend your first day or two doing what comes naturally: lounging at the hotel pool, playing in the waves, and going out for dinner and drinks. If you start to feel restless your second day, you can head to the Ruinas del Rey, go tequila tasting at La Destileria, or take a ride into El Centro (downtown Cancún) to browse the shops and open-air markets along Avenida Tulum and grab some real Mexican food.

Day 3: Cozumel or Isla Mujeres

Spend the day visiting one of the islands off Mexico's Caribbean Coast. If beachcombing and a laid-back meal of fresh seafood under a *palapa* (thatch roof) sound appealing, take a ferry from the Embarcadero Dock at Playa Linda and make the 30-minute trip to Isla Mujeres. If you like underwater sea life, drive or take a bus south from Cancún to Playa del Carmen, where you can catch a boat over to Cozumel. There are more than 100 scuba and snorkeling outfits on the

island, all of which run trips out to the spectacular Mesoamerican Barrier Reef.

Day 4: Playa del Carmen and Xcaret

In the morning, pack your bathing suit and take a bus from your hotel (M$388) to the magical Xcaret nature park. You can easily spend an entire day here snorkeling through underwater caves, visiting the butterfly pavilion, sea-turtle nursery, and reef aquarium, and bonding with dolphins (if you reserve a spot early). Alternatively, get up early and take a rental car south along Carretera 307 toward Playa del Carmen, about 1½ hours away. Once you arrive, head to Avenida 5, where you can choose from dozens of waterfront lunch spots. Then spend the afternoon either wandering among the shops and cafés or relaxing at a beach club. Since Xcaret is only a 10-minute drive south, ambitious types can tick that box, too.

Days 5 and 6: Tulum and Cobá

If you have the time, it's worth spending a day at each of these beautiful Mayan ruins south of Playa del Carmen; they are entirely different from one another. Cobá, which is about a half-hour's drive west of Tulum, is a less visited but spectacular ancient city that's completely surrounded by jungle. Tulum, the only major Mayan site built right on the water, has less stunning architecture but a dazzling location overlooking the Caribbean. After picking through the ruins, you can take a path down from the cliffs and laze for a while on the fabulous beach below. Be warned, though: since Tulum is just a 45-minute drive south from Playa, it's the Yucatán's most popular Mayan site.

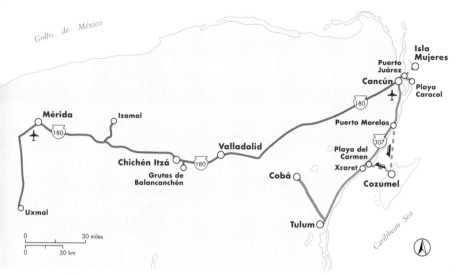

YUCATÁN AND THE MAYAN INTERIOR

If you have more than a week to spend on the peninsula, you're in luck. You'll have time to visit some of the most beautiful—and famous—ruin sites in the country, and to explore some authentically Mexican inland communities that feel worlds away from the more touristy coast.

Day 7: Valladolid and Chichén Itzá

Get up early, check out of your hotel, and make the drive inland along Carretera 180D toward the world-renowned Chichén Itzá ruins. Stop en route for a late breakfast or early lunch in Valladolid, about 2½ hours from Cancún. One of the best places to go is the casual eatery at Cenote Zaci, where you can also swim in the lovely jade-green cenote. Continue another half hour to Chichén Itzá and check into one of the area hotels (the Hacienda Chichén is a terrific choice), then spend the afternoon exploring the site before it closes at 5 pm. Visit El Castillo; check out the former marketplace, steam bath, observatory, and temples honoring formidable Mayan gods; then turn in after dinner at your hotel.

Days 8 and 9: West to Mérida

Either take an easterly detour for an on-the-hour tour at the limestone caverns of Grutas de Balancanchén, or head immediately west on Carretera 180D for the 1½-hour drive to Mérida. After checking into a hotel in the city (Casa Azul is an especially delightful option), wander the zócalo (main plaza) and surrounding streets. Spend the next day shopping, visiting museums, and enjoying Mérida's vibrant city scene.

Days 10 and 11: East to Cancún and Departure

The drive from Mérida back to Cancún will take you about 4½ hours, so if you're flying out of Cancún airport the same day, get an early start. Otherwise, if you can afford to take your time, stop at Izamal on the way back. At this charming town, famous for its bright yellow buildings, you can take a horse-drawn carriage tour of artisans' shops, visit the stately 16th-century church, or climb to the top of crumbling Kinich Kakmó pyramid. Arrive in Cancún in the afternoon, take a last swim on the sugar-sand beach before dinner, and get a good night's sleep at your hotel before your departure the next day.

THE PEOPLE OF THE YUCATÁN PENINSULA

The Maya people, whose ancient ruins have made the Yucatán a world-renowned attraction, also make up the bulk of the area's population.

The Maya are the single largest indigenous group on the entire North American continent. Although predominantly located on the Yucatán, members of this group have also settled in other Mexican states such as Campeche, Quintana Roo, Tabasco, and Chiapas. Outside of Mexico, the Maya can be found in Guatemala, Belize, Honduras, and El Salvador. Their total population is estimated at about 7 million, with 1.2 million living on the Yucatán Peninsula.

The Maya are rightfully proud of their history, which dates back to a period immediately following the rise of the Olmec culture. After the fall of the Olmecs, the Maya rose to power and settled in the Yucatán Peninsula, where they developed several city-states including that of Chichén Itzá.

Mayan architecture, much of it ceremonial in nature, has been archaeologically classified as dating back some 3,000 years. Well-preserved hieroglyphics found in the Yucatán trace the presence of the Maya to 200 BC or before. More than 100 ancient Maya ruins still exist today, many of them drawing travelers from around the world to the Yucatán each year.

These ancient and mysterious ruins clearly show that the Maya were once a regional superpower, and that Maya nobles had widespread influence. This remarkable group inhabited the Yucatán Peninsula long before the arrival of the Spanish.

The Spanish fought to colonize the Yucatán well into the 1500s. The first attempt took place in 1527, but it was only 20 years later, in 1546, that the Spanish saw victory. But long before the Spanish arrived, the once-powerful Mayan civilization was in decline, and no one really knows why—possibly disease, war, or famine.

Linguists have associated 24 distinct indigenous languages among the Maya. Many of the Maya in this area speak "Yucatec Maya" and use Spanish only as a second language.

The Maya continue to blend the elements of their ancient worship practices and rituals (minus the human sacrifice) with more contemporary religious practices. Many still wear traditional clothing, and construct the oblong, thatch-roof houses of their forebears. The Mayan passion to preserve their long history can be seen in the highly valued handicrafts that they create with the same skill and artistry as their ancestors.

CANCÚN

WELCOME TO CANCÚN

TOP REASONS TO GO

★ **Dancing the night away:** Salsa, cumbia, reggae, mariachi, hip-hop, and electronic music dizzy the air of the Zona Hotelera's many nightclubs.

★ **Exploring the nearby Mayan ruins:** Trips to remarkable sites like Tulum, Cobá, and Chichén Itzá can easily be accomplished in a day.

★ **Getting wild on the water:** Rent a Wave Runner, jungle boat, stand-up paddleboard, or kayak, then skim across the sea or Laguna Nichupté.

★ **Browsing for Mexican crafts:** The colorful stalls of Mercado Veintiocho and Coral Negro will certainly hold something that catches your eye.

★ **Indulging in local flavor:** Dishes like lime soup and *poc chuc* (pork in a sour orange sauce) and drinks like tamarind margaritas pay respect to traditional cuisine.

1 **El Centro.** Cancún's mainland commercial center provides an authentic glimpse into modern-day Mexico and a colorful alternative to the Zona Hotelera. Many of the restaurants scattered throughout this downtown area offer surprising bursts of culture and Mexican flavor. With more than 800,000 permanent residents, Cancún is full of shops, cafés, and open-air markets that cater mainly to locals. Although the majority of tourists choose to bask on the beaches, those who venture into the heart of El Centro will be glad they did—prices are much more reasonable and the food is outstanding.

2 **Punta Sam.** A separate strip called Punta Sam, north of Puerto Juárez, is sometimes referred to as the Zona Hotelera Norte (Northern Hotel Zone) or Playa Mujeres. This area is quieter than the main Zona, but there are some newer resorts, marinas, restaurants, and a golf course. This is also a good launch point for those heading to the nearby Isla Mujeres.

3 **Zona Hotelera.** The Hotel Zone is structured along a 25-km (15½-mile) stretch known as Kukulcán Boulevard. On the Caribbean side, dozens of resorts and condominiums tightly line the beachfront like a row of Legos. On the inland side, Laguna Nichupté is home to water sports, shopping malls, restaurants, and golf courses. At the northern tip of this main thoroughfare, near Punta Cancún, is a pack of nightclubs, discos, and bars—a nighttime favorite for those who like to party. For quiet accommodations, opt for a hotel near Punta Nizuc (at the southern tip of Kukulcán Boulevard) or Pok-Ta-Pok (a small inlet halfway between Punta Cancún and El Centro).

GETTING ORIENTED

Over the past four decades, Cancún has turned into the Miami of the south, with international investors pouring money into property development. The main attractions for most visitors lie along the Zona Hotelera, a barrier island shaped roughly like the number 7. To the east is the Caribbean, and to the west you'll find a system of lagoons, the largest of which is Laguna Nichupté. Downtown Cancún—aka El Centro—is 4 km (2½ miles) west of the Zona Hotelera on the mainland.

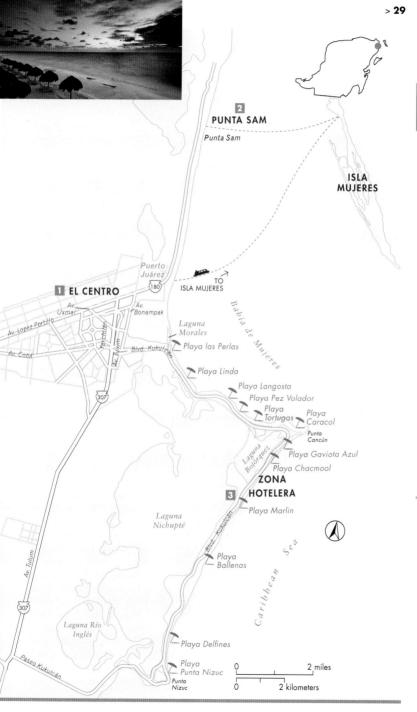

2

2

PUNTA SAM

Punta Sam

ISLA MUJERES

Puerto Juárez

1 EL CENTRO

180

TO
ISLA MUJERES

Av. Uxmal

Av. Bonampak

Av. López Portillo

Av. Cobá

307

Bahía de Mujeres

Laguna Morales

Playa las Perlas

Blvd. Kukulcán

Playa Linda

Playa Langosta

Playa Pez Volador

Playa Tortugas

Playa Caracol

Punta Cancún

Laguna Bojórquez

Playa Gaviota Azul

Playa Chacmool

ZONA

3 HOTELERA

Playa Marlin

Laguna Nichupté

Av. Tulum

Blvd. Kukulcán

Playa Ballenas

Caribbean Sea

307

Laguna Río Inglés

Playa Delfines

Paseo Kukulcán

Playa Punta Nizuc

Punta Nizuc

0   2 miles

0   2 kilometers

MEXICAN FOOD PRIMER

Regional culinary characteristics make it difficult to define "Mexican food" as a whole. Its complexity is a direct result of the different ingredients that are available within each region.

Still, there are overlapping items used throughout much of the county. The most frequently used spices are chile powder, cumin, oregano, cilantro, epazote, cinnamon, and cocoa. *Chipotle*, a smoke-dried jalapeño chile, is common, as are tomatoes, garlic, onions, and peppers. Rice is the most common grain, but corn, beans, and chiles are considered the cornerstones of Mexican cuisine.

The Spanish introduced rice, wheat, olive oil, nuts, cinnamon, wine, and parsley, and a variety of animals including cattle, chickens, goats, sheep, and pigs. These ingredients were incorporated with indigenous corn-based dishes, beans, turkey, fish, vanilla, chocolate, and fruits such as guava, pineapple, and papaya, giving us what we now know as Mexican food.

JUST DESSERTS

Locally grown fruits like mango, mamey, cherimoya, pomegranate, *tuna* (cactus apple), and strawberries are delicious alone or served with a dollop of cream and sugar. Stewed peaches and guavas are refreshing on a hot summer day, especially with a side of *nieves* (sherbet or sorbet). Among Mexico's most common desserts are *tres leches* (sponge cake soaked in three types of milk), churros (fried-dough pastry), and *arroz con leche* (rice cooked in milk with sugar and cinnamon). *Capirotada* (Mexican bread pudding), traditionally eaten during Lent, is made from French bread soaked in syrup, sugar, cheese, raisins, and walnuts.

REGIONAL CUISINES

Mexican food is much more than burritos, tacos, and rice and beans. Traditional recipes reach far beyond these stereotypical dishes, varying by region as a result of the climate, geography, local ingredients, and cultural differences among the inhabitants.

Yucatán Peninsula. The cuisine of the Yucatán Peninsula has both strong European and Mayan influences. Specialties of the region include *cochinita pibil* (seasoned pork colored with annatto seed and wrapped in banana leaves), turkey with black stuffing, and *papadzules* (tortillas filled with hard-boiled eggs and topped with a pumpkin seed sauce). Unique to Yucatán's cooking is the earthen pit oven where meats are slowly cooked with *recado negro* or *chilmole* (a blend of dried chiles that are set aflame and ground with spices to create a paste).

Mexico City and Environs (including Puebla). Largely influenced by the rest of the country, Mexico City still has original dishes such as *carnitas* (braised or roasted pork), *menudos* (tripe stew), and *pozole* (pork and hominy soup). Mexico City is also known for its incredible cheeses, tamales, and yellow-corn tortillas. The favored *mixiote* (mutton wrapped in maguey leaves) is slowly steam-baked in a pit oven. Puebla produces various species of cacti including

maguey and nopal, which can be eaten as a vegetable (de-spined, of course) or used to make juices and sorbets. Puebla is best known for *mole poblano* (thick, chocolate-tinged sauce) and *chiles en nogada* (stuffed chiles topped with a walnut cream sauce).

Oaxaca. With a strong pre-Hispanic influence, the state of Oaxaca has the second-highest percentage of indigenous residents in Mexico, exceeded only by the Yucatán. *Gusanos de maguey* (worms) and *chapulines* (grasshoppers), originally indigenous foods, are fried and eaten like roasted peanuts or sprinkled onto tacos. Oaxaca takes pride in its assortment of chiles, including yellow and black *chilhuacles, costeños,* and the large, light green *chiles de agua.*

Veracruz. Spanning the coast of the Gulf of Mexico, the cuisine here is characterized geographically by fish and seafood. It is also one of the most versatile agricultural regions of Mexico. Nut- and seed-based sauces are very popular, as are spicy chicken and vegetable dishes. Spanish influence is evident in the *pescado a la veracruzana,* fish made with tomato sauce, capers, and olives.

(Left) Cancún's famous seafood (Top) Steaming white pozole (Bottom) Salsa verde goes with just about everything.

Updated by Marlise Kast-Myers

Cancún is a great place to experience 21st-century Mexico, because it has everything you'd want in a vacation: shopping, sports, spas, and beaches. Here you'll find five-star resorts, exceptional food, Mexican culture, and natural beauty, all within day-trip distance of the world-famous Mayan ruins. That said, there isn't much that's quaint or historic in this distinctively modern city.

The locals—most of whom have embraced the accoutrements of urban middle-class life—typically live on the mainland in a part of the city called El Centro, but they work in the Zona Hotelera's tourist hub. The zone's main drag is Boulevard Kukulcán, and kilometer markers along it indicate where you are, from Km 1 near El Centro to Km 25 at the southern tip of Punta Nizuc. The area in between consists entirely of hotels, restaurants, shopping complexes, marinas, and time-share condominiums. Most travelers base themselves in this 25-km (15½-mile) stretch of paradise.

The party atmosphere of Zona Hotelera has inevitably earned it the title "Spring Break Capital of the World." Dozens of bars and nightclubs cater to college students just south of Punta Cancún at Km 9. Fortunately, this late-night/early-morning scene is contained within a small area, far from the larger resorts. Cancún, though, isn't just a magnet for youth on the loose. Adults with more sophisticated tastes appreciate its posh restaurants and world-class spas, while families are drawn to the limitless water sports and a plethora of children's activities.

If you believe that local flavor trumps the Zona Hotelera's pristine beaches, El Centro beckons. Although it is less visited by vacationers, the downtown area holds cultural gems that will remind you that you really are in Mexico. Hole-in-the-wall cantinas promise authentic regional food; evocative markets offer bargain-priced goods; and the hotels, while much more modest in terms of scale and amenities, provide true Mexican ambience.

PLANNING

2

TIMING

There's a lot to see and do in Cancún—if you can force yourself away from the beach, that is. Understandably, many visitors stay here a week, or longer, without ever leaving the silky sands and seductive comforts of their resorts. If you're game to do some exploring, though, it's a good idea to allow an extra two or three days for day trips to nearby eco-parks and archaeological sites.

WHEN TO GO

The sun shines an average of 253 days a year in Cancún. During High Season (late November to early April), the weather is nearly perfect, with temperatures hovering around 29°C (84°F) during the day and 18°C (64°F) at night. Hotel prices hit their peak between December 15 and January 5. If you plan to visit during Christmas, Spring Break, or Easter, you should book at least three months in advance.

Vacationers with travel-date flexibility can avoid the crowds and save 20% to 50% on accommodations during the remaining months. Be advised, though, that May through September are hot and humid, with temperatures that can top 36°C (97°F). The rainy season starts in mid-September and lasts until mid-November, bringing afternoon downpours that can last anywhere from 30 minutes to two hours. El Centro's streets often get flooded during these storms, and traffic can grind to a halt.

GETTING HERE AND AROUND

AIR TRAVEL

Located 16 km (9 miles) southwest of the heart of Cancún and 10 km (6 miles) from the Zona Hotelera's southernmost point, Cancún Aeropuerto Internacional receives direct scheduled flights from many cities, including New York, Boston, Washington, D.C., Houston, Dallas, Miami, Chicago, Los Angeles, Orlando, Ft. Lauderdale, Charlotte, and Atlanta. An increasing number of direct charter flights from other locales are also available. Hourly buses link the airport to downtown Cancún; taxis, *colectivos* (minibuses), hotel shuttles, and rental cars are other options. (⇨ *Check out our Travel Smart chapter for more on air travel and ground transportation.)*

BICYCLE TRAVEL

Cancún is not the sort of place you can get to know on foot, although there's a cycling and walking path that starts downtown at the beginning of the Zona Hotelera and continues through to Punta Nizuc. The beginning of the path parallels a grassy strip of Boulevard Kukulcán decorated with reproductions of ancient Mexican art.

BUS TRAVEL

For travel within the Zona Hotelera, buses R1, R2, R15, and R27 stop every five minutes along Boulevard Kukulcán and cost a flat MX$10 no matter where you get on or off. The R2 and R15 continue to El Centro's Wal-Mart and Mercado Veintiocho; the R1 goes as far as Puerto Juarez and the main bus terminal in El Centro.

Buses for farther-flung destinations leave from El Centro's terminal. One of the oldest bus lines in Mexico, ADO has first-class buses that stop incrementally at Puerto Morelos, Playa del Carmen, Tulum, Felipe Carrillo Puerto, Limones, and Chetumal; the full trip (concluding in Chetumal) takes 5 hours and 45 minutes and costs MX$354. Fifteen buses make the trip daily, departing between 6 am and midnight. Mayab, a division of ADO, has second-class buses leaving for destinations along the Riviera Maya every hour.

Bus Contacts ADO ☎ *555/133–2424* ⊕ *www.ado.com.mx.* **Terminal de Autobuses** ⊠ *Corner of avs. Tulum and Uxmal, El Centro* ☎ *998/884–5552.*

CAR TRAVEL

If you are planning to visit only Cancún, you don't need to (and probably shouldn't) rent a car. But if you want to explore the region, a car can be convenient if expensive. Be sure to read our extensive guidelines regarding road conditions, insurance requirements, and costs (*see ⇨ Car Travel in Travel Smart*) so that you can make an informed decision.

TAXI TRAVEL

It's easy and cheap to get around Cancún by bus; if you prefer traveling by taxi, however, you can always find one. Cab rides cost MX$135–MX$270 within the Zona Hotelera and MX$67–MX$135 within El Centro. Fares between the two run around MX$270. A ride to the ferries at Punta Sam or Puerto Juárez will set you back MX$330 or more. Make sure you check the fare before accepting a ride; a list of rates can be found in the lobby of most hotels or you can ask the concierge.

HOTELS

You might find it bewildering to choose among Cancún's many hotels, not least because brochures and websites make them sound—and look—almost exactly alike. For luxury and amenities, the Zona Hotelera is the place to stay. In the modest Centro, local color outweighs facilities. The hotels here are more basic and much less expensive than those in the Zona. If you want to be in the heart of the action, northern hotels near Punta Cancún are within walking distance of the nightclubs. Quieter properties are located at the southern end of Boulevard Kukulcán and in the residential streets between El Centro and the Zona Hotelera at Laguna Nichupté near the Pok-Ta-Pok Golf Course.

Many hotels have all-inclusive packages, as well as theme-night parties complete with food, beverages, activities, and games. Take note: generally the larger the all-inclusive resort, the blander the food (and the more watered-down the cocktails). For more memorable meals, you may need to dine off-site and essentially pay for food you're not consuming.

Many of the larger and more popular all-inclusives will no longer guarantee an ocean-view room when you make your reservation. If this is important to you, check that all rooms have ocean views at your chosen hotel, or book only at places that will guarantee one. Be sure to bring your confirmation information with you to prove you paid for an ocean-view room. Also be careful about lost wristbands and unreturned towels, since many resorts have started charging up to $150 per day for the former and $25 for the latter. When checking out, make sure the hotel hasn't tacked on excessive phone or minibar charges, as some tend to do. ■TIP→ At check-in, ask if your "all-inclusive" rate includes tips—some resorts are now automatically adding 15% gratuities—and "resort fees," which tend to be hidden supplementary charges.

Hotel reviews have been condensed for this book. For expanded reviews, facilities, and current deals, visit Fodors.com.

RESTAURANTS

Large breakfast and brunch buffets are among the most popular meals in the Zona Hotelera, with prices ranging from MX$165 to MX$338 per person. Most local restaurants open for lunch around 2 pm and generally stay open until midnight. When choosing one, be aware that those lining avenidas Tulum and Yaxchilán are often noisy and crowded, and gas fumes make it hard to enjoy meals alfresco. Many of the finer options are on Avenida Bonampak. Eateries in the Parque de las Palapas, just off Avenida Tulum, serve expertly prepared Mexican food. Deeper into the city center, you can find fresh seafood and traditional fare at Mercado Veintiocho (Market 28). Dress is casual in Cancún, but many restaurants do not allow bare feet, short shorts, or bathing suits. Even at the fanciest places, suggested attire is "resort elegant," meaning long pants, collared shirts, and closed shoes for gentlemen. For women, a dress or skirt and blouse with chichi sandals or heels will suffice. ⚠ Upscale resorts in the Zona Hotelera typically purify their tap water; however, ask in advance whether it's safe to drink.

DINING AND LODGING PRICES IN DOLLARS AND PESOS			
	$	$$	$$$	$$$$
Restaurants	under MX$135	MX$135–MX$200	MX$201–MX$350	over MX$350
Hotels in dollars	under $100	$100–$200	$201–$300	over $300
Hotels in pesos	under MX$1450	MX$1450–MX$2900	MX$2901–MX$4400	over MX$4400

Restaurant prices are the average price for a main course at dinner; or if dinner is not served, at lunch. Hotel prices are for a standard double room in high season, including taxes.

SAFETY

Cancún is one of the safest cities in Mexico. Reported violence generally takes place 2,090 km (1,300 miles) from Cancún on the northern border of Mexico, the same distance from New York to Texas. Don't be surprised to see Tourist Police patrolling the Zona Hotelera, especially during the holidays and high season when security is increased. The C4 Surveillance and Rescue Center monitors the tourist area through video cameras installed in strategic points throughout the city, and an emergency 911 call center is available. Visitors are still advised to exercise caution and use common sense while traveling.

TOURS

GENERAL TOURS

Gray Line Cancún. Cancún's Gray Line office can customize your vacation, offering everything from luxury airport transportation and dolphin adventures to sunset dinner cruises and tours of Chichén Itzá. ☎ 877/240–5864, 998/887–2495, 01800/719–5465 *toll-free in Mexico* ⊕ *www.graylinecancun.com* ✉ *From MX$680.*

Olympus Tours. Specializing in outings around Cancún, this agency's options run the gamut from ATV and horseback tours to cenote excursions and cultural encounters. It will also book reservations for Xcaret, Xel-Há, and other area adventure parks. ⊠ *Av. Yaxchilán, Sm 17, Lote 13, Mza 2, El Centro* ☎ *998/881–9030, 786/338–9358 in the U.S.* ⊕ *www.olympus-tours.com* ✉ *From MX$750.*

BOAT TOURS

AquaWorld. In addition to Nichupté lagoon tours and Isla Mujeres day trips, AquaWorld's sightseeing menu includes unusual options like the B.O.B. Adventure. Short for Breathing Observation Bubble, B.O.B. lets you steer through the reefs on a machine that resembles an underwater motor scooter (a pressurized helmet allows for normal breathing). Tours on the Paradise SubSee are another alternative. This "floating submarine" is a glass-bottom boat that submerges halfway into the water. On the short journey to Punta Nizuc, you'll see turtles, fish, coral, and a few statues in the Underwater Museum. ⊠ *Blvd. Kukulcán, Km 15.2, Zona Hotelera* ☎ *998/848–8327, 877/730–4054* ⊕ *www.aquaworld. com.mx* ✉ *B.O.B. MX$920, SubSee Explorer from MX$544, other tours from MX$817.*

Asterix Tours. This is one of the only companies permitted to depart from the Zona Hotelera on tours to Isla Contoy and the underwater gardens of Isla Mujeres. Trips to the former leave at 9 am and return at 5 pm on Tuesday, Thursday, and Saturday; those to the latter leave on Wednesday and Friday. Day- and nighttime fishing trips run three times a week. ⊠ *Blvd. Kukulcán, Km 5.5, Zona Hotelera* ☎ *998/886–4270* ⊕ *www.contoytours.com* ✉ *Isla Contoy tours MX$1827, Isla Mujeres tours MX$1287, fishing trips MX$1111.*

Kolumbus Tours. Excursions to Isla Contoy are available Thursday and Sunday on a double-decker trawler; you can also choose a daily catamaran tour that combines Isla Contoy and Isla Mujeres. ⊠ *Punta Conoco 36, Sm 24, El Centro* ☎ *998/884–5333, 01800/715–3375 toll-free in Mexico* ⊕ *www.kolumbustours.com* ✉ *From MX$1294.*

Sea Passion Catamaran. Day trips to Isla Mujeres (which include a buffet lunch, open bar, and snorkel equipment) are available by reservation. ⊠ *Chac-Chi Marina, Blvd. Kukulcán, Km 3.2, Zona Hotelera* ☎ *998/849–5573* ⊕ *www.seapassion.net* ✉ *From MX$1089.*

ECOTOURS

Eco Colors. Bike tours, butterfly- and bird-watching adventures, as well as kayaking, diving, and eco-oriented snorkeling trips can be booked through Eco Colors. They also specialize in cultural programs and volunteer opportunities. ⊠ *Calle Camarón 32, Sm 27, El Centro* ☎ *998/884–3667* ⊕ *www.ecotravelmexico.com* ✉ *From MX$1361.*

VISITOR INFORMATION

Cancún Convention and Visitors Bureau (*CVB*). The civic tourist office has lots of information about area accommodations, restaurants, and attractions. ⊠ *Zona Hotelera, Blvd. Kukulcán, Km 9, El Centro* ☎ *998/881–2745* ⊕ *www.cancun.travel.*

EXPLORING

Taxis from the Zona to El Centro cost around MX$270 each way. A more affordable alternative is to catch a north-bound public bus to the Kukulcán–Bonampak intersection, which marks the beginning of El Centro (MX$10). From here, you can explore by foot or flag down a taxi to your area of choice. If you want to get a taste of downtown culture, start at the colorful Mercado Veintiocho or Parque de las Palapas. To return to the Zona Hotelera, take a taxi to the Chedraui on Avenida Tulum and then catch a bus that passes every few minutes toward the Zona. (Don't be alarmed if a man in a clown suit roams the aisle in search of tips: at night the buses come alive with all sorts of amateur performers, from accordionists to jugglers, hoping to earn a few pesos.)

South of Punta Cancún, Boulevard Kukulcán becomes a busy road and is difficult for pedestrians to cross. It's also punctuated by steeply inclined driveways that turn into the hotels, most of which are set back at least 100 yards from the road. The lagoon side of the boulevard consists of scrubby stretches of land alternating with marinas, shopping centers, and restaurants. ■ TIP➔ **Because there are so few sights, there are no orientation tours of Cancún: just do the local bus circuit to get a feel for your surroundings. Buses run until midnight, and you'll rarely have to wait more than five minutes.**

When you first visit El Centro, the downtown layout might not be self-evident. It's not based on a grid but rather on a circular pattern. The whole city is divided into districts called Super Manzanas (abbreviated "Sm" in this book), each with its own central square or park. In general, walks through downtown are somewhat unpleasant, with whizzing cars, corroded pathways, and overgrown weeds. Sidewalks disappear for brief moments, forcing pedestrians to cross grassy inlets and thin strips of land separating four lanes of traffic. Few people seem to know exactly where anything is, even the locals who live in El Centro. When exploring on foot, expect to get lost at least once and enjoy it—you may just stumble on a courtyard café or a lively cantina.

Fodor'sChoice
★
Cancún Underwater Museum. Locally known as MUSA, Cancún's Underwater Museum is made up of more than 400 lifelike statues sculpted by Jason de Caires Taylor. The stunning artworks, located off the shores of Punta Cancún, Punta Nizuc, and Manchones Reef near Isla Mujeres, create an artificial habitat for marine life that can be viewed by divers, snorkelers, and passengers on glass-bottom-boat tours. ⊠ *Punta Cancún, Punta Nizuc, and Manchones Reef, Isla Mujeres* ⊠ *Free.*

El Centro. Two decades ago, downtown Cancún was the place to be after a day at the beach. The once-barren Zona Hotelera had very limited dining options, so tourists strolled the active streets of avenidas Tulum

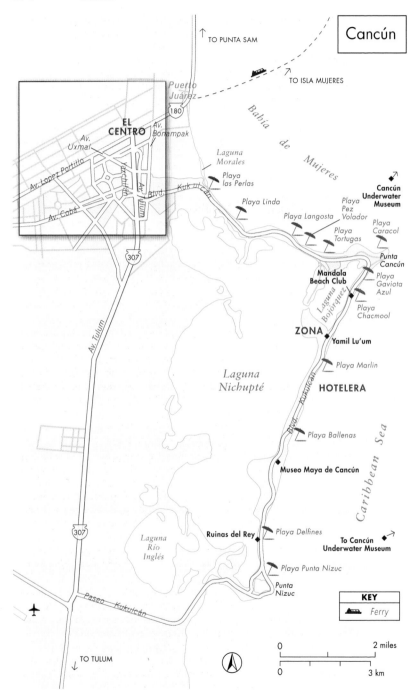

Cancún

TO PUNTA SAM

TO ISLA MUJERES

Puerto Juárez

Bahía de Mujeres

EL CENTRO

Av. Bonampak

Av. Uxmal

Av. López Partillo

Av. Cobá

Laguna Morales

Playa las Perlas

Playa Linda

Playa Langosta

Playa Pez Volador

Playa Tortugas

Cancún Underwater Museum

Playa Caracol

Punta Cancún

Mandala Beach Club

Playa Gaviota Azul

Laguna Bojórquez

Playa Chacmool

ZONA

Yamil Lu'um

Playa Marlin

HOTELERA

Laguna Nichupté

Av. Tulum

Blvd. Kukulcán

Playa Ballenas

Museo Maya de Cancún

Caribbean Sea

Ruinas del Rey

Playa Delfines

To Cancún Underwater Museum

Laguna Río Inglés

Playa Punta Nizuc

Punta Nizuc

Paseo Kukulcán

TO TULUM

KEY

Ferry

0   2 miles
0   3 km

and Yaxchilán, and the Parque de las Palapas. With the emergence of luxury resorts and mass tourism, a major shift brought the focus back to the Zona. Today many visitors are unaware that the downtown area even exists, while others consider "downtown" to be the string of flea markets near the convention center. In reality, El Centro's malls and markets offer a glimpse of Mexico's urban lifestyle. Avenida Tulum, the main street, is marked by a huge sculpture of shells and starfish in the middle of a traffic circle. This iconic Cancún sight, which many locals refer to as "el ceviche," is particularly dramatic at night when the lights are turned on. El Centro is also home to many restaurants and bars, as well as **Mercado Veintiocho** (Market 28), an enormous crafts market just off avenidas Yaxchilán and Sunyaxchén. For bargain shopping, hit the stores and small strip malls along Avenida Tulum.

Museo Maya De Cancún. Opened in December 2012, this modern museum in the Zona Hotelera sits in the middle of a small, lush jungle with 14 excavated ruins. Air-conditioned second-floor exhibits, accessible by elevator, showcase Mayan artifacts such as pottery, jewelry, and stone-carved scripts from various eras of civilization. While there is much to see, signposting is mostly in Spanish. On a sunny day, leave time to wander the grounds adjacent to the museum. ■ TIP➜ **The admission fee is taken in Mexican pesos, so be sure to have proper currency.** ✉ *Blvd. Kukulcán, Km 16.5, Zona Hotelera* ☎ *998/885–3842* ⊕ *www.inah.gob. mx* ✍ *MX$59* ☉ *Tues.–Sun. 9–5.*

Ruinas el Rey. Large signs on the Zona Hotelera's lagoon side, roughly opposite Playa Delfines, point out the Ruins of the King. Although much smaller than famous archaeological sites like Tulum and Chichén Itzá, this site (commonly called "El Rey") is worth a visit and makes for an interesting juxtaposition of Mexico's past and present. First entered into Western chronicles in a 16th-century travelogue, the ruins weren't explored by archaeologists until 1910, and excavations didn't begin until 1954. In 1975, archaeologists began restoration work on the 47 structures with the help of the Mexican government.

Dating to the 3rd and 2nd centuries BC, El Rey is notable for having two main plazas bounded by two streets. (Most other Mayan cities contain only one plaza.) Originally named Kin Ich Ahau Bonil (Mayan for "king of the solar countenance"), the site was linked to astronomical practices. The pyramid is topped by a platform, and inside its vault are paintings on stucco. Skeletons interred at the apex and at the base indicate the site may have been a royal burial ground. In 2006, workmen unearthed an ancient Mayan skeleton on the outskirts of the park. ✉ *Blvd. Kukulcán, Km 17, Zona Hotelera* ☎ *998/849–2880* ✍ *MX$43* ☉ *Daily 8–4:30.*

Yamil Lu'um. Located on Cancún's highest point (the name means "hilly land"), this archaeological site is on the grounds of the Park Royal Cancún and Westin Lagunamar, which means that nonguests can only visit from the beach side. The concierges at either hotel may let you enter through their property if you ask nicely, but otherwise head to Playa Marlín and admire the ruins from a distance. Although it consists of two structures—one probably a temple, the other probably a lighthouse—this is the smallest of Cancún's ruins. Discovered in 1842 by John Lloyd Stephens, the ruins date from the late 13th or early 14th century. Keep an eye out for roaming iguanas. ⊠ *Blvd. Kukulcán, Km 12, Zona Hotelera* ⊑ *Free* ◷ *Daily 9–5.*

BEACHES

All beaches can be reached by public transportation; just let the driver know where you are headed. Those not maintained by hotels will have seaweed on their shores. If you're traveling with young children, it's best to choose beaches facing Bahía de Mujeres at the top of the "7." They tend to be less crowded and more sheltered than ones on the Caribbean side. Wide beaches and shallow waters make the northern tip ideal for those wanting to snorkel or swim. Forming the right side of the "7" are beaches facing the Caribbean Sea. Here riptides and currents can be somewhat dangerous, especially when the surf is high. For snorkeling, it's best to head to the southern end of Boulevard Kukulcán near the Westin Hotel. In the saltwater lagoon, jungle boats and Wave Runners rule the waters by day and adult crocodiles wade the banks by night.

The beaches listed here are organized by location, beginning on the northwest side of the "7" facing Bahía de Mujeres and continuing down along the Caribbean side toward Punta Nizuc.

■TIP→ Don't swim when the black danger flag flies; a red or yellow flag indicates that you should proceed with caution; and a green flag means the waters are calm. Most likely, you will always see a red or yellow flag posted on the shores.

Playa Ballenas. "Whale Beach" is a raw stretch of sand and crystal water at Km 14.5 between the Hard Rock Hotel and Secrets The Vine. Jet Skiers often zoom through the water, and the strong wind makes the surf rough. The beach is open to the public; parking and beach access are at Calle Ballenas. Food and drinks are available at any of the resorts along this stretch, including the Hard Rock, Secrets The Vine, and Sandos Cancun—but keep in mind these all-inclusives cater only to hotel guests. **Amenities:** parking (no fee); water sports. **Best for:** walking; windsurfing. ⊠ *Blvd. Kukulcan, Km 14.5, Zona Hotelera.*

Playa Caracol. The last "real beach" along the east–west stretch of the Zona Hotelera is near Plaza Caracol and the Xcaret dock. Located at Km 8.5, the whole area has been eaten up by development, in particular the high-rise condominium complex next to the entrance. Playa Caracol (or "Snail Beach") is also hindered by the rocks that jut out from the water to mark the beginning of Punta Cancún, where Boulevard Kukulcán turns south. There are several hotels along here and a few sports rental outfits. It's also the launching point for trips to Contoy Island. ■TIP→ Closer to the Fiesta Americana Grand Coral Beach hotel, the water is calm because of the jetty that blocks the wind and waves. **Amenities:** food and drink; water sports. **Best for:** swimming; windsurfing. ⊠ *Blvd. Kukulcán, Km 8.5, Zona Hotelera.*

Playa Chacmool. Located at Km 10 on Boulevard Kukulcán, Playa Chacmool can be accessed through the beach entrance across the street from

Señor Frog's. As at Playa Caracol, development has greatly encroached on Chacmool's shores. There are a lot of rocks, but the water is a stunning turquoise; moreover, the beach is close to shopping centers and the party zone, so there are plenty of restaurants nearby. The short stretch to the south has gentler waters and fewer rocks. Public changing rooms and limited free parking are also available. The clear, shallow water makes it tempting to walk far out, but be careful—there's a strong current and undertow. Lifeguards are on duty until 5 pm. The closest hotel to Playa Chacmool is Le Blanc Resort. **Amenities:** food and drink; lifeguards; parking (no fee); toilets. **Best For:** partiers. ⊠ *Blvd. Kukulcán, Km 10, Zona Hotelera.*

Playa Delfines. Near Ruinas del Rey, where Boulevard Kukulcán curves into a hill, "Dolphin Beach" is one of the last before Punta Nizuc. Hotels have yet to dominate this small section of coastline, and there's an incredible lookout over the ocean with a huge "Cancún" sign, making for a great photo op. On a clear day you can see at least four shades of blue in the water, though swimming is treacherous unless a green flag is posted. This resort-free area has plenty of sand and waves, and it's one of the few places in Cancún you'll see a surfer (during a wind swell). Even during hurricane season, waves seldom hit "epic" status; at best, you might find choppy, inconsistent surf. **Amenities:** lifeguard; parking (no fee); toilets. **Best For:** solitude; surfing. ⊠ *Blvd. Kukulcán, Km. 18, Zona Hotelera.*

Playa Gaviota Azul (*Blue Seagull Beach*). Heading down from Punta Cancún onto the long, southerly stretch of the island, Playa Gaviota Azul (literally "Blue Seagull Beach," but also commonly called "City Beach" or "Forum Beach") is the first on the Caribbean's open waters. Closer to Km 9, the waves break up to six feet during hurricane season, making it one of the few surfing spots in Cancún; lessons are offered by the 360 Surf School (⊕ *www.360surfschoolcancun.com*). If you'd rather just relax, ascend a short flight of steps to Mandala Beach Club at Km 9.5, where you can enjoy the full resort experience without booking into a hotel. There is paid parking at Plaza Forum plus minimal street parking. The closest hotels—Krystal Grand Punta Cancun and Aloft—are across the street from the beach. **Amenities:** food and drink; parking (fee); toilets; water sports. **Best for:** partiers; surfing; swimming. ⊠ *Blvd. Kukulcán, Km 9.5, Zona Hotelera.*

FAMILY **Playa Langosta.** Small, placid "Lobster Beach" has safe waters and gentle waves that make it a popular swimming spot for families and Spring Breakers alike. On weekends, you'll be lucky if you can find a space on the sand. There's an entrance to the beach at Boulevard Kukulcán's Km 5. A dock juts out in the middle of the water, but swimming areas are marked off with ropes and buoys. Next to the beach is a small building with a restaurant, an ice-cream shop, and an ATM. **Amenities:** food and drink; toilets. **Best for:** swimming. ⊠ *Blvd. Kukulcán, Km 5, Zona Hotelera.*

FAMILY **Playa las Perlas.** "Pearl Beach" is the first heading east from El Centro along Boulevard Kukulcán. Located at Km 2.5, between the Cancún mainland and the bridge, it's a relatively small beach on the protected waters of the Bahía de Mujeres, and is popular with locals. There are several restaurants lining the sand, but most of the water-sports activities are only available to those staying at the nearby lodgings like the Imperial las Perlas. There's a small store beside that resort where you can buy sandwiches and drinks if you want to have a beach picnic. **Amenities:** food and drink; lifeguards; water sports. **Best For:** swimming. ⊠ *Blvd. Kukulcán., Km 2.5, Zona Hotelera.*

Playa Linda. At Km 4 on Boulevard Kukulcán, "Pretty Beach" is where the ocean meets the freshwater Laguna Nichupté to create the Nichupté Channel. Restaurants and changing rooms are available near the launching dock. Playa Linda is situated between the Barceló Costa Cancun and Sotavento Hotel. There's lots of boat activity along the channel, and the ferry to Isla Mujeres leaves from the adjoining Embarcadero marina, so the area isn't safe for swimming. It is, however, a great place to people-watch, with a 300-foot rotating scenic tower nearby that offers a 360-degree view. **Amenities:** food and drink; parking (no fee); toilets. **Best For:** solitude. ⊠ *Blvd. Kukulcán, Km 4, Zona Hotelera.*

Playa Marlin. Accessible via a road next to Kukulcán Plaza, "Marlin Beach" is a seductive stretch of sand in the heart of the Zona Hotelera at Km. 13. Despite its turquoise waters and silky sands, the waves are strong and the currents are dangerous. If this beach is crowded, you can walk in either direction to find quieter spots. There's also a small tent where you can rent boogie boards, snorkel gear, and motorized sports equipment. Although there are currently no public facilities, you can always walk over to Kukulcán Plaza if you need a restroom. **Amenities:** water sports. **Best For:** snorkeling; surfing; walking. ⊠ *Blvd. Kukulcán, Km. 13, Zona Hotelera.*

FAMILY **Playa Pez Volador.** The calm surf and relaxing shallows of Playa Pez Volador make it an aquatic playground for families with young children. Marked by a huge Mexican flag at Km 5.5, the wide beach is popular with locals, as many tourists tend to head to the more active Playa Langosta. Sea grass occasionally washes ashore here, but by early morning it is cleared away by the staff of the neighboring Casa Maya Hotel. **Amenities:** none. **Best For:** swimming. ⊠ *Blvd. Kukulcan, Km 5.5, Zona Hotelera.*

Playa Punta Nizuc. You'll find Cancún's most isolated and deserted beach on the southern tip of the peninsula. Far from the crowds and party scene, Playa Punta Nizuc has few amenities other than those available to guests at the nearby Wet 'n Wild Waterpark (Km. 25), Nizuc Resort (Km. 21), or Club Med (Km 21.5). The lack of beach traffic helps keep the white sands clean and the waters sparkling, except when sea grass washes up. Bordered by jungle to the south, Playa Punta Nizuc can be accessed directly from Boulevard Kukulcán, so there's plenty of street parking. There are few aminities, though, so make sure you bring water, snacks, sunscreen, and an umbrella for shade. ■TIP➔ This is a great place to collect shells or swim, since waves crash only on stormy days. **Amenities:** parking (no fee). **Best for:** solitude; swimming; snorkeling; walking. ⊠ *Blvd. Kukulcán, Km 24Zona Hotelera.*

Playa Tortugas. Don't be fooled by the name—this spot is seldom frequented by *tortugas*. It's the opportunity to swim, snorkel, kayak, paraglide, and ride Wave Runners that really brings folks to "Turtle Beach." The water is deep, but the beach itself (the nicest section of which is on the far right, just past the rocks) can get very crowded. Passengers usually grab a drink or snack here before catching the ferry to Isla Mujeres, and locals from El Centro will spend their entire weekend on the sand. So if you are looking for isolation, it's best to head elsewhere. **■ TIP→ There's an over-the-water bungee jumping tower where your head will actually touch the water.** **Amenities:** food and drink; water sports. **Best for:** partiers; snorkeling; swimming. ✉ *Blvd. Kukulcán, Km 6.5, Zona Hotelera.*

WHERE TO EAT

ZONA HOTELERA

$$$ ARGENTINE

🍴 **Cambalache.** This Argentine steakhouse is rustic yet elegant, with dark wooden tables and arched brick ceilings. The house cocktail, *clericot,* made from red wine, sparkling cider, and fresh fruit, is prepared at your table. For starters, try traditional empanadas. Not surprisingly, steak is the most popular main; however, the local fish and lamb skewers grilled over a brick fire are also delicious. Be sure to leave room for *alfajor,* a crisp pastry layered with caramel and pecans. The tango music coupled with views of Coral Negro Market give this restaurant international flair (and help you forget you're inside a mall). With room for 350 people, the dining room tends to get rather loud at night, and there's no outdoor seating. [$] *Average main: 338 MP* ✉ *Plaza Forum, Blvd. Kukulcán, Km 9, Zona Hotelera* ☎ *998/883–0902* 🌐 *www.cambalacherestaurantes.com* ✣ *1:D2.*

$$$$ EUROPEAN

🍴 **Casa Rolandi.** The secret to this restaurant's success is its creative handling of Italian and Swiss cuisine—which explains why both *carpaccio de pulpo* (thin slices of fresh octopus) and cheese fondue appear on the menu. Appetizers are tempting: there's puff bread from a wood-burning oven plus a salad and antipasto bar. For something with more local flavor, try the black ravioli stuffed with lobster or Casa Rolandi's specialty, Gamberoni dei Re Maya: jumbo shrimp baked in banana leaves and topped with a special Mayan sauce. Entrées are served under silver domes. The restaurant also has an extensive wine list. The beautiful dining room, attentive service, and pleasant lagoon views from the spacious patio encourage you to linger. [$] *Average main: 406 MP* ✉ *Blvd. Kukulcán, Km 13.5, in front of Royal Sands, Zona Hotelera* ☎ *998/883–2557* 🌐 *www.rolandi.com* ✣ *1:C3.*

$$$$ SEAFOOD

🍴 **Casitas.** Sink your toes into the sand at Cancún's only on-the-beach restaurant where impeccable service matches an incredible setting. The romantic ambience caters to couples, and many of the seafood dishes are created for two. Silk curtains drape palapas, each centered with an illuminated table adorned with seashells. For a delicious sampling, try the seafood platter of shrimp, oysters, tuna tartare, king crab, and lobster tail. A variety of steaks and salads are also available. The mini

CLOSE UP

Cancún's History

The Maya, Cancún's original inhabitants, arrived centuries ago, and their descendants live in the area to this day. During the golden age of Mayan civilization, called the Classic Period, this part of the coast remained sparsely populated as other parts of the peninsula were developing trade routes and building enormous temples and pyramids. Consequently, Cancún never grew into a major Mayan center. Excavations of ruins at El Rey in what is now the Zona Hotelera have shown that the Maya communities that lived here around AD 1200 simply used this area for burial sites. Even the name given to the area was not inspiring: Cancún means "nest of snakes" in Mayan.

When the Spanish conquistadors began to arrive in the early 1500s, much of the Mayan culture was already in decline. Over the next three centuries the Spanish largely ignored coastal areas like Cancún, which consisted mainly of low-lying scrub, mangroves, and swarms of mosquitoes, and focused instead on settling inland where there was more economic promise.

Although it received a few refugees from the Caste War of the Yucatán, which engulfed the entire region in the mid-1800s, Cancún remained more or less undeveloped until the middle of the 20th century. By the 1950s, Acapulco had become the number-one tourist attraction in the country—and had given the Mexican government its first taste of tourism dollars. When Acapulco's star began to fade in the late 1960s, the government hired a market-research company to determine the perfect location for developing Mexico's next big tourist destination. Guess where they picked?

In April 1971, Mexico's president, Luis Echeverría Alvarez, authorized the Ministry of Foreign Relations to buy the island offshore of Cancún and the surrounding region. With a $22 million development loan from the World Bank and the Inter-American Development Bank, the transformation of Cancún began. At the time there were just 120 residents, most of whom worked at a coconut plantation. By 1979 Cancún had become a resort of 40,000, attracting more than 2 million tourists a year. Today, more than 800,000 people live here, and the city has become Mexico's most lucrative source of tourism income. The recently opened Museo Maya showcases the evolution of the region and its archaeological timeline. Set in the middle of the bustling hotel zone, attractions include both indoor exhibits and outdoor ruins.

dessert shooters are the perfect way to extend your dinner-with-a-view; head to the oceanfront beds after your meal to relax and digest. Call ahead, since the restaurant is at the mercy of the weather. There's live saxophone music Thursday through Sunday. [$] *Average main: 1299 MP* ✉ *Ritz-Carlton Cancún, Retorno del Rey 36, off Blvd. Kukulcán, Km 13.5, Zona Hotelera* ☎ *998/881–0808* 🌐 *www.ritzcarlton.com* ✍ *Reservations essential* 🕘 *No lunch* ✣ *1:C3.*

$$$$ ITALIAN 🍴 **Cenacolo.** Brick-oven pizza and pasta, handmade in full view, have made this fine Italian restaurant a favorite. Appetizers include beef or octopus carpaccio that practically melts in your mouth, and a light

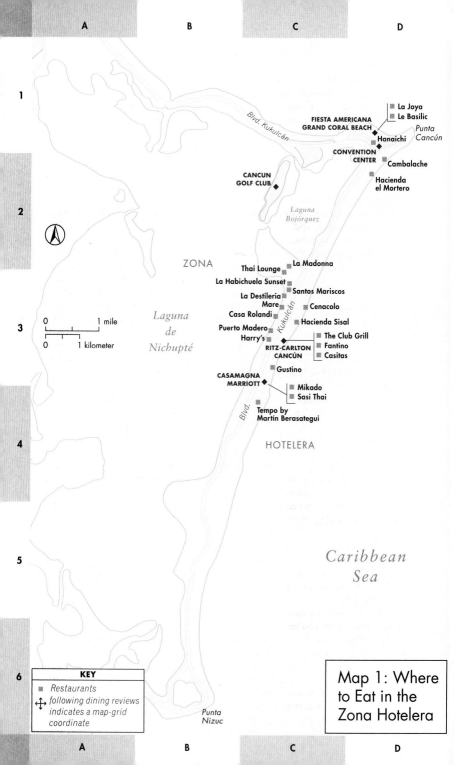

Map 1: Where to Eat in the Zona Hotelera

calamari. Stellar pasta dishes include a delicious lobster ravioli filled with ricotta cheese and served in a white-wine sauce. Cenacolo also has a small wine cave with a romantic table for two (reserve this section in advance). Although it's inside a mall, the restaurant's main dining room is elegant, with stained-glass panels on the ceiling and live piano music. If you're coming by for lunch, note that it opens at 2 pm. ■ TIP→ There's now a second location at Plaza Peninsula on Avenida Bonampak in El Centro. $ *Average main: 379 MP* ⊠ *Kukulcán Plaza, Blvd. Kukulcán, Km 13, Zona Hotelera* ☎ *998/885–3603* ⊕ *www. cenacolo.com.mx* ✢ *1:C3.*

$$$$
INTERNATIONAL
Fodor's Choice
★

✕ **The Club Grill.** Details like a martini lounge, tuxedoed waiters, and live jazz help recreate a swank 1960s ambience at the Club Grill. The romantic dining room is quietly elegant, with rich wood, fresh flowers, crisp linens, and courtyard views. The contemporary menu changes every six months, but might include starters like tuna tartare and mains like tequila duck; a five-course tasting menu, paired with boutique Mexican wines, is available, too. For dessert, try the soufflé trio served with cups of liquid chocolate, coconut cream, and Grand Marnier sauce. Like a waiters' ballet, the delivery of domed silver platters is synchronized among the servers, making the entire dining experience memorable. To cap the evening, women are given a red rose and a box of truffles. ■ TIP→ Reservations are recommended, and a collared dress shirt for men is required. $ *Average main: 676 MP* ⊠ *Ritz-Carlton Cancún, Retorno del Rey 36, off Blvd. Kukulcán, Km 13.5, Zona Hotelera* ☎ *998/881–0822* ⊕ *www.ritzcarlton.com* ☾ *No lunch* ✢ *1:C3.*

$$$$
MEDITERRANEAN

✕ **Fantino.** Reflecting Mexico's rich Spanish heritage, this Mediterranean restaurant lives up to its reputation. Grandeur hits a peak in a ballroom setting, with long-stem roses and hand-painted ceiling frescoes that subtly match the fine china; the velvet walls mounted with candelabras are only overshadowed by the red satin curtains and ocean views. Each course is paired with its own wine. Designed to play with the senses, appetizers moisten the palate in preparation for the seven-course tasting menu. Dishes include watermelon salad with buffalo mozzarella, sautéed foie gras with berries, and vanilla braised veal cheek with squash gnocchi. All ingredients are hand-selected from local farms or air-freighted to the hotel. Just when you think you've seen it all, the waiter wheels over the candy cart, featuring 10 glass towers of handmade sweets. Reservations are recommended, and suggested attire is "resort elegant." $ *Average main: 1016 MP* ⊠ *Ritz-Carlton Cancún, Blvd. Kukulcán, Km 13.5, Zona Hotelera* ☎ *998/881–0822* ⊕ *www. ritzcarlton.com* ⌖ *Reservations essential* ⌂ *Jacket required* ☾ *No lunch* ✢ *1:C3.*

$$$$
ITALIAN

✕ **Gustino.** As soon as you walk down the dramatic entrance staircase, you know you're in for a memorable experience. The circular dining room has artistic lighting and views of the wine cellar and open-air kitchen. The *gamberetti al aglio* appetizer (sautéed shrimp with garlic) is a standout, as are the tagliatelle in truffle sauce and seafood risotto entrées. Other memorable dishes include the sea bass baked in wax paper and the braised veal with prosciutto and wild mushrooms. The service here is impeccable, and saxophone music adds a dash of romance. ■ **TIP→ A private dining area can hold up to 14 guests.** [$] *Average main: 677 MP* ✉ *JW Marriott Resort, Blvd. Kukulcán, Km 14.5, Zona Hotelera* ☎ *998/848–9600, 998/848–9600* 🌐 *www.gustinocancun.com* ✍ *Reservations essential* ⏲ *No lunch* ⊕ *1:C3.*

$$$$ MEXICAN 🍴 **Hacienda el Mortero.** The main draw at one of Cancún's first restaurants is the setting: a replica of a 17th-century hacienda, complete with courtyard fountain, flowering garden, and strolling mariachi band. Although there's nothing outstanding on the traditional Mexican menu, the tortilla soup is very good and the chicken fajitas and ribeye steaks are tasty. Fish lovers may also like the *pescado Veracruzana* (fresh grouper prepared Veracruz-style with olives, garlic, and fresh tomatoes). Sunday brunch is served from 9 to 2. This is a popular restaurant for large groups, so it can get boisterous—especially once guests begin sampling the 110 types of tequila. There's live mariachi music nightly from 7 to 10:30 pm. [$] *Average main: 610 MP* ✉ *Blvd. Kukulcán, Km 9, Zona Hotelera* ☎ *998/848–9800* 🌐 *www.restaurantehaciendaelmortero.com* ⏲ *No lunch Mon.–Sat.* ⊕ *1:D2.*

$$$ MEXICAN 🍴 **Hacienda Sisal.** Built to resemble a sprawling hacienda, this restaurant is warm and intimate, with comfortable high-backed chairs and Mexican paintings. Menu highlights include the goat cheese and mango salad, Tampico chicken breast, New York steak with stuffed pepper, and annatto-seasoned grilled pork chops. Traditional dances from Mexico and the Caribbean are performed on various weeknights in the restaurant's patio section. Children under 12 eat free on Tuesday night. There's a breakfast buffet from 8 to 2 on Sunday, which is the only day when Hacienda Sisal opens early. [$] *Average main: 338 MP* ✉ *Blvd. Kukulcán, Km 13.5, next to Royal Sands Resort, Zona Hotelera* ☎ *998/848–8220* 🌐 *www.haciendasisal.com* ⏲ *No lunch* ⊕ *1:C3.*

$$ SUSHI Fodor's Choice ★ 🍴 **Hanaichi.** It might look like a hole-in-the-wall, but this small Japanese restaurant has some of Cancún's best sushi and is frequented by some of Mexico's best chefs. Expect sashimi, nigiri, and every type of sushi roll imaginable; house specialties include the Copan Roll (deep fried shrimp wrapped in cucumber) and the Cancún Roll (stuffed with eel and scallops). There is a sushi bar on the ground floor and an intimate dining area with a few tables upstairs. Granted, you may not hear crashing waves, but you'll have an authentic Japanese experience for a fraction of what you might pay down the road. ■ **TIP→ It's best to know your sushi if you dine here as the menu is written only in Spanish and Japanese.** [$] *Average main: 203 MP* ✉ *Blvd Kukulcan, Km 9, across from Plaza Caracol, Zona Hotelera* ☎ *998/883–2804* 🌐 *www.hanaichicancun.com* ⊕ *1:D1.*

$$$$ STEAKHOUSE 🍴 **Harry's.** On the lagoon across from the Ritz-Carlton, this contemporary steakhouse is easy to spot: look for the line of luxury cars at valet parking. High-profile locals and visitors alike are drawn to its Vegas–meets–Beverly Hills style. The dimly lit interior is dominated by white stone, with cedar beams adding a touch of warmth. The spectacular menu features glazed duck, Maine lobster, and Kobe beef served with aged Vermont cheddar cheese. If you can get past the glass meat cooler in the lobby, the concept is impressive—steaks are aged in-house for 21–28 days, then grilled and broiled to perfection. Save room for Mini

2

Indulgences, six tasty desserts served in shot glasses. Waiters deliver a tower of cotton candy with the check (try not to faint when you see the total). ■ TIP→ The stone interior creates echoes, so outdoor seating is recommended. $ *Average main: 677 MP* ⊠ *Blvd. Kukulcán, Km 14.2, across from Ritz-Carlton, Zona Hotelera* ☎ *998/840–6550* ⊕ *www. harrys.com.mx* ✦ *1:C3.*

$$$ ✕ **La Destileria.** Be prepared to have your perceptions of tequila changed
MEXICAN forever. In what looks like a Mexican hacienda, complete with an *alambique* (tequila distillery), you can sample from a list of 100 varieties—in shots or superb margaritas—and also visit the on-site tequila museum and store. The traditional Mexican menu focuses on fresh fish and seafood. Other highlights include the *molcajete de arrachera* (a thick beef stew served piping hot in a mortar), and the Talla-style fish fillet from a traditional Acapulco recipe. Midday (1–5 pm) diners can enjoy tequila tastings, appetizers, and a house cocktail for MX$244. Be sure to leave room for the caramel crêpes, a signature Mexican dessert. Reservations are recommended. $ *Average main: 311 MP* ⊠ *Blvd. Kukulcán, Km 12.65, across from Plaza Kukulcán, Zona Hotelera* ☎ *998/885–1086, 998/885–1087* ⊕ *www.ladestileria.com.mx* ✦ *1:C3.*

$$$$ ✕ **La Habichuela Sunset.** Following up on its success in El Centro, this
CARIBBEAN lagoonside eatery opened a second outpost in the bustling Zona Hotelera. Catering to tourists with its Mayan live music show (complete with fire eaters) on Monday, Wednesday, and Friday at 8, the multilevel dining area features a dramatic staircase leading down to an archaeological dig covered by a glass floor. Blending modern and Mayan designs, the restaurant has an outdoor patio with a small stream and illuminated trees. Popular dishes include soft-shell crab tacos, garlic shrimp, and breaded fish served with tamarind and mango sauce. Although known for fresh fish, La Habichuela Sunset also offers chicken, steak, and pasta at inflated prices. Dessert lovers will enjoy the butterscotch crêpes and Mayan coffee. $ *Average main: 406 MP* ⊠ *Blvd. Kukulcán, Km 12.6, Zona Hotelera* ☎ *988/840–6240* ⊕ *www.lahabichuela.com* ✦ *1:C3.*

$$$$ ✕ **La Joya.** Soaring stained-glass windows, a fountain, artwork, and
MEXICAN beautiful furniture from the central part of the country lend drama to this restaurant in the Fiesta Americana Grand Coral Beach. Like the décor, the Mexican food is traditional but creative. The grilled Tampiqueña-style beef is especially popular, as is the sea bass wrapped in maguey leaves. Dishes like chicken mole and cactus leaf with roasted grasshoppers from Oaxaca will appeal to more adventurous eaters, while those with light appetites will appreciate the sampler of mini cochinita pibil–style tacos. Performances by folk dancers and a mariachi band (Tues.–Sat. 7:30–8:30 pm) add to the ambience. $ *Average main: 406 MP* ⊠ *Fiesta Americana Grand Coral Beach, Blvd. Kukulcán, Km 9.5, Zona Hotelera* ☎ *998/881–3200* ⊕ *www.fiestamericanagrand.com* ⊘ *Closed Mon. No lunch* ✦ *1:D1.*

$$$$ ✕ **La Madonna.** This dramatic-looking, three-story restaurant is a great
ITALIAN place to enjoy a selection of 180 martinis, as well as Italian food with a "creative Swiss twist." For starters, try the pan-seared mozzarella wrapped in prosciutto. You can also enjoy classics like fettuccine with shrimp in a grappa sauce, mussels in white wine with saffron cream,

and veal parmigiana served on a bed of homemade basil pasta. Gluten-free pastas are available. Cheese and chocolate lovers can order one of the chef's traditional fondues. In addition to the ground-level patio, there's a pleasant terrace on the third floor. [$] *Average main: 540 MP* ✉ *La Isla Shopping Village, Blvd. Kukulcán, Km 12.5, Zona Hotelera* ☎ *998/883-2222* ⊕ *www.lamadonna.com.mx* ✛ *1:C2.*

$$$$ ✕ **Le Basilic.** If heaven had a restaurant, this would be it: arched bay
MEDITERRANEAN windows, checkered marble floors, live jazz, and exquisite garden
Fodor's Choice views create a stunning backdrop. Fourteen chestnut tables surround a
★ sunken gazebo where orchids bloom. Doubling as a gallery, Le Basilic displays paintings by local artists, and, each Friday and Saturday (by request), an artist paints while you dine. The dishes here—created by French chef Henri Charvet—are served beneath silver domes by tuxedoed waiters. The menu changes every four months but always features fine French-Mediterranean cuisine. As a keepsake, guests are presented with a box of French truffles and refined recipe cards recapping the bill of fare. Note that the dress code is "resort elegant," reservations are recommended, and children are not allowed. ■ TIP→ Since this restaurant is rather intimate, expect quality service, meaning that some people might feel uncomfortable being watched by the attentive waiters. [$] *Average main: 474 MP* ✉ *Fiesta Americana Grand Coral Beach, Blvd. Kukulcán, Km 9.5, Zona Hotelera* ☎ *998/881-3200* ⊕ *www.lebasiliccancun.com* ⌁ *Reservations essential* ⋔ *Jacket required* ☾ *Closed Sun. No lunch* ✛ *1:D1.*

$$$$ ✕ **Mare.** This Italian restaurant from the creators of Cenacolo takes
ITALIAN great pride in its handmade pasta—that's evident as you pass the chef
Fodor's Choice rolling out dough before cutting it into strands with a *chitarra* ("pasta
★ guitar"). Traditional Italian and bold Mediterranean flavors emerge in dishes like the squid ink pasta, lobster risotto, spaghetti with seafood, and garden ravioli with artichoke and zucchini. Mare's stylish setting is equally appealing: everything here is stark white, including the stone facade, grand piano, and even the brick oven, where fresh bread is baked. Come early to watch the sunset, and snag a table on the back terrace overlooking the lagoon. [$] *Average main: 474 MP* ✉ *Blvd. Kukulcán, Km 12.5, Zona Hotelera* ☎ *998/885-2746* ⊕ *www.restaurantemare.com* ✛ *1:C3.*

$$$$ ✕ **Mikado.** Sit around the teppanyaki tables and watch the utensils fly
JAPANESE as the showmen chefs here prepare steaks, seafood, and vegetables.
FAMILY The menu includes Japanese specialties such as *futo-maki* (large sushi rolls) and pan-fried sea bass. The sushi, tempura, grilled salmon, and beef teriyaki are all feasts fit for a shogun. For added flavor, several dishes are infused with sake or braised with Sapporo beer, like the oriental short ribs served with crispy onions. Unlike most restaurants in Cancún, however, there's no outdoor seating or scenic view. ■ TIP→ If you're looking for a quiet, romantic meal, consider going elsewhere—this is a lively place that's popular with families. [$] *Average main: 610 MP* ✉ *CasaMagna Marriott, Blvd. Kukulcán, Km 14.5, Zona Hotelera* ☎ *998/881-2036* ⊕ *www.mikadocancun.com* ☾ *No lunch* ✛ *1:C3.*

$$$$ STEAKHOUSE Fodor's Choice ★

🍴 **Puerto Madero.** Modeled after the dock warehouses that have been converted into modern eateries in Argentina's Puerto Madero, this steak-and-seafood house gets rave reviews from locals. The grilled octopus seasoned with paprika is exceptional, as is the Alaskan halibut prepared with white wine, shallots, and fresh pepper. No matter what you order, request a side of soufflé potatoes (potatoes fried until they're puffed)—bite down and they crackle on your tongue. A new sushi menu lists swanky appetizers. Adding to the cosmopolitan ambience is a fun-loving staff, most of whom have been here over 15 years. If the restaurant is too loud inside, ask for a table outside on the patio overlooking the lagoon. Reservations are recommended on weekends. [$] *Average main: 474 MP* ✉ *Blvd. Kukulcán, Km 14.1, Zona Hotelera* ☎ *998/885–2829* 🌐 *www.puertomaderorestaurantes.com* ✥ *1:C3.*

$$ MEXICAN

🍴 **Santos Mariscos.** This kitschy cantina, marked by a string of Christmas lights dangling over the patio, is a tribute to masked wrestling champion El Santo. Just south of La Isla Shopping Village, its reasonable prices, retro décor (picture rainbow lawn chairs and sculptures of the Virgin Mary holding plastic roses), plus surprisingly good food attract locals who work in the Zona. Menu highlights include fried cheese tacos and shrimp tacos with seven types of sauces. Tamarindo margaritas are also very refreshing. A bright red bar dominates the downstairs, and upstairs there's a dining area with a small outdoor patio. ■ **TIP→ This isn't a fine-dining spot, so don't be surprised if the one waiter on staff serves you in stages.** [$] *Average main: 162 MP* ✉ *Blvd. Kukulcán, Km 12.7, Zona Hotelera* ☎ *998/840–6300* ✥ *1:C3.*

$$$$ THAI

🍴 **Sasi Thai.** Despite the street-facing views, this open-air restaurant has one of the most pleasant settings in Cancún. Six thatch-roof cabanas—each housing four tables—are staggered on a hill and dimly lighted with cubed candles and marble lanterns. Plank floors lead to a bamboo bar where fruity mojitos and martinis are prepared. The menu features traditional Thai cuisine such as spring rolls, pork dumplings, red duck curry, and pad thai with chicken or shrimp. The mango crème brûlée with ginger sorbet makes it worth a special visit. [$] *Average main: 474 MP* ✉ *Casa Magna Marriott, Blvd. Kukulcán, Km 14.5, Zona Hotelera* ☎ *998/881–2092* 🌐 *www.sasi-thai.com* ⏲ *No lunch* ✥ *1:C3.*

$$$$ ECLECTIC Fodor's Choice ★

🍴 **Tempo by Martin Berasategui.** This elegant restaurant in the Paradisus Cancún is the latest Caribbean offering from acclaimed Spanish chef Martin Berasategui. Its stylish white dining room is enhanced by mirrored columns, leather chairs, orchid accents, and white-glove service. The adults-only culinary experience includes a seven-course tasting menu and wines from around the world, chosen by sommelier Carlos Duarte. Although the tasting menu changes regularly, it might contain dishes like fennel pearls in emulsified risotto, warm foie gras with potatoes, and suckling pig with papaya and citrus purée; à la carte options such as beef tenderloin with Swiss chard and Camembert bonbons or grilled white tuna with mango and capers are also available. Save room for the requisite finishing touch: delectable petit fours. [$] *Average main: 542 MP* ✉ *Paradisus Cancún, Blvd. Kukulcán, Km 16.5, Zona Hotelera* ☎ *998/881* 🌐 *www.paradisus.com* ✍ *Reservations essential* ⏲ *No lunch* ✥ *1:C4.*

$$$$ THAI 🍴 **Thai Lounge.** Expect a unique dining experience from the minute you enter this garden oasis. After all, not many restaurants have a dolphin aquarium in the bar area. The individual huts with thatch roofs provide an intimate setting to sample spicy Thai dishes like roasted duck in coconut red curry or the house favorite, a deep-fried fish fillet prepared with ginger, garlic, and a tamarind chile sauce. The bill of fare also features such traditional items as shrimp curry, Thai salad, and spicy chicken soup. Amp up the romance quotient by calling ahead to reserve one of the palapa casitas perched over the water on stilts. ■ **TIP→ There are only seventeen tables, so reservations are highly recommended.** [$] *Average main: 338 MP* ✉ *Plaza la Isla, Blvd. Kukulcán, Km 12.5, Zona Hotelera* ☎ *998/176–8070* 🌐 *www.thai.com.mx* 🕑 *No lunch* ✥ *1:C3.*

EL CENTRO

$$ VEGETARIAN 🍴 **100% Natural.** You'll be surrounded by plants and modern Mayan sculptures when you eat at this open-air restaurant. Start the day with one of the signature omelets and a *bebida inteligente* ("intelligent drink") which combines fruit juice with ginseng. The menu has soups, salads, pastas, and other vegetarian items. Sandwiches, soy burgers, and stuffed pitas are prepared with fresh-baked breads; for those craving meat, there's grilled chicken done fajita-style. Mexican and Italian specialties are also available. The neighboring 100% Integral shop sells whole-wheat breads and other goodies. [$] *Average main: 135 MP* ✉ *Av. Sunyaxchén 62, Sm 25, El Centro* ☎ *998/884–0102* 🌐 *www.100natural.com* ✥ *2:A3.*

$$$$ ARGENTINE 🍴 **Bandoneon.** Entering Bandoneon you might think you've taken a right turn and ended up in Buenos Aires. Every detail replicates the streets of Argentina, right down to the cobblestone floors and dramatic tango music. Walls are adorned with antique *bandoneons* (concertinas, similar to accordions) and paintings of tango dancers. In the center of the restaurant, two enormous lighthouse structures guard more than 500 bottles of wine. The broad menu features starters like smoked marlin and charcoal-grilled provolone cheese; mains include pasta, fish, and chicken, but steak is the star. The sizzling ribeye is extremely tender; however, health-conscious dinners should request a leaner cut. If you still have room, order the brandy-soaked cake roll with caramel filling for dessert. ■ **TIP→ With 160 seats, this place can be a bit chaotic; reservations are recommended Thursday through Saturday.** [$] *Average main: 406 MP* ✉ *Av. Bonampak at Nichupté, El Centro* ☎ *998/889–9500* 🌐 *www.bandoneonrestaurantes.com* ✥ *2:D6.*

$$$$ FRENCH Fodor's Choice ★ 🍴 **duMexique.** Discreetly located on bustling Avenida Bonampak, this hidden gem created by Chef Alain Grimond and his wife, Sonya, has an intimate dinner-party feel. Doubling as a gallery, the dining room features modern art, a grand piano, red velvet chairs, and a crystal chandelier that casts spectrums of light onto the ceiling. Accommodating only 20 guests per evening, duMexique is a dream come true for foodies, as Chef Alain marshals his 55 years of culinary experience to prepare each dish with passion. The French menu (featuring five appetizers, five entrées, and four desserts) changes daily; selections might

include foie gras, duckling with risotto, or entrecôte with wine sauce. By calling ahead, you can request *soufflé de huitlacoche,* a delicacy made from mushrooms that grow on cornstalks. The crème brûlée is magnifique! ■ TIP➜ Visit the kitchen, where the master chef's awards are displayed. Ⓢ *Average main: 542 MP* ✉ *Av. Bonampak 109, Sm 3, El Centro* ☏ *998/884–5919* ✍ *Reservations essential* ⊗ *Closed Sun. No lunch* ✛ *2:D3.*

$ ✕ **El Cejas.** The seafood is fresh at this open-air eatery, and the clientele
SEAFOOD   is lively—often joining in song with the musicians who stroll among the tables. If you've had a wild night, try the *vuelva a la vida,* or "return to life" (conch, oysters, shrimp, octopus, calamari, and fish with a hot tomato sauce). The kitchen serves crab (stuffed, steamed, or fried) and whole-fried fish that's crispy outside and moist inside. The ceviche and spicy shrimp soup are also good, though the quality can be inconsistent. Located at the bustling Mercado Veintiocho, this no-frills local favorite is open from 9 to 7. Ⓢ *Average main: 130 MP* ✉ *Mercado Veintiocho, Sm. 26, Loc 90–100, El Centro* ✛ *2:A3.*

$$ ✕ **El Oasis.** This aptly named eatery is a welcome respite from El Cen-
SEAFOOD   tro's busy streets. A small wooden bridge leads into a palapa, which is colorfully decorated with turquoise chairs, mosaic flooring, seashell lamps, and a bamboo bar. Diners can relax to the sounds of a cascading waterfall, skirted by palm trees and tropical plants. House specials include grilled seafood with rice, fish fillet with coconut cream, and smaller dishes like ceviche or *aguachiles* (spicy lime shrimp). Many of the dishes can be prepared with your choice of mango, tamarind, or guava salsa. Open only from 1 to 7, El Oasis is popular with the locals. Note that menus are in Spanish, and the staff don't speak much English. Ⓢ *Average main: 140 MP* ✉ *Av. Yaxchilan, Sm 17, Mza 2, Lote 3, across from Costco, El Centro* ☏ *998/884–4106* ⊕ *www.eloasismariscos.com* ⊗ *No dinner* ✛ *2:B6.*

$$ ✕ **Labná.** Yucatecan cuisine reaches new and exotic heights at this
MEXICAN   Mayan-theme restaurant, with fabulous dishes prepared by Chef Elviro
Fodor'sChoice   Pol. The *papadzules* (tortillas stuffed with eggs and covered with pump-
★   kin seed sauce) are a delicious starter; for an entrée, try the *poc chuc* (tender pork loin in a sour orange sauce) or *longaniza de Valladolid* (traditional sausage from the city of Valladolid). The "Yucatan Tour" sampler will give you a little taste of everything. Finish off your meal with some *maja blanco* (white pudding), and Xtabentun-infused Mayan coffee. Weekdays from 12 to 5, there's a buffet (MX$200) that's popular with locals. Owned by the same team as La Habichuela, this spot serves the most authentic regional food. Ⓢ *Average main: 140 MP* ✉ *Av. Margaritas 29, Sm 22, El Centro* ☏ *998/892–3056* ⊕ *www.labnaonline. com* ✛ *2:A3.*

$$$ ✕ **La Dolce Vita.** The grande dame of Cancún restaurants delivers on
ITALIAN   the promise of its name (which means "the sweet life" in Italian). In
Fodor'sChoice   business since 1983, this local favorite has candlelit tables and discreet
★   waiters who will make you feel as if you've been transported to Italy. The fare includes homemade pizzas and pastas such as Bolognese-style lasagna; veal scaloppini and calamari steak in shrimp and lobster sauce are other options. The wine list is excellent, and the dessert truffle is

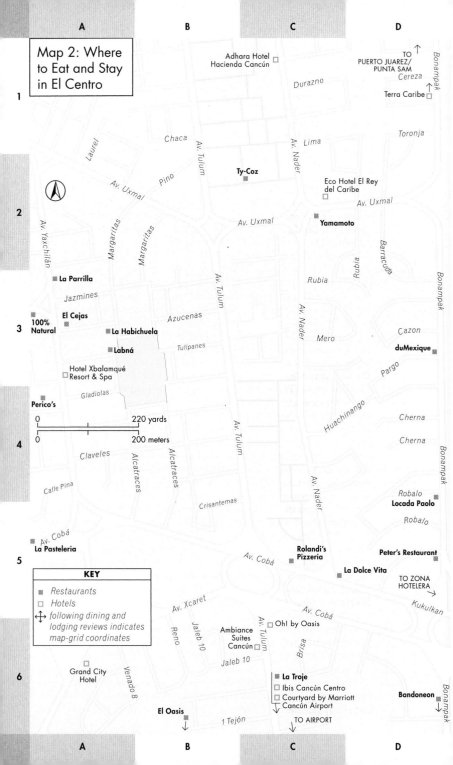

Map 2: Where to Eat and Stay in El Centro

A   **B**   **C**   **D**

Adhara Hotel Hacienda Cancún

Durazno

TO PUERTO JUAREZ/ PUNTA SAM

Cereza

Bonampak

Terra Caribe

1

Chaca

Av. Tulum

Av. Nader

Lima

Toronja

Laurel

Pino

Ty-Coz

Eco Hotel El Rey del Caribe

Av. Uxmal

Av. Uxmal

Av. Uxmal

Av. Uxmal

Yamamoto

2

Av. Yaxchilán

Margaritas

Margaritas

Av. Tulum

Rubia

Rubia

Barracuda

Bonampak

La Parrilla

Jazmines

Azucenas

Av. Nader

Mero

Cazon

100% Natural

El Cejas

La Habichuela

duMexique

3

Labná

Tulipanes

Pargo

Hotel Xbalamqué Resort & Spa

Gladiolas

Huachinango

Cherna

Perico's

0   220 yards

0   200 meters

Av. Tulum

Cherna

Bonampak

4

Claveles

Alcatraces

Alcatraces

Av. Nader

Calle Pina

Robalo

Crisantemas

Locada Paolo

Robalo

Av. Cobá

La Pasteleria

Rolandi's Pizzeria

Peter's Restaurant

5

Av. Cobá

La Dolce Vita

TO ZONA HOTELERA

Kukulkan

KEY

■ Restaurants

□ Hotels

⟷ following dining and lodging reviews indicates map-grid coordinates

Av. Xcaret

Reno

Jaleb 10

Ambiance Suites Cancún

Av. Tulum

Brisa

Av. Cobá

Oh! by Oasis

Jaleb 10

Grand City Hotel

Venado 8

La Troje

Ibis Cancún Centro

Courtyard by Marriott

Cancún Airport

Bandoneon

Bonampak

6

El Oasis

1 Tejón

TO AIRPORT

A   **B**   **C**   **D**

a must for chocolate lovers. Be patient when waiting for your order, though, as good food takes time to prepare. $ *Average main: 338 MP* ✉ *Av. Cobá 87, Sm 3, El Centro* ☎ *998/884–3393* ⊕ *www.ladolcevita cancun.com* ✛ *2:D5.*

$$$ ✕ **La Habichuela.** Open since 1977, the much-loved "Green Bean" has an
CARIBBEAN elegant yet cozy indoor dining room plus an outdoor area full of Mayan sculptures and local flora. Seafood lovers can satisfy their cravings by ordering Caribbean lobster tail or giant shrimp prepared 10 different ways. The menu also features chicken, pasta, and grilled kabobs. Finish off your meal with *xtabentún*, a Mayan liqueur made with honey and anise. If you prefer to stay in the Zona Hotelera, there is a second location (dubbed La Habichuela Sunset) on Boulevard Kukulcán, but the prices there are slightly higher. $ *Average main: 271 MP* ✉ *Av. Margaritas 25, Sm 22, El Centro* ☎ *998/884–3158* ⊕ *www.lahabichuela. com* ✛ *2:A3.*

$$$ ✕ **La Parrilla.** With its flamboyant live mariachi music and energetic
MEXICAN waiters, this place is a Cancún classic. The menu isn't fancy, but it offers good, basic Mexican food—including the sizzling fajitas, thick burritos, and 30 different taco dishes. Two reliably tasty choices are the mixed grill (with chicken, beef, and shrimp) and the Tampiqueña-style steak. Combining entertainment and cuisine, waiters flame broil lobster, salmon, shrimp, and filet mignon directly at your table. There's also a wide selection of tequilas to accompany your meal. $ *Average main: 216 MP* ✉ *Av. Yaxchilán 51, Sm 22, El Centro* ☎ *998/287–8118* ⊕ *www.laparrilla.com.mx* ✛ *2:A3.*

$ ✕ **La Pasteleria.** This cheery café and bakery has comfortable *equipales*
CAFÉ (rustic Mexican chairs) to plop into as you sample terrific soups, salads, and fish dishes. The eggs Benedict and crêpes are what keep locals coming back (the turkey breast crepe makes a perfect lunch). For travelers with a sweet tooth, a variety of delectable desserts is baked on site. Somewhat difficult to find, this downtown gem is on bustling Avenida Cobá near Wal-Mart. $ *Average main: 108 MP* ✉ *Plaza Malecon las Americas, Av. Cobá 7, Sm 25, El Centro* ☎ *998/193–1150* ⊕ *www. pasteleria.com.mx* ✛ *2:A5.*

$$$ ✕ **La Troje.** From the moment you enter the garden patio, you'll feel as if
ECLECTIC you've stumbled onto a local hideaway. A brick staircase leads into the main dining area, where Chef Ana Cano and her daughters prepare a vast menu that melds French, Italian, and Mexican flavors. Homemade pastas, pizzas, and crêpes are served along with various meat dishes (try the grilled chicken stuffed with spinach, apricots, and cream cheese). You can also choose from among 21 salads, all with the distinctive flavors of fruits, nuts, cheeses, and tangy dressings. ■TIP➔ **There's a 30% discount on food and wine on Tuesday. Come for the cuisine and setting, not the service—waitstaff can be rather inhospitable.** $ *Average main: 203 MP* ✉ *Av. Acanceh, Sm 15, Mza 3, Lote 3, El Centro* ☎ *998/887–9556* ⊕ *www.latrojedecancun.com* ✛ *2:C6.*

$$$ ✕ **Locanda Paolo.** Flowers and artwork lend warmth to this sophisticated
ITALIAN Italian restaurant, where the cuisine includes linguine with lobster, angel hair pasta with seafood, specialty lasagnas, plus assorted meat and fish dishes. Despite the formal setting, the waiters are laid-back and seem to

know everyone who walks in the door (most patrons are locals who've been dining here for more than 20 years). On any given night, many of Chef Paolo Ceravolo's offerings are colorful and innovative specials that do not appear on the menu. The international wines are another major draw. **■ TIP→ If you're coming for lunch, plan on a late one: Locanda Paolo opens at 2 pm daily.** [$] *Average main: 257 MP* ✉ *Av. Bonampak 145, Sm 3, corner of Calle Jurel, El Centro* ☎ *998/887–2627* 🌐 *www.locandapaolo.com* ✥ *2:D5.*

$$$ MEXICAN 🍴 **Perico's.** Okay—it's a tourist trap. But it's a really fun, albeit dated, one. Bar stools are topped with saddles, and waiters dressed as revolutionaries serve flaming drinks and desserts while mariachi and marimba bands play (loudly). Every so often everyone jumps up to join the conga line; your reward for galloping through the restaurant and nearby streets is a free shot of tequila. With 300 seats, this place can sometimes feel a bit empty. The Mexican menu (tacos, seafood, fajitas, and such) is passable—the real reason to come is the nonstop party. For a photo op, stop in the lobby, where you can try on traditional Mexican clothing and pose with props like sombreros and ponchos. [$] *Average main: 271 MP* ✉ *Av. Yaxchilán 61, Sm 25, El Centro* ☎ *998/884–3152* 🌐 *www.pericos.com.mx* ⏲ *No lunch* ✥ *2:A4.*

$$$ INTERNATIONAL Fodor'sChoice ★ 🍴 **Peter's Restaurant.** Conveniently located at the gateway to El Centro, this family-run fine dining establishment is one of the best deals in Cancún. Although it has only six tables, Peter's Restaurant has an impressive menu that gives international dishes a Mexican twist—think foie gras with hibiscus or grilled salmon with potato-chipotle mash. Portions are generous, and the flavors are outstanding. For something lighter, try the Claudia Salad, a mix of field greens with raspberry vinaigrette named after personable Chef Peter's lovely wife. The key lime pie with tequila sorbet provides a refreshing finish, but, for a local's secret, request the off-the-menu chocolate brownie and ice cream drizzled with habañero honey. [$] *Average main: 271 MP* ✉ *Av. Bonampak, Sm 3, between Robalo and Sierra, El Centro* ☎ *998/251–9310* ⏲ *Closed Mon. June–Nov. No lunch* ✥ *2:D5*

$$ PIZZA 🍴 **Rolandi's Pizzeria.** A Cancún landmark for more than 35 years—with outposts in nearby Isla Mujeres, Cozumel, and Playa del Carmen—Rolandi's continues to draw crowds with its scrumptious wood-fired pizzas. There are 20 varieties to choose from; the most popular, Pizza Del Patrón, is topped with tomatoes, prosciutto, arugula, and mascarpone cheese. The calzones are smothered with olive oil and packed with fresh ingredients like asparagus, mushrooms, and ham. Homemade pasta dishes like the veal-stuffed ravioli or vegetable lasagna are also very good. **■ TIP→ Check the website for discounts.** [$] *Average main: 189 MP* ✉ *Av. Cobá 12, Sm 5, El Centro* ☎ *998/884–4047* 🌐 *www.rolandipizzeria.com* ✥ *2:B5.*

$ CAFÉ 🍴 **Ty-Coz.** Tucked behind the Comercial Mexicana grocery store and across from the bus station on Avenida Tulum, this inexpensive restaurant serves croissants and freshly brewed coffee that make a delicious breakfast combo. At lunchtime, stop in for a huge sandwich stuffed with all the deli classics, but be prepared to wait a while since lines can get long. There are also a few vegetarian items on the menu. The company has recently branched out to offer "Ty-Coz Express" locations, usually connected to local gas stations or convenience stores. $ *Average main: 81 MP* ✉ *Av. Tulum, Sm 2, El Centro* ☎ 998/884–6060 ⊕ *www. tycozmexico.com.mx* ▬ *No credit cards* ☉ *Closed Sun.* ✛ 2:C2.

$$$

JAPANESE

✕ **Yamamoto.** As the oldest Japanese restaurant in Cancún, Yamamoto has some of the best sushi in El Centro. In addition to sashimi, there's a menu of traditional Japanese dishes like chicken teriyaki and tempura for those who prefer their food cooked. Large groups can order combination platters of sushi, sashimi, *kushikatsu*, and *gyoza*. The dining room is tranquil, with Japanese art and bamboo accents, but you can also call to have food delivered to your hotel room. ■TIP➔ **If you're used to an early lunch or late dinner, take note that this restaurant is open from 1:30 to 8 pm.** $ *Average main: 230 MP* ✉ *Av. Uxmal 31, Sm 3, El Centro* ☎ 998/887–3366 ⊕ *www.yamamoto-cancun.com* ✛ 2:C2.

WHERE TO STAY

PUNTA SAM

The area north of Cancún is slowly being developed into an alternative hotel zone, known informally as the Zona Hotelera Norte or Playa Mujeres. This is an ideal area for a tranquil beach vacation, because the shops, eateries, and nightlife of Cancún are about 30 minutes away by cab. If you decide against an all-inclusive plan, be sure to factor in about MX$540 in cab fees (each way) from Punta Sam to Cancún restaurants.

$$$$

ALL-INCLUSIVE

Fodor'sChoice

★

▥ **The Beloved Hotel.** One of the area's only boutique-style all-inclusives, this modern sugar-cube-like structure is stylishly decorated in creams and whites, and offers the perfect balance between luxury and comfort. **Pros:** great food; Wi-Fi signal reaches beach; personalized service; tequila tastings. **Cons:** narrow beach lined with sea grass; swim-up bar is in the shade; one-way cab fare to Cancún is MX$480. $ *Rooms from: $549* ✉ *Vialidad Paseo Mujeres, Sm 3, Mza 1, Lote 10, Zona Continental de Isla Mujeres* ☎ 998/872–8730 ⊕ *www.belovedhotels. com* ⤳ *109 rooms* ⦿*All-inclusive* ✛ 3:A1.

$$$$

ALL-INCLUSIVE

▥ **Excellence Playa Mujeres.** North of mainland Cancún, this adults-only resort lends luxury to the all-inclusive concept. **Pros:** beautiful property; never feels crowded; doesn't operate as a time-share. **Cons:** $40 charge for spa facilities; 15-minute drive to El Centro, 30-minute drive to Zona Hotelera; no children under 18. $ *Rooms from: $480* ✉ *Prolongacíon Bonampak s/n, Sm 003, Mza 001, Lote Terrenos 001, Zona Continental de Isla Mujeres* ☎ 866/540–2585, 998/872–8600 ⊕ *www.excellence-resorts.com* ⤳ *450 rooms* ⦿*All-inclusive* ✛ 3:A1.

$$$$

RESORT

▥ **Villa del Palmar.** Blending Mayan and modern architecture, this five-star resort makes you feel right at home. **Pros:** free non-motorized sports equipment; on-site minimart; complimentary Cancún shuttle; walking distance to Isla Mujeres ferry; great service. **Cons:** mosquitoes; seaweed in water; time-share pitch. $ *Rooms from: $310* ✉ *Carretera Punta Sam, Km 5.2, Zona Continental de Isla Mujeres* ☎ 998/193–2600, 877/845–3795 ⊕ *www.villapalmarcancun.com* ⤳ *125 rooms, 290 suites* ⦿*Multiple meal plans* ✛ 3:A1.

ZONA HOTELERA

$$ HOTEL 🏨 **Aloft Cancún.** Near the convention center, this hip Starwood property has a fresh, modern concept that generates quite a social scene. **Pros:** free parking and Wi-Fi; pet- and child-friendly; within walking distance to main clubs. **Cons:** small rooms; not on beach; meals not included. [$] *Rooms from: $138* ✉ *Blvd. Kukulcán, Km 9, across from Fiesta Americana Grand Coral, Zona Hotelera* ☎ *998/848–9900* 🌐 *www.starwoodhotels.com* 🛏 *177 rooms* 🍴 *No meals* ✥ *3:C2.*

$$$$ ALL-INCLUSIVE FAMILY 🏨 **Barceló Costa Cancún.** Ferries to Isla Mujeres are just steps away from this active resort near El Embarcadero; however, the location also means the beach here is quite small and there are often boats passing by. **Pros:** great for kids; close to Embarcadero; good water-sports center. **Cons:** no a/c in lobby; small beach area; check-in/check-out times are chaotic in the lobby area; charge for Wi-Fi. [$] *Rooms from: $300* ✉ *Blvd. Kukulcán, Km 4.5, Zona Hotelera* ☎ *998/849–7100, 800/227–2356* 🌐 *www.barcelo.com* 🛏 *358 rooms* 🍴 *All-inclusive* ✥ *3:B1.*

$$$ ALL-INCLUSIVE 🏨 **Barceló TuCancún Beach.** Just behind the massive Kukulcán Plaza and a short distance from La Isla, this lively resort is an ideal location for mall addicts; however, there's enough to keep nonshoppers occupied, too—including volleyball games and water-polo matches in the activities pool. **Pros:** near two of Cancún's biggest malls; wide range of activities for children and adults; four handicapped-accessible rooms. **Cons:** extra fees for using Wi-Fi, safes, and such; only half the rooms have water views; hotel feels dated; chaotic lobby during check-in/check-out times. [$] *Rooms from: $204* ✉ *Blvd. Kukulcán, Km 13.5, Zona Hotelera* ☎ *998/891–5900, 800/227–2356* 🌐 *www.barcelo.com* 🛏 *316 rooms, 16 villas* 🍴 *All-inclusive* ✥ *3:C3.*

$$ HOTEL 🏨 **Beach Scape Kin-Ha Villas & Suites.** This condo hotel is a wonderful place for families thanks to its tranquil beach and relaxed atmosphere. **Pros:** all rooms have balconies; peaceful location; one of Cancún's best beaches. **Cons:** three-story hotel has no elevator; no children's programs; meals not included. [$] *Rooms from: $186* ✉ *Blvd. Kukulcán, Km 8.5, Zona Hotelera* ☎ *998/891–5400* 🌐 *www.beachscape.com.mx* 🛏 *49 rooms, 47 suites* 🍴 *No meals* ✥ *3:C2.*

$$ RESORT 🏨 **The Bel Air Collection Cancún.** On the south end of Boulevard Kukulcán, this chic resort is aimed at adults looking for a tranquil hideaway. **Pros:** all-inclusive plan available; aesthetically pleasing design. **Cons:** no kids under 12; open-air lobby can be very wet and windy in rainy season; patchy Wi-Fi; rooms need work. [$] *Rooms from: $150* ✉ *Blvd. Kukulcán, Km 20.5, Zona Hotelera* ☎ *998/193–1770* 🌐 *www.belaircollection.com* 🛏 *149 rooms, 19 suites* 🍴 *Multiple meal plans* ✥ *3:B6.*

$$$ RESORT FAMILY 🏨 **CasaMagna Marriott Cancún Resort.** The sweeping grounds and arched walkways that lead up to this six-story, hacienda-style building will make you forget you're at a Marriott. **Pros:** more culturally traditional than most Marriotts; excellent Thai restaurant; gorgeous views from most rooms; newly remodeled rooms. **Cons:** geared to groups and conventions, which account for 60% of the business; no designated children's pool; Wi-Fi (MX$245 per day) can be spotty. [$] *Rooms from: $235* ✉ *Blvd. Kukulcán, Km 14.5, Zona Hotelera* ☎ *998/881–2000,*

800/900–8800 🌐 www.marriott.com ⇆ 414 rooms, 38 suites 🍴 Multiple meal plans ✥ 3:C4.

$$$$ ALL-INCLUSIVE FAMILY **Fiesta Americana Condesa Cancún.** More laid-back than the Fiesta Americana Grand Coral Beach, this sister property is easily recognized by the 118-foot-tall palapa that covers its lobby. **Pros:** friendly staff; scheduled activities on the hour; smaller pools designated for children. **Cons:** halls get slippery when it rains; sound carries between floors; popular with convention-goers and tour groups. [$] *Rooms from: $430 ✉ Blvd. Kukulcán, Km 16.5, Zona Hotelera ☎ 998/881–4200 🌐 www.fiestaamericana.com/cancun ⇆ 476 rooms, 26 suites 🍴 All-inclusive ✥ 3:B4.*

$$$$ RESORT Fodor's Choice ★ **Fiesta Americana Grand Coral Beach.** Luxury lovers will feel at home in this distinctive all-suites hotel, which boasts both an award-winning restaurant (Le Basilic) and Latin America's largest spa (the 40,000-square-foot Gem). **Pros:** stellar spa and restaurant; enormous pool with swim-up bars; complimentary kids' club; business center with private offices; excellent service. **Cons:** chilly pool water; too big for some. [$] *Rooms from: $550 ✉ Blvd. Kukulcán, Km 9.5, Zona Hotelera ☎ 998/881–3200 🌐 www.fiestamericanagrand.com ⇆ 602 suites 🍴 No meals ✥ 3:D2.*

$$$ ALL-INCLUSIVE **Golden Parnassus Resort & Spa.** Accommodations at this all-inclusive, adults-only resort are decorated with rich wood furnishings and a cream-and-plum palette. **Pros:** free shuttle to sister property Great Parnassus Resort & Spa; evening entertainment; great tiki bar. **Cons:** no kids under 18; charge for Wi-Fi; thin towels and poor lighting; dated common areas. [$] *Rooms from: $200 ✉ Blvd. Kukulcán, Km 14.5, Retorno San Miguelito, Lote 37, Zona Hotelera ☎ 998/287–1400 🌐 www.parnassusresorts.com ⇆ 214 rooms 🍴 All-inclusive ✥ 3:C3.*

$$$$ ALL-INCLUSIVE FAMILY **Gran Caribe Real.** There's no such thing as a standard room at this all-suite resort, where the most basic option is a spacious junior suite with a sofa bed, sitting area, flat-screen TV, stocked minibar, and balcony. **Pros:** wide array of activities; gym has yoga and spin classes; access to four sister properties in Playa del Carmen and Cancún. **Cons:** mediocre restaurants; pools tend to get crowded and rowdy. [$] *Rooms from: $329 ✉ Blvd. Kukulcán, Km 11.5, Zona Hotelera ☎ 998/881–5500, 800/760–0944 🌐 www.realresorts.com ⇆ 487 suites 🍴 All-inclusive ✥ 3:C2.*

$$$$ ALL-INCLUSIVE **Grand Oasis Cancún.** Comprising a main building (simply called "Pyramid") and two flanking ones, the Grand Oasis sits next door to sister property and Spring Break mecca the Oasis Cancún. **Pros:** enormous pool area; lively atmosphere. **Cons:** MX$82 charge for room safe; large grounds require fair amount of walking; too boisterous for some; staff lack attention to detail and service. [$] *Rooms from: $350 ✉ Blvd. Kukulcán, Km 16.5, Zona Hotelera ☎ 888/774–0040, 998/881–7000 🌐 www.grandoasiscancunresort.com ⇆ 765 rooms 🍴 All-inclusive ✥ 3:B4.*

$$ ALL-INCLUSIVE **Grand Park Royal Cancún Caribe.** There's a wide variety of accommodations at the Grand Park Royal, including the newest category of beachfront villas with a private beach area and personal concierge. **Pros:** most rooms face ocean; excellent pool areas. **Cons:** Wi-Fi and gym

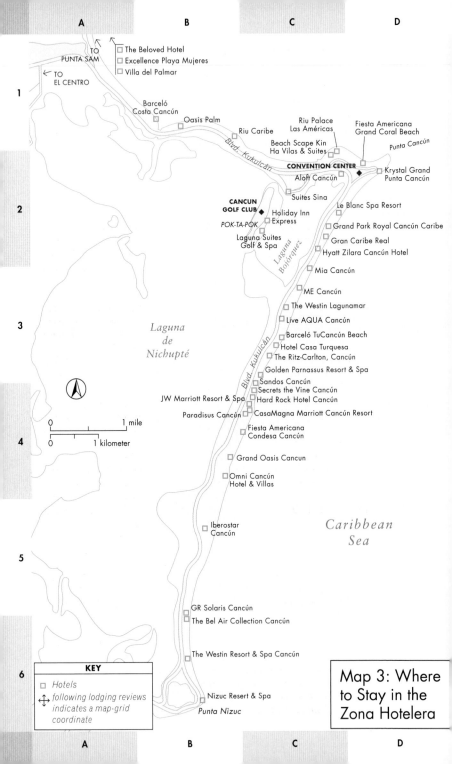

Map 3: Where to Stay in the Zona Hotelera

cost extra; reservations required at restaurants. $ *Rooms from: $190* ✉ *Blvd. Kukulcán, Km 10.5, Zona Hotelera* ☎ 998/848–7800 ⊕ *www. park-royalhotels.com* ⤳ *311 rooms* |○| *All-inclusive* ✢ 3:C2.

$$$
ALL-INCLUSIVE

⬚ **GR Solaris Cancún.** More upscale than its Cancún sister properties (the Royal Solaris and GR Caribe), this resort has a lively atmosphere but offers a few quiet spots that are off-limits to children, including an adults-only pool and outdoor massage area. **Pros:** lighted tennis court; 24-hr room service. **Cons:** noisy pool area; loud music in common areas; Jacuzzis lack privacy; Wi-Fi costs extra. $ *Rooms from: $267* ✉ *Blvd. Kukulcán, Km 18.5, Zona Hotelera* ☎ 998/848–8400 ⊕ *www. hotelessolaris.com* ⤳ *306 rooms* |○| *All-inclusive* ✢ 3:B5.

$$$$
ALL-INCLUSIVE
FAMILY

⬚ **Hard Rock Hotel Cancún.** This resort's focus on music and entertainment fits right into Cancún's energetic atmosphere. **Pros:** activities for children and teens; two tennis courts; excellent Japanese restaurant; friendly staff. **Cons:** some rooms lack ocean views; no water sports; time-share sales pitch; rock-hard beds. $ *Rooms from: $450* ✉ *Blvd. Kukulcán, Km 14.5, Zona Hotelera* ☎ 998/881–3600 ⊕ *www.hrhcancun.com* ⤳ *601 rooms, 24 suites* |○| *All-inclusive* ✢ 3:C4.

$$
HOTEL

⬚ **Holiday Inn Express.** Within walking distance of the Pok-Ta-Pok Golf Club, this 1980's hotel caters to tourists seeking an affordable alternative to pricey resorts. **Pros:** good rates; free entrance to Cocos Beach Club; largest Holiday Inn pool in Mexico. **Cons:** simple, dated rooms; no elevator; not on the beach. $ *Rooms from: $80* ✉ *Paseo Pok-Ta-Pok, lotes 21 and 22, off Blvd. Kukulcán, Km 7.5, Zona Hotelera* ☎ 998/883–2200, 888/465–4329 ⊕ *www.hiexpress.com/cancunmex* ⤳ *119 rooms* |○| *Breakfast* ✢ 3:C2.

$$$$
HOTEL

⬚ **Hotel Casa Turquesa.** Perched on a hill overlooking the ocean, this all-suites boutique hotel doubles as an impressive gallery showcasing works by famous artists. **Pros:** lighted tennis court; 24-hr room service; intimate, personalized feel. **Cons:** ground-floor rooms lack full ocean views; not child-friendly; MX$340 charge for Wi-Fi. $ *Rooms from: $350* ✉ *Boulevard Kukulcán, Km. 13.5, Zona Hotelera* ☎ 998/193–2260 ⊕ *www.casaturquesa.com* ⤳ *29 rooms* |○| *Multiple meal plans* ✢ 3:C3.

$$$$
ALL-INCLUSIVE
Fodor's Choice
★

⬚ **Hyatt Zilara Cancún Hotel.** Luxury is the focus at this high-end, adults-only resort, where every room has mahogany furniture, Jacuzzis, ocean views, balconies with hammocks, and "magic boxes" that allow room service to be delivered without ever opening the door. **Pros:** two-person Jacuzzis in suites; ocean view from all suites; turtle release program Oct.–Nov.; bike tours. **Cons:** no children under 16; time-share sales pitch; sleepless nights for rooms near the pool and lobby. $ *Rooms from: $500* ✉ *Blvd. Kukulcán, Km 11.5, Zona Hotelera* ☎ 998/881–5600 ⊕ *www.cancun.zilara.hyatt.com* ⤳ *307 suites* |○| *All-inclusive* ✢ 3:C2.

$$$$
ALL-INCLUSIVE

⬚ **Iberostar Cancún.** Since every standard room has an ocean view, the Caribbean plays a central role at this all-inclusive resort. **Pros:** beachfront villas renovated in 2014; all standard rooms are ocean-view; angled pool area gets all-day sunshine. **Cons:** only one heated pool; some villas lack ocean views. $ *Rooms from: $500* ✉ *Blvd. Kukulcán, Km 17, Zona Hotelera* ☎ 998/881–8000 ⊕ *www.iberostar.com* ⤳ *426 rooms, 23 suites, 82 villas* |○| *All-inclusive* ✢ 3:B5.

$$$$ RESORT
🏨 **JW Marriott Cancún Resort & Spa.** Plush is the name of the game at this towering beach resort, where manicured lawns are threaded with an expansive maze of pools, and large vaulted windows let sunlight stream into a lobby that features marble floors and beautiful flower arrangements. **Pros:** top-notch service; huge spa; artificial reef. **Cons:** lacks the festive mood of other hotels on the strip; breakfast buffet costs MX$408; extra charge for Wi-Fi and Kids' Club. [$] *Rooms from: $358* ✉ *Blvd. Kukulcán, Km 14.5, Zona Hotelera* ☎ *998/848–9600, 888/813–2776* 🌐 *www.marriott.com* 🛏 *448 rooms, 74 suites* 🍴 *No meals* ⊕ *3:C4.*

$$$ RESORT
🏨 **Krystal Grand Punta Cancún.** On the tip of Punta Cancún, this contemporary 14-story hotel—formerly the Hyatt Regency—offers some of the Hotel Zone's best views; west-facing rooms can enjoy the sunset and both lagoon and bay vistas, while east-facing ones can watch the sunrise over Isla Mujeres. **Pros:** excellent views; on-site beauty salon and car rental; great restaurants. **Cons:** bathrooms have showers only; extra charge for Kids' Club and Wi-Fi; neighboring construction through 2015. [$] *Rooms from: $288* ✉ *Blvd. Kukulcán, Km 8.5, Zona Hotelera* ☎ *998/891–5555* 🌐 *www.krystal-hotels.com* 🛏 *287 rooms, 8 suites* 🍴 *Multiple meal plans* ⊕ *3:D2.*

$$$ HOTEL
🏨 **Laguna Suites Golf & Spa.** Framing the fairway of Pok-Ta-Pok Golf Course, this tranquil resort is comprised of 12 white-stucco buildings, each housing four spacious suites. **Pros:** free hourly shuttle to the beach; quiet location; access to golf course; all-inclusive plan available; neighboring laundromat is convenient. **Cons:** menu is very repetitive if you select all-inclusive package; no children's activities; bathrooms have showers only; mosquitoes in common areas. [$] *Rooms from: $280* ✉ *Paseo Pok Ta Pok 3, Zona Hotelera* ☎ *998/891–5252* 🌐 *www.lagunasuites.com.mx* 🛏 *47 suites* 🍴 *Multiple meal plans* ⊕ *3:C2.*

$$$$ ALL-INCLUSIVE
Fodor's Choice ★
🏨 **Le Blanc Spa Resort.** An airy, modern hotel with a minimalist white-and-beige décor, Le Blanc Spa is the most upscale of the Palace Resort properties and perhaps the most luxurious all-inclusive resort in Cancún. **Pros:** aesthetically pleasing design; excellent spa; butler service; great food. **Cons:** no kids; pricey; some rooms have small French balconies only; chilly, heavily chlorinated pool. [$] *Rooms from: $600* ✉ *Blvd. Kukulcán, Km 10, Zona Hotelera* ☎ *998/881–4740* 🌐 *www.leblancsparesort.com* 🛏 *222 rooms, 38 suites* 🍴 *All-inclusive* ⊕ *3:C2.*

$$$$ ALL-INCLUSIVE
Fodor's Choice ★
🏨 **Live AQUA Cancún.** From the aromatherapy and ambient music to the water features and welcome hand massage, everything about Live AQUA lends it a relaxing, spa-like quality. **Pros:** huge suites; all rooms have ocean views; gratuities included; free yoga classes. **Cons:** no kids under 16; no nightly entertainment; MX$1,361 fee for a beach- or poolside cabana; some hallway noise carries into rooms. [$] *Rooms from: $600* ✉ *Blvd. Kukulcán, Km 12.5, Zona Hotelera* ☎ *998/881–7600, 888/782–9722* 🌐 *www.liveaqua.com* 🛏 *325 rooms, 36 suites* 🍴 *All-inclusive* ⊕ *3:C3.*

$$$$ ALL-INCLUSIVE
🏨 **ME Cancún.** The ME takes the chic flavor of a trendy boutique hotel and blows it up to the grand scale of a large resort. **Pros:** great for young couples; pet-friendly; 24-hr gym. **Cons:** not ideal for kids; watered-down cocktails; $150 charge for lost all-inclusive wristband. [$] *Rooms*

Cancún's beautiful JW Marriott resort is the only local property designed to withstand a category-five hurricane.

from: $450 ✉ *Blvd. Kukulcán, Km 12, Zona Hotelera* ☎ 998/881–2500 ⊕ *www.me-cancun.com* ⏎ *348 rooms, 71 suites* ⦿ *All-inclusive* ✛ *3:C3.*

$$

HOTEL

▦ **Mia Cancún.** Amid the big, sleek resorts lining the Zona Hotelera, this spot (formerly the Avalon Baccara) stands out for its small size and rustic design. **Pros:** refreshing homelike setting; artistically unique. **Cons:** small pool and patios; steep driveway can be dangerous; only three parking spaces. $ *Rooms from:* $112 ✉ *Blvd. Kukulcán, Km 11.5, Zona Hotelera* ☎ 998/881–3900 ⊕ *www.hotelmiacancun.com* ⏎ *12 rooms, 15 suites* ⦿ *Breakfast* ✛ *3:C2.*

$$$$

RESORT

Fodor's Choice

★

▦ **Nizuc Resort & Spa.** Tucked away on a beach sheltered by mangroves and facing the Mesoamerican Barrier Reef, the stylish 29-acre Nizuc Resort has the most secluded and spectacular location in Cancún. **Pros:** opened in 2013; only private beach in Cancún; top-tier restaurants; excellent service; all-inclusive plan available. **Cons:** occasional airplane noise; 18% service charge added to bill; sprawling property means long walks or golf cart trips. $ *Rooms from:* $726 ✉ *Blvd. Kukulcán, Km 21.26, Zona Hotelera* ☎ 998/891–5700 ⊕ *www.nizuc.com* ⏎ *274 rooms* ⦿ *Multiple meal plans* ✛ *3:B6.*

$$

ALL-INCLUSIVE

FAMILY

▦ **Oasis Palm.** Within walking distance of El Embarcadero, this all-inclusive family resort sits in a prime location if you're looking to take a boat to Isla Mujeres, and it's the most affordable Oasis property in Cancún. **Pros:** great value; access to Grand Oasis Cancún golf course; good for families. **Cons:** pool is shaded most of the day; the only Jacuzzi is at the spa and it costs extra; dated rooms. $ *Rooms from:* $140

The Nizuc Resort & Spa has a beautiful infinity pool looking out onto Punta Nizuc.

✉ *Blvd. Kukulcán, Km 4.5, Zona Hotelera* ☎ *998/848–7500* 🌐 *www.oasishotels.com* 🛏 *470 rooms* 🍴 *All-inclusive* ✥ *3:B1.*

$$$$ ALL-INCLUSIVE **Omni Cancún Hotel & Villas.** A relaxed atmosphere and accommodating staff give this 12-story all-inclusive added appeal. **Pros:** tons of scheduled activities; educational programs at Kid's Club; four handicapped-accessible rooms. **Cons:** crowded pool area; time-share sales pitches; dark lobby is uninviting. [$] *Rooms from: $395* ✉ *Blvd. Kukulcán, Km 16.5, Zona Hotelera* ☎ *998/881–0600* 🌐 *www.omnihotels.com* 🛏 *259 rooms, 19 suites, 23 villas* 🍴 *All-inclusive* ✥ *3:B4.*

$$$$ ALL-INCLUSIVE **Paradisus Cancún.** Resembling a modern Mayan temple, this enormous beachfront property comes complete with atriums topped by pyramid-shape skylights. **Pros:** three play zones for babies, kids, and teens; privacy of Royal Service; free golf course exclusively for guests. **Cons:** no children allowed at several restaurants; top-shelf alcohol and Tempo restaurant not part of the all-inclusive plan; time-share sales pitch. [$] *Rooms from: $300* ✉ *Blvd. Kukulcán, Km 16.5, Zona Hotelera* ☎ *998/881–1100* 🌐 *www.paradisus.com* 🛏 *668 suites* 🍴 *All-inclusive* ✥ *3:C4.*

$$$$ RESORT Fodor's Choice ★ **The Ritz-Carlton, Cancún.** Outfitted with crystal chandeliers, beautiful antiques, and oil paintings, this hotel's style is so European you may forget you're in Mexico. **Pros:** cultural and environmental kids programs; tennis center; impeccable service; turtle-release program July–Nov. **Cons:** conservative atmosphere; expensive; slightly dated and not up to Ritz-Carlton standards. [$] *Rooms from: $459* ✉ *Retorno del Rey 36, off Blvd. Kukulcán, Km 13.5, Zona Hotelera* ☎ *998/881–0808* 🌐 *www.ritzcarlton.com* 🛏 *363 rooms, 50 suites* 🍴 *No meals* ✥ *3:C3.*

$$$$
ALL-INCLUSIVE

Riu Caribe. After renovations in 2012, this hotel ditched its Mayan theme for a more modern motif that includes bright orange balconies overlooking the white pyramid-shape lobby. **Pros:** tennis courts; large beach and pools; use of facilities at neighboring Riu Cancún. **Cons:** beach and pool areas can get crowded; no room service; Wi-Fi in common areas only; a far walk to the clubs and shops. $ *Rooms from: $300* ✉ *Blvd. Kukulcán, Km 5.5, Zona Hotelera* ☎ *998/848–7850* ⊕ *www.riu.com* ➹ *445 rooms, 61 suites* ⏐◯⏐ *All-inclusive* ✛ *3:B1.*

$$$$
ALL-INCLUSIVE

Riu Palace Las Américas. The most upscale of Cancún's four Riu properties, this colossal eight-story resort at the north end of the Zona is visually stunning. **Pros:** spacious suites; access to sister properties in Cancún and Playa del Carmen. **Cons:** small pools and tiny beach; not much sun by the pool or beach by late afternoon; some rooms smell musty. $ *Rooms from: $450* ✉ *Blvd. Kukulcán, Km 8.5, Zona Hotelera* ☎ *998/891–4300* ⊕ *www.riu.com* ➹ *470 suites* ⏐◯⏐ *All-inclusive* ✛ *3:C1.*

$$$$
ALL-INCLUSIVE

Sandos Cancún. High on a hill off the main boulevard, this refined yet relaxed hotel (formerly Le Méridien Cancún) is gaining recognition for its personalized service under Sandos's management. **Pros:** near one of Cancún's best malls; good fitness facilities; all rooms have water views; tastefully decorated. **Cons:** shady pool by early afternoon; time-share sales pitch; not all rooms have balconies. $ *Rooms from: $500* ✉ *Retorno del Rey, Lote 37, Mza 53, off Blvd. Kukulcán, Km 14, Zona Hotelera* ☎ *998/881–2200, 866/336–4083* ⊕ *www.sandos.com* ➹ *214 rooms* ⏐◯⏐ *All-inclusive* ✛ *3:C4.*

$$$$
ALL-INCLUSIVE

Secrets The Vine Cancún. Opened in 2013, this adults-only resort boasts "unlimited luxury," so even butler service, international calls, 24-hour room service, taxes, and gratuities are included in the rate. **Pros:** great restaurants; free fitness classes; no dinner buffets; access to Riviera Maya sister properties. **Cons:** thin walls; understaffed; only suites have full ocean view; no children under 18. $ *Rooms from: $450* ✉ *Retorno del Rey, Mza 13, lotes 38 and 38B, off Blvd. Kukulcan, Km 14.5, Zona Hotelera* ☎ *998/848–9400* ⊕ *www.secretsresorts.com/vine-cancun* ➹ *478 rooms, 17 suites* ⏐◯⏐ *All-inclusive* ✛ *3:C4.*

$
HOTEL

Suites Sina. On a quiet residential street off Boulevard Kukulcán, these economical suites are in front of Laguna Nichupté and close to the Pok-Ta-Pok golf course. **Pros:** ideally situated on the lagoon; affordable; MX$68 access to beach club at Ocean Spa Hotel. **Cons:** 10-min walk from beach; no elevator; loud a/c. $ *Rooms from: $80* ✉ *Club de Golf, Calle Quetzal 33, Zona Hotelera/El Centro* ✛ *Turn right at Blvd. Kukulcán, Km 7.5, after golf course* ☎ *998/883–1017* ⊕ *www.suitessina cancun.com* ➹ *4 rooms, 32 suites* ⏐◯⏐ *No meals* ✛ *3:C2.*

$$$$
RESORT
FAMILY

The Westin Resort & Spa Cancún. Subtle hints of pampering are what make this hotel so extraordinary, like the white-tea mist that periodically sprays in the lobby and the "heavenly beds" so luxurious that some guests buy them for their own homes. **Pros:** two beaches; natural reef great for snorkeling; all-inclusive plan available; one of closest resorts to the airport. **Cons:** extra charge for Wi-Fi; driving distance to off-site shops and restaurants; only odd-numbered rooms have ocean views. $ *Rooms from: $351* ✉ *Blvd. Kukulcán, Km 20, Zona Hotelera*

☎ *998/848–7400* 🌐 *www.westin.com/cancun* 🛏 *361 rooms, 18 suites* 🍴 *Multiple meal plans* ✥ *3:B6.*

$$$ RESORT FAMILY **The Westin Lagunamar.** Renovated in 2010, this timeshare–resort is centrally located across from La Isla shopping center. **Pros:** beautiful infinity pool; all the comforts of home; great for families. **Cons:** timeshare pitch; spotty Wi-Fi in areas; no all-inclusive plan. [$] *Rooms from: $269* ✉ *Blvd Kukulcan, Km 12.5, Zona Hotelera* ☎ *998/891–4200* 🌐 *www.starwoodhotels.com* 🛏 *592 rooms* 🍴 *No meals* ✥ *3:C3.*

EL CENTRO

$$ HOTEL **Adhara Hacienda Cancún.** A stimulating change from the street on which it sits, this hacienda-style building is strikingly hip and sleek. **Pros:** state-of-the-art gym equipment; business center; beach shuttle; one handicapped-accessible unit. **Cons:** east-facing rooms tend to have street noise; lights in rooms are movement triggered; popular breakfast buffet not included in room rate. [$] *Rooms from: $100* ✉ *Av. Náder 1, El Centro* ☎ *998/881–6500* 🌐 *www.adharacancun.com* 🛏 *173 rooms at Adhara, 74 rooms at Margarita wing* 🍴 *No meals* ✥ *2:C1.*

$$ HOTEL **Ambiance Suites Cancún.** Branding itself as "your home and office," this modern hotel caters mostly to business executives. **Pros:** convenient El Centro location; good value. **Cons:** unfriendly staff; far from the beach. [$] *Rooms from: $100* ✉ *Av. Tulum 227, Sm 20, El Centro* ☎ *998/892–0392* 🌐 *www.ambiancecancun.com* 🛏 *48 rooms* 🍴 *Breakfast* ✥ *2:C6.*

$$ HOTEL **Courtyard by Marriott Cancún Airport.** The draw of this deluxe property is that it's five minutes from the airport and offers free round-trip airport shuttle service. **Pros:** free Wi-Fi; free shuttle to airport and beach club; 24-hr gym. **Cons:** high phone charges; far from Cancún center; some rooms face the parking lot. [$] *Rooms from: $109* ✉ *Blvd. Luis Donaldo Colosio, Km 12.5, Carretera Cancún-Aeropuerto* ☎ *998/287–2200* 🌐 *www.marriott.com/cuncy* 🛏 *195 rooms, 6 suites* 🍴 *No meals* ✥ *2:C6.*

$ HOTEL Fodor's Choice ★ **Eco Hotel El Rey del Caribe.** Thanks to the use of solar energy, a water-recycling system, and composting toilets, this tranquil hotel has little impact on the environment—and its luxuriant garden blocks the heat and noise of downtown. **Pros:** walking distance to El Centro's shops and restaurants; eco-friendly; affordable spa; free Wi-Fi. **Cons:** simple and musty rooms; no elevator; mosquitoes in common areas. [$] *Rooms from: $88* ✉ *Av. Uxmal 24, Sm 2A, at Náder, El Centro* ☎ *998/884–2028* 🌐 *www.elreydelcaribe.com* 🛏 *31 rooms* 🍴 *Breakfast* ✥ *2:C2.*

$ HOTEL Fodor's Choice ★ **Grand City Hotel.** This downtown budget hotel offers large, pleasant rooms, each with a flat-screen TV, W-Fi, iPod dock, minibar, safe, and microwave. **Pros:** best budget hotel in Cancún; kids under 12 stay free. **Cons:** noise from neighboring biker bar; restaurant closes early; no early check-ins. [$] *Rooms from: $74* ✉ *Av. Yaxchilán 154, Sm 20, across from Red Cross, El Centro* ☎ *998/193–3580* 🌐 *www.grandcity-hotel.com* 🛏 *18 rooms* 🍴 *Breakfast* ✥ *2:A6.*

$ HOTEL **Hotel Xbalamqué Resort & Spa.** This refreshing retreat from El Centro's bustling streets reflects Mayan culture through murals, statues, and reliefs; it forms part of a complex that also includes two restaurants and a snack shop, which are open to the general public. **Pros:** small on-site spa and beauty salon; good El Centro location; kids under 11 stay free. **Cons:** street noise audible from front rooms; intermittent hot water; patchy Wi-Fi. $ *Rooms from: $80* ✉ *Av. Yaxchilan 31, Sm 22, Mza 18, El Centro* ☎ *998/193–2720* ⊕ *www.xbalamque.com* ☛ *80 rooms, 11 suites* ⭐ *Breakfast* ✛ *2:A3.*

$ ☲ **Ibis Cancún Centro.** Within walking distance of Las Américas Shopping
HOTEL Center and next to a grocery store, this hotel is perfect for mixing business with pleasure at a very reasonable price. **Pros:** 15 minutes from airport; clean, bright rooms; free underground parking; car rental agency and tour operator on site. **Cons:** no pool; mainly caters to business and budget travelers; hotel will not sell alcohol on Sunday. $ *Rooms from: $65* ✉ *Avs. Tulum and Nichupté, Sm 11, El Centro* ☎ *998/272–8500* ⊕ *www.ibishotel.com* ☛ *190 rooms* ⭐ *No meals* ✛ *2:C6.*

$ ☲ **Oh! By Oasis.** This fresh, hip hotel greets guests with a pop art–style
HOTEL lobby and vibrant hallways, which lead to guest rooms with marble floors, iPod docks, 42" flat-screen TVs, minibars, and small balconies. **Pros:** full renovation in 2014; lovely pool area. **Cons:** no spa; not on the beach; not suitable for families. $ *Rooms from: $78* ✉ *Av. Tulum, Sm 4, corner of Brisa, El Centro* ☎ *998/848–8600* ⊕ *www.oh-by-oasis. com* ☛ *58 rooms* ⭐ *No meals* ✛ *2:C6.*

$ ☲ **Terracaribe Hotel.** Midway between El Centro and Punta Sam, this
HOTEL Mediterranean-style hotel may not have the best location, but the prices are outstanding and rooms are spotless; all have air-conditioning, safes, flat-screen TVs, free Wi-Fi, and strong water pressure—rarities in the area's budget digs. **Pros:** rooms renovated in 2014; comfy beds; polite staff. **Cons:** no views; far from the beach and the Zona Hotelera; weak Wi-Fi. $ *Rooms from: $63* ✉ *Av. Lopez Portillo 70, at Av. Bonampak, El Centro* ☎ *998/880–0448* ⊕ *www.terracaribe.com* ☛ *55 rooms* ⭐ *Breakfast* ✛ *2:D1.*

NIGHTLIFE

We're not here to judge: we know that most people come to Cancún to party. If you want fine dining and dancing under the stars, you'll definitely find it here. But if your tastes run more toward bikini contests, all-night chug-a-thons, or cross-dressing Cher impersonators, rest assured: Cancún has plenty of those, too.

▧ **TIP**➜ **If you want to avoid rowdy Spring Breakers, stay clear of "open-bar" establishments and chain restaurants like Señor Frog's. They'll likely be packed with party animals on the loose.**

BARS

ALL-PURPOSE BARS
Many of these spots daylight as restaurants, but after sunset the party kicks up with pulsating music and waiters who don't so much encourage crowd participation as demand it. Just remember: it's all in good fun.

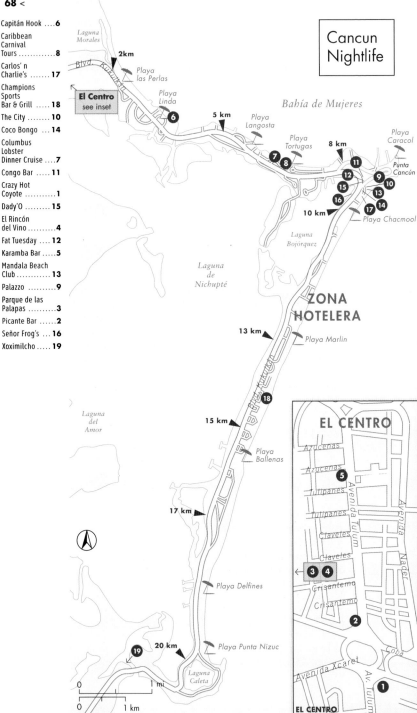

Cancun Nightlife

Carlos 'n Charlie's. Waiters here will occasionally abandon their posts to start singing or performing comical skits. It's not unusual for them to rouse everyone from their seats to join a conga line before going back to serving food and drinks. ⊠ *Forum-by-the-Sea, Blvd. Kukulcán, Km 9, Zona Hotelera* ☎ *998/883–4468* ⊕ *www.carlosandcharlies.com/cancun.*

Fat Tuesday. With a large daiquiri bar plus live and piped-in club music, Fat Tuesday is another place to dance the night away. For MX$300, you can drink unlimited alcohol slushies. ⊠ *Blvd. Kukulcán, Km 9.5, Zona Hotelera* ⊕ *www.fat-tuesday.com.*

Señor Frog's. Known for its over-the-top drinks, Señor Frog's serves up foot-long funnel glasses filled with margaritas, daiquiris, or beer, which you can take home as souvenirs once you've chugged them dry. Needless to say, Spring Breakers adore this place and often stagger back night after night. Expect to pay a MX$474 cover or MX$813 for the open-bar option. ⊠ *Blvd. Kukulcán, Km 9.5, across from Coco Bongo, Zona Hotelera* ☎ *998/883–3454* ⊕ *www.senorfrogscancun.com.*

GAY BARS

Karamba Bar. This large open-air disco and club is known for its stage performers. A variety of drag shows with the usual lip-synching celebrity impersonations are put on every Wednesday and Thursday. On Friday night the Go-Go Boys of Cancún entertain, and strip shows run on weekends. The bar opens at 10:30 pm and the party goes on until dawn. Cover charges range from MX$67 to MX$108. ⊠ *Av. Tulum 9, corner of Azuenas, Sm 22, El Centro* ⊕ *www.karambabar.net* ⊗ *Closed Mon.*

Picante Bar. The oldest gay bar in Cancún has been operating for over 15 years. Doors open at 10 pm and close at 7 am, and there's no cover. ⊠ *Plaza Galerias, Av. Tulum 20, Sm 5, El Centro* ⊗ *Closed Mon. and Tues.*

SPORTS BARS

Champions Sports Bar & Grill. With a giant TV screen and 26 smaller monitors, Champions Sports Bar & Grill is a place to watch all kinds of sporting events. You can also play pool here, dig in to American-style grub, or enjoy karaoke at night. ⊠ *CasaMagna Marriott Cancún Resort, Blvd. Kukulcán, Km 14.5, Zona Hotelera* ☎ *998/881–2000* ⊕ *www.championscancun.com.*

WINE BARS

El Rincón del Vino. You can enjoy the sounds of live *trova*, rumba, flamenco, and jazz music at this popular wine and tapas bar. Open from 6 pm to midnight, Monday through Saturday, it has 250 varieties of *vino* hailing from the world's top winemaking regions, plus tapas like *tortilla española* (a potato omelet) and *chistorra* (a Spanish sausage). ⊠ *Av. Náder 88, El Centro* ☎ *998/883–9284, 998/168–8752 (evening only)* ⊕ *www.elrincondelvino.com.mx* ⊗ *Closed Sun. No lunch.*

DANCE CLUBS

Cancún wouldn't be Cancún without glittering clubs, which generally start jumping around midnight (though most open at 9:30) and often carry on until 6 am. As the hours roll on, clothes peel off and frenzied dancing seems to quake the building and the floor beneath. Most offer open-bar tickets (MX$540–MX$1084) that cover admission and unlimited drinks until 3 am. If you stay past 3, however, you'll have to pay for beverages. You can also pay a lower cover charge of MX$135–MX$470 and buy drinks separately. Typical prices range from MX$40 for a shot to MX$135 for a cocktail. The most popular clubs include Coco Bongo, Dady'O, the City, and Palazzo, but every place seems to be pumping by midnight—especially during Spring Break. ■ TIP➔ The **Mandala Group owns nearly every club on the strip, meaning that your ticket to one might be valid for entry at another.**

The City. Open only on Friday nights, the City is a giant party complex with several large bars selling overpriced drinks and a cavernous dance floor with stadium seating. Dancing and live shows are the main draw during the legendary foam parties. This is by far the loudest club in the Zona Hotelera, so don't be surprised if you go home with your ears ringing. Doors open at 10:30 pm; expect to pay a MX$408 cover or MX$817 for open-bar entry. ⊠ *Blvd. Kukulcán, Km 9.5, Zona Hotelera* ☎ *998/848–8385* ⊕ *www.thecitycancun.com.*

Coco Bongo. The wild, wild Coco Bongo has no chairs, but there are plenty of tables that everyone dances on and capacity for 1,800 people. There's also a popular show billed as "Las Vegas meets Hollywood," featuring celebrity impersonators and an amazing gravity-defying acrobatic performance accompanied by a 12-piece orchestra. After the shows, the techno gets cranked to full volume and everyone gets up to get down. Doors open at 10:30 pm. Tickets (MX$881–MX$1,016 for open bar and shows) include free entrance to Congo Bar, a sister club. ⊠ *Forum-by-the-Sea, Blvd. Kukulcán, Km 9.5, Zona Hotelera* ☎ *01800/841–4636 toll-free in Mexico, 998/883–2373* ⊕ *www.coco bongo.com.mx.*

Congo Bar. Brought to you by the makers of the famed Coco Bongo, Congo Bar is hard to miss. This spot stops traffic due to the scantily clad women who dance on open platforms that line the street. Expect Jell-O shots, confetti showers, go-go dancers, and loud music. An open-bar ticket costs MX$408. ⊠ *Blvd Kukulcán, Km 9, diagonally across from Coco Bongo, Zona Hotelera* ☎ *01800/841–4636 toll-free in Mexico* ⊕ *www.cocobongo.com.mx.*

Crazy Hot Coyote. If you don't want to deal with the long lines or hefty entrance fees at Coco Bongo, Crazy Hot Coyote (or CHC) is El Centro's best spot for music, dancing, and entertainment. The MX$200 cover charge converts into a food or drink credit. There are burlesque shows every Thursday, Friday, and Saturday. ⊠ *Oh! by Oasis, Ave. Tulum, Sm 4, corner of Brisa, El Centro* ☎ *998/848–8600* ⊕ *www. oh-by-oasis.com.*

Continued on page 78

TEQUILA AND MEZCAL—¡SALUD!

If God were Mexican, tequila and mezcal would surely be our heavenly reward, flowing in lieu of milk and honey. Before throwing back your first drink, propose a toast in true Mexican style and wave your glass accordingly—"¡Arriba, abajo, al centro, pa' dentro!" ("Above, below, center, inside!")

Historians maintain that, following Spanish conquest and the introduction of the distillation process, tequila was adapted from the ancient Aztec drink *pulque*. Whatever the true origin, Mexico's national drink long predated the Spanish, and is considered North America's oldest spirit.

When you think about tequila, what might come to mind are spaghetti-Western-style bar brawls or late-night teary-eyed confessions. But tequila is more complex and worldly than many presume. By some accounts it's a digestive that reduces cholesterol and stress. Shots of the finest tequilas can cost upward of $100 each, and are meant to be savored as ardently as fine cognacs or single-malt scotches.

Just one of several agave-derived drinks fermented and bottled in Mexico, tequila rose to fame during the Mexican Revolution when it became synonymous with national heritage and pride. Since the 1990s tequila has enjoyed a soaring popularity around the globe, and people the world over are starting to realize that tequila is more than a one-way ticket to (and doesn't necessitate) a hangover.

Harvesting agave in Jalisco.

TEQUILA AND MEZCAL 101

Harvesting blue agave to make tequila.

WHICH CAME FIRST, TEQUILA OR MEZCAL?

Mezcal is tequila's older cousin. Essentially, all tequila is mezcal but only some mezcal is tequila. The only difference between tequila and mezcal is that the tequila meets two requirements: 1) it's made only from blue agave (but some non-agave sugar can be added) and 2) it must be distilled in a specific region in Jalisco or certain parts of neighboring Guanajuato, Michoacán, Nayarit, and Tamaulipas. Unlike tequila, all mezcal must be made from 100 percent agave and must be bottled in Mexico.

CHOOSE YOUR LIQUOR WISELY

Your first decision with tequila is whether to have a *puro* or a *mixto*. You'll know if a bottle is *puro* because it will say so prominently on the label; if the words "100% de agave" don't appear, you can be sure you're getting mixto. Don't be fooled by bottles that say, "Made from agave azul," because all tequila is made from agave azul; that doesn't mean that cane sugar hasn't been added. Popular wisdom holds that puro causes less of a hangover than mixto, but we'll leave that to your own experimentation.

Even among *puros*, there's a wide range of quality and taste, and every fan has his or her favorite. For sipping straight (*derecho*), most people prefer *reposado*, *añejo*, or extra *añejo*. For mixed drinks you'll probably want either a *blanco* or a *reposado*.

Herradura

TEQUILA TIMELINE

Aztec ritual human sacrifice as portrayed on the Codex Magliabechiano.

Pre-Columbian	Aztecs brew pulque for thousands of years; both priests and the sacrificial victims consume it during religious rituals.
1600	The first commercial distillery in New Spain is founded by Pedro Sanches de Tagle, the father of tequila, on his hacienda near the village of Tequila.
1740	*Mezcal de Tequila* earns an enthusiastic following and King Philip V of Spain grants José Antonio Cuervo the first royal license for a mezcal distillery.

THE MAKING OF MEZCAL

1 To make both mezcal and tequila, the agave may be cultivated for as long as ten years, depending on growing conditions and the variety of plant.

2 When the agave is ripe, the leaves, or *pencas*, are removed and the heavy core (called a *piña*, Spanish for "pineapple," because of its resemblance to that fruit) is dug up, **3** cut into large chunks, and cooked to convert its starches into sugars.

4 The *piñas* are then crushed and their juice collected in tanks; yeast is added and the liquid ferments for several days.

After the fermentation, the resulting *mosto* generally measures between 4 and 7 percent alcohol. **5** Finally it's distilled (usually twice for tequila, once for mezcal). This process of heating and condensing serves to boost the alcohol content. **6** And finally, the alcohol is aged in barrels.

While the process is the same, there are a few critical differences between tequila and mezcal: mezcal is made in smaller distilleries and still retains more of an artisanal quality; mezcal magueys are grown over a wider area with more diverse soil composition and microclimate, giving mezcals more individuality than tequila; and lastly, the *piñas* for mezcal are more likely to be baked in stone pits, which imparts a distinctive smoky flavor.

The World's Columbian Fair in Chicago, 1893.

1800s	As the thirst for mezcal grows, wood (used to fire the stills) becomes scarce and distilleries shift to more efficient steam ovens.
1873	Cenobio Sauza exports mezcal to the United States via a new railroad to El Paso, Texas.
1893	*Mezcal de Tequila* (now simply called tequila) receives an award at Chicago's Columbian Exposition.

TEQUILA COCKTAILS

Margarita: The original proportions at Rancho La Gloria were reportedly 3 parts tequila, 2 parts Triple Sec, and 1 part lime juice, though today recipes vary widely. In Mexico an orange liqueur called Controy is often substituted for the Triple Sec. The best margaritas are a little tart and are made from fresh ingredients, not a mix. Besides deciding whether you want yours strained, on the rocks, or frozen, you have dozens of variations to choose from, many incorporating fruits such as strawberry, raspberry, mango, passion fruit, and peach. To salt the rim or not to salt is yet another question.

Sangrita: The name meaning "little blood," this is a very Mexican accompaniment, a spicy mixture of tomato and orange juice that's sipped between swallows of straight tequila (or mezcal).

Tequila refresca: Also very popular in Mexico, this is tequila mixed with citrus soft drinks like Fresca, or Squirt. Generally served in a tall glass over ice.

Tequila Sunrise: Invented in the 1950s, this is a distant runner-up to the margarita, concocted from tequila, orange juice, and grenadine syrup. The grenadine sinks to the bottom, and after a few refills you might agree that the resulting layers resemble a Mexican sky at dawn.

Bloody Maria: One to try with brunch, this is a bloody Mary with you-know-what instead of vodka.

DID YOU KNOW?

Aging mezcal and Tequila imparts a smoothness and an oaky flavor, but over-aging can strip the drink of its characteristic agave taste.

TEQUILA TIMELINE

Mexican revolutionaries

1910–1920	During the Mexican Revolution, homegrown tequila becomes a source of national pride, associated with the hard-riding, hard-drinking rebels.
1930s	Federal land reforms break up the great haciendas and Mexico's agave production slumps by two thirds. To make up for the shortfall, the government allows distillers to begin mixing non-agave sugars into their tequila. This blander drink, called mixto, is better suited to American tastes and sales surge.

TEQUILA AND MEZCAL VOCABULARY

pulque: an alcoholic drink made by the Aztecs

mexcalmetl: Nahuatl word for agave

mixto: a type of tequila that is mixed with non-agave sugars

puro: tequila made with no non-agave sugars

reposado: aged between two months and a year

añejo: aged between one and three years

extra añejo: aged longer than three years

blanco: tequila that is aged less than two months

joven: young tequila, usually a mixto with colorings and flavors

caballito: tall shot glass

pechuga: mezcal flavored with raw chicken breast

cremas: flavored mezcal

aguamiel: agave juice

piña: the agave core

salmiana: a type of agave

pencas: agave leaves

mosto: fermented agave before it is distilled

gusano: the larva found in mescal bottles

WHAT'S WITH THE WORM?

Some mezcals (never tequila) are bottled with a worm (*gusano*), the larva of one of the moths that live on agave plants. Rumor has it that the worm was introduced to ensure a high alcohol content (because the alcohol preserves the creature), but the truth is that the practice started in the 1940s as a marketing gimmick. The worm is ugly but harmless and the best mezcals are not bottled *con gusano.*

Agave

Early 1940s | The history of mixology was forever altered when Carlos Herrera invented the margarita for American starlet Marjorie King.

2004 | The agave fields around Tequila become a UNESCO World Heritage Site.

2006 | A one-liter bottle of limited-edition premium tequila sold for $225,000. The most expensive bottle ever sold according to The Guiness World Records.

CHOOSING A BOTTLE

Reposado (rested)

Silver

Añejo (mature)

Corralejo

BUYING TEQUILA

There are hundreds of brands of tequila, but here are a baker's half dozen of quality *puros* to get you started; generally these distillers offer blanco, reposado, añejo, and extra añejo.

Corralejo—An award winner from the state of Guanajuato, made on the historic hacienda once owned by Pedro Sanchez de Tagle, "the father of tequila" and birthplace of Miguel Hidalgo, the father of Mexican independence.

Corzo—Triple distilled, these tequilas are notably smooth and elegant.

Don Julio—This award-winning tequila, one of the most popular in Mexico, is known for its rich, smooth flavor; the *blanco* is especially esteemed.

Espolón—A relative newcomer founded only in 1998, this distiller has already won several international awards.

Herradura—This is a venerable, popular brand known for its smoky, full body.

Patrón—Founded in 1989, this distiller produces award-winning tequilas. The *añejo* is especially noteworthy for its complex earthiness.

Siete Leguas—Taking their name ("Seven Leagues") from the horse of Pancho Villa, a general in the Mexican Revolution, these quality tequilas are known for their big, full flavor.

TYPES OF TEQUILA AND MEZCAL

Three basic types of tequila and mezcal are determined by how long they've been aged in oak barrels.

Blanco (white) is also known as *plata* or silver. It's been aged for less than two months.

Reposado ("rested") is aged between two months and a year.

añejo ("mature") is kept in barrels for at least a year and perhaps as long as three. Some producers also offer an extra *añejo* that is aged even longer.

Herradura

Don Julio

Gusano Rojo

BUYING MEZCAL

As for enjoying mezcal, it can be substituted in any recipe calling for tequila. But more often it's drunk neat, to savor its unique flavor. Like tequila, straight mezcal is generally served at room temperature in a tall shot glass called a *caballito*.

Some producers now add flavorings to their mezcals. Perhaps the most famous is *pechuga*, which has a raw chicken breast added to the still, supposedly imparting a smoothness and subtle flavor. (Don't worry, the heat and alcohol kill everything.) Citrus is also a popular add-in, and *cremas* contain flavorings such as peaches, mint, raisins, or guava, along with a sweetener such as honey or *aguamiel* (the juice of the agave).

Part of the fun of mezcal is stumbling on smaller, less commercial brands, but here are a few recognized, quality producers. Most make *blancos*, *reposados*, and *añejos*, and some offer extra *añejos*, flavored mezcals, and *cremas* as well.

El Señorio—Produced in Oaxaca the traditional way, with stone ovens and a stone wheel to crush the *piñas*.

El Zacatecano—Founded in 1910 in the northern state of Zacatecas; in a recent competitive tasting, their añejo was judged the best in its category.

Gusano Rojo—This venerable Oaxaca distillery makes the number-one-selling mezcal in Mexico. Yes, there's a worm in the bottle.

Jaral de Berrio—From Guanajuato, this distiller uses the *salmiana* agave. Their *blanco* recently garnered a silver medal.

Real de Magueyes—From the state of San Luis Potosí, these fine mezcals are also made from the local *salmiana* agave. Try the flavorful añejo.

Scorpion—More award-winning mezcals from Oaxaca. Instead of a worm, there's a scorpion in the bottle.

Dady'O. Cancún's original dance club is still very "in" with the younger set. A giant screen projects music videos above the always-packed dance floor, while laser lights whirl across the crowd. During Spring Break, Hawaiian Bikini contests make the place even livelier. The cover charge (waived for women on Friday) is MX$474, and the open-bar option is MX$813. ⊠ *Blvd. Kukulcán, Km 9.5, across from Coco Bongo, Zona Hotelera* ☎ *998/883–3333* ⊕ *www.dadyo.com.mx* ☽ *Closed Tues., Wed., and Sun.*

Mandala Beach Club. This Balinese-style party place is a buzzing beach retreat by day and a more upscale nightclub after dark. Both have bikini contests, DJs, pool parties, and bottle service. Expect to pay a MX$474 cover or MX$813 for an open bar. ⊠ *Blvd. Kukulcán, Km 9, Zona Hotelera* ☎ *998/848–8380* ⊕ *www.mandalabeach.com.*

Palazzo. Dress to impress at this upscale dance club where it's all about bottle service, VIP treatment, fog machines, and go-go dancers covered in neon body paint. The purple décor, chandeliers, and stripper poles that look like lamps set the stage for dance music and a dazzling light show. Naturally, this place is popular with Spring Breakers. Note that Palazzo operates only on Wednesday and Saturday nights. Open-bar entry costs MX$885. ⊠ *Blvd. Kukulcán, Km 9, next to Krystal Cancún Hotel, Zona Hotelera* ☎ *998/848–8380* ⊕ *www.palazzodisco.com.*

DINNER CRUISES

Sunset boat cruises that include dinner, drinks, music, and sometimes dancing are popular in Cancún—especially among couples looking for a romantic evening and visitors who'd rather avoid the carnival atmosphere of the clubs and discos.

FAMILY **Capitán Hook.** Watch a show aboard a replica of an 18th-century Spanish galleon, then enjoy a lobster or steak dinner and drinks as the ship cruises around at sunset. Capitán Hook's three-hour trip runs daily from 7:30 to 10:30 pm, but you must arrive 30 minutes before departure. ⊠ *Blvd. Kukulcán, Km 5, Zona Hotelera* ☎ *998/849–4451, 998/884–5386* 🖃 *MX$1342–MX$1545.*

FAMILY **Caribbean Carnival Tours.** Board a two-level catamaran for a cruise to Isla Mujeres. There's an open bar on the trip over, and on shore you're treated to a dinner buffet and theme show. Weekdays the theme is Caribbean carnival; Saturday sailings are all about pirates. ⊠ *Playa Tortugas, Blvd. Kukulcán, Km 6.5, Zona Hotelera* ☎ *998/884–3760* ⊕ *www.caribbeancarnaval.com* 🖃 *MX$1125* ☽ *Mon.–Sat. noon–5 and 7–11:30.*

Columbus Lobster Dinner Cruise. This company offers couples-only cruises on a 62-foot galleon. Advertised as a "romance tour," it has some elements of a booze cruise (including watered-down cocktails). But it's still worth it for the fresh lobster and sunset views over Laguna Nichupé; the boat trip continues after dinner so you can stargaze. No children under 14. ⊠ *Agua Tours Marina, Blvd. Kukulcán, Km 6.5, in front of Playa Tortugas, Zona Hotelera* ☎ *866/393–5158 in the*

U.S., 01800/727–5391 toll-free in Mexico ⊕ *www.thelobsterdinner.com* ✉ *MX$1626* ☾ *Daily at 5 and 8 pm.*

Fodor's Choice **Xoximilco.** Brought to you by the creators of Xcaret, this dinner cruise
★ experience combines culture, cuisine, music, and dancing for a fiesta like
no other. Set sail aboard a colorful *trajinera* (gondola-like boat) named
after one of the Mexican states. While cruising down the freshwater
canals, passengers are treated to live music, an open bar (tequila and
beer), and various dishes from around the country. Three-hour tours
begin at 6 pm. ■TIP➔ Bring mosquito spray. ✉ *Carretera 307, Km 338,
5 mins from airport, Carretera Cancún-Aeropuerto* ☏ *998/883–3143*
⊕ *www.xoximilco.com* ✉ *MX$1206* ☾ *Closed Sun.*

LIVE MUSIC

Parque de las Palapas. To mingle with locals and hear great music for
free, head to the Parque de las Palapas. Every Friday night at 7:30
there's live music ranging from jazz to salsa; lots of locals show up to
dance. On Sunday afternoon the Cancún Municipal Orchestra plays.
✉ *Bordered by avs. Tulum, Yaxchilán, Uxmal, and Cobá, Sm 22, El
Centro.*

SHOPPING AND SPAS

The *centros comerciales* (malls) in Cancún are fully air-conditioned and
as well kept as similar establishments in the United States or Canada.
Like their northerly counterparts, they also sell just about everything:
designer clothing, beachwear (including raunchy T-shirts aimed at the
Spring Break crowd), sportswear, jewelry, music, electronics, household
items, shoes, and books. Some even have the same terrible mall food
that's standard north of the border. Prices are fixed in shops. They're
also generally—but not always—higher than in the markets, where bargaining is a given. Perfumes in Cancún are considerably less expensive
than at home (and even than at the duty-free shops at the airport). Of
course tequila is a bargain here as well, but make sure you buy at the
supermarket rather than at a souvenir shop.

There are many duty-free stores selling designer goods at reduced prices,
sometimes as much as 30% or 40% below retail. You can find hand-
woven textiles, leather goods, and handcrafted silver jewelry, although
prices are higher than in other cities and the selection is limited.

Monday through Saturday, shopping hours are generally 10–1 and 4–7,
although more stores are staying open throughout the day rather than
closing for siesta. Many are now opening on Sunday afternoon as well.
Centros comerciales tend to be open daily from 9 or 10 am to 8 or 9 pm.

GALLERIES

Casa de Cultura. Serious collectors visit Casa de Cultura for regular
shows featuring Mexican artists. ✉ *Prolongación Av. Yaxchilán, Sm
25, El Centro* ☏ *998/884–8364* ⊕ *www.culturaencancun.blogspot.com.*

El Pabilo. This downtown café showcases Mexican painters and photographers on a rotating basis. It's open only in the evening, Monday through Saturday from 5 pm to 1 am. ⊠ *Av. Yaxchilán 31, Sm 7, El Centro* ☎ *998/884–4949* ⊗ *Closed Sun.*

GROCERY STORES

■ TIP→ The few grocery stores in the Zona Hotelera tend to be expensive. It's better to shop for groceries downtown.

Chedraui. With several locations in El Centro, this popular superstore has a large selection of local and American products. ⊠ *Av. Tulum 57, at Av. Cobá, El Centro* ☎ *998/884–1024* ⊕ *www.chedraui.com.mx.*

Costco. If you're a member in the States, you can visit Costco in Mexico. ⊠ *Avs. Kabah and Yaxchilán, Sm 21, El Centro* ☎ *998/881–0265* ⊕ *www.costco.com.mx.*

> ### AVOID TORTOISESHELL
>
> Refrain from buying anything made from tortoiseshell. The *carey,* or hawksbill turtle from which most of it comes, is an endangered species, and it's illegal to bring tortoiseshell products into the United States and several other countries. Also be aware that there are some restrictions regarding black coral. For one, you must purchase it from a recognized dealer.

Mega Comercial Mexicana. One of the major Mexican grocery-store chains, Mega Comercial Mexicana has multiple locations. The most convenient is at avenidas Tulum and Uxmal, across from the bus station; its largest store, farther north on Avenida Kabah, is open 24 hours. ⊠ *Avs. Tulum and Uxmal, Sm 2, El Centro* ☎ *998/884–3330* ⊕ *www.comercialmexicana.com.mx.*

Sam's Club. You'll find plenty of bargains on groceries and souvenirs at Sam's Club. ⊠ *Paseo Kukulcán, Sm 21, Mza 2, Lote 2, between Palenque and Yaxchilán, El Centro* ☎ *998/881–0200* ⊕ *www.samsclub.com.*

Super Aki. This is a smaller grocery store downtown. ⊠ *Av. Centenario, Sm 227, Lote 083, Mza 73, El Centro* ☎ *998/889–5034.*

Wal-Mart. As in the U.S., Wal-Mart is a popular place to pick up beach supplies, snacks, and necessities you forgot to pack. ⊠ *Av. Cobá, Sm 21, Lote 2, El Centro* ☎ *998/884–1383* ⊕ *www.wal-mart.com.mx.*

MARKETS AND MALLS

ZONA HOTELERA

Coral Negro. Next to the convention center, this open-air market has about 50 stalls selling crafts and souvenirs. Everything here is overpriced, and vendors can be pushy; however, bargaining does work. Stalls deeper in the market tend to have better deals than those around the periphery. ⊠ *Blvd. Kukulcán, Km 9, Zona Hotelera* ⊗ *Daily 9–9.*

Forum-by-the-Sea. This three-level entertainment and shopping plaza in the Zona features brand-name restaurants, upscale clothing boutiques, a food court, and chain stores, all in a circuslike atmosphere. For Spring Breakers, the main draws are the nightclubs, Coco Bongo and Carlos 'n Charlie's. The bungee trampolines set up here during high season are especially popular with children. You will also find several ATMs on site. ✉ *Blvd. Kukulcán, Km 9.5, Zona Hotelera* ☎ *998/883–4425* ⊕ *www.forumbythesea.com.mx.*

Fodor's Choice
★

La Isla Shopping Village. The glittering, ultratrendy, and ultra-expensive La Isla Shopping Village is on the Laguna Nichupté under chic, white canopies. A series of canals and small bridges is designed to give the place a Venetian look. In addition to more than 200 designer shops, the mall has a marina, restaurants, and movie theaters. There's also an interactive aquarium where you can swim with the dolphins and feed the sharks. ✉ *Blvd. Kukulcán, Km 12.5, Zona Hotelera* ☎ *998/883–5025* ⊕ *www.laislacancun.com.mx.*

Plaza Caracol. North of the convention center, the two-story Plaza Caracol has 100-odd retail options, including chain stores (like Sunglass Island, Benetton, and Ultrafemme), souvenir shops, jewelry boutiques, and pharmacies. If you work up an appetite, it also has a food court. ■ TIP→ Free Wi-Fi is available at the Häagen-Dazs ice cream shop. ✉ *Blvd. Kukulcán, Km 8.5, Zona Hotelera* ☎ *998/883–4760* ⊕ *www. caracolplaza.com* ⊘ *Closed weekends*

Plaza El Zócalo. It may look small from the entrance, but Plaza El Zócalo has a few dozen stalls where you can find traditional Mexican handicrafts, silver jewelry, and handmade sandals. It also houses four restaurants—including Mextreme, which still sports a banner announcing its claim to fame as a filming location for the 1980s movie *Cocktail.* ✉ *Blvd. Kuckulcán, Km 9, Zona Hotelera.*

Plaza Flamingo. Around 80 shops that sell mainly clothing, jewelry, and souvenirs fill this small mall, but the Outback Steakhouse and Bubba Gump restaurants are the main attraction for many visitors. ✉ *Blvd. Kukulcán, Km 11.5, Zona Hotelera* ☎ *998/883–2855* ⊕ *www.flamingo. com.mx.*

Plaza Kukulcán. This upscale mall houses about 100 shops and four restaurants. Plaza Kukulcán's Luxury Avenue section offers brand names like Cartier, Fendi, Burberry, and Coach. The mall also hosts art exhibits and other cultural events; there's even a tequila museum with free tastings. ■ TIP→ While parents shop, kids can enjoy the game arcade and play area. ✉ *Blvd. Kukulcán, Km 13, Zona Hotelera* ☎ *998/193–0161.*

Plaza la Fiesta (*Mexican Outlet*). In from the convention center, Plaza la Fiesta has 20,000-square feet of showroom space and more than 100,000 different products for sale. Probably the widest selection of Mexican goods in the Zona, it includes leather items, jewelry, clothing, handicrafts, alcohol, and assorted souvenirs. There are some good bargains, but be prepared to pay sticker price as this is not a place to haggle. ✉ *Blvd. Kukulcán, Km 9, Zona Hotelera.*

EL CENTRO

There are lots of interesting shops downtown along Avenida Tulum between avenidas Cobá and Uxmal; however, by and large, stores in El Centro are geared toward the needs of locals rather than tourists. The most interesting shops for travelers may be in Plaza Bonita; otherwise, there are better options available in the Zona Hotelera.

Cancún Gran Plaza. Mainly frequented by El Centro residents, Cancún Gran Plaza has jewelry shops, fashion boutiques, and major department stores such as Sanborns and Walmart. There are on-site cinemas and eateries, too. ☒ *Av. Nichupté, Sm 51, Mza 18, Lote 1, Locs 24, 30 and 62A, El Centro* ☎ *998/206–1705* ⊕ *www.granplazacancun.com* ⊙ *Daily 9–9.*

Ki Huic. The oldest and largest of Cancún's crafts markets is Ki Huic. Open daily from 9 to 9, it houses about 100 vendors. ☒ *Av. Tulum 17, Sm 3, between Bancomer and Bital banks, El Centro* ☎ *998/884–3347.*

Fodor's Choice ★ Mercado Veintiocho (*Market 28*). Just off avenidas Yaxchilán and Sunyaxchén, Mercado Veintiocho is Cancún's largest open-air market. In addition to a few small restaurants, it has about 100 stalls where you can buy many of the same items found in the Zona Hotelera at a fraction of the cost. Expect to be bombarded by aggressive vendors trying to coax you into their shop. This is a great place to haggle, and usually you can end up paying half of the initial asking price. ☒ *Off avs. Yaxchilán and Sunyaxchén, next to Wal-Mart, El Centro.*

Parque Lumpkul. Vendors sell their wares Wednesday through Sunday at this small park, but Friday and Saturday are the best nights to go. Although there are only about 20 tables, you can find bargains on beautiful handmade jewelry with unusual stones, as well as hand-painted clothing. Parque Lumpkul has a hippy vibe and sometimes hosts music and artistic performances on market days. ☒ *Parque Lumpkul, Sm 22, between Av. Margaritas and Calle Azucenas, El Centro.*

Paseo Cancún. Developed by the company that owns La Isla in the Zona Hotelera, Paseo Cancún has the same open-air design as its sister property with modern white canopies throughout. It houses approximately 60 stores, plus a small ice-skating rink, a movie theater, a bowling alley, and a food court. ☒ *Av. Andrés, Sm 39, El Centro* ☎ *998/872–3735.*

Plaza Bonita. A small outdoor plaza attached to Mercado Veintiocho, Plaza Bonita has many wonderful specialty shops carrying Mexican goods and crafts. ☒ *Av. Xel-Há 1 and 2, Sm 28, El Centro* ☎ *998/884–6812* ⊕ *www.plazabonita.com.mx.*

Plaza Hollywood. You'll find several small boutiques and eateries at this strip mall. Starbucks fans can get their coffee fix here, and wine connoisseurs can visit La Europea Wine Market, which carries a wide selection of Mexican reds, plus imported cheeses and meats. ☒ *Av. Xcaret 35, at Rubi Cancún, El Centro.*

Plaza Hong Kong. With its massive pagoda structure, Plaza Hong Kong seems strikingly out of place in Cancún; inside, however, the shops sell Mexican handicrafts and souvenirs. ■ TIP➔ The mall has a babysitting service available. ☒ *Between Labná and Av. Xcaret, Sm 35, Mza 2, Lote 6, El Centro.*

Plaza Las Américas. This is the largest shopping center in downtown Cancún. Its 50-plus shops, three restaurants, two movie theaters, video arcade, fast-food outlets, and several big department stores will—for better or worse—make you feel right at home. The mall is intolerably crowded on weekends. ⊠ *Av. Tulum, Sm 4 and Sm 9, El Centro.*

Plaza Las Avenidas. Far from the Hotel Zone, this shopping area is most convenient for those staying in El Centro. There are gift shops, fast-food restaurants, cafés, nightclubs, and a karaoke bar. You'll also find a drugstore and a bakery on the premises. ⊠ *Av. Yaxchilán, Sm 35, El Centro* ☎ 998/887–7552.

SPAS

Fodor's Choice
★

Gem Spa. At Latin America's largest spa, the experience begins with a 10-step hydrotherapy ritual that detoxifies the skin through contrasts of warm and cool temperatures combined with high and low water pressures. Gem Spa treatments—ranging from a diamond dust body exfoliation to an amber and gold facial—are inspired by the healing energy of gemstones. The 80-minute Seventh Wonder Luxury Massage, during which quartz crystals are placed on the seven corresponding chakras, is worth the splurge. A day pass to the hydrotherapy circuit will set you back MX$1152. ⊠ *Fiesta Americana Grand Coral Beach, Blvd. Kukulcán, Km 9.5, Zona Hotelera* ☎ 998/881–3200 ⊕ *www.gem spacancun.com.*

JW Marriott Spa. This 35,000-square-foot spa has breathtaking ocean views and Mayan-inspired treatments like chocolate massages, ground corn exfoliations, and chaya detoxifications. Choose from one of 13 invigorating facials including the pumpkin enzyme treatment or the cucumber–green tea facial. Women will enjoy "Precious Stones and Flowers," which begins with a detoxifying marine mask followed by flower petals and crystals placed over energy points to bring balance and harmony to the body. The JW Spa even offers specialized treatments for men, golfers, couples, and teens. ⊠ *JW Marriott, Blvd. Kukulcán, Km 14.5, Zona Hotelera* ☎ 998/848–9700 ⊕ *www.jwmarriottcancun resort.com.*

Kayantá Spa. The intimate Kayantá Spa at the Ritz-Carlton offers a "Deep Blue Peel," a massage and body-scrub combo that involves marine extracts, seaweed, bergamot, and jojoba oil. The avocado and yogurt wrap will leave your skin feeling silky smooth, but you won't go wrong with a plain, old massage. ⊠ *Ritz-Carlton, Retorno del Rey 36, Blvd. Kukulcán, Km 13.5, Zona Hotelera* ☎ 998/881–0808 ⊕ *www. ritzcarlton.com/cancun.*

Le Blanc Spa. This massive facility takes pampering to a whole new level. Arrive early and linger in one of the many dimly lighted relaxation rooms, nibble on fresh cookies and sip *agua fresca* flavored with hibiscus or cucumber, or take a circuit in the hydrotherapy pools. A vast array of treatments—from facials and body wraps to intensive four-handed couples massages—are offered in oversized suites. ■TIP➔ Nonguests can use the resort on a day pass when booking treatments at the spa. ⊠ *Le Blanc Resort, Blvd. Kukulcán, Km 10, Zona Hotelera* ☎ 998/881–4740 ⊕ *www.leblancsparesort.com.*

Spa Aqua. It may be one of the smaller spas in the Zona Hotelera, but Spa Aqua has talented, veteran therapists who attract repeat clients from neighboring resorts. Treatments begin with a foot bath, hand massage, and your choice of chlorophyll water or green tea. A hydrotherapy ritual is included with treatments like the coffee exfoliation, coconut-chocolate wrap, and honey scrub. For the ultimate in pampering, request a caviar facial with 100% caviar and pearl dust, followed by a fusion massage that integrates techniques from around the world. ⊠ *Live Aqua, Blvd. Kukulcán, Km 12.5, Zona Hotelera* ☎ *998/881–7600* ⊕ *www.spaaqua.net.*

SPORTS AND THE OUTDOORS

BOATING AND SAILING

AquaWorld. Aside from organizing assorted on-the-water excursions, this outfit rents two-person speedboats for jungle tours. Wave Runners and cool water toys like the Flyboard (picture a marine jet pack that can shoot you 45 feet out of the water) are available, too. ⊠ *Blvd. Kukulcán, Km 15.2, Zona Hotelera* ☎ *998/848–8327* ⊕ *www.aquaworld.com.mx* ⌑ *From MX$680.*

El Embarcadero. The marina complex at Playa Linda, El Embarcadero is the departure point for ferries to Isla Mujeres and several tour boats. ⊠ *Playa Linda, Blvd. Kukulcán, Km 4, Zona Hotelera* ☎ *998/849–7343.*

Marina Barracuda. Jungle boats for two to four passengers can be rented through Marina Barracuda. Big-game fishing trips can also be arranged. ⊠ *Blvd. Kukulcán, Km 14.1, in front of Ritz-Carlton, Zona Hotelera* ☎ *998/885–2444 for marina, 998/884–1617 for fishing charters* ⊕ *www.marinabarracuda.com* ⌑ *Rentals from MX$935, fishing trips from MX$5862.*

Marina Punta del Este. Wave Runner rentals, catamaran tours, and self-drive speedboat trips through Nichupté Lagoon are all available through Marina Punta del Este. ⊠ *Blvd. Kukulcán, Km 10.3, in front of the Grand Park Royal Cancún Caribe, Zona Hotelera* ☎ *998/883–1210* ⊕ *www.puntaestemarina.com* ⌑ *From MX$899.*

FISHING

Some 500 species—including sailfish, wahoo, bluefin, marlin, barracuda, and red snapper—live in the waters off Cancún. You can charter deep-sea fishing boats for four to eight hours; rates generally include a captain and first mate, gear, bait, and beverages.

Charter Fishing Cancún. This outfit offers sportfishing trips between the mainland and Isla Mujeres. Possible catches include mahimahi, sailfish, barracuda, king mackerel, wahoo, tunas, grouper, snapper, and shark. Boats, ranging in size from 31 to 46 feet, can be chartered for four, six, or eight hours. Shared boats with a maximum of six anglers are also available. ⊠ *Marina Aquatours, Blvd. Kukulcán, Km 6.5, Zona*

CLOSE UP

Water Sports in Cancún

With the Caribbean on one side and the still waters of Laguna Nichupté on the other, it's no wonder that Cancún is one of the world's water sports capitals. The top activities are snorkeling and diving along the coral reef just off the coast.

Kiteboarding and windsurfing are also popular, although the waves are not as constant as on Mexico's Pacific coast. For the beach-break surfer, the sandbars are best at Playa Gaviota Azul and Playa Delfines, but waves are generally choppy and created by wind swells. Thirty-two kilometers (20 miles) south of Cancún are several point breaks off the coast of Puerto Morelos and Punta Brava.

If you want to view the mysterious underwater world but don't want to get your feet wet, a glass-bottom boat or "submarine" is the ticket. You can also go fishing, parasailing, or try your balancing skills on a stand-up paddleboard. Paddleboats, kayaks, catamarans, and banana boats are readily available, too.

Because the beaches along the Zona Hotelera can have a strong undertow, always respect the flags posted in the area. A black flag means no swimming at all. A red flag means you can swim but only with extreme caution. Yellow means approach with caution, while green means water conditions are safe. You'll most likely always see a red or yellow flag, even when the water is calm.

Unfortunately, there's very little wildlife in the Laguna Nichupté, so most advertised jungle tours are glorified Jet Ski romps where you drive around fast, make a lot of noise, and don't see many animals. American crocodiles still reside in these waters though, so don't stand or swim in the lagoon.

Although the coral reef in this area is not as spectacular as farther south, there's still marine life. It's quite common to spot angelfish, parrotfish, blue tang, sea turtles, and the occasional moray eel. To be a good world citizen, follow the six golden rules for snorkeling or scuba diving:

1. Don't throw any garbage into the sea, as the marine life will assume it's food, an often lethal mistake.

2. Never stand on the coral.

3. Secure all cameras and gear onto your body so you don't drop anything onto the fragile reef.

4. Never take anything from the sea.

5. Don't feed any of the marine animals.

6. Avoid applying sunblock, tanning lotion, or mosquito repellent just before you visit the reef.

Hotelera ☎ *998/200–3240* ⊕ *www.charterfishingcancun.com* ✉ *From MX$2110.*

Scuba Cancún. In addition to diving trips, Scuba Cancún offers deep-sea fishing expeditions that last from four to eight hours. ⊠ *Playa Langosta, Blvd. Kukulcán, Km 5, Zona Hotelera* ☎ *998/849–7508, 998/849–4736* ⊕ *www.scubacancun.com.mx* ✉ *From MX$7997.*

GO-CARTS

FAMILY **Exotic Rides.** About 10 minutes south of Cancún, speed demons can get their fix at Exotic Rides. It has a racetrack where Honda-engine go-carts reach speeds of up to 80 kph or 50 mph (there are also slower carts for children). For the experienced driver, Ferraris, Porsches, Audis, and V8 Nascars are available, too. ⊠ *Carretera Cancún–Aeropuerto, Km 7.5, Residencial Campestre* ☎ *998/882–0558, 998/882–1246* ⊕ *www. exoticridescancun.com* ⊠ *Go-carts from MX$325 for 15 mins, cars from MX$3605 for 5 laps* ⊗ *Thurs.–Tues. 6–11 pm.*

GOLF

Cancún Golf Club at Pok-Ta-Pok. Cancún's oldest golf course has fine views of both sea and lagoon but is showing its age with tired greens and rock-hard bunkers. The lack of upkeep means it's seldom crowded, plus it's not as challenging as some of the other courses in the area. Its 18 holes were designed by Robert Trent Jones Jr. It also has two practice greens, three tennis courts, a pro shop, and a restaurant. The green fees include your cart, food, and beverages. ⊠ *Blvd. Kukulcán, Km 7.5, Zona Hotelera* ☎ *998/883–1230* ⊕ *www.cancungolfclub.com* ⊠ *$160 for 18 holes* ⅄ *18 holes. 7051 yards. Par 72.*

Fodor'sChoice **Iberostar Cancún.** The only 18-hole championship course in Cancún is
★ at the Iberostar. Designed by legendary golfer Isao Aoki, it lies along the Nichupté Lagoon. The course has a practice facility with driving range and putting green. Four sets of tees stretch from 5,000 yards to 6,800 yards over 150 lush acres; you're likely to see all kinds of wildlife including crocodiles, birds, and iguanas as you play. Other than a few holes lined by jungle and lagoon, the course is wide open and the fairways are fast. The 16th hole overlooks the Mayan Ruinas del Rey. Hotel guests receive 60% off green fees, which include carts, food, and drinks. ⊠ *Iberostar, Blvd. Kukulcán, Km 17, Zona Hotelera* ☎ *998/881–8016* ⊕ *www.iberostar.com* ⊠ *$199 for 18 holes* ⅄ *18 holes. 6734 yards. Par 72.*

Moon Spa & Golf Club. This Jack Nicklaus–designed course features four sets of tees and is lined with jungle, wetlands, and strategically placed bunkers. Skilled golfers will welcome the challenge of Hole 17, a 151-yard par 3 that plays downwind to an island green. Other course highlights include Hole 6 (a drivable par 4 that plays 336 yards but crosses over water), and the last hole (a tough par 4 that plays 446 yards). The 18-hole green fee includes a cart, food, and drink service. If you're staying at any of the Palace Resorts, inquire about all-inclusive golf packages. Lessons are available. ⊠ *Moon Palace Golf & Spa Resort, Carretera Cancún–Chetumal, Km 340, about 15 mins from airport* ☎ *998/881–6000* ⊕ *www.palaceresorts.com* ⊠ *$303 for 18 holes* ⅄ *18 holes. 7165 yards. Par 72.*

Playa Mujeres Golf Club. Designed by Greg Norman, Cancún's newest course is challenging due to the daily trade winds and waterways on most holes. The game gets serious on Hole 11, a par 3 protected by bunkers, framed on the right by water, and 197 yards into the breeze. Yet

Cancún may not be the best destination for serious golfers, but it has several beautiful and challenging courses.

the toughest par 4 on the back nine is Hole 12, which has more water on the right all the way, plus the breeze and enormous beach bunker protecting the green; the 446 yards make it difficult to keep the ball dry. Green fees include a cart, bottled water, and balls. ⊠ *Playa Mujeres Beach Resort, Prolongación Bonampak, Punta Sam* ☎ *998/887–7322, 998/800–3892* ⊕ *www.playamujeresgolf.com.mx* ⊠ *$179 for 18 holes* ⚐ *18 holes. 7218 yards. Par 72.*

Puerto Cancún Golf. Designed by British Open Champion Tom Weiskopf, this 18-hole course is in Puerto Cancún, midway between the Zona Hotelera and El Centro. It stretches over 185 acres and has ocean views plus two holes that play on the marina. The winding fairways will test your skills on distance and short game swing, and the strategically placed bunkers demand a great deal of accuracy. Stay focused on the final hole, as it is located on an island in the middle of a canal. The course offers access to the Puerto Cancún youth golf program. ⊠ *Blvd. Kukulcán, Km 1.5, Zona Hotelera* ☎ *998/898–3306* ⊕ *www. puertocancun.com* ⊠ *$93 for 18 holes* ⚐ *18 holes. 7107 yards. Par 72* ⊘ *Closed Mon.*

Riviera Cancún Golf. Designed by Jack Nicklaus, this 18-hole golf course has ocean views and a Mexican-style clubhouse that's surrounded by mangroves, dunes, bridges, and lakes. The beautifully manicured course requires a certain level of strategic bunkering, straight shots, and skill, especially off the tee. The back nine are more challenging than the front nine. Bring more balls than you think, as you'll encounter water at nearly every hole. This course is not associated with a specific hotel. ⊠ *Blvd. Kukulcán, Km. 25, near Punta Nizuc, Zona Hotelera*

☎ 998/848–7777 ⊕ www.playgolf.mx ⌨ $200 for 18 holes ⚌ 18 holes. 7060 yards. Par 72.

SCUBA DIVING AND SNORKELING

The snorkeling is best at Punta Nizuc, Punta Cancún, and Playa Tortugas, although you should be careful of the strong currents at Tortugas. You can rent gear from many of the diving places as well as at many hotels.

Scuba diving is popular in Cancún, though it's not as spectacular as in Cozumel. Look for a company that will give you lots of personal attention. (Smaller outfits are often better at this than larger ones.) Regardless, ask to meet the dive master, and check the equipment and certifications thoroughly. ■TIP→ A few words of caution about one-hour courses that many resorts offer for free: such courses do not prepare you to dive in the open ocean—only in shallow water where you can easily surface without danger. If you've caught the scuba bug and want to take deep or boat dives, prepare yourself properly by investing in a full certification course.

FAMILY **Aqua Fun.** Sign on with Aqua Fun for a two-hour tour of the mangroves that includes snorkeling at the Punta Nizuc reef. Tours go daily at 9, noon, and 3; advance reservations are required. ✉ Blvd. Kukulcán, Km 16.5, Zona Hotelera ☎ 998/885–2930 ⊕ aquafun.com.mx ⌨ MX$953.

FAMILY **AquaWorld.** If you want to visit the underwater museum, AquaWorld runs both snorkeling excursions and scuba trips to the site. Dive explorations of boat wrecks are also organized. ✉ Blvd. Kukulcán, Km 15.2, Zona Hotelera ☎ 998/848–8327 ⊕ www.aquaworld.com.mx ⌨ Snorkeling trips MX$610, dive trips from MX$881, wreck dives MX$1043.

Marina Punta del Este. Located right in front of the Grand Park Royal Cancún Caribe, Marina Punta del Este has dives that last from 3½ to 4 hours. If you need a lesson, they begin daily at 9 am and 1 pm. ✉ Blvd. Kukulcán, Km 10.3, Zona Hotelera ☎ 998/883–1210 ⊕ www.puntaestemarina.com ⌨ Dives from MX$1030.

Scuba Cancún. Tomás Hurtado, who has more than 60 years of experience, operates Scuba Cancún. His outfit specializes in diving trips and offers PADI instruction. ✉ Playa Langosta, Blvd. Kukulcán, Km 5, Zona Hotelera ☎ 998/849–7508 ⊕ www.scubacancun.com.mx ⌨ Dives from MX$840.

Solo Buceo. In addition to PADI instruction, Solo Buceo offers one- and two-tank dives; special twilight dives are scheduled on Tuesday and Thursday. ✉ Blvd. Kukulcán, Km 9.5, Zona Hotelera ☎ 998/883–3979 ⊕ www.solobuceo.com ⌨ Dives from MX$881, instruction from MX$1423.

ISLA MUJERES

WELCOME TO ISLA MUJERES

TOP REASONS TO GO

★ **Getting away from the crowd:** Although Isla Mujeres is just across the bay from Cancún, the peace and quiet make it seem like another universe.

★ **Exploring the southeastern coast:** Bump along in a golf cart where craggy cliffs meet the blue Caribbean.

★ **Eating freshly grilled seafood:** For some reason it always tastes best under a beachfront *palapa* (thatch roof) at lovely Playa Norte.

★ **Diving with "sleeping sharks":** Plunge into the underwater caverns off Isla, where these gentle giants sleep.

★ **Taking a boat trip to Isla Contoy:** On this even smaller island, more than 150 species of birds make their home.

1 The Western Coast. Midway along the western coast of Isla you can glimpse the lovely Laguna Makax. At the lagoon's southeastern end are the shady stretches of Playa Tiburón and Playa Lancheros. At Isla's southernmost tip is El Garrafón National Park.

2 Playa Norte. With its waist-deep turquoise waters and wide soft sands, Playa Norte is the northernmost beach on Isla Mujeres, and the most beautiful. The bulk of the island's resorts and hotels are located here, and the town center and historic cemetery are both just a short walk away.

3 El Pueblo. Directly in front of the ferry piers, El Pueblo is Isla's only town. It extends the full width of the island's northern end, sandwiched between sand and sea to the south, west, and northeast. The *zócalo* (main square) is the hub of *isleño* life.

GETTING ORIENTED

Isla Mujeres is still quiet by Riviera Maya standards, with a small-town feel that makes it a great escape from Cancún. (Don't mention that to locals, who will tell you that the influx of big hotels has changed it forever.) Just 8 km (5 miles) long and 1 km (½ mile) wide, its landscapes include flat sandy beaches in the north and steep rocky bluffs to the south. The liveliest activities here are swimming, snorkeling, exploring the remnants of the island's past, drinking cold beer, eating fresh seafood, and lazing under palapas.

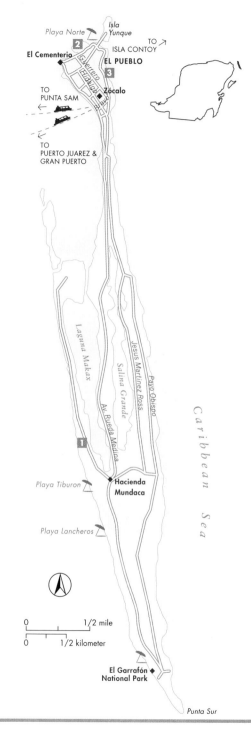

Isla Yunque

Playa Norte

2

El Cementerio ◆

EL PUEBLO

3

Zócalo ◆

TO ISLA CONTOY

Guerrero

Hidalgo

Juárez

TO PUNTA SAM

TO PUERTO JUAREZ & GRAN PUERTO

Laguna Makax

Salina Grande

Jesus Martinez Ross

Payo Obispo

Av. Rueda Medina

1

Playa Tiburon

Hacienda Mundaca ◆

Playa Lancheros

Caribbean Sea

| 0 | 1/2 mile |
| 0 | 1/2 kilometer |

El Garrafón National Park ◆

Punta Sur

Updated
by Marlise
Kast-Myers

Once a small fishing village, colorful Isla Mujeres (meaning "Island of Women") has become a favorite for travelers seeking natural beauty, island serenity, and a slower pace of life—all without compromising its cultural traditions. Winter months offer excellent sportfishing, and the calm surrounding waters are great for snorkeling and swimming year-round.

During high season, boatloads of visitors pop over from Cancún for a taste of the island life. The midday rush is a boon for vendors and hagglers offering every kind of service from hair braiding to beach massages. By late afternoon, though, the masses disappear and return to their big-city nightlife and the comforts of the mainland. Those who stay behind discover that on Isla Mujeres, worldly concerns fade with the setting sun.

Isla has about 16,000 permanent residents, many of whom earn a living selling fish at the docks or plates of food outside their homes. There are plenty of opportunities to practice your Spanish, and you'll find that most locals beam when you try. Taxi drivers are genuinely interested in sharing details of the island's history and telling you about their families who were born and raised here.

The minute you step off the boat, you'll get a sense of how small Isla is. The sights and properties are strung along the coasts, and there's not much to the interior except for two saltwater marshes where the Maya harvested salt centuries ago.

PLANNING

TIMING

Although most mainland travelers visit Isla only for the day, it's definitely worth spending the night if you're looking for a mix of culture, tranquility, good food, and island ambience. In a single afternoon you can visit all the best beaches and major attractions. You may even have enough time to snorkel or swim.

3

WHEN TO GO

When you factor in an international contingent of vacationers seeking winter sunshine and the day-tripping college students who flock in from neighboring Cancún during Spring Break, it's easy to see why high season here extends from late November (American Thanksgiving) straight through Easter. Other months qualify as low season, and prices may be cut in half. Some of the best deals can be found from late October to mid-November, after the rainy season has passed but before the crowds have arrived.

Isla enjoys its best weather between November and May, when temperatures usually hover around 27°C (80°F). June, July, and August are the hottest and most humid months, with daytime highs routinely over 35°C (95°F). A few festivals and holidays are worth keeping in mind while you're planning your trip: Carnaval in either February or March (the week before Lent); the Sol a Sol Regatta in late April; Founder's Day on August 17; the Day of the Virgin de la Caridad del Cobre, patron saint of local fishermen, on September 9; the Day of the Dead from October 31 to November 2; and the Feast of the Immaculate Conception from December 1 to 8. Be sure to book well in advance if you're planning to visit on any of these days.

GETTING HERE AND AROUND

BOAT AND FERRY TRAVEL

Isla ferries are typically two-story passenger cruisers that run between the mainland and the island's main dock.

Magana Express makes the crossing in just under 20 minutes. A one-way ticket from Puerto Juárez costs MX$78, and daily boats leave every 30 minutes from 5:30 am to 8:30 pm; there's a late ferry at 11:30 pm for those returning from partying in Cancún. The company also operates a slower open-air ferry from 5 am to 6 pm. It takes about 45 minutes but costs only MX$40 per person.

Between 9:30 and 5:30, Ultramar ferries to Isla's main dock depart from three locations in Cancún's Zona Hotelera: El Embarcadero marina complex at Playa Linda, Playa Tortugas, and Playa Caracol. The voyage costs MX$182 one-way and takes about 30 minutes.

Although you don't need a car on Isla Mujeres, the Naviera Contoy Vehicle Ferry leaves from Punta Sam, a dock north of Puerto Juárez. The ride takes about 45 minutes, and the fare is MX$15 per person and MX$185–MX$275 per vehicle, depending on the size of your car. If you're staying at Zoëtry Villa Rolandi or Isla Mujeres Palace, transportation on a private yacht is included in your room rate.

Contacts Magana Express ⊠ *Puerto Juarez Terminal, Av. Lopez Portillo, Sm 85, Cancún* ☏ *998/877–0254, 998/877–0088.* **Naviera Contoy Vehicle Ferry** ⊠ *Punta Sam Ferry Dock, Carretera Punta Sam, Km 5.2, past the Navy Base, Punta Sam, Cancún* ☏ *998/887–0065.* **Ultramar** ⊠ *Gran Puerto Cancún, Av. Lopez Portillo, Sm 84, Cancún* ☏ *998/881–5890* ⊕ *www.granpuerto.com.mx.*

GOLF CART TRAVEL

Golf carts are a fun way to get around the island, especially if you're traveling with kids. Due to *topes* (speed bumps) and potholes, they're a much safer option than exploring by moped or bike. There are more than a dozen rental agencies, although not all golf carts are created equal. Bypass the rusty cream-color carts, and opt for those with thick tires made by familiar brands like Jeep Wrangler. Most companies allow prebooking online and will deliver your golf cart directly to your hotel. This, however, limits your ability to haggle over the price. Rates start at approximately MX$802 for 24 hours depending on the season.

Contacts Golf Carts Indios *(Apache's).* ⊠ *Av. Rueda Medina, Sm 1, Mza 2, Lote 19, between avs. Lopez Mateos and Matamoros* ☎ *998/274-0392* ⊕ *www. indios-golfcarts.com.* **Prisma** ⊠ *Av. Ruida Medina, one block north of Ultramar ferry dock* ☎ *998/183-9971* ⊕ *www.islamujeresgolfcartrentals.com.* **Rentadora Ciro's** ⊠ *Av. Guerrero Norte 14, at Av. Matamoros* ☎ *998/877-0568* ⊕ *www. islamujeresgolfcartrentals.com.*

MOPED AND BICYCLE TRAVEL

Rueda Medina, directly across from the dock, is lined with shops where you can rent mopeds; most charge MX$535 a day or MX$200 per hour, but the final price will depend on the vehicle's make and condition and your own haggling skills. Some also offer bike rentals, with daily rates starting at MX$200 for beaters and MX$267 for mountain bikes. If are interested in cycling, be advised that it's hot here and you'll encounter plenty of speed bumps. Don't ride at night, since many roads don't have streetlights, and make sure your bike comes with a lock to keep it from wandering off. ⚠ **Before leaving the rental agency, check your moped or golf cart for scratches and dings. You may even want to take a photo for additional proof of the original condition. Otherwise, you'll pay dearly for any damage that was not noted prior to your rental agreement.**

HOTELS

Hotels here range from B&Bs and boutique properties to all-inclusive resorts; even the largest of the latter are small compared to what you might find on the mainland, and, with so many restaurants around, it's not worth paying for an all-inclusive package unless you'd rather not venture off site. Places on the north end near El Pueblo are within walking distance of shops, eateries, and the calm waters of Playa Norte; budget digs can be found in the center of town—just bear in mind they get street noise from the pedestrian traffic on Avenida Hidalgo. Lodgings elsewhere on the island are more private but aren't as convenient and might lack beaches. Many of Isla's smaller hotels don't accept credit cards, and some add a 5%–10% surcharge if you use one. Hoteliers here have also been tightening up cancellation policies, so inquire about fees for changing reservations. ■ TIP→ **Before paying, always ask to see your room to make sure everything is satisfactory—especially at the smaller hotels.**

Vacation rentals are an alternative to hotels, and several agencies can help you find one: ⊕ *www.islabeckons.com*, for example, lists fully equipped apartments and houses (and also handles reservations for hotel rooms); ⊕ *www.morningsinmexico.com* offers less expensive properties.

For expanded reviews, facilities, and current deals, visit Fodors.com.

RESTAURANTS

Dining on Isla is a casual affair, and much more affordable than in neighboring Cancún. Restaurants tend to serve simple food like seafood, pizza, salads, and Mexican dishes. Fresh ingredients and hospitable waiters make up for the island's lack of elaborate menus and master chefs. It's cash-only in most restaurants. If credit cards are accepted, you'll most likely pay an additional 5% service charge. It's customary in Mexico for the waiter to bring the bill only when you ask for it (*"la cuenta, por favor"*). Always check to make sure you didn't get charged for something you didn't order, and to make sure the addition is correct. The "tax" on the bill is often a service charge, a sort of guaranteed tip.

Though informal, most indoor restaurants do request that you at least wear a shirt and shoes. Some outdoor terrace and palapa restaurants also require shoes and some sort of cover-up over your bathing suit.

DINING AND LODGING PRICES IN DOLLARS AND PESOS			
	$	$$	$$$	$$$$
Restaurants	under MX$135	MX$135–MX$200	MX$201–MX$350	over MX$350
Hotels in dollars	under $100	$100–$200	$201–$300	over $300
Hotels in pesos	under MX$1450	MX$1450–MX$2900	MX$2901–MX$4400	over MX$4400

Restaurant prices are the average price for a main course at dinner, or if dinner is not served at lunch. Hotel prices are for a standard double room in high season, including taxes.

BANKS AND CURRENCY EXCHANGE

Isla Mujeres banks rarely change U.S. dollars into Mexican pesos, but there are many *casas de cambio* (exchange houses) that will; there's also one at the Ultramar ferry dock in Cancún if you want to come prepared. Alternatively, you can withdraw pesos at several on-island ATMs, including those at the Super Express store on the town square, the Banamex at the corner of Juarez and Morelos, and the HSBC across from the ferry port. Note, however, that these machines tend to have long lines and can run out of money on busy weekends and holidays. While most businesses accept U.S. dollars, you should expect to get change back in pesos at a subjective exchange rate. A minority of establishments accept credit cards (mostly MasterCard and Visa, and often with a 5% service fee attached), though this number is growing.

SAFETY

There's little crime on this small island, making it an excellent choice for visitors traveling alone. But common sense precautions do apply: stay clear of drugs; don't leave personal items unattended on the beach or in a golf cart; and lock your hotel room when you leave. Dehydration is one of the biggest safety concerns, so drink plenty of bottled water

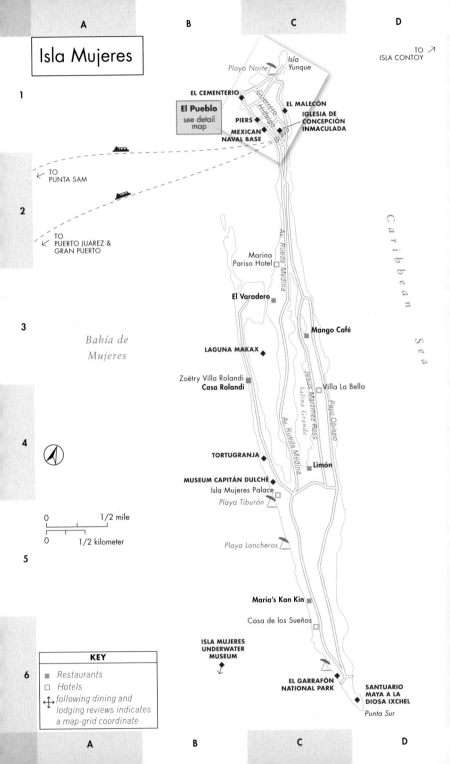

Isla Mujeres

A **B** **C** **D**

1

TO ↗
ISLA CONTOY

Isla
Yunque
Playa Norte

EL CEMENTERIO

EL MALECÓN

El Pueblo
see detail
map

**IGLESIA DE
CONCEPCIÓN
INMACULADA**

PIERS

**MEXICAN
NAVAL BASE**

Guerrero · Hidalgo · Juárez

← TO
PUNTA SAM

2

← TO
PUERTO JUAREZ &
GRAN PUERTO

Marina
Pariso Hotel

Av. Rueda Medina

El Varadero

Caribbean

3

*Bahía de
Mujeres*

Mango Café

LAGUNA MAKAX

Zoëtry Villa Rolandi
Casa Rolandi

Jesús Martínez Ross

Salina Grande

Villa La Bella

Payo Obispo

Sea

4

TORTUGRANJA

Av. Rueda Medina

Limón

MUSEUM CAPITÁN DULCHÉ

Isla Mujeres Palace
Playa Tiburón

Playa Lancheros

5

Maria's Kan Kin

Casa de los Sueños

**ISLA MUJERES
UNDERWATER
MUSEUM**

6

KEY

■ *Restaurants*
□ *Hotels*
⊕ *following dining and
lodging reviews indicates
a map-grid coordinate*

**EL GARRAFÓN
NATIONAL PARK**

**SANTUARIO
MAYA A LA
DIOSA IXCHEL**

Punta Sur

0 ___ 1/2 mile
0 ___ 1/2 kilometer

A **B** **C** **D**

and order beverages without ice unless you're at a restaurant that uses purified water. Be careful when driving along the narrow roads, especially since many have gravel surfaces and potholes.

VISITOR INFORMATION

Contacts **Tourist office.** Located directly across from the ferry pier, the tourist office is open weekdays 9–4 and has lots of general information about the island. ⊠ *Av. Rueda Medina 130* ☎ *998/877–0307, 998/877–0767* ⊕ *www.isla mujeres.gob.mx.*

EXPLORING

To get your bearings, picture the island as a long fish: the head is the southeastern tip, the tail is the northwest prong. Eight kilometers (5 miles) long and 1 km (½ mile) wide, Isla Mujeres is easy to explore in a single day. If you take your time, however, you'll discover that the island is not a destination to be rushed. Mopeds and golf carts are the most popular modes of transportation on Isla's virtually car-free dirt roads. If you're staying at one of the remote hotels on the southern tip, a taxi will take you from one end of the island to the other for MX$88 or roughly MX$210 per hour.

If you're interested in taking a DIY driving tour of Isla Mujeres, start by looping the island's perimeter, stopping midway at the southernmost tip. Here you can walk down to the rocky shores where waves crash at your feet. The views from Punta Sur are magnificent, and the temple of Goddess Ixchel is worth a visit. Head back north and explore colorful neighborhoods on the outskirts of town, with a stop at the excellent Mango Café for lunch. If you prefer the beach, relax at peaceful Playa Lancheros on the island's west side and see the area's dolphins, turtles, or nurse sharks before enjoying a traditional Mayan lunch at Playa Tiburón. Finish your tour with a sunset cocktail at Playa Norte before going downtown for dinner and live music.

TOP ATTRACTIONS

FAMILY **El Garrafón National Park.** Despite the widely-publicized "Garrafón Reef Restoration Program," much of the coral at this national marine park is dead—the result of hurricanes, boat anchors, and too many careless tourists. There are still colorful fish, but many of them will come near only if bribed with food. Although there's not much for snorkelers anymore, the park does have kayaks, restaurants, ziplines, bathrooms, and a gift shop. Be prepared to spend MX$1,164 for the basic package called "Royal Garrafón," which includes snorkeling gear, breakfast, lunch, kayaks, transportation from Cancún, a bike tour, and an open bar. Another option is "Dolphin Discovery" (MX$1,324–MX$2,341), which lets you use the park amenities and swim with dolphins. ■TIP→ The Beach Club Garrafón de Castilla next door is a much cheaper alternative; the snorkeling is at least equal to that available in the park, and a day pass is just MX$50. You can take a taxi from town. El Garrafón National Park is home to the **Santuario Maya a la Diosa Ixchel,** the sad vestiges of a Mayan temple once dedicated to

Who Was Ixchel?

CLOSE UP

Ixchel (ee-*shell*) is a principal figure in the pantheon of Mayan gods. Sometimes called Lady Rainbow, she is the goddess of childbirth, fertility, and healing, and is said to control the tides and all water on earth. Originally married to the earth god Voltan, Ixchel fell in love with the moon god Itzamna, considered the founder of the Maya because he taught them how to read, write, and grow corn. When Ixchel became his consort, she gave birth to four powerful sons known as the Bacabs, who continue to hold up the sky in each of the four directions.

Often portrayed as a wise crone, Ixchel can be seen wearing a skirt decorated with crossbones and a crown of serpents while carrying a jug of water. The crossbones are a symbol of her role as the giver of new life and keeper of dead souls. The serpents represent her wisdom and power to rejuvenate, and the water jug alludes to her dual role as both a benign and destructive deity. Although she gives mankind the continual gift of water—the most essential element of life—according to Mayan myth Ixchel also sent floods to cleanse the earth of wicked people who had stopped thanking the gods. She is said to give special protection to those making the sacred pilgrimage to her sites on Cozumel and Isla Mujeres.

the goddess Ixchel. This southern point is where the sun first rises in Mexico, meaning that thousands of travelers make a pilgrimage to the temple on New Year's to see the country awaken. A lovely walkway around the area remains, but the natural arch beneath the ruin has been blasted open and "repaired" with concrete badly disguised as rocks. The views are spectacular, though: you can look to the open ocean, where waves crash against dramatic cliffs on one side and the Bahía de Mujeres (Bay of Women) on the other. On the way to the temple there's a cutesy Caribbean-style shopping center selling overpriced jewelry and souvenirs, as well as a park with brightly painted abstract sculptures. The ruins (open daily 9–5) are near the old lighthouse, where the road turns northeast into the Corredor Panorámico. It costs MX$30 to visit just the ruins and sculpture park, but this is included with admission to El Garrafón. ✉ *Punta Sur, southeast of Playa Lancheros, Carretera El Garrafón, Km 6, Sm 9, Mza 41, Lote 12* ☎ *998/193–3360 for call center, 866/393-5158 toll-free in the U.S., 998/877–1100 for park office* ⊕ *www.garrafon.com* 💲 *MX$1164* ⊙ *Daily 10–5; closed Sat. May–Nov.*

OFF THE BEATEN PATH

When exploring the southeastern tip of Isla Mujeres, be sure to visit the unique shell-shape house located on Corredor Panorámico. Owned by artist Octavio Ocampo, it resembles an enormous conch shell both inside and out.

Iglesia de Concepción Inmaculada (*Church of the Immaculate Conception*). In 1890 local fishermen landed at a deserted colonial settlement known as Ecab, where they found three identical statues of the Virgin Mary, each carved from wood with porcelain face and hands. No one knows where the statues came from, but it's widely believed they were gifts from the Spanish during a visit in 1770. One statue went to the city of Izamal in the Yucatán, and another was sent to Kantunikin in Quintana Roo. The third remained on the island. It was housed in a small wooden chapel while this church was being built; legend has it that the chapel burst into flames when the statue was removed. Some islanders still believe the statue walks on the water around the island from dusk until dawn, looking for her sisters. You can pay your respects daily 10–11:30 am and 7–9 pm, or attend prayer services (in both English and Spanish) throughout the week. ⊠ *Avs. Morelos and Bravo, south side of the zócalo* ⊠ *Free.*

NEED A BREAK? It's a little island, but there are several shops selling gelato and homemade ice cream.

Gelateria Monte Bianco. Run by an Italian couple who have lived on the island since 2005, Gelateria Monte Bianco serves a wide variety of gelatos, as well as tasty desserts like tiramisù. ⊠ *Av. Matamoros 20* ☐ *No credit cards* ☉ *Closed Sun. and Sept.–Oct.*

Panna e Cioccolato. For a cool treat on a hot day, stop by this small shop— it has more than 50 flavors of ice cream. ⊠ *Av. Hildago at corner of Calle Abasolo* ☎ *984/142-1935 (mobile)* ⊕ *www.pannaecioccolato.com.mx.*

Fodor's Choice ★ **Isla Mujeres Underwater Museum.** Combining art and nature, sculptor Jason de Caires Taylor (⊕ *www.underwatersculpture.com*) has created "underwater museums" off the shores of Punta Cancún, Punta Nizuc, and Manchones Reef near Isla Mujeres. Locally known as MUSA (Museo Subacuático de Arte), his main work features more than 400 lifelike statues that serve as artificial reefs to attract marine life. Within the 12 galleries is a full-scale VW Beetle made from eight tons of concrete. The displays have conveniently been placed in shallow areas for viewing by divers, snorkelers, and glass-bottom boats. The unusual artificial habitat also helps restore the natural reefs that have suffered damage over the years. Most local dive shops can organize excursions to the site for about MX$1,000. ⊠ *Punta Cancún, Punta Nizuc, and Manchones Reef in Isla Mujeres* ☎ *998/578-7097* ⊕ *www.musaislamujeres. com* ⊠ *Free.*

Museum Capitán Dulché. The island's only museum gives a glimpse into the life of famed ocean explorers Ramón Bravo, Jacques Cousteau, and Captain Ernesto Dulché Escalante, who founded the 5th Naval Region of Isla Mujeres. A collection of photographs, model ships, anchors, buoys, lanterns, and other maritime tools also showcases Isla's seafaring history. The museum is part of a beach club, so you can reminisce about the past before enjoying the present with a cold beer under the shade of a palapa. ⊠ *Carretera Garrafón, Km 4.5* ☎ *998/849-7594* ⊕ *www. capitandulche.com* ⊠ *Free* ☉ *Daily 10:30–7:30.*

FAMILY **Tortugranja** (*Turtle Farm*). This scientific station, run by the Mexican government in partnership with private funding, works to conserve the endangered sea turtle. You can see rescued hatchlings in three large pools or watch larger turtles in sea pens. There's also a small section with seahorses, crabs, and other marine life. ■ **TIP**➔ **May through October, you can join the staff in collecting and hatching eggs; in the fall you can help release baby turtles.** ⊠ *Carretera Sac Bajo, Km 5* ✛ *Take Av. Rueda Medina south of town; about a block southeast of Hacienda Mundaca, take right fork (smaller road that loops back north called Sac Bajo); entrance is about ½ km (¼ mile) farther on left* ☎ *998/888–0705* 🖵 *MX$30* ⊗ *Daily 9–5.*

WORTH NOTING

El Cementerio. Isla's cemetery is on Avenida López Mateos, the road that runs parallel to Playa Norte. Many of the century-old gravestones are covered with carved angels and flowers, with the most elaborate and beautiful marking the graves of children. Hidden among them is the tomb of the notorious Fermín Mundaca de Marechaja, a 19th-century slave trader—often billed more glamorously as a pirate—who carved his own skull-and-crossbones gravestone with the ominous epitaph: "As you are, I once was; as I am, so shall you be." Ironically, his remains actually lie in Mérida, where he died. The monument is tough to find, so ask a local to point out the unidentified marker. ⊠ *Av. Lopez Mateos.*

Laguna Makax. Pirates are said to have anchored their ships in this lagoon while waiting to ambush hapless vessels crossing the Spanish Main. Today it houses a local shipyard and provides a safe harbor for boats during hurricane season. ⊠ *Off Av. Rueda Medina, about 2½ km (1½ miles) south of town.*

BEACHES

Despite being surrounded by water, Isla Mujeres really has only three beaches suitable for visitors: Playa Norte on the north end, and Playa Lancheros and Playa Tiburón on the west side. With its crystal-clear water, Playa Norte is generally tranquil and better for swimming than eastern beaches facing the Caribbean, which are rocky and susceptible to strong winds and riptides. Western beaches always have a subtle south-to-north current, which can be dangerous if you're not alert. The southern part of the island has several secluded beaches, but they too have exposed reefs and strong currents and are often littered with sea grass and ocean debris.

In 2009, high winds and stormy seas stole nearly 30 yards of Isla's sandy beaches. Because of potential environmental impact, the government made minimal efforts to replenish the sand, which never fully recovered. More recently, property owners have worked to minimize erosion with geotubes placed along Playa Norte's shores.

FAMILY **Playa Lancheros** (*Boatman's Beach*). On the western side of the island, this stretch between Laguna Makax and El Garrafón National Park is a popular spot with an open-air restaurant where locals gather to eat freshly grilled *tikin xic* (whole fish marinated with *adobo de achiote* and sour oranges, then wrapped in a banana leaf and cooked over an open flame). Playa Lancheros has grittier sand than Playa Norte but more palm trees. Calm water makes it good for children, although it's

Isla's History

The name Isla Mujeres means "Island of Women," although no one knows who dubbed it that. Many believe it was the ancient Maya, who were said to use the island as a religious center for worshipping Ixchel (aka Lady Rainbow), the tide-controlling Mayan goddess of fertility, childbirth, and healing. Another popular legend has it that the Spanish conquistador Hernández de Córdoba named the island when he landed here in 1517 and found hundreds of female-shape clay idols dedicated to Ixchel and her daughters. Still others say the name dates from the 1600s, when visiting pirates stashed their women on Isla before sailing out to pillage merchant ships. (Reputedly both Henry Morgan and Jean Lafitte buried treasure here, although no one has ever found any pirate's gold.)

It wasn't until 1821, when Mexico became independent, that people really began to settle on Isla. In 1847, refugees from the Caste War of the Yucatán fled to the island and built its first official village of Dolores, which was welcomed into the newly created territory of Quintana Roo in 1850. By 1858 a slave-trader-turned-pirate named Fermín Mundaca de Marechaja began building an estate that took up 40% of the island. By the end of

the century the population had risen to 651, and residents had begun to establish trade with the mainland, mostly by supplying fish to the owners of chicle and coconut plantations on the coast. In 1949, the Mexican navy built a base on Isla's northwestern coast. Around this time the island also caught the eye of some wealthy Mexican sportsmen, who began using it as a vacation spot.

Tourism flourished on Isla during the latter half of the 20th century, partly due to the island's most famous resident, Ramón Bravo (1927–98). A diver, cinematographer, ecologist, and colleague of Jacques Cousteau, Bravo was the first underwater photographer to explore the area. He contributed to the discovery of the now-famous Cave of the Sleeping Sharks and produced dozens of underwater documentaries for American, European, and Mexican television. Bravo's efforts to maintain the ecology on Isla have helped keep development here to a minimum. Even today, Bravo remains a hero to many *isleños* (ees-*lay*-nyos); his statue can be found where Avenida Rueda Medina becomes the Carretera El Garrafón, and there's a museum named after him on nearby Isla Contoy.

best if they stay close to shore as the bottom drops off steeply. Souvenir stands here are fairly low-key, and most bars and restaurants will give you access to their beach facilities provided you order a drink. The closest hotel is Isla Mujeres Palace, an all-inclusive resort open to hotel guests only. ■TIP→ There's a small pen with tame tiburones gatos (nurse sharks). You can swim with them or just get your picture taken for a MX$20 tip. **Amenities:** food and drink; parking (no fee). **Best for:** snorkeling. ⊠ *Carretera El Garrafon, Km 4.6, near Hacienda Mundaca.*

Fodor'sChoice **Playa Norte** (*North Beach*). Playa Norte is easy to find: simply head ★ north on any of the north–south streets in town until you hit it. The turquoise sea is as calm as a lake here, though developers have built

Playa Norte is a superb beach for strolling in the sun.

along most of the coast. The small cove between Mia Reef Resort and the Caribbean is the nicest section. Relatively shallow, the water flows directly from the open sea, so it's clean and good for snorkeling; tour guides often lure the fish with food. A food or drink purchase from **Cafe del Mar** gives you access to beach beds and changing facilities at Privilege Aluxes Resort. Alternately, you can enjoy a libation at one of the palapa bars where wooden swings take the place of bar stools; **Buho's** is especially popular, as MX$60 lounge chairs and MX$200 beach beds come with a free drink ticket. At **Sunset Grill,** lounge chairs, umbrellas, towels, toilets, and showers are included when you spend MX$300 on food or drink. **Amenities:** food and drink; showers; toilets. **Best for:** snorkeling; sunset; swimming. ⊠ *Calle Zazcil-Há, along the north end of the island, just before Mia Reef Resort.*

Playa Tiburón (*Shark Beach*). Like Playa Lancheros, this beach on the west side of the island faces Bahía de Mujeres, so the water is exceptionally calm. Once a respite from the crowds, it has become more developed, with a large restaurant (through which you actually enter the beach) that serves burgers, hot dogs, and fish. There are several souvenir stands selling handmade seashell jewelry. On certain days you can find women who will braid your hair or give you a henna tattoo. Many people visit to swim or take photos with tame nurse sharks (MX$50), but the tiny pen entrapping the large creatures is rather sad. ■ **TIP →** Although there are public restrooms, you have to pay for toilet paper. **Amenities:** food and drink; toilets. **Best for:** swimming. ⊠ *Carretera Sac Bajo, near the turtle farm.*

CLOSE UP

Isla's Salt Mines

The ancient salt mines in Isla's interior were worked during the postclassic period of Mayan history (roughly AD 1000–1500). Salt was an important commodity for the Maya, who used it not only for preserving and flavoring food but also for making armor. Since the Maya had no metal, they soaked cotton cloth in salt until it formed a hard coating.

There's little to see today: simply two shallow marshes called Salina Chica (Small Salt Mine) and Salina Grande (Big Salt Mine) with murky water and quite a few mosquitoes at dusk. But since both of the island's main roads (Avenida Rueda Medina and the Corredor Panorámico) pass by them, you can have a look on your way to other parts of Isla.

3

WHERE TO EAT

EL PUEBLO

$ CAFÉ 🍴 **Aluxes Coffee House.** Open from 7 am to 10 pm, this spot is equally good for an early-morning cappuccino, afternoon tea, or nighttime cocktail. It also has terrific smoothies and bakery items (the New York–style cheesecake and triple-fudge brownies are especially decadent). For a hearty alternative, try the egg and chorizo fajitas. **■ TIP→ If you want the café's famous banana bread, get here early—loaves usually sell out by 10 am.** [$] *Average main: 93 MP* ✉ *Av. Matamoros 87, between avs. Hidalgo and Guerrero* ☎ *998/218–5843* 💳 *No credit cards* 🕒 *Closed Tues.* ✥ *C3.*

$$ ECLECTIC 🍴 **Amigos.** Although it used to be known mainly for its superb pizza, this easy-to-miss eatery offers a little bit of everything from fish and meat to pastas and vegetarian dishes. Breakfasts, featuring delicious omelets and strong coffee, are also served. Big portions, drink specials, and a convivial vibe make Amigos a local favorite; once you settle in at one of the streetside tables, the staff treat you like an old friend. [$] *Average main: 147 MP* ✉ *Av. Hidalgo 19, between avs. Matamoros and Abasolo* ☎ *998/877–0624* ✥ *C4.*

$$$ ITALIAN 🍴 **Angelo.** Named for its Italian chef Angelo Sanna, this charming bistro on Hidalgo's busy main strip is done up with soft lighting and a wood-fired oven. Come for the pizza; they have a thin crispy crust and are quite delicious. A large selection of Italian classics round out the menu. Try their famous wood-oven lasagna or mussels steamed in white wine. Angelo, who has lived and worked in Isla Mujeres for more than 18 years, is a hospitable host and a great source of local information. **■ TIP→ Open late, Angelo will serve pizzas to the local bars if you're hungry at the end of a long night.** [$] *Average main: 267 MP* ✉ *Av. Hidalgo 14* ☎ *998/877–1273* 🕒 *Closed Sept. No lunch* ✥ *B4.*

$$ BISTRO 🍴 **Bistro Français.** The name of this casual restaurant is somewhat deceiving. Though French dishes like chicken *cordon bleu* or *coq au vin* can

be found on the menu, the grilled fish and pasta specials are the real reason to visit. Breakfast is particularly good, featuring tasty fruit salads and fluffy French toast. The apple crêpes with maple cream might just inspire repeat trips. Victor, the owner, makes it a point to ensure that each of his diners has a good experience. The deck overlooks the bustling street, so you can watch the world go by. [$] *Average main: 187 MP* ✉ *Av. Matamoros 29, between avs. Juárez and Hidalgo* ☎ *998/877–0123* 💳 *No credit cards* ✣ *B4.*

SAFETY FIRST

Unlike Cancún and Cozumel, Isla Mujeres does not use the colored safety flag system, and there are no lifeguards to keep watch over swimmers. Therefore it's best to venture out near familiar beaches like Playa Norte, Playa Lancheros, and Playa Tiburón only on calm days when winds are light. Be wary of strong currents and riptides, especially on the east and west sides of the island.

If you plan to spend a day at the beach, bring fresh drinking water and use sunscreen or wear protective clothing to avoid overexposure.

$ CAFÉ 🍴 **Café Cito.** Opened in 1988, this cheery, seashell-decorated place was one of Isla's first cafés, and it's still among the best breakfast spots on the island. The menu includes pancakes, waffles, fruit-filled crêpes, and egg dishes, as well as great cappuccino and espresso. Every breakfast comes with complimentary coffee or tea, and the fresh-squeezed OJ is a great way to start the day. Don't miss the pineapple-coconut marmalade. Lunch specials are also available daily. [$] *Average main: 80 MP* ✉ *Avs. Juárez and Matamoros* ☎ *998/877–1470* 💳 *No credit cards* 🕒 *No dinner* ✣ *B4.*

$$ ECLECTIC 🍴 **Café Mogagua.** Whether you're sitting at one of the wooden tables, on a comfortable couch, or on a street-facing lounger, you'll enjoy the relaxed vibe at this open-air café. Packed for breakfast and lunch, its menu ranges from Mexican classics like chilaquiles and *huevos divorciados* (eggs with chile sauce) to pizza, grilled meats, and fish later in the day. If you feel like lingering, you can play board games, have a glass of wine with a friend, or spend quality time with your laptop (Wi-Fi is free) while enjoying a cup of organic coffee from Chiapas. [$] *Average main: 160 MP* ✉ *Av. Juárez at Madero, El Pueblo* ☎ *998/877–0127* ✣ *C4.*

$$ ECLECTIC 🍴 **ComoNo at El Patio** (*El Patio*). This low-key establishment is a peaceful oasis in the heart of El Pueblo. On the ground level, chit palms and ocean grape trees decorate the open-air restaurant, each branch wrapped in fairy lights and adorned with seashell lanterns. House specialties like steak and shrimp wrapped in prosciutto are smoked over a bed of coals and served with grilled vegetables and a baked potato. The menu also features tapas and vegetarian dishes including couscous, veggie spring rolls, and roasted beet salad. ■ **TIP→ Head to the rooftop lounge for live jazz and frozen mojitos.** [$] *Average main: 200 MP* ✉ *Av. Hidalgo 17, El Pueblo* ☎ *998/243–4475* 🌐 *www.islamujeresdining.com* 💳 *No credit cards* 🕒 *Closed Sun.* ✣ *C4.*

$$ MEXICAN 🍴 **Don Chepo.** Resembling a small hacienda, lively Don Chepo serves some of the island's best Mexican food. The *arrachera,* a fine cut of beef grilled to perfection and served with rice, salad, baked potato, warm

tortillas, and beans, is a reliably excellent choice, as is the chile relleno. Tables outside are perfect for watching all the downtown action. Inside, the focal point is a large, well-stocked bar, where you can chat with other visitors or enjoy mariachi music. The cocktails are strong and pair well with ceviche; a two-for-one happy hour lasts all day long. $ *Average main: 160 MP* ⊠ *Avs. Hidalgo and Francisco Madero* ☎ *998/877–0165* ✛ *C4.*

$$$
MEXICAN

✕ **Fenix.** Next to the trendy Na Balam Hotel, Fenix offers beachside dining under big, shady palms, with tiki torches and beach beds (MX$200 food or drink minimum). For a more intimate alternative, you can ask to be seated under a palapa. Tapas, ranging from garlic shrimp to peppers stuffed with goat cheese, are the focus at lunch. Later in the day the kitchen serves innovative vegetarian fare plus dishes like coconut curry, paella, shrimp ravioli, and pad thai. ■ TIP➔ **Musicians from Mexico, Cuba, and elsewhere in the Caribbean often play during the weekends, turning the restaurant into an after-hours island hotspot.** $ *Average main: 227 MP* ⊠ *Calle Zazil-Há 118* ☎ *998/274–0073* ⊕ *www.fenixisla.com* ✛ *B2.*

$$
MEXICAN

✕ **Fredy's Restaurant & Bar.** This family-run restaurant specializes in simple fish, seafood, and Mexican dishes like fajitas and oven-baked shrimp. There isn't much here in the way of décor—think plastic chairs and tables—but the staff is friendly, the food is fresh, the beer is cold, and the value is good. The tasty daily specials are a bargain and attract both locals and visitors. $ *Average main: 147 MP* ⊠ *Av. Hidalgo between avs. Matamoros and Lopez Mateo* ☎ *998/190–8183* ⊕ *www. fredys.myislamujeres.com* ⊘ *Closed Tues. No lunch* ✛ *B4.*

$$$
CARIBBEAN

✕ **Lola Valentina.** Lori Dumm, former executive chef of Mango Cafe, has brought her talents to the heart of El Pueblo. Providing a unique take on Caribbean-fusion cuisine, she creates all of her own recipes and makes every menu item from scratch. Start with blue corn empanadas served with tamarind dipping sauce. The shrimp-stuffed red snapper is topped with creamy poblano peppers, and the chicken kabobs are bathed in a peanut-coconut sauce. Breakfasts of coconut French toast and eggs Benedict are equally divine. Those with dietary constraints will appreciate the variety of vegetarian and gluten-free options, including a vegan chocolate cake. $ *Average main: 240 MP* ⊠ *N. Av. Hidalgo 27* ☎ *998/159–2187* ⊕ *www.lolavalentina.blogspot.com* ⊟ *No credit cards* ⊘ *No lunch* ✛ *B4.*

$
MEXICAN
Fodor'sChoice
★

✕ **Loncheria La Lomita.** Don't judge a restaurant by its setting. This hole-in-the-wall, with its red plastic tables and chairs, is a perennial local favorite. Expect enormous portions, starting with the beloved *sopa de frijoles* (black bean soup made with onions, tomatoes, lime and fresh cheese). Fish fillets are moist, and the chicken mole is the best on the island. But if you only try one dish, make it the *chiles rellenos*: stuffed chiles lightly battered, fried, and served with a side of pickled cabbage and rice. Late diners should note that Loncheria La Lomita closes at 9 pm. $ *Average main: 110 MP* ⊠ *Av. Juárez Sur 25-B, at Av. Allende, El Pueblo* ☎ *998/179–9431* ⊟ *No credit cards* ✛ *D5.*

$$
SEAFOOD

✕ **Minino's Cocteleria.** If you're looking to dine on the waterfront with sand between your toes, head for Minino's. This no-frills spot serves fresh fish tossed in ceviche or simply grilled. During the afternoon, you can watch local fisherman bring their catch back to shore while you sip on a beer and lazily nosh on small plates like fish tacos and shrimp cocktails. The grilled octopus and lobster are both outstanding. For those who like it hot: the *pico de gallo* is delicious but incredibly spicy, so watch how much you add to your plate. **TIP→ There's live music nightly from 4 to 8.** [$] *Average main: 160 MP* ✉ *Av. Rueda Medina, El Pueblo* ☎ *998/274–0159* ✥ *B5.*

$$ MEDITERRANEAN Fodor's Choice ★

🍴 **Olivia.** The delightful dishes at this sexy Mediterranean restaurant are combinations of Moroccan, Greek, and Turkish flavors based on owners Lior and Yaron Zelzer's family recipes. Everything from the freshly baked spanakopita to the flaky baklava is made in the open-air kitchen. Start with the Greek or Moroccan tapas and move onto house favorites like the *shawarma* pita wrap filled with grilled chicken, hummus, tahini, and fried eggplant, or the *mafrum,* a blend of potatoes stuffed with ground beef in a Moroccan red sauce. The setting is casual yet romantic, with tiki torches lighting the way to a tropical garden where rustic tables sit beneath a palapa. No visit is complete without a bowl of homemade cherry ice cream. [$] *Average main: 160 MP* ✉ *Matamoros 11, between avs. Juárez and Rueda Medina, El Pueblo* ☎ *998/877–1765* 🌐 *www.olivia-isla-mujeres.com* 🕓 *Closed Sun., and Mon. Apr.–Dec.; closed 3–4 wks Sept.–Oct. No lunch* ✥ *B4.*

$$ SEAFOOD

🍴 **Picus Cocktelería.** Kick off your shoes and settle back with a beer at this charming beachside restaurant near the ferry docks. You can watch the fishing boats come and go while you wait for some of the island's freshest seafood. The grilled fish and lobster with garlic butter are both excellent, as are the shrimp fajitas—but the real showstopper is the ceviche, which might include conch, shrimp, abalone, fish, or octopus. For a traditional Yucatan dish, try *pescado tikin-xic* seasoned with achiote, orange, and garlic, then topped with pickled red onions. [$] *Average main: 147 MP* ✉ *Av. Rueda Medina, 1 block northwest of ferry docks* ☎ *998/129-6011* 🕓 *Closed Tues.* ✥ *B5.*

$ CUBAN Fodor's Choice ★

🍴 **Qubano.** This delightful restaurant is owned by vivacious chef Vivian Reynaldo, who seems to know everyone in town. Her rich Hungarian potatoes, a recipe handed down from her mother, have been known to leave customers speechless, while the grilled *tostones* sandwiches, which use fried plantains instead of bread, are topped with a finger-licking onion-and-orange sauce. Meat lovers will relish the juicy hamburgers stuffed with goat cheese and served with yucca fries. Several vegetarian dishes are also available, and lunch salads are topped with fresh ingredients like garbanzo beans, avocado, and jicama. **TIP→ By night, Qubano morphs into a tapas bar, operated by the talented neighboring chef, Angelo.** [$] *Average main: 80 MP* ✉ *Av. Hidalgo, across from Angelo* ☎ *998/214–2118* ✥ *B4.*

$$$ ITALIAN

🍴 **Sardinian Smile.** Despite the cheesy name (there's an outpost in Sardinia), this cozy spot on busy Avenida Hidalgo is the island's most authentic Italian restaurant, serving handmade pastas like fettuccine with clams or a spicy arrabbiata sauce to happy crowds. Pesto linguini, lobster ravioli, and rich tiramisù dusted with cocoa powder make it hard to forget that you're not in Italy. Meat and cheese platters add protein to a carbohydrate-rich menu. Always ask about the daily catch; the snapper baked in wine and olive oil is divine. Though service can be slow, it's worth it when the food arrives; just order a glass of Italian wine and await your feast while listening to live music (8–10 pm). [$] *Average main: 240 MP* ✉ *Av. Hidalgo, near the zócalo, El Pueblo* ☎ *998/163–6850* ⏲ *Closed Mon. Sept.–Nov. No lunch* ✥ *C4.*

$$$ SEAFOOD 🍴 **Sunset Grill.** With an enormous menu to appease every appetite and a prime location on Playa Norte, this elegant palapa restaurant is the perfect place to savor the sunset. A wall-less dining terrace overlooks the sea, while soft music and candlelight add to the romantic ambience. Grab a table in the sand and you can take a dip in the ocean between courses. The wide range of dinner dishes includes grilled tuna, coconut shrimp, paella, and grouper in a creamy dill and wine sauce; homemade coconut pie provides a sweet finish. At lunch, the kitchen offers Mexican favorites like tacos and quesadillas, plus plenty of vegetarian options. **■ TIP→ If you're traveling with tykes, there's also a menu for kids.** [$] *Average main: 227 MP* ✉ *Condominios Nautibeach, Av. Rueda Medina, Playa Norte* ☎ *998/877–0785* 🌐 *www.sunsetgrill.com.mx* ✥ *A4.*

ELSEWHERE ON THE ISLAND

Listings in this section appear on the Isla Mujeres map.

$$$ NORTHERN ITALIAN 🍴 **Casa Rolandi.** This quietly sophisticated hotel restaurant has an open-air dining room connected to a deck overlooking the water. Tables are set with beautiful linens, china, and cutlery, making Casa Rolandi the most upscale and romantic restaurant on the island. A northern Italian menu includes wonderful carpaccio *di tonno alla Giorgio* (thin slices of tuna with extra-virgin olive oil and lime juice), along with excellent pastas. Even the simplest dishes, such as angel-hair pasta in tomato sauce, are delicious. For something different, try the saffron risotto or *costolette d'agnello al forno* (lamb chops with a thyme infusion). The sunset views, of course, are spectacular. [$] *Average main: 267 MP* ✉ *Zoëtry Villa Rolandi, Fracc. Laguna Mar, Sm 7, Mza 75, Lotes 15 and 16* ☎ *866/754–0452, 998/999–2000* ✥ *C3.*

$$ CUBAN 🍴 **El Varadero.** Located off the beaten path in a weathered, palapa-topped fisherman's cottage, this local favorite is the perfect place for delicious, reasonably priced seafood. It's known for fresh mojitos, but the family-style plates of grilled or fried fish are an even bigger draw. The day's catch changes regularly, ranging from grouper to lobster (order them with creole sauce if it's being served). Cuban specialties like tostones and sandwiches round out the menu. [$] *Average main: 173 MP* ✉ *Laguna Makax, Colonia Electricistas, Calle de Septiembre Lt. 14* ☎ *998/877–1600* ⏲ *Closed Mon.* ✥ *C3.*

$$ MEXICAN FUSION 🍴 **Limón.** Situated smack dab in the center of the island, Limón is more about taste than location. Inspired by "mom's recipes," Chef Sergio makes freshness a top priority—nothing here is ever frozen. The Mexican-fusion menu starts with slightly sweet hibiscus-filled tacos and impressive zucchini towers with grilled panela cheese. The shrimp with a four-chile sauce has the right amount of kick, and the local fish cooked Mayan-style in a banana leaf is unbelievably moist. Fish and steaks are

grilled on the garden patio just steps from your table, as is the pineapple flambé with vanilla ice cream. $ *Average main: 200 MP* ⊠ *Colonia la Gloria, Calle Lizeta 159, near Super Express* ☎ 998/130–1924 ▭ *No credit cards* ⊗ *Closed Tues. No lunch* ⊹ *C4.*

$ ✕ **Mango Cafe.** Warm and inviting with wooden tables and colorful chalkboards announcing the day's *aguas frescas*, this 10-table hotspot is a must if you're looking for an unbeatable breakfast or lunch. The owner, Polo Avila, serves up playfully inspired takes on classic dishes using Mexican ingredients and flavors. Standouts are a bacon-egg-and-cheese-stuffed poblano chile and eggs Benedict topped with local *chaya* (a cousin of spinach). Portions are massive, so be sure to come hungry. A self-serve coffee bar guarantees you always have a full cup of joe. Once you move on to cold beers and mango mimosas, it's difficult to leave, but plan accordingly—Mango Cafe closes at 3 pm daily. $ *Average main: 120 MP* ⊠ *Payo Obispo, Lot 1, No 725, across from Guadalupe Church* ☎ 998/274–0118 ⊗ *No dinner* ⊹ *D5.*

ECLECTIC
Fodor'sChoice
★

$$$ ✕ **Maria's Kan Kin.** The difference between a memorable evening here and an unforgettable one is reserving a table for two at the water's edge. Otherwise, you'll be sitting beneath a palapa overlooking an infinity pool and the crystal bay, which is, of course, a spectacular runner-up. The minimal menu presents the best local seafood in dishes like red snapper with herb sauce; shrimp skewers with lime; and grouper with tomatoes, olives, and basil. For something meaty, try the ribeye or grilled lobster. Cap your meal by ordering caramel lava cake with homemade mango sorbet. Note that this little haven is reached via a dark, steep driveway. $ *Average main: 240 MP* ⊠ *Carretera El Garrafón, Km 4.5* ☎ 998/877–0015 ⊕ *www.mariaskankin.com* ▭ *No credit cards* ⊹ *C5.*

SEAFOOD

WHERE TO STAY

EL PUEBLO

$ ⊞ **Casa el Pio.** Off the town square, this boutique hotel is bursting with character, charm, and creativity. **Pros:** unlimited fresh drinking water; spotless property; excellent rates. **Cons:** no meals; no housekeeping or check-ins on Sunday. $ *Rooms from: $75* ⊠ *Av. Hidalgo 3, between Bravo and Allende* ☎ 998/152–8669 ⊕ *www.casaelpio.com* ⤵ *5 rooms* ⫽⊙⫽ *No meals* ⊹ *D4.*

HOTEL
Fodor'sChoice
★

$ ⊞ **Hotel Belmar.** Cozy rooms in this hacienda-style hotel feature Mexican artwork, saltillo tile floors, and French doors that lead to small balconies. **Pros:** clean and comfortable; near shops and restaurants; master suite has a private Jacuzzi. **Cons:** some street noise; rooms vary in size. $ *Rooms from: $77* ⊠ *Av. Hidalgo Norte 110, between avs. Madero and Abasolo* ☎ 998/877–0429, 998/877–0430 ⊕ *www.hotelbelmarisla.com* ⤵ *10 rooms, 1 suite* ⫽⊙⫽ *Breakfast* ⊹ *C4.*

B&B/INN

$ ⊞ **Hotel Frances Arlene.** One block from downtown and one block from the beach, this perennial favorite has rooms surrounding a pleasant courtyard; all are outfitted with bamboo furniture and refrigerators, some come with kitchenettes, and those on the top floors have ocean

HOTEL

views. **Pros:** reasonable rates; friendly staff; one of the few hotels that accommodates wheelchairs. **Cons:** some street noise; not all rooms have balconies or a/c; lots of mosquitoes. ⓢ *Rooms from: $75* ⊠ *Av. Guerrero 7* ☎ *998/877–0310* ⊕ *www.francisarlene.com* ⤵ *26 rooms* ⦿ *No meals* ✦ *C4.*

$$ 🛏 **Hotel Playa la Media Luna.** This breezy palapa-roofed hotel lies along
HOTEL Half Moon Beach, just south of Playa Norte. **Pros:** some deluxe rooms have Jacuzzis; nearby beach is calm and shallow. **Cons:** pool bar seldom open; hotel needs renovating; lost safe key costs $50, lost towel costs $10. ⓢ *Rooms from: $140* ⊠ *Half Moon Beach, Sección Rocas, Lote 9/10* ☎ *998/877–0759* ⊕ *www.playamedialuna.com* ⤵ *20 rooms* ⦿ *Multiple meal plans* ✦ *C2.*

$$ 🛏 **Hotel Rocamar.** You can smell, hear, and see the ocean from the starkly
HOTEL minimalist, blue-and-white rooms at this hotel: located right on the eastern *malecón* (boardwalk), it's one of the few on the island that overlooks the Caribbean. **Pros:** steps from the water; helpful staff; communal lounge with TV and library. **Cons:** bathrooms lack privacy; no elevator; Wi-Fi in common areas only. ⓢ *Rooms from: $120* ⊠ *Avs. Nicolas Bravo and Abasolo* ☎ *998/877–0101* ⊕ *www.rocamar-hotel. com* ⤵ *31 rooms, 1 suite* ⦿ *No meals* ✦ *D4.*

$$$ 🛏 **Hotel Secreto.** Intimate and contemporary, Hotel Secreto is one of
HOTEL Isla's only luxury boutique hotels. **Pros:** reasonably priced in-room massage and facials; pool overlooks ocean; private and secure; great fitness center. **Cons:** no elevator or restaurant; rocky beach; property could use renovation. ⓢ *Rooms from: $259* ⊠ *Half Moon Beach, Sección Rocas, Lote 11* ☎ *998/877–1039* ⊕ *www.hotelsecreto.com* ⤵ *12 rooms* ⦿ *Breakfast* ✦ *C2.*

$$ 🛏 **Ixchel Beach Hotel.** The location of these privately owned condos—on
RENTAL a beach with clear, calm water—is unbeatable. **Pros:** beautiful location; reasonable rates; on-site restaurant; complimentary beach chairs. **Cons:** small pool; no meals; some rooms are very humid. ⓢ *Rooms from: $155* ⊠ *Playa Norte, Calle Guerrero, Sm 1* ☎ *998/999–2010, 800/638–5061* ⊕ *www.ixchelbeachhotel.com* ⤵ *117 rooms* ⦿ *No meals* ✦ *A3.*

$$ 🛏 **Na Balam.** Elegant without being pretentious, this tranquil hotel is
HOTEL a true sanctuary with sandy pathways winding through a jungle setting that spills onto the beach. **Pros:** good restaurant; beautiful beach; 24-hr security. **Cons:** not all rooms are on the beach; lots of mosquitoes; Wi-Fi in common areas only. ⓢ *Rooms from: $200* ⊠ *Calle Zazil-Há 118* ☎ *998/881–4770* ⊕ *www.nabalam.com* ⤵ *35 rooms* ⦿ *Multiple meal plans* ✦ *B2.*

$$ 🛏 **Privilege Aluxes.** Perched on the sugary shores of Playa Norte, this
RESORT five-story resort is the island's largest and one of the few to offer an all-inclusive plan. **Pros:** excellent location; Wi-Fi on the beach. **Cons:** some rooms have cemetery views and noise from neighboring school; standard rooms lack tubs. ⓢ *Rooms from: $170* ⊠ *Playa Norte, Av. Adolfo Lopez Mateos* ☎ *998/848–8470* ⊕ *www.privilegehotels.com* ⤵ *124 rooms* ⦿ *Multiple meal plans* ✦ *A4.*

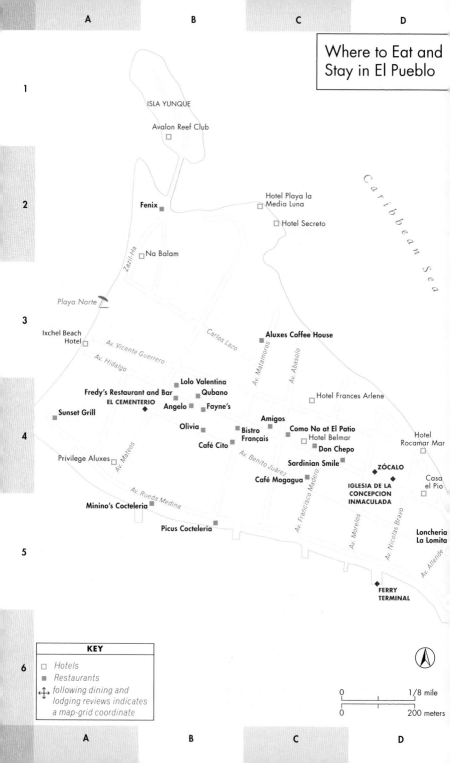

Where to Eat and Stay in El Pueblo

ISLA YUNQUE

Avalon Reef Club

Caribbean Sea

Fenix

Hotel Playa la Media Luna

Hotel Secreto

Na Balam

Zazil-Ha

Playa Norte

Ixchel Beach Hotel

Av. Vicente Guerrero

Carlos Lazo

Aluxes Coffee House

Av. Hidalgo

Av. Matamoros

Av. Abasolo

Lolo Valentina

Qubano

Fredy's Restaurant and Bar
EL CEMENTERIO

Angelo

Fayne's

Hotel Frances Arlene

Sunset Grill

Olivia

Amigos

Como No at El Patio

Bistro Français

Hotel Belmar

Don Chepo

Café Cito

Av. Benito Juárez

Hotel Rocamar Mar

Av. Mateos

Privilege Aluxes

Sardinian Smile

ZÓCALO

Café Mogagua

Av. Rueda Medina

Av. Francisco Madero

IGLESIA DE LA CONCEPCION INMACULADA

Casa el Pio

Minino's Cocteleria

Av. Morelos

Av. Nicolas Bravo

Loncheria La Lomita

Picus Cocteleria

Av. Allende

FERRY TERMINAL

KEY

☐ Hotels
■ Restaurants
↔ following dining and lodging reviews indicates a map-grid coordinate

0   1/8 mile

0   200 meters

ELSEWHERE ON THE ISLAND

Listings in this section appear on the Isla Mujeres map.

$$$ HOTEL Fodor's Choice ★ **Casa de los Sueños.** Walking into the open-air sunken lobby of this gorgeous hotel feels like walking into a friend's fabulous vacation hacienda; it's colorful and cozy, yet modern and chic. **Pros:** intimate atmosphere; exceptional breakfast served until noon; free use of bikes; philanthropic owners. **Cons:** not child-friendly; far from town; no beach. [$] *Rooms from: $275* ✉ *Fracc. Turquesa, lotes 9A and B* ☎ *998/877–0708, 877/372–3993* 🌐 *www.casasuenos.com* 🛏 *8 rooms, 2 suites* 🍴 *Breakfast* ✣ *C6.*

$$$$ ALL-INCLUSIVE **Isla Mujeres Palace.** Fine all-inclusive dining, a blissful beach and pool, plus an on-site spa and dive center make Palace's island outpost a tempting vacation choice. **Pros:** large pool; comfortable rooms; great service. **Cons:** far from downtown; no children under 18; only one restaurant. [$] *Rooms from: $500* ✉ *Carretera Garrafón, Km 4.5, Sm 8, Mza 62* ☎ *998/999–2020* 🌐 *www.palaceresorts.com* 🛏 *62 rooms* 🍴 *All-inclusive* ✣ *C4.*

$$ HOTEL **Marina Pariso Hotel.** Far enough away to feel secluded but within walking distance of El Pueblo, this hotel—made up of white two-story buildings—has a private marina, an infinity pool, and a well-regarded restaurant (Barlito). **Pros:** excellent restaurant; caters to divers; accommodating staff. **Cons:** no beach; Wi-Fi in common areas only; not all rooms have ocean views. [$] *Rooms from: $108* ✉ *Av. Rueda Medina, Prol. Aeropuerto 491* ☎ *998/877–0252* 🌐 *www.marinaparaiso-islamujeres.com* 🛏 *16 rooms, 4 suites* 🍴 *No meals* ✣ *C2.*

$$ B&B/INN **Villa La Bella.** This romantic, laid-back B&B on the east coast has fantastic sea views and funky designs—bungalow rooms are equipped with king-size beds, conch shower heads, and bamboo faucets; rooms with palapas have beds swinging from ropes; and the grounds feature remarkable stonework. **Pros:** welcoming owners; relaxing atmosphere; tasty breakfasts. **Cons:** taxi ride from downtown; kids under 18 not allowed. [$] *Rooms from: $150* ✉ *Carretera Perimetral al Garrafón* ☎ *998/888–0342* 🌐 *www.villalabella.com* 🛏 *5 rooms, 1 suite* 🍴 *Breakfast* ✣ *C3.*

$$$$ ALL-INCLUSIVE **Zoëtry Villa Rolandi.** The luxury starts with a private yacht that delivers you to this all-inclusive hotel from Cancún's Embarcadero Marina, and it continues throughout your stay. **Pros:** attentive staff; great views; luxurious amenities. **Cons:** expensive; must drive to main town; children under 13 not allowed. [$] *Rooms from: $500* ✉ *Fracc. Laguna Mar, Sm 7, Mza 75, lotes 15 and 16* ☎ *998/999–2000* 🌐 *www.zoetryresorts.com/mujeres* 🛏 *35 suites* 🍴 *All-inclusive* ✣ *C3.*

NIGHTLIFE

This sleepy island has a surprisingly healthy nightlife scene, with a variety of options to choose from. Most bars close by midnight, but the party continues at the nightclubs until 2 am. The majority of venues are within downtown's four-block radius, with a few others along Playa Norte. The proximity makes barhopping on foot perilously convenient.

Isleños also celebrate many holidays and festivals in El Pueblo, usually with live entertainment. Carnaval, held annually in February or March (the week before Lent), turns sleepy Isla Mujeres into party central with music, dancing, and colorful parades in the zócalo. In Mardi Gras–like fashion, locals dressed in costumes liven up the island with decorated golf carts and dance performances. Other popular events include Founder's Day (August 17), which marks the island's official founding by the Mexican government. From October 31 to November 2, locals head to the cemetery to honor their dearly departed during Día de los Muertos (Day of the Dead) celebrations.

BARS

Buho's. From 10 am to midnight, you can grab a swing or hammock, order a cold drink, and let the hours roll by at Buho's palapa beach bar. For MX$60, you can also rent a Buho's lounge chair on Playa Norte, which includes a free nonalcoholic beverage. ⊠ *Cabanas Marina del Mar, Playa Norte, Av. Carlos Lazo 1* ☎ 998/877–0179.

Café del Mar. Designed by renowned architect Lluís Güell, Café del Mar is an Ibiza-inspired beach bar that plays chill-out music by day and has live music at night. The fish tacos are a perfect cerveza accompaniment. Try to stop by for the gorgeous sunset. ⊠ *Privilege Aluxes, Playa Norte, Av. Adolfo Lopez Mateos* ☎ 998/848–8473.

Jax Bar & Grill. When you're looking for live music, cold beer, good bar food, and a satellite TV that's always tuned to the current game, make tracks for Jax. It is open daily, 9 am to 11 pm. ⊠ *Av. Adolfo Lopez Mateos 42, near lighthouse* ☎ 998/887–1218 ⊘ *Closed Sept.*

La Adelita Tequileria. Connoisseurs can sample more than 150 varieties of tequila and cigars at this popular spot. ⊠ *Av. Hidalgo Norte 12A.*

DANCE CLUBS

Fayne's. Best known for its terrific cocktails and live music, Fayne's is a brightly painted place with a hip, energetic personality. The party kicks off nightly at 8 pm with everything from American rock to Caribbean rhythms providing the soundtrack. Bring your dancing shoes. ⊠ *Av. Hidalgo 12A, between avs. Mateos and Matamoros* ☎ 998/877–0528 ⊕ *www.faynesbarandgrill.com* ⊘ *Closed Sept.–Oct. 15.*

SHOPPING

Although Isla produces few local crafts, the streets are filled with souvenir shops selling cheap T-shirts, garish ceramics, and seashells glued onto a variety of objects. Amid all the junk you may find good Mexican folk art, hammocks, textiles, and silver jewelry. Most stores are small family operations that don't take credit cards, but almost everyone gladly accepts American dollars. Stores that do take credit cards sometimes tack on a fee to offset the commission they must pay. Hours are generally Monday through Saturday 10–1 and 4–7, although many stores stay open during siesta hours (1–4).

CLOTHING

Gladys Galdamez Swimwear. Galdamez's eponymous shop carries Isla-designed and manufactured clothing and accessories for both men and women, as well as bags and jewelry. Select something off the rack, or bring a photograph of your dream bikini and she'll sew a bespoke version for you. ✉ *Mariano Abasolo 40* ☎ *998/877–0071* ⊘ *Closed weekends*

CRAFTS

Isla Mujeres Artist Fair. Held on the first Thursday of the month, November through April, this community event profiles the work of resident artists, designers, authors, and even palm readers. It's a great place to find jewelry, clothing, and artwork, while benefiting local nonprofits. Food vendors and musicians also take part in the fair, which runs from 4 to 9 pm. ✉ *Zócalo, between Avs. Morelos and Brava.*

Women's Beading Cooperative (*Taller Artesanias de Mujeres*). Nearly 60 local women are part of this beading cooperative, which creates hand-crafted jewelry for a very reasonable price. It's worth the drive to the middle of the island to see these talented artisans at work. ✉ *Colonia La Gloria, Av. Huachinango, next to Red Cross and across from Catholic church* ☎ *998/161–9659* ⊘ *Closed Sun.*

GROCERY STORES

Chedraui. Selling everything from food and clothing to appliances and medicine, this Mexican grocery chain is about as close as you can get to the Wal-Mart experience. ✉ *Mid-island, at Salina Chica, south of the hospital, near the baseball field* ☎ *01800/925–1111 toll-free in Mexico* ⊕ *www.chedraui.com.mx.*

Mercado Municipal (*Mercado Audomaro Magaña*). For fresh produce, the Mercado Municipal is your best bet. It's open daily from 6 am until 2 pm. ■ TIP➔ A second market (Mercado Javier Rojo Gomez) operates during the same hours on Avenida Guerrero between avenidas Mateos and Matamoros. ✉ *Col. Cañotal.*

Super Express. One of two main grocery stores on the island, Super Express is well stocked with all the basics and is a good in-town option if you can't make it out to Chedraui. ✉ *Av. Morelos 3, between avs. Hidalgo and Guerrero, El Pueblo.*

JEWELRY

Jewelry on Isla ranges from tasteful to tacky. Bargains are available, but beware of street vendors—most of their wares, especially the amber, are fake.

Galeria de Arte Mexicano. Bypass the street vendors and come directly to this lovely shop for the best quality silver in town. It also sells Talavera and custom-made jewelry at amazing prices. ■ TIP➔ Don't be afraid to haggle. ✉ *Av. Guerrero 3* ☎ *998/877–1272.*

Galeria L'Mento Arte. For authentic made-in-Isla gifts—including wooden boxes, hand-carved sculptures, and ceramics—head to Galeria L'Mento Arte. Jewelry is another top draw: pick your stone, setting, and clasp, then watch the masters make a custom piece before your eyes. ✉ *Av. Hidalgo, at Plaza los Almendros* ☎ *998/158–4277.*

Joyería Maritza. Reasonably priced jewelry from Taxco (Mexico's silver capital) and crafts from Oaxaca are sold at Joyería Maritza. ✉ *Av. Hidalgo 14, between avs. Morelos and Francisco Madero* ☎ *998/168–6880.*

Silver Factory Taxaco. For jewelry, check out the Silver Factory, which specializes in pieces made in Taxco. ✉ *Avs. Juárez and Morelos* ☎ *998/877–1316.*

SPORTS AND THE OUTDOORS

BOATING

Villa Vera Puerto Isla Mujeres. This full-service marina includes a fuel station, a 150-ton lift, customs assistance, 24-hour security, plus laundry and cleaning services. Docking prices depend on the length of your stay and the size of your boat (it can accommodate vessels up to 175 feet). ✉ *Puerto de Abrigo, Laguna Makax* ☎ *998/877–0330* ⊕ *www.puerto islamujeres.com.*

FISHING

Jax Sport Fishing. Year-round, you can charter a 29-foot custom boat through Jax Sport Fishing. Captain Michael has more than 20 years' experience in offshore fishing, and the catch of the day might include sailfish, blue marlin, white marlin, or mahimahi. ✉ *Av. Adolfo Mateos 42, near lighthouse* ☎ *998/877–1254, 214/295–7104* ⊕ *www.jaxsport fishing.com* 🖃 *MX$12,713 per day.*

Keen M International Blue Water Encounters. Captain Anthony Mendillo Jr. runs specialized fishing trips from December to June aboard several vessels, which range from 34 to 41 feet. ✉ *Av. Arq. Carlos Lazo 1* ☎ *998/877–0759* ⊕ *www.islamujeressportfishing.com* 🖃 *From MX$14,970 per day.*

Sea Hawk Divers. If you're interested in either offshore or deep-sea fishing, try Sea Hawk Divers. It has trips daily from 9 am to 1 pm. ✉ *Av. Arq. Carlos Lazo, near Playa Norte* ☎ *998/877–1233* ⊕ *www. seahawkislamujeres.com* 🖃 *From MX$4014.*

Sociedad Cooperativa Turística. This fishermen's cooperative rents boats for a maximum of four hours and six people; tours to the underwater museum (lunch included) are also available. ✉ *Contoy Pier, Av. Rueda Medina* ☎ *998/887–0800* 🖃 *Boat rentals MX$2676, tours MX$602 per person.*

CLOSE UP

In Search of the Dead

El Día de los Muertos (the Day of the Dead) is often described as a Mexican version of Halloween, but it's much more than that. The festival, which runs from October 31 to November 2, is a hybrid of pre-Hispanic and Christian beliefs that honors the cyclical nature of life and death. Local celebrations are as varied as they are dynamic, often laced with warm tributes and dark humor.

To honor departed loved ones at this time of year, families and friends create *ofrendas*, altars adorned with photos, flowers, candles, liquor, and other items whose colors, smells, and potent nostalgia are meant to lure spirits back for a family reunion. The favorite foods of the deceased are prepared with extra spice so that the souls can absorb the essence of the offerings. Although the ofrendas and the colorful *calaveritas* (sugar skulls and skeletons) are common everywhere, the holiday is observed in so many ways that a definition of it depends entirely on what part of Mexico you visit. In the Yucatán Peninsula, the cultural center of Mérida is where most people gather to honor the dead.

On Isla Mujeres, reverence is paid at the historic cemetery, where locals like Marta rest on a fanciful tomb in the late-afternoon sun. "She is my sister," Marta says, motioning toward the teal-and-blue tomb. "I painted this today." Instead of mourning, she's smiling, happy to be spending the day with her sibling.

Nearby, Juan puts the final touches— vases made from shells he's collected—on his father's colorful tomb. A glass box holds a red candle and a statue of the Virgin Mary, her outstretched arms pressing against the glass as if trying to escape the flame. "This is all for him," Juan says, motioning to his masterpiece, "because he is a good man."

—David Downing

SNORKELING AND SCUBA DIVING

Most local dive spots are described in detail in *Mexicandiver* magazine, available in many local shops. Coral reefs at El Garrafón National Park have suffered tremendously from a variety of factors, some unavoidable (hurricanes) and some all-too-avoidable (boats dropping anchors onto soft coral, a practice now outlawed). Some good snorkeling can be found near Playa Norte on the north end.

Isla is a good place for learning to dive, since dive areas are close to shore. Offshore, there is excellent diving and snorkeling at Xlaches (pronounced *ees*-lah-chays) reef, due north on the way to Isla Contoy. One of Contoy's most alluring dives is a cave full of sharks off the northern tip. Discovered in 1969 by a local fisherman, the cave was extensively explored by Ramón Bravo, a local diver, cinematographer, and Mexico's foremost expert on sharks. It's a fascinating 150-foot dive for experienced divers only.

At 30–40 feet deep and 3,300 feet off the southwestern coast, the coral reef known as **Manchones** is a good dive site. During the summer of 1994, an ecological group hoping to divert divers and snorkelers from

Some impressive catches are to be had off the coast of the island.

El Garrafón commissioned a 1-ton, 9¾-foot bronze cross, which was later sunk here. Named the Cruz de la Bahía (Cross of the Bay), it's a tribute to everyone who has died at sea. Another option is the Barco L-55 and C-58 dive, which visits World War II boats 20 minutes off Isla Mujeres's coast.

Most dive shops offer a variety of packages with rates depending on the time of day, location, and the number of tanks.

Carey Diving. You can sign on for one-tank reef dives, deep dives, and two-tank cenote dives at this popular PADI dive shop. Whale-watching, fishing, and snorkeling excursions are offered as well. ⊠ *Av. Matamoros 13-A, off Av. Juárez* ☎ *998/877–0763* ⊕ *www.careydivecenter.com* 🖃 *Dives from MX$736.*

Cruise Divers. This company organizes two-tank reef dives, shipwreck dives, and nighttime dives. ⊠ *Carretera Garrafón–Miraflores, Km. 3.6* ☎ *998/274–0247* ⊕ *www.scubaislamujeres.com.mx* 🖃 *From MX$869.*

Sea Hawk Divers. In addition to highly regarded PADI courses, Sea Hawk Divers offers one- and two-tank dives plus special excursions to the more exotic shipwrecks and underwater museum. For nondivers, snorkel trips depart daily at 8:30 and 2:30. ⊠ *Av. Arq. Carlos Lazo, near Playa Norte* ☎ *998/877–1233* ⊕ *www.seahawkislamujeres.com* 🖃 *Dives from $M936.*

Searious Diving. Venture into the heart of whale shark territory with Searious Diving from June 1 to September 15. Owner Ramon Guerrero Garcia is a professional diver who has dedicated more than 20 years to researching these gentle giants. Included in the boat trip are beverages,

CLOSE UP

Shhh . . . Don't Wake the Sharks

The underwater caverns off Isla Mujeres attract reef sharks, a dangerous species. Once the sharks swim into the caves, though, they enter a state of relaxed nonaggression seen nowhere else. Naturalists have two explanations, both involving the composition of the water inside the caves, which contains more oxygen, more carbon dioxide, and less salt than usual.

According to the first theory, the decreased salinity causes the parasites that plague sharks to loosen their grip, allowing the remora fish (sharks' personal vacuum cleaners) to eat the parasites more easily. Perhaps the sharks relax to make the cleaning easier, or maybe it's the aftereffect of a good scrubbing. Another theory is

that the caves' combination of fresh- and saltwater produces a euphoria similar to the "nitrogen narcosis" scuba divers experience on deep dives.

Whatever the sharks experience while "sleeping" in the caves, they pay a heavy price for it. A swimming shark breathes automatically and without effort as water flows through its gills, but a stationary shark must laboriously pump water to continue breathing. If you dive in the Cave of the Sleeping Sharks, be cautious: many are reef sharks, the species responsible for the largest number of attacks on humans. Dive with a reliable guide and be on your best underwater behavior.

a light snack, snorkel gear, and time at the reef and beach. Tours last approximately five hours and must be prebooked online. Ramon is available to answer questions via email at ✑ *seariousdiving@yahoo. com* or in person at Adrian's Internet Cafe in town. ⊠ *Adrian's Internet Cafe, Av. Morelos, between avs. Guerrero and Hidalgo* ☎ *998/735– 7360* ⊕ *www.islawhalesharks.com* ✑ *MX$1,672.*

Squalo Adventures. One of the more experienced dive shops on the island, this PADI-certified outfit offers full scuba courses, as well as one- and two-tank dives to local sites including the underwater museum. ⊠ *Av. Hidalgo, Sm 1, Mza 18, Lote 27, between Matamoros and Playa Norte* ☎ *998/274–1644* ⊕ *www.squaloadventures.com* ✑ *Dives from MX$976.*

SIDE TRIP TO ISLA CONTOY

30 km (19 miles) north of Isla Mujeres.

The national wildlife park and bird sanctuary of Isla Contoy (Isle of Birds) is just 6 km (4 miles) long and less than 1 km (about ½ mile) wide. The whole island is a protected area, with visitor numbers carefully regulated to safeguard the flora and fauna. Isla Contoy has become a favorite among nature lovers who come to enjoy its unspoiled beauty. Sand dunes rise as high as 70 feet along the east coast, which is edged by black rocks and coral reefs. The west coast is fringed with sand, shrubs, and coconut palms.

More than 150 bird species—including gulls, pelicans, petrels, cormorants, cranes, ducks, flamingos, herons, doves, quail, spoonbills, and hawks—fly this way in late fall, some to nest and breed. Although the number of species is diminishing, partly as a result of human traffic, Isla Contoy remains a treat for bird-watchers.

The island is rich in sea life as well. Snorkelers will see brilliant coral and fish, while 5-foot-wide manta rays are visible in the shallow waters. All around the island are large numbers of shrimp, mackerel, barracuda, flying fish, and trumpet fish. In December, lobsters pass through in great (though diminishing) numbers on their southerly migration.

GETTING HERE AND AROUND

The trip to Isla Contoy takes 45 minutes to 1½ hours, depending on the weather and the boat, and costs MX$1017. Everyone landing has to purchase a MX$80 authorization ticket, though this is usually included in the price of a guided tour. The standard excursion begins with a fruit breakfast on the boat and a stopover at Xlaches reef on the way to Isla Contoy for snorkeling (gear is included). As you sail, your crew trolls for the lunch it will cook on the beach: anything from barracuda to snapper (beer and soda are also included). While the catch is being barbecued, you have time to explore the island, snorkel, check out the small museum and biological station, or just laze under a palapa.

The island is officially open to visitors daily 9–5:30, and overnight stays aren't allowed. Other than the birds and the dozen or so park rangers who live here, the island's only residents are iguanas, lizards, turtles, hermit crabs, and boa constrictors. You can read more about Isla Contoy at ⊕ *www.islacontoy.org.*

TOURS

Captain Ricardo Gaitan. A local Isla Contoy expert, Captain Ricardo Gaitan also provides an excellent tour for large groups (6–20 people) aboard his 36-foot boat *Estrella del Norte.* ⊠ *Contoy Pier, Av. Rueda Medina* ☎ *044–998/894–0771 (mobile)* ✆ *MX$1021 per person.*

Captain Tony Garcia. Board the *Guadalupana,* Captain Tony Garcia's tour boat, for a trip to Isla Contoy. While you snorkel around the island, he and his crew will prepare a delicious feast for you. One of the most dependable tour operators, Tony is also an expert on local wildlife. ⊠ *Calle Matamoros 7A, Isla Mujeres* ☎ *998/877–0229* ⊕ *www.isla-mujeres.net/capttony/home* ✆ *MX$813.*

Sociedad Cooperativa Isla Mujeres. Daily boat trips from Isla Mujeres to Isla Contoy for 6–12 people are available through the Sociedad Cooperativa Isla Mujeres. ⊠ *Contoy Pier, Av. Rueda Medina* ☎ *998/877–0800* ✆ *MX$1021 per person.*

4

THE RIVIERA
MAYA

WELCOME TO THE RIVIERA MAYA

TOP REASONS TO GO

★ **Tulum:** Only an hour south of Playa del Carmen, the ruins are a dramatic remnant of a sophisticated pre-Columbian people overlooking the Caribbean—one of Mexico's classic views.

★ **Casting for bonefish:** These elusive shallows-dwellers, off the Chinchorro Reef near the Reserva de la Biósfera Sian Ka'an, can match wits with even the most seasoned fly-fisher.

★ **Relaxing at a spa:** The Riviera Maya is flush with luxurious spas, some incorporating native ingredients and ancient rituals into their treatments.

★ **Snorkeling and diving outer reefs and cenotes:** The Mesoamerican Barrier Reef, Banco Chinchorro, and freshwater *cenotes* (cavernous sinkholes) are teeming with marine life.

★ **Soaking up local culture:** Cradled between mangrove and sea, the quaint fishing village of Puerto Morelos has maintained its authenticity despite neighboring growth.

1 North of Playa del Carmen. Coastal locales between Cancún and Playa del Carmen run the gamut from sleepy fishing villages like Puerto Morelos to glitzy resort enclaves like Mayakoba.

2 Playa del Carmen. As one of the fastest growing cities in Latin America, this lively community has a plethora of shops, hotels, restaurants, and beach clubs, all within a trendy pedestrian zone.

3 South of Playa del Carmen. Whether you want to tick off bucket-list adventures at an eco theme park, find your bliss on a quiet beach, or just enjoy American-style amenities, you can do it here.

4 Tulum and Cobá. Eco-friendly Tulum combines breathtaking ruins with hippie-chic beach hangouts. The less visited (but more impressive) pyramids at Cobá are surrounded by jungle.

5 Reserva de la Biósfera Sian Ka'an. Coastal mangrove forests dotted with cenotes give way to dense inland vegetation in Mexico's second-largest wilderness reserve.

6 The Costa Maya. Although droves of cruise passengers descend on Mahahual, much of the Costa Maya is still an unspoiled region that appeals to nature lovers, divers, and off-the-grid enthusiasts.

184

Caobas

Rio Bec

Kohunlich

CAMPECHE

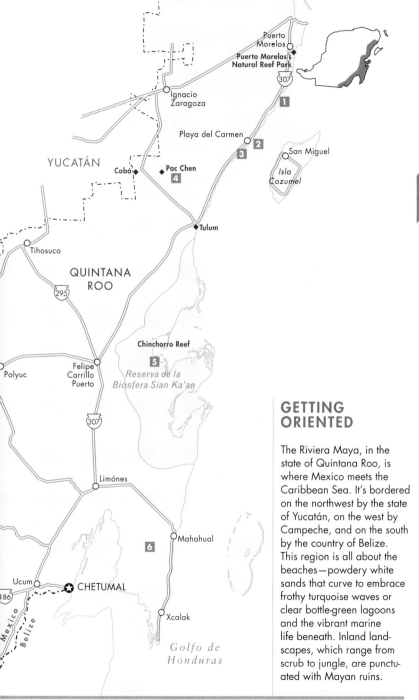

Puerto
Morelos

Puerto Morelos's
Natural Reef Park

307

1

Playa del Carmen

2

3

San Miguel

YUCATÁN

Cobá ◆   ◆ Pac Chen

4

Isla
Cozumel

◆ Tulum

Tihosuco

QUINTANA
ROO

295

Chinchorro Reef

5

Polyuc

Felipe
Carrillo
Puerto

Reserva de la
Biosfera Sian Ka'an

307

Limónes

Mahahual

6

Ucum

CHETUMAL

86

Xcalak

Mexico

Belize

Golfo de
Honduras

4

GETTING
ORIENTED

The Riviera Maya, in the
state of Quintana Roo, is
where Mexico meets the
Caribbean Sea. It's bordered
on the northwest by the state
of Yucatán, on the west by
Campeche, and on the south
by the country of Belize.
This region is all about the
beaches—powdery white
sands that curve to embrace
frothy turquoise waves or
clear bottle-green lagoons
and the vibrant marine
life beneath. Inland landscapes, which range from
scrub to jungle, are punctuated with Mayan ruins.

Updated
by Marlise
Kast-Myers

Mexico's Caribbean coast is full of treasures, from spectacular white-sand beaches and offshore reefs to some of the Yucatán Peninsula's most beautiful Mayan ruins. Unsurprisingly, much of the region is also full of tourists, who come from around the world to bask in the sun and soak up the unique Mayan-Mexican culture. From Bahía Petempich in the north down to Punta Allen in the south, it has more than 23,000 hotel rooms, plus countless restaurants, shops, and other tourist amenities.

The entire area can essentially be divided into three types of terrain: developed coast, national reserve, and wild coast. The top stretch from Bahía Petempich to Tulum has the greatest concentration of sights and services, and includes some of the Yucatán's most memorable ruins and cenotes. The bottom stretch, from the southern border of Sian Ka'an to Xcalak (and inland to Chetumal), is where civilization thins out. Here in the "Costa Maya" you'll find the most alluring landscapes. Sandwiched between the two is the sprawling wilderness of the Reserva de la Biósfera Sian Ka'an: a pristine preserve that is both a shelter for myriad species of wildlife (including jaguars and manatees) and a window to a time before resort development changed this coast forever.

Discovering the Riviera Maya is easy. One road, the Carretera 307, cuts all the way through to the border of Belize and will take you everywhere you want to go. The well-paved conduit is a convenient way to cover long distances between sights, but on your journey there's little to see beyond road signs and the monumental resort entrances marking access roads. Although exploring the region is about the soft sway of palms along sparkling sands, it's also about the highway miles you'll cover to get there.

PLANNING

WHEN TO GO

Peak Season is November through April. The coastal weather is heavenly, with temperatures of 27°C (80°F) and near-constant ocean breezes. Hotel rates reflect increased demand from sun-starved northerners, especially in Playa del Carmen. During Christmas week, they often increase by 50% and hoteliers request a minimum five-night stay. If you're planning a Christmas vacation, you'd do well to book six months in advance.

June, September, and October are low season. September and October bring the worst weather, with frequent rain, mosquitoes, and the risk of hurricanes. There's also often rain in June. Breezes disappear, and humidity soars, especially inland. But if you're looking for a spa getaway and don't mind the weather outside, you'll be able to find real deals on accommodations during these months. Just keep in mind that some of Riviera Maya's best restaurants and boutique hotels shut down during September, while larger resorts undergo renovation.

In May, July, and August, off-season prices and sunny skies make late spring and midsummer a great time to save on airfares and hotels, while having the beach to yourself.

TIMING

Five days will give you enough time to enjoy the beach and explore many of the best parts of the Riviera Maya. If you use Playa del Carmen as a base, you can easily take day trips to the Xcaret theme park or Tulum's beachfront Mayan ruins. Don't miss swimming in one of the numerous cenotes along Carretera 307. The beaches at Paamul and Xpu-Há are also within driving distance, as is the Mayan village of Pac Chen, the ruins at Cobá, and the Reserva de la Biósfera Sian Ka'an.

GETTING HERE AND AROUND

BUS TRAVEL

Fifteen first-class ADO buses per day depart from Cancún between 6 am and midnight, stopping incrementally at Puerto Morelos, Playa del Carmen, Tulum, Felipe Carrillo Puerto, Limones, and Chetumal. The full trip from Cancún to Chetumal takes just under six hours and costs MX$354.

Bus Contacts ADO ☎ 984/873–0109 in Playa del Carmen, 983/832–5110 in Chetumal ⊕ www.ado.com.mx.

CAR TRAVEL

Discovering the Riviera Maya by car is easy. The entire coast from Cancún to Chetumal is connected by one highway, the Carretera 307. Between Cancún and Tulum it's four divided lanes, and after Tulum it's two, but it's in excellent condition the whole way. (A section of the highway sometimes is not referred to as the 307 but by the towns it connects: Carretera Playa del Carmen–Tulum, Carretera Tulum–Chetumal.) Because this is the only road linking cities, towns, parks, and jungle attractions, expect to spend a lot of time on it to see the region. Addresses along the highway but outside of towns are usually referred to by kilometer markers on small, white, upright signs at the side of the road.

If you want to explore beyond your accommodations, you'll need a rental car. Be aware that some roads off the highway are bumpy or potholed, and the road between Mahahual and Xcalak in the extreme south can be challenging after heavy rain.

Driving: The most dangerous place on the Caribbean Coast may be the road. Carretera 307 is in excellent shape, but secondary roads can develop a serious case of the potholes. Combine that with poor lighting, unexpected speed bumps, and the occasional big crab skittering across the road, and you've got ample reason to drive slowly and carefully. Speed bumps, called *topes,* deserve special mention: they range from well-built and -marked tarred hills to a simple but effective thick rope laid across the tarmac. When they're marked, you'll see a yellow or white sign showing bumps or reading "TOPE." Often, however, they're not, so use caution and watch the road.

Obey speed limits: Police radar and sudden decreases in speed limits are easy traps for travelers. Should you get pulled over, hand over your license and expect to get it back the next day, when you pay your ticket at the police station. Most police officers are honest, but some will pull you over just to see if you'll pay them a small "tip" to avoid the hassle— don't fall for it. In many cases you'll get off with a warning when you make it clear you're prepared for the official paperwork. (⇨ *Check out our Travel Smart chapter for rules of the road and information on rental car agencies if you plan on driving.)*

Precautions: Before your trip, purchase travel insurance, monitor the weather, and notify your embassy and credit card company of your whereabouts. Make a copy of your passport and leave your travel itinerary with a friend or family member. To avoid unwanted situations, steer clear of remote locations, travel with a partner, and refrain from driving long distances at night.

HOTELS

There's lodging for every taste and budget here, from giant all-inclusive luxury resorts to small family-run cabanas on the beach. Most are in remote areas off Carretera 307. If your accommodation choice doesn't provide good shuttle service, you may want to rent a car to visit off-site attractions or restaurants. Staying at beach areas in Playa del Carmen, Akumal, or Tulum will allow you to explore on foot from your hotel.

Hotel reviews have been condensed. For full reviews, see Fodors.com.

RESTAURANTS

Restaurants here vary from quirky beachside affairs with outdoor tables and palapas to more elaborate and sophisticated establishments. Dress is casual at most places, so leave your tie and jacket at home. Smaller eateries may not accept credit cards, especially in remote beach villages. Bigger ones and those in hotels normally accept plastic. Many restaurants add *propinas* (tips) to the bill; look for a charge for "*servicio.*" If tips aren't included, a 15% gratuity is standard. It's best to order fresh local fish—grouper, dorado, red snapper, and sea bass—rather than shellfish like shrimp, lobster, and oysters, since the latter are often flown in frozen from the Gulf. Playa del Carmen has the largest selection of restaurants.

DINING AND LODGING PRICES IN DOLLARS AND PESOS			
	$	$$	$$$	$$$$
Restaurants	under MX$135	MX$135–MX$200	MX$201–MX$350	over MX$350
Hotels in dollars	under $100	$100–$200	$201–$300	over $300
Hotels in pesos	under MX$1450	MX$1450–MX$2900	MX$2901–MX$4400	over MX$4400

Restaurant prices are the average price for a main course at dinner, or if dinner is not served at lunch. Hotel prices are for a standard double room in high season, including taxes.

SAFETY

With its massive resorts and tourist-oriented beach towns, the Riviera Maya is free of most big-city dangers. Though increasingly urban, Playa del Carmen is generally safe in tourist areas, and extensive police patrols keep it that way. Between 2011 and 2013, Playa del Carmen experienced a slight rise in crime outside the major resort areas, most of it associated with criminal groups. Regardless of this, Playa del Carmen is still more secure than most North American cities and remains among the safest areas in Mexico for vacationers. Resorts all have 24-hour security guards, and most have in-room safes. Thanks to advances in water purification, food safety has made great strides in the last decade, but Mexicans drink bottled water and you should, too. However, there's no need to worry about ice—it's made from purified water virtually everywhere. Look for the barrel-shaped, industrial ice cubes, just to be sure.

TOURS

Alltournative. Offering eco-friendly adventures for travelers of all ages and fitness levels, Alltournative will have you feeling like Indiana Jones in no time. You can kayak through a lagoon, snorkel in a cenote, or zipline above a lush jungle. The company also organizes visits to Mayan communities on expeditions to Cobá. ⊠ *Carretera 307, Km 287, near Playacar, Playa del Carmen* ☎ *984/803–9999, 877/437–4990* ⊕ *www.alltournative.com* ⚑ *From MX$935.*

Hilario Hiler. For customized tours of Mayan villages, ruins, and the jungle, contact Hilario Hiler. He is fluent in Spanish, Mayan, and English. ⊠ *La Jolla, Casa Nai Na, 3rd fl., Akumal* ☎ *984/875–9066* ✐ *hilario-hiler@gmail.com.*

Maya Sites Travel Services. This outfit uses archaeologists and other experts to lead inexpensive tours of ancient Mayan sites. ☎ *505/255–2279, 877/620–8715* ⊕ *www.mayasites.com.*

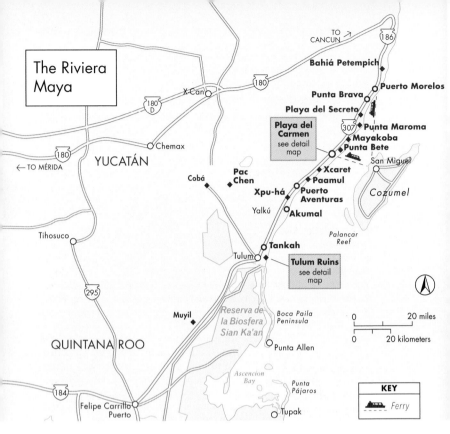

The Riviera Maya

Bahía Petempich
180
X-Can
180 D
Puerto Morelos
Punta Brava
Playa del Secreto
Playa del Carmen see detail map
Punta Maroma
307
Mayakoba
Chemax
Punta Bete
YUCATÁN
San Miguel
← TO MÉRIDA
180
Cobá
Pac Chen
Xcaret
Paamul
Xpu-há
Puerto Aventuras
Cozumel
Yalkú
Akumal
Tihosuco
Palancar Reef
Tankah
Tulum
Tulum Ruins see detail map
295
Reserva de la Biosfera Sian Ka'an
Muyil
Boca Paila Peninsula
0   20 miles
0   20 kilometers
QUINTANA ROO
Punta Allen
Ascencion Bay
Punta Pájaros
184
KEY
Felipe Carrillo Puerto
Tupak
Ferry

VISITOR INFORMATION

Online resources can help you plan your trip. Meaning "white road" in Maya, Sac-Be.com covers everything from local beaches to environmental issues. TravelYucatan.com has information on transportation, hotels, and attractions, plus travel tips for both novice and veteran travelers. If you're looking for updated info on Playa del Carmen and surrounding areas, click Playa.info.

NORTH OF PLAYA DEL CARMEN

Riviera Maya's stretch of coastline starts south of Cancún at Bahía Petempich, where the party atmosphere fades and a feeling of tranquility takes hold. Encountering this area for the first time via monotonous Carretera 307, travelers might ask, "I came all this way for this?" But just wait—beyond those towering security gates, access roads lead to an enviable collection of resorts and, ultimately, to white sandy strands. Other than the fishing village of Puerto Morelos, the "towns" north of Playa del Carmen aren't much more than vacation complexes dotting postcard beaches. ■TIP→ It's worth noting that while all beaches in Mexico are open to the public, access is not guaranteed. This means that when a resort snatches a prime beachfront site, it can effectively block access to nonguests.

BAHÍA PETEMPICH (PUNTA TANCHACTÉ)

44 km (27 miles) north of Playa del Carmen, 23 km (14 miles) south of Cancún.

The Riviera Maya region technically begins at Bahía Petempich (also known as Punta Tanchacté), where long expanses of sand are lapped by turquoise waters. Historically a fishing village, this area has recently been overtaken by Puerto Morelos's growth, and now there are new hotels and resorts here as well. Just 20 minutes south of Cancún, Bahía Petempich is quieter than neighboring towns but still close to the action.

GETTING HERE AND AROUND

Driving north on Carretera 307, turn right at Km 328. Heading south on Carretera 307, turn left at Km 27.5. The entrance is marked by a large gate reading "Bahía Petempich." This community of resorts does not offer any facilities other than those that are available within the hotels. The nearest shops, restaurants, banks, and clinics are in Cancún and Puerto Morelos.

WHERE TO STAY

$$$
ALL-INCLUSIVE
FAMILY

🏨 **Azul Beach Hotel.** Situated on a beautiful beach, this all-inclusive hotel has ocean views, lush grounds, palapa-covered walkways, and several categories of rooms, all of which were remodeled in 2014. **Pros:** intimate setting; excellent service; good food. **Cons:** Wi-Fi extra; lots of seaweed on the beach; proximity to mangroves can produce an unpleasant sulfur odor and attract mosquitoes. $ *Rooms from: $268* ✉ *Carretera 307, Km 27.5, Punta Tanchacté* 🕿 *998/872–8080* ⊕ *www. karismahotels.com* ⟿ *145 rooms, 2 villas* ⏀ *All-inclusive.*

$$$$
ALL-INCLUSIVE

🏨 **Zoëtry Paraíso de la Bonita.** A pair of stone dragons guards the entrance to this eclectic resort, where the spacious rooms—all with sweeping sea and jungle views—are elegantly styled after seven destinations, Africa, Mexico, Bali, and Asia among them. **Pros:** attentive staff; tasteful room design; every room has ocean view. **Cons:** no evening entertainment; mediocre lunch; no kids' club. $ *Rooms from: $688* ✉ *Carretera 307, Km 328, Punta Tanchacté* ⟿ *Turn on hwy. at signs for Paraiso de la Bonita; follow rd. about 3 km (2 miles) for gate to Zoetry.* 🕿 *998/872–8301* ⊕ *www.zoetryparaisodelabonita.com* ⟿ *90 suites* ⏀ *All-inclusive.*

SPAS

Thalasso Center & Spa. The 22,000-square-foot spa at the Zoëtry Paraíso de la Bonita resort is the only certified thalassotherapy spa in the Riviera Maya, meaning many of its treatments use seawater to wash your cares away. The extensive menu features body wraps, holistic treatments, saltwater hydrotherapy, and proto-Mayan *temezcal* rituals. Although most treatments involve getting wet, you'll also find healing dry remedies like wraps, facials, massages, and acupuncture. Spa products infused with sea kelp and marine mud are said to eliminate toxins. Acupuncture, tai chi, yoga, and Mayan healing practices are available upon request.

Zoëtry Paraíso de la Bonita is unique: a truly luxurious all-inclusive resort.

✉ *Zoetry Paraiso de la Bonita Resort, Carretera 307, Km 328, Punta Tanchacté* ☎ *984/872–8320* ⊕ *www.zoetryresorts.com/wellness-spa.*

SPORTS AND THE OUTDOORS

Snorkeling Adventure (*Restaurant La Plage*). Snorkeling tours at Bahia Petempich last from 1½ to 7 hours and include gear, a buffet lunch, and a trip to the second longest coral reef in the world. ✉ *Carretera 307, Km 27.5 Sm 12, off dirt road to Azul Beach Hotel and Zoetry Paraiso, Punta Tanchacté* ☎ *800/983–4057 in the U.S., 01800/681–8121 toll-free in Mexico* ⊕ *www.cancunsnorkelingadventure.com* 🖅 *From MX$610.*

PUERTO MORELOS

32 km (20 miles) north of Playa del Carmen.

At the edge of a mangrove-tangled jungle pushing up to the shore, Puerto Morelos is one of the few coastal towns on this stretch of the Riviera Maya that's maintained a measure of authenticity. Although it's become a favorite of Canadian and American expat artists, painters, and poets, it's still essentially a salty Mexican seaside village. Nothing here has been prettied up for the gringos, and tourist traps are few and far between. With a wide selection of restaurants, a variety of nearby hotels, and a good road connecting the town with the highway, it makes a great base.

Environmental laws and building restrictions have so far kept growth under tight control. This has prevented Puerto Morelos from becoming the next Cancún or Playa del Carmen—which many locals consider a blessing. The waters here are calm and safe; however, if a spectacular beach is a key part of your vacation plans, consider staying at a resort north or south of town.

Where Puerto Morelos shines is out at sea: the superb Mesoamerican Barrier Reef, only 1,800 feet offshore, is an excellent place to explore with a snorkel or scuba tank. The reef is healthy, meaning you'll see plenty of marine life; but it and the surrounding mangrove forests are a protected national park, so you'll need to visit with a licensed guide and purchase a mandatory MX$300 conservation bracelet. Home to many species of birds, the park is also a draw for bird-watchers. (The mangroves are a haven for mosquitoes, too—bring repellent, especially after dusk.) ■TIP➜ **Architecture fans shouldn't miss the bizarre cartoon castle at the corner of Niños Heroes and Morelos, a carved, curvy, leaning tree-house fantasy that has to be seen to be believed.**

GETTING HERE AND AROUND

Puerto Morelos is the first major town on Carretera 307. When the center of the road rises up to an overpass, motorists should stay right and turn left underneath, then just follow the road 2 km (1 mile) east. This will take you directly to the town square and lighthouse. You can also reach Puerto Morelos by turning at the paved road at Croco-Cun Zoo off Carretera 307 at Km 31. This paved road dead-ends at the entrance to Excellence Resort, where you will turn right and follow the road along the mangroves to the center of town. ADO (⊕ *www. ado.com.mx*) links Cancún, Puerto Morelos, Playa del Carmen, Tulum, Felipe Carrillo Puerto, Limones, and Chetumal by bus.

Downtown, which can be explored by foot, is essentially the sprawling town square, bordered by Avenida Rafael Melgar at the beach, Avenida Rojo Gomez parallel, and avenidas Tulum and Morelos to the south and north respectively. The square verges on the water, where you'll find a fisherman's shack (for boat tours) next to Pelicanos restaurant. Steps to the left take you down to the beach. The taxi stand is at the northeast corner of the square at Morelos and Rojo Gomez. Avenida Niños Heroes is the next street inland, parallel to Avenida Rojo Gomez.

Taxi Contacts Taxi Service ☏ *998/871–0090.*

EXPLORING

FAMILY **Croco-Cun Zoo.** The biologists running the Croco-Cun Zoo, an animal farm just north of Puerto Morelos, have collected specimens of many of the reptiles and some of the mammals indigenous to the area. They offer immensely informative tours—you may even get to handle a baby crocodile or feed a monkey. Be sure to wave hello to the 500-pound crocodile secure in his deep pit. ⊠ *Carretera 307, Km 31* ☏ *998/850–3719* ⊕ *www.crococunzoo.com* ⊠ *MX$366* ⊗ *Daily 9–5.*

Yaax Che Jardín Botánico del Dr. Alfredo Barrera Marín (*Dr. Alfredo Barrera Marín Botanical Garden*). This 150-acre botanical garden is the largest in Mexico. Named for a local botanist, it exhibits the peninsula's plants and flowers, which are labeled in English, Spanish, and Latin. The park features a 130-foot suspension bridge, three observation towers, and a library equipped with reading hammocks. There's also a tree nursery, a remarkable orchid and epiphyte garden, an authentic

Mayan house, and an archaeological site. A nature walk goes directly through the mangroves for some great birding; more than 220 species have been identified here (be sure to bring bug spray, though). Spider monkeys can usually be spotted in the afternoons, and a treehouse lookout offers a spectacular view—but the climb isn't for those afraid of heights. ✉ *Carretera 307, 1 km (½ mile) south of Puerto Morelos* ✣ *Enter from northbound side of highway. From southbound side, turn around after town.* ☎ *998/206–9233* 🎟 *MX$150* ⏲ *Dec.–April, daily 8–4; May–Nov., Mon.–Sat. 8–4.*

> **BEACH SAFETY**
>
> Deserted beaches invite thieves—never leave anything visible in your car. Remember that even the calmest-looking waters can have currents and riptides. Take note that waves are most powerful during December, and that hurricane season lasts from June into November. If visiting isolated beaches, bring sunscreen and drinking water to avoid overexposure and dehydration.

BEACHES

Puerto Morelos Main Beach. Newcomers to Puerto Morelos might be disappointed by the rocky beaches, blankets of seaweed, and boats that dock ashore—after all, this place is more about snorkeling on the reef than sunning on the sand. Your best bet is to head for the narrow stretch of beach two blocks north of the square in front of Ojo de Agua Hotel. Park on the town square or adjacent streets. You can walk just north of the hotel for better snorkeling. **Amenities**: food and drink; parking (no fee). **Best for**: snorkeling. ✉ *North of town square.*

WHERE TO EAT

$$ SOUTH AMERICAN 🍴 **Al Chimichurri.** The smoky aromas of a South American *parillada* waft down the street from this Uruguayan barbecue joint. Heaping portions of short ribs, flank steak, and chorizo, start you off; crêpes with "flaming apple" or *dulce de leche* finish nicely. Tables are set off the street, in a pleasant walled courtyard. [$] *Average main: 140 MP* ✉ *Av. Javier Rojo Gomez, between avs. Tulum and Isla Mujeres* ☎ *1998/192–1129 (mobile), 998/252–4666* 🌐 *www.alchimichurri.com* 💳 *No credit cards* ⏲ *Closed Mon. and Sept. No lunch.*

$$$ INTERNATIONAL 🍴 **John Gray's Kitchen.** Next to the jungle, this restaurant draws a regular crowd of Cancún and Playa residents. Using only the freshest ingredients—from local fruits and vegetables to seafood right off the pier—the chefs work their magic in a comfortable, contemporary setting that feels more Manhattan than Mayan. Don't miss the tender roasted duck breast with tequila, chipotle, and honey; another great option is *coronado,* a local white fish grilled to perfection and served with pesto and cilantro. The menu changes weekly, so repeat guests are always in for a treat. [$] *Average main: 271 MP* ✉ *Av. Niños Heroes, 1 block north of Av. Morelos, on jungle side* ☎ *998/871–0665* ⏲ *Closed Sun. No lunch.*

$ MEXICAN 🍴 **La Playita.** Two blocks north of the town square, this "restaurant" is actually made up of plastic tables and chairs shaded by mini palapas and tarps. What it lacks in charm is more than made up for by the food and prices. La Playita is where locals go for seafood soup, fried fish, shrimp tacos, ceviche, and fresh guacamole—but plan to either practice your

Spanish or use sign language because this family-run business focuses more on quality cooking than customer service. You should plan to eat early, too, as it closes at 8. ■ **TIP➔ La Playita is the perfect place to sink your toes in the sand and enjoy a refreshing rice-milk horchata.** ⓈⒶ *Average main: 110 MP* ⊠ *Av. Rafael Melgar, Sm 2, Mza 3, Lote 2.*

$$$
INTERNATIONAL
Fodor'sChoice
★

✕ **La Sirena.** Overlooking the town square, La Sirena serves an eclectic mix of dishes ranging from mini-sliders and grilled grouper to hearty plates of BBQ pulled pork with shoestring fries. If you like Mediterranean food, opt for Greek specialties prepared by Chef Anthony Chalas, who credits his skills to his years spent in Greece. The dip sampler—with homemade hummus and tzatziki—is completely understated, as is the Greek salad topped with a block of feta and Kalamata olives. The *keftedes* (Greek meatballs) are outstanding. You can taste the quality here, reflecting Anthony's effort to buy only organic and fresh ingredients. There's live music nightly in high season. Ⓢ *Average main: 230 MP* ⊠ *Jose Maria Morelos* ☎ *998/254–1314* ⊕ *www.lasirenapm.com.*

$
BAKERY

✕ **Le Café D'Amancia.** This colorful hangout on the corner of the main plaza is the best place in town to watch the world go by (or take advantage of free Wi-Fi) while lingering over coffee and a pastry. The fruit smoothies are delicious, as are the croissants. Most items are organic. Ⓢ *Average main: 67 MP* ⊠ *Av. Tulum at Av. Rojo Gomez* ☎ *998/206–9242* ⊟ *No credit cards* ☾ *Closed Mon.*

$$
ECLECTIC

✕ **Pangea.** Abutting the plaza at the beach, Pangea has it all: breakfast, lunch, and dinner served on an umbrella-shaded terrace overlooking the sea, plus live music and entertainment until late. Daily menus—all prepared with organic ingredients and without preservatives—may include grilled fresh tuna, vegetarian lasagna, or shrimp kebabs, and there's fresh ginger-lemongrass tea and pancakes for breakfast. Evening menus are themed according to the show—thus, Middle Eastern food for belly-dancing night and Spanish tapas for flamenco. The owners came from Mexico City in the early 1990s and are a great source for tourist tips and local gossip. Ⓢ *Average main: 162 MP* ⊠ *Av. Morelos at the water* ☎ *1998/159–5241 (mobile).*

$$$
SEAFOOD

✕ **Pelicanos.** Enjoy fresh seafood on the shaded patio of this family-owned restaurant in the heart of town. Try fish prepared *al ajo* (in a garlicky butter sauce), breaded, grilled, or *tikin–xic* style (marinated with adobo de achiote and sour oranges). The fried shrimp, served in a coconut shell, melds sweet and salty, while the massive margaritas pack a powerful punch. ■ **TIP➔ Pelicanos also offers a variety of four-hour excursions that include fishing, snorkeling, then cooking the daily catch at the restaurant (from MX$3,388).** Ⓢ *Average main: 244 MP* ⊠ *Av. Rafael Melgar at Av. Tulum* ☎ *998/871–0014.*

WHERE TO STAY

$$
B&B/INN
Fodor'sChoice
★

▦ **Casa Caribe.** Five minutes from the town square and opposite the main beach, this charming hacienda-style B&B has large rooms with king-size beds plus private ocean-view terraces. **Pros:** free beach chairs and umbrellas provided; great breakfasts; lovely staff. **Cons:** not all rooms have a/c; proximity to the mangroves attracts bugs; no pool; four-night minimum. Ⓢ *Rooms from: $135* ⊠ *Av. Rojo Gómez 768*

☎ *998/251–8060, 512/410–8146* 🌐 *www.casacaribepuertomorelos.com* 🛏 *5 rooms* 🍴 *Breakfast.*

$$$$ ALL-INCLUSIVE FAMILY 🏨 **Dreams Riviera Cancún.** This sprawling resort offers a wide range of activities and a good (albeit expensive) spa. **Pros:** family-friendly; children under 12 stay free; hydrotherapy circuit at the spa garden for Preferred Members. **Cons:** only 60% of rooms have ocean views; hallway noise can be heard in rooms; sea grass on the beach. [$] *Rooms from: $450* ✉ *Calle 55, Sm 11, Mza 4, Puerto Morelos* ☎ *998/872–9200* 🌐 *www.dreamsresorts.com* 🛏 *486 rooms* 🍴 *All-inclusive.*

$$$$ ALL-INCLUSIVE 🏨 **Excellence Riviera Cancún.** Just 15 minutes from Cancún Airport, this luxurious, adults-only resort is centered on an indulgent spa and six meandering pools. **Pros:** caters to honeymooners; plenty of pool lounging space; rooms have private hot tubs for two. **Cons:** thin walls; mediocre food; no children under 18. [$] *Rooms from: $454* ✉ *Carretera 307, Km 324, north of Puerto Morelos* ☎ *998/872–8500* 🌐 *www.excellence-resorts.com* 🛏 *440 rooms* 🍴 *All-inclusive.*

SHOPPING

BOOKS

Alma Libre Bookstore. There are more than 20,000 titles in stock at Alma Libre. You can buy outright or trade in your own books for 25% of their cover price and replenish your holiday reading list. Owners Robert and Joanne Birce are also great sources of local information. ✉ *Av. Tulum 3* 🌐 *www.almalibrebooks.com* 🕒 *Daily 10:30–6.*

CRAFTS AND FOLK ART

Colectivo de Artesanos de Puerto Morelos. The Puerto Morelos Artists' Cooperative is a series of palapa-style buildings where local artisans sell their jewelry, hand-embroidered clothing, hammocks, and other items. You can sometimes find real bargains. ✉ *Av. Javier Rojo Gómez at Av. Isla Mujeres* 🕒 *Daily 8 am–dusk.*

Ixchel Jungle Market & Spa. This nonprofit organization generates income for Maya women and their families. From December through April, a Sunday market features traditional dances, regional foods, and handmade crafts sold by Maya women wearing embroidered dresses. Year-round, the spa offers traditional Mayan treatments such as deep-tissue massage and body wraps with aloe vera or chocolate fresh from the cacao; it's open by appointment only, with bookings at 10, noon, 2, and 4. ✉ *Calle 2* ☎ *998/208–9148* 🌐 *www.mayaecho.com* 🕒 *Market: Dec.–Apr., Sun. 10:30–1. Spa: Jan.–Mar., daily; Apr.–Dec., Tues.–Sat. 10:30–1.*

SPORTS AND THE OUTDOORS

ADVENTURE TOURS

FAMILY **Selvática.** Just outside Puerto Morelos, Selvática offers tours over the jungle on more than 3 km (2 miles) of zip-lines. The full trip—including zip-lines, aerial bridges, dirt buggies, a bungee swing, a cenote swim, lunch, and transfers—takes five hours. Advance reservations are required. ✉ *Carretera 307, Km 321, 19 km (12 miles) from turnoff* ☎ *998/898–4312, 866/552–8826* 🌐 *www.selvatica.com.mx* 🎟 *MX$2697* 🕒 *Closed Sun.*

Xenotes Oasis Maya. Operated by Experiencias Xcaret, Xenotes Oasis Maya includes a trip to four cenotes where you can kayak, zip-line, rappel, and snorkel. Tours begin at 9 am and take about nine hours, including transfers. Transportation, lunch, and equipment are included. ☎ *998/883–3143, 855/326–2969* 🌐 *www.xenotes.com* 🎟 *MX$1627* 🕒 *Closed Sun.*

COOKING SCHOOLS

The Little Mexican Cooking School. Learn how to cook authentic Mexican cuisine from the trained chefs at Casa Caribe's culinary school. After participating in the hands-on making of seven to eight dishes, you can enjoy the meal you've just prepared. Classes are offered Tuesday through Saturday, from 10 to 3:30, by reservation only. ✉ *Casa Caribe, Av. Rojo Gomez 768, 3½ blocks north of town square* ☎ *998/251–8060, 512/410–8146 in the U.S.* 🌐 *www.thelittlemexicancookingschool.com* 🎟 *MX$1735.*

SCUBA DIVING AND SNORKELING

Almost Heaven Adventures. The oldest dive shop in the area is the only one owned and operated by locals. Options here include reef and wreck diving; night tours are especially popular in summer, so book at least a day in advance. Almost Heaven Adventures also has snorkeling trips. ✉ *Av. Javier Rojo Gómez, Mza 2, Lote 10* ☎ *998/846–8009, 998/871–0230* 🌐 *www.almostheavenadventures.com* 🎟 *Snorkeling from MX$745, diving from MX$948.*

Diving Dog Tours. Snorkeling trips at various sites on the Great Mesoamerican Reef are organized by Diving Dog. ✉ *Av. Jose Ma. Morelos* ☎ *998/848–8819* 🌐 *www.puertomorelosfishing.com* 🎟 *MX$406.*

PUNTA BRAVA

24 km (15 miles) north of Playa del Carmen.

Punta Brava is a long, winding sweep of sand strewn with seashells. The only direct access to this beach area is through the security gate at the Grand Velas or El Dorado Royale resort. Past the entrance is a tropical jungle and more than 1½ km (1 mile) of coastline at Punta Brava Beach. In an effort to calm the powerful waves, artificial sandbars have been built along the shore. Not only are these burlap sacks an eyesore, but also they have eliminated one of the few spots in the area where bodysurfing was once possible.

GETTING HERE AND AROUND

If you're heading north from Playa del Carmen, turn right into El Dorado Royale gate at Km 45. Currency exchange is available within El Dorado Royale Resort. Otherwise, the nearest banks, medical facilities, and police stations are 8 km (5 miles) north in Puerto Morelos.

WHERE TO STAY

$$$$ RESORT ALL-INCLUSIVE

🏨 **El Dorado Royale.** Although this beachfront property has been overshadowed by its newer neighbors, the location—amid 500 acres of lush jungle—is as alluring as ever. **Pros:** on-site health bar and ATM; sprawling property; green practices. **Cons:** rocky beach with sea grass; slow room service; no kids under 18; slippery bathroom tile. [$] *Rooms from:*

$450 ⊠ *Carretera 307, Km 45* ☎ *998/872–8030* ⊕ *www.eldorado-resort.com* ↘ *478 rooms* ❍ *All-inclusive.*

PLAYA DEL SECRETO

23 km (14½ miles) north of Playa del Carmen.

The secret is out—the ½-km (1-mile) stretch of white sand at Playa del Secreto is one of the most beautiful in the Riviera Maya. Surrounded by jungle and Caribbean waters, the protected shores are a favorite nesting ground for giant leatherback sea turtles, weighing up to 300 pounds. From May through October, early risers can watch baby turtles struggle from their shells and skitter down to the sea. The bordering jungle is home to foxes, deer, crocodiles, wild boars, and coatimundis. Bird-watching is excellent here, with species ranging from wild parrots and hawks to kingfishers and black-necked stilts. This coastal community is midway between Cancún and Playa del Carmen, meaning that nightclubs, shopping, and restaurants are less than 20 minutes away.

GETTING HERE AND AROUND

From Playa del Carmen, drive approximately 20 minutes north on Carretera 307 and turn right at Km 312. The entrance for Playa del Secreto is just past the Cirque du Soleil Theater. From Cancún, take Carretera 307 south. Approximately 10 km (6 miles) past Puerto Morelos, turn left at Km 312 onto the Playa del Secreto road that leads to the beach. For those staying at the Valentin resort, there's a designated entrance off Carretera 307 at Km 311. Because only private villas and a resort make up this beach community, there are no restaurants, shops, or services available. The nearest are north in Puerto Morelos.

BEACHES

Playa del Secreto. Free of rocks, sea grass, and drop-offs, Playa del Secreto is perfect for swimming, kayaking, or snorkeling. On windy days, the waves are large enough for boogie boarding or bodysurfing. At the nearby reef, divers can get down with lobster, octopus, crabs, and turtles. The powdery white sand makes it great for long walks. The stretch near Valentin Imperial Maya is especially clean, with clear warm water where fish come to eat out of your hand. Dotting the shore are vacation rentals and a private community of homeowners, meaning that there is no public access to this beach other than through the private roads off Carretera 307. Despite the fact this is a public beach, non–hotel guests will be turned away at security gates. That also means that there are no public facilities other than those offered exclusively to guests. **Amenities:** none. **Best for:** snorkeling; swimming; walking. ⊠ *Carretera 307, Km 311, 15 mins south of Cancún Airport.*

WHERE TO STAY

$$$$
ALL-INCLUSIVE

▦ **Valentin Imperial Maya.** Nestled in thriving mangrove forests, this adults-only all-inclusive is one of the few in the region that still embraces Mexican tradition. **Pros:** good service; enormous pools; authentic Mexican coffee; pillow menu. **Cons:** evening entertainment disappointing; no kids under 18; slippery hallways during rainy season; main pool gets crowded. Ⓢ *Rooms from: $454* ⊠ *Carretera 307, Km*

311.5 ☎ *984/206–3660* 🌐 *www.valentinmaya.com* 🛏 *524 rooms, 16 suites* 🍴 *All-inclusive.*

NIGHTLIFE

JOYÀ by Cirque du Soleil. From the creators of Cirque du Soleil, this whimsical show follows the adventures of a rebellious teenage girl swept away to a mysterious jungle. Several ticket packages are available. ✉ *Carretera 307, Km 48, near Mayan Palace Resort* ☎ *800/247–7837, 984/206–4036* 🌐 *www.cirquedusoleil.com* 🎟 *From MX$971* 🕒 *Closed Sun. and Mon.*

PUNTA MAROMA

23 km (14 miles) north of Playa del Carmen.

The waters of this protected bay stay calm even on blustery days, and the enchanting beach ranks among Mexico's finest. A string of resorts has taken advantage of its enviable position—including the Belmond Maroma Resort & Spa, the Blue Diamond Resort, and Secrets Maroma. Unfortunately, nonguests will not be able to access the beach since the only entry point is through the security gate.

GETTING HERE AND AROUND

Driving north from Playa del Carmen, turn right into the Punta Maroma gate at Km 51. Heading south from Cancún, take Carretera 307 to the east (left) turnoff at Km 306.5. Signs (and a security guard) will point you to your resort. Blue Diamond Resort is accessed by way of a private entrance at Km 298.8 off Carretera 307. Because Punta Maroma is a gated community, the only available facilities are within the resorts themselves. The closest shops, restaurants, banks, and emergency facilities are 10 minutes south in Playa del Carmen.

BEACHES

Punta Maroma. One of Mexico's most beautiful beaches has deep white sand that feels like powdered sugar and crystalline water that's free of rocks. The small waves crashing onshore make it great for bodysurfing; 10 minutes off the coast of the Blue Diamond Resort, you'll find terrific diving, too. Hotels supply lounge chairs and offer activities like volleyball, yoga, and even remote-control boat racing for guests. Unfortunately, this beach can only be accessed by way of the security gate on Carretera 307 that leads to Secrets Maroma, Catalonia Playa Maroma, and Belmond Maroma Resort & Spa. Unless you plan to visit by boat or stay at one of these resorts, you're probably out of luck. **Amenities:** food and drink; toilets (for resort guests only). **Best for:** walking. ✉ *Carretera 307, Km 306.*

WHERE TO STAY

$$$$ RESORT Fodor's Choice ★

🏨 **Belmond Maroma Resort & Spa.** Connecting jungle and beach, a labyrinth of paths threads through the grounds at this elegant Mayan-themed hotel, where butterflies and parrots fly and the scent of flowers fills the air. **Pros:** most rooms have ocean views; exceptional beach; great place to escape the crowds; programs for children. **Cons:** not much entertainment; difficult to find from highway. [$] *Rooms from: $765* ✉ *Carretera 307, Km 306* ⊕ *From Carretera 307, look for the peacock mural and the Burger*

Bar restaurant just outside the security entrance (there's no other sign) ☎ *998/872–8200, 866/454–9351* ⊕ *www.belmond.com* ⇱ *30 rooms, 34 suites, 1 villa* ○| *Multiple meal plans.*

$$$$
ALL-INCLUSIVE
⊤ **Blue Diamond Riviera Maya.** Midway between Punta Bete and Punta Maroma, this all-inclusive resort is on the south end of Maroma Beach. **Pros:** golf carts and bikes available; huge rooms; excellent service. **Cons:** strict dress code at some restaurants; lots of mosquitoes; no children under 18. $ *Rooms from: $364* ⊠ *Carretera 307, Km 298* ☎ *984/206–4100* ⊕ *www.bluediamond-rivieramaya.com* ⇱ *128 rooms* ○| *All-inclusive.*

$$$$
ALL-INCLUSIVE
⊤ **Secrets Maroma Beach Riviera Cancún.** Strip away the gourmet restaurants, elegant rooms, and 18 swimming pools, and you're still basking on Mexico's best beach. **Pros:** romantic property; unlimited luxury; swim-up rooms; peaceful for the size. **Cons:** dress code at all restaurants; no children under 18. $ *Rooms from: $600* ⊠ *Carretera 307, Km 306.5* ☎ *984/877–3600* ⊕ *www.secretsresorts.com* ⇱ *412 rooms* ○| *All-inclusive.*

SPAS

Kinan Spa. Signature treatments at the Belmond Maroma's spa include the Kinan Ritual (a wrap and exfoliation), the Aphrodisiac Chocolate Invigoration (a wrap and massage with cacao), Janzu (water therapy), and the Mayan Temazcal Ritual (combining ancient traditions, chants, and meditation). The alignment of treatment rooms is based on celestial energies. But if you're looking for something less ethereal, medical treatments (such as Botox) are available, too. ⊠ *Belmond Maroma Resort & Spa, Carretera 307, Km 51* ☎ *998/872–8200* ⊕ *www.belmond.com.*

Spa at Blue Diamond. Exclusively for guests of the Blue Diamond resort, this 25,000-square-foot spa merges ancient Mayan philosophy with Asian healing rituals. Both the design and philosophy are inspired by the Mayan healing elements of water, air, fire and earth. Signature treatments include Four Hand Harmony (a four-hands massage), Temazcal Ceremony (a ritual guided by a Mayan Shaman), and Peace Stone Ritual (a stone massage to balance energy levels). Scrubs and wraps made with chocolate and coffee are also popular. Body treatments, ranging from 1 to 6 hours, take place in jungle palapas, Thai suites, or garden villas. ■ **TIP→** Travelers who've spent too long basking in the sun can try the sunburn remedy wrap and hydrating facial. ⊠ *Blue Diamond Riviera Maya, Carretera 307, Km 298, Punta Bete* ☎ *984/206–4100* ⊕ *www. bluediamond-rivieramaya.com.*

MAYAKOBA

10 km (6 miles) north of Playa del Carmen.

Mayakoba (meaning "village of water") is home to three of the world's most exclusive resorts—the Banyan Tree Mayakoba, Fairmont Mayakoba, and Rosewood Mayakoba. They are connected by a network of canals that inspire the property's tagline, "the Venice of the Caribbean." Aside from luxury lodgings, this 1,600-acre enclave supports mangrove forests, freshwater lagoons, beach dunes, and sunken cenotes; and the resident wildlife includes monkeys, turtles, crocodiles, and 160 species of birds. Here, spas are perched amid jungle treetops, and thatch-roof boats drift between limestone waterways.

GETTING HERE AND AROUND

The only way to reach this resort community is by car. From Playa del Carmen, head north on Carretera 307 for approximately 15 minutes; after passing the entrance for Grand Velas, turn right at Km 298 into Mayakoba. From Cancún, take Carretera 307 south to the east turnoff at Km 298. The entrance is marked by a large metal gate with silver lettering. Security guards will direct you to the property of your choice. Access to hotels, restaurants, spas, and the golf course are permitted by reservation only. Cars are banned, but guests can explore the jungle habitat by golf cart or bike (a paved trail connects the three properties); there's also a complimentary eco-boat that cruises through 11 km (7 miles) of waterways.

WHERE TO EAT

$$$ ✕ **Agave Azul.** There's more to Agave Azul than those sweeping lagoon
SUSHI and mangrove views. The glass-walled restaurant at the elegant Rosewood Mayakoba is hands down the best place to go for fresh sushi and premium tequila. Housing more than 120 labels of the latter (and 40 of mezcal), it hosts weekly tequila and sushi pairings. In addition to ceviche, sashimi, and maki rolls, the dinner menu here includes Asian-inspired entrées like chicken yakitori, yellow curry, and pad thai. The coconut flan with strawberry tapioca pearls is the perfect accompaniment to more tequila. ■ TIP➜ Kick off your night by sampling dangerously smooth cocktails infused with fresh cucumber, watermelon, and jalapeños. $ *Average main: 338 MP* ⊠ *Rosewood Mayakoba, Carretera 307, Km 298* ☎ *984/875–8000* ⊕ *www.rosewoodhotels.com* ☾ *No lunch.*

WHERE TO STAY

$$$$ 🏨 **Banyan Tree Mayakoba.** This Thai chain has brought its own traditions
RESORT to Mexico's Riviera with stunning results: in addition to vaulted ceilings, lounge areas, dining rooms, private gardens, and Talavera earthenware sinks, all rooms have outdoor bathtubs and private 376-foot swimming pools—a unique perk. **Pros:** all-villa resort; top-notch spa; excellent food; world-class service. **Cons:** no sign of Mexico; small kids' club; fee to use bicycles on property; not many activities. $ *Rooms from: $619* ⊠ *Carretera 307, Km 298* ☎ *984/877–3688* ⊕ *www.banyantree.com* ☞ *117 rooms* ❘○❘ *No meals.*

$$$$ 🏨 **Fairmont Mayakoba.** Set under a mangrove canopy, this sprawling
RESORT luxury resort sets new standards in the Riviera Maya for sustainability and comfort. **Pros:** all-inclusive plan available Oct.–May; free shuttle to neighboring properties; bird-watching tours; cooking classes and beer tastings. **Cons:** Internet costs $20 per day; some rooms lack water views; 20-min walk from lobby to ocean. $ *Rooms from: $399* ⊠ *Carretera 307, Km 298* ☎ *984/206–3000* ⊕ *www.fairmont.com/mayakoba* ☞ *367 rooms, 34 suites* ❘○❘ *No meals.*

$$$$ 🏨 **Rosewood Mayakoba.** From the moment you set foot on the palapa-
RESORT covered boat that brings you to your room's private dock, the Rosewood
FAMILY transports you to an exotic world. **Pros:** free kids' club; complimen-
Fodor's Choice tary bottle of tequila; extraordinary spa; check-in takes place on the
★ boat. **Cons:** narrow beach; limited food options; no meals included;

The Rosewood Mayakoba is one of the Riviera Maya's most elegant resorts.

7-night minimum stay during holidays. $ *Rooms from: $750* ⊠ *Carretera 307, Km 298* ☎ *984/875–8000* ⊕ *www.rosewoodmayakoba.com* ↩ *130 suites* ¡○¡ *No meals.*

SPAS

Banyan Tree Spa. Built over freshwater lagoons, the Banyan Tree Spa draws on centuries-old Asian traditions. The therapists (most of whom are from Thailand) begin with a heavenly footbath, followed by your choice of Asian-flavored healing treatments, including scrubs with turmeric, lemongrass, or green tea. Treatments take place in private pavilions, each with its own steam room, shower, and outdoor Jacuzzi enclosed by bamboo walls. Unique to Banyan Tree are its signature Rainmist Steam Bath and the romantic couples' Rainforest Experience, that combines hydrotherapy with infrared light to release tension and revitalize the body. ⊠ *Banyan Tree Resort, Carretera 307, Km 298* ☎ *984/877–3688* ⊕ *www.banyantree.com.*

Fodor'sChoice ★ **Sense Spa.** Rosewood's 17,000-square-foot spa is on its very own jungle-covered island. Wooden walkways lead to a swimming pool and limestone cenote, which is fed by subterranean springs. Many treatments, such as the *temazcal* ritual and the Mayakoba ancient massage, incorporate the Mayan tradition of aligning the energies of the body in rhythmic harmony. The chaya-mojito body scrub and anti-aging facial are both heavenly. Nonguests can book a treatment, then enjoy the spa facilities, including the gym, sauna, Jacuzzi, plunge pool, and the eucalyptus steam room for free. Without a treatment, a day pass costs MX$500. ⊠ *Rosewood Mayakoba, Carretera 307, Km 298* ☎ *984/875–8000* ⊕ *www.rosewoodhotels.com.*

Willow Stream Spa. It's easy to lose yourself (literally) within the 20,000-square-foot spa at the Fairmont Mayakoba. Signature treatments include the Mexican stone massage, the Mayan clay massage, and the Cha Chac Rain ritual (a massage that takes place on a seven-jet Vichy table). Weary travelers will want to try the Deep Sleep treatment, a massage that purports to reverse the negative effects of flying and time zone changes. After a gym workout, ease your muscles at the rooftop vitality pool. ⊠ *Fairmont Mayakoba, Carretera 307, Km 298* ☎ *984/206–3038* ⊕ *www.willowstream.com.*

SPORTS AND THE OUTDOORS

El Camaleón Mayakoba. Designed by the legendary Greg Norman, El Camaleón's 18-hole course is set amid jungle, mangrove, and sea. It is home to Mexico's only PGA tour event—the OHL Classic at Mayakoba, held in November. The layout is exceptional, from the first hole with a cenote in the middle of the fairway to the par 3s on the back with ocean views. Throughout the perfectly manicured course, each hole has a minimum of five tee blocks, so there is distance for every skill level. Holes 7 and 15 skirt the ocean; Hole 17 plays directly between a limestone canal and the Fairmont Mayakoba Resort. ⊠ *Carretera 307, Km 298* ☎ *984/206–3088* ⊕ *www.mayakobagolf.com* ⊇ *$279 for 18 holes* ⏴ *18 holes. 7024 yards. Par 72.*

PUNTA BETE (XCALACOCO)

6 km (4 miles) north of Playa del Carmen.

Beyond Punta Maroma, a river spills into the sea, dividing the coastline. South of the split, Playa Xcalacoco (scala-coco) is a 7-km-long (5½-mile-long) beach dotted with bungalows; small, exclusive resort hotels; and thatch-roof restaurants, backing into dense jungle. The beach is beautiful, a more natural extension of Playa del Carmen, but the shore can be rocky. Some hotels here supply water shoes for swimming, and the Viceroy has a dock to enter deeper water.

GETTING HERE AND AROUND

Driving north from Playa del Carmen, turn right at the Coca-Cola factory and follow the road east. Heading south from Cancún on Carretera 307, turn at the huge sign for the Princess Resort at Km 296 to reach Petit Lafitte, Cocos Cabanas, the Viceroy, and the beach. (To reach Le Rêve, you'll have to take the road about 100 yards south, marked with a blue sign for Azul Fives condos.) Punta Bete has few shops, bars, or restaurants outside of the hotels; however, there is a convenience store and a pizzeria on the way to Le Rêve.

BEACHES

If long walks on the beach are your thing, you'll love the 6-km (4-mile) stretch from Playa Xcalacoco to Playa del Carmen. Although delightfully deserted, the beach itself is not the area's best; the sand is somewhat coarse and often draped in sea grass. There's decent snorkeling, however, and the isolation is unbeatable. Plus, it's a way to explore Playa from Xcalacoco without bumping over the jungle road.

WHERE TO STAY

$
B&B/INN
$\boxed{\cdot}$ **Cocos Cabanas.** Tranquility and seclusion are the name of the game in these bright, cozy bungalows located a stone's throw from the beach. **Pros:** good pizza; friendly staff; gorgeous beach. **Cons:** patchy Wi-Fi; not on beach; tons of mosquitoes; tiny pool. $\boxed{\$}$ *Rooms from: $95* $\boxtimes$ *Carretera 307, Km 296, Playa Xcalacoco* ✛ *Take the paved road at Princess Resort and follow signs. Turn left onto the dirt road. Cocos Cabanas will be on your right.* ☏ *998/874–7056* ⊕ *www.cocoscabanas.com* ⟿ *6 rooms* †◯| *Breakfast.*

> **TEQUILA TASTINGS**
>
> Viceroy Riviera Maya (☏ *800–578–0281* ⊕ *www.viceroyhotelsandresorts.com*) offers tequila tastings at 5, 6, and 9 daily. Top-shelf brands like Don Julio and Herradura are paired with four types of ceviche. The resort's maestro *tequilero* will reveal the secrets and history behind this local favorite, and can prepare mezcal tastings upon request. By reservation only.

$$$$
HOTEL
$\boxed{\cdot}$ **Le Rêve Hotel & Spa.** At the end of a short, bumpy dirt road, this secluded little resort seems tailor-made for a romantic getaway. **Pros:** stylish feel; all rooms have balcony or garden; all-inclusive meal plan available; free use of kayaks, iPad, and snorkel gear. **Cons:** dirt access road full of potholes; small resort means few amenities; time-share sales pitch. $\boxed{\$}$ *Rooms from: $320* $\boxtimes$ *Playa Xcalacoco Fracc. 2A, Carretera 307, Km 295, Playa del Carmen* ✛ *From Carretera 307, turn at Azul Fives hwy. sign and follow signs* ☏ *984/109–5660* ⊕ *www.hotellereve.com* ⟿ *25 rooms* †◯| *Multiple meal plans.*

$$$$
RESORT
FAMILY
$\boxed{\cdot}$ **Petit Lafitte.** Named after the famous pirate, this warm and family-friendly resort has multi-unit cabanas plus freestanding bungalows on the beach's north end that are more private and charming. **Pros:** peaceful atmosphere; kids love the small animal refuge; fabulous staff. **Cons:** rocky beach, mosquitoes; no TVs in bungalows. $\boxed{\$}$ *Rooms from: $295* $\boxtimes$ *Carretera 307, Km 296, Punta Bete* ✛ *From Carretera 307, turn onto the paved road for the Princess Resort and follow the signs to Petit Lafitte* ☏ *984/877–4000* ⊕ *www.petitlafitte.com* ⟿ *30 rooms, 20 bungalows* †◯| *Some meals.*

$$$$
RESORT
Fodor's Choice
★
$\boxed{\cdot}$ **The Viceroy Riviera Maya.** Punta Bete's most luxurious jungle-beach resort is as romantic and exotic as ever. **Pros:** romantic and private; great food; luxurious villas; several meal plans available. **Cons:** bugs in jungle setting; hidden service charges; rocky beach; no children under 14. $\boxed{\$}$ *Rooms from: $685* $\boxtimes$ *Playa Xcalacoco, Carretera 307, Km 296, Punta Bete* ✛ *From Carretera 307, turn onto the paved road for Princess Resort and follow the signs to the Viceroy* ☏ *800/578–0281* ⊕ *www.viceroyrivieramaya.com* ⟿ *41 villas* †◯| *Multiple meal plans.*

SPAS

Wayak Spa. Although not as grandiose as most spas in the Riviera Maya, this small spot (meaning "the dreamer") utilizes natural surroundings to create a unique pampering experience. From the shaman who greets you with a purifying waft of cobal smoke to the treatment rooms oriented toward sun, moon, and stars, the Wayak Spa makes a point of reminding you that you're in the land of the Maya. Opt for massages in jungle palapa huts surrounded by waterfalls (and mosquito curtains) or a purifying steam bath with a heavenly oculus. Client favorites include the honey-citrus scrub and seaweed body wrap. The black-lava treatment infuses minerals in a three-step process including a body scrub, hydration, and a heated wrap. ⊠ *Viceroy Riviera Maya Resort, Carretera 307, Km 296, Playa Xcalacoco* ✢ *From Carretera 307, turn onto the paved road at Princess Resort and follow the signs to the Viceroy.* ⊕ *www.viceroyhotelsandresorts.com.*

PLAYA DEL CARMEN

68 km (42 miles) south of Cancún.

Welcome to the party! "Playa," currently Latin America's fastest-growing community, has a population of more than 150,000 and an international flavor lent by the *estadounidenses* (United States citizens), Canadians, and Europeans who have been moving here since the early 1990s. Full of lively bars, restaurants, beach clubs, shops, and hotels, its eminently walkable downtown is one of the few places on the Riviera Maya where you can have a car-free vacation.

Sunbathe and swim at trendy beach clubs by day, then drink and dance at nightclubs until the sun comes up and start all over again. In between, there's an enjoyable array of diversions along Avenida 5, a pedestrian-only cobbled street that is the town's main drag. Its southern section, from about Calle 4 to Constituyentes, is busy, noisy, and sometimes rowdy—the place to go for nightlife, tequila shots, and souvenir shopping. Its quieter, more upscale northern end, north of Constituyentes up to about Calle 38, is the place for chic cafés and stylish boutiques. Rapid development means a decline in Mexican culture, with chain stores and cheap souvenirs emerging on every corner (Starbucks junkies can easily get their fix.) It also means businesses open and close monthly, surviving on the hope they can offer a better service than their neighbors.

Although building-height restrictions have helped to keep Playa from turning into the next Cancún, you'll have to leave town to get off the beaten path. Much of the area is developed, most recently by a slew of all-inclusive resorts opening up on the city's outskirts. If you plan on leaving the town center, be aware of your surroundings. A slight increase in criminal activity was reported between 2011 and 2013, most of which occurred outside major resort areas.

GETTING HERE AND AROUND

Driving from Cancún airport, follow the signs on Carretera 307. Shortly before town, take the overpass up and descend at the Avenida Constituyentes exit. Turn left under the overpass and follow Constituyentes into town. The trip takes about an hour. Note that there are several rather intimidating police checkpoints as you approach Playa del Carmen from the highway. Officers occasionally check vehicles at random, especially at night.

If you are coming from Cancún by taxi, expect to pay MX$813–MX$1220. Shared vans from the airport generally cost MX$338 per

person; if you're traveling with a group or even find some other Playa-bound travelers at the airport, a van can be a good way to go.

Buses traveling south from Cancún stop at Playa del Carmen's bus terminal at Avenida 20 and Calle 12, a short walk from downtown and the main drag, Avenida 5 (known as "la Quinta"). Buses headed to Cancún from Playa del Carmen use the main bus terminal at Avenida Juárez and Avenida 5. ADO (⊕ www.ado.com.mx) runs express, first-class, and second-class buses to major destinations.

The town is set up on a grid system that's easy to navigate, if you know the rules. North–south avenidas are numbered in multiples of five, with Avenida 1 along the beach, and then moving westward through Avenidas 5, 10, 15, 20, and so on. East–west calles are even numbers only, starting with Calle 2 and progressing northward through 4, 6, 8, and so on. The Playacar resort development is south of the numbered calles, starting at Avenida Juárez. To get there from Cancún, stay on the highway past the Constituyentes exit and turn left after the overpass at the Playacar sign. ■ TIP➜ In Playa del Carmen, parking is prohibited at yellow curbs. If you're ticketed, your license plate will be taken to a nearby police station and returned only after the fine has been paid.

BEACHES

Playa del Carmen is famous for its pristine beaches, which have various access points staggered between the hotels on Avenida 5. Of course, it is equally famous for its thriving nightlife, and the trendy beach clubs here—all located in central Playa del Carmen—offer the best of both. The combination of DJ music, cocktails, and twentysomethings makes these open-air bars a can't-miss for young singles. Outside of resorts, they're also the only places you'll find beach amenities.

There are beach clubs all the way from Calle 8 to Calle 46, the hottest being at Mamita's and Kool beach between calles 26 and 30. (In between, you can also find little ad hoc massage places for about MX$542 per hour.) Coco Beach, where Calle 46 meets the ocean at Canibal Royal Beach Club, is popular with snorkelers drawn to the outer Chunzubul Reef. For deserted strands, head even farther north, where the waves are small and the water is shallow.

The southern beaches of Playacar extending to the ferry dock at Avenida Benito Juárez are shored up against erosion with buried sandbags, but there's still a sharp drop-off from the beach level to the water; beaches north of the ferry dock are more level. Although all local strands are technically open to the public, those in Playacar are difficult to access since they are dominated by all-inclusive resorts. You also won't find any beach clubs in Playacar.

Although Playa's beaches lack protective outer reefs, the strong wind and waves make these areas great for water sports. For an underwater adventure, organize a tour with one of the local dive companies that will take you to outer reefs and cenotes.

Mamita's Beach. This stretch of beach north of the ferry dock, from Constituyentes to Calle 38, is known to locals as Mamita's, although it also encompasses Kool beach club and the Royal and Mahekal hotels. Independent of the main beach's drop-off (and the sandbags that are sometimes visible there), it's a lovely straight stretch of flat sand and clear water, which you'll share with lots of other visitors. The tradeoff is that Wave Runners, which are largely absent from the main beach, are very present here. It's a good spot for fun in the sun, not seclusion. **Amenities:** food and drink; toilets; water sports. **Best for:** partiers; swimming. ⊠ *Between Constituyentes and Calle 38.*

Playa del Carmen Main Beach. The community's most central section of beach stretches from the ferry docks up to Calle 14 at Gran Porto Real, a swath of deep white sand licked by turquoise water. The beach and water are clean, but there is some boat traffic that makes swimming less idyllic. Snorkelers aren't likely to see much here, but you can't beat the beach for convenience: countless bars and restaurants are a short walk away on Fifth Avenue, masseurs compete (discreetly) to knead out your kinks, and it's easy to find a dive shop ready to take you out to sea. The closer you get to the docks, the more people you'll find. If you're looking for seclusion, head farther north outside Playa del Carmen. **Amenities:** food and drink; water sports. **Best for:** swimming; walking. ⊠ *Between ferry docks and Calle 14.*

BEACH CLUBS

Canibal Royal. Playa's most urbane beach club is set apart from the crowd in more ways than one. It's north of town at Calle 48, and its retro-1960s architecture and eclectic music selection make it a destination in itself. The beach area is equipped with plenty of lounge chairs, and there's a rooftop bar with a plunge pool and sundeck. Expect to pay around MX$200 for a chair and umbrella; fees are generally waved for those who spend a minimum of MX$200 on food or drinks. For a stylish lunch, try braised octopus or a tarte flambé. There's also a juice bar and full cocktail menu featuring the signature rosemary *caipiroska* (vodka with lime and sugar). **Amenities:** food and drink; toilets. **Best for:** partiers. ⊠ *Calle 48, in front of Elements Condominiums and next to Grand Coco Bay* ☎ *984/859–1441, 984/859–1443* ⊕ *www.canibal-royal.com* ⊠ *MX$200 food/drink minimum* ⊙ *Daily 10–7.*

Indigo Beach. Cure your morning hangover with the breakfast buffet (MX$150) at this beach club beside El Taj Condo Hotel. The restaurant serves fresh fusion cuisine that blends Italian, Asian, and Mexican dishes. Lounge chairs and beach beds are abundant, and there are changing rooms, outdoor showers, and oversize towels for your convenience. A section of beach is used as a launching point by small fishing boats, but the view is still lovely and there is plenty of space to relax. As you enter the water, you'll feel about 20 feet of coral stone before the bottom transitions to smooth sand. The morning yoga and tai chi classes are a great way to start the day. **Amenities:** food and drink; showers; toilets. **Best for:** walking. ⊠ *Calle 14, beside El Taj Condo Hotel* ☎ *984/803–2222* ⊕ *www.indigobeach.com.mx* ⊠ *Free with food or drink purchase* ⊙ *Daily 8–5:30.*

Kool Beach. Private cabanas, a fashionable restaurant, a happening bar, and a vast terrace with a view make this one of Playa's favorite beach clubs. Guests can relax in the VIP area while a DJ spins trance and techno beside the freshwater pool. With two bars, a massage palapa, supply store, and a private catamaran, this place caters to the pampered traveler. A day pass isn't cheap, but it includes food, drinks, and club amenities. Kool Beach is next to Mamita's; both are main venues for the occasional festivals that draw international DJs to town. **Amenities:** food and drink; toilets. **Best for:** partiers. ⊠ *Calle 28* 🕾 *984/803–1961* ⊕ *www.koolbeachclub.com.mx* 🖃 *Day pass MX$975* ⊗ *Daily 9–5.*

Mamita's Beach Club. Accessible by way of Calle 28, this is Playa's hottest spot to catch some rays. You can rent an umbrella or chair for MX$30; MX$200 will get you a king-size bed in the sand. A day in the sun can get pricey though; expect to pay around MX$160 for a cocktail and MX$65 for a beer while listening to a famous DJ or conversing with young singles. Facilities include a dive shop, swimming pool, lounge bar, and dressing room. Guests can also enjoy beach volleyball or swim in the small pool. **Amenities:** food and drink; toilets; water sports. **Best for:** partiers. ⊠ *Calle 28, Playa del Carmen* 🕾 *984/803–2867* ⊕ *www.mamitasbeachclub.com* 🖃 *Free with food or drink purchase* ⊗ *Daily 9–6.*

Mosquito Beach Club. An extension of the Mosquito Beach Hotel, this trendy hot spot is often utilized by guests from neighboring hotels without beach access or swimming pools. For a flat MX$200 fee you can lounge on a comfy beach bed, nap under a huge umbrella, or take a dip in the pool. Expect amazing views of the water and a restaurant that serves Mexican food until 4 (the bar is open until 7 pm). DJs spin chill-out music throughout the day, but unlike some other loud beach clubs, you can still have a conversation here. ■**TIP**➔ Towels and lockers are not offered. **Amenities:** food and drink; showers; toilets. **Best for:** swimming; walking. ⊠ *Calle 8* 🕾 *984/873–0001 for Mosquito Beach Hotel* ⊕ *www.mosquitoblue.com* 🖃 *MX$200* ⊗ *Daily 8–7.*

Zenzi. This beach club and restaurant is one of the few open every day from morning (8 am) to late (2 am). Take a dip in the ocean and then catch some rays on one of the sun beds or chaise longues. When the sun goes down, there is live music, shows, and salsa lessons (Monday, Thursday, and Saturday) on the beach. The fish tacos and daily drink specials make it difficult to ever leave. **Amenities:** food and drink; toilets. **Best for:** partiers; swimming. ⊠ *Calle 10* 🕾 *984/803–5738* ⊕ *www.zenzi-playa.com* 🖃 *Free with food or drink purchase.*

WHERE TO EAT

$$$
MODERN
MEXICAN
✕**Aldea Corazón.** Playa's most dramatically sited restaurant sits atop a small cenote in a vast jungly garden full of strangler vines and Mayan ruins—right in the middle of Avenida 5. Designed in accordance with Maya building practices, it's a feast for the eyes, with living "green walls" covered with plants, a bar built on a stone wall, and a park in back that makes for a romantic setting at night (bring bug spray). The menu full of dressed-up Playa standards—fresh fish, chicken mole, jicama tacos, guacamole—isn't as memorable, but it's a worthwhile meal nonetheless. ■**TIP**➔ Come by between noon and 6 for 2-for-1

margaritas. [$] *Average main: 230 MP* ✉ *Av. 5 between calles 14 and 16* ☎ *984/803–1942* 🌐 *www.aldeacorazon.com* ✥ *C4.*

$$$$ ECLECTIC 🍴 **Alux Restaurant & Lounge.** Although this restaurant is a 10-minute drive from downtown, its location in an underground cavern makes it extremely popular. A candlelit rock stairway leads to a setting that's part Carlsbad Caverns, part *The Flintstones*. Some of the "cavernous" rooms are for lounging, some for drinking, some for eating, some for dancing. Creative lighting casts the stalactites and stalagmites in pale shades of violet, blue, and pink. Although the setting is the highlight, the food—including the cenote duck, chile Mexico lindo, lobster, and steak—is also quite good. With a packed house, this place can get rather musty and humid. [$] *Average main: 338 MP* ✉ *Av. Juarez between calles 65 and 70* ☎ *984/206–2589* 🌐 *www.aluxrestaurant.com/en* 🕓 *No lunch* ✥ *A1.*

$$ THAI 🍴 **Babe's Noodles & Bar.** Photos and paintings of old Hollywood pin-up models share décor space with a large stone Buddha at this Swedish-owned Thai restaurant. It's known for fresh, interesting fare cooked to order. Try the spring rolls with peanut sauce and Korean sesame noodles, then wash it all down with a refreshing lemonade, blended with ice and mint. If you're traveling during low season, note that this restaurant usually closes from mid-September through early October. [$] *Average main: 135 MP* ✉ *Calle 10 between avs. 5 and 10* ☎ *984/879–3569* 🌐 *www.babesnoodlesandbar.com* 🕓 *Closed Mon.* ✥ *C3*

$ FRENCH Fodor's Choice ★ 🍴 **Chez Céline.** Take one bite of Céline's chocolate croissants, and you'll think you've died and gone to Paris. Fresh-baked breads and pastries bring honor to France, especially exquisite desserts like the lemon tart and crème brûlée. Classic bistro fare—including quiche Lorraine and vols-au-vent—make for a light lunch *comme il faut*. Streetside tables on Avenida 5 are great for people watching. Chez Céline stays open until 11 pm daily, and there's free Wi-Fi for patrons. [$] *Average main: 81 MP* ✉ *Av. 5 at Calle 34* ☎ *984/308–3480* 🌐 *www.chezceline.com.mx* ✥ *C6.*

$$$ MEDITERRANEAN 🍴 **Como Como.** This small, intimate Mediterranean restaurant is where locals and travelers in the know go for perfectly al dente homemade pasta. Top orders range from squid ink tagliatelle with clams to seared tuna with tamarind sauce. For an imaginative starter, try the white tuna carpaccio topped with apple, ginger, beet, fresh mint, and lime salad. Most dishes can be modified for vegetarians. Prepare for the triumphant moment when a chocolate fondant reaches your table, resulting in the inevitable words, "I shouldn't really, but I'm on vacation." [$] *Average main: 230 MP* ✉ *Av. 10, at the corner of Calle 14, next to La Tortuga Hotel* ☎ *984/859–1646* 🌐 *www.comocomo.mx* ✥ *C4.*

$$$ CARIBBEAN Fodor's Choice ★ 🍴 **El Muelle.** "The Pier" resembles a Caribbean fish market with its wooden plank floors, whitewashed tables, and pilings strung with rope. A chalkboard features the catch of the day; it's delivered from local fishermen every morning and simply yet flavorfully prepared one of five ways or sold by the gram to go. El Muelle opens at 4 pm, so come before dinner for a strawberry-lemon spritzer and mixed ceviche made Peruvian-style with *Leche de Tigre*. From that point on, you're hooked, and you'll soon find there isn't a mediocre dish on the menu. **TIP→ This darling, ocean-to-table restaurant is not to be confused**

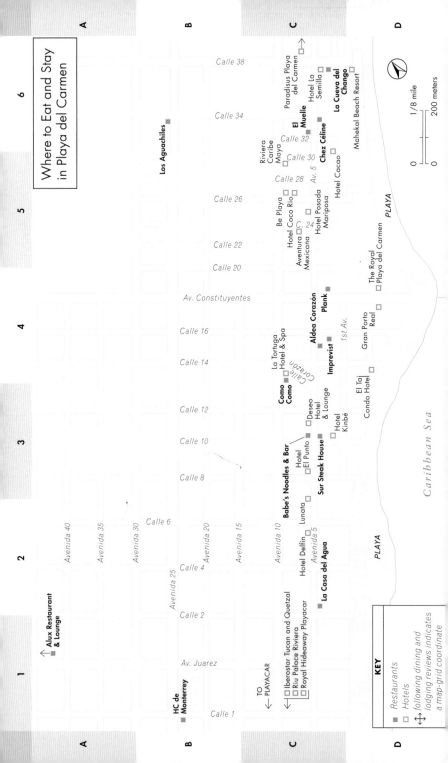

Where to Eat and Stay in Playa del Carmen

Caribbean Sea

PLAYA

Restaurants and Hotels

- Alux Restaurant & Lounge
- HC de Monterrey
- Los Aguachiles
- Iberostar Tucan and Quetzal
- Riu Palace Riviera
- Royal Hideaway Playacar
- La Casa del Agua
- Hotel Delfin
- Lunata
- Babe's Noodles & Bar
- Hotel El Punto
- Sur Steak House
- Como Como
- La Tortuga Hotel & Spa
- Deseo Hotel & Lounge
- Hotel Kinbé
- Aldea Corazón
- Plank
- Imprevist
- El Taj Condo Hotel
- Gran Porto Real
- Be Playa
- Hotel Coco Rio
- Aventura Mexicana
- Hotel Posada Mariposa
- The Royal Playa del Carmen
- Riviera Caribe Maya
- Chez Céline
- Hotel Cacao
- El Muelle
- Paradisus Playa del Carmen
- Hotel La Semilla
- La Cueva del Chango
- Mahekal Beach Resort

Streets
Av. Juarez, Avenida 40, Avenida 35, Avenida 30, Avenida 25, Avenida 20, Avenida 15, Avenida 10, Avenida 5, 1st Av., Av. Constituyentes, Calle Corazón, Calle 1, Calle 2, Calle 4, Calle 6, Calle 8, Calle 10, Calle 12, Calle 14, Calle 16, Calle 20, Calle 22, C. 24, Calle 26, Calle 28, Calle 30, Calle 32, Calle 34, Calle 38

TO PLAYACAR

KEY

- Restaurants
- Hotels
- following dining and lodging reviews indicates a map-grid coordinate

0   1/8 mile
0   200 meters

with Muelle 3 right around the corner. $ *Average main: 271 MP* ⊠ *Av. 5 and Calle 32* ☎ *984/803–0073* ⊕ *www.elmuelledeplaya.com* ⊗ *Closed Mon. No lunch* ⊹ *C6.*

$ ✕ **HC de Monterrey.** Follow your nose to this Mexican grill, where locals
MEXICAN gather for some of the best-tasting steak in town. Far from romantic, the open-air restaurant is filled with the sounds of mariachi music
blaring from the radio; a mounted bull's head hangs above the plastic
tables and chairs. The main draws are the huge cuts of beef, pork, and
chicken served with baskets of corn tortillas, baked potatoes, and ripe
avocados. This might just be the tastiest *arrachera* you'll find on your
vacation. There is a second location on Constituyentes, between avenidas 25 and 30. $ *Average main: 81 MP* ⊠ *Calle 1, between avs. 20 and
25* ☎ *984/803–4727* ⊕ *www.hcdemonterrey.com* ⊹ *B4.*

$$$ ✕ **Imprevist.** The name means "unexpected," and—thanks to the inter-
ASIAN FUSION national dishes created by executive chef Juan Diego Solombrino—this
Fodor's Choice place is truly a surprise. At breakfast, you can order hangover-healing
★ eggs Benedict, Belgian waffles, or old-fashioned French toast; later,
Imprevist pulls out all the stops with a hint of molecular gastronomy
in the tuna tartare with lime and sake foam, and the chilled beetroot
soup with goat cheese croquettes, truffle oil, and thyme cream. Risotto
choices include a seafood number with squid ink and shaved fennel. The
fish cooked in parchment is unbelievably moist, and the beef filet with
foie gras mousse practically melts in your mouth. The cool cocktails and
sticky date cake will leave you longing for a siesta. Seating is available at
sidewalk tables and in an intimate underground dining room. $ *Aver-
age main: 244 MP* ⊠ *Av. 1, between calles 14 and 16* ☎ *984/168–7025*
⊕ *www.imprevist.mx* ⊗ *No lunch Sun.* ⊹ *C4.*

$$$ ✕ **La Casa del Agua.** From the street-level bistro, a dramatic staircase
SEAFOOD leads up to a small cocktail bar and dining room overlooking Avenida
5. A stone waterfall is the focal point of the latter, and an open layout
provides nearly every table with a breeze from the water. Start with
crispy scallops marinated in lime and served over Champagne risotto,
then follow up with favorite mains like sesame-seared blue-fin tuna
with Portobello mushrooms or *cocinita pibil* ravioli (a lighter take on
Yucatecan achiote-roasted pork). Remarkably flavorful short ribs are
cooked for 8 hours in black beer, Dijon mustard, red wine, and honey.
$ *Average main: 338 MP* ⊠ *Av. 5 and Calle 2* ☎ *984/803–0232* ⊕ *www.
lacasadelagua.com* ⊗ *No lunch* ⊹ *C2.*

$ ✕ **La Cueva del Chango.** This Playa institution, in a funky jungle garden
MEXICAN with fountains, palmettos, and a rambling koi pond, is a favorite breakfast spot. The well-prepared, authentic Mexican selections include soft
enchiladas with an excellent mole; homemade empanadas with *huitlacoche* corn truffle; a seductively spicy habanero cream soup; and classic *chilaquiles*, a tortilla-and-egg scramble that will have you skipping
lunch. It's popular for lunch and dinner as well. $ *Average main: 108
MP* ⊠ *Calle 38, between Av. 5 and the beach* ☎ *984/147–0271* ⊕ *www.
lacuevadelchango.com* ⊟ *No credit cards* ⊗ *No dinner Sun.* ⊹ *C6.*

$$ ✕ **Los Aguachiles.** This upscale taquería is an anchor of Playa's alterna-
MEXICAN tive culinary scene, reimagining tacos sautéed in olive oil and topped
with cucumber or strawberry-habanero salsa. Local favorites include

shrimp tacos with "black gold" (beans), fish ceviche with green salsa, and fish tacos wrapped in your choice of corn tortilla, flour tortilla, or a giant leaf of Bibb lettuce. It's an in-the-know spot for lunch or (since it closes at 7) a very early dinner. You'll find other Los Aguachiles locations on Avenida Constituyentes (between avenidas 1 and 5) and the Canibal Royal Beach Club. $ *Average main: 138 MP* ⊠ *Calle 34 at Av. 25* ☎ *984/859–1442, 984/803–1583* ⊕ *www.losaguachiles.mx* ▭ *No credit cards* ✛ *B6.*

$$$
STEAKHOUSE

✕ **Plank.** The name says it all at this New York–inspired restaurant where entrées are grilled on wooden planks or Himalayan salt blocks. The smoky flavors of cedar, maple, hickory, and oak come through in signature dishes like grilled salmon or Beef Wellington encased in braided dough. Sides of mashed potatoes and Portobello mushrooms are served in mini cast-iron skillets, and flatbreads are topped with goat cheese, figs, and arugula leaves. Cocktails such as the "Musty Mojito" add smolder to your meal. ■TIP➔ This is the place to celebrate birthdays, as the entire staff will burst out in song with cake and sparklers. $ *Average main: 220 MP* ⊠ *Calle 16, between avs. 5 and 1* ☎ *984/803–0108* ⊕ *www.plank.mx* ☒ *No lunch* ✛ *C4.*

$$$
ARGENTINE

✕ **Sur Steak House.** Focusing on food from the Pampas region of Argentina, this trendy corner spot has tables on Avenida 5 and second-story seating overlooking the action below. Entrées come with four sauces, dominant among them is *chimichurri*, made with oil, vinegar, and finely chopped herbs. Start off with empanadas or Argentine sausage, follow up with a sizzling half-pound *vacio* (flank steak) served on a cast-iron skillet, then finish your meal with chocolate fondant and ice cream. $ *Average main: 271 MP* ⊠ *Av. 5 at Calle 10* ☎ *984/803–2995* ⊕ *www.grupoazotea.com* ✛ *C3.*

WHERE TO STAY

PLAYA DEL CARMEN

$$
HOTEL

⌂ **Aventura Mexicana.** This small inn three blocks from the beach is a work of art, with Mexican décor, batik wall hangings, and rustic wood-frame beds. **Pros:** spotless; friendly staff; spacious rooms. **Cons:** uncomfortable beds; unimaginative breakfasts; no ocean views. $ *Rooms from: $115* ⊠ *Calle 24, between avs. 5 and 10* ☎ *984/873–1876* ⊕ *www.aventuramexicana.com* ⤴ *49 rooms* �|○| *Breakfast* ✛ *C5.*

$$
HOTEL

⌂ **Be Playa.** This funky boutique hotel melds retro vintage with a touch of modern, from the red vinyl couches in the lobby all the way up to the exceedingly cool rooftop pool bar, where tables and chairs wade in the water. **Pros:** creative design; good views from rooftop bar; free use of bikes. **Cons:** four blocks from beach; rooms don't have ocean views; bland breakfast. $ *Rooms from: $130* ⊠ *Calle 26, between avs. 5 and 10* ☎ *984/803–2243* ⊕ *www.beplaya.com* ⤴ *23 rooms* �|○| *Breakfast* ✛ *C5.*

$$$
HOTEL

⌂ **Deseo Hotel & Lounge.** This trendy but comfortable adults-only hotel is known for its cutting-edge design. **Pros:** contemporary décor; friendly staff; comfortable beds; excellent pool bar. **Cons:** small pool; no kids under 16; can't control a/c in some rooms. $ *Rooms from: $265* ⊠ *Av.*

5 and Calle 12 ☎ *984/879–3620* 🌐 *www.hoteldeseo.com* 🛏 *12 rooms, 3 suites* 🍴 *Breakfast* ✥ *C3.*

$$$ RENTAL Fodor's Choice ★ 🏨 **El Taj Condo Hotel.** This pair of curvaceous buildings contains stylish condo rentals with luxurious furnishings imported from Bali. **Pros:** on or near beach; private kitchens; free access to neighboring fitness club. **Cons:** units are mostly two- and three-bedroom; oceanfront units have water views, but not all beachside ones do; 2-night minimum stay. [$] *Rooms from: $295* ✉ *Calle 14* ☎ *984/879–3918, 866/479–2738* 🌐 *www.eltaj.com* 🛏 *57 units* 🍴 *Breakfast* ✥ *D4.*

$$$ ALL-INCLUSIVE FAMILY 🏨 **Gran Porto Real.** The family-friendly sister hotel to the Royal (which is across the street) has downtown Playa's best accommodations for the schoolyard set. **Pros:** lots of amenities for kids; central location; good breakfast buffet. **Cons:** gaudy style; touts in lobby; least attractive part of beach. [$] *Rooms from: $280* ✉ *Av. Constituyentes 1, at the beach* ☎ *984/873–4000* 🌐 *www.realresorts.com* 🛏 *287 rooms* 🍴 *All-inclusive* ✥ *D4.*

$$ HOTEL 🏨 **Hotel Cacao.** Opened in late 2014, this hotel—named for the bean-like seeds from which chocolate is made—is a sweet vision. **Pros:** new and stylish; great value; central location. **Cons:** cold pool; rooms facing Av. 5 can be noisy; not oriented to children. [$] *Rooms from: $200* ✉ *Av. 1, between calles 30 and 32* ☎ *984/803–0485* 🌐 *www.hotelcacao.com.mx* 🛏 *60 rooms* 🍴 *Breakfast* ✥ *C5.*

$$ HOTEL 🏨 **Hotel Coco Rio.** A tropical garden beckons near the entry to this small, quiet hotel on a tree-lined street in Playa's north end. **Pros:** pleasant staff; charming setting; great value. **Cons:** no breakfast; no ocean views; 3-story hotel with no elevator; patchy Wi-Fi in top level rooms. [$] *Rooms from: $112* ✉ *Calle 26, between avs. 5 and 10* ☎ *984/879–3361* 🌐 *www.hotelcocorio.com* 🛏 *13 rooms, 5 suites* 🍴 *No meals* ✥ *C5.*

$ B&B/INN 🏨 **Hotel Delfín.** This simple, ivy-covered hotel is a good option for budget travelers who don't need to be directly on the beach. **Pros:** quiet setting; central location. **Cons:** no common areas; no restaurant or bar; lots of steps (and no elevator). [$] *Rooms from: $70* ✉ *Av. 5 and Calle 6* ☎ *984/873–0176, 518/227–4208 in the U.S.* 🌐 *www.hoteldelfin.com* 🛏 *15 rooms* 🍴 *No meals* ✥ *C2.*

$$$ HOTEL 🏨 **Hotel El Punto.** The glass-floored corridors of this modern hotel, each inlaid with strips of bamboo, lead to well-appointed rooms with king-size beds (illuminated from beneath) that have enormous headboards and bathrooms made of marble and sapote wood. **Pros:** contemporary décor; first floor rooms have espresso machines; free Wi-Fi and breakfast. **Cons:** not all rooms have ocean views; no elevator; no kids under 15; no restaurant or bar. [$] *Rooms from: $200* ✉ *Av. 5 and Calle 8* ☎ *984/803–0288* 🌐 *www.hotelelpunto.com* 🛏 *16 rooms* 🍴 *Breakfast* ✥ *C3.*

$ HOTEL 🏨 **Hotel Kinbé.** An interesting fusion of Mayan and contemporary décor, the stylish Kinbé (which means "path to the sun") is set in a tropical garden steps from the beach. **Pros:** great value; free access to nearby Indigo Beach Club; in the heart of Playa. **Cons:** small rooms; some street noise; strict cancellation policy. [$] *Rooms from: $85* ✉ *Calle 10 Norte,*

La Tortuga Hotel & Spa

between avs. 1 and 5 ☎ *984/873–0441, 984/873–0443* 🌐 *www.kinbe.com* 🛏 *19 rooms, 10 suites* 🍴 *Breakfast* ✥ *C3.*

$$ B&B/INN Fodor's Choice ★ 🏨 **Hotel La Semilla.** "The Seed" of perfection is apparent at this boutique hotel where hospitality, comfort, and style collide. **Pros:** beautiful design; outstanding breakfasts; lush garden setting; free use of bikes. **Cons:** tons of mosquitoes; street noise; no kids under 18; no phones or TVs. [$] *Rooms from: $180* ✉ *Calle 38 Norte, between Av. 5 and the beach* ☎ *984/147–3234* 🌐 *www.hotellasemilla.com* 🛏 *9 rooms* 🍴 *Breakfast* ✥ *C6.*

$$ HOTEL 🏨 **Hotel Posada Mariposa.** Although it has few facilities, this hotel is still a great value, with impeccable rooms set around an open-air garden courtyard where trees grow past the third floor. **Pros:** cozy setting; discount to Mamita's Beach Club. **Cons:** hard beds; Wi-Fi only in lobby; no pool or gym. [$] *Rooms from: $150* ✉ *Av. 5, No. 314, between calles 24 and 26* ☎ *984/873–3886* 🌐 *www.mariposagrouphotels.com* 🛏 *18 rooms, 5 suites* 🍴 *Breakfast* ✥ *C5.*

$$ B&B/INN Fodor's Choice ★ 🏨 **La Tortuga Hotel & Spa.** Mosaic stone paths wind through lovely gardens, and colonial-style hardwood furnishings gleam throughout at this inn on a side street. **Pros:** some rooms have rooftop terraces; lovely grounds; outstanding breakfast. **Cons:** late-night street noise; no kids under 16; a few showers overflow and cause flooding. [$] *Rooms from: $140* ✉ *Av. 10, at the corner of Calle 14* ☎ *984/873–1484, 866/550–6878* 🌐 *www.latortugahotelspa.com* 🛏 *45 rooms, 6 jr. suites* 🍴 *Breakfast* ✥ *C4.*

$$ B&B/INN 🏨 **Lunata.** An elegant entrance, Spanish-tile floors, and hand-tooled furniture from Guadalajara greet you at this classy inn. **Pros:** prime location; impeccable rooms; intimate setting. **Cons:** street-facing rooms tend

to be noisy; mediocre breakfast; no pool; mosquitoes in common areas. [$] *Rooms from: $145* ✉ *Av. 5, between calles 6 and 8* ☎ *984/873–0884* 🌐 *www.lunata.com* 🛏 *10 rooms* 🍴 *Breakfast* ⊕ *C3.*

$$$ ALL-INCLUSIVE FAMILY 🏨 **Paradisus Playa del Carmen.** This all-inclusive offers flash and class in a Vegas-meets-cruise-ship environment with 14 restaurants, 11 bars, and nearly 1,000 rooms scattered between two buildings. **Pros:** complimentary cell phones; beautiful swim-up rooms; plenty of children's activities. **Cons:** hot tubs are cold; rocky beach; 10-min drive from downtown Playa; not all restaurants are open to children. [$] *Rooms from: $289* ✉ *Av. 5 and Calle 112* ☎ *984/877–3900* 🌐 *www.paradisus.com* 🛏 *512 rooms at Esmeralda, 394 rooms at La Perla* 🍴 *All-inclusive* ⊕ *C6.*

$ HOTEL 🏨 **Riviera Caribe Maya.** It may not have the bells and whistles of other Playa hotels, but this small property, on a quiet street two blocks from the beach, is very pleasant. **Pros:** breezy rooms; outstanding pool area; huge bathrooms. **Cons:** hard mattresses; Wi-Fi in common areas only; minimal street noise. [$] *Rooms from: $80* ✉ *Av. 10 and Calle 30* ☎ *984/873–1193* 🌐 *www.hotelrivieramaya.com* 🛏 *21 rooms, 4 suites* 🍴 *No meals* ⊕ *C5.*

$$$$ RESORT ALL-INCLUSIVE 🏨 **THE Royal Playa del Carmen.** If you are looking for the royal treatment, this place has everything from butler service and iPad check-in to in-room Jacuzzis and liquor bars. **Pros:** on Playa's best beach; live entertainment evenings; great spa; access to Gran Porto resort across the street. **Cons:** most rooms face the garden; no kids under 16. [$] *Rooms from: $550* ✉ *Av. Constituyentes 2* ☎ *984/877–2900* 🌐 *www.realresorts.com* 🛏 *513 rooms* 🍴 *All-inclusive* ⊕ *D4.*

PLAYACAR

South of downtown Playa del Carmen, the upscale gated community of Playacar is home to a string of all-inclusive resorts, beachfront condos, and rental properties. It also features an 18-hole golf course and the small open-air mall (Plaza Playacar) but is of little interest otherwise. A paved bike path skirts the tree-lined streets of the development, past private neighborhoods, all the way north to downtown Playa and south to the adventure parks Xplor and Xcaret.

$$ ALL-INCLUSIVE FAMILY 🏨 **Iberostar Tucan and Quetzal.** This unique all-inclusive resort has preserved its natural surroundings—among the resident animals are flamingos, turtles, toucans, peacocks, and monkeys. **Pros:** tropical setting; bicycles for guests; tax and tips included in rate. **Cons:** food lacks variety; old gym equipment; water at swim-up bar can be chilly; Wi-Fi costs extra. [$] *Rooms from: $147* ✉ *Av. Xamanha, Playacar* ☎ *984/877–2000* 🌐 *www.iberostar.com* 🛏 *730 rooms* 🍴 *All-inclusive* ⊕ *C1.*

$$$$ ALL-INCLUSIVE 🏨 **Riu Palace Riviera Maya.** This enormous all-inclusive serves its luxury with an extra helping of glitz, but its breathtaking beach and exceptional service are what really shine. **Pros:** sports bar open nonstop; friendly staff; lots of scheduled activities. **Cons:** reservations needed for certain restaurants; no poolside service; hallways echo at night; always seem to be piles of luggage in the lobby; some rooms smell musty. [$] *Rooms from: $339* ✉ *Av. Xaman-Ha, lotes 9 and 10, Playacar* ☎ *984/877–2280* 🌐 *www.riu.com* 🛏 *460 rooms* 🍴 *All-inclusive* ⊕ *C1.*

$$$$ ALL-INCLUSIVE 🏨 **Royal Hideaway Playacar Resort.** Art and antiques from around the world fill the lobby, and streams, waterfalls, and fountains fill the

4

grounds of this 13-acre resort on a stretch of pristine beach. **Pros:** romantic setting; attentive service; taxes and gratuities included. **Cons:** no children under 13; pool service can be slow. [$] *Rooms from: $430* ✉ *Av Xaman-Ha, Lote 6, Playacar* ☎ *984/873–4500, 800/858–2258* 🌐 *www.royalhideaway.com* 🛏 *194 rooms, 6 suites* 🍴 *All-inclusive* ✥ *C1.*

NIGHTLIFE

The club scene is a major draw in the South Beach of Mexico. The action is on Calle 12, lined with nightclubs and lively young things ready to set the night afire. Most clubs are open-air, so this part of town gets very noisy until very late—something to keep in mind if you're planning to stay downtown and actually want to sleep. By day, Playa's lively beach clubs are packed with travelers lounging in the sun or dancing to the sounds of a live DJ. The Riviera Maya Jazz Festival (🌐 *www.rivieramayajazzfestival.com*) splashes cool on Playa's music scene every year during the last week of November.

Alux. Inside a cavern, Alux has a bar, disco, wine cellar, and restaurant. There's a MX$100 drink minimum. ✉ *Av. Juárez, between avs. 65 and 70, Mza 217, Lote 2* ☎ *984/206–2589* 🌐 *www.aluxrestaurant.com.*

Bar Ranita. Attached to the Rana Cansada Hotel, Bar Ranita is a favorite among rowdy expats. The prices are unbeatable, and the margaritas pack a powerful punch. ✉ *Rana Cansada Hotel, Calle 10, between avs. 5 and 10* ☎ *984/873–0389* 🌐 *www.ranacansada.com.*

CoCo Bongo. Following the success of its sister property in Cancún, CoCo Bongo has flying acrobats, bar-top conga lines, live bands, and DJs mixing everything from rock to hip-hop. The cover charge includes unlimited drinks. ✉ *Calle 10 at Av. 10* ☎ *984/803–5939* 🌐 *www.cocobongo.com.mx* 🎟 *MX$881* ⏲ *Closed Sun.*

Deseo Lounge. DJs spin chill-out music as black-and-white Mexican film classics are projected on the wall at the rooftop Deseo Lounge (otherwise known as the Hotel Deseo's pool bar). It's famous for its icy-cool cucumber martinis. ✉ *Hotel Deseo, Av. 5 and Calle 12* ☎ *984/879–3620* 🌐 *www.hoteldeseo.com.*

Diablito Cha Cha Cha. Miami-chic with retro white patent leather chairs and a palapa, Diablito Cha Cha Cha serves up sushi and DJ tunes as late as 3 am. ✉ *Calle 12, between avs. 5 and 1* ☎ *984/803–3695* 🌐 *www.diablitochachacha.com.*

Kartabar. Hookah-smokers here puff on fruit-flavored tobacco that wafts away into the open tropical night. On weekends, belly dancers weave their way between the tables. ✉ *Calle 12 at Av. 1, Playa del Carmen* ☎ *984/873–2228* 🌐 *www.kartabar.com.mx.*

Kitxen. An anchor of Playa's live music scene, cool Kitxen features bands from Mexico and the Caribbean playing everything from rock to reggae. Cash only. ✉ *Av. 5 between Calle 20 and Av. Constituyentes.*

La Bodeguita del Medio. Graffiti'd La Bodeguita del Medio, a franchise of the famous Havana outpost, features live Cuban music

Tuesday to Sunday. ⊠ *Av. 5 and Calle 34* ☎ *984/803–3951* ⊕ *www. labodeguitadelmedio.com.mx.*

La Santanera. International DJs and a young, cosmopolitan crowd groove to electronic music until very late at this "underground disco cantina." For a breath of fresh air, head upstairs to the rooftop lounge for cool drinks and chill-out music. ⊠ *Calle 10, Mza 29, Lote 1* ☎ *984/803–2856* ⊕ *www.lasantanera.com* ⌐ *MX$100* ⊘ *Closed Mon.*

Mandala. The biggest, loudest and most expensive party spot on Calle 12, trendy Mandala is divided into a street-level bar, a rooftop terrace, and a dance club; each has its own DJ spinning anything from house and hip-hop to disco and techno. ⊠ *Calle 12, between Avs. 1 and 5* ☎ *984/879–4189* ⊕ *www.mandalanightclub.com* ⌐ *Cover MX$33; open bar MX$677.*

SHOPPING

Avenida 5 between Calles 4 and 38 has the Riviera Maya's best shopping. Small galleries sell original folk art from around Mexico, clothing boutiques offer everything from chic bikinis to tacky tees, and there are stores dedicated to Mexican specialties as varied as silver, chocolate, and tequila. Mexico's upscale Liverpool department store puts in an appearance at Calle 14, and you'll find international brand names like Diesel and Havaianas scattered up and down the avenue.

BOOKS

Librería Mundo. This spot has an extensive selection of books on Mayan culture, along with used English-language books. Profits from all English-language tomes are donated to Mexican schools to buy textbooks. ⊠ *Plaza las Américas, Carretera 307* ☎ *984/109–1566.*

CRAFTS

Fodor'sChoice **Ah Cacao.** This modish chocolate shop sells Mexico's finest—in bars,
★ tablets, soaps, massage oils, and brownies. There's another branch at the corner of Avenida 5 and Calle 30. ⊠ *Avs. 5 and Constituyentes* ☎ *984/803–5748* ⊕ *www.ahcacao.com.*

Artevelas. The outsize, handmade candles that you see lighting the night so elegantly in Playa's restaurants and hotels are sold at Artevelas. ⊠ *Av. 1, between calles 14 and 16* ☎ *984/267–3420* ⊕ *www.artevelas. com* ⊘ *Closed Sun.*

Hacienda Tequila. Over 750 different types of tequila plus an assortment of kitschy Mexican crafts and souvenirs are sold at Hacienda Tequila. Free tastings are available, and there's an exhibit that walks you through the world of agave booze. ⊠ *Av. 5 and Calle 14* ☎ *984/873–1202.*

La Hierbabuena Artesanía. Owner Melinda Burns offers a collection of fine Mexican clothing and crafts at La Hierbabuena Artesanía. ⊠ *Av. 5, between calles 8 and 10* ☎ *984/873–1741.*

JEWELRY

Ambar Mexicano. Come here for jewelry crafted of Chiapan amber by a local designer. ⊠ *Av. 5, between calles 4 and 6* ☎ *984/873–2357.*

MALLS

Paseo del Carmen. Upscale, open-air Paseo del Carmen has numerous boutiques—including Diesel, Ultrafemme, and American Apparel. Seattle-coffee lovers can get their fix at the Starbucks that dominates the center of the mall. A cobblestone path makes this one of the area's most popular and pleasant shopping destinations. ⊠ *Av. 10 and Calle 1* ☎ *984/803–3789.*

Plaza Las Américas. This family-friendly mall features restaurants, shops, and cinemas. ⊠ *Carretera 307* ☎ *984/109–2161.*

Plaza Playacar. This Mexican colonial–style outdoor mall in Playacar sells handcrafts, clothes, jewelry, and specialty items like tequila and cigars. Of course, there is also a Starbucks. ⊠ *Paseo Xaman-Ha, past the main entrance of Playacar* ☎ *984/873–0006* ⊕ *www.plazaplayacar. com.*

Quinta Alegría. This three-story plaza on Playa's main drag houses Sanborn's department store, Victoria's Secret, Forever 21, Nike, Bebe Clothing, Levi's, and much more. There's even a Häagen-Dazs where you can cool off with an ice cream before more shopping. ⊠ *Av. 5 at Av. Constituyentes* ☎ *984/803–2358* ⊕ *www.quintaalegria.com.mx.*

SPORTS AND THE OUTDOORS

ADVENTURE TOURS

Punta Venado. Just below Playa del Carmen, Punta Venado offers adventure tours in all-terrain vehicles or on horseback. The 4 km (2½ miles) of isolated coastline are great for snorkeling and kayaking. ⊠ *Carretera 307, Km 278, Calica* ☎ *984/158–8912, 855/325–9060* ⊕ *www. puntavenado.com* ⊠ *From MX$406.*

FITNESS CENTERS

The Gym. Playa's most complete workout is to be had at this vast and well-equipped gym, which offers a full complement of cardio, weights, and classes from spinning to yoga. ⊠ *Av. 1 Norte, No. 255, between Av. Constituyentes and Calle 16* ☎ *984/873–2098* ⊕ *www.thegym.com. mx* ⊠ *Day passes MX$200.*

GOLF

Grand Coral Golf Course. This 18-hole championship course was designed by Nick Price. Not as busy (or expensive) as neighboring courses at Mayakoba or Playacar, Grand Coral is challenging without being overly intimidating. You'll face a good amount of bunkers and water on the holes. The greens are slow, but the course is well maintained. If you can swing it, opt for the all-inclusive package that covers food and drink. Otherwise green fees cover only the cart, bottled water, and golf tees. ⊠ *Grand Coral Riviera Maya, Carretera 307, Km 294* ☎ *984/109–6025* ⊕ *www.grandcoralgolf.com* ⊠ *$175 for 18 holes* ⌘ *18 holes. 7043 yards. Par 71.*

Playacar Golf Club. The 18-hole course at the Playacar Golf Club is considered to be one of the most challenging in the Riviera Maya. There's not a ton of water here, but watch out for sand traps and tricky Hole 14. Signature holes are Hole 13 (342 yards, par 4) and Hole

18 (530 yards, par 5). Included in the green fee are food and drink, which is delivered cartside every few shots. Plan to lose a few balls during your game as the greens are tight and narrow. The fairways are well manicured and full of wildlife. If it gets too challenging, swing on over to the practice area complete with a driving range and putting green with its own chipping, pitching, and greenside bunker areas. ■TIP➔ Come after 1 pm for the twilight rate. ⊠ *Paseo Xaman-Ha, near Riu Palace, Playacar* ☎ *984/873–4990* ⊠ *$180 for 18 holes* ⅀ *18 holes. 7144 yards. Par 72.*

> ### NAVIGATING XCARET
>
> You can easily spend at least a full day at Xcaret. This place is big, so it's a good idea to check the daily activities against a map of the park to organize your time. Plan to be in the general area of an activity before it's scheduled to begin—you'll beat the crowds and avoid having to sprint across the property.

SCUBA DIVING AND SNORKELING

Abyss. PADI and SSI-affiliated Abyss offers introductory courses and dive trips. They also run dives in Tulum under the name Cenote Dive Center. ⊠ *Av. 1, between calles 10 and 12* ☎ *984/873–2164* ⊕ *www.abyssdiveshop.com* ⊠ *From MX$745.*

Mexico Blue Dream. Custom snorkel tours in Playa, Laguna Yal-Ku, Akumal, and nearby cenotes are available through Mexico Blue Dream; dive trips to Cozumel are also arranged. ⊠ *Between Av. 1 and Mamita's Beach* ☎ *984/803–0660* ⊕ *www.mexicobluedream.com* ⊠ *From MX$474.*

Tank-Ha Dive Center. Playa's original dive outfit has PADI-certified teachers and runs diving and snorkeling excursions to the reefs and caverns. Dive packages and Cozumel trips are available, too. ⊠ *Calle 10, between avs. 5 and 10* ☎ *984/873–0302* ⊕ *www.tankha.com* ⊠ *From MX$610.*

Yucatek Divers. PADI-affiliated Yucatek Divers offers cenote dives, dive packages, and instruction. A one-tank introductory course costs MX$1,355; the four-day, five-dive beginner certification course is MX$5,557. ⊠ *Av. 15, between calles 2 and 4* ☎ *984/803–2836* ⊕ *www.yucatek-divers.com* ⊠ *Dives from MX$820.*

SKYDIVING

Skydive Playa. Adrenaline junkies can take the plunge high above Playa in a tandem sky dive (where you're hooked up to an instructor the whole time). Jumps take place every hour; reserve at least one day in advance. ■TIP➔ For an extra MX$2155, SkyDive Playa will shoot video of your free fall. ⊠ *Plaza Marina 32, next to Señor Frog's, at Cozumel ferry* ☎ *984/873–0192* ⊕ *www.skydive.com.mx* ⊠ *MX$3646.*

SOUTH OF PLAYA DEL CARMEN

South of Playa, the atmosphere is calm and the pristine beaches along this 61-km (38-mile) section become even more beautiful the closer you get to Tulum. Combining cultural activities and ecological theme parks, the area around Xcaret offers much more than sun and sand. Solitude and tranquility abound on the barren coastlines at Xpu-Há and Tankah, where the favorite past time is swinging in a hammock. The towns of Puerto Aventuras and Akumal, both Americanized beach communities, promise good snorkeling plus plenty of hotels and restaurants with all the creature comforts you'd expect back home.

XCARET

6 km (4 miles) south of Playa del Carmen.

Once a sacred Mayan city and port, Xcaret (pronounced *ish*-car-et) is now home to two popular parks on a gorgeous stretch of coastline. The 250-acre ecological theme park, simply known as "Xcaret," is the Riviera Maya's most heavily advertised attraction. Billed as "nature's sacred paradise," it has its own published magazines plus a collection of stores. Just 2 km (1 mile) away is Xplor; half the size of Xcaret, this sister property is targeted at extreme-adventure seekers.

GETTING HERE AND AROUND

If you're driving, the entrance for both parks and the Occidental Grand Xcaret Resort is at Km 282 on Carretera 307. Organized day trips from Cancún will also take you to Xcaret; a cab ride from nearby Playa del Carmen will cost about MX$220.

EXPLORING

FAMILY **Xcaret.** Among the most popular attractions are the Paradise River raft tour that takes you on a winding, watery journey through the jungle; the Butterfly Pavilion, where thousands of butterflies float dreamily through a botanical garden while New Age music plays in the background; and an ocean-fed aquarium where you can see local sea life drifting through coral heads and sea fans.

The park has a Wild Bird Breeding Aviary, nurseries for both abandoned flamingo eggs and sea turtles, and a series of underwater caverns that you can explore by snorkeling or snuba (a hybrid of snorkeling and scuba). A replica Mayan village includes a colorful cemetery with catacomb-like caverns underneath; traditional music and dance ceremonies (including performances by the famed Voladores de Papantla—the Flying Birdmen of Papantla) are performed here at night. But the star performance is the evening "Spectacular Mexico Night Show," which tells the history of Mexico through song and dance.

The list of Xcaret's attractions goes on and on: you can visit a dolphinarium, a bee farm, a manatee lagoon, a bat cave, an orchid and bromeliad greenhouse, an edible-mushroom farm, and a small zoo. You can also visit a scenic tower that takes you 240 feet up in the air for a spectacular view of the park.

The entrance fee covers only access to the grounds and the exhibits; all other activities and equipment—from sea treks and dolphin tours to lockers and swim gear—are extra. The Plus Pass includes park entrance, lockers, snorkel equipment, food, and drinks. You can buy tickets from any travel agency or major hotel along the coast. ⊠ *Carretera 307, Km 282* ☎ *01800/292–2738 toll-free in Mexico, 888/922–7381* ⊕ *www.*

There's plenty to do and see in Xcaret.

xcaret.com ✉ *Basic Pass MX$1348, Plus Pass MX$1757* ⊘ *Daily 8:30 am–9:30 pm*

FAMILY **Xplor.** Designed for thrill-seekers, this 125-acre park features underground rafting in stalactite-studded water caves and cenotes. Swim in a stalactite river, ride in an amphibious vehicle, or soar across the park on 13 of the longest zip-lines in Mexico. The price includes all food, drink, and equipment. ✉ *Carretera 307, Km 282* ☎ *984/147–6560, 888/922–7381* ⊕ *www.xplor.travel* ✉ *MX$1613* ⊘ *Mon.–Sat. 8:30–5*

WHERE TO STAY

$$$$ 🏨 **Occidental Grand Xcaret.** In such an enormous all-inclusive, it's sur-
ALL-INCLUSIVE prising to find the excellent service that you get here. **Pros:** pleasant lagoon; minimum 3-night stay includes free entrance to Xcaret; free scuba course. **Cons:** time-share sales reps give you the hard sell; small beach; squawking parrots in the lobby. 💲 *Rooms from: $309* ✉ *Carretera 307, Km 282* ☎ *984/871–5400* ⊕ *www.occidentalhotels.com* 🛏 *724 rooms, 45 suites* ⑩ *All-inclusive.*

PUERTO AVENTURAS

26 km (16 miles) south of Playa del Carmen.

The most Americanized of all the Riviera Maya's resorts is a 900-acre gated community and golf course more reminiscent of coastal Florida than Mexico. This has its advantages if you want to speak English exclusively and have the option to eat American food. Fatima Bay (the beach in front of the Omni hotel) is glorious, but the town itself is not particularly scenic. The main marina is closed off to boat traffic and is instead home to Dolphin Discovery's dolphins and sea lions, which are fun to watch from the waterside restaurants and benches.

GETTING HERE AND AROUND

Puerto Aventuras is a 20-minute drive south of Playa del Carmen along Carretera 307. Its orientation around a small marina makes it very walkable—it's the sort of place where you can let older kids go off by themselves for the afternoon. Taxis are stationed at the small parking area near the marina outside the Omni hotel. You can also find them outside all major hotels. Taxis from Playa del Carmen cost about MX$338.

EXPLORING

Museo CEDAM. Here you'll see coins, nautical devices, clay dishes, and other artifacts from 18th-century sunken ships, recovered by members of the Mexican Underwater Expeditions Club. The club was established in 1959 by Pablo Bush Romero, who later went on to found the nearby town of Akumal. ⊠ *North end of marina* 🖃 *By donation* ☉ *Mon.–Sat. 9–1 and 2:30–5:30.*

**OFF THE
BEATEN
PATH**

Cenotes Kantún Chi. This Maya-owned and -operated eco-park has cenotes and a few beautiful underground caverns that are great for snorkeling and diving, as well as some small Mayan ruins. The place is low-key—a nice break from the crowds. Bring natural mosquito repellent. ⊠ *Carretera 307, Km 266, in front of Barceló Hotel* ☎ *984/803–0143* ⊕ *www.kantunchi.com* 🖃 *MX$799* ☉ *Daily 9–5.*

BEACHES

Fatima Bay (*Omni Beach*). Although the marina is the main focus here, Puerto Aventuras' beaches are naturally stunning and seldom crowded. The main one, Fatima Bay, commonly referred to as "Omni Beach," stretches nearly 3 km (2 miles) south between Chac Hal Al condominiums and the Grand Peninsula residence. Its shallow, calm waters are kid-friendly, especially inside the breakwater. Further out the temperature drops, making for a refreshing swim. To the north is a smaller bay, known as Chan Yu Yum, used by guests of the Catalonia Resort; better beaches lie just south of Puerto Aventuras in the community of Xpu-Há. **Amenities:** food and drink. **Best for:** snorkeling; swimming. ⊠ *Behind the Omni Hotel.*

Paamul Beach. Beachcombers, campers, and snorkeling snowbirds love Paamul (pronounced pah-*mool*), a crescent-shape lagoon 21 km (13 miles) south of Playa del Carmen with clear, placid waters sheltered by a coral reef. Shells, sand dollars, and even glass beads—some from the sunken, 18th-century Spanish galleon *Mantanceros*, which lies off nearby Akumal—wash up onto the sandy parts of the beach. (There's a sandy path into deeper water in front of the restaurant—on the rocks, watch out for sea urchins.) Sea turtles hatch here June through November. ■ TIP→ If you'd like to stay on this piece of paradise, Paamul Hotel and Cabañas is a laid-back option. **Amenities:** food and drink; toilets. **Best for:** snorkeling; swimming; walking. ⊠ *Paamul Bay, Carretera 307 Cancun–Chetumal, Km 85, between Xcaret and Puerto Aventuras, Paamul.*

Continued on page 166

ANCIENT ARCHITECTS
THE MAYA

Visiting the Yucatán Peninsula and not touring any Mayan sites is like going to Greece and not seeing the Acropolis or the Parthenon. One look at the monumental architecture of the Maya and you might feel transported to another world. The breathtaking structures are even more impressive when you consider that they were built 1,000 to 2,000 years ago or more without iron tools, wheels, pulleys, or beasts of burden—and in terrible heat and difficult terrain.

El Castillo, Tulum

THE ARCHITECTURAL PERIODS

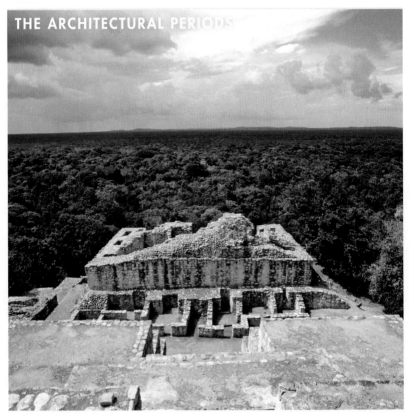

Calakmul

PRECLASSIC PERIOD: Petén

Between approximately 2000 BC and AD 100, the Maya were centered around the lowlands in the south-central region of Guatemala. Their communities were family-based, and governed by hereditary chiefs; their worship of agricultural gods (such as Chaac, the rain god), who they believed controlled the seasons, led them to chart the movement of heavenly bodies. Their religious beliefs also led them to build enormous temples and pyramids—such as El Mirador, in the Guatemalan lowlands—where sacrifices were made and ceremonies performed to please the gods.

The structures at El Mirador, as well as at the neighboring ruin site of Tikal, were built in what is known today as the Petén style; pyramids were steeply pitched, built on stepped terraces, and decorated with large stucco masks and ornamental (but sometimes "false" or unclimbable) stairways. Petén-style structures were also often roofed with corbeled archways. The Maya began to move northward into the Yucatán during the late part of this period, which is why Petén-style buildings can also be found at Calakmul, just north of the Guatemalan border.

EARLY CLASSIC PERIOD: Río Usumacinta

The Classic Period, often referred to as the "golden age," spanned from about AD 100 to AD 1000. Maya civilization expanded northward and became much more complex. A distinct ruling class emerged and hereditary kings ruled over densely populated jungle cities, filled with increasingly impressive-looking palaces and temples.

During the early part of the Classic Period, Maya architecture began to take on some distinctive characteristics. Build-ers placed their structures on hillsides or crests, and the principal buildings were covered with bas-reliefs carved in stone. The pyramid-top temples had vestibules and rooms with vaulted ceilings; many chamber walls were carved with scenes recounting important events during the reign of the ruler who built the pyramid. Some of the most stunning examples of this style are at the ruins of Palenque, near Chiapas.

Palenque

Chicanná

MID-CLASSIC PERIOD: Río Bec and Chenes

It was during the middle part of the Classic Period (roughly between AD 600 and AD 800) that the Maya pres-ence exploded into the Yucatán Pen-insula. Several Maya settlements were established in what is now Campeche state, including Chicanná and Xpujil, near the southwest corner of the state. The architecture at these sites was built in what is now known as the Río Bec style. As in the earlier Petén style, Río Bec pyramids had steeply pitched sides and ornately decorated founda-tions. Other Río Bec-style buildings, however, were long, one-story affairs incorporating two or sometimes three tall towers. These towers were typi-cally capped by large roof combs that resembled mini-temples.

During the same part of the Classic Period, a different architectural style, known as Chenes, developed in some of the more northerly Maya cities, such as Hochob. While some Chenes-style structures share the same long, single-story construction as Río Bec buildings, others have strik-ingly different characteristics—like door-ways carved in the shape of huge Chaac faces with gaping open mouths.

Chichén Itzá

The fusion of two distinct Maya groups—the Chichén Maya and the Itzás—produced another striking architectural style. This style, known as Northeast Yucatán, is exemplified by the ruins at Chichén Itzá. Here, columns and grand colonnades were introduced. Palaces with row upon row of columns carved in the shape of serpents looked over grand patios, platforms were dedicated to the planet Venus, and pyramids were raised to honor Kukulcán (the plumed serpent god borrowed from the Toltecs, who called him Quetzalcoátl). Northeast Yucatán structures also incorporated carved stone Chacmool figures—reclining statues with offering trays carved in their midsections for sacrificial offerings.

Some of the Yucatán's most spectacular Mayan architecture was built between about AD 800 and AD 1000. By this time, the Maya had spread into territory that is now Yucatán state, and established lavish cities at Labná, Kabah, Sayil, and Uxmal—all fine examples of the Puuc architectural style. Puuc buildings were beautifully proportioned, often designed in a low-slung quadrangle shape that allowed for many rooms inside. Exterior walls were kept plain to show off the friezes above—which were embellished with stone-mosaic gods, geometric designs, and serpentine motifs. Corners were edged with gargoyle-like, curved-nose Chaac figures.

▼
Between 2000 BC and AD 100, the Maya are based in lowlands of south-central Guatemala, and governed by hereditary chiefs.

Uxmal

2000 BC   1000

PETÉN

PRECLASSIC

POSTCLASSIC PERIOD: Quintana Roo Coast

Although Maya culture continued to flourish between AD 1000 and the early 1500s, signs of decline also began to take form. Wars broke out between neighboring city-states, leaving the region vulnerable when the Spaniards began invading in 1521. By 1600, the Spanish had dominated the Maya empire.

Mayan architecture enjoyed its last hurrah during this period, mostly in the region along the Yucatán's Caribbean coast. Known as Quintana Roo Coast architecture, this style can be seen today at the ruins of Tulum. Although the

structures here aren't as visually arresting as those at earlier, inland sites, Tulum's location is breathtaking: it's the only major Maya city overlooking the sea.

Tulum

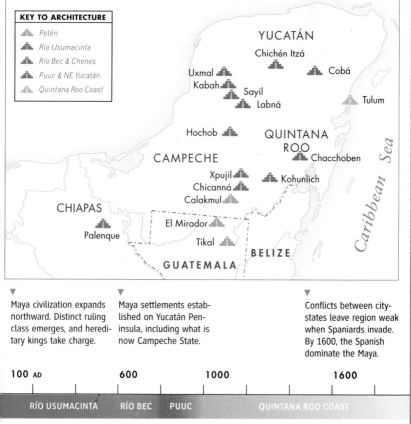

KEY TO ARCHITECTURE

- Petén
- Río Usumacinta
- Río Bec & Chenes
- Puuc & NE Yucatán
- Quintana Roo Coast

YUCATÁN

Chichén Itzá

Uxmal · · · Cobá
Kabah
Sayil
Labná · · · Tulum

Hochob

QUINTANA ROO

CAMPECHE · · · Chacchoben

Xpujil · · · Kohunlich
Chicanná
Calakmul

CHIAPAS

El Mirador

Palenque · · · Tikal

BELIZE

GUATEMALA

Caribbean Sea

4

IN FOCUS ANCIENT ARCHITECTS: THE MAYA

▼ Maya civilization expands northward. Distinct ruling class emerges, and hereditary kings take charge.

▼ Maya settlements established on Yucatán Peninsula, including what is now Campeche State.

▼ Conflicts between city-states leave region weak when Spaniards invade. By 1600, the Spanish dominate the Maya.

100 AD	600	1000	1600

RÍO USUMACINTA · RÍO BEC · PUUC · QUINTANA ROO COAST

CLASSIC · POSTCLASSIC

WHERE TO EAT

$$ SEAFOOD 🍴 **Café Olé International.** The laid-back hub of Puerto Aventuras is a terrace café with a varied menu, including coconut shrimp and chicken with a chimichurri sauce made from red wine, garlic, onion, and fine herbs. If you (and the local fishermen) get lucky, the nightly specials might include fresh-caught fish in garlic sauce. Cheesecakes and pies, all homemade by owner Gaylita, are delicious. ■ **TIP→ There's live music on Sunday, Wednesday, and Friday in high season.** [$] *Average main: $10* ✉ *Across from Omni hotel* ☎ *984/873–5125* 🕒 *Closed Sept., and Mon. in Oct. No lunch.*

WHERE TO STAY

$$$$ ALL-INCLUSIVE FAMILY 🏨 **Hard Rock Hotel Riviera Maya.** Focused on music, this 85-acre all-inclusive resort lets you live out your rock star fantasies while getting pampered by Hard Rock hospitality. **Pros:** great entertainment; gratuities included; gracious staff; access to neighboring golf course. **Cons:** timeshare sales pitch; artificial beach; theme isn't for everyone. [$] *Rooms from: $547* ✉ *Carretera 307, Km 72, 3 km (2 miles) north of Puerto Aventuras* ☎ *984/875–1100, 800/346–8225* 🌐 *www.hrhrivieramaya.com* 🛏 *1,264 rooms* 🍽 *All-inclusive.*

$$$$ RESORT 🏨 **Omni Puerto Aventuras.** Atop the main beach and in the center of the action, the Omni is the focal point of Puerto Aventuras, but its low-key luxury is a cut above the town's other resorts. **Pros:** pretty beach; sushi restaurant; nearby marina with dolphins; decent golf course. **Cons:** food choices could be better; no elevator; extra charge for beach amenities. [$] *Rooms from: $350* ✉ *Calle Punta Celis* ☎ *984/875–1950* 🌐 *www.omnihotels.com* 🛏 *30 rooms* 🍽 *Breakfast.*

$$ HOTEL 🏨 **Paamul Hotel and Cabañas.** Located in Paamul, south of Playa del Carmen, this rustic resort sits on a perfect white-sand beach. **Pros:** on the beach; some lovely views; rooms have spacious balconies; in-room Wi-Fi. **Cons:** need car to get around; somewhat pricey restaurant with mediocre food. [$] *Rooms from: $175* ✉ *Paamul, Carretera Cancún-Tulum, Km 85, 19 km (12 miles) south of Playa del Carmen* ☎ *984/875–1053, 612/353–6825 in the U.S.* 🌐 *www.paamulcabanas.com* 🛏 *13 rooms, 10 cabanas, 220 RV sites, 30 campsites* 🍽 *Breakfast.*

SHOPPING AND SPAS

Rock Spa. With 75 treatment rooms, steam baths, and hydrotherapy pools, the Rock Spa is one of the largest in the Caribbean. In keeping with Hard Rock's music theme, massage therapists synchronize movements with an expertly curated playlist. From facials to wraps, each treatment connects the healing power of music with the power of touch and relaxation. There's also a yoga temple, beauty salon, and fitness center, but the Mayan temazcal is the big draw; only resort guests have access to the spa. ✉ *Hard Rock Hotel Riviera Maya, Carretera 307, Km 72, 3 km (2 miles) north of Puerto Aventuras* ☎ *984/875–1100* 🌐 *www.hrhrivieramaya.com.*

SPORTS AND THE OUTDOORS
DOLPHIN SWIMS

FAMILY **Dolphin Discovery.** You can swim with dolphins in the closed-off waters of the marina—or get up close and personal with manatees, stingrays, and sea lions—at Dolphin Discovery. Programs are available daily from 9 to 3:30. ⊠ *On the marina, Calle Bahia Xcacel* ☎ *998/193–3360, 866/393–5158* ⊕ *www.dolphindiscovery.com* ✆ *From MX$1206.*

SCUBA DIVING AND SNORKELING

Aquanuts. The reef here invites exploration. Aquanuts, a full-service dive shop, specializes in open-water dives, cenote dives, multitank dives, and certification courses. ⊠ *Calle Punta Celis, by the marina* ☎ *984/873–5041, 877/623–2491 in U.S.* ⊕ *www.aquanutsdiveshop.com* ✆ *Dives from MX$813; courses from MX$6100.*

XPU-HÁ

Fodor's Choice *31 km (19 miles) south of Playa del Carmen.*
★
Located 20 minutes south of Playa del Carmen and 20 minutes north of Tulum, Xpu-Há is the perfect base to relax and get away from the crowds. The beach is startling white, with soft clean sand that is raked by the few boutique hotels and villas that dot the shores. Other than the Catalonia Royal Tulum, you won't find sprawling resorts taking over the area. But this stellar stretch has recently brought in several beach clubs and restaurants, which means this hush-hush haven is now officially on the map.

GETTING HERE AND AROUND

The Xpu-Há entrance is just south of Puerto Aventuras at Km 265, after the Barceló Resort. If you're coming from the south, make a U-turn at the retorno across from the Pemex gas station; if you're coming from the north, individual signs for Al Cielo, Esencia, and Catalonia Royal mark the three entrances on the east side of the highway. Bumpy dirt roads will drop you in paradise. Since Xpu-Há is simply a beach community comprising of hotels and villas, the closest services are in Puerto Aventuras to the north and Akumal to the south.

BEACHES

Chan Yu Yum. North of Tulum is a smaller bay, known as Chan Yu Yum, edging the Catalonia Royal Tulum. While it's marginally less protected than Omni Beach, it's also delightfully calm, with flat white sands melting into shallow waters great for snorkeling. Divers are likely to spot turtles, stingrays, toadfish, and perhaps even a nurse shark; however, underwater currents can make diving a challenge. **Amenities:** none. **Best for:** snorkeling; swimming. ⊠ *Bahia Xcacel, near Catalonia Royal Tulum, off Carretera 307, Km 264.5, Xpu-há.*

La Playa. Located at Playa Xpu-Há, this beach club is open year-round from 11 to 6. Guests of nearby villas are often lured here by the plethora of amenities—including showers, lockers, hammocks, umbrellas, chaise longues, and a rental shop that has snorkeling gear, Wave Runners, boogie boards, and kayaks. In full beach club tradition, there's a restaurant and a bar with swings instead of stools. You can burn off your lunch with a game of volleyball, or opt for hair braids and henna tattoos. **Amenities:** food and drink; showers; toilets; water sports. **Best for:** partiers; swimming; walking. ✉ *Carretera 307, Km 265, Xpu-há* ☎ *984/106–0024* 🌐 *www.laplayaxpuha.com* 🎟 *MX$40 entry and MX$120 drink minimum.*

Xpu-Há Beach. Other than the occasional villa and resort, including Royal Catalonia Tulum smack dab in the center, this stretch of white sand is fairly isolated. South of here are a few spots where you can grab a midday snack, like La Playa Beach Club. There are no hidden rocks in shallow areas, so many people come to swim or snorkel, especially when the winds are calm; the sugary sand is raked, making it a good place for an unobstructed stroll, too. Unlike many beaches, this one isn't blocked by resort security. You can access it through La Playa or by having lunch at the Al Cielo Hotel. **Amenities:** food and drink; showers; toilets; water sports. **Best for:** partiers; snorkeling; swimming; walking. ✉ *Carretera 307, Km 265, at the entrance to La Playa Beach Club, Xpu-há.*

WHERE TO STAY

$$$ B&B/INN

🏨 **Al Cielo Hotel.** On the powdery shores of Xpu-Há, this boutique inn has four chic rooms named after the four elements, all with hardwood floors, palapas, and beds draped in white curtains. **Pros:** great restaurant; hospitable staff; excellent beach; intimate hotel. **Cons:** Wi-Fi in restaurant only; not child-friendly; no TVs; restaurant open to public. [$] *Rooms from: $270* ✉ *Carretera 307, Km 118, Xpu-há* ☎ *984/840–9012* 🌐 *www.alcielohotel.com* 🛏 *3 villas, 5 suites* 💳 *No credit cards* 🍴 *Multiple meal plans.*

$$$ ALL-INCLUSIVE

🏨 **Catalonia Royal Tulum.** This lavish, adults-only resort was designed around the surrounding jungle and has a great beach and terrific food for a resort in its price range; however, it may not be the place for you if you don't want a nonstop environment. **Pros:** excellent beach; great diving classes; enthusiastic staff. **Cons:** time-share sales pitch; no kids under 18; no elevator; no pool bar. [$] *Rooms from: $259* ✉ *Carretera 307, Km 264.5, Xpu-há* ☎ *984/875–1800* 🌐 *www.hoteles-catalonia.com* 🛏 *288 rooms* 🍴 *All-inclusive.*

$$$$ HOTEL Fodor'sChoice ★

🏨 **Hotel Esencia.** Situated on 50 acres of jungle, this sprawling estate—once the home of an Italian duchess—has been converted into one of the Riviera Maya's most luxurious hotels. **Pros:** blackout shades; tips included; stunning beach; daily yoga; remarkable food. **Cons:** small section of the beach is rocky; not all rooms have ocean views; no gym. [$] *Rooms from: $320* ✉ *Carretera 307, Km 265, Predio Rústico Xpu-Há, lotes 18 and 19, Xpu-há* ☎ *984/873–4830, 877/528–3490* 🌐 *www.hotelesencia.com* 🛏 *29 rooms* 🍴 *Multiple meal plans.*

SPORTS AND THE OUTDOORS

KITEBOARDING

Morph Kiteboarding. These certified IKO instructors offer three-hour lessons that can be tailored to all levels. Based in Xpu-Há, they'll pick you up at your hotel and take you to the nearest kite-friendly location. ✉ *Carretera 307, Km 265, Xpu-há* ☎ *984/114–9524* 🌐 *www.morphkiteboarding.com* 🎟 *From MX$3050.*

SCUBA DIVING AND SNORKELING

Zero Gravity Dive Center. This dive shop rents equipment and has a staff of experienced instructors that specialize in cave diving. ☒ *Carretera 307, Km 265, in front of Hotel Maeva, Xpu-há* ☎ *1984/840–9030 (mobile)* ⊕ *www.zerogravity.com.mx* ✉ *From MX$2188* ⊙ *Closed Sun.*

AKUMAL

37 km (23 miles) south of Playa del Carmen.

In Mayan, Akumal (pronounced ah-koo-*maal*) means "place of the turtle," and this portion of coast is a storied nesting ground, especially at Half Moon Bay. Akumal first attracted international attention in 1926, when explorers discovered the *Mantanceros*, a Spanish galleon that sank there in 1741; then, in the 1960s, diver Pablo Bush Romero established the Hotel Akumal Caribe. The rest is history.

Today Akumal is an Americanized beach community, home to divers, fishermen, and laid-back expats from the U.S. and Canada. It's essentially a long string of upscale homes and condos along three bays. Akumal Bay is the best base for visits, with a good selection of hotels and restaurants plus the best all-around beach for swimming and snorkeling. Half Moon Bay, just beyond, has decent snorkeling and more condos for rent, but the beach is narrow and rocky. Laguna Yalku is a protected snorkeling lagoon.

■ TIP→ Bypass the vendors at Akumal's entrance offering snorkel gear for rent. Although their rates are slightly less than you'll pay elsewhere, once you tack on conservation fees, parking, and a guide, you're better off going through an official dive shop.

GETTING HERE AND AROUND

The entrance to town is on the east side of the highway, so coming from the north you'll have to make a U-turn at the well-marked retorno; coming from the south, exit at Km 264 off Carretera 307. From either direction, follow the signs to "Akumal Playa." Getting around is easy as there's only one road. It runs from the highway through the Arch—the town's gateway, at Hotel Akumal Caribe—and along Akumal Bay past Half Moon Bay to Laguna Yalku, a distance of about 10 minutes by car. Unlike many beach communities, this one can be entered even when a guard is stationed. Simply explain that you're heading to the beach. Akumal's tourist office is a small booth on the main road before the Arch as you enter town.

EXPLORING

FAMILY **Aktun-Chen** (*Indiana Joes*). The name is Mayan for "the cave with cenotes inside," and these amazing underground caverns—estimated to be about 5 million years old—are the area's largest. You walk through the underground passages, past stalactites and stalagmites, until you reach the cenote with its various shades of deep green. There's also an on-site canopy tour and one cenote where you can take a swim. ■ TIP→ **This top family attraction isn't as crowded or touristy as Xplor, Xel-Há, and Xcaret.** ☒ *Carretera 307, Km 107, opposite Bahia Principe resort, between Akumal and Xel-Há* ☎ *998/806–4962 for park, 984/109–2061*

Fodor's Choice
★

for office ⊕ *www.aktun-chen.com* ✉ *Cave tour MX$447, cenote tour MX$447, canopy tour MX$596* ⊘ *Mon.–Sat. 9–5.*

FAMILY   **Laguna Yal-kú** (*Yal-kú Lagoon*). Devoted snorkelers may want to follow the unmarked dirt road to Laguna Yal-kú, about 3 km (2 miles) north of Akumal town center. A series of small mangrove-edged lagoons that gradually reach the ocean, Yal-kú is an eco-park that's home to schools of parrot fish in clear water with visibility to 160 feet in winter and spring. Snorkeling equipment can be rented in the parking lot; the site also has toilets, lockers, changing rooms, outdoor showers, and a snack bar. ■ TIP➡ Sunscreen is not allowed, so bring a T-shirt to keep from getting burned. ✉ *End of main rd., just past Half Moon Bay* ✉ *MX$200* ⊘ *Daily 8–5:30.*

FAMILY   **Xel-Há.** Part of the Xcaret nature-adventure park group, Xel-Há (pronounced shel-*hah*) is a natural aquarium made of coves, inlets, and lagoons cut from the limestone shoreline. The name means "where the water is born," and a natural spring here flows out to meet the salt water, creating a unique habitat for tropical marine life. There's enough to impress novice snorkelers, though there seem to be fewer fish each year, and the mixture of fresh and salt water can cloud visibility. Low wooden bridges over the lagoons allow for leisurely walks around the park, and there are spots to rest, swim, cliff-jump, zip-line, or swing from ropes over the water.

Xel-Há gets overwhelmingly crowded, so come early. The grounds are well equipped with bathrooms and restaurants. At the entrance you'll receive specially prepared sunscreen that won't kill the fish; other sunscreens are prohibited. The entrance fee (MX$1,206) includes a meal, towel, locker, inner tubes, and snorkel equipment; other activities like scuba diving, zip-lining, swimming with the dolphins, and spa treatments, are available at additional cost. ■ TIP➡ Discounts are offered when you book online. ✉ *Carretera 307, Km 240, Xel-Há* ☎ *984/875–6000, 888/922–7381* ⊕ *www.xelha.com* ✉ *MX$1206* ⊘ *Daily 8:30–7.*

BEACHES

Akumal Bay. Known for the sea turtles that swim in its waters, Akumal Bay is sheltered by an offshore reef—sadly only about 30% of it is alive. It's best to explore the waters with a certified guide available through dive shops in town. A MX$122 conservation fee is tacked on to all tours. Do not wear sunscreen in the water as it can harm the reef, and, above all, do not touch the wildlife or coral. Be careful to stay clear of the red "fire reef" since excessive contact can be fatal. When you drag yourself away from the snorkeling, there are plenty of palm trees for shade, as well as a variety of waterfront shops, restaurants, and cafés. If you continue on the main road, you'll reach Half Moon Bay and Laguna Yalkú, also good snorkeling spots. **Amenities:** food and drink; lifeguards; water sports. **Best for:** snorkeling. ✉ *Entrance at Hotel Akumal Caribe.*

Half Moon Bay. The crescent bay on the north end of Akumal has shallow waters and almost no current, making it a safe swimming spot for children; the snorkeling is also good here (you might even see the occasional sea turtle). Beach chairs and hammocks line the shore at La

Buena Vida restaurant, which has a pool, restrooms, and limited street parking for patrons. The area near Casa Maya is protected by an outer reef; however, the entry point is rocky, so bring water shoes. Bring an umbrella, too—Half Moon Bay is known for its white sand and clear waters, but the lack of trees means you'll have trouble finding shade. **Amenities:** food and drink; toilets. **Best for:** snorkeling; swimming. ⊠ *Beach Rd., Lote 35, North Akumal.*

X'cacel Beach. About 10 km (6 miles) south of Akumal, this beach (also written "Xca-Cel"), has white powdery sand and a nearby cenote that can be accessed through a jungle path to your right. Snorkeling is best on the beach's north end. To reach it from Carretera 307, turn at the dirt road that runs between Chemuyil and Xel-Há. The route is blocked by a guard who will charge you MX$30 to enter; after paying, simply continue on to the beach itself. From May through November, this area is reserved for turtle nesting. Avoid stepping on any raised mounds of sand as they could be turtle nests. Note that the beach road is open daily from 9 to 5. **Amenities:** parking (no fee); toilets. **Best for:** snorkeling; solitude. ⊠ *Carretera 307, Km 248.*

WHERE TO EAT

$$
MEXICAN

✕ **La Buena Vida.** With driftwood tables overlooking Half Moon Bay, swings at the lively bar, and salsa music keeping things moving, this might be the perfect beach restaurant. The usual Mexican fare—quesadillas, empanadas, burritos, and fish tacos with handmade tortillas—is perfectly fine, but the food isn't the point. It's all about the location. Directly on the beach, this place takes full advantage with two big upstairs terraces that provide sweeping views of the water. Lounge chairs are scattered on the sand for customers' use, and there's a small pool to keep the kids busy while you have another margarita. Climb the ladder to the two-seater tower table, 15 feet above the sand, where your drinks are delivered in a bucket on a rope. $ *Average main: 176 MP* ⊠ *Half Moon Bay, Lote 35, North Akumal* ☏ 984/875–9061 ⊕ *www. labuenavidarestaurant.com.*

$$
SEAFOOD

✕ **La Cueva del Pescador.** Dig your toes in the sand floor and enjoy the catch of the day at La Cueva del Pescador. A crowd of easygoing expats hunker down for the afternoon to feast on octopus, shrimp, or conch ceviche prepared with lime juice and flavored with cilantro—usually with a generous helping of beer on the side. Great grilled garlic shrimp and simple quesadillas are also served. Portions are sizeable, and prices are moderate. There's a pool table here plus a TV that's typically tuned to sports. $ *Average main: 135 MP* ⊠ *Plaza Ukana, main rd., Akumal Bay* ☏ 984/875–9002 ▭ *No credit cards.*

$
CAFÉ

✕ **Turtle Bay Café & Bakery.** This funky café serves Akumal's best breakfast, with a vast menu spanning açai bowls, eggs Benedict, pancakes, and fruit plates. For lunch and dinner, you'll find blackened fish tacos, lamb burgers, and vegetable wraps. Set back from the little plaza, the garden is a pleasant place to have a coffee, and its location by the ecological center makes it the closest thing Akumal has to a downtown. Smoothies, homemade ice cream, and fresh-baked goods like the chocolate–peanut butter cheesecake are tempting. If you fall in love with a local stray, the owner has set up an animal rescue program that will ship a pet directly to your home. The restaurant is open until 9 pm and has free Wi-Fi. [$] *Average main: 81 MP* ✉ *Plaza Ukana, main rd., Akumal Bay* ☎ *984/875–9138* 🌐 *www.turtlebaycafe.com.*

WHERE TO STAY

$$$ ALL-INCLUSIVE 🏨 **Grand Bahía Principe** (*Bahia Principe Riviera Maya*). This all-inclusive mega-complex consists of four upscale hotels (Akumal, Cobá, Tulum, and Sian Ka'an) with extensive shared facilities reachable by shuttle. **Pros:** on the beach; attentive staff; good food. **Cons:** beach is rocky; some rooms are worn; difficult to get a booking at some restaurants. [$] *Rooms from: $230* ✉ *Carretera 307, Km 250* ✥ *Access the property through the resort gate off Carretera 307, rather than the main entrance into Akumal town* ☎ *984/875–5000, 866/282–2442* 🌐 *www.bahiaprincipeusa.com* 🛏 *Akumal 630 rooms, Cobá 1080, Tulum 915, Sian Ka'an 420* 🍴 *All-inclusive.*

$$ HOTEL 🏨 **Hotel Akumal Caribe.** Back in the 1960s, Pablo Bush Romero established this resort as a place for his diving buddies to crash, and it still offers pleasant accommodations and a congenial staff. **Pros:** reasonable rates; on the beach; easy snorkeling. **Cons:** sometimes a bit noisy; no elevator; bungalows lack ocean views. [$] *Rooms from: $185* ✉ *Akumal Arch, main rd., Akumal Bay* ☎ *984/206–3500, 800/351–1622* 🌐 *www.hotelakumalcaribe.com* 🛏 *21 rooms, 40 bungalows, 4 villas, 1 condo* 🍴 *Breakfast.*

$$ RESORT 🏨 **Vista Del Mar.** Each small room in the main building here has an ocean view, a private terrace, and colorful Guatemalan-Mexican accents; next door are more expensive condos with Spanish-colonial touches. **Pros:** on beach; all rooms have Wi-Fi and ocean views; well-kept grounds. **Cons:** beach is a little rocky; beds aren't very comfortable; no meals. [$] *Rooms from: $110* ✉ *Half Moon Bay, Lote 40A* ☎ *984/875–9060, 505/992–3333, 866/425–8625* 🌐 *www.akumalinfo.com* 🛏 *16 rooms, 16 condos* 🍴 *No meals.*

SHOPPING AND SPAS

CRAFTS AND FOLK ART

Galería Lamanai. A laid-back spot under a palapa, Galería Lamanai carries a real mix of folk and fine art from Mexican and international artists. ✉ *Hotel Akumal Caribe, Akumal Bay* ☎ *984/875–9055* 🌐 *www.galerialamanai.mfbiz.com.*

Mexicarte. This little shop sells high-quality crafts from around the country. ✉ *Main rd., Akumal Bay, next to Hotel Akumal Caribe* ☎ *984/875–9115* 🌐 *www.akumalart.com.*

SPAS

Budha Gardens Spa. This small day spa in Akumal offers Swedish massage, reflexology, facials, body scrubs, wraps, manicures, and pedicures. After a day in the sun, try the popular Mayan clay mask, said to firm the skin and draw out impurities. Body scrub options range from mango-ginger to bamboo-walnut, while the cooling body wraps incorporate local ingredients like cucumber and lavender to rehydrate the skin. Each wrap and scrub is accompanied by a mini-facial and head massage. ✉ *Past Akumal Arch on main rd., next to Hotel Akumal Caribe* ☎ *984/745–4942, 984/137–6947* 🌐 *www.budhagardensspa.com.*

SPORTS AND THE OUTDOORS

BICYCLING

Akumal Guide. The small booth inside Hotel Akumal Caribe rents bikes for MX$108, as well as golf carts for MX$542 per day. Golf carts are a very popular way to get around Akumal. ⊠ *Hotel Akumal Caribe, Akumal Bay* ☎ *984/875–9251, 984/875–9115* ⊕ *www.akumal guide.com.*

SCUBA DIVING AND SNORKELING

Akumal Dive Center. The area's oldest dive operation offers reef or cenote diving as well as one-hour snorkeling tours; the latter includes gear, lockers, showers, guides, and the MX$122 conservation wristbands. Three-hour fishing trips for up to four people can also be arranged. Take a sharp right at the Akumal Arch and you'll see the dive shop on the beach. ⊠ *Hotel Akumal Caribe, Akumal Bay* ☎ *984/875–9025* ⊕ *www.akumaldivecenter.com* ◊ *Dives from MX$542, snorkeling tours MX$406, fishing trips MX$2440.*

FAMILY
Fodor's Choice
★

Akumal Dive Shop. You can go snorkeling with turtles or diving at cenotes with the Akumal Dive Shop. Certification courses as well as specialized programs for kids are also available. If boating is more your thing, it runs daytime and sunset catamaran cruises, too. ⊠ *Plaza Ukana, North Akumal Bay* ☎ *984/875–9030, 984/875–9031* ⊕ *www. akumaldiveshop.com* ◊ *Snorkeling tour MX$460 diving trip MX$1897 cruises MX$1287.*

Centro Ecológico Akumal. The ecological center in Akumal has exhibits and a video about the bay and turtles that is worth watching before you venture into the water. Snorkeling tours are available through the center, and proceeds go to turtle conservation. ⊠ *Carretera 307, Km 104* ☎ *984/875–9095* ◊ *Ecological center free, snorkeling MX$300.*

TANKAH

56 km (35 miles) south of Playa del Carmen.

If you plan on staying in the Cobá area, nearby Tankah is a good option—especially if you want to avoid the Tulum crowds. In ancient times Tankah was an important Mayan trading city. A number of small, reasonably priced hotels have cropped up here over the past few years, and several expats who own villas in the area rent them out year-round. Often overlooked by travelers, this spectacular stretch of coastline offers great snorkeling, diving, and best of all, isolation. A cenote that tunnels under the beach road and spills into the sea makes the area even more unique.

GETTING HERE AND AROUND

To reach the coastal road in Tankah, turn east off Carretera 307 at Km 237 (a sign for Blue Sky Hotel and a peacock mural mark the turn). At the end of the long, pitted road, turn left (north) where a string of villas and small hotels parallel the beach. The closest medical clinics, grocery stores, and emergency services are 4 km (2½ miles) south in Tulum.

BEACHES

Tankah Bay. Nestled in a protected cove, this wide stretch of beach is popular with divers and snorkelers due to the outer reef that keeps waters calm. The fine sand is perfect for a barefoot stroll, but the shallow waters have sharp rocks just below the surface. Across the road from Casa Cenote Restaurant is Manatee Cenote, an underwater cave that spills from the mangroves into the sea. This freshwater pool, coupled with the outer reef, make Tankah a snorkeler's paradise. The main draw is that the area is relatively isolated since most sun worshipers tend to bask on the shores of Playa del Carmen. **Amenities:** food and drink; toilets. **Best for:** snorkeling; solitude; walking. .

4

WHERE TO EAT

$$$ ECLECTIC

🍴 **Restaurante Oscar y Lalo.** This wonderful palapa restaurant with a pebble floor and peaceful garden is actually a couple of miles outside Tankah on Carretera 307. The seafood is excellent, although a bit pricey. Lalo's Special (a dish made with local lobster, shrimp, conch, and fish) and the chicken fajitas are standouts. The ceviche made of fresh fish and lobster, and the *caracoles* (snails) with citrus juice are also exceptional. Many come just for the grilled octopus seasoned with paprika. You're likely to either have this place all to yourself or be lost in a crowd of travelers arriving by tour bus. [$] *Average main: 203 MP* ✉ *Bahia de Soliman, Carretera 307, Km 241* ✣ *Look for large billboard* ☎ *1984/127–1587 (mobile), 1984/115–9965 (mobile)* 🌐 *www.oscarandlalo.com.*

WHERE TO STAY

$$$ HOTEL

🏨 **Blue Sky Hotel.** This boutique beach property—complete with oceanfront pool and exquisite accommodations just steps from the secluded white sand—underwent a thorough renovation in 2013 that made it one of the area's best. **Pros:** sublime beachfront setting; excellent restaurant; stunning rooms. **Cons:** need car to get around; one room lacks full ocean view. [$] *Rooms from: $280* ✉ *Bahía Tankah, past Casa Cenote* ☎ *998/800–1371* 🌐 *www.blueskyhotel.com.mx* 🛏 *9 rooms* 🍽 *Breakfast.*

$$ B&B/INN

🏨 **Casa Cenote Hotel.** Across from the cenote for which it's named, this peaceful property offers multiple lodging choices. **Pros:** on the beach; close to cenote; excellent food; new suites; on-site dive shop and grocery store. **Cons:** need a car to get around; Wi-Fi in common areas only; breakfast, kayaks, and maid service included only in casitas and suite rates. [$] *Rooms from: $150* ✉ *Interior Fracc. Tankah, Mza 3, Lote 32, across from Cenote Manatee* ☎ *984/115–6996* 🌐 *www.casacenote.com* 🛏 *7 casitas, 1 villa, 4 suites, 2 bungalows* 🍽 *Multiple meal plans.*

$$$ HOTEL FAMILY Fodor's Choice ★

🏨 **Jashita.** This sophisticated little hotel at the northern end of Soliman Bay has style in spades. **Pros:** kid-friendly; clear, calm bay; very private. **Cons:** mediocre, expensive restaurant; poor Wi-Fi; bay too shallow for swimming in some places; only seven ocean-view rooms. [$] *Rooms from: $210* ✉ *Bahia de Soliman, Tankah Rd. IV, across Carretera 307 from Restaurante Oscar y Lalo* ☎ *1984/139–5131 (mobile)* 🌐 *www.jashitahotel.com* 🛏 *16 rooms* 🍽 *Breakfast.*

SPORTS AND THE OUTDOORS

Due to the outer reef, calm bay, and connecting cenote, Tankah has become a popular dive spot. The closest dive shop is Maya Dive Center; however, most dive shops along Riviera Maya can organize trips to Tankah.

KITEBOARDING

Extreme Control Kite School. All levels of kitesurfing lessons and the latest equipment are available through Extreme Control Kite School. Led by IKO (International Kiteboarding Organization) instructor Marco Cristofanelli, courses take place at Caleta Tankah Beach Club, about five minutes from Tulum. The outfit operates on the beach from 9 am to sunset every day unless there is absolutely no wind (call ahead to check conditions). Paddle boarding, diving, and snorkeling are also offered. ✉ *Caleta Tankah Beach Club, Carretera 307, Km 230* ☎ *1984/130–1596 (mobile), 1984/745–4555 (mobile)* ⊕ *www.extremecontrol.net* 🖅 *From MX$830.*

SCUBA DIVING AND SNORKELING

Cenote Manatee (*Casa Cenote*). Directly across from Casa Cenote Hotel, this open lagoon (often referred to as Casa Cenote) is popular with experienced cave divers since a freshwater tunnel—dropping below the main road—connects directly to the ocean. Here two ecosystems collide with both fresh and saltwater, offering a maximum diving depth of 26 feet. The constant currents draw in a variety of marine life including parrotfish, swimming crabs, moray eels, juvenile barracuda, and tarpon. Only skilled divers should enter the underwater cave since the distance between the cenote and ocean is dangerously long. There is a small parking lot, and a shack renting snorkeling equipment, but no facilities other than those at neighboring hotels and restaurants. ✉ *Interior Fracc. Tankah, Mza 3, Lote 32* 🖅 *MX$40.*

Gorgonian Gardens. Located about 60 feet below the outer reef, the Gorgonian Gardens have made Tankah a destination for divers. From southern Tankah to Bahía de Punta Soliman, the sand-free ocean floor has allowed for the proliferation of Gorgonians, or soft corals—sea fans, candelabras, and fingers that can reach 5 feet in height—as well as a variety of colorful sponges. Fish love to feed here, and so many swarm the gardens that some divers compare the experience to being surrounded by clouds of butterflies. Although this underwater habitat goes on for miles, Tankah is the best place to access it. ✉ *In front of Tankah Inn, just south of Casa Cenote.*

TULUM AND COBÁ

Tulum is home to the Yucatán Peninsula's most visited Mayan ruins, but stunning beaches, a colorful pueblo, jungle-chic bungalows, and organic restaurants give visitors another reason to come to this eco-friendly town. About 30 minutes inland, the ancient ruins of Cobá might not be perched above turquoise waters like those in Tulum; however, the solitude you'll find among towering temples overgrown with flora is worth the trip. Birds and monkeys calling overhead add to the ambience at this under-appreciated site.

TULUM

61 km (38 miles) south of Playa del Carmen.

It used to be that Tulum was simply known as dusty little town with a stellar archaeological site and a few palapa huts. No longer. Discovered by the international eco-set, it now has whitewashed, solar-powered bungalow hotels that line the spectacular beach 2 km (1 mile) east of town. Locals speak of a battle for Tulum's bohemian soul, and although first-time visitors may not notice the changes, it's indisputable that the free-spirited hippie days are over.

Tulum is divided into three main areas: the downtown pueblo, south from the shore along Carretera 307 (here known as Avenida Tulum); the Mayan ruins to the north on the coast; and the beach (Zona Hotelera), which extends down from the ruins.

Those ancient structures were the town's original draw, and Tulum (meaning "wall" in Mayan) now lures more than 2 million people annually. Even if you couldn't care less about history, the site's waterfront location elevates it to the sublime. The pueblo, conversely, is a jumble of food stalls, souvenir shops, budget hostels, and cheap eateries, some catering to tourists, some to locals, and some to both. Although it's more appealing to stay at the beach, the town offers an authentic slice of Mexico.

Tulum's irresistible beach begins just east on the Boca Paila road. (Technically there's beach all the way from the ruins down to Sian Ka'an, but the coast by the ruins, and south to Zamas restaurant, is a series of rocky coves. The endless powdery sand you came for is south of the bridge and police checkpoint after Zamas.) Miles of magnificent white sand sparkle before the aquamarine waves, backed by eco-hotels on one side of the narrow road, and tropical hipster restaurants, yoga centers, and the odd spa on the other.

Tulum's ongoing transformation has brought new services, including a 24-hour hospital, four gas stations, and a Chedraui supermarket. But there's still no community power supply, so eco-resorts—both rustic and chic—rely on wind turbines, solar energy, recycled water, and generators and/or candlelight. Rooms are void of TVs and phones, and they seldom have Wi-Fi or 24-hour air-conditioning (although this is slowly changing); it's also worth noting that some hotels draw water from cenotes, which might result in a salty shower and low water pressure.

GETTING HERE AND AROUND

Tulum is a 20-minute drive from Akumal and a 45-minute drive from Playa del Carmen. You can hire a taxi from Cancún for approximately MX\$1,355. Tucan Kin has a direct (shared) shuttle service from Cancún airport for MX\$596 per person one-way. Roberto Solis of Bob Transfers offers transportation between Cancún and Tulum for MX\$1,355 one-way (up to five passengers). Buses operated by ADO (⊕ *www.ado.*

com.mx) link Cancún, Puerto Morelos, Playa del Carmen, Tulum, Felipe Carrillo Puerto, Limones, and Chetumal.

From the pueblo, you can walk the 2 km (1 mile) to the archaeological site entrance, rent a bike, or catch one of the shuttles that pass every few minutes. Within the hotel zone, travelers must rely on taxis, cars, or bikes to get around. If you plan on driving, watch carefully for the large beach crabs that cross the roads after dark. To reach the beachfront Zona Hotelera, head south on Carretera 307 and turn left (east) at the second stoplight in Tulum. Shortly after passing the fire station, you'll come to a "T" in the road. There you'll find dozens of signs directing travelers to hotels; the best beach is to the right, and the ruins are to the left. A taxi from the pueblo to the Zona costs MX$130.

Taxi Contacts Bob Transfers ☎ *1984/133–5774 (mobile_).* **Tucan Kin** ☎ *984/871–3538* ⊕ *www.tucankin.com.*

EXPLORING

Fodor's Choice
★
Tulum Ruins. Tulum is one of the few Mayan cities known to have been inhabited when the conquistadors arrived in 1518. In the 16th century it was a trade center, a safe harbor for goods from rival Mayan factions who considered the city neutral territory. Tulum reached its height when its merchants, made wealthy through trading, for the first time outranked Maya priests in authority and power. But when the Spaniards arrived, they forbade the Maya traders to sail the seas, and commerce among the Maya died.

Tulum has long held special significance for the Maya as a symbol of resistance and independence. A key city in the League of Mayapán (AD 987–1194), it was never conquered by the Spaniards, although it was abandoned by the Maya about 75 years after the conquest of the rest of Mexico. For 300 years thereafter it symbolized the defiance of an otherwise subjugated people, and it was one of the last outposts of the Maya during their insurrection against Mexican rule in the Caste Wars, which began in 1847. Uprisings continued intermittently until 1935, when the Maya ceded Tulum to the Mexican government.

▪TIP➜ At the entrance to the ruins you can hire a guide for MX$474, but keep in mind that some of their information is more entertainment than historical accuracy. (Disregard the stuff about virgin sacrifices.) Although you can see the ruins thoroughly in two hours, you might want to allow extra time for a swim or a stroll on the beach.

The first significant structure is the two-story **Templo de los Frescos,** to the left of the entryway. The temple's vault roof and corbel arch are examples of classic Mayan architecture. Faint traces of blue-green frescoes outlined in black on the inner and outer walls depict the three worlds of the Maya and their major deities, and are decorated with stellar and serpentine patterns, rosettes, and ears of maize and other offerings to the gods. One scene portrays the rain god seated on a four-legged animal—probably a reference to the Spaniards on their horses. Unfortunately, the frescos are difficult to see from the path to which visitors are restricted.

The largest and most-photographed structure, the **Castillo** (Castle), looms at the edge of a 40-foot limestone cliff just past the Temple of the Frescoes. Atop it, at the end of a broad stairway, is a temple with stucco ornamentation on the outside and traces of fine frescoes inside the two chambers. (The stairway has been roped off, so the top temple is inaccessible.) The front wall of the Castillo has faint carvings of the Descending God and columns depicting the plumed serpent god, Kukulcán, who was introduced to the Maya by the Toltecs. To the left of the Castillo, facing the sea, is the **Templo del Díos Descendente**—so called for the carving over the doorway of a winged god plummeting to earth.

A few small altars sit atop a hill at the north side of the cove, with a good view of the Castillo and the sea. **TIP→ To avoid the longest lines, be sure to arrive before 11 am. Outside the entrance are dozens of vendors selling Mexican crafts, so bring some extra cash for souvenirs.** ✉ *Carretera 307, Km 133* ☎ *983/837–2411* 🎫 *MX$59 entrance, MX$54 parking, MX$67 video fee, MX$27 shuttle from parking to ruins* 🕓 *Daily 8–4:30.*

BEACHES

Tulum Beach. Extending 11 km (7 miles), Tulum's main beach is a tropical paradise comprising glassy water and powdery sand, set off from the jungle by dunes and, increasingly, low-slung bungalow hotels where the yoga set take their virtuous rest. It's divided by a bridge and rocky promontory into two main sections, similar to each other, although the farther south you go on the Carretera Tulum-Boca Paila beach road, the more secluded and lovelier it gets. The beach is bordered on the south by the Sian Ka'an biosphere reserve, whose coast is even more deserted. To the north, you'll find the Tulum ruins. **Amenities:** food and drink; toilets; water sports. **Best For**: swimming; walking. ✉ *Carretera Tulum–Boca Paila.*

Tulum Ruins Beach. Talk about a beach with a view! At Tulum's archeological site, the Caribbean's signature white sand and turquoise waters are framed by a backdrop of Mayan pyramids. The small cove can get crowded, especially during peak season when travelers flock to the ruins for a day of sightseeing. The south end by the rocks tends to have more breathing room. Only those who purchase a ticket to the ruins can access this beach, unless of course you approach the shores by boat. **Amenities**: none. **Best for:** swimming. ✉ *Carretera 307, Km 130* 🎫 *MX$59 for entrance via ruins.*

WHERE TO EAT

$ SEAFOOD

🍴 **El Camello Jr.** By the time you get to this local favorite at the very end of Tulum's downtown strip, you'll think you've already left town. In fact, you've just arrived. Called "Camellito" by locals, it's famed for having Tulum's freshest seafood—and the jammed parking lot is testament to its enduring popularity. Fish or shrimp tacos are light and fresh, but the full splendor of the place is expressed by its whole grilled or fried fish, served with generous mounds of rice, beans, and plátanos. Come hungry. The lively scene and tropical ambience are a Mexican original. [$] *Average main: 81 MP* ✉ *Avs. Tulum and Luna, at back end of town* 💳 *No credit cards* 🕓 *Closed Wed.*

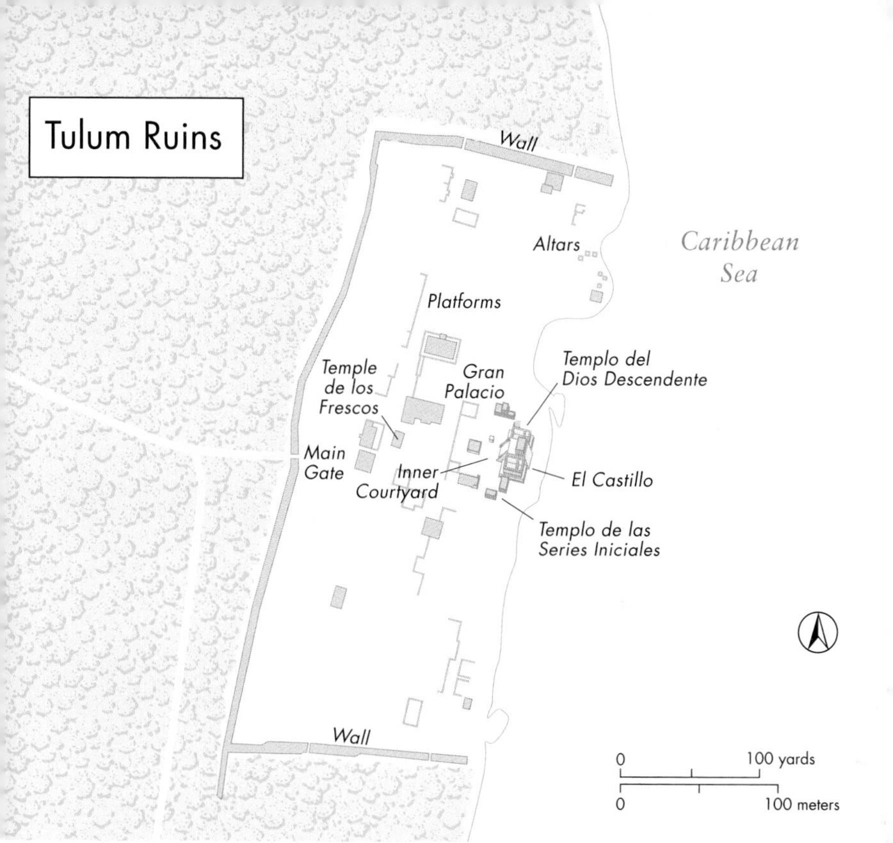
Tulum Ruins
Wall
Altars
Caribbean Sea
Platforms
Temple de los Frescos
Gran Palacio
Templo del Dios Descendente
Main Gate
Inner Courtyard
El Castillo
Templo de las Series Iniciales
Wall
0
100 yards
0
100 meters

$$$ MODERN MEXICAN 🍴 **El Tábano.** This jungleside hangout run by Barcelona chef Laura Brea brings imaginative cuisine to a rustic garden. You could spend the day here at a country-kitchen table: farm-fresh eggs and homemade bread with mango honey jam for breakfast; papaya tomato gazpacho for lunch; and fresh grouper in a *pipian* (pumpkin-seed) sauce or *chile ancho* stuffed with shrimp and nuts, served in a steaming clay pot, for dinner. Paying tribute to local blends is the wine list, on which 80% of the bottles are from Mexico. An international crowd of locals, expat residents, and in-the-know vacationers makes for a lively scene, especially at night. For large parties, book ahead. [$] *Average main: 220 MP* ✉ *Carretera Tulum–Boca Paila, Km 5.7* ☎ *984/125–7172 (mobile), 984/134 –8725* 🌐 *www.eltabanorestaurant.com* 💳 *No credit cards.*

$$$$ ECLECTIC Fodor's Choice ★ 🍴 **Hartwood.** New York chefs cooking New York food for New York prices—in a wood-fired jungle lot, open to the night sky—that's Hartwood. Big-city transplants Mya Henry and Eric Werner opened this solar-powered restaurant in 2011, and it has been drawing a full house ever since. Try slow-roasted pork ribs, cooked overnight, or a marinated beet and Gorgonzola salad. Or go local with jicama, Caribbean lobster, or sea bass just a few hours out of the ocean. Chef Werner has added farming to his list of talents and serves his own chipotle rabbit sausage. The setting of picnic tables on a white pebble floor is remarkably charming, as is the presentation of dishes served in cast-iron skillets and mason jars. The open kitchen and massive oven make for a dramatic, fiery show when the sun goes down. But in high season, get here when the restaurant opens at 6, or risk a New York–style wait, too. [$] *Average main: 406 MP* ✉ *Carretera Tulum–Boca Paila, Km 7.6* 🌐 *www.hartwoodtulum.com* ▭ *No credit cards* 🕒 *Closed Mon., Tues., and Sept. 1–Oct. 15. No lunch.*

$$ THAI 🍴 **Mezzanine Thai.** People come from Playa del Carmen for the zingy flavors of this authentic Thai restaurant. Overseeing the menu is Thai Chef Dim Geefay, a well-known teacher and TV cooking personality. Recipes start with basil, chile, mint, and lemongrass, which are homegrown from seeds brought over from Thailand. The spiciness of the soups and curries (created with homemade coconut milk) are rated as "Tourist," "Expatriate," and "Truly Thai." For something a bit milder, try the sweet-and-sour chicken, fish, or shrimp. Also available are salads, Thai noodles, and grilled fish wrapped in banana leaves. [$] *Average main: 185 MP* ✉ *Carretera Tulum–Boca Paila, Km 1.5, Zona Hotelera* ☎ *1984/131–1596 (mobile)* 🌐 *www.mezzanine.com.mx.*

$$$ INTERNATIONAL Fodor's Choice ★ 🍴 **Unico.** As competitive as the culinary scene has become in Tulum, this restaurant by Chef Brian Sernatinger truly is *único* (unique), with every dish made from scratch. Brian's 15 years as a chef in Spain, followed by training in France, come through in dishes like ravioli filled with smoked bacon and sweet-pea puree or whiskey chicken with hand-cut fries. The fried goat cheese with local honey is an exceptional starter. Vegetarians and gluten-free travelers will appreciate the vegetable lasagna—made with zucchini instead of pasta, it's a flavorful stack of roasted tomatoes, carrots, pesto, and whipped ricotta. The ocean views at this poolside restaurant invite lingering, so stick around for dessert (it's delivered with a shot of D'aristi). [$] *Average main: 270 MP* ✉ *Hotel Mi Amor, Carretera Tulum–Boca Paila, Km 2, Zona Hotelera* ☎ *984/188–4273* 🌐 *www.unicotulum.com.*

$$$ MODERN MEXICAN 🍴 **Ziggy's Restaurant.** With tables under a palapa and on the beach, this restaurant is a perfect place to sink your toes in the sand while dining. Chef Jorge Hidalgo offers understated appetizers like tuna nachos (tuna tartare and avocado with tortilla strips) or coconut shrimp (dipped in piña colada sauce). Veggie fans will love salads made with jicama, beets, and paprika-lemon vinaigrette. The fish is about as fresh as it gets—if you're an angler, the kitchen will even cook up your catch. By day, the menu focuses on sandwiches and wraps; by night the attention turns to beef filet with black truffles and short ribs cooked for 8 hours. **TIP→ There's Mexican wine tasting on Thursday and live jazz on Friday.** [$] *Average main: 271 MP* ✉ *The Beach Tulum, Carretera Tulum–Boca Paila, Km 7, Zona Hotelera* ☎ *984/157–5569* 🌐 *www.thebeach-tulum.com.*

WHERE TO STAY

$$$$ HOTEL Fodor's Choice ★ 🏨 **Ahau Tulum.** Named after the Mayan sun god, Kin Ahau, this environmentally conscious property has rooms ranging from simple Bali huts to palapa suites with 20-foot vaulted ceilings, enormous decks, and two-person hammocks that make you forget the day of the week. **Pros:** yoga and aerial dance classes; romantic property; all furnishings built on-site by locals. **Cons:** Bali huts don't have a/c; meals not

included. $ *Rooms from: $350* ⊠ *Carretera Tulum–Boca Paila, Km 7.5, Zona Hotelera* ☎ *984/802–5632* ⊕ *www.ahautulum.com* ⬎ *17 rooms, 2 huts* ⧀ *No meals.*

$$$$ ⌁ **The Beach Tulum.** As Tulum's only property with swim-up rooms, this
HOTEL upscale, adults-only boutique hotel raised the bar on beachfront luxury when it opened in 2013. **Pros:** excellent breakfast; all rooms are oceanfront; private rooftop decks; discounts at Ziggy's. **Cons:** added charge for yoga and bikes; a/c isn't 'round-the-clock; no kids under 18. $ *Rooms from: $350* ⊠ *Carretera Tulum–Boca Paila, Km 7, Zona Hotelera* ☎ *984/157–5569* ⊕ *www.thebeach-tulum.com* ⬎ *20 rooms* ⧀ *Breakfast.*

$$$$ ⌁ **Be Tulum.** Designed by owner-architect Sebastian Sas, this chic beach-
HOTEL front hotel is like stepping onto a beautifully executed canvas—each room is a pure work of art, with Brazilian wood floors, cowhide rugs, marble bathrooms, and outdoor showers. **Pros:** free use of bikes and Wi-Fi; garden showers; excellent restaurant. **Cons:** no kids under 12; ground-level rooms get noise from above; only two rooms have ocean views. $ *Rooms from: $443* ⊠ *Carretera Tulum–Boca Paila, Km 10, Zona Hotelera* ☎ *984/132–6215* ⊕ *www.behoteles.com* ⬎ *20 rooms* ⧀ *Breakfast.*

$$$ ⌁ **El Pez.** Perched on the shores of Turtle Cove, this chic boutique hotel
HOTEL has elevated rooms with private balconies that catch the ocean breeze.
Fodor's Choice **Pros:** unlimited bottled water; gourmet breakfast included; saltwater
★ pool. **Cons:** some rooms get street noise; several open-plan bathrooms don't have doors; beach not great for swimming. $ *Rooms from: $285* ⊠ *Carretera Tulum–Boca Paila, Km 5.5, at Turtle Cove, Zona Hotelera* ☎ *984/116–3357, 303/800–1943* ⊕ *www.tulumhotelpez.com* ⬎ *4 rooms, 6 cabanas, 2 houses* ⧀ *Breakfast.*

$$ ⌁ **La Vita e Bella Beachfront Bungalows.** Perched on sand dunes above
RESORT the sea, this small Italian resort has lodgings that are rustic but very comfortable. **Pros:** on the beach; laid-back atmosphere; nice restaurant. **Cons:** electricity is limited; mosquitoes at dusk; needs a renovation; Wi-Fi in common areas only. $ *Rooms from: $176* ⊠ *Carretera Tulum Ruinas, Km 1.5, Zona Hotelera* ☎ *984/177–4404* ⊕ *www.lavitaebella-tulum.com* ⬎ *22 bungalows* ⧀ *Breakfast.*

$$$ ⌁ **La Zebra.** This jungle-chic, environmentally conscious hotel on a pris-
RESORT tine beach underwent a full renovation in late 2014, doubling the size of its cabanas and adding four two-story "pods" (with four rooms each) in the process. **Pros:** authentic Mexican food; on-site tequila bar; eco-friendly; free salsa lessons 6 to 7 pm on Sunday. **Cons:** usually booked three months in advance; plan to build 36 more rooms might lessen intimate feel. $ *Rooms from: $250* ⊠ *Carretera Tulum–Boca Paila, Km 8.2, Zona Hotelera* ☎ *303/800–1943 in the U.S., 984/115–4726 for reception, 984/115–4728 for reservations* ⊕ *www.lazebratulum.com* ⬎ *15 rooms, 9 cabanas* ⧀ *No meals.*

$$$ ⌁ **Mezzanine.** On the quieter side of Tulum's beachfront, this small,
HOTEL hip hotel is a 25-minute walk from the ruins along a powdery stretch of white sand. **Pros:** great Thai restaurant; DVD library; two-for-one margaritas daily from 1 to 4; rates drop 50% in low season. **Cons:** small pool area gets crowded; some rooms lack view; no kids under 16;

some late night noise from pool bar. $ *Rooms from: $250* ✉ *Carretera Tulum–Boca Paila, Km 1.5, Zona Hotelera* ☎ *984/136–9154* ⊕ *www. mezzaninetulum.com* ⤺ *7 rooms, 2 suites* ⦿ *No meals.*

$$ ⊤ **Zamas.** On wild Punta Piedra (Rock Point), Zamas has small, rustic
HOTEL   cabanas with palapas and ocean views as far as the eye can see; comfortable beds, tile bathrooms, and bright Mexican colors make them a chic-bohemian alternative for budget travelers. **Pros:** great restaurant; unspoiled views; on-site dive center; one of the least dense properties in Tulum. **Cons:** rocky beach; some traffic noise; tiny rooms; Wi-Fi in restaurant only. $ *Rooms from: $195* ✉ *Carretera Tulum–Boca Paila, Km 5, Zona Hotelera* ☎ *984/877–8523* ⊕ *www.zamas.com* ⤺ *20 cabanas, 1 house* ⦿ *No meals.*

NIGHTLIFE

Gitano. This trendy jungle bar boasts handcrafted cocktails, mezcals from Oaxaca, and cool beats that come compliments of a live DJ. Bring a loaded wallet as drinks are pricey but powerful. ■ **TIP➡ Night owls take note, this place shuts down around midnight.** ✉ *Boca Paila Rd, Km 7, jungle side, next to Hartwood, Zona Hotelera* ☎ *984/745–9068* ⊕ *www.gitanotulum.mx.*

La Zebra. Get your hips ready for "Salsa Sundays" at this beachfront hot spot, where you can hear live music and enjoy cocktails made with their own sugar cane. Brush up on your dance moves with free salsa lessons at 6 pm. ✉ *Carretera Tulum–Boca Paila, Km 8.2, Zona Hotelera* ☎ *303/800–1943, 984/115–4726* ⊕ *www.lazebratulum.com.*

Papaya Playa Project. Party people gather at this beachfront nightclub where DJs spin electronic and house music on Saturday nights. It's especially renowned for its monthly full moon parties. Papaya Playa Project doubles as a hotel, but most people come here to simply kick off their flip-flops and dance among the trees. ✉ *Carretera Tulum–Boca Paila, Km 4.5, Zona Hotelera* ☎ *984/116–3774* ⊕ *www.papayaplaya project.com.*

SPORTS AND THE OUTDOORS

BICYCLING

Punta Piedra Bike Rental. Daily bike rentals are the focus at this small shop—but don't be fooled by the name. It rents boogie boards (MX$67), scooters (MX$542), and snorkel gear (MX$135), too. The owner, Felix, can also organize two-hour snorkeling tours for MX$406. Cash only. ✉ *Carretera Tulum–Boca Paila, Km 4, Zona Hotelera* ☎ *984/157–4248 cell* ⤺ *Bikes MX$135 per day* ⊙ *Daily 7:30–6.*

KITEBOARDING

Mexican Caribbean Kitesurf & Paddlesurf. Located in front of the Ahau Tulum, this school gives lessons in kitesurfing and paddleboarding. Its popular stand-up paddleboard tours take you to a cenote, a reef, or a gorgeous lagoon in the Sian Ka'an Biosphere. ✉ *Carretera Tulum–Boca Paila, Km 7.5, Zona Hotelera* ☎ *984/168–1023* ⊕ *www.mexican caribbeankitesurf.com* ⤺ *Paddleboard lessons from MX$690, kitesurf lessons from MX$760, tours from MX$1106.*

COBÁ

42 km (26 miles) northwest of Tulum.

Near five lakes and between coastal watchtowers and inland cities, Cobá (pronounced ko-*bah*) once exercised economic control over the region through a network of at least 16 *sacbéob* (white-stone roads)—one, measuring 100 km (62 miles), is the longest in the Mayan world. The city covered 70 square km (27 square miles), making it a note-worthy sister to Tikal in northern Guatemala, with which it had close cultural and commercial ties. Cobá is noted for its massive temple-pyramids, including the largest and highest one in northern Yucatán (it stands 138 feet tall). Although often overlooked by visitors who opt for better-known Tulum, Cobá is less crowded, giving you a chance to immerse yourself in ancient culture.

4

GETTING HERE AND AROUND

Cobá is a 35-minute drive northwest of Tulum, along a road that leads straight through the jungle. Taxis from Tulum cost about MX$338. ADO (⊕ *www.ado.com.mx*) runs buses here from Playa del Carmen and Tulum at least three times a day: expect to pay about MX$95 between Cobá and Playa, MX$85 between Cobá and Tulum.

EXPLORING

Fodor'sChoice
★

Cobá Ruins. Mayan for "water stirred by the wind," Cobá flourished from AD 800 to 1100, with a population of as many as 55,000. Now it stands in solitude, and the jungle has overgrown many of its buildings—the silence is broken only by the occasional shriek of a spi-der monkey or the call of a bird. Most of the trails here are pleasantly shaded; processions of huge army ants cross the footpaths as the sun slips through openings between the tall hardwood trees, ferns, and giant palms. Cobá's ruins are spread out and best explored on a bike, which you can rent for MX$40 a day. Taxi-bike tours are available for MX$70. If you plan on walking instead, expect to cover 5 to 6 km (3 to 4 miles).

The main groupings of ruins are separated by several miles of dense vegetation, but you can scale one of the pyramids to get a sense of the city's immensity. ▪TIP➜ Don't be tempted by the narrow paths that lead into the jungle unless you have a qualified guide with you. It's easy to get lost here, so stay on the main road, wear comfortable shoes, and bring insect repellent and drinking water. Inside the site, there are no restrooms and only one small hut selling water (cash only).

The first major cluster of structures, to your right as you enter the ruins, is the **Cobá Group,** whose pyramids are around a sunken patio. At the near end of the group, facing a large plaza, is the 79-foot-high temple, which was dedicated to the rain god, Chaac. Some Maya still place offerings and light candles here in hopes of improving their harvests. Around the rear, to the left, is a restored ball court, where a sacred game was once played to petition the gods for rain, fertility, and other blessings.

Farther along the main path to your left is the **Chumuc Mul Group,** little of which has been excavated. The principal pyramid here is covered with the remains of vibrantly painted stucco motifs (*chumuc mul* means "stucco pyramid"). A kilometer (½ mile) past this site is the **Nohoch Mul Group** (Large Hill Group), the highlight of which is the pyramid of the same name, the tallest at Cobá. It has 120 steps—equivalent to 12 stories—and shares a plaza with Temple 10. The Descending God (also seen at Tulum) is depicted on a facade of the temple atop Nohoch Mul, from which the view is excellent.

Beyond the Nohoch Mul Group is the **Castillo,** with nine chambers that are reached by a stairway. To the south are the remains of a ball court, including the stone ring through which the ball was hurled. From the main route, follow the sign to **Las Pinturas Group,** named for the still-discernible polychrome friezes on the inner and outer walls of its large, patioed pyramid. An enormous stela here depicts a man standing with his feet on two prone captives. Take the minor path for 1 km (½ mile) to the **Macanxoc Group,** not far from the lake of the same name. The main pyramid at Macanxoc is accessible by a stairway. ✉ *42 km (26 miles) northwest of Tulum* 🎟 *MX$59* 🕓 *Daily 8–5.*

OFF THE BEATEN PATH

Pac Chen. This Maya jungle settlement is home to about 200 people who still live in round thatch huts and pray to the gods for good crops. **TIP→ You can only visit on trips organized by Alltournative, an eco-tour company based in Playa del Carmen. The "Cobá Maya Encounter" includes transportation, entrance to Cobá ruins, lunch, and Maya guides within Pac-Chen, which accepts no more than 120 visitors on any given day.** Alltournative pays the villagers a monthly stipend to protect the land; this money has made the village self-sustaining, and has given the inhabitants an alternative to logging and hunting, which were their main means of livelihood before.

The half-day tour starts with a trek through the jungle to a cenote where you grab onto a harness and zip-line to the other side. Next is the Jaguar Cenote, set deeper into the forest, where you must rappel down the cavelike sides into a cool underground lagoon. You'll eat lunch under an open-air palapa overlooking another lagoon, where canoes await. The food includes such Mayan dishes as grilled *achiote* (annatto seed) chicken, fresh tortillas, beans, and watermelon. ☎ *877/437–4990, 984/803–9999* 🌐 *www.alltournative.com* 🎟 *MX$1884.*

WHERE TO EAT

$$ MEXICAN

🍴 **Ki-Janal.** You can't get any closer to the ruins than this two-story restaurant. Adding color to the palapa setting are Mexican blankets draped over wooden tables. Some of the more traditional selections include fish prepared Yucatán-style, chicken in banana leaves, and cochinita pibil. You can also find soups, salads, and pastas. Plan to stay a while: Ki-Janal doesn't have the best service, but it's the only restaurant anywhere near Cobá. [$] *Average main: 160 MP* ✉ *To the right of the Cobá ruins entrance* 💳 *No credit cards* 🕓 *No dinner.*

WHERE TO STAY

$$ HOTEL

🏨 **La Selva Mariposa.** Halfway between Tulum's beaches and Cobá's ruins, this jungle sanctuary provides the perfect escape for travelers wanting the best of both worlds. **Pros:** owners live on site; peaceful retreat; delightful breakfast; bikes for exploring. **Cons:** two-night

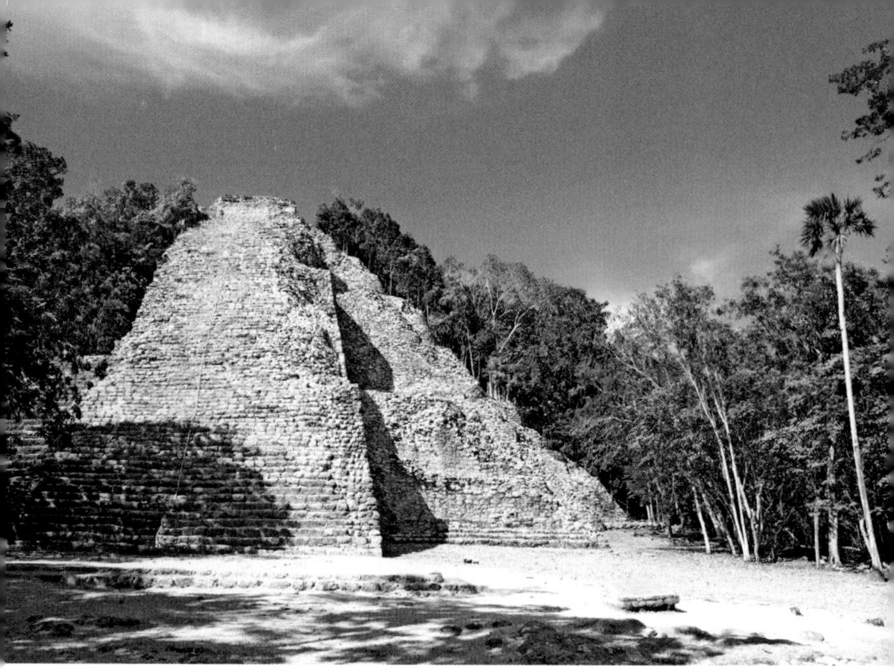

The ruins of Cobá are best explored by bike.

minimum stay; 20 minutes from beach; advance reservations required; not all rooms allow children. [$] *Rooms from: $175* ✉ *Carretera Tulum–Coba, Km 20, Macario Gomez* ✥ *On road to Cobá, turn right at Km 20 after first speed bump, just past the small store with "SOL" sign. Follow signs to hotel.* ☎ *1984/133–3695 (mobile), 1984/133–3696 (mobile)* 🌐 *www.laselvamariposa.com* 🛏 *4 rooms* 🍴 *Breakfast.*

RESERVA DE LA BIÓSFERA SIAN KA'AN

15 km (9 miles) south of Tulum to Punta Allen turnoff, 252 km (156 miles) north of Chetumal.

Wildlife has understandably been affected by the development of coastal resorts; however, thanks to the federal government's foresight, 1.3 million acres of coastline and jungle have been set aside for protection as the Reserva de la Biósfera Sian Ka'an. Whatever may happen elsewhere along the coast, this pristine wilderness preserve (Mexico's second-largest after the Reserva de la Biósfera Calakmul) remains a haven both for thousands of species of wildlife and for travelers who seek the Yucatán of old.

GETTING HERE AND AROUND

To explore on your own, follow the beach road past Boca Paila to the secluded 35-km (22-mile) coastal strip of land that's part of the reserve. You'll be limited to swimming, snorkeling, and camping on the beaches, as there are no trails into the surrounding jungle. The narrow, rough dirt roads down the peninsula are filled with monstrous potholes,

Caste Wars

When Mexico won independence from Spain in 1821, there wasn't much for Maya to celebrate. They continued to be treated as second-class, "lower-caste" citizens, just as they had under centuries of Spanish rule, and the new government refused to return confiscated lands. In Valladolid in 1847, the Maya rose up in a coordinated rebellion. Within a year, hundreds of Mexicans were dead, and the Caste War of the Yucatán was on.

Help for the embattled Mexicans arrived with a vengeance from Mexico City, Cuba, and the United States. By 1850 the tables had turned, and as many as 200,000 Maya—nearly half the population—were killed. Survivors fled to the jungles and held out for decades, until government troops finally withdrew in 1915. The Maya controlled Quintana Roo from Tulum, their headquarters, but were finally forced to accept Mexican rule in 1935.

completely impassable after a rainfall. In rainy season, don't attempt it without a four-wheel-drive vehicle.

The archaeological ruins at Muyil sit on the northwestern edge of Sian Ka'an, about 16 km (10 miles) south of Tulum on Carretera 307.

TOURS

Visit Sian Ka'an. Local guide Aldo Ancona offers various tours of Sian Ka'an, including bird-watching, fly-fishing, snorkeling, and wildlife excursions. The popular Nature Encounter Tour includes a boat trip into the lagoons of Boca Paila and Campechen in search of crocodiles, birds, and manatees. ⊠ *Coastal rd. Tulum–Boca Paila–Punta Allen, Km 15.8* ☎ *984/141–4245, 984/108–8853* ⊕ *www.visitsiankaan.com* 🖼 *From MX$1203.*

Sian Ka'an Visitor Center. The biosphere's visitor center is 9 km (6 miles) south of Tulum, just past the archway on the coastal road toward Boca Paila. Several kinds of tours, including bird-watching by boat and night kayaking to observe crocodiles, are offered on-site. A rickety observation tower offers the best view—just don't look down. ☎ *998/887–1969 for National Commission of Natural Protected Areas, 1984/141–4245 (mobile at Visitor Center), 1984/108–8853 (mobile at Visitor Center)* ⊕ *www.cesiak.org.*

EXPLORING

Muyil (*Chunyaxché*). This photogenic archaeological site at the northern end of the Sian Ka'an biosphere reserve is underrated. Once known as Chunyaxché, it's now called by its ancient name, Muyil (pronounced moo-*hill*). It dates from the late preclassic era, when it was connected by road to the sea and served as a port between Cobá and the Mayan centers in Belize and Guatemala. A 15-foot-wide *sacbé*, built during the postclassic period, extended from the city to the mangrove swamp and was still in use when the Spaniards arrived.

Structures were erected at 400-foot intervals along the white limestone road, almost all of them facing west, but there are only three still standing. At the beginning of the 20th century the ancient stones were used to build a *chicle* (gum arabic) plantation, which was managed by one of the leaders of the Caste Wars. The most notable site at Muyil today is the remains of the 56-foot **Castillo**—one of the tallest on the Quintana Roo coast—at the center of a large acropolis. During excavations of the Castillo, jade figurines representing the goddess Ixchel were found. Recent excavations at Muyil have uncovered some smaller structures.

The ruins stand near the edge of a deep-blue lagoon and are surrounded by almost impenetrable jungle—so be sure to bring insect repellent. You can drive down a dirt road on the side of the ruins to swim or fish in the lagoon. The bird-watching is also exceptional here; come at dawn, before the site officially opens (there's no gate) to make the most of it. ✉ *Carretera 307, 16 km (10 miles) south of Tulum* ⊕ *muyil.smv.org* 💲 *MX$50* 🕙 *Daily 8–5.*

FAMILY **Sian Ka'an.** One of the last undeveloped stretches of coastline in North
Fodor's Choice America, Sian Ka'an was declared a wildlife preserve in 1986, and a
★ UNESCO World Heritage Site in 1987. The 1.3-million-acre reserve accounts for 10% of the land in the state of Quintana Roo and spans 100 km (62 miles) of coastline. It's amazingly diverse, encompassing freshwater and coastal lagoons, mangrove swamps, cayes, savannas, tropical forests, and a barrier reef. Hundreds of species of local and migratory birds, fish, animals, and plants share the land with fewer than 1,000 Maya residents. The area was first settled by the Maya in the 5th century AD—the name Sian Ka'an translates to "where the sky is born." There are approximately 32 ruins (none excavated) linked by a unique canal system—one of the few of its kind in Mayan Mexico. There's a MX$29 entrance fee for the park, but to see much of anything, you should take a guided tour.

Many species of the once-flourishing wildlife have fallen into the endangered category, but the waters here still teem with roosterfish, bonefish, mojarra, snapper, shad, permit, sea bass, and crocodiles. Fishing the flats for wily bonefish is popular, and the peninsula's few lodges also run deep-sea fishing trips.

■ TIP➔ Most fishing lodges along the way close for the rainy season in August and September, and accommodations are hard to come by. The road ends at Punta Allen, a fishing village whose main catch is spiny lobster, which was becoming scarce until ecologists taught the local fishing cooperative how to build and lay special traps to conserve the species. There are several small, expensive guesthouses. If you haven't booked ahead, start out early in the morning so you can get back to civilization before dark. ✉ *Coastal Road Tulum–Boca Paila–Punta Allen, Km 15.8, just beyond the Arco Maya (arch entrance)* ☎ *998/887–1969, 983/834–0265* ⊕ *www.cesiak.org.*

WHERE TO STAY

$$$$ 🏨 **Boca Paila Fishing Lodge.** Home of the "grand slam" (fishing lingo
ALL-INCLUSIVE for catching three different kinds of fish in one trip), this charming lodge has nine bungalows, each with air-conditioning, two double beds,

couches, bathrooms, and screened-in porches. **Pros:** on beach; attentive staff; great fishing. **Cons:** not much to do besides fish; drinks not included; three-night minimum. $ *Rooms from: $718* ⊠ *Boca Paila Peninsula* ☎ *724/935–1577 in the U.S., 800/245–1950 for reservations (Frontiers management company), 998/185–3570* ⊕ *www.bocapaila. com* ↯ *9 bungalows* ⦿ *All-inclusive.*

$$$$
ALL-INCLUSIVE

🕾 **Casa Blanca Lodge.** This fishing lodge is on a rocky outcrop on remote Punta Pájaros Island, reputed to be one of the best places in the world for light-tackle saltwater fly-fishing. **Pros:** remote location; comfortable rooms; Mayan ruins on the island. **Cons:** one-week minimum stay; far from anywhere else; all-inclusive package doesn't cover drinks. $ *Rooms from: $659* ⊠ *Punta Pájaros* ☎ *724/935–1577 in the U.S., 800/245–1950 for reservations (Frontiers management company), 877/261–8867* ⊕ *www.casablancafishing.com* ↯ *10 rooms* ⦿ *All-inclusive.*

THE COSTA MAYA

The coastal area south of Sian Ka'an is more purely Maya than anything in the resort-rich coast north to Cancún. Fishing collectives and close-knit communities carry on ancient traditions here, and the proximity to Belize lends a Caribbean flavor, particularly in Chetumal, where you'll hear both Spanish and a Caribbean patois. Although cruise ships disgorge droves of passengers in Mahahual and resort development is creeping in, a multimillion-dollar government initiative is attempting to support ecotourism and sustainable development projects in the area.

FELIPE CARRILLO PUERTO

156 km (97 miles) north of Chetumal.

Felipe Carrillo Puerto, the Costa Maya's first major town, is named for the governor of Yucatán in 1920, who was hailed as a hero after instituting a series of reforms to help the impoverished *campesinos* (peasants). Midway between Tulum and the beaches of the Costa Maya, the town itself has very little to offer visitors; however, Chacchoben, a little-explored archaeological site, isn't far.

GETTING HERE AND AROUND

You guessed it—Carretera 307, known locally as Avenida Benito Juárez, runs right through the center of town. Just drive straight and you can't miss it. ADO (⊕ *www.ado.com.mx*) links Cancún, Puerto Morelos, Playa del Carmen, Tulum, Felipe Carrillo Puerto, Limones, and Chetumal by bus. Taxis drive up and down the street if you arrive without your own wheels. The tourist office is at the corner of Avenida Juárez and Avenida Santiago Pacheco Cruz. As you enter town, there's an HSBC bank with an ATM and a Pemex gas station (it's one of the few places to fuel up between here and Chetumal).

EXPLORING

Chacchoben. Excavated in 2005, Chacchoben (pronounced *cha*-cho-ben) is an ancient city that was a contemporary of Kohunlich and the most important trading partner with Guatemala north of the Bacalar Lagoon

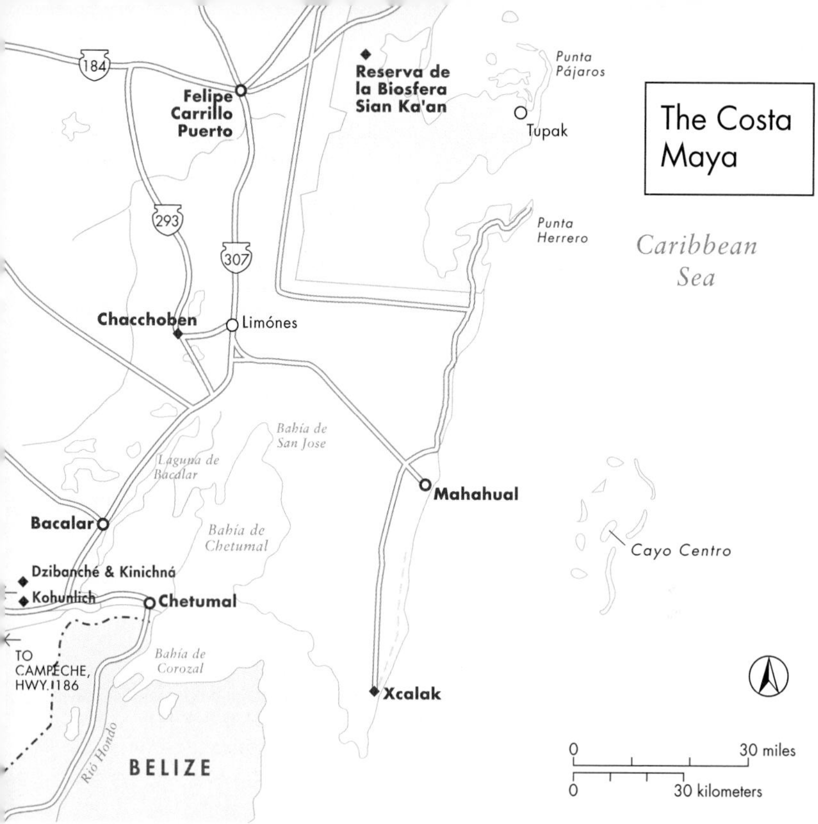

The Costa Maya
184
Felipe Carrillo Puerto
Reserva de la Biosfera Sian Ka'an
Punta Pájaros
Tupak
293
307
Punta Herrero
Caribbean Sea
Chacchoben
Limónes
Bahía de San Jose
Laguna de Bacalar
Mahahual
Bacalar
Bahía de Chetumal
Cayo Centro
Dzibanché & Kinichná
Kohunlich
Chetumal
TO CAMPECHE, HWY. 186
Bahía de Corozal
Xcalak
Río Hondo
BELIZE
0
30 miles
0
30 kilometers

area. Several newly unearthed buildings are still in good condition. The lofty **Templo Uno,** the site's main temple, was dedicated to the Mayan sun god Itzamná, and once held a royal tomb. (When archaeologists found it, though, it had already been looted.) Most of the site was built around AD 200, in the Petén style of the early classic period, although the city could have been inhabited as early as 200 BC. It's thought that inhabitants made their living growing cotton and extracting chewing gum and copal resin from the trees. ✣ *From Carretera 307, turn right on Carretera 293 south of Cafetal, continue 9 km (5½ miles) passing Lázaro Cardenas town* 🌐 *www.chacchobenruins.com* 🎫 *MX$48* 🕓 *Daily 8–5.*

WHERE TO STAY

$ HOTEL 🏨 **El Faisán y El Venado.** If you absolutely need a place to stay in the area, then this simple three-story hotel is really your only remotely acceptable option. **Pros:** best place to stay in town; central location; strong a/c. **Cons:** no-frills rooms; staff speak little English; Wi-Fi in common areas only. [$] *Rooms from: $44* ✉ *Av. Benito Juárez, Lote 781* ☎ *983/834–0702, 983/834–0043* 🛏 *37 rooms* 🍴 *No meals.*

BACALAR

40 km (25 miles) northwest of Chetumal.

Founded in AD 435, Bacalar (pronounced *baa*-ka-lar) is one of Quintana Roo's oldest settlements. The town's most notable feature is a cenote-fed lake of the same name—Laguna de Bacalar. The mix of freshwater and salt water that intensifies its color has earned this long, narrow body of water the nickname "Lago de los Siete Colores" (Lake of the Seven Colors). Marking the entrance to Bacalar is Cenote Azul, a crystalline cenote that's 300 feet deep and 600 feet across. The water is clean and the diving is excellent here.

GETTING HERE AND AROUND

Bacalar is 30 minutes north of Chetumal, just off Carretera 307. If you're coming from Cancún, follow the well-marked signs. Upon entering the town, you'll cross over two huge speed bumps. Pass the Catholic church on your right, take a left at the first corner, and continue straight to the town square (Bacalar has no bank, but there is an ATM on this square); to your left will be the Fort of San Felipe. Northbound drivers should take Carretera 106 to 307 and enter at Km 34, marked by a sign for "Cenote Azul." Just past the cenote is a paved road that parallels Laguna de Bacalar and eventually leads to the town center.

EXPLORING

Fuerte de San Felipe Bacalar (*San Felipe Fort*). This 17th-century stone fort was built by the Spaniards using stones from the nearby Mayan pyramids. It was originally constructed as a haven against pirates and marauding bandits, then was transformed into a Maya stronghold during the War of the Castes. Today the monolithic structure, which overlooks the enormous Laguna de Bacalar, houses government offices and a museum with exhibits on local history (ask for someone to bring a key if museum doors are locked). ☎ 983/832–6838 *for museum* 🖃 MX$67 ☉ *Tues.–Sun.* 9–7.

Laguna de Bacalar (*Lago de los Siete Colores*). Some 42 km (26 miles) long but no more than 2 km (1 mile) wide, Laguna de Bacalar is the town's focal point. The lake is renowned for both its vibrant green-and-blue waters and for the age-old limestone formations (stromatolites) that line its shores. Fed by underground cenotes, the mix of freshwater and saltwater here creates ideal conditions for a refreshing swim. Most hotels along Laguna de Bacalar rent kayaks and paddleboats; however, there are no beaches or amenities other than those found in rental properties or hotels. English-speaking guide Victor Rosales (☎ 983/733–6712 ⊕ *vkrosales.simdif.com*), who organizes custom excursions throughout the Costa Maya, offers a particularly fascinating tour of the lake's 3½-billion-year-old stromatolites. ⊠ *Bacalar Coastal Rd.*

WHERE TO EAT

$$$

SEAFOOD

✕ **Restaurant Cenote Azul.** Perched on the rim of the 300-foot-deep cenote, this palapa restaurant charges a MX$10 entrance fee to access the site. Busloads of tourists come to dine on chicken, pork, and fish dishes, as well as house specialties like the seafood platter and shrimp

The Laguna de Bacalar is known for its giant stromatolites—limestone formations that are estimated to be 3½ billion years old.

kebab. Although the setting surpasses food, it's still worth lingering over a meal while gazing out over the deep blue waters. After your food digests, enjoy a swim off the dock. There's also a souvenir shop popular with tour groups. $ *Average main: 203 MP* ⊠ *Carretera 307, Km 34* ☎ *983/834–2460* ☉ *Daily 9–6.*

WHERE TO STAY

$$$
B&B/INN
🛏 **Akalki** (*Centro Holistico Akalki*). Considered the most upscale property on Laguna de Bacalar, Akalki offers nine luxurious cabanas built over the water, each with a private dock and direct access to the enchanting turquoise waters. **Pros:** romantic setting; immaculate rooms; closest thing to a Bora Bora experience. **Cons:** rooms have electricity only at night; Wi-Fi in common areas only; no outlets in the rooms; tons of mosquitoes. $ *Rooms from: $258* ⊠ *Carretera 307, Km 12.5* ☎ *1983/106–1751 (mobile)* ⊕ *www.akalki.com* ⇗ *9 rooms* ⏍ *Multiple meal plans.*

$$
HOTEL
Fodor's Choice
★
🛏 **Rancho Encantado.** On the shores of Laguna Bacalar, Rancho Encantado's property is dotted with freestanding Mayan-theme casitas; each is uniquely decorated with murals and hammocks and can comfortably sleep four people. **Pros:** great location on lagoon; friendly staff; huge Jacuzzi; Wi-Fi in restaurant. **Cons:** some traffic noise; need car to get around; low water pressure; mosquitoes. $ *Rooms from: $200* ⊠ *Carretera 307, Km 24 (look for turnoff sign)* ☎ *998/884–2071, 877/229–2046* ⊕ *www.encantado.com* ⇗ *10 casitas, 6 suites* ⏍ *Breakfast.*

CHETUMAL

328 km (283 miles) southeast of Playa del Carmen.

At times, Chetumal—the capital city of Quintana Roo—feels more Caribbean than Mexican; this isn't surprising, given its proximity to Belize. A population that includes Afro-Caribbean and Middle Eastern immigrants creates a melting pot of music (reggae, salsa, calypso) and cuisines (Yucatecan, Mexican, Lebanese). Because this is the closest major community to Bacalar, Mahahual, and Xcalak, many residents from neighboring towns come here to do banking and stock up on supplies. Traffic can get very congested, but you will see very few tourists. Nevertheless, this small city has a number of parks on a waterfront that's as pleasant as it is long: the Bay of Chetumal surrounds the city on three sides. Tours will also take to the fascinating nearby ruins of Kohunlich, Dzibanché, and Kinichná, a trio dubbed the "Valley of the Masks."

GETTING HERE AND AROUND

Aeropuerto Internacional Chetumal (CTM), on the city's southwestern edge, has daily Interjet flights to and from Mexico City. Chetumal's main bus terminal, at Avenida Salvador Novo 179, is served mainly by ADO (⊕ *www.ado.com.mx*). The bus trip from Cancún takes 5 hours 45 minutes, with stops along the way in Puerto Morelos, Playa del Carmen, Tulum, Felipe Carrillo Puerto, and Limones; tickets costs MX$354. There's an ATM at the bus station. On Avenida Insurgentes, there's a bank and ATM in the center of the shopping mall. If you're driving here, be sure to fill up at the Pemex station in Felipe Carrillo Puerto, one of the few stations along this stretch of Carretera 307.

VISITOR INFORMATION

Contacts **Chetumal Tourist Information** ⊠ *Calles 28 de Enero and Reforma* ☎ *983/832–6647.*

EXPLORING

Dzibanché. The alliance between sister cities Dzibanché and Kinichná was thought to have made them the most powerful cities in southern Quintana Roo during the Mayan classic period (AD 100–1000). The fertile farmlands surrounding the ruins are still used today as they were hundreds of years ago, and the winding drive deep into the fields makes you feel as if you're coming upon something undiscovered. Archaeologists have been making progress in excavating more and more ruins, albeit slowly.

At Dzibanché ("place where they write on wood," pronounced zee-ban-*che*), several carved wooden lintels have been found; the most perfectly preserved sample is in a supporting arch at the **Plaza de Xibalba**. Also at the plaza is the **Templo del Búho** (Temple of the Owl), atop which a recessed tomb was discovered—only the second of its kind in Mexico (the first was at Palenque in Chiapas). In the tomb were magnificent clay vessels painted with white owls—messengers of the underworld gods. More buildings and three plazas have been restored as excavation continues. Several other plazas are surrounded by temples, palaces, and pyramids, all in the Petén style. The carved stone steps at **Edificio 13** and

Edificio 2 (Buildings 13 and 2) still bear traces of stone masks. A copy of the famed lintel of **Templo IV**, with eight glyphs dating from AD 618, is housed in the Museo de la Cultura Maya in Chetumal. (The original was replaced in 2003 because of deterioration.) Four more tombs were discovered at **Templo I**. ⊠ *Carretera 186 (Chetumal–Escárcega), 80 km (50 miles) west of Chetumal* ⊕ *Following Carretera 186, turn north at Km 58 and pass through town of Morocoy; continue 2 km (1 mile) farther, and turn right at the sign for Dzibanché. The entrance is 7 km (4½ miles) away.* ⊠ *MX$48 (includes Kinichná)* ⊙ *Daily 8–5.*

Kinichná. After you see Dzibanché, make your way back to the fork in the road and head to Kinichná ("House of the Sun," pronounced kin-itch-*na*). At the fork, you'll see the restored **Complejo Lamai** (Lamai Complex), the administrative buildings of Dzibanché. Kinichná consists of a two-level pyramidal mound split into Acropolis B and Acropolis C, apparently dedicated to the sun god. Two mounds at the foot of the pyramid suggest that the temple was a ceremonial site. Here a giant Olmec-style jade figure was found. At its summit, Kinichná affords one of the finest views of any archaeological site in the area. ⊠ *Carretera 186 (Chetumal–Escárcega), 80 km (50 miles) west of Chetumal* ⊕ *Following Carretera 186, turn north at Km 58 and pass through town of Morocoy; continue 2 km (1 mile) further, and turn right at the sign for Dzibanche. The entrance for both ruins is 7 Km (4½ miles) away. Pass Dzibanche, and veer left toward the hill where Kinichná is located.* ⊠ *MX$48 (includes Dzibanché)* ⊙ *Daily 8–5.*

Kohunlich. Kohunlich (pronounced *ko*-hoon-lich) is renowned for the giant stucco masks on its principal pyramid, the **Edificio de los Mascarones** (Mask Building). It also has one of Quintana Roo's oldest ball courts and the remains of a great drainage system at the **Plaza de las Estelas** (Plaza of the Stelae). Masks that are about 6 feet tall are set vertically into the wide staircases at the main pyramid, called **Edificio de las Estelas** (Building of the Stelae). First thought to represent the Mayan sun god, they're now considered to be composites of Kohunlich's rulers and important warriors. Another giant mask was discovered in 2001 in the building's upper staircase.

Kohunlich was built and occupied during the classic period by various Mayan groups. This explains the eclectic architecture, which includes the Petén and Río Bec styles. Although there are 14 buildings to visit, it's thought that there are at least 500 mounds on the site waiting to be excavated. Digs have turned up 29 individual and multiple burial sites inside a residence building called **Temple de Los Viente-Siete Escalones** (Temple of the Twenty-Seven Steps). This site doesn't have a great deal of tourist traffic, so it's surrounded by thriving flora and fauna. ⊠ *Off Carretera 186, 65 km (46 miles) west of Chetumal* ⊕ *Follow Carretera 186 west of Chetumal for 65 km (40 mi); continue another 9 km (5.5) south on side road to ruins.* ⊠ *MX$57* ⊙ *Daily 8–5.*

FAMILY **Museo de la Cultura Maya.** Dedicated to the complex world of the Maya, this interactive museum is outstanding. Exhibits in Spanish and English trace Mayan architecture, social classes, politics, and customs. The most impressive display is the three-story Sacred Ceiba Tree, a symbol used by the Maya to explain the relationship between the cosmos and the earth. The first floor represents the tree's roots and the Mayan underworld, Xibalba; the middle floor is the tree trunk, known as Middle World, home to humans and all their trappings; on the top floor, leaves and branches evoke the 13 heavens of the cosmic otherworld. ⊠ *Av. Héroes and Calle Mahatma Gandhi* ☎ *983/832–6838* 🖃 *MX$62* ⊗ *Tues.–Sun. 9–7.*

Oxtankah. The small ruins at Oxtankah are worth a visit if you're in the Chetumal area. Named for the Ramon trees ("ox" in Mayan) that populate the grounds, they're in a parklike setting and take about an hour to explore. The ruins include a Spanish mission, a pyramid, and several other structures. Archaeologists believe this city's prosperity peaked between AD 200 and 600. Maya groups returned to the area during the 15th and 16th centuries, using old stone to build new structures. There are toilets, free parking, and a tiny museum on site but no food or drink available, so come prepared. ⊠ *Calderitas, 16 km (10 miles) north of Chetumal* ✛ *Take Carretera Chetumal–Calderitas (Av. Héroes) north of town and continue on the paved road bordering the bay; 4.5 km (3 miles) to the north is the sign that marks access to the archaeological zone.* 🖃 *MX$43* ⊗ *Daily 8–5.*

BEACHES

Chetumal Bay. Several grassy beach parks, including Punta Estrella and Dos Mulas, surround the bay. The latter is presently not recommended due to maintenance and cleanliness issues. But Punta Estrella has parking, toilets, volleyball courts, and a small boat marina. The water here is calm, if cloudy, and there's plenty of shade from trees and little palapa-topped picnic tables. Popular with fishermen, the bay itself is shallow and the flats go on for miles. **Amenities:** food and drink; parking (no fee); toilets. **Best for:** walking.

WHERE TO EAT

$ ✕ **Restaurant Encuentro.** In addition to 12 kinds of coffee, this bright café
CAFÉ   serves fresh salads, pastas, sandwiches, and chicken dishes. Early risers can enjoy a house omelet stuffed with *chaya* (tree spinach), tomatoes, and salsa verde. It's a great place to quickly escape the busy streets outside. $ *Average main: 68 MP* ⊠ *Av. Alvaro Obregón 193* ☎ *983/833–3013* ⊗ *Closed Sun.*

$$$ ✕ **Sergio's Restaurant & Pizzas.** Locals rave about the grilled steaks and
PIZZA   garlic shrimp at Sergio's—one of the nicest restaurants in Chetumal. The barbecued chicken (made with the owner's special sauce) and smoked-oyster or seafood pizzas are equally tasty. When you order the delicious Caesar salad for two, a waiter prepares it at your table. This place also offers a huge breakfast menu plus a variety of lunchtime pasta dishes. You can order takeout or have food delivered, but the gracious staff and free Wi-Fi give you an added incentive to eat in. $ *Average main: 203 MP* ⊠ *Av. Alvaro Obregón 182, at Av. 5 de Mayo* ☎ *983/832–2991, 983/832–0882.*

WHERE TO STAY

$$$$

ALL-INCLUSIVE

Fodor'sChoice

★

The Explorean Kohunlich. Forty minutes outside Chetumal, at the edge of the Kohunlich ceremonial grounds, this ecological luxury resort lets you feel adventurous without really roughing it. **Pros:** attentive staff; excellent food; tours, meals and transportation included. **Cons:** expensive; no Internet; no children under 14. $ Rooms from: $400 ⊠ Carretera Chetumal–Escarega, Km 5.6, on road to ruins ☎ 55/5201–8350 in Mexico City, 877/397–5672, 800/343–7821 ⊕ www.theexplorean. com ⇨ 40 suites ⦿ All-inclusive.

$

HOTEL

Hotel Los Cocos. Large and modern by Chetumal's standards, Hotel Los Cocos has a pool framed by a pleasant garden (a boon on sweltering days) plus rooms that are clean, if not especially stylish; some have balconies or outside sitting areas. **Pros:** reasonable rates; strong water pressure; good location; free Wi-Fi in rooms. **Cons:** uncomfortable beds; loud a/c; staff speaks minimal English; no English-language TV channels. $ Rooms from: $76 ⊠ Av. Héroes 134, at Calle Chapultepec ☎ 983/835–0430 ⊕ www.hotelloscocos.com.mx ⇨ 134 rooms, 3 suites ⦿ No meals.

MAHAHUAL

143 km (89 miles) northwest of Chetumal via Carreteras 186 and 307.

Tiny Mahahual (also spelled Majahual) has something of a split personality. With a population of only 600, it's a quiet beachfront outpost with clear, calm waters, good snorkeling and diving, and not a whole lot to do. That's just the way its Mexican and expat U.S. and Canadian residents like it. When the cruise ships are in port, however, this sleepy spot gets a locally unwelcome shot in the arm. Passengers flood its waterside palapa restaurants, beach clubs, and the boardwalk fronting the town's few blocks; it's lively but can be overwhelming. That's when locals and savvy overnight visitors retreat to the handful of delightfully remote beachfront hotels and inns on Mahahual's outskirts, waiting out the crowds in a hammock, beach book in hand.

GETTING HERE AND AROUND

If you're coming by car, take Carretera 307 to Carretera 10, approximately 2½ km (1½ miles) past dusty little Limones (you can't miss the road; it's marked "Mahahual"). Continue for 50 km (30 miles) until you reach the coast; then turn right at the lighthouse and follow the road into town, where a string of hotels and restaurants line the beach. If you're staying at the Almaplena Beach Resort (halfway between Mahahual and Xcalak), turn right at the paved road toward Xcalak and continue for 16 km (10 miles) until you see a sign for Punta Herradura; turn left on this bumpy road and follow the signs to the resort. To reach the port area of New Mahahual, turn left at Km 55, just past the mayor's office.

Be advised that the beach road south of town is rough and potholed. After it rains driving here can be an adventure. If you're planning to drive south, check with locals for road conditions, and plan plenty of time.

A stay at the luxurious Almaplena Resort may be just what the doctor ordered if you are looking for a prescription for relaxation.

There's a taxi stand at the corner of Avenida Mahahual and Calle Rubic. A full day of transportation with a private driver can be arranged for around MX$1355. Otherwise, you can expect to pay around MX$10 per km (½ mile). Additional taxis are parked on the west side of the soccer field. Always ask to see a rate card before agreeing to a price.

BEACHES

The three cruise ships that stop here daily have made Mahahual's beach the liveliest place in town. Seaside restaurants dish out cerveza and ceviche, and several vendors offer boat tours and rental equipment like glass-bottom kayaks. The main beach in the center of town has fine sand and calm waters, great for swimming and snorkeling. Some hotel owners have opened beach clubs to cater to cruise passengers looking for a day (and a drink) in the sun.

BEACH CLUBS

Fodor's Choice ★ **Nacional Beach Club.** Many travelers stumble on this colorful beach club and end up staying past sunset. For just MX$135, you get a beach chair, umbrella, and access to the pool, showers, and changing facilities. Margaritas can be delivered to you beachside, or you can escape the heat by grabbing a bite in the enclosed patio. The MX$40 Coronas and free Wi-Fi make this a popular spot to while away the day. There's decent snorkeling right out front, and equipment is available next door at Gypsea Divers. Even if you don't get in the water, the four shades of turquoise are breathtaking. Movies are shown under the stars Wednesday at 6. There are also six bungalows (MX$950) for rent if you feel like staying the night. Cash only. **Amenities:** food and drink; showers; toilets. **Best for:** partiers; snorkeling; swimming. ⊠ *Av. Mahahual*

☎ *983/834–5719* 🌐 *www.nacionalbeachclub.com* 🎟 *MX$135* 🕒 *Daily 8–5.*

Nohoch Kay Beach Club. This beachfront restaurant on the boardwalk doubles as a beach club, offering an open bar, lunch, beach chairs, umbrellas, kayaks, and snorkeling gear for a flat MX$677 per person fee. There are restrooms, showers, and an on-site massage therapist ready to work her magic for MX$406 per half-hour. The restaurant cooks up ceviche, tacos, sandwiches, and nachos, but most people opt for the fresh fish served with tortillas and homemade tartar sauce. Between tanning sessions, you can head to the outer reef on a private catamaran for a snorkeling tour. Cruise passengers flock to this all-you-can-drink hotspot, so reserve ahead if you want to be part of the action. **Amenities:** food and drink; showers; toilets; water sports. **Best For:** partiers; snorkeling. ✉ *Malecón, between calles Liza and Cazón* ☎ *983/125–6610* 🎟 *MX$677.*

4

WHERE TO EAT

$$ MEXICAN

🍴 **100% Agave.** Fernando's friendly, homey restaurant—which serves as a sort of ersatz visitors bureau—seems to change locations often but remains a Mahahual institution. The affordable menu features Mexican and Yucatecan specialties with a generous splash of "gringo." Should you be in the market for a margarita, don't be shy; as suggested by the name, this is the place for expert guidance on all things agave. You can even buy a bottle of Fernando's homemade tequila to go. If the indoor party scene isn't lively enough for you, head to the outside tables, where cruise passengers are known to do shots. [$] *Average main: 135 MP* ✉ *Plaza Martillo, between Coronado and Martillo, north of the soccer field* ☎ *983/834–5609* 🕒 *Closed Mon.*

$ CAFÉ

🍴 **Cafe Karlita's.** The smell of fresh-baked goods wafts onto Mahahual's boardwalk from this central café. The towers of cookies, pastries, and muffins under glass domes make you forget caloric intake with the honest excuse, "I'm on vacation." For something lighter, opt for the bagel with salmon, a fruit smoothie, or organic tea. Karlita brews her own brand of coffee into cappuccinos, frappuccinos, and any other -inos you can think of. Open 8 to 8, this air-conditioned pink nook has free Wi-Fi plus $1-per-minute phone calls for cruise passengers wanting to call home. If you happen to fall in love during your travels, Karlita makes wedding cakes too. [$] *Average main: 40 MP* ✉ *Malecón, next to Port Captain office* ☎ *983/834–5709.*

$ INTERNATIONAL

🍴 **Ibiza Sunset.** It may be far from Ibiza, but this trendy beachfront spot hits the mark with food like garlic fish and vegetables wrapped in foil, pineapple stuffed with seafood, black pepper–crusted tuna, and chicken breast with panela cheese. The lunch menu is less gourmet but equally good (think tacos, fajitas, and whole fried fish). Martini and tapas options add an urban touch, as do sides like ginger-curry mashed potatoes. In true Ibiza style, you'll find leather couches and party music—the difference is the palapa roof and the fact you're in a remote location where time stands still. [$] *Average main: 125 MP* ✉ *Av. Principal, at end of the boardwalk, near Hotel Luna de Plata* ☎ *983/154–2293.*

WHERE TO STAY

$$ RESORT Fodor's Choice ★ **Almaplena Resort.** One of only two fully green eco-hotels in the area, Almaplena Resort also happens to be the most luxurious, with rustic-chic rooms featuring textiles from Chiapas, rugs from Michoacan, wood from Yucatán, and iron from Jalisco. **Pros:** spotless rooms; great snorkeling out front; stunning views from rooftop terrace. **Cons:** no TV; cash only; low water pressure; bland breakfast. [$] *Rooms from: $175* ✉ *Carretera Mahahual–Xcalak, Km 12.5* ☎ *1983/137–5070 cell* 🌐 *www.almaplenabeachresort.com* 🛏 *10 rooms* 💳 *No credit cards* 🍴 *Breakfast.*

$ HOTEL **Balamku.** Ecologically sensitive Balamku, located 5 km (3 miles) south of town, sits on a stretch of pristine private beach where you can lose all track of time. **Pros:** beachfront location; rooms remodeled in 2014; excellent breakfast; friendly owner. **Cons:** far from town; no air-conditioning; seagrass on rocky beach. [$] *Rooms from: $95* ✉ *Carretera Mahahual–Xcalak, Km 5.7* ☎ *983/732–1004* 🌐 *www.balamku.com* 🛏 *10 rooms* 🍴 *Breakfast.*

$ HOTEL **El Caballo Blanco.** Since El Caballo Blanco can be accessed only by walking along the beach, there isn't much standing in the way of you and the ocean. **Pros:** great views; rooftop bar and pool; fantastic restaurant. **Cons:** small bathrooms; back room lacks full ocean view; meals not included. [$] *Rooms from: $95* ✉ *Av. Mahahual, Mza 12, Lote 1* ☎ *983/126–0319* 🌐 *www.hotelelcaballoblanco.com* 🛏 *7 rooms* 🍴 *No meals.*

$ HOTEL **La Posada de los 40 Cañones.** Ocean breezes sweep through this hotel adorned with wicker-basket pendant lamps and queen-size beds that swing from ropes. **Pros:** reasonably priced; covered parking; comfortable beds; good restaurant. **Cons:** no pool; reservations require nonrefundable payment; not all rooms have ocean view. [$] *Rooms from: $70* ✉ *Calle Huachinango* ☎ *983/123–8591* 🌐 *www.40canones.com* 🛏 *26 rooms* 🍴 *No meals.*

$$ B&B/INN **Maya Luna.** Far from the boardwalk, this small inn on the beach is a quiet, relaxing place. **Pros:** beachfront location; nice restaurant open to the public; relaxed atmosphere. **Cons:** no a/c; 40-minute walk to town; Wi-Fi in common areas only. [$] *Rooms from: $120* ✉ *Carretera Mahahual–Xcalak, Km 5.2* ☎ *983/836–0905* 🌐 *www.hotelmayaluna.com* 🛏 *4 rooms* 🍴 *Breakfast.*

$$ B&B/INN Fodor's Choice ★ **Mayan Beach Garden.** There isn't another hotel for miles, so this solar-powered B&B offers blessed isolation. **Pros:** optional all-inclusive plan; custom tours available; huge movie and book library; free use of bikes, kayaks, paddle boards, and snorkels. **Cons:** minimum three-night stay in high season; bumpy dirt road means 30-minute drive to town; only two rooms have a/c; no kids under 12 during high season (Christmas to April). [$] *Rooms from: $140* ✉ *Carretera Mahahual–Punta Herrera, 20 km (12½ miles) north of Mahahual town* ☎ *983/130–8568, 206/905–9665 in the U.S.* 🌐 *www.mayanbeachgarden.com* 🛏 *2 cabanas, 5 rooms, 1 suite* 🍴 *Multiple meal plans.*

$ B&B/INN **Posada Pachamama.** This simple, charming hotel is just across the street from the beach on Mahahual's main boardwalk. **Pros:** central beachfront location; good rates; rooftop deck. **Cons:** no pool; tiny rooms; no meals; ground-floor rooms lack ocean views. $ *Rooms from: $90* ⊠ *Calle Huachinango s/n* ☎ *983/834–5762, 1983/134–3049 (mobile)* ⊕ *www.posadapachamama.net* ⌁ *10 rooms.*

SPORTS AND THE OUTDOORS

ADVENTURE TOURS

Native Choice. Ivan and David know all there is to know about Costa Maya sites like Chacchoben, Kohunlich, and Dzibanché. Aside from archaeology-themed outings, their company has tours that focus on adventure and contemporary Maya culture, too. ⊠ *Paseo del Puerto 1021, corner of Chinchorro, Nuevo Mahahual* ☎ *983/103–5955, 998/869–3346* ⊕ *www.thenativechoice.com* ⌁ *From MX$810.*

FISHING

Western Caribbean Fly Fishing School. Based out of Nohoch Kay Beach Club, this fly-fishing school offers trips to the Sian Ka'an biosphere, Xcalak, Chetumal Bay, or local cenotes in search of tarpon and snook. Fly-fishing instructor Nick Denbow leads beginners and experts through the fine arts of fly-tying and casting; he also customizes trips for individuals and groups. ⊠ *Nohoch Kay Beach Club, Malecón between calles Liza and Cazón* ☎ *1983/732–3144 (mobile)* ⊕ *www. westerncaribbeanflyfishing.com* ⌁ *From MX$2570.*

SCUBA DIVING AND SNORKELING

Dreamtime Dive Resort. This PADI resort has snorkeling tours plus an assortment of one- to three-tank dive trips managed by some of the most experienced divers in the area. It's one of the only operators licensed to organize trips to Banco Chinchorro. Rental gear is available. ⊠ *Av. Mahahual, Km 2.5, south of town* ☎ *983/124–0235, 904/669–2403 in the U.S.* ⊕ *www.dreamtimediving.com* ⌁ *Snorkeling tours MX$477, dives from MX$682.*

Gypsea Divers. Owners Catherine and Abel offer both dive trips and snorkeling tours. Group discounts are available. ⊠ *Av. Mahahual, next to Nacional Beach Club* ☎ *983/130–3714, 983/111–2563* ⊕ *www. gypseadivers.com* ⌁ *Dives from MX$813, snorkeling tours $M328.*

XCALAK

180 km (111 miles) southwest of Chetumal.

The southernmost town in Quintana Roo, Xcalak (pronounced *ish-ka-lack*) is only 11 km (7 miles) from the Belize border by water, and a little of both places is evident in local life. Spanish is still the primary language, although most people speak English, and you'll sometimes hear a Caribbean patois. Getting here is an adventure, but it's worth the effort. After all, this remote area offers excellent saltwater fly-fishing; flowers, birds, and butterflies are abundant; and the terrain is marked by savannas, marshes, streams, and island-dotted lagoons. You'll also find fabulously deserted beaches and a small town center comprised of bars, restaurants, and a few food shops.

The entire coast in this area is a designated National Marine Park, and all construction near Xcalak is bound by stringent environmental laws, which protect the natural beauty. By extension, electricity isn't

Mayan Beach Garden Inn

very dependable and tourist amenities are few; the community has no nightlife, and hotels (the majority of which close down during hurricane season) cater mostly to rugged outdoorsy types.

Since there are no standard phones here and cell service is very limited, visitors should plan on being out of touch, or doing as the locals do and keep connected via email or Skype. The lack of phone lines means no one accepts credit cards either; moreover, there are no banks or ATMs in or near Xcalak—the closest ATMs are 64 km (40 miles) north in Mahahual—so bring plenty of cash for your entire stay.

GETTING HERE AND AROUND

Following Carretera 10, turn right at the intersection 2 km (1 mile) before Mahahual and continue along the rough and tricky road until you reach Xcalak, about 61 km (37 miles) away. Pass the soccer field and turn left onto the bumpy beach road, now heading north toward "Zona Hotelera," a 14-km (9-mile) stretch of properties lining the beach. Your hotel will probably be within this main area. If you arrive in Xcalak without a car, don't rely on taxi service or local transportation. Consider staying close to town or in a hotel that offers bicycles. Note that this is a great launching point for day trips to Belize and for diving trips to Banco Chinchorro, a coral atoll and national park some two hours northeast by boat. ■ TIP➔ On a map, the 55 km (34 miles) of bay separating Chetumal from Xcalak looks like an easy boat trip. Unfortunately, shallow sections of the bay make it impassable.

SAFETY

Make sure you have a full tank before you drive south. Although there is a Pemex gas station in Mahahual, it is sometimes closed for no apparent reason. Unlike the trafficked roads along Riviera Maya, the two-lane stretch near Belize is seldom visited by tourists. It's always best to travel with a partner and to drive during daylight hours. Drive with caution and be careful of wild animals and potholes. Once you leave the paved road and enter Xcalak, the road goes from bad to worse. Be sure to rent a car that can handle pitted dirt roads.

Xcalak's growing expat community includes several nurses, who are always willing to help if health issues arise. There's a small clinic in the center of town; however, the "medic" (not always a doctor) is seldom around. Usually, a local can point you in the right direction for rudimentary first aid until you can reach the nearest staffed clinic in Bacalar. The closest small hospital (Carranza Clinic) is in Chetumal.

BEACHES

Playa Xcalak. This remarkably tranquil strand stretches for miles, and the isolated location means you might have it all to yourself. Much of the white sand has been eaten away by past hurricanes, narrowing the beach and making strolling a chore; however, the waters are pristine and placid. As a result, this is one of the area's best spots for swimming or kayaking. Sections of the beach connect to a network of protected mangroves frequented by manatees. Moreover, the offshore reef of nearby Banco Chinchorro is great for snorkeling, diving, and fishing. **Amenities:** food and drink. **Best for:** snorkeling; swimming.

WHERE TO EAT

$$$
SEAFOOD
Fodor's Choice
★

✕ **The Leaky Palapa.** Nobody expected the kind of sophisticated flavors that the Leaky Palapa brought to town, but this little 11-table palapa restaurant done up in twinkling lights has quickly become *the* place to meet, enjoy a beer, and eat like kings. Feast on lobster bisque or seared shrimp on bean cakes with tamarind salsa. Although homemade pasta isn't the first thing that comes to mind when you think tropical beach, the ravioli with corn truffle will convince you. Canadian owners Linda and Marla believe in using local ingredients as much as possible, so the menu changes weekly, depending on what fishermen bring to the dock. Hours (and months) vary—check the website before arrival. $ *Average main: 203 MP* ⊠ *Calle Pedro Moreno, just past the lighthouse, in the big red house on the left* ⊕ *www.leakypalaparestaurant.com* ⊟ *No credit cards* ⊘ *Closed Mon–Thurs., and Sept. and Oct. No lunch.*

$$
EUROPEAN

✕ **The Mayan Grill.** Unlike most restaurants in Xcalak, this beachside eatery is open daily for breakfast, lunch, and dinner. Start the morning with a ham and cheese "O'Mayalete" (omelet) served with beans and potatoes. The child-friendly lunch menu offers everything from tacos and nachos to hotdogs and quesadillas. For something a bit more gourmet, drop by at night for delectable dishes like fresh lobster, shrimp brochettes, or chicken stuffed with poblano and cheese. Dinner prices include an appetizer, soup, entrée, and dessert. The open-air palapa, right on the water's edge, is a great place to spend the day. $ *Average main: 162 MP* ⊠ *Hotel Tierra Maya, 3 km (2 miles) past the soccer* *field on the beach road* ☎ *330/735–3072* 🌐 *www.tierramaya.net* 💳 *No credit cards.*

$ MEXICAN 🍴 **Toby's.** Near the entrance to Xcalak, this modest Mexican restaurant is made up of a few plastic tables and chairs. Stop by for Toby's famous fajitas, fried fish, coconut shrimp, and chicken quesadillas. The place comes alive on Monday night, when locals gather for the daily special and live music. This is one of the few spots in town where Wi-Fi is available (free with food). [$] *Average main: 108 MP* ✉ *Leona Vicario s/n, across from parking lot and volleyball court* ☎ *1983/107–5426 (mobile)* 💳 *No credit cards* ⏲ *Closed Sun.*

WHERE TO STAY

$$ B&B/INN 🏨 **Casa Carolina.** This small hotel is a wonderful place to stay if you want to dive, snorkel, kayak, fly-fish, or just relax in one of the hammocks. **Pros:** on a nice beach; private fishing dock; kayaks and bikes available; renovations in 2014. **Cons:** no restaurant; no a/c. [$] *Rooms from: $120* ✉ *Carretera Majahual–Xcalak, Km 48* ✣ *Beach road, 2 km (1 mile) north of Xcalak town* ☎ *678/630–7080 in the U.S.* 🌐 *www.casacarolina.net* 🛏 *4 rooms* 💳 *No credit cards* 🍽 *Breakfast.*

$ B&B/INN Fodor's Choice ★ 🏨 **Sin Duda Villas.** Poised on a lovely beach, this property has several types of accommodations, all adorned with Mexican pottery and other collectibles. **Pros:** solar-powered; all rooms have Wi-Fi; world-class snorkeling; credit cards accepted via PayPal. **Cons:** getting here isn't easy; no restaurant. [$] *Rooms from: $90* ✉ *Xcalak Peninsula, 60 km (33 miles) south of Majahual, 5½ km (4 miles) north of Costa de Cocos* ☎ *306/500–3240 in U.S.* 🌐 *www.sindudavillas.com* 🛏 *3 rooms, 1 studio, 2 apartments* 🍽 *Breakfast.*

SPORTS AND THE OUTDOORS

FISHING

Costa de Cocos. Xcalak's only full-service fishing resort offers half- and full-day fly-fishing trips plus all-inclusive, multinight packages. Scuba diving is also available. ✣ *Head north on beach road, through Xcalak town, past the lighthouse and pier; turn left at two-story white building (Captain's Office) and then right at next street. Cocos is less than 1 km (½ mile) north of the bridge.* 🌐 *www.costadecocos.com* 🎟 *Fly-fishing from MX$2438, diving from MX$697.*

SCUBA DIVING AND SNORKELING

XTC Dive Center. This is the town's sole full-service dive shop and one of the few outfits licensed to take passengers to Chinchorro. In addition to recreational diving, it provides DAN and PADI instruction; fly-fishing, snorkeling, and boat excursions to Belize can also be arranged. Serious divers might be interested in renting one of the basic rooms attached to the property. Cash only. ✉ *Camino Costero Mahahual–Xcalak, Km 54, 650 ft. north of the main bridge in Xcalak* ☎ *1983/120–5804 (mobile)* 🌐 *www.xtcdivecenter.com* 🎟 *Dives from MX$820.*

COZUMEL

WELCOME TO COZUMEL

TOP REASONS TO GO

★ **Diving the Great Mayan Reef:** Tropical fish, coral, and other marine creatures enliven the 1,000-km-long (621-mile-long) Mesoamerican Barrier Reef, which stretches from Cozumel to Central America.

★ **Slowing down:** Stroll along a white-sand beach, then explore the gardens above and below the waters at Chankanaab. Or just grab a table at a sidewalk café and watch the world go by.

★ **Savoring local life:** San Miguel's Plaza Central is a Sunday-evening hot spot for locals who gather for music and dancing. On any major holiday you'll see parades, processions, and food stands with seasonal treats.

★ **Visiting Mayan sites:** Take a refresher course on Mayan culture past and present at the Museo de la Isla de Cozumel, then explore the temples dedicated to Ixchel, the Mayan goddess of childbirth, fertility, and healing, at San Gervasio.

1 The Northwest Coast. Broad beaches and the island's only golf course occupy the quiet northwest tip of Cozumel. The sand sometimes gives way to limestone shelves jutting over the water. Dive operations regularly visit this area to coincide with the annual eagle ray migrations.

2 San Miguel. Though cruise ships loom over the piers during the day and souvenir shops line the streets, Cozumel's only town still retains some of the flavor of a Mexican village. On weekend nights, musicians and food vendors gather in the main square and attract lively crowds.

3 The Southwestern Beaches. Proximity to Cozumel's best reefs makes the beaches south of San Miguel a prime destination for divers and snorkelers. An inviting string of hotels, beach clubs, commercial piers, and dive shops line the shore here.

4 The Southern Nature Parks. Cozumel's natural treasures are protected both above and below the sea. At Punta Sur, mangrove lagoons and beaches shelter nesting sea turtles. Chankanaab, one of Mexico's first marine parks, is superb for snorkeling.

5 The Windward Coast. The rough surf of the Caribbean pounds against the limestone shore here, creating pocket-size beaches that seem tailor-made for solitary sunbathing. The water can be rough, though, so pay attention to tides, currents, and sudden drop-offs in the ocean floor.

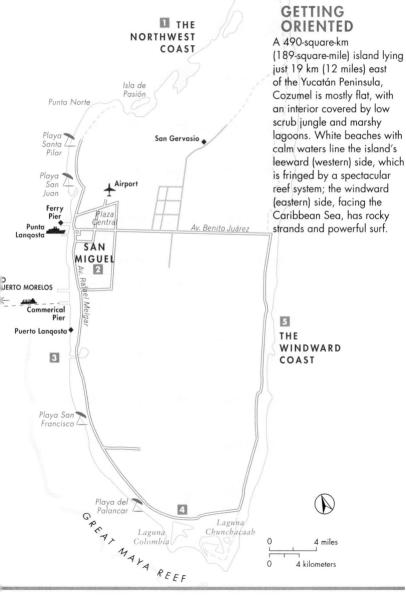

Punta Molas

GETTING ORIENTED

A 490-square-km (189-square-mile) island lying just 19 km (12 miles) east of the Yucatán Peninsula, Cozumel is mostly flat, with an interior covered by low scrub jungle and marshy lagoons. White beaches with calm waters line the island's leeward (western) side, which is fringed by a spectacular reef system; the windward (eastern) side, facing the Caribbean Sea, has rocky strands and powerful surf.

1 THE NORTHWEST COAST

Isla de Pasión

Punta Norte

Playa Santa Pilar

San Gervasio ◆

Playa San Juan

✈ Airport

Ferry Pier

Punta Lanqosta

Plaza Central

SAN MIGUEL 2

Av. Rafael Melgar

Av. Benito Juárez

UERTO MORELOS

Commerical Pier

Puerto Lanqosta ◆

3

5 THE WINDWARD COAST

Playa San Francisco

Playa del Palancar

4

Laguna Colombia

Laguna Chunchacaab

GREAT MAYA REEF

| 0 | | 4 miles |
| 0 | | 4 kilometers |

5

Updated by Mark S. Lindsey

It's not another Cancún yet, but Cozumel's days as a rustic divers' hangout are history. Whether arriving at the airport or the gleaming ferry terminal, visitors soon realize there's nothing deserted about this island.

That has its advantages. It's rare to find such stunning natural beauty, crystal-clear aquamarine seas, and vast marine life combined with top-flight visitor services and accommodations. As a result, Cozumel's devotees are legion. Divers sharing stories of lionfish and sharks sit table-to-table with families tanned from a day at the beach club, while Mexican couples spin and step to salsa music in the central plaza. But the elephant in Cozumel's big and bountiful room is the throngs of cruise-ship passengers who take over the countless craft and jewelry stores along the seaward boulevard downtown any day there are ships in port—which is to say, just about every day except Sunday. But take just a few steps off the beaten path and you'll soon see that the country's third-largest island offers big rewards. Windswept beaches, wild and vibrant natural parks, and miles of coral reef are still yours for the discovering.

Irregularly shaped, Cozumel is, at most, 48 km (30 miles) long and 15 km (9 miles) wide. Plaza Central, or just "El Centro," is the heart of San Miguel, directly across from the ferry docks that serve Playa del Carmen. Residents congregate here in the evening, especially on weekends, when free concerts begin at 8 pm. Heading inland (east) takes you away from the tourist zone and toward residential areas of town. Most of the island's restaurants, hotels, stores, and dive shops are concentrated downtown and along the two hotel zones that fan out on the leeward coast to the north and south of San Miguel. Cozumel's solitude-seeking windward side has a few beach-bar restaurants, one hotel, and miles of deserted beaches.

PLANNING

WHEN TO GO

When choosing vacation dates, keep in mind that the weather here is more extreme than you might expect on a tropical island.

High season extends from December until mid-April, with prices spiking around Christmas and Easter. Spring, being warm and dry, has the optimal conditions. If you're coming in winter, *nortes* (north winds) occasionally blow through, churning the sea and lowering temperatures, so pack a shawl or jacket for the comparatively chilly 18°C (65°F) evenings. Note that the windward side is calmer in winter than the leeward one, and the interior is warmer than the coast.

June through October is the rainy season. Summer is generally hot and humid. But crowds disperse and prices drop in the low season—and, if you're a diver, warm water and the year's-best visibility might be enough to induce you to brave the heat. Mid-April through May is the sweet spot. With a lull in tourist business and the fine weather that precedes the rainy season, late spring might be your all-around best bet. November is another good option, provided you avoid Thanksgiving weekend.

GETTING HERE AND AROUND

AIR TRAVEL

A few national and international flights land at the Aeropuerto Internacional de Cozumel (CZM), 3 km (2 miles) north of San Miguel, but flights to Cancún are usually less expensive. A small airline called Mayair offers comfortable twin turbo-prop service between Cancún and Cozumel; one-way flights start at about MX$905, and luggage is limited to 20 kg (44 pounds) per passenger. A budget alternative is to take a bus from the Cancún airport to Playa del Carmen and then the ferry to Cozumel. If everything runs on schedule, the trip should cost less than MX$350 and take about three hours.

The Cozumel airport is less than 10 minutes from downtown. On arrival, take a *colectivo* (a van seating up to eight) to your hotel; fares range from MX$100 to MX$350 per person depending on where you're going.

Contacts Mayair. ✉ *Cozumel Airport, Blvd. Aeropuerto at Av. 65* ☎ *987/872–3609* ⊕ *www.mayair.com.mx.*

BOAT AND FERRY TRAVEL

Passenger-only ferries bound for Cozumel leave Playa del Carmen's dock about every other hour on the hour, from 6 am to 11 pm. On the return trip, they leave Cozumel's main pier approximately every other hour from 5 am to 10 pm. The crossing takes 45 minutes and costs about MX$210 each way. The number of trips per day varies by season, so be sure to check ferry websites for times. The lone car ferry leaves from Calica; it charges MX$500 per vehicle and MX$71 for each person after the driver.

Contacts Car ferry from Calica ☎ *987/872–7688* ⊕ *www.transcaribe.net/default.cfm.* **Mexico Waterjets** ☎ *984/879–3112* ⊕ *www.mexicowaterjets.com.* **Ultramar.** ☎ *998/881–5890* ⊕ *www.granpuerto.com.mx.*

BUS TRAVEL

Bus service on Cozumel is basically limited to San Miguel's residential areas and mostly used by locals, so you'll need a rental car or taxi to explore. Though it's tempting to drive on Cozumel's dirt roads (which lead to the least crowded beaches), most car-rental companies have a policy that voids your insurance once you leave the paved roadway.

CAR TRAVEL

If you want to explore Cozumel (particularly the eastern side) at your own pace, you can rent a car. Fuel is available at any of the four government-owned Pemex stations around the island. *(⇨ Check out our Travel Smart chapter for rules of the road and information on rental car agencies if you plan on driving.)*

MOPED TRAVEL

Mopeds are popular, but heavy traffic, potholes, and hidden stop signs make them a risky option. Mexican law requires all riders to wear helmets (it's a MX$350 fine if you don't). If you do decide to rent a moped, drive slowly, check for oncoming traffic, and don't ride when it's raining or you've been drinking. Mopeds rent for about MX$495 per day or MX$285 for a half day, including insurance. A small rental car is almost the same price and significantly safer.

Contacts Ernesto's Rental ⊠ *Carretera Costera Sur, Km 4* ☎ *1987/871–1223 cell* ⊕ *www.ernestosrental.com.*

TAXI TRAVEL

Cabs wait at all the major hotels, and you can hail them on the street. The fixed rates run about MX$45–MX$70 within town; MX$70–MX$125 between town and the north hotel zone; MX$115–MX$350 between town and the south hotel zone; MX$140–MX$425 from most hotels to the airport; and MX$210–MX$350 from the northern hotels or town to Parque Chankanaab or Playa San Francisco. The cost from the Puerta Maya cruise-ship terminal by El Cid La Ceiba to San Miguel is about MX$140.

HOTELS

Small, one-of-a-kind hotels have long been the norm in Cozumel. Most of the island's accommodations are on the leeward (western) and south sides of the island, but there's one peaceful hideaway on the windward (eastern) side. The larger resorts are north and south of San Miguel, while the less expensive places are found in town. Cozumel also has a growing condo rental market. Rates are competitive, and condos are easily found via any of the numerous vacation rental websites.

Hotel reviews have been condensed, for full reviews, see Fodors.com.

RESTAURANTS

Dining options on Cozumel reflect the island's laid-back attitude: breezy and relaxed, with casual dress and no reservations the rule at most places. Generally, restaurants emphasize fresh ingredients, simple presentation, and amiable service. As befits an island, there's lots of just-caught seafood on the menu. Yucatecan cuisine is harder to come by; you're more likely to find standard Mexican fare like tacos, enchiladas, and huevos rancheros. For budget meals, head into the untouristed part of downtown, because they're few and far between elsewhere. Although some restaurants are turning out creative cuisine to suit the most demanding of palates, most visitors say their best dining experiences are in little family-owned spots that seem to have been here forever. While many restaurants accept credit cards, café-type places generally don't. ■TIP→ Cab drivers are often paid to shill for restaurants, so take their dining suggestions with a grain (or two) of salt.

DINING AND LODGING PRICES IN DOLLARS AND PESOS			
	$	$$	$$$	$$$$
Restaurants	under MX$135	MX$135–MX$200	MX$201–MX$350	over MX$350
Hotels in dollars	under $100	$100–$200	$201–$300	over $300
Hotels in pesos	under MX$1450	MX$1450–MX$2900	MX$2901–MX$4400	over MX$4400

Restaurant prices are the average price for a main course at dinner, or if dinner is not served at lunch. Hotel prices are for a standard double room in high season, including taxes.

BANKS AND CURRENCY EXCHANGE

San Miguel is dotted with bank offices, and ATMs are abundant—including a few that dispense U.S. dollars; some major hotels and resorts along the northern and southern hotel zones also have ATMs on site. However, it's best to stick with bank-affiliated machines and withdraw only pesos since independent ones offering U.S. dollars charge exorbitant fees. If you'd prefer to pay by credit card, ask first as not all businesses accept them.

SAFETY

Cozumel is very safe; the most trouble you're likely to get in has four wheels and a motor (drive carefully). If you plan to try water sports, make sure that your health or travel insurance has a sports rider.

TOURS

Tours of the island's sights, including the San Gervasio ruins, El Cedral, Parque Chankanaab, and the Museo de la Isla de Cozumel, cost about MX$710 per person and can be arranged through travel agencies; most larger hotels have an on-site agency or tour operator. Another option is to take a private tour of the island via taxi, which costs about MX$1130 for a half day.

VISITOR INFORMATION

The website ⊕ *www.thisiscozumel.com* has up-to-date news items and info on all things Cozumel. The site ⊕ *www.cozumelmycozumel.com*, edited by full-time island residents, has insider tips on activities, sights, and places to stay and eat. There's also a bulletin board where you can post questions.

Contacts **Cozumel Tourist Information Office** ⊠ *Plaza del Sol, Calle 2 Norte No. 299-B* ☎ *987/872–7585* ⊕ *www.cozumel.travel.*

EXPLORING COZUMEL

Unless you want to stick around your hotel or downtown San Miguel for your whole stay, you'll do well to rent a car. Most worthwhile sites, such as the island's Mayan ruins and pristine windward beaches, are readily accessible only with wheels. Taxi fares can be astronomical, and after just a few trips a rental car is clearly a better deal.

San Miguel is Cozumel's only town. Wait until the cruise ships sail toward the horizon before strolling the *malecón,* or boardwalk. The waterfront has been taken over by large shops selling jewelry, imported rugs, leather boots, and souvenirs to cruise-ship passengers, but the northern end of the malecón, past Calle 10 Norte, is a pleasant area lined with sculptures of Mayan gods and goddesses that draws more locals than tourists. The town feels increasingly traditional as you head inland to the pedestrian streets around the plaza, where family-owned restaurants and shops cater to residents and savvy travelers.

San Miguel's heart is the plaza, where families gather Sunday nights to stroll, snack, and dance to live music around the central *kiosko,* or bandstand. There are plenty of benches for watching the action. Facing the square is an artisan's market, a good stop for souvenirs. Renovated in late 2014, the plaza has lost some of its rustic charm but remains a place to see and be seen.

TOP ATTRACTIONS

FAMILY **Cozumel Pearl Farm.** Poised on a private northern beach and surrounded
Fodor's Choice by turquoise waters, this place raises Caribbean pearl oysters. Con-
★ ceived as a research and development project, the rustic Cozumel Pearl Farm opened in 2012. Groups of up to 12 people per day can learn how to grow a pearl, as well as snorkel and relax on the white sand beach. Accessible only by boat, the farm will make you feel like a castaway on a desert island during the six-hour experience, which runs from 10 am to 4 pm. Transportation (from San Miguel Pier or other meeting point), gear, lunch, beer, and soft drinks are included in the price. ⊠ *Punta Norte* ☎ *987/119–9417, 984/114–9604 in the U.S.* ⊕ *www. cozumelpearlfarm.com* ☒ *MX$1320.*

FAMILY **Museo de la Isla de Cozumel.** Filling two floors of a former hotel, Cozumel's museum has displays on natural history—the island's origins, endangered species, topography, and coral-reef ecology—as well as human history during the pre-Columbian and colonial periods. The photos of the island's transformation over the 20th and 21st centuries are especially fascinating, as is the exhibit of a typical Mayan home. Guided tours are available. ⊠ *Av. Rafael E. Melgar, between calles 4 and 6 Norte* ☎ *987/872–1475* ⊕ *www.cozumelparks.com/esp/museo_isla. cfm* ☒ *MX$54* ☉ *Mon.–Sat. 9–5, Sun 9–4.*

QUICK
BITES

✕ **Restaurante del Museo.** On the terrace off the second floor of the Museo de la Isla de Cozumel, the Restaurante del Museo serves breakfast, lunch, and dinner from 7 am to 11 pm. The Mexican fare is enhanced by a great waterfront view, and the café is popular with locals as well as

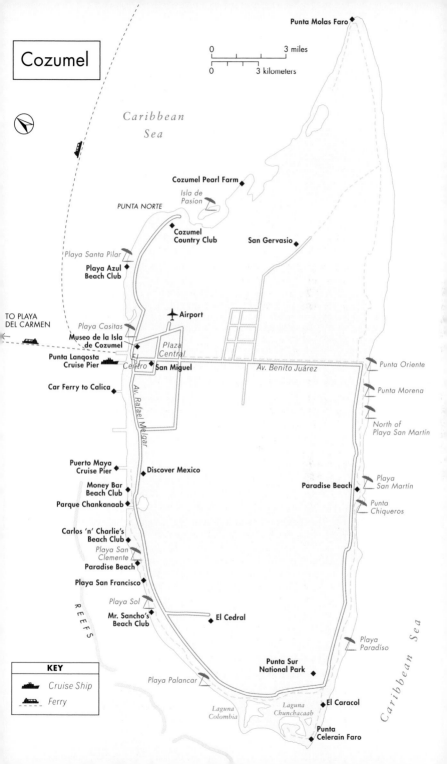

Cozumel is a favorite cruise-ship destination.

tourists. ⊠ *Museo de la Isla de Cozumel, Av. Rafael E. Melgar, between calles 4 and 6 Norte* ☎ *987/120-2255.*

FAMILY **Parque Chankanaab.** The National Park of Chankanaab, translated as "small sea," consists of a saltwater lagoon, an archaeological park, and a botanical garden, with reproductions of a Mayan village and Olmec, Toltec, Aztec, and Mayan stone carvings scattered throughout. You can swim at the beach, plus there's plenty for snorkelers and divers to see beneath the surface—picture underwater caverns, a sunken ship, crusty old cannons and anchors, and a sculpture of La Virgen del Mar (Virgin of the Sea), all populated by parrotfish and sergeant majors galore. To preserve the ecosystem, rules forbid touching the reef or feeding the fish. You'll find dive shops, restaurants, gift shops, a snack stand, and dressing rooms with lockers and showers right on the sand. Parque Chankanaab also has a Dolphin Discovery facility where true *Flipper* fans can swim with the much-loved marine mammals (⊕ *www.dolphindiscovery. com*). ⊠ *Carretera Sur, Km 9* ☎ *987/872-0093* ⊕ *www.cozumelparks. com/eng/chankanaab.cfm* 📷 *MX$286* ⊙ *Daily 8–4.*

Punta Molas Faro (*Molas Point Lighthouse*). The lighthouse at Cozumel's northernmost point is a solitary, beautiful sight. The rutted road to Punta Molas is open for four-wheel-drive vehicles and dune buggies only, but the scenery is awe-inspiring no matter how far you're able to go. Some dive boats travel out this way, providing a photo op from the sea.

San Gervasio. Rising from the jungle, these temples make up Cozumel's largest remaining Mayan and Toltec site. San Gervasio was the island's capital and ceremonial center, dedicated to the fertility goddess Ixchel.

The classic- and postclassic-style buildings and temples were continuously occupied from AD 300 to 1500. Typical architectural features include limestone plazas and arches atop stepped platforms, as well as stelae and bas-reliefs. Be sure to see the temple "Las Manitas," with red handprints all over its altar. ■TIP→ Plaques in Mayan, Spanish, and English clearly describe each structure, but it's worth hiring a guide to fully appreciate the site. ⊠ *Benito Juarez Transversal Rd., Km 7.5* ✥ *From San Miguel, take cross-island road east to San Gervasio access road; turn left and follow road 7 km (4½ miles)* ☎ *987/872–0093* ⊕ *www.cozumelparks.com/eng/san_gervasio.cfm* ⊠ *MX$129* ⊙ *Daily 8–3:45.*

WORTH NOTING

FAMILY **Discover Mexico.** Want to see all of Mexico while staying on the island? This theme park purports to show you the country's archaeological sites, important architectural landmarks, and cultures, without leaving Cozumel. The scale models of temples, pyramids, monasteries, and more have kitsch value, but a slickly produced film about the country and high-quality folk art exhibits begin to touch on the real thing. An outdoor café serves tasty fruit sorbets and light meals; you can also reserve in advance for the daily tequila tasting. ■TIP→ The gift shop has an array of beautiful Mexican folk art for sale. ⊠ *Carretera Sur, Km 5.5* ☎ *987/875–2820* ⊕ *www.discovermexico.org* ⊠ *MX$272* ⊙ *Mon.–Sat. 8–4.*

El Cedral. Spanish explorers discovered this site—once the hub of Mayan life on Cozumel—in 1518, and in 1847 it became the island's first official city. Today it's a farming community with small, well-tended houses and gardens. Conquistadores tore down much of the Mayan temple, so there's little in the way of actual ruins apart from one small stone arch; if you're in the market for souvenirs, however, vendors around the main plaza display embroidered blouses and hammocks. ⊠ *Off Carretera Sur* ✥ *Turn at Km 17.5 off Carretera Sur or Av. Rafael E. Melgar, then drive 3 km (2 miles) inland to site* ⊠ *Free.*

FAMILY **Punta Sur National Park.** This 247-acre national preserve is a protected habitat for numerous birds and animals, including crocodiles, flamingos, egrets, and herons. At the park's (and Cozumel's) southernmost point stands the **Faro de Celarain,** a lighthouse that's now a museum of navigation. Climb the 134 steps to the top for the best view on the island. Spot birds from observation towers near **Laguna Colombia** or **Laguna Chunchacaab,** or visit the ancient Mayan lighthouse **El Caracol,** which was designed to whistle when the wind blows in a certain direction. Beaches here are wide and deserted, and there's great snorkeling offshore; snorkeling equipment is available for rent, as are kayaks. Leave your car at the Faro and take a park shuttle or rental bike to the beach. If you're coming by cab, expect to pay about MX$585 for a round-trip ride from San Miguel. ⊠ *Carretera Costera Sur, Km 30* ⊕ *www.cozumelparks.com/eng/punta_sur.cfm* ⊠ *MX$163* ⊙ *Daily 8–4.*

DID YOU KNOW?

Parque Chankanaab has a number of good reproductions of Olmec, Toltec, Aztec, and Mayan stone carvings. A visit lets you dip into the diverse artistic styles throughout the centuries.

BEACHES

Cozumel's beaches range from broad strands and secluded coves to pockets of sand collected between parts of ancient, exposed reefs. The best of the bunch lie at northern end of the island's leeward side, and the numerous private beach clubs and public beaches extending the full length of this coast all promise a day of sun and sea. The windward coast has stretches of spectacular isolated beaches, some rocky, some sandy. Prevailing winds create rip-currents that make swimming dangerous when the surf is up, so stay close to shore if you feel inclined to enter the water.

LEEWARD BEACHES

Wide, sandy beaches washed with shallow waters are typical at the far north and south ends of Cozumel's west coast. The topography changes between the two, with small sandy coves interspersed with limestone outcroppings. ■ TIP➜ Generally, the best snorkeling from shore is wherever piers or rocky shorelines provide a haven for sergeant majors and angelfish. However, shore diving and snorkeling took a hit with Hurricane Wilma in October 2005, from which they have not yet fully recovered. While they're improving gradually, you'll still find the greatest undersea life at the reef, reachable only by boat.

Isla de Pasión. Off Punta Norte on the northwest coast, private Isla de Pasión has one of Cozumel's loveliest beaches. Most guests arrive on organized excursions (from MX$1,090), but you can also get to the Isla dock independently (it's at the end of the bumpy dirt road to Punta Norte) and come over for MX$885. Either way, your visit includes the short round-trip boat ride, a buffet lunch, soft drinks, some alcoholic drinks, and use of the extensive facilities. You can easily spend a whole day here strolling the strand, floating in the shallow water, swinging in a hammock, playing volleyball, indulging in a massage (for an extra fee), or even getting married in the island's chapel. This is a favorite stop for hordes of cruise-shippers, but the beach stretches for 4 km (2½ miles), so you can still escape the crowds. **Amenities:** food and drink; showers; toilets. **Best For:** swimming; walking. ⊠ *Bahia Ciega Lagoon* ☎ *987/105–9791* ⊕ *www.isla-pasion.com* ⊠ *From MX$885.*

FAMILY **Playa las Casitas.** Hugely popular with locals, Playa las Casitas has several large palapa-style restaurant-bars, small palapas for shade, calm waters, and a long stretch of beach. Swim out 50 yards from the north end to enjoy the fish-filled artificial reefs. Windsurfers and stand-up paddleboards are also available for rent. The beach is fairly deserted on weekdays but completely packed on Sunday, the traditional day for family outings. **Amenities:** food and drink; parking (no fee); toilets; water sports. **Best for:** snorkeling; sunsets; swimming. ⊠ *Carretera Norte at Blvd. Aeropuerto* ⊠ *Free.*

Playa Palancar. South of the resorts, down a rutted road and way off the beaten path, lies serene Playa Palancar—a long, walkable beach with hammocks hanging under coconut palms. The on-site dive shop can outfit scuba enthusiasts for trips to the famous Palancar and Columbia reefs, just offshore; boats will take snorkelers out every two hours from

Cozumel's History

Cozumel's name is believed to have come from the Mayan "Ah-Cuzamil-Peten" ("Land of the Swallows"). For the Maya, who lived here intermittently between about AD 600 and 1200, the island was not only a center for trade and navigation but also a sacred place. Pilgrims from all over Mesoamerica came to honor Ixchel, the goddess of fertility, childbirth, and healing. The mother of all other gods, Ixchel (also known as Lady Rainbow) was often depicted with swallows at her feet. Maya women, who were expected to visit her site at least once in their lives, made the dangerous journey from the mainland by canoe. Cozumel's main exports were salt and honey, both of which at the time were considered more valuable than gold.

In 1518 Spanish explorer Juan de Grijalva arrived on the island in search of slaves. His tales of treasure inspired Hernán Cortés, Mexico's most famous Spanish explorer, to visit the following year. There he met Gerónimo de Aguilar and Gonzalo Guerrero, Spaniards who had been shipwrecked years earlier. Initially enslaved by the Maya, the two were later accepted into the community. Aguilar joined forces with Cortés, helping set up a military base on the island and using his knowledge of the Maya to defeat them. Guerrero, in contrast, died defending his adopted people, and the Maya still consider him a hero. By 1570 most Maya islanders had been massacred by the Spanish or killed by disease, and by 1600 the island was abandoned.

In the 17th and 18th centuries, pirates found Cozumel to be the perfect hideout. The notorious buccaneers Jean Lafitte and Henry Morgan favored the island's safe harbors and hid their treasures in Mayan catacombs and tunnels. By 1843 Cozumel had again been abandoned. Five years later, 20 families fleeing Mexico's brutal Caste War of the Yucatán resettled the island, and their descendants still live there today.

By the early 20th century the island began capitalizing on its abundant supply of *zapote* (sapodilla) trees, which produce *chicle*, a chewy substance prized by the chewing-gum industry. (Now you know how Chiclets got their name.) Shipping routes began to include Cozumel, whose natural harbors made it a perfect stop for large vessels. Jungle forays in search of chicle led to the discovery of ruins, and soon archaeologists began visiting the island as well. Meanwhile, Cozumel's importance as a seaport diminished as air travel grew, and the demand for chicle dropped off with the invention of synthetic chewing gum.

For decades Cozumel was another backwater where locals fished, hunted alligators and iguanas, and worked on coconut plantations to produce *copra*, the dried kernels from which coconut oil is extracted. Cozumeleños subsisted largely on seafood, still a staple of the local economy. During World War II, the U.S. Army paid to have an airstrip built to hunt the German U-boats that were sinking Mexican ships. Then, in the 1960s, the underwater explorer Jacques Cousteau helped make Cozumel famous by featuring its reefs on his television show. Today, Cozumel is among the world's most popular diving destinations.

9 to 5. There's also a nice open-air restaurant-bar here if you'd rather just relax. **Amenities:** food and drink; parking (no fee); showers; toilets; water sports. **Best for:** snorkeling; swimming; walking. ⊠ *Carretera Sur, Km 19.5* ▢ *Free.*

Playa Santa Pilar. Running along the northern hotel strip where the Melia and El Cozumeleño hotels are located, you'll find long stretches of sand and shallow water that encourage leisurely swims. Beach hotels have all the facilities you would need, but most are exclusive and don't allow nonguests on the premises. If you're not staying at one, bring your own shade and slip onto the beach between properties. ■**TIP**→ **Kite- boarders gather in this area when the winds are good, offering hours of entertaining acrobatics; equipment can be rented nearby from De Lille Sports.** **Amenities:** food and drink (for guests only); parking (no fee). **Best for:** swimming; walking. ⊠ *Carretera San Juan, just south of Punta Norte* ▢ *Free.*

BEACH CLUBS

Carlos 'n' Charlie's Beach Club. Easily accessible by cab from downtown or the cruise piers, this spot at Playa San Francisco is a rowdy affair with a restaurant and bar where waiters break into song and draw customers into line dances. The food is typical of the chain—burgers, barbecued ribs, tacos—and the alcohol flows generously. While there's a wide array of water sports offered, the water is shallow and not always clear. **Amenities:** food and drink; parking (no fee); showers; toilets; water sports. **Best for:** partiers. ⊠ *Carretera Costera Sur, Km 14* ☎ *987/564–0960 (mobile)* ⊕ *www.carlosandcharliesbeachclub.com* ▢ *Entry free with food or drink purchase* ⊙ *Mon.–Sat. 9–5, Sun. 11–5.*

FAMILY **Money Bar Beach Club.** Situated on Dzul-Ha reef, the island's most upscale beach club has a small sandy beach, sunset views, and great food. Entry is free; once inside, you can pay for individual activities or choose an all-inclusive package that might cover anything from meals and massages to guided snorkel tours. (If you snorkel the fish-filled reef on your own, watch out for sea urchins on the rocks). A water-sports center rents snorkel gear, kayaks, and small sailboats. Mingle with locals and sip frothy cocktails during the sunset happy hour. ■**TIP**→ **There's danceable live music on weekend nights.** **Amenities:** food and drink; parking (no fee); showers; toilets; water sports. **Best for:** snorkeling; sunset; swimming. ⊠ *Carretera Sur, Km 6.5* ☎ *987/869–5141* ⊕ *www. moneybarbeachclub.com* ▢ *Free; all-inclusive packages from MX$562* ⊙ *Mon.–Thurs. 7 am–9 pm, Fri.–Sun. 7 am–10 pm.*

FAMILY **Mr. Sancho's Beach Club.** There's always something going on at Mr. San- cho's. Scores of vacationers come here to swim, snorkel, drink, and ride around on Jet Skis. The restaurant, which offers a number of meal options, holds a lively, informative tequila seminar at lunchtime. Grab a swing seat under the palapa and sip a mango margarita, or opt for a massage. Lockers are available and souvenirs are for sale. This is one of the few bars on the west side that is free to enter and also offers an all- inclusive package. **Amenities:** food and drink; parking (no fee); show- ers; toilets; water sports. **Best for:** partiers; swimming. ⊠ *Carretera Sur,*

Km 15 ☎ *1987/871–9174 (mobile)* ⊕ *www.mrsanchos.com* ✉ *Free; all-inclusive packages from MX$749* ⊙ *Daily 8:30–5.*

FAMILY **Paradise Beach.** Home to one of the largest heated pools on the island, this club charges MX$36 for lounge chairs; a Fun Pass (MX$225) gives you all-day use of kayaks, and snorkel gear, plus numerous large floats in the water. Parasailing equipment and Jet Skis are available for rent. Food at each of the club's three bar-restaurants is expensive, and the minimum per-person consumption cost (MX$120) is easily reached. **Amenities:** food and drink; parking (no fee); showers; toilets; water sports. **Best for:** swimming. ⊠ *Carretera Sur, Km 14.5* ☎ *987/120–0027* ⊕ *www.paradise-beach-cozumel.com* ✉ *Entry MX$42.*

Playa Azul Beach Club. This club sits just north of the hotel of the same name. The beach is actually pockets of soft sand between limestone shelves; there's also a pool at the hotel that is open to club guests. The restaurant beneath a large palapa serves delicious ceviche and bountiful club sandwiches with a side of fries, and there's free Wi-Fi to boot. Live music on Sunday afternoon draws a crowd of fun-loving people. ▉**TIP**➔ A hotel is being built next door, with construction set to be complete in late 2015. Construction noise is nominal. **Amenities:** food and drink; parking (no fee); showers; toilets. **Best For:** snorkeling; sunsets; swimming. ⊠ *Carretera Norte, Km 4* ☎ *987/869–5160* ⊕ *www.playa-azul.com/eng/beach-club.cfm* ✉ *Free* ⊙ *Daily 9–5.*

Playa San Francisco. This busy but inviting 5-km (3-mile) expanse of sand is among the longest and finest on Cozumel. Encompassing the beaches Maya and Santa Rosa, it's typically packed with cruise-ship passengers in high season. On Sunday, locals flock here to eat fresh fish. Amenities include two outdoor restaurants, a bar, dressing rooms, gift shops, beach chairs, massage treatments, and water-sports equipment rentals. **Amenities:** food and drink; parking (no fee); showers; toilets; water sports. **Best for:** walking; swimming. ⊠ *Carretera Costera Sur, Km 14* ✉ *Free (MX$136 minimum for food and drink).*

Playa UVAS. Sitting on narrow sandy beach, UVAS caters to small cruise-ship groups and independent tourists. On-site amenities include a dive shop, kayak rentals, massages, and more. The basic entrance fee gets you one beverage and the use of beach umbrellas and lounge chairs, but additional food and drink purchases can quickly run up your tab; all-inclusive packages are also available. ▉**TIP**➔ Phone or online reservations are required, since the club limits the number of guests. **Amenities:** food and drink; parking (no fee); showers; toilets; water sports. **Best for:** swimming. ⊠ *Carretera Sur, Km 8.5* ☎ *987/872–5876* ⊕ *www.playauvas.com* ✉ *Entry MX$144, packages from MX$324.*

WINDWARD BEACHES

The east coast of Cozumel presents a splendid succession of deserted rocky coves and narrow powdery beaches poised dramatically against the turquoise Caribbean. ⚠ Swimming can be treacherous here if you go out too far—in some places the strong undertow can sweep you out to sea in minutes. These beaches are perfect for solitary sunbathing.

Cozumel's best beaches and reefs are on the leeward side.

Several casual restaurants dot the coastline; they all close around sunset as there is no electricity on this side of the island.

Beyond Punta Oriente, the sandy road beside Mezcalitos leading to the wild northeast coast is sometimes open and sometimes gated—a shame, because the beaches there are superb. Other than ATV outings there are no tours to this part of the coast, and the road is too rutted for rental cars. Rumors abound as to this area's future—some say there will be a small-scale resort here someday, while others hope it will become an ecological reserve. A small navy bivouac at the Punta Molas lighthouse is the only settlement on the road for now, though some of the scrub jungle is divided into housing lots.

North of Playa San Martín. About 1 km (½ mile) to the north of Playa San Martín the island road turns hilly and offers panoramic ocean views. **Coconuts,** a hilltop palapa restaurant, is a prime lookout spot that also serves decent food. One hundred yards away, **Ventanas al Mar** (the only hotel on the windward coast) attracts travelers who value solitude. Locals picnic on the long beach directly north of the hotel. When the water is calm, there's good snorkeling around the rocks beneath Ventanas al Mar, but steer clear if it's rough. **Amenities:** food and drink; parking (no fee), toilets. **Best For:** solitude; snorkeling; surfing. ⌂ *Carretera C-1, Km 43.5* ▢ *Free.*

Playa de San Martín. Not quite 3 km (2 miles) north of Punta Chiqueros, a long stretch of beach begins along the Chen Río Reef. Turtles come to lay their eggs on the section known as Playa de San Martín. Soldiers or ecologists sometimes guard the beach during full moons from May to September to prevent poaching. This is a particularly good spot for

The Quieter Side of Cozumel

Blazing-white cruise ships parade in and out of Cozumel like a regatta of floating apartment buildings. Sundays aside, there's at least one on the horizon every day of the year; some days the island gets six. The day-trippers they carry pack the tourist-trap souvenir shops and bars on San Miguel's waterfront every afternoon, making the place feel more like a suburban shopping mall than a small Mexican town.

Luckily, there's plenty of Cozumel to go around. If you're fortunate enough to overnight on the island, try these tricks to avoid the crowds.

1. Keep a low profile. Stick close to the beach and pool when more than two ships are in port.

2. Time your excursions. Go into San Miguel for early breakfast and errands, then stay out of town for the rest of the day. Wander back after you hear the ships blast their departure warnings around 5 or 6 pm.

3. Dive in. Hide from the hordes by slipping underwater. But be sure to choose a small dive operation that travels to less popular reefs.

4. Drive on the wild side. Rent a car and cruise the windward coast, still free of rampant construction. You can picnic and sunbathe on private beaches hidden by limestone outcroppings, and watch the waves roll in. Use caution when swimming, though, since the surf can be rough.

5. Frequent the "other" downtown. Most of Cozumel's residents live and shop far from San Miguel's waterfront. Avenidas 15, 20, and 25 are packed with taco stands, *papelerías* (stationery stores), and neighborhood markets. While driving here can be messy, so park on a quieter side street and explore the shops and neighborhoods to see a whole different side of Cozumel.

swimming when the water is calm (and the turtles aren't nesting). When the wind is blowing from the south though, the water is best for kiteboarders and windsurfers. When you're ready to kick back, **La Palapa de St. Martin** serves cold drinks and seafood. **Amenities:** food and drink; lifeguards (part-time); parking (no fee). **Best for:** swimming; solitude. ⊠ *Carretera C-1, Km 41* 🖾 *Free.*

FAMILY **Punta Chiqueros.** Sheltered by an offshore reef, this half-moon cove is the first popular swimming area as you drive north on the coastal road. Part of a longer beach that some locals call Playa Bonita, it has fine sand, clear water, and moderate waves. At lunchtime, you can linger over fried fish at a casual eatery that's also named **Playa Bonita. Amenities:** food and drink; parking (free); toilets. **Best For:** walking; sunsets; surfing; swimming. ⊠ *Carretera C-1, Km 38* 🖾 *Free.*

Punta Morena. Surfers, kiteboarders, and boogie boarders have made Punta Morena one of their official hangouts—and for good reason: it has great waves and a restaurant serving surfer-friendly burgers, fries, and nachos. ■ TIP→ If you are away from the main palapa, ask the waiter for a beverage service flag; use pesos when paying, as the conversion rate is used to their advantage. **Amenities:** food and drink; parking (no fee); toilets. **Best for:** surfing. ✉ *Carretera C-1, Km 46* 🎟 *Free.*

Punta Oriente. This typical eastside beach is great for beachcombing but unsuitable for swimming due to the currents. It's nicknamed "Playa Mezcalitos" after the much-loved **Mezcalito Café,** which serves seafood and beer and can get pretty rowdy. Señor Iguana's is the other restaurant option here. **Amenities:** food and drink; parking (no fee). **Best For:** partiers; nudists (to the north); walking. ✉ *Carretera C-1, Km 49* 🎟 *Free.*

WHERE TO EAT

ZONA HOTELERA SUR

$$$ ITALIAN 🍴 **Alfredo di Roma.** The opportunity to dine graciously amid crystal and candlelight (and blessedly cool air-conditioning) is just one reason to book a special dinner at Alfredo's. The pastas are made fresh daily, and cheeses are flown in from Italy so that the chef can prepare the house special—authentic fettuccine Alfredo—at your table. The carpaccio, spaghetti with lobster, and Chilean sea bass in white wine and tomato sauce are all superb, and the wine cellar is the largest on the island. Book a table for early evening and enjoy the sunset view through floor-to-ceiling windows. Note that diners not staying at the hotel must have advance reservations. [$] *Average main: 300 MP* ✉ *Presidente InterContinental Cozumel, Carretera Chankanaab, Km 6.5* ☎ *987/872–9500* 🌐 *www.alfredodiroma.com.mx* ✍ *Reservations essential* 🕒 *No lunch* ✣ *B4.*

SAN MIGUEL

$ MEXICAN Fodor's Choice ★ 🍴 **Burritos Gorditos.** If you've got a hankering for a hole-in-the-wall place that serves cheap, delicious meals, Burritos Gorditos fits the bill. The made-to-order shrimp burritos are excellent and big enough to split; a solid assortment of tacos and salads is also available, but no alcohol is served. Seating is limited (which is why locals call ahead for takeout). ■ **TIP→ If the tables are full, place your order and wait for one to open up, or eat outside on the wall.** [$] *Average main: 54 MP* ✉ *Av. Norte 5A, between calles 2 and 4, San Miguel* ☎ *987/120–0237* ✍ *Reservations not accepted* 💳 *No credit cards* ✣ *C2.*

$ MEXICAN 🍴 **Casa Denis.** This little yellow house near the plaza has been satisfying cravings for Yucatecan favorites like *cochinita pibil* (spiced pork baked in banana leaves) since 1945. Locals tend to stop in between 8:30 and 1 for cheap breakfast and lunch menus that highlight tacos and empanadas. *Tortas* (sandwiches) are also a real bargain. In the evening, Casa Denis is a place to see and be seen—if you're seeking more privacy, opt for a seat in the quiet garden courtyard to the rear. [$] *Average main: 130 MP* ✉ *Calle 1 Sur 132, between avs. 5 and 10, San Miguel* ☎ *987/872–0067* 🌐 *www.casadenis.com* ✍ *Reservations not accepted* ✣ *B3.*

$$$ MEXICAN FAMILY 🍴 **Casa Mission.** Part private home, part restaurant (and owned by the same family since the 1980s), this place evokes a country hacienda in mainland Mexico. The on-site botanical garden has mango and papaya

CLOSE UP

Island Dining

There's no shortage of dining choices on Cozumel, where restaurateurs from Mexico, the U.S., and Europe bring every visitor a taste of home. The narrow streets of San Miguel are filled with the aromas of grilling steaks and smoking shrimp, as waiters deliver platters of enchiladas and pizza to sidewalk tables and passersby eye the tables full of food, trying to choose where to eat. At rooftop restaurants, groups gather over Italian feasts; along the shoreline, lobster and fresh fish are the catch of the day. All over the island, there is a bias toward tourist taste buds. Yucatecan dishes such as cochinita pibil, *queso relleno* (Gouda cheese stuffed with ground meat), and *sopa de lima* (lime soup) rarely appear on menus aimed at foreign visitors; however, you will still find authentic regional cuisine at San Miguel's small family-owned eateries, which are often simply a cluster of wobbly tables in a tiny café.

Although there are a growing number of restaurants that serve fine cuisine, even the island's top chefs tend to emphasize natural flavors and simple preparations. The same spirit holds for the dining room, where casual clothes are the rule and a shirt with buttons qualifies as dressed up. (There are a few places here where you can let your sartorial excellence shine.)

trees and a small zoo with caged birds. The setting, with tables lining the veranda, outshines the food, which caters to the tourist palate. Nonetheless, stalwart fans rave about huge platters of fajitas and grilled fish. Casa Mission also has two more centrally located sister restaurants, La Mission and Parilla Mission. [$] *Average main: 327 MP* ✉ *Av. 55, between avs. Juárez and Calle 1 Sur, San Miguel* ☎ *987/872–1641* 🌐 *www.missioncoz.com* ✣ *D3.*

$ MEXICAN 🍴 **El Foco.** Popular among locals, this *taquería* has moved a few blocks down from its original location; however, it's still charming and remains open late (until 2 am daily). The soft tacos stuffed with pork, chorizo, cheese, or beef aren't the cheapest on the island, but they're tasty and filling. [$] *Average main: 95 MP* ✉ *Av. 5, between calles 5 and 7 Sur, San Miguel* ✍ *Reservations not accepted* 💳 *No credit cards* ✣ *B3.*

$$ MEXICAN Fodor's Choice ★ 🍴 **El Moro.** You'll have to work hard to find El Moro, but your perseverance will be rewarded with one the better meals in Cozumel. This family-owned, open-air restaurant has been feeding hungry locals and tourists for years. Brothers Ray, Efren, and Heiser strive to make you feel welcome, so the service is excellent—and the portions are large. A wide range of seafood and beef dishes offers something for everyone. After dinner, try a taste of *xtabentún*, a traditional Yucatecan liqueur made of fermented honey and aniseed. [$] *Average main: 163 MP* ✉ *75 Bis Norte 124, between calles 2 and 4, San Miguel* ✣ *Head east on Calle 4 from Av. 65; take the 4th right turn onto 75 Bis (no street signs). It's in the middle of the block on the right* ☎ *987/872–3029* ✍ *Reservations not accepted* 🕒 *Closed Thurs.* ✣ *D3.*

$$$ ITALIAN 🍴 **Guido's.** Chef Yvonne Villiger works wonders with fresh fish—if the wahoo with capers and black olives is on the menu, don't miss it—but Guido's is best known for pizzas that are baked in a wood-burning oven

and served by an incredibly attentive staff. Enjoy a pitcher of delicious sangria in the pleasant, roomy courtyard. $ *Average main: 299 MP* ✉ *Av. Rafael E. Melgar 23, between calles 6 and 8 Norte, San Miguel* ☎ *987/872–0946* ⊕ *www.guidoscozumel.com* ☾ *No lunch Sun.* ✛ *C1.*

$$$
MEXICAN
Fodor's Choice
★

✕ **Kinta.** It's easy to overlook the entrance to this upscale spot (look for a bright orange facade on the west side of the street); however, once you've discovered the blissfully air-conditioned dining room, romantic outdoor garden, and impressive menu, you'll likely return. The personable owner, Chef Kris Wallenta, whips up sophisticated interpretations of classic Mexican fare in his open kitchen. The menu is updated often, but favorites dishes include savory black bean soup, pork in a smoky *pasilla* chile sauce, and filet mignon with *huitlaoche* (a corn truffle) and cheese. Hand-crushed mojitos and fruity sangria add a refreshing lilt, and the *budín de la abuelita* (bread pudding with Mexican chocolate and caramel sauce) is a fitting end to a stellar meal. $ *Average main: 217 MP* ✉ *Av. 5 No. 148B, between Calles 2 and 4, San Miguel* ☎ *987/869–0544* ⊕ *kintacozumel.com* ☖ *Reservations essential* ☾ *Closed Mon. No lunch* ✛ *C2.*

$$$
MEXICAN

✕ **Kondesa.** You can't miss the hot pink and turquoise exterior of Chef Kris Wallenta's second restaurant—it features a palapa-covered bar that opens onto a dimly lit garden dining area. Wallenta puts modern spins on classic flavors, and this menu centers on fresh-caught fish. Favorites include the Kondesa *kake* (an interpretation of crab cakes made with lion fish) and enchiladas filled with seafood. A full cocktail list complements any meal, so if you can't make it for dinner, stop in for a drink. $ *Average main: 266 MP* ✉ *Av. 5 No. 456, between Calles 5 and 7, San Miguel* ☎ *987/869–1086* ⊕ *kondesacozumel.com* ☾ *Closed Mon. No lunch* ✛ *A3.*

$
CUBAN

✕ **La Casa del Mojito.** Considering Cuba is less than 257 km (160 miles) away, it's not surprising that it would exert some influence on Cozumel's cuisine. You'll certainly feel it at this open-air, Cuban-style eatery. Enjoy a pork loin sandwich, fried plantains, or the signature sandwich (aptly named "The Cuban") while sipping one of the best made-from-scratch mojitos on the island. Alex, the owner, and his staff work hard to make your experience memorable. $ *Average main: 130 MP* ✉ *Av. 5, between Calles 3 and Adolfo Rosado Salas, San Miguel* ✛ *B3.*

$
MEXICAN

✕ **La Choza.** Locals and expats gather here for breakfasts of *migas* (scrambled eggs with bits of bacon and tortilla) and the daily lunchtime *comida corrida* (a set-priced meal with a choice of appetizers and entrées); the latter is a great deal considering that the à la carte menu is almost double the price. Favorite dishes include *pollo con mole poblano* (chicken in a smooth, earthy chile sauce), chile relleno *de camarón* (chile stuffed with shrimp), and pork with pumpkin seed sauce. You can sample an array of *agua frescas* in flavors like hibiscus, but remember to leave room for the chilled avocado pie. $ *Average main: 122 MP* ✉ *Av. 10, between Calles 3 and Adolfo Rosado Salas, San Miguel* ☎ *987/872–0958* ✛ *B3.*

$$$
MEDITERRANEAN
Fodor's Choice
★

✕ **La Cocay.** This casually sophisticated dining room and garden is a local favorite. Although the menu changes frequently, you can expect to find salads laced with fruits, pastas dishes, steaks, and seafood entrées like seared sashimi-grade tuna. Consider sharing several small plates

Cozumel's main town, San Miguel, is full of casual, local restaurants.

from the tapas menu (the blue-cheese phyllo rolls with black-cherry sauce, salmon meatballs, and octopus with garlic are top picks). Also on offer are reasonably priced wines by the glass from Argentina, Chile, and Mexico. As everything is made fresh, popular menu items tend to run out, but everyone seems to leave happy. $ *Average main: 272 MP* ✉ *Calle 8 Norte 208, between avs. 10 and 15, San Miguel* ☎ *987/872–5533, 987/872-5533* ⊕ *www.lacocay.com* ✛ *C1.*

$$$
ECLECTIC
✕ **Le Chef.** Dining is an all-day affair at this tiny café and restaurant, which features six tables inside and another six outside. At breakfast, you can have a full meal for less than MX$135; at lunch you can linger over the must-have lobster BLT sandwich, assorted soups, salads, or special pizzas. As the sun sets, Le Chef's ambience skews toward cozy as the lights dim and the menu expands to include a daily list of specials. ■ **TIP→ You'll find an excellent selection of wines to accompany your meal.** $ *Average main: 218 MP* ✉ *Av. 5 No. 378, at Calle 5, San Miguel* ☎ *987/878–4391* ⊙ *Closed Sun.* ✛ *B3.*

$$$
MEXICAN
✕ **Pancho's Backyard.** Marimbas play beside a bubbling fountain in the charming courtyard behind one of Cozumel's best folk-art shops. Though Pancho's is always busy, the waitstaff is patient and helpful. Cruise-ship passengers seeking a taste of Mexico pack the place at lunch; dinner is a bit more serene. The American-style, English menu is geared toward tourists, but regional ingredients like smoky chipotle chile make even the standard steak stand out. Other stars include the cilantro cream soup and shrimp flambéed with tequila. $ *Average main: 218 MP* ✉ *Av. Rafael E. Melgar, between calles 8 and 10 Norte, San Miguel* ☎ *987/872–2141* ⊕ *www.panchosbackyard.com* ⊙ *No lunch Sun.* ✛ *C1*

$$$$ STEAKHOUSE 🍴 **Pepe's Steak and Seafood House.** This popular second-story restaurant has a casual yet elegant steakhouse feel. The air-conditioned dining room's tall windows allow for fantastic sunset and ocean views. Classic cuts of meat—including filet mignon, T-bone, and prime rib—please American palates, though some say they aren't up to U.S. steakhouse standards. **■ TIP→ Check the website for daily specials.** [$] *Average main: 450 MP* ✉ *Av. Rafael E. Melgar and Calle Adolfo Rosado Salas, San Miguel* ☎ *987/872–0213* 🌐 *www.pepesgrillcozumel.com* ✣ *B3.*

$ ECLECTIC 🍴 **Rock 'n Java Caribbean Bar & Grill.** The extensive breakfast menu here includes whole-wheat French toast and cheese crêpes. For lunch or dinner try the vegetarian tacos, linguine with clams, or choose from more than a dozen salads. Pies, cakes, and pastries are baked on-site daily. You can savor your healthy meal or sweet snack (and take advantage of free Wi-Fi) while enjoying a sea view through the back windows. New Rock 'n Java spots—Noodle Bar & Sushi and Tex-Mex Island Grill (both in the nearby Mega Shopping Center)—round out the offerings of this popular Cozumel brand. [$] *Average main: 123 MP* ✉ *Av. Rafael E. Melgar, No. 602-6, San Miguel* ☎ *987/872–4405* 🌐 *www.rocknjavacozumel.com* ✣ *A3.*

5

WINDWARD COAST

$$ MEXICAN 🍴 **Coconuts.** The T-shirts and bikinis hanging from the palapa of this hilly, windward hangout are good indicators of its party-time atmosphere. Classic rock and reggae tunes play in the background while crowds down cervezas, fish, fajitas, and garlic shrimp. The meals may not be good enough to write home about, but they are good enough to keep the crowds coming. Be sure to stroll out to the quieter, outer edges of the dining area and admire the stunning view. The party closes at sunset, and the carved coral steps going downhill can be tricky: use caution. [$] *Average main: 163 MP* ✉ *Carretera C-1, Km 43* 🌐 *www.coconutscozumel.com* 💳 *No credit cards* ✣ *C4.*

$$ MEXICAN 🍴 **Playa Bonita.** Locals gather on Sunday afternoons at this casual beach café. The water here is usually calm, and families alternate between swimming and lingering over long lunches of fried fish. Weekdays are quieter, making it a good place to spend the day if you want access to food, drinks, and showers but aren't into the loud beach-club scene. [$] *Average main: 136 MP* ✉ *Punta Chiqueros, Carretera C-1, Km 38* ☎ *987/872–4868* 💳 *No credit cards* 🕒 *No dinner* ✣ *C4.*

WHERE TO STAY

ZONA HOTELERA NORTE

$$ RESORT FAMILY 🏨 **Coral Princess Hotel and Resort.** Good snorkeling off the rocky shoreline and a relaxed family feel makes this resort, which offers both hotel rooms and apartmentlike units, a north-coast favorite. **Pros:** snorkeling right off beach; decent, well-priced meals; family-friendly, short cab ride to town. **Cons:** can be noisy at pool; some rooms lack bathtubs. [$] *Rooms from: $115* ✉ *Carretera Costera Norte, Km 2.5*

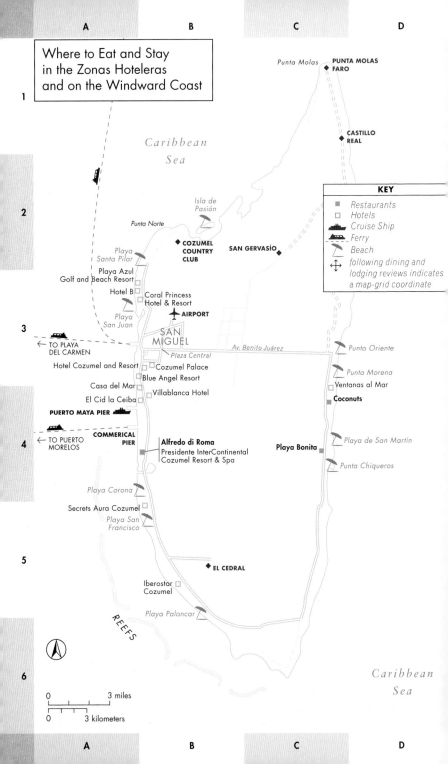

Where to Eat and Stay in the Zonas Hoteleras and on the Windward Coast

Caribbean Sea

Punta Molas

PUNTA MOLAS FARO

CASTILLO REAL

Isla de Pasión

Punta Norte

COZUMEL COUNTRY CLUB

SAN GERVASÍO

Playa Santa Pilar

Playa Azul Golf and Beach Resort

Hotel B

Coral Princess Hotel & Resort

AIRPORT

Playa San Juan

SAN MIGUEL

Av. Benito Juárez

Plaza Central

← TO PLAYA DEL CARMEN

Hotel Cozumel and Resort

Cozumel Palace

Blue Angel Resort

Casa del Mar

Villablanca Hotel

El Cid la Ceiba

PUERTO MAYA PIER

← TO PUERTO MORELOS

COMMERICAL PIER

Alfredo di Roma Presidente InterContinental Cozumel Resort & Spa

Punta Oriente

Punta Morena

Ventanas al Mar

Coconuts

Playa de San Martín

Playa Bonita

Punta Chiqueros

Playa Corona

Secrets Aura Cozumel

Playa San Francisco

EL CEDRAL

Iberostar Cozumel

Playa Palancar

REEFS

Caribbean Sea

KEY

- ■ Restaurants
- □ Hotels
- 🚢 Cruise Ship
- 🛥 Ferry
- 🏖 Beach
- ⊕ following dining and lodging reviews indicates a map-grid coordinate

0 3 miles
0 3 kilometers

☎ 987/872–3200 🌐 www.coralprincess.com 🛏 142 rooms 🍴 Breakfast ✥ B3.

$$$ HOTEL — 🏨 **Hotel B.** The latest entry in the northern hotel zone, this sleek boutique property has quickly become the preferred lodging choice for a discerning, young crowd. **Pros:** on-site dive center; nice spa; sleek design; close to town and marina; bikes available. **Cons:** rocky beach; spotty in-room Wi-Fi. [$] *Rooms from: $270 ✉ Playa San Juan, Km 2.5 ☎ 987/872–0300 🌐 www.hotelbcozumel.com 🛏 45 rooms 🍴 Breakfast ✥ A3.*

$$ HOTEL — 🏨 **Playa Azul Golf and Beach Resort.** Playa Azul feels like a charming, understated Mexican hacienda—there's elegance in its simplicity. **Pros:** intimate; excellent spa; green fees included; good snorkeling. **Cons:** rocky beach entry; major construction project on the adjacent north side of property through 2015. [$] *Rooms from: $185 ✉ Carretera Costera Norte, Km 4 ☎ 987/869–5160 🌐 www.playa-azul.com 🛏 36 rooms, 16 suites, 1 house 🍴 Multiple meal plans ✥ A3.*

5

ZONA HOTELERA SUR

$$ HOTEL — 🏨 **Blue Angel Resort.** A 2009 makeover turned this homey, diver-friendly hangout into a real gem; the guest rooms are clean and bright, and all have balconies or terraces with hammocks and racks for drying dive gear. **Pros:** friendly feel; close to town; on-site PADI outfit; incredible sunsets. **Cons:** small pool; busy street behind the hotel. [$] *Rooms from: $109 ✉ Carretera Sur, Km 2.2 ☎ 987/872–0819 🌐 www.blueangelresort.com 🛏 22 rooms 🍴 Breakfast ✥ B3.*

$ HOTEL — 🏨 **Casa del Mar.** All rooms at this diver-oriented hotel are enlivened by Mexican artwork, but those with sea-facing balconies are lighter, airier, and don't cost that much more. **Pros:** good dive shop; optional, reasonably priced all-inclusive plan. **Cons:** air-conditioning weak in some rooms; beach is across the street. [$] *Rooms from: $79 ✉ Carretera Sur, Km 4 ☎ 987/872–1900 🌐 www.casadelmarcozumel.com 🛏 98 rooms, 8 cabanas 🍴 No meals ✥ B4.*

$$$$ ALL-INCLUSIVE FAMILY — 🏨 **Cozumel Palace.** At times, the Cozumel Palace seems more like a cruise ship than an upscale all-inclusive hotel; the tight confines of the pool deck area, when combined with music and flowing drinks, can create a raucous outdoor atmosphere. **Pros:** on-site spa and dive shop; stocked fridges; walking distance to downtown. **Cons:** time-share reps; pool and lobby get noisy at happy hour. [$] *Rooms from: $389 ✉ Av. Rafael E. Melgar, Km 1.5 ☎ 987/872–9430, 877/325–1537 🌐 www.palaceresorts.com 🛏 175 rooms 🍴 All-inclusive ✥ B3.*

$$ RESORT FAMILY — 🏨 **El Cid la Ceiba.** Next door to the Puerta Maya cruise pier and shopping center, this smallish resort is a comfortable choice, with large condo-style rooms that come equipped with kitchenettes. **Pros:** comfy accommodations; reasonably priced all-inclusive option available. **Cons:** pool area is small and the scene can be boisterous; heavy boat traffic in snorkel areas. [$] *Rooms from: $135 ✉ Carretera Chankanaab, Km 4.5 ☎ 987/872–0844, 800/733–7308 🌐 www.elcid.com 🛏 60 rooms 🍴 Multiple meal plans ✥ B4.*

$$ RESORT FAMILY — 🏨 **Hotel Cozumel and Resort.** In high season, families and revelers surround the enormous pool at this bright orange hotel, while activity directors enliven the crowd with games and loud music. **Pros:** 15-minute walk

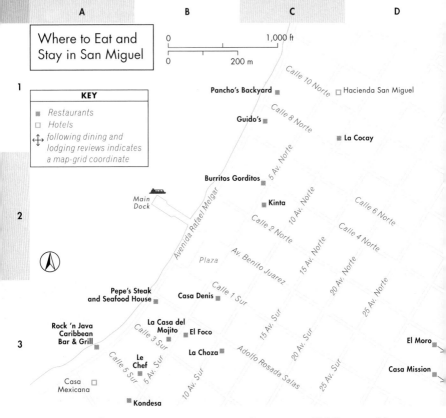

Where to Eat and Stay in San Miguel

KEY

■ Restaurants
□ Hotels
✛ following dining and lodging reviews indicates a map-grid coordinate

Pancho's Backyard ■   □ Hacienda San Miguel

Calle 10 Norte

Guido's ■

Calle 8 Norte

■ La Cocay

Calle 6 Norte

Burritos Gorditos ■

Main Dock

■ Kinta

Calle 2 Norte

Av. Benito Juarez

Plaza

Pepe's Steak and Seafood House ■   Casa Denis ■

Calle 1 Sur

Rock 'n Java Caribbean Bar & Grill ■

La Casa del Mojito ■   ■ El Foco

Calle 3 Sur

■ La Choza

El Moro ■

Le Chef ■

Adolfo Rosada Salas

Casa Mission ■

Casa Mexicana □

Kondesa ■

---

from town; near grocery stores and restaurants; 10 fully-accessible rooms; breakfast-only option available. **Cons:** rocky beach area; poolside entertainment loud and annoying; Wi-Fi unreliable; average food. **$** *Rooms from: $155* ⊠ *Carretera Costera Sur, Km 17* ☎ *987/872–9020* ⊕ *www.hotelcozumel.com.mx* ⤴ *181 rooms* ❑ *Multiple meal plans* ✛ *B3.*

$$$
ALL-INCLUSIVE
FAMILY

☷ **Iberostar Cozumel.** Jungle greenery surrounds this all-inclusive resort at Cozumel's southernmost point. **Pros:** friendly, personal service; large pool area with plenty of lounge chairs. **Cons:** rocky beach; murky water; so-so food; expensive cab ride to town. **$** *Rooms from: $280* ⊠ *Carretera Chankanaab, Km 17, past El Cedral turnoff* ☎ *987/872–9900, 888/923–2722* ⊕ *www.iberostar.com* ⤴ *300 rooms, 6 suites* ❑ *All-inclusive* ✛ *B5.*

$$$
RESORT
FAMILY
Fodor's Choice
★

☷ **Presidente InterContinental Cozumel Resort and Spa.** The InterContinental owns the luxury resort market on Cozumel, offering top-notch service, expansive lawns, pristine beaches, and spacious, modern rooms. **Pros:** High-quality beds and linens; iPod docking stations, impeccable service. **Cons:** pricey food; timeshare pitches in the lobby; far from town. **$** *Rooms from: $295* ⊠ *Carretera Chankanaab, Km 6.5* ☎ *987/872–9500, 800/327–0200* ⊕ *www.intercontinentalcozumel.com* ⤴ *183 rooms, 37 suites* ❑ *No meals* ✛ *B4.*

$$$$
ALL-INCLUSIVE

☷ **Secrets Aura Cozumel.** Part of the Secrets brand, the elegant, all-inclusive Aura raises the bar for the south coast's string of swish beach properties.

The Presidente InterContinental Cozumel Resort & Spa

Pros: high-tech; luxurious amenities (rare on Cozumel); intimate, sophisticated ambience. **Cons:** far from town; offshore snorkeling not very good; no kids allowed; some rooms need updating. [$] *Rooms from: $500* ✉ *Carretera Costera Sur, Km 12.9* ☎ *01800/413–3886 toll-free in Mexico, 800/467–3273* 🌐 *www.secretsresorts.com* 🛏 *168 suites* 🍴 *All-inclusive* ⊕ *B5.*

$ HOTEL 🏨 **Villablanca Hotel.** The landscaped grounds here are lovely, as are most rooms; befitting the price, though, there is a certain budget-hotel sparseness to the place. **Pros:** lush gardens around pool; good value; package deals available. **Cons:** no dressers in standard rooms; 3 km (2 miles) from town. [$] *Rooms from: $83* ✉ *Carretera Chankanaab, Km 3* ☎ *987/872–0730* 🌐 *www.villablanca.net* 🛏 *45 rooms and suites, 1 penthouse, 3 villas* 🍴 *No meals* ⊕ *B4.*

SAN MIGUEL

$ HOTEL Fodor's Choice ★ 🏨 **Casa Mexicana.** Although not on the beach, this distinctive and inexpensive hotel overlooks the water; oceanfront rooms, with comfortable balconies from which to enjoy the views, are worth the added cost. **Pros:** near restaurants and shops; friendly staff; substantial breakfast; all rooms have balconies. **Cons:** no beach; tiny pool; some street noise. [$] *Rooms from: $70* ✉ *Av. Rafael E. Melgar 457, between calles 5 and 7 Sur, San Miguel* ☎ *987/872–9090, 877/228–6747* 🌐 *www.casamexicanacozumel.com* 🛏 *90 rooms* 🍴 *Breakfast* ⊕ *A3.*

$ B&B/INN 🏨 **Hacienda San Miguel.** Five blocks south of San Miguel's main plaza, this small inn consists of two-story buildings set around a lush courtyard; second-floor rooms get far more air and light than those at ground level, but all have coffeemakers, purified water, and bathrobes. **Pros:** quiet but central; plenty of great restaurants nearby; courtyard gardens make it feel like a private home. **Cons:** no parking or pool; a/c can be noisy; musty smell; free Wi-Fi in courtyard only. [$] *Rooms from: $94* ✉ *Calle 10 Norte 1500, at Av. 5* ☎ *987/872–1986* 🌐 *www.haciendasanmiguel.com* 🛏 *7 studios, 3 suites, 1 townhouse* 🍴 *Breakfast* ✥ *C1.*

SPRING FESTIVAL

If you're here in April, tap your toes to some traditional dance during the **Fería del Cedral**, a fair held in the settlement of El Cedral around the last weekend of the month. Park in dirt lots nearby or take one of many available buses. To get here, turn at Km 17.5 off Carretera Sur or Avenida Rafael E. Melgar, then drive 3 km (2 miles) inland to the site.

WINDWARD COAST

$$ B&B/INN **Ventanas al Mar.** The lights of San Miguel are a distant glow on the horizon when you look west from the only hotel on the windward coast. **Pros:** blissful solitude; long beach for morning walks. **Cons:** spotty electricity; limited food and drink options. [$] *Rooms from: $110* ✉ *Carretera C-1, Km 43.5* ☎ *987/105–2684* 🌐 *www.ventanasalmar.com.mx* 🛏 *12 rooms, 2 suites* 🍴 *Breakfast* ✥ *C4.*

NIGHTLIFE

Not so long ago, Cozumel's already low-key nightlife shut down by midnight, perhaps thanks to the many dive excursions leaving at the crack of dawn. The cruise-ship passengers mobbing the bars seemed to drink enough for the whole island, and the rowdiest action sometimes took place in the afternoon, when mojito-slinging revelers pulled out the stops before reboarding. These days, visitors staying up late will be rewarded by a thriving live music scene at haunts that are frequented by locals and tourists alike. Many remain open to 4 am. Even if you're not a night a night owl, you'll find excellent salsa, jazz, acoustic, and rock bands playing downtown at places like Wet Wendy's and Viva Mexico. Money Bar Beach Club has a live band Friday and Saturday around sunset with happy hour specials. As an alternative, do like the locals and head for the *zócalo* (main square) to hear mariachis and Caribbean-style bands on Sunday evenings from 8 to 10.

BARS

Fat Tuesday. On the northwest corner of the square, this rowdy spot draws mostly cruise-ship crowds during the day and vacationers staying on the island at night. Expect frozen daiquiris, ice-cold beers, and blaring rock. There is a second location at Puerta Maya. ✉ *Av. Juárez 2, between Av. Rafael E. Melgar and Calle 3 Sur, San Miguel* 🌐 *fattuesday.cozumel.net.*

Señor Frog's. The *Animal House* ambience at Señor Frog's includes loud music and a bar-dancing, bead-throwing, balloon hat–wearing, anything-goes drinking scene. The pub grub is better than you'd expect, and the waiters are always entertaining. ⊠ *Punta Langosta, Av. Rafael E. Melgar, between calles 7 and 11* ☎ *987/869–1651, 987/869–1648* ⊕ *www.senorfrogs.com.*

Viva Mexico. Live bands and DJs play dance music into the wee hours at Viva Mexico. An extensive food menu with the expected items (burgers, quesadillas, and such) helps make this second-floor bar/restaurant popular day and night. Happy hour generally runs from 6 to 8 pm. ∎ TIP➜ The best seats overlook the waterfront and the sunset. ⊠ *Av. Rafael E. Melgar, at Calle Adolfo Rosado Salas, San Miguel* ☎ *987/872–0799* ☾ *Closed Sun.*

Fodor'sChoice **Wet Wendy's Margarita House.** You'll find the best and largest frozen ★ margaritas in town at Wet Wendy's. Sit at the bar and down one of the potent concoctions, or grab a table in the outdoor garden to dine on remarkably good food and dance to the salsa, rock, and jazz bands that play here several nights a week. Service is friendly, so don't be surprised if the bartender asks you if you want "the usual" on your second visit. ⊠ *Plaza Quinta 53, San Miguel* ⊕ *www.wetwendys.com* ⌕ *Reservations not accepted* ☾ *Closed Sun.*

DANCE CLUBS

Tiki Tok. A second-floor, tiki-theme bar and restaurant by day, this spot is reborn as a dance club after dark. On Friday and Saturday, local group Explosión Latina draws salsa aficionados of all stripes from 10:30 pm to about 4 am; a DJ spins '70s and '80s hits, rock, Latin, and reggaeton (a blend of West-Indian and Latin beats) the rest of the week. ⊠ *Av. Rafael E. Melgar 13, between calles 2 and 4 Norte, San Miguel* ☎ *987/869–8119* ⊕ *www.tikitokcozumel.com.*

MOVIES

Cinepolis. On a sweltering afternoon, slip into Cinepolis. The modern, multiscreen theater shows current hit films in Spanish and English at afternoon matinees and nightly shows. ⊠ *Av. Rafael E. Melgar 1001, between calles 15 and 17 Sur, San Miguel* ☎ *987/869–0799* ⊕ *www.cinepolis.com/cartelera/cozumel.*

SHOPPING

Cozumel's main souvenir-shopping area is downtown on or near the waterfront; tourist-trap malls at the cruise-ship piers sell jewelry, perfume, sportswear, and low-end souvenirs at high-end prices.

Most downtown shops accept U.S. greenbacks, and many goods are priced in dollars. But to get better prices, pay with pesos and stick to cash—some shops tack a hefty surcharge on credit-card purchases. Shops, restaurants, and streets are always crowded between 10 am and 2 pm, but slow down in the evening. Traditionally, stores are open from 9 to 9, although most do close on Sunday morning.

CLOSE UP

A Ceremonial Dance

Women regally dressed in embroidered, lace-trimmed dresses and men in their best guayabera shirts carry festooned trays on their heads during the Baile de las Cabezas de Cochino (Dance of the Pig's Head) at the Fería del Cedral, held in El Cedral. The trays are festooned with trailing ribbons, *papeles picados* (paper cutouts), piles of bread and, in some cases, the head of a barbecued you-know-what.

The pig is a sacrificial offering to God, who is said to have saved the founders of this tiny Cozumel settlement during the 19th-century Caste War, when Yucatán's Maya rose up against their oppressors. The enslaved Maya killed most of the *mestizos* (those of mixed European and indigenous heritage) in the mainland village of Sabán. Casimiro Cárdenas, a wealthy young mestizo, survived while clutching a small wooden cross, and later promised he would establish an annual religious festival once he found a new home.

Today the original religious vigils and novenas blend into the more secular fair, which usually runs through the last weekend in April. Festivities include horse races, bullfights, and carnival rides, and food stands sell hot dogs, corn on the cob, and cold beer. Celebrations peak with the ritual dance, usually held on the final day.

The music begins with a solemn cadence as families enter the stage, surrounding one member bearing a multitiered tray. The circular procession proceeds, with participants showing off their costumes and offerings. Gradually the beat quickens and the dancing begins. Grabbing the ends of ribbons trailing from the trays, children, parents, and grandparents twirl in ever-faster circles until the scene becomes a whirl of laughing faces and bright colors.

■ TIP➔ When you shop for souvenirs, be sure you don't buy anything made with black coral. Not only is it overpriced, it's also an endangered species, and you may be barred from bringing it to the United States and other countries.

MARKETS

FAMILY **Crafts Market.** On the east side of the downtown square, a crafts market sells a respectable assortment of Mexican wares. Practice your bartering skills—start low, compromise, smile—while shopping for blankets, T-shirts, hammocks, and pottery. Most shops are cash only. ⊠ *Between calles 1 and Juárez, San Miguel* ⊗ *Daily 9–9.*

Mercado Municipal. For fresh produce, fish, chiles, and a taste of local life, stop by the Mercado Municipal. ⊠ *Calle Adolfo Rosado Salas, between avs. 20 and 25 Sur, San Miguel* ☎ *987/872–0771* ⊗ *Daily 6:30–3.*

SHOPPING MALLS

Forum Shops. This flashy marble-and-glass mall has loads of perfumes, jewelry, and watches glistening in glass cases, plus an overabundance of eager sales clerks. Note: you'll pay top dollar for purchases, so negotiate

hard and be prepared to walk away when you realize you can find the same thing for the same amount back home. ⊠ *Av. Rafael E. Melgar and Calle 10 Norte, San Miguel* ☎ *987/869–1687.*

Puerta Maya. A pedestrian mall geared to cruise passengers, Puerta Maya has branches of many of downtown's most popular shops, restaurants, and bars. It's close to the ships at the end of a huge parking lot. ⊠ *Carretera Sur, Km 4, at the southern cruise dock* ⊕ *www.puertamaya.com.*

Punta Langosta. This fancy, multilevel shopping mall is across from the downtown cruise-ship dock. A covered pedestrian walkway leads over the street from the ships to the center, which houses several jewelry, sportswear, and souvenir stores, as well as ice cream shops and chain restaurants. ⊠ *Av. Rafael E. Melgar 551, at Calle 7, San Miguel* ⊕ *www.centrocomercial-puntalangosta.com.mx.*

RECOMMENDED STORES

CLOTHING

Exotica. Look for high-quality sportswear, swimwear, and shirts with nature-themed designs at Exotica. ⊠ *Av. Juárez at the plaza, San Miguel* ☎ *987/872–5880.*

Island Outfitters. Mexican crafts, sportswear, beach towels, and sarongs are among the offerings at Island Outfitters. ⊠ *Av. Rafael E. Melgar at the plaza, San Miguel* ☎ *987/872–0132.*

Mr. Buho. Black-and-white clothing (picture well-made guayabera shirts and cotton dresses) is Mr. Buho's specialty. ⊠ *Av. Rafael E. Melgar, between calles 3 and 5, San Miguel* ☎ *987/872–1601* ⊕ *www.mrbuho.com.mx.*

CRAFTS

Balam Mayan Feather. Artists here create intricate paintings on feathers from local birds. There's a second location at Plaza Vista Del Mar near Punta Langosta. ⊠ *Av. 5 and Calle 2 Norte, San Miguel* ☎ *987/869–0548.*

Galería Azul. At Cozumel's best art gallery, Greg Dietrich creates and shows his engraved blown glass along with paintings, jewelry, photography, and other works by local artists. It's open weekdays from 11 to 7 (others times by appointment). ⊠ *Av. 15 Norte, No. 449, between calles 8 and 10, San Miguel* ☎ *987/869–0963* ⊕ *www.cozumelglassart.com.*

FAMILY
Fodor's Choice
★
Los Cinco Soles. This is the best one-stop shop in Cozumel for Mexican crafts. Numerous display rooms, covering almost a block, are filled with clothing, furnishings, home-décor items, quality tequilas, and jewelry. There are smaller branches at Puerta Maya, the Cozumel airport, and Punta Langosta. ⊠ *Av. Rafael E. Melgar and Calle 8 Norte, San Miguel* ☎ *987/872–9004* ⊕ *www.loscincosoles.com.*

Viva Mexico. Upstairs from the bar of the same name, Viva Mexico sells souvenirs and handicrafts from all over Mexico; it's a great place to find vanilla, T-shirts, household goods, art, and assorted trinkets. There is also a branch at the Puerta Maya. ⊠ *Av. Rafael E. Melgar at Calle Adolfo Rosado Salas, San Miguel* ☎ *987/872–5466.*

GROCERY STORES

Chedraui. Open daily from 7 am to 10 pm, this big, full-service grocery store also carries clothing, kitchenware, appliances, and furniture. Brand-name suntan lotions, while expensive, are available. ■**TIP**➔ **The deli and bakery are excellent places to stock up on picnic provisions; coolers and ice are sold here, too.** ⊠ *Av. Rafael E. Melgar between calles 15 and 17 Sur, San Miguel* ☎ *987/872–5404.*

Mega. A supermarket, pharmacy, and department store all under one big roof, Mega has a huge enclosed parking lot and pretty much anything you would need for a short or extended stay on Cozumel. It's open daily from 7:30 am to 10:30 pm; alcohol sales on Sunday cease at 3. ⊠ *Av. Rafael E. Melgar and Calle 11, San Miguel.*

JEWELRY

Diamonds International. You can custom-design pieces of jewelry from a collection of loose diamonds, emeralds, rubies, sapphires, or tanzanite at Diamonds International. There is also a broad range of watches to choose from. The shop and its affiliates, Tanzanite International and Silver International, have multiple locations along the waterfront and in the shopping malls—in fact, it's hard to avoid them. ⊠ *Av. Rafael E. Melgar Sur 131, at Calle 2* ☎ *987/872–5330* ⊕ *www.diamonds international.com.*

Luxury Avenue (Ultrafemme). High-end goods—including watches and perfume—are the highlights here. ⊠ *Av. Rafael E. Melgar 341, San Miguel* ☎ *987/872–0025.*

Pama. A trusted longtime business on the island, Pama offers a wide array of imported jewelry, perfumes, watches, and glassware. ⊠ *Av. Rafael E. Melgar Sur 9, San Miguel.*

Sergio Bustamante. The renowned artist's wild sculpture and jewelry collections are sold at this gallery on Cozumel's main drag. ⊠ *Av. Rafael Melgar at Calle 4 Norte, San Miguel* ⊕ *www.sergiobustamante.com.mx.*

SPORTS AND THE OUTDOORS

Not surprisingly, water sports—most notably scuba diving, snorkeling, and fishing—are Cozumel's biggest draw. Services and equipment rentals are available throughout the island, especially through major hotels and at the beach clubs.

FISHING

The waters off Cozumel teem with more than 230 species of fish, making this one of the world's best deep-sea fishing destinations. During billfish migration season from late April through June, blue marlin, white marlin, and sailfish are plentiful, and world-record catches aren't uncommon.

The larger sportfishing boats are located in the Puerto Abrigo marina just north of San Miguel. Fishing boats are also located at **La Caleta,** the marina on the south side, beside the Presidente InterContinental resort. Some sportfishing companies are affiliated with dive shops and offer a full range of water activities. Hotels can help arrange daily charters—some offer special deals, with boats leaving from their own docks.

3 Hermanos. This outfit specializes in deep-sea and fly-fishing trips. It also offers scuba-diving excursions. Boats are available for group charters, allowing you to move at your own pace. ⊠ *Puerto Abrigo Marina, Av. Rafael E. Melgar Norte, Puerto Abrigo* ☎ *987/107–0655* ⊕ *www. cozumelfishing.com* ✉ *From MX$4775 for 6 people.*

Albatros Deep Sea Fishing. Half- and full-day outings that include boat and crew, tackle and bait, plus libations and lunch (quesadillas or your own fresh catch) are organized by Albatros Deep Sea Fishing. Customized dive trips are also available. ⊠ *Puerto Abrigo Marina, Av. Rafael E. Melgar Norte, Puerto Abrigo* ☎ *987/872–7904, 888/333–4643* ⊕ *www. albatroscharters.com* ✉ *From MX$6070 for 6 people.*

Ocean Tours. All equipment and tackle, lunch with beer, and, of course, the boat and crew are included in Ocean Tours' full-day rates. Half-day tours are also offered, and discounts are given for cash payments. ⊠ *Cozumeleno Beach Resort, Playa Santa Pilar, Zona Hotelera Norte, Km 4.5* ☎ *987/872–9530* ⊕ *www.cozumel-diving.net/oceantur* ✉ *From MX$6002 for 6 people.*

Sand Dollar Sports. Both bottom- and deep-sea fishing trips can be arranged through Sand Dollar; ditto for diving and snorkeling excursions. Charter rates for one to six people include beer, soda, water, and snacks. ⊠ *Carretera Sur, Km 6.2* ☎ *987/872–0793* ⊕ *www.sanddollar sports.com* ✉ *MX$5400 for 4 hours.*

Fodor'sChoice **Spearfishing Today.** The blue waters of Cozumel are a great place to learn
★ to spearfish. After a short lesson with this outfit's certified instructors, you'll launch out from Puerto Abrigo on a four-hour boat trip. Expect to get shots off at grouper, snapper, or trigger fish. Snacks, water, soft drinks, and all equipment are included. The crew will also clean your catch and provide names of restaurants that will cook it for you. ⊠ *Carretera Costa Norte, Km 1.5, Puerto Abrigo* ☎ *987/876-0862* ⊕ *www. spearfishingtoday.com* ✉ *From MX$3527.*

GOLF

Cozumel Country Club. The 18-hole, par-72 championship golf course at the Cozumel Country Club is the work of the Nicklaus Design Group. The lush fairways amid mangroves and a lagoon have been declared an Audubon nature reserve, and it's a favorite spot for bird-watching. Green fees (reduced after 1:30 pm) include a golf cart for your party, and rental clubs are available. Some hotels, including Playa Azul, offer golf packages here. Tee times are generally required, and reservations can be made online. ■TIP➜ **Duffers should bring lots of balls as the fringe areas are notorious for eating them; the crocodiles in the water hazards are real—so use caution when looking for balls.** ⊠ *Carretera Costera Norte, Km 6.5* ☎ *987/872–9570* ⊕ *www.cozumelcountryclub. com.mx* ✉ *MX$1890 for 18 holes* ⅄ *18 holes. 6734 yards. Par 72.*

Continued on page 245

COZUMEL DIVING AND SNORKELING

First comes the giant step, a leap from a dry boat into the warm Caribbean Sea. Then the slow descent to white sand framed by rippling brain coral and waving purple sea fans. If you lean back, you can look up toward the sea's surface. The water off Cozumel is so clear you can see puffy white clouds in the sky even when you're submerged 20 feet under.

With more than 30 charted reefs whose depths average 50–80 feet and water temperatures around 24°C–27°C (75°F–80°F) during peak diving season (June–August, when hotel rates are coincidentally at their lowest), Cozumel is far and away the place to dive in Mexico. More than 60,000 divers come here each year.

Because of the diversity of coral formations and the dramatic underwater peaks and valleys, divers consider Cozumel's Palancar Reef (promoters now call it the Maya Reef) to be one of the top five in the world. Sea turtles headed to the beach to lay their eggs swim beside divers in May and June. Fifteen-pound lobsters wave their antennae from beneath coral ledges; they've been protected in Cozumel's National Marine Park for so long they've lost all fear of humans. Long, green moray eels still appear rather menacing as they bare their fangs at curious onlookers, and snaggle-toothed barracuda look ominous as they swim by. But all in all, diving off Cozumel is relaxing, rewarding, and so addictive you simply can't do it just once.

Hurricane Wilma damaged the reefs during her 2005 attack and rearranged the underwater landscape. Favorite snorkeling and diving spots close to shore were affected, and the fish may not be as abundant as they were in the past.

The reef is home to brain coral and huge sponges.

DIVE SITES

(left and right) Felipe Xicotencatl (C-53 Wreck)

Cozumel's reefs stretch for 32 km (20 mi), beginning at the international pier and continuing to Punta Celarain at the island's southernmost tip. Following is a rundown of Cozumel's main dive destinations.

◤ **Chankanaab Reef.** This inviting reef lies south of Parque Chankanaab, about 350 yards offshore. Large underground caves are filled with striped grunt, snapper, sergeant majors, and butterfly fish. At 55 feet, there's another large coral formation that's often filled with crabs, lobster, barrel sponges, and angelfish. If you drift a bit farther south, you can see the Balones de Chankanaab, balloon-shaped coral heads at 70 feet.

◤ **Colombia Reef.** Several miles off Palancar, the reef reaches 82–98 feet and is best suited for experienced divers. Its underwater structures are as varied as those of Palancar Reef, with large canyons and ravines to explore. Clustered near the overhangs are large groupers, jacks, rays, and an occasional sea turtle.

◤ **Felipe Xicotencatl (C-53 Wreck).** Sunk in 2000 specifically for scuba divers, this 154-foot-long minesweeper is located on a sandy bottom about 80 feet deep near Tormentos and Chankanaab. Created as an artificial reef to decrease some of the traffic on the natural reefs, the ship is open so divers can explore the interior and is gradually attracting schools of fish.

◤ **Maracaibo Reef.** Considered one of the most difficult reefs, Maracaibo is a thrilling dive with strong currents and intriguing old coral formations. Although there are shallow areas, only advanced divers who can cope with the current should attempt Maracaibo.

◤ **Palancar Reef.** About 2 km (1 mi) offshore, Palancar is actually a series of varying coral formations with about 40 dive locations. It's filled with winding canyons, deep ravines, narrow crevices, archways, tunnels, and caves. Black and red coral and huge elephant-ear, and barrel sponges are among the attractions. At the section called Horseshoe, a series of coral heads form a natural horseshoe

shape. This is one of the most popular sites for dive boats and can become crowded.

◤ **Paraíso Reef.** About 330 feet offshore, running parallel to the international cruise-ship pier, this reef averages 30–50 feet. It's a perfect spot to dive before you head for deeper drop-offs. There are impressive formations of star and brain coral as well as sea fans, sponges, sea eels, and yellow rays. It's wonderful for night diving.

◤ **Paseo El Cedral.** Running parallel to Santa Rosa reef, this flat reef has gardenlike valleys full of fish, including angelfish, grunt, and snapper. At depths of 35–55 feet, you can also spot rays.

◤ **San Francisco Reef.** Considered Cozumel's shallowest wall dive (35–50 feet), this 1-km (1/2-mi) reef runs parallel to Playa San Francisco and has many varieties of reef fish. You'll need to take a dive boat to get here.

◤ **Santa Rosa Wall.** North of Palancar, Santa Rosa is renowned among experienced divers for deep dives and drift

Chankanaab Reef

Young yellow sponges, Palancar Reef.

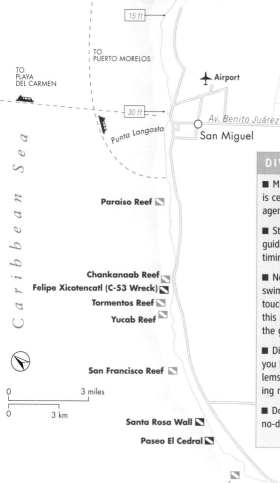

15 ft

TO
PUERTO MORELOS

TO
PLAYA
DEL CARMEN

✈ Airport

30 ft

Punta Langosta

Av. Benito Juárez

San Miguel

Caribbean Sea

Paraíso Reef ◣

Chankanaab Reef ◣
Felipe Xicotencatl (C-53 Wreck) ◣
Tormentos Reef ◣
Yucab Reef ◣

San Francisco Reef ◣

0 — 3 miles
0 — 3 km

Santa Rosa Wall ◣
Paseo El Cedral ◣

Palancar Reef ◣
◣
Colombia Reef ◣

Laguna
Colombia
Laguna
Chunchacaab

Parque Punta Sur

Punta Celarain

Maracaibo Reef ◣

30 ft
50 ft

dives; at 50 feet there's an abrupt yet sensational drop-off to enormous coral overhangs. The strong current drags you along the tunnels and caves, where there are huge sponges, angelfish, groupers, and rays—and sometime even a shark or two.

◣**Tormentos Reef.** The abundance of sea fans, sponges, sea cucumbers, arrow crabs, green eels, groupers, and other marine life—against a terrifically colorful backdrop—makes this a perfect spot for underwater photography. This variegated reef has a maximum depth of around 70 feet.

◣**Yucab Reef.** South of Tormentos Reef, this relatively shallow reef is close to shore, making it an ideal spot for beginners. About 400 feet long and 55 feet deep, it's teeming with queen angelfish and sea whip swimming around the large coral heads. The one drawback is the strong current, which can reach two or three knots.

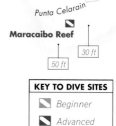

KEY TO DIVE SITES

◣ *Beginner*

◣ *Advanced*

It's important to choose a dive shop that suits your expectations. Beginners are best off with the more established, conservative shops that limit the depth and time spent underwater. Experienced divers may be impatient with this approach, and are better suited to shops that offer smaller group dives and more challenging dive sites. More and more shops are merging these days, so don't be surprised if the outfit you dive with one year has been absorbed by another the following year. Recommending a shop is dicey. The ones we recommend are well-established and also recommended by experienced Cozumel divers.

Because dive shops tend to be competitive, it's well worth your while to shop around. Many hotels have their own on-site operations, and there are dozens of dive shops in town. Before signing on, ask experienced divers about the place, check credentials, and look over the boats and equipment. Shops can have specialties, so if you have special needs (for example, kids) look for an outfitter comfortable with family dives.

(top) Felipe Xicotencatl (C-53 Wreck). (bottom) Coral, coral and more coral.

WHAT IT COSTS	
Regulator & BC	$15–$25
Underwater camera	$35–$45
Video camera	$75
Pro videos of your dive	$160
Two-tank boat trips	$60–$90
Specialty dives	$70–$100
One-tank afternoon dives	$35–$45
Night dives	$35–$45
Marine park fee	$2

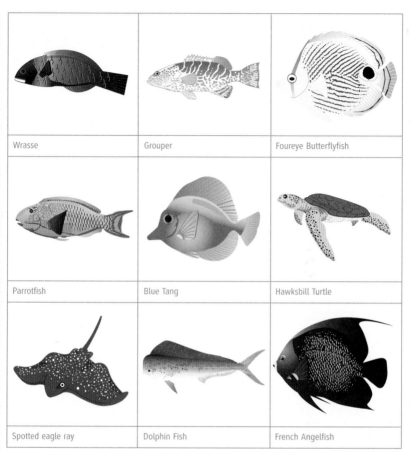

Wrasse	Grouper	Foureye Butterflyfish
Parrotfish	Blue Tang	Hawksbill Turtle
Spotted eagle ray	Dolphin Fish	French Angelfish

SNORKELING TIPS

Snorkeling equipment is available at nearly all hotels and beach clubs as well as at Parque Chankanaab, Playa San Francisco, and Parque Punta Sur. Gear rents for less than $10 a day. Snorkeling tours run about $60 and take in the shallow reefs off Palancar, Chankanaab, Colombia, and Yucab.

■ Never turn your back on the ocean, especially if the waves are big.

■ Ask about rip tides before you go in.

■ Enter and exit from a sandy beach area.

■ Avoid snorkeling at dusk and never go in the water after dark.

■ Wear lots of sunscreen, especially on your back and butt cheeks.

■ Don't snorkel too close to the reef. You could get scratched if a wave pushes you.

■ Be mindful of boats.

SCUBA DIVING

There's no way anyone can do all the deep dives, drift dives, shore dives, wall dives, and night dives in one trip, never mind the theme dives focusing on ecology, archaeology, sunken ships, and photography.

Many hotels and dive shops offer introductory classes in a swimming pool. Most include a beach or boat dive. Resort courses cost about $60–$80. Many dive shops also offer full open-water certification classes, which take at least four days of intensive classroom study and pool practice. Basic certification courses cost about $350, while advanced and specialty certification courses cost about $250–$500. You can also do your classroom study at home, then make your training and test dives on Cozumel.

DIVING SAFELY There are more than 100 dive shops in Cozumel, so look for high safety standards and documented credentials. The best places offer small groups and individual attention. Next to your equipment, your dive master is the most important consideration for your adventure. Make sure he or she has PADI or NAUI certification (or FMAS, the Mexican equivalent). Be sure to bring your own certification card; all reputable shops require customers to show them before diving. If you forget, you may be able to call the agency that certified you and have the card number faxed to the shop.

Keep in mind that much of the reef off Cozumel is a protected National Marine Park. Boats aren't allowed to anchor in certain areas, and you shouldn't touch the coral or take any "souvenirs" from the reefs when you dive there. It's best to swim at least three feet above the reef—not just because coral can sting or cut you, but also because it's easily damaged and grows very slowly; it has taken 2,000 years to reach their present size.

There are two reputable recompression chambers in Cozumel if you need emergency medical attention: **Medicina Hiperbarica Integral** (⊠ Calle 5 Sur 21B ☎ 987/872–1430 24-hr hotline); and **Costamed Cozumel** (⊠ Calle Primera sur 101, Adolfo López Mateos ☎ 9400 or 987/872–5050). These chambers, which aim for a 35-minute response time from reef to chamber, treat decompression sickness, commonly known as "the bends," which occurs when you surface too quickly and nitrogen bubbles form in the bloodstream. Recompression chambers are also used to treat nitrogen narcosis, collapsed lungs, and hypothermia.

You may also want to consider buying dive-accident insurance from the U.S.-based **Divers Alert Network** (DAN) (☎ 800/446–2671, 919/684–9111 emergency hotline ⊕ www.diversalertnetwork.org) before embarking on your dive vacation. DAN insurance covers dive accidents and injuries, and their emergency hotline can help you find the best local doctors, hyperbaric chambers, and medical services. They can also arrange for airlifts.

Diver on the Paradise Reef.

KITEBOARDING AND PADDLEBOARDING

De Lille Sports. Cozumel native Raul De Lille—a former world windsurf champion and national kiteboard champion—offers two- to three-hour classes in both stand-up paddleboarding (SUP) and kiteboarding. Multiday courses, rental equipment, and sport-oriented tours are available, too. ■ TIP→ If the winds are calm, inquire about De Lille's private snorkeling tour to the northern tip of the island. ☎ *987/103–6711 (mobile)* ⊕ *www.delillesports.com* ✉ *From MX$2120 for a 2- to 3-hr class.*

SNORKELING AND SCUBA DIVING

Aldora Divers. Make the most of your trip by exploring the undersea environment with Aldora Divers. Although it also works with neophytes, this outfit caters to experienced divers. Its all-day, three-tank nitrox trip gets you up close to reef sharks, eagle rays, and huge lionfish. ■ TIP→ Ask about Aldora's afternoon lionfish hunting trip to the north end of the island. ⊠ *Calle 5 Sur, between avs. 5 and Rafael E. Melgar, San Miguel* ☎ *987/872–3397, 210/569–1203* ⊕ *www.aldora. com* ✉ *Two-tank dives from MX$1213.*

Aquatic Sports and Expeditions. Sergio Sandoval gets rave reviews from his clients, many of whom are repeat customers. In addition to the usual excursions, he'll take you out for wreck dives, underwater photo safaris, or lionfish hunting. He also charters his boat for full- and half-day fishing trips. ⊠ *Carretera Sur, Km 6.5* ☎ *987/112–5002, 1987/111–1172 (mobile)* ⊕ *www.cozumeldivingwithsergio.com* ✉ *Two-tank dives from MX$1023.*

Blue Angel Scuba School. The combo dive-and-snorkel excursions arranged by Blue Angel allow family members to have fun together, even if not all are scuba enthusiasts. Dedicated dive trips to local reefs and PADI courses are also offered. ⊠ *Blue Angel Resort, Carretera Sur, Km 2.2* ☎ *987/872–1631* ⊕ *www.blueangelscubaschool.com* ✉ *Snorkel trips from MX$532, two-tank dives from MX$1078.*

Del Mar Aquatics. In operation since 1987, Del Mar Aquatics offers PADI and DAN certified dive trips as well as certification courses. Their boats are larger and slower, but have an onboard head (toilet). ⊠ *Casa Del Mar Hotel, Carretera Sur Km 4.5* ☎ *987/872–5949* ⊕ *www. delmaraquaticsstore.com* ✉ *Two-tank dives from MX$1092.*

Eagle Ray Divers. Snorkeling trips and dive instruction are available through Eagle Ray Divers. (The three-reef snorkel trip lets non-divers explore beyond the shore.) As befits their name, the company keeps track of the eagle rays that appear off Cozumel from December to February and runs trips for advanced divers to walls where the rays congregate. Beginners can also see rays around some of the reefs. ⊠ *La Caleta Marina, near the Presidente InterContinental* ☎ *987/872–5735, 866/465–1616* ⊕ *www.eagleraydivers.com* ✉ *Two-tank dives from MX$1023.*

Fury Catamarans. Vacationers who can't decide between snorkeling and partying can combine the two by boarding one of Fury's 65-foot catamarans. Boats visit the reef en route to a private stretch of beach south of town. Rates include equipment, lunch, soft drinks, beer, and margaritas, plus access to assorted beach toys. A sunset booze cruise is also offered, and there are numerous pick-up points along the west coast. ✉ *Carretera Sur, Km 3.5, beside Casa del Mar Hotel* ☎ *987/872–5145* ⊕ *www.furycozumel.com* ✉ *From MX$805.*

Fodor's Choice ★   **Scuba Du.** Dive magazines regularly rate Scuba Du among the best dive shops in the Caribbean. Along with the requisite Cozumel reef dives, it organizes night dives and an advanced trip to walls off Punta Sur, as well as snorkeling and fishing trips. The Presidente InterContinental Hotel, Casa Mexicana, and Hotel B offer lodging and dive packages. ✉ *Presidente InterContinental Hotel, Carretera Sur, Km 6* ☎ *987/872–9500, 310/684–5556* ⊕ *www.scubadu.com* ✉ *Two-tank dives from MX$1214.*

Fodor's Choice ★   **ScubaTony.** Diving with ScubaTony is like diving with friends you've known for years. The personalized trips include tanks, weights, fresh fruit, and drinks. If you're new to the sport or have a few years between dives, introductory and refresher courses are available; PADI certified instructors will also work with you to obtain additional certifications (such as nitrox). ✉ *Puerto Caleta, Carretera A Chankanaab, Km 6* ☎ *987/113–3706, 310/272–9943* ⊕ *www.scubatony.com* ✉ *Two-tank dives from MX$1220.*

Fodor's Choice ★   **Tiger's Adventures.** Tiger Aguilar leads one of the island's more enjoyable snorkel-and-party excursions. In the water, you might encounter harmless nurse sharks in addition to turtles, fish, and starfish; aboard the boat, you can indulge in adult beverages, sodas, and fresh snacks. Trips run from 11 to 4:30, with passengers departing from Money Bar Beach Club bound for the shallow lagoon, "El Cielo." ✉ *Carretera Costa Sur, Km 6.5* ☎ *987/871–0897* ⊕ *www.tigers-adventures.com* ✉ *MX$846 (cash only), reservations required.*

SUBMARINE TOURS

FAMILY   **Atlantis Submarine.** If you're curious about what's underneath Cozumel's waters but don't like getting wet, Atlantis Submarine has 1½-hour submarine rides that explore the Chankanaab Reef and surrounding area. Subs descend about 100 feet—deeper than most scuba dives go—but be warned: claustrophobes may not be able to handle the sardine-can conditions. All passengers must be at least 36" tall and over 4 years old. ✉ *Carretera Sur, Km 4, across from Hotel Casa del Mar* ☎ *987/872–5671* ⊕ *www.atlantissubmarines.travel* ✉ *MX$1432.*

YUCATÁN AND CAMPECHE STATES

WELCOME TO YUCATÁN AND CAMPECHE STATES

TOP REASONS TO GO

★ **Visiting spectacular Mayan ruins:** Chichén Itzá and Uxmal are two of the largest, most beautiful sites in the region.

★ **Living like a wealthy hacendado:** You can stay in a restored *henequen* (sisal) plantation-turned-hotel and delight in its old-world charm.

★ **Browsing at fantastic craft markets:** This region is known for its handmade *hamacas* (hammocks), piñatas, and other local handicrafts.

★ **Swimming in pristine freshwater cenotes:** These sinkholes, like portals to the underworld, are scattered throughout the inland landscape.

★ **Tasting diverse flavors:** Yucatecan specialties served in restaurants here include Mayan-originated dishes like *cochinita pibil* (pork cooked in banana leaves).

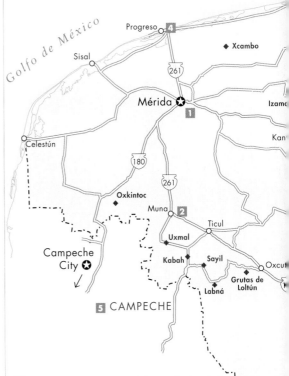

1 Mérida. Fully urban, and bustling with foot and car traffic, Mérida was once the main stronghold of Spanish colonialism in the peninsula. Tucked among the restaurants, museums, and markets are grand, old, ornamented mansions and civic buildings that recall the city's heyday as the wealthiest capital in Mexico.

2 Uxmal and the Ruta Puuc. South of Mérida, beautiful Uxmal is less well known (and typically far less crowded) than Chichén Itzá. Many other smaller archaeological sites—some hardly visited—lie along the Ruta Puuc.

3 Chichén Itzá and the Mayan Interior. Yucatán's spectacular Mayan ruins are famous all over the world. The best-known is Chichén Itzá, a magnificent and mysterious site that draws more than a million visitors every year.

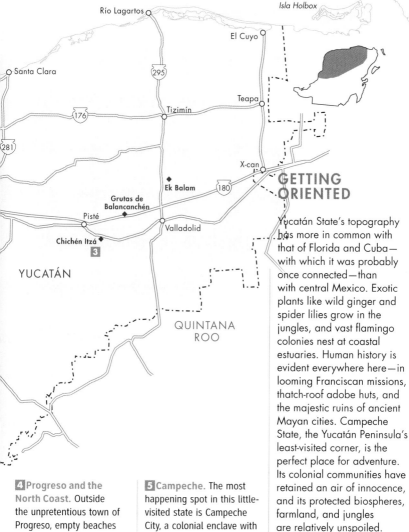

Río Lagartos

Isla Holbox

El Cuyo

Santa Clara

295

Teapa

176

Tizimín

281

X-can

Ek Balam

180

**GETTING
ORIENTED**

Grutas de
Balancanchén

Pisté

Valladolid

Chichén Itzá

3

YUCATÁN

**QUINTANA
ROO**

6

Yucatán State's topography
has more in common with
that of Florida and Cuba—
with which it was probably
once connected—than
with central Mexico. Exotic
plants like wild ginger and
spider lilies grow in the
jungles, and vast flamingo
colonies nest at coastal
estuaries. Human history is
evident everywhere here—in
looming Franciscan missions,
thatch-roof adobe huts, and
the majestic ruins of ancient
Mayan cities. Campeche
State, the Yucatán Peninsula's
least-visited corner, is the
perfect place for adventure.
Its colonial communities have
retained an air of innocence,
and its protected biospheres,
farmland, and jungles
are relatively unspoiled.
Campeche City, the state's
most accessible spot, makes
a good hub for exploring
other areas, many of which
have only basic restaurants
and primitive lodgings.

4 **Progreso and the
North Coast.** Outside
the unpretentious town of
Progreso, empty beaches
stretch for miles in either
direction—punctuated only
by fishing villages, estuaries, and salt flats. Bird-
watchers and nature lovers
flock to Celestún and Río
Lagartos to admire one of
the hemisphere's largest
colonies of pink flamingos.

5 **Campeche.** The most
happening spot in this little-
visited state is Campeche
City, a colonial enclave with
the dreamy air of bygone
times. Elsewhere are Mayan
villages that maintain their
traditional ways. To the
south, along the Guate-
malan border, the Reserva
de la Biósfera Calakmul is
home to thousands of birds,
butterflies, and plants.

YUCATÁN CUISINE

Chefs in Mexico skillfully combine ingredients and techniques from the New World and Old, but the cuisines here vary dramatically from region to region. The flavors of Yucatán are subtle, unique, and not to be missed.

(*Above and top right*) The presentation of cochinita pibil can vary from restaurant to restaurant. (*Bottom right*) Huevos motuleños

In terms of culinary traditions, the country can be divided into four regions. Foods from the north tend to be unpretentious; here you'll find dishes that were originally served on ranches and haciendas. On both coasts, seafood takes center stage. The central region includes the area in and around Mexico City, where many of the country's most characteristic plates were invented in convent kitchens during colonial times. Foods from the south, including the Yucatán, are singular within Mexico. This region was once a difficult area to access, so the culinary traditions that developed on the isolated peninsula were quite different from those in other areas of the country. At the same time, centuries of commercial and cultural trade with Cuba, Europe (especially France), and New Orleans have left their mark on Yucatecan cuisine. More recent Middle Eastern influences are also visible.

AGUA

In the Yucatán's warm weather, nothing satisfies like a cool *agua fresca* (fruit-infused water). One drink that you won't want to miss is *agua de chaya*. Chaya, sometimes called "tree spinach," is a nutritious leafy green that's used in a wide variety of recipes, including soups, omelets, tamales, and a sweet agua fresca.

REGIONAL CUISINES

Visitors to the Yucatán often discover a wide variety of dishes they've never seen before. This is because Yucatán cuisine is not often served in Mexican restaurants north of the border, or even in other areas of the country. Here are some of the most typical dishes—all of them well worth a try.

Huevos motuleños. This is a popular breakfast dish that originated in Motul, a small town east of Mérida, where the ancient Mayan city of Zacmotul once stood. Eggs, sunny side up, are covered with black beans and cheese and served on a crispy tortilla. Other ingredients like red salsa, ham, and green peas are usually heaped on top. Fried plantains are often served on the side.

Sopa de lima. This soup is traditionally prepared with turkey, indigenous to the Yucatán, and includes pieces of tomatoes, sweet chile or green pepper, and lime juice. It's garnished with strips of lightly fried tortilla.

Queso relleno. Legend has it that in the 19th century a boat from Holland was forced to dock on the peninsula because of bad weather, and the people in Mérida were delighted with the cargo of Dutch cheese. From this trip, a typical Yucatecan dish made with Gouda or Edam cheese was born. A salty cow's-milk cheese is stuffed with spiced ground meat and served with

two sauces: a tomato-caper sauce and a milder creamy sauce.

Cochinita pibil. This is perhaps the most representative dish in the Yucatecan repertoire. The word *pibil* means "roasted in the hole," which describes just how this dish is classically prepared. The Maya used to roast venison in this way, but the Spanish-introduced pork is now the standard. The meat is first marinated in a mixture of bitter orange juice (from the Seville oranges that grow in this region), *achiote* (an intensely peppery paste that some describe as having a nutmeglike flavor, made from annatto seeds), oregano, salt, and pepper. Next, it's wrapped in banana leaves and placed in a hole lined with stones that have been heated with fire. The meat cooks slowly. These days, this dish is often made in a pot on the stove or slow-roasted in the oven. It's usually served in tacos with pickled onions called *cebollas en escabeche*.

Updated by Jeffrey Van Fleet

In sharp contrast to the resort lifestyle of Cancún and the Riviera Maya, the Yucatán and Campeche states cater to a more tranquil traveler who is looking to avoid the Spring Break atmosphere. Here you'll find innumerable natural and historic wonders, including mangrove forests, unspoiled beaches, quaint colonial villages, and more than 50% of Mexico's bird species.

Unlike Quintana Roo, Yucatán and Campeche states have few international residents, and there's much less emphasis on beachside activities. With the largest indigenous population in the country, these states are defined by Mayan culture and traditions; the area's history, people, and food set it apart from the rest of Mexico.

One of the Yucatán State's biggest draws is its capital, Mérida. It is the handsome regional hub of art and culture, and locals and travelers alike gather in the main square for weekend performances. Izamal, the oldest town in the Yucatán, will take you back in time with its cobblestone streets, iron lampposts, yellow-painted buildings, and horse-drawn carriages. Near the state's eastern border, the budding cosmopolitan town of Valladolid offers excellent bird-watching and freshwater cenotes where you can explore underwater caves.

More than 2,000 Mayan ruins lie within these two states, but only a handful have been restored for tourism. Nestled amid rampant jungles are the magnificent archaeological sites of Uxmal, Kabah, Labná, Sayil, Dzibilchaltún, and Chichén Itzá, a UNESCO Natural World Heritage Site. Roughly one hour southeast of Uxmal, the Grutas de Loltún show signs of human civilization dating as far back as 800 BC. At these natural caverns, illuminated pathways meander past stalactites, stalagmites, and limestone formations.

The beach town of Celestún offers nature lovers a chance to ogle huge flocks of pink flamingos. To combine wildlife with adventure, head to Río Lagartos where you can kayak through the mangroves. Off the coast of Isla Holbox, diving with whale sharks is possible from June through August. This small island, void of cars, is one of the area's best spots to relax and enjoy beach life. Near Mérida, the sand-rimmed community of Progreso is another coastal favorite.

Campeche, the more remote neighboring state, is known for its haciendas and colonial towns. The state's capital (also called Campeche) sits within a 26-foot wall that served as a protective border against pirates in the 17th century. Today this harbor city is centered by colorful buildings and a charming plaza where people gather to admire the cathedral, browse the market, or enjoy *pan de cazón*, a traditional casserole made with shredded shark meat. For a mellow alternative, you can explore the coastline by boat or spend a day bird-watching at the Calakmul Biosphere Reserve.

PLANNING

WHEN TO GO

As with many other places in Mexico, high season begins in late November and continues until early April. The weeks around Christmas and Easter are peak times for visiting; making reservations up to a year in advance is common. Fortunately, the Yucatán doesn't get the Spring Break crowds like Cancún, but you may see a slight increase in travelers (and prices) during August, when most Europeans take their vacations.

If you're traveling off-season, May is usually the hottest month of the year; rainfall is heaviest between June and October, bringing with it an uncomfortable humidity. Provided you can avoid Thanksgiving weekend, November is one of your best bets for good weather and affordable rates. This time of year, the rainy season is over, the humidity has faded, and temperatures are pleasantly cool—plus you also won't have to deal with holiday hordes, which means properties and airlines will most likely be offering discounted rates.

GETTING HERE AND AROUND

AIR TRAVEL

Aeroméxico and Interjet fly from Mexico City to both Aeropuerto Manuel Crescencio Rejón (MID) in Mérida and Aeropuerto Internacional Alberto Acuña Ongay (CPE) in Campeche City. Volaris also links Mérida to Mexico City, and Mayair, a small regional airline, connects it to Cancún daily. International flights land in Mérida as well. United comes nonstop daily from Houston, and Aeroméxico flies in from Miami.

BUS TRAVEL

ADO runs direct buses to many coastal cities and ruins from Mérida. They depart from the first-class CAME bus station. Regional bus lines to intermediate or more out-of-the-way destinations leave from the second-class terminal just across the street.

CAR TRAVEL

From Mérida, highways radiate in every direction. To the east, Carreteras 180D *cuota* and 180 *libre* are, respectively, the toll and free roads to Cancún; driving the full length of the former (⊕ *www.sct. gob.mx*) costs about MX$414. The toll road has exits for the famous

Chichén Itzá ruins and the low-key colonial city of Valladolid; the free road passes through these and many smaller towns. Although it's a dull drive, the toll road is faster, better maintained, and void of detours. Heading south from Mérida on Carretera 261 (Carretera 180 until the town of Umán), you come to Uxmal and the Ruta Puuc, a series of small ruins of relatively uniform style (most have at least one outstanding building). Carretera 261 north from Mérida takes you to the port and beach resort of Progreso. To the west, the laid-back fishing village of Celestún—which borders protected wetland—can be accessed by a separate highway from Mérida. *(⇨ Check out our Travel Smart chapter for rules of the road and information on rental car agencies if you plan on driving.)*

■ TIP➜ If you're independent and adventurous, hiring a rental car is a great way to explore. Daily rental rates are low, but full-coverage car insurance (by Mexican law) will cost you about $45 per day. Be sure to check the lights, windshield wipers, and spare tire before taking off. Carry plenty of bottled water, fill up the gas tank whenever you see a station, and try to avoid driving at night.

RESTAURANTS

Expect a superb variety of cuisines—primarily Yucatecan, of course, but also Lebanese, Italian, French, Chinese, vegetarian, and Mexican—at very reasonable prices. Reservations are advised for the pricier restaurants on weekends and in high season. Beach towns, such as Progreso, Río Lagartos, and Celestún, tend to serve fresh, simply prepared seafood. The regional cuisine of Campeche is renowned throughout Mexico. Specialties include fish and shellfish stews, cream soups, shrimp cocktail, squid and octopus, and *panuchos* (chubby rounds of fried cornmeal covered with refried beans and topped with onion and shredded turkey or chicken).

Mexicans generally eat lunch in the afternoon—certainly not before 2. If you want to eat at noon, call ahead to verify hours. In Mérida the locals make a real event of late dinners, especially in summer. Casual (but neat) dress is acceptable at all restaurants. Avoid wearing shorts or casual sandals in the more expensive places, and anywhere at all—especially in the evening—if you don't want to look like a tourist. Although food servers at most local restaurants are kind and hospitable, they don't always show it like they do in the States. Be patient and realize that, for many, the language barrier may cause them to be more reserved but not necessarily unfriendly. ■ TIP➜ It's common practice for restaurants to include gratuity and tax in the total bill, so double-check your bill before adding a tip.

HOTELS

Yucatán State has around 8,500 hotel rooms—a little over a third of what Cancún has. Try to check out the interior before booking a room; the public spaces in Mérida's hotels are generally better kept than the guest quarters. Most hotels have air-conditioning, and even many budget hotels have installed it in at least some rooms—but it's best to ask ahead.

> ■TIP→ If you plan to spend most of your time enjoying downtown Mérida, stay near the main square or along Calle 60. If you're a light sleeper, however, opt for one of the high-rises along or near Paseo Montejo, about a 20-minute stroll (but an easy cab ride) from Plaza Grande.

Inland towns such as Valladolid and Ticul are good options for a look at the slow-paced countryside. There are several charming hotels near the major archaeological sites Chichén Itzá and Uxmal, and a growing number of small beachfront hotels in Progreso. Campeche City has a few interesting lodgings converted from old homes (and in some cases mansions), as well as newer, large hotels along the *malecón* (boardwalk) and near the town center.

The hotel reviews in this book have been condensed. For more detailed reviews, see Fodors.com.

DINING AND LODGING PRICES IN DOLLARS AND PESOS			
$	**$$**	**$$$**	**$$$$**
Restaurants	under MX$135	MX$135–MX$200	MX$201–MX$350	over MX$350
Hotels in dollars	under $100	$100–$200	$201–$300	over $300
Hotels in pesos	under MX$1450	MX$1450–MX$2900	MX$2901–MX$4400	over MX$4400

Restaurant prices are the average price for a main course at dinner, or if dinner is not served at lunch. Hotel prices are for a standard double room in high season, including taxes.

TIMING

You should plan to spend at least five days in the Yucatán. It's best to start your trip with a few days in Mérida. (Weekends, when some streets are closed to traffic and there are lots of free outdoor performances, are a great time to visit.) You should also budget enough time to day-trip to the sites of Chichén Itzá and Uxmal; visiting Mérida without traveling to at least one of these sites is like driving to the beach and not getting out of the car.

VISITOR INFORMATION

Oficina de Turismo de Yucatán. The main branch of the state tourism office is on the ground floor of the Palacio del Gobierno in Mérida; there's also a branch office in the city's Teatro Peón Contreras. ⊠ *Palacio del Gobierno, Calle 61 between calles 60 and 62, Col. Centro, Mérida* ☎ *999/930–3101 for main office, 999/954–9290 for branch office* ⊕ *www.yucatan.gob.mx* ⊙ *Daily 8–8.*

MÉRIDA

307 km (184 miles) west of Cancún.

Bustling streets, lively parks, a tropical version of the Champs-Elysées, endless cultural activities, and a varied nightlife: Mérida is the beating urban heart of the Yucatán. The hubbub of the city can seem frustrating—especially if you've just spent a peaceful few days on the coast or visiting Mayan sites—but as the cultural and intellectual hub of the peninsula, Mérida is rich in art, history, and tradition.

Most streets here are one-way and the bus routes are not all that direct, so you're better off parking your car downtown and walking to the local sites and attractions. Most are located around Plaza Grande (the *zócalo* or main square), bordered by calles 60–63. Using this as your starting point is a great way to get to know the layout of the city. If you need extra help getting oriented, stop by the tourism offices on the square; the friendly, helpful staff have loads of information.

Plaza Grande itself is in the oldest part of town, the Centro Histórico. On Saturday night and Sunday, practically the entire population of the city gather in the parks and plazas surrounding it to socialize and watch live entertainment. Calle 60 between Parque Santa Lucía and Plaza Grande gets especially lively. Restaurants set out tables in the streets, which quickly fill with patrons enjoying the free tango, salsa, or jazz performances. On Sunday mornings, downtown streets are closed for pedestrians and cyclists from Parque de la Ermita through Plaza Grande to Paseo Montejo.

■TIP→ Most streets in Mérida are numbered, not named, and most run one-way. North–south streets have even numbers, which descend from west to east; east–west streets have odd numbers, which ascend from north to south. Street addresses are confusing because they don't progress in even increments by blocks, for example, the 600s may occupy two or more blocks. A particular location is therefore usually identified by indicating the street number and the nearest cross street, as in "Calle 64 and Calle 61," or "Calle 64 between calles 61 and 63," which is written "Calle 64 x 61 y 63."

GETTING HERE AND AROUND

AIR TRAVEL

Mérida's airport, Aeropuerto Manuel Crescencio Rejón, is 7 km (4½ miles) west of the city on Avenida Itzáes. Getting from it to the downtown area usually takes 20 to 30 minutes by taxi, and the fare will be about MX$180.

BUS TRAVEL

Municipal buses charge about MX$6 for trips around Mérida; having the correct change is helpful but not required. Riding the red, double-decker **Turibus** is a fun and informative alternative. You can buy your ticket (MX$120) on board the open-roof vehicle and get on and off as you please at seven key stops, enjoying recorded commentary along the way. The full route takes 1 hour 45 minutes to complete, and buses operate from 9:05 am until 9 pm. A smaller bus operator, **Carnavalito**, visits many of the same sites. The upside to this tour is that it's given by real people (in both Spanish and English), so you can ask questions; the downside is that you can't hop on and off at will. Tours cost MX$100 and last around two hours, with a 20-minute break at a small shopping center where you can stretch your legs or buy a drink. The colorful Carnavalito bus takes off from Parque Santa Lucía Monday to Saturday at 10, 1, 4, and 7; Sunday departures are at 1 and 3.

Contacts Carnavalito ☎ *999/927–6119* ⊕ *www.carnavalitocitytour.com.mx.*
Turibus ☎ *999/920–7636, 55/5563–6693 in Mexico City* ⊕ *www.turibus.com.mx.*

CARRIAGE TRAVEL

One of the best ways to get a feel for the city is to hire a *calesa,* or horse-drawn carriage. You can hail one of these at Plaza Grande or, during the day, at Palacio Cantón, site of the archaeology museum on Paseo Montejo. Choose your horse and driver carefully, as some of the animals look dispirited, but others are fairly well cared-for. Drivers charge about MX$200 for an hour-long circuit around downtown and up Paseo de Montejo, pointing out notable buildings and providing a little historic background along the route (note the drivers' English-language proficiencies run the gamut from capable to halting); an extended tour costs about MX$350.

TAXI TRAVEL

Regular taxis in Mérida charge beach-resort prices, and most don't use meters. Ones that do have a sign that reads "*taxímetro*" on the roof; these are recommended because they offer fair rates. Expect to pay MX$15 to MX$25 for a trip around Centro and MX$50 between Centro and Paseo Montejo.

TOURS

Mérida has more than 50 tour operators, and they generally take you to the same places. Because there are so many reputable, reasonably priced companies, there's no reason to opt for the less predictable *piratas* ("pirates") who sometimes lurk outside tour offices offering to sell you a cheaper trip and don't necessarily have much experience or your best interests at heart.

EcoTurismo Yucatán. A good mix of day trips, overnight tours, and customized excursions throughout the region is available through EcoTurismo Yucatán, which is based in Mérida. Their Calakmul tour includes several nights' camping in the biosphere reserve for nature spotting, as well as visits to Calakmul, Chicanná, and other area ruins. A daylong biking adventure packs includes cycling plus brief visits to two archaeological sites, a cave, a hacienda, and two cenotes. ⊠ *Calle 3, No. 235, between calles 32A and 34, Col. Pensiones* ☎ *999/920–2772, 954/242–0007 in the U.S.* ⊕ *www.ecoyuc.com* ✉ *From MX$875.*

Gray Line Yucatán. This familiar name offers a bit of everything—from a city tour of Mérida to archaeology-themed outings in Chichén Itzá, Uxmal, or Kabah. Other options include bird-watching, cenote swims, and hacienda visits. Airport transfers, private transportation, and overnight packages are available, too. The Yucatán operation is based in Mérida, and most tours leave from there, but they visit the entire region. ☎ *998/887–2495, 01800/719–5465 toll-free in Mexico* ⊕ *www.graylineyucatan.com* ✉ *Tours from MX$712.*

Mérida English Library. If you enjoy walking, the Mérida English Library conducts 2½-hour home and garden tours every Tuesday morning from November through April. Meet at the library at 9 am for registration. ⊠ *Calle 53, No. 524, between calles 66 and 68, Col. Centro* ☎ *999/924–8401* ⊕ *www.meridaenglishlibrary.com* ✉ *MX$200.*

Municipal Tourist Office Tours. Free 90-minute walking tours are offered year-round by the city's tourist office (Oficina de Turismo de Mérida). They depart from City Hall, on the main plaza, at 9:30 am Monday through Saturday; in July, evening tours are added at 7:30. The office also conducts a fun, spooky guided walk through the municipal cemetery every Wednesday evening. It's free as well, but advance reservations are required. All tours are conducted in Spanish and English. ■ TIP→ DIY types can rent gear for a four-hour audio tour of the city (MX$80). ⊠ *Palacio Municipal, Calle 62 between calles 61 and 63, Col. Centro* ☎ *999/942–0000* ⊕ *www.merida.gob.mx.*

VISITOR INFORMATION

Contacts **Oficina de Turismo de Mérida** ⊠ *Palacio Municipal, Calle 62 between calles 61 and 63, Col. Centro* ☎ *999/942–0000* ⊕ *www.merida.gob.mx* ⊙ *Daily 8–8.*

EXPLORING

TOP ATTRACTIONS

Casa de Montejo. Three Franciscos de Montejo—father, son, and nephew—conquered the peninsula and founded Mérida in January of 1542, and they completed construction of this stately home on the south side of the central plaza in 1549. It's the city's oldest and finest example of colonial plateresque architecture, a Spanish architectural style popular in the 16th century and typified by the kind of elaborate ornamentation you'll see here. A bas-relief on the doorway—the facade is all that remains of the original house—depicts Francisco de Montejo the younger, his wife, and daughter, as well as Spanish soldiers standing on the heads of the vanquished Maya. The building now houses a branch of the Banamex bank and the **Museo de Sitio**, with interesting exhibits of Meridano life in the 19th century. ⊠ *Calle 63, No. 506, Col. Centro* ☎ *999/923–0633* ⊕ *www.museocasamontejo.com* 🖭 *Free* ⊙ *Tues.–Sat. 10–7, Sun. 10–2.*

Catedral de Mérida. Begun in 1561, Mérida's archdiocesan seat is the oldest cathedral on the North American mainland (though an older one can be found in the Dominican Republic). It took several hundred Maya laborers, working with stones from the pyramids of the ravaged Mayan city, 37 years to complete it. Designed in the somber Renaissance style by an architect who had worked on the Escorial in Madrid, its facade is stark and unadorned, with gunnery slits instead of windows, and faintly Moorish spires. Inside, the black *Cristo de las Ampollas* (Christ of the Blisters) occupies a side chapel to the left of the main altar. At 23 feet tall, it's the tallest Christ figure inside a Mexican church. The statue is a replica of the original, which was destroyed during the revolution in 1910, which is also when the gold that typically decorated Mexican cathedrals was carried off. According to one of many legends, the Christ figure burned all night yet appeared the next morning unscathed—except that it was covered with the blisters for which it's named. You can hear the pipe organ play at the 11 am Sunday Mass. ⊠ *Calles 60 and 61, Col. Centro* ☎ *999/924–7777* ⊕ *www.arquidiocesisdeyucatan.com.mx* 🖭 *Free* ⊙ *Daily 7–11:30 and 4:30–8.*

FAMILY **Centro Cultural de Mérida Olimpo.** Referred to as simply the "Olimpo," this is the best venue in town for free cultural events. The beautiful porticoed cultural center was built adjacent to City Hall in late 1999, occupying what used to be a parking lot. The marble interior is a showcase for top international art exhibits, classical-music concerts, conferences, and theater and dance performances. The adjoining 1950s-style movie house shows classic art films by directors like Buñuel, Fellini, and Kazan. The center also houses a planetarium with 60-minute shows explaining the solar system (narration is in Spanish); they run Tuesday through Sunday at 6 pm and Sunday at 10, 11, noon, 6, and 7—be sure to arrive 15 minutes early, as nobody is allowed to sneak in once the show has begun. ⊠ *Calle 62, between calles 61 and 63, Col. Centro* ☎ *999/942–0000* ⊕ *www.merida.gob.mx/planetario* ▱ *Free; MX$56 for planetarium* ☉ *Tues.–Sun. 9–3 and 5–8.*

FAMILY

Fodor's Choice

★

Gran Museo del Mundo Maya. Whether or not the "Grand Museum of the Mayan World" lives up to its lofty name depends on your taste and expectations, but the institution has certainly made a big architectural splash. The starkly modern building was designed to resemble a giant ceiba tree, sacred to the Maya, and it looms over the northern outskirts of town on the highway to Progreso. (Plan on a MX$100 taxi ride from downtown to get here.)

Inaugurated the night of Dec. 21, 2012 (the reputed end of the world according to the Mayan calendar), the museum showcases an amazing collection of 1,100 Mayan artifacts previously housed at the Palacio Cantón, where there was limited room for displays. Here, exhibitions wind through four themed halls: The Mayab, Nature, & Culture; Ancestral Maya; Yesterday's Maya; and Today's Maya. Much of the exhibit space is given over to multimedia presentations, and therein lies the problem for some museum purists. The interactive screens *are* enormously popular, especially with younger visitors. (One all-the-rage panel of screens lets you tap in your birth date, convert it to the corresponding date on the Mayan calendar, and email yourself your Mayan horoscope.) Museum officials have responded to criticisms about the inclusion of modern technology by saying that Mayan culture isn't merely an artifact of the past but an evolving way of life that has adapted to modern times—why not adapt a museum's teaching methods to modernity, too?

Everything here—artifact labeling and multimedia narration—is trilingual (Spanish, English, and Maya). An outdoor sound-and-light show depicting Mayan themes is projected onto the building's exterior on weekend nights. With 34 changing screens, the spectacle is billed as Latin America's largest such show. An adjoining theater, named the Mayamax, screens films, and a concert hall hosts some of the biggest names in Latin American showbiz. ⊠ *Calle 60 Norte, Unidad Revolución* ☎ *999/341–0430* ⊕ *www.granmuseodelmundomaya.com* ▱ *MX$170* ☉ *Wed.–Mon. 8–5; sound-and-light show Fri.–Sun. at 8:30 pm.*

Paseo Montejo. North of downtown, this 10-block-long street was *the* place to reside in the late 19th century, when wealthy plantation owners sought to outdo each other with the opulence of their elegant mansions.

Mérida

They typically opted for the decorative styles popular in New Orleans, Cuba, and Paris—imported Carrara marble, European antiques—rather than any style from Mexico. The broad boulevard, lined with tamarind and laurel trees, has lost much of its former panache; many of the mansions are now used as office buildings, while others have been or are being restored as part of a citywide, privately funded beautification program. But the street is still a lovely place to explore on foot or in a horse-drawn carriage.

Plaza Grande. Mérida's main square is wired as a Wi-Fi hotspot, but don't be so glued to your smartphone that you fail to take in the passing parade of activity in one of Mexico's loveliest town centers. Locals traditionally refer it as the "Plaza Grande" or "Plaza de la Independencia"; you'll also hear it called "zócalo," primarily among foreigners. Whichever name you prefer, it's a good place to start a city tour, watch dance performances, listen to music, or chill in the shade of a laurel tree. Plaza Grande was laid out in 1542 on the ruins of T'hó, the Mayan city demolished to make way for Mérida, and it's still the focal point around which the most important public buildings cluster. *Confidenciales* (S-shape benches) invite intimate tête-à-têtes, and lampposts keep the park beautifully illuminated at night. ⊠ *Bordered by calles 60, 62, 61, and 63, Col. Centro.*

Teatro Peón Contreras. This 1908 Italianate theater was built along the same lines as grand turn-of-the-20th-century European theaters and opera houses. In the early 1980s, the marble staircase, dome, and frescoes were restored. Today, in addition to being a performing arts venue, the theater houses a branch of the **Oficina de Turismo** (tourist information office) for the state of Yucatán. The theater's most popular attraction, however, is the café-bar spilling out into the street facing Parque de la Madre. ⊠ *Calle 60 between calles 57 and 59, Col. Centro* ☎ *999/924–3954* ⊕ *www.culturayucatan.com* ☉ *Daily 9–9.*

WORTH NOTING

Aké. This compact archaeological site east of Mérida offers the unique opportunity to view architecture spanning two millennia in one sweeping vista. Standing atop a ruined Mayan temple built more than a thousand years ago, you can see the incongruous sight of workers processing sisal in a rusty-looking factory, which was built in the early 20th century. To the right of this dilapidated building are the ruins of the old Hacienda and Iglesia de San Lorenzo Aké, both constructed of stones taken from the Mayan temples.

Experts estimate that Aké was populated between AD 250 and 900; today many people in the area have Aké as a surname. The city seems to have been related to the very important and powerful one at present-day Izamal; in fact, the two cities were once connected by a *sacbé* (white road) 43 feet wide and 33 km (20 miles) long. All that has been excavated so far are two pyramids, one with rows of columns (35 total) at the top, reminiscent of the Toltec columns at Tula, north of Mexico City. ⊠ *Near Tixkokob, 32 km (19 miles) east of Mérida* ⊠ *MX$42* ☉ *Daily 9–5.*

Ermita de Santa Isabel. Several blocks south of the city center stands the restored Hermitage of St. Isabel, also known as the Hermitage of the Good Trip. Completed in 1748 as part of a Jesuit monastery, the beautiful edifice served as a resting place for colonial-era travelers heading to Campeche. It's one of the most peaceful places in the city and a good destination for a ride in a horse-drawn carriage. Behind the hermitage are huge, lush tropical gardens, with a waterfall and footpaths, which are usually unlocked during daylight hours. ⊠ *Calles 66 and 77, La Ermita* ⊠ *Free* ⊙ *Hrs vary; church open only during Mass.*

Iglesia de la Tercera Orden de Jesús. Just north of Parque Hidalgo is one of Mérida's oldest buildings and the first Jesuit church in the Yucatán. It was built in 1618 from the limestone blocks of a dismantled Mayan temple, and faint outlines of ancient carvings are still visible on the west wall. Although a favorite place for society weddings due to its antiquity, the church interior is not ornate.

The former convent rooms in the rear of the building now host the **Pinoteca Juan Gamboa Guzmán,** a small but interesting art collection. The most engaging pieces here are the striking bronze sculptures of indigenous Maya crafted by celebrated 20th-century sculptor Enrique Gottdiener Soto. On the second floor are about 20 forgettable oil paintings, mostly of past civic officials. ⊠ *Calle 60 between calles 57 and 59, Col. Centro* ☎ *999/924–9712* ⊕ *www.inah.gob.mx* ⊠ *Free* ⊙ *Tues.–Fri. 7–noon and 6–8, Sat. 7–noon and 6–8:30, Sun. 8–1 and 6:30–9:30.*

Museo Fernando García Ponce—MACAY. Originally designed as an art school and used until 1915 as a seminary, this enormous, light-filled building now showcases the works of contemporary Yucatecan artists such as Gabriel Ramírez Aznar and Fernando García Ponce, and hosts a variety of temporary exhibits. If you want to explore beyond the outside plaza, be sure to sign in first. ⊠ *Plaza Grande, Pasaje de la Revolución 1907, between calles 58 and 60, Col. Centro* ☎ *999/928–3236* ⊕ *www. macay.org* ⊠ *Free* ⊙ *Wed.–Mon. 10–5:30.*

Museo de Arte Popular de Yucatán. This museum offers a comprehensive introduction to different kinds of Mexican arts and crafts including ceramics, textiles, stonework, woodwork, and glass. Leave time to peruse the on-site gift shop, which sells shawls, baskets, dolls, and masks. Prices are a bit high, but so is the quality of the items; even if you don't buy anything here, a look around will inform your purchases at area markets. ⊠ *Calle 50, No. 487, between calles 57 and 59, Col. Centro* ☎ *999/928–5263* ⊕ *www.culturayucatan.com* ⊠ *Free* ⊙ *Tues.– Sat. 10–5, Sun 10–3.*

Palacio Cantón. The most compelling of the mansions on **Paseo Montejo,** this stately palacio was built as the residence for General Francisco Cantón between 1909 and 1911. Designed by Enrique Deserti, who also did the blueprints for the Teatro Peón Contreras, the building has a grandiose air that seems more characteristic of a mausoleum than a home: there's marble everywhere, as well as Doric and Ionic columns and other Italianate beaux-arts flourishes. Temporary exhibits brighten the home. ⊠ *Paseo Montejo 485, at Calle 43, Paseo Montejo*

☎ *999/928–6719*   ⊕ *www.palaciocanton.inah.gob.mx*   ▣ *MX$56* ⊙ *Tues.–Sun. 8–5.*

Palacio del Gobierno. Visit the seat of state government on the north side of Plaza Grande. You can see Fernando Castro Pacheco's murals of the bloody history of the conquest of the peninsula, painted in bold colors and influenced by the Mexican muralists José Clemente Orozco and David Alfaro Siquieros. On the main balcony (visible from outside on the plaza) stands a reproduction of the Bell of Dolores Hidalgo, on which Mexican independence rang out on the night of September 15, 1810, in the town of Dolores Hidalgo in Guanajuato. On the anniversary of the event, the governor rings the bell to commemorate the occasion. There's a branch of the state tourist office on the ground floor. ⊠ *Calle 61, between calles 60 and 62, Col. Centro* ☎ *999/930–3101* ⊕ *www.yucatan.gob.mx* ▣ *Free* ⊙ *Daily 8–8.*

Palacio Municipal. The west side of the main square is occupied by City Hall, or Ayuntamiento, a 17th-century building trimmed with white arcades, balustrades, and the national coat of arms. Originally erected on the ruins of the last surviving Mayan structure, it was rebuilt in 1735 and then completely reconstructed along colonial lines in 1928. It remains the headquarters of the local government. On the ground floor, you'll find the Oficina de Turismo de Mérida (municipal tourist office). ⊠ *Calle 62, between calles 61 and 63, Col. Centro* ☎ *999/928–2020* ⊕ *www.merida. gob.mx* ▣ *Free* ⊙ *Palacio daily 9–8; tourist office daily 8–8.*

NEED A BREAK?

El Colón Sorbetes y Dulces Finos. The homemade ice cream and sorbet at El Colón have been keeping locals cool since 1907. Served up in a pyramid-shape scoop, the tropical fruit flavors (like *chico zapote*, a brown fruit native to Mexico that tastes a little like cinnamon and comes from a tree used in chewing-gum production) are particularly refreshing. The shop also sells cookies and fresh candies—the meringues are exceptional. The tables inside are under whirling fans that make it a comfortable spot on a hot afternoon. ⊠ *Calle 62, No. 500, between calles 59 and 61, Col. Centro* ▤ *No credit cards.*

Parque Hidalgo (*Plaza Cepeda Peraza*). A half block north of the main plaza is this small cozy park, officially known as Plaza Cepeda Peraza. Historic mansions, now reincarnated as hotels and sidewalk cafés, line its south side, and at night the area comes alive with marimba bands and street vendors. On Sunday the streets are closed to vehicular traffic, and there's free live music performed throughout the day. ⊠ *Calle 60, between calles 59 and 61, Col. Centro.*

FAMILY   **Parque Zoológico El Centenario.** Mérida's top children's attraction is the large Parque Zoológico El Centenario, which features pleasant wooded paths, playgrounds, inexpensive amusement-park rides, an inline skating rink, a small lake you can row on, and a little train that circles the property. It also includes cages that house more than 300 native animals as well as exotic ones like lions and tigers (a modern zoo this is not, so you mightn't approve of those cages). At the exit, you'll find snack bars and vendors; there are on-site picnic areas, too. The French

Renaissance–style arch commemorates the 100th anniversary of Mexican independence. ✉ *Av. Itzáes, between calles 59 and 65 (entrances on calles 59 and 65), Col. Centro* ☎ *999/928–5815* 🌐 *www.merida.gob.mx/centenario* 🎟 *Entry free, activities extra* 🕒 *Tues.–Sun. 8–6.*

WHERE TO EAT

With more than 250 restaurants (not to mention the markets and street-food stands), Mérida has plenty of dining options to choose from. Regional cuisine is the staple, but the flavors and preparations don't stop there. You can find places serving burgers and sandwiches if you're craving something familiar.

$$ MEXICAN Fodor's Choice ★ 🍴 **Amaro.** The romantic patio of this historic home glows with candlelight in the evening; during the day things look a lot more casual. Meat, fish, and shellfish are served here in moderation, but the emphasis is on vegetarian dishes like avacodo pizza and *chaya* soup (made from a green plant similar to spinach), and healthful juices. Other local favorites include stuffed mushrooms, spinach lasagna, cochinita pibil, and butterfly chicken breast in a cream sauce. Prices are reasonable, and the service is always excellent. Amaro stays open until 2 am from Monday to Saturday. Expect live music in the open-air courtyard daily between 8:30 pm and midnight. [$] *Average main: 155 MP* ✉ *Calle 59, No. 507, between calles 60 and 62, Col. Centro* ☎ *999/928–2451* 🌐 *www.restauranteamaro.com* ✣ *B6.*

$$ ITALIAN 🍴 **Café Lucía.** Music floats above black-and-white tile floors in the dining room of this century-old restaurant in the Hotel Casa Lucía near the main plaza. Meals are relatively heavy, like the steak cooked in sherry and the Fettuccini Lucia with cream, cheese, and mushrooms. Pizzas, salads, and calzones are the linchpins of the Italian menu, and pecan pies, cakes, and cookies beckon from behind the glass dessert case. **■ TIP→ Breakfasts are about half the price of the lunch and dinner menu, so drop by early for a great value.** [$] *Average main: 155 MP* ✉ *Hotel Casa Lucía, Calle 60, No. 474A, between calles 53 and 55, Col. Centro* ☎ *999/928–0740* 🌐 *www.casalucia.com.mx* ✣ *B5.*

$ CAFÉ FAMILY 🍴 **Dante's.** Couples, groups of students, and lots of families crowd this bustling coffeehouse at the Centro Cultural Dante, just above Mérida's largest bookshop. The house specialty is crêpes: there are 10 varieties with either sweet or savory fillings. Light entrées such as sandwiches, burgers, pizzas, and *molletes* (large open-face rolls smeared with beans and cheese and then broiled) are also served, along with cappuccino, specialty coffees, beer, and wine. The restaurant has more traditional Yucatecan dishes like sopa de lima, too. [$] *Average main: 84 MP* ✉ *Calle 17, No. 138B, at Prolongación Paseo Montejo, Paseo Montejo* ☎ *999/927–7676* 🌐 *www.editorialdante.com* 🕒 *Closed Sun.* ✣ *D1.*

$ MEXICAN 🍴 **Eladio's.** Part bar, part restaurant, and part theater, this lively venue is often crammed with locals. There's an ample dance floor and a free, supervised children's play area—you can also buy ceramic figures for them to paint while you dance. The full menu includes tasty Yucatecan dishes like *papadzules* (hard-boiled eggs wrapped in warm tortillas and covered with a thick pumpkin-seed sauce). Free appetizers, which are actually just smaller portions of the dishes on the menu, come with your beer. From 2 to 6:30 pm you'll hear live salsa, cumbia, and other Latino tunes. The attached sports bar offers 2-for-1 beers Monday through Friday. Around 7:30 most families disappear, and singles and couples arrive to watch whatever football or boxing match is on TV. This place is known to get lively, loud, and hot. [$] *Average main: 127 MP* ✉ *Calle 24, No. 101C, at Calle 59, Col. Itzimná* ☎ *999/927–2126* 🌐 *www.eladios.com.mx* ✣ *B1.*

$$ MEXICAN Fodor's Choice ★ 🍴 **Hacienda Teya.** A former henequen-producing site dating back to 1683, this beautiful hacienda just outside Mérida serves some of the best regional food around. It has also attracted big names including Vicente Fox (when he was president, he'd order the queso relleno to go) and Hillary Clinton. Most patrons are well-to-do meridanos enjoying a leisurely lunch, so don't wear beach clothes (in fact, men wearing tank tops will be asked to change). Hacienda Teya is open from noon to 6 daily, and a guitarist serenades diners between 2 and 5 on weekends. Start with sopa de lima, then move on to standout mains like poc chuc or cochinita pibil (both served with homemade tortillas). The restaurant has the Yucatán's largest wine selection, and desserts come with a complimentary digestif. After your meal stroll through the gardens where peacocks roam. If you want to spend the night, the hacienda has six handsome suites ($$), but you'll need to book ahead for long weekends and holidays. [$] *Average main: 170 MP* ✉ *Carretera 180, Kanasín, 12.5 km (8 miles) east of Mérida* ☎ *999/988–0800* 🌐 *www.haciendateya.com* ⏲ *Closed Dec. 25–Jan 1. No dinner* ✣ *B6.*

$$$ MODERN MEXICAN 🍴 **Kuuk.** Meaning "sprout" in Mayan, Kuuk offers Mérida's most unique dining experience. The cutting-edge menu features eight courses, each prepared using molecular gastronomy and fresh ingredients, most of them grown on-site. Many of the Yucatecan dishes are cooked in the custom built "pibil" oven, a modernized version of the underground cooking method that gives food that smoky flavor. Although small, each course is a work of art—picture dollops of baby pumpkin dusted with goat cheese the texture of powdered snow or transparent potatoes as thin as tissue paper. Desserts are sprinkled with dehydrated berries, honey-soaked seeds, and cilantro pieces that look more like Skittles. Kuuk is chic in every sense of the word, from the cutlery and décor to the wine cellar and suave waiters. **■ TIP→ Plan to stay a while since dining takes between two and three hours.** [$] *Average main: 338 MP* ✉ *Calle 30, No. 313, between calles 37 and 39, San Ramon Norte* ☎ *999/944–3377* 🌐 *www.kuukrestaurant.com* ⏲ *Closed Mon. No dinner Sun.* ✣ *C1.*

$$ MEXICAN 🍴 **La Casa de Frida.** Chef-owner Gabriela Praget puts a healthful, cosmopolitan spin on Mexican fare. Traditional dishes like *chiles en nogada* (stuffed pepper in a walnut sauce) or duck in a dark, rich mole sauce share the menu with gourmet vegetarian cuisine. Standouts include potato and cheese tacos, ratatouille in puff pastry, and crêpes made with *huitlacoche* (a delicious trufflelike corn fungus). The dining room—a casual covered patio decorated with plants, copies of Frida Kahlo self-portraits, several Frida dolls, and other art—is a comfortable place to enjoy a leisurely meal. Praget prepares all the dishes herself and

is usually on hand to greet guests. Don't be alarmed if "Coco," her little white rabbit, hops between the tables. Note that a 15% service charge is automatically added to your bill. $ *Average main: 183 MP* ✉ *Calle 61, No. 526, at Calle 66, Col. Centro* ☎ *999/928–2311* ⊕ *www. lacasadefrida.com.mx* ▭ *No credit cards* ⊗ *Closed Sun. No lunch* ⊹ *A6*

$ ✕ **La Tradición.** This family restaurant is a top choice among locals—in

MEXICAN fact, many say it's their favorite restaurant in town. It's also one of the most formal places serving regional cuisine, but you'll still fit right in wearing jeans. Dishes are prepared with a charcoal stove, like your grandma might have used (if you were from around here). Portions are huge, and just about everything you'll try is tasty—including the *queso relleno* (hollowed-out cheese, stuffed with a meat-vegetable mixture) and cochinita pibil—but you might not want to pass up the cream of chaya soup, since you won't find it in many other restaurants. This original northside location serves only lunch; however, the newer downtown branch (Calle 60, No. 468) serves dinner, too. $ *Average main: 127 MP* ✉ *Calle 60, No. 293, at Calle 25, three blocks north of Fiesta Americana, Col. Alcalá Martin* ☎ *999/925–2526* ⊕ *www.latradicionmerida. com* ⊗ *No dinner* ⊹ *B1.*

$$$ ✕ **La Tratto.** Although the open design of this popular family-owned Ital-

ITALIAN ian eatery does make it a nice place to enjoy the cool evening weather, the food isn't spectacular, and the prices are pretty high by Mérida standards. Still, the salads are generous, almost all of the thin-crust pizzas come with four cheeses, and there are 2-for-1 pastas on Wednesday; there's usually some kind of deal on the excellent wine list, too (check the website for promotions). Happy hour runs weekdays from 7 to 9 pm, and you can drink in the activity on Paseo Montejo from the bar. The original La Tratto opens only for dinner, but a newer outlet on Calle 60 near the Parque Santa Lucía serves lunch as well. $ *Average main: 226 MP* ✉ *Prolongación Paseo Montejo 479C, Paseo Montejo* ☎ *999/927–0434* ⊕ *www.latrattomerida.com* ⊗ *No lunch* ⊹ *C1.*

$$ ✕ **Los Almendros.** A vintage Yucatecan restaurant with high colonial

MEXICAN ceilings and an elegant atmosphere, Los Almendros is a longtime local favorite. The *combinado yucateco* (Yucatecan combination plate) is a great way to try different dishes: cochinita pibil, *longaniza asada* (grilled pork sausages), *escabeche de Valladolid* (turkey with chiles, onions, and seasonings in an acidic sauce), and *poc chuc* (slices of pork in a sour-orange sauce). In fact, Los Almendros invented some dishes that have become Yucatecan classics—including the cheese soup, which is also spectacular. A live trio performs daily from 2 to 5 pm. $ *Average main: 197 MP* ✉ *Calle 50A, No. 493, between calles 57 and 59, facing Parque La Mejorada, Col. Centro* ☎ *999/928–5459* ⊕ *www. restaurantelosalmendros.com.mx* ⊹ *C6.*

$$$ ✕ **Pancho's.** In the evening this patio restaurant is bathed in candlelight

MEXICAN and the glow from tiny white lights decorating the tropical shrubs. Much of the menu, as well as the décor, is geared toward tourists—you can even buy a Pancho's T-shirt on your way out. Although you won't find authentic Yucatecan dishes at this lively spot, the tasty tacos, fajitas, burritos, and other dishes will be pleasantly recognizable to those familiar with Mexican food served north of the border. Waiters—dressed

6

in white muslin shirts and pants of the Revolution era—recommend the shrimp flambéed in tequila, and the tequila in general. Happy hour is weekdays from 6 to 8 pm. $ *Average main: 225 MP* ⊠ *Calle 59, No. 509, between calles 60 and 62, Col. Centro* ☎ *999/923–0942* ⊕ *www.panchosmerida.com* ⊘ *No lunch* ⊕ *B6.*

$ × **Rescoldos.** This small, cozy Mediterranean bistro (whose name means "burning embers") was the dream of Canadian owners Jake and Rae Ann. Food is served in a courtyard where Jake mans the Pompeii pizza oven that they converted from an old cement water cistern. Rae Ann puts her own spin on traditional Italian dishes like fried raviolis with apple and walnut and thick-crust pizza piled high with sausage, spinach and provolone. Equally satisfying are Greek selections like spanakopita and falafel. Vegetarians have plenty of options, including vegetable lasagna, roasted veggies, and a selection of tasty salads. Don't leave without trying the memorable homemade gelato. $ *Average main: 127 MP* ⊠ *Calle 62, No. 366, between calles 41 and 43, Col. Centro* ☎ *999/286–1028* ⊕ *www.rescoldosbistro.com* ⊟ *No credit cards* ⊘ *Closed Sun.–Tues. No lunch* ⊕ *B4.*

MEDITERRANEAN

$$ × **Ristorante Bologna.** You can dine alfresco or inside at this beautifully restored old mansion, a few blocks off Paseo Montejo. Tables have fresh flowers and cloth napkins, walls are adorned with pictures of Italy, and there are plants everywhere. Most menu items are ordered à la carte; among the favorites are the shrimp pizza and pizza *diabola*, topped with salami, tomato, and chiles. The beef filet—served solo or covered in cheese or mushrooms—comes with a baked potato and a medley of sautéed vegetables. $ *Average main: 155 MP* ⊠ *Calle 21, No. 117A, between calles 24 and 24A, Col. Itzimná* ☎ *999/926–2505* ⊘ *Closed Tues.* ⊕ *C1.*

ITALIAN

$$$$ × **Rosas & Xocolate Restaurant.** A tribute to the owner's mother Rosa and to Mayan chocolate, this trendy restaurant is beautifully designed in hues of pink and brown, with long-stem roses on every table. Choose from the formal dining room, the more casual open-air patio, or the rooftop bar. Chef David Segovia's culinary creations are categorized by "Land" and "Sea." The menu changes regularly but you might find top selections like ribeye with cardamom-seasoned eggplant or tuna with a black-sesame crust. There is also a six-course tasting menu as well as a reasonably priced lunch menu offering pasta, burgers, and sandwiches. $ *Average main: 367 MP* ⊠ *Paseo Montejo, No. 480, at Calle 41, Col. Centro* ☎ *999/924–2992* ⊕ *www.rosasandxocolate.com* ⊕ *C4.*

ECLECTIC

MARKET SNACKS

Parque Santa Ana. The simple market in Parque Santa Ana is a popular breakfast spot where you'll find locals happily starting their day with regional dishes and fresh juices at plastic tables. The tamales are good and the *tortas de cochinita*, pork sandwiches flavored with a few drops of sour-orange chile sauce, are heavenly. Most vendors here close around 1:30 in the afternoon, but some reopen to sell snacks between 7 pm and midnight. ⊠ *Calle 60 between calles 45 and 47, Centro.*

$$$ STEAKHOUSE 🍴 **Trotter's.** One of Mérida's most upscale eateries is beautifully designed with indoor-outdoor dining rooms separated by a glass wall. Although less formal, the outdoor patio is surrounded by lush vegetation, helping you forget that you are on a bustling avenue. Catering to foreigners and locals alike, the staff speak perfect English and will gladly explain house favorites like the tuna steak with black-pepper crust or the Angus beef served with a side of rosemary potatoes. Although steaks are the specialty here, you'll also find plenty of delicious tapas and salads. In fact, the starters alone make Trotter's worth visiting; try the octopus carpaccio or foie gras. [$] *Average main: 338 MP* ✉ *Circuito Colonias between calles 34 and 36, Paseo Montejo* ☎ *999/927–2320* 🌐 *www.trottersmerida.com* ⏲ *No dinner Sun.* ✣ *C1.*

WHERE TO STAY

Mérida has a wide range of lodgings, from old haciendas and converted colonial homes to big corporate hotels and little B&Bs. Generally, you'll find smaller options in the downtown area, within walking distance of most sights; nights are inevitably a little louder here, especially if your room faces the street. Note that small lodgings usually sport small, easy-to-miss signs; you may need to spin around the block a time or two in your taxi or rental vehicle to find your hotel. A few larger chain hotels around the Paseo de Montejo offer quiet rooms, and are still near major streets, and only a short ride from downtown.

$ HOTEL 🏨 **Best Western Maya Yucatán.** The only U.S. chain hotel in the city center combines a familiar name with local touches. **Pros:** terrific rates; business amenities; familiar name. **Cons:** even with local touches, still a U.S. chain; business-oriented. [$] *Rooms from: $70* ✉ *Calle 58, No. 483, between calles 55 and 57, Col. Centro* ☎ *999/923–7070, 800/564–2515* 🌐 *www.hotelmayayucatan.com.mx* 🛏 *72 rooms, 6 suites* 🍽 *No meals* ✣ *B5.*

$$$ B&B/INN Fodor's Choice ★ 🏨 **Casa Azul.** Declared a historical monument and a Yucatán Heritage site, the French-style "Blue House" is notable for its extraordinary antiques, luxurious fabrics, rose-filled bouquets, and superior service. **Pros:** sterling service; modern comforts in colonial home; filtered tap water; conveniently located off Paseo Montejo. **Cons:** small pool; some street noise; no children under 12. [$] *Rooms from: $250* ✉ *Calle 60, No. 343, between calles 35 and 37, Col. Centro* ☎ *999/925–5016* 🌐 *www.casaazulhotel.com* 🛏 *8 rooms* 🍽 *Breakfast* ✣ *B3.*

$ HOTEL 🏨 **Casa del Balam.** This pleasant hotel has an excellent location two blocks from the zócalo in downtown's best shopping area. **Pros:** easy walk to many sights; spacious rooms; great restaurant service. **Cons:** slow elevator; street noise can be a problem. [$] *Rooms from: $81* ✉ *Calle 60, No. 488, at Calle 57, Col. Centro* ☎ *999/924–8844, 800/624–8451* 🌐 *www.casadelbalam.com* 🛏 *43 rooms, 8 suites* 🍽 *Breakfast* ✣ *B6.*

$$$ B&B/INN Fodor's Choice ★ 🏨 **Casa Lecanda.** From the moment you step off the busy streets into Casa Lecanda's cool lobby, you're wrapped in European grandeur; wrought-iron chandeliers and antique furniture pay tribute to a bygone era in Mérida's most luxurious boutique hotel, while the photographs of the modern-day city bring you back to the present. **Pros:** local flavor; elegant atmosphere; excellent service. **Cons:** must reserve dinner

6

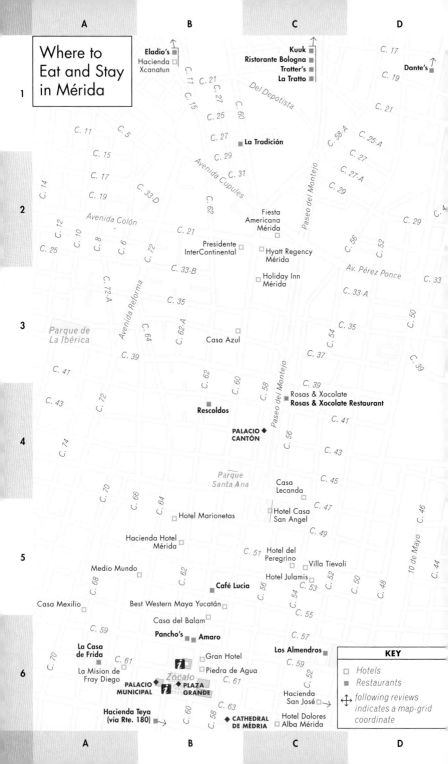

Where to Eat and Stay in Mérida

A

Eladio's ■
Hacienda □
Xcanatun

C. 11 *C. 21*

C. 11

C. 5

C. 15

C. 14

C. 17

C. 19

C. 33-D

Avenida Colón

C. 12
C. 10
C. 8
C. 6

C. 25

C. 72

Parque de
La Ibérica

C. 41

C. 43

C. 72

Avenida Reforma

C. 74

C. 64

C. 62-A

C. 39

C. 70
C. 66
C. 64

Hacienda Hotel
Mérida □

Medio Mundo □

C. 68
C. 62

Casa Mexilio □

Best Western Maya Yucatán □

C. 59

La Casa
de Frida ■

C. 70
C. 61

La Mision de
Fray Diego □

PALACIO ◆
MUNICIPAL

Hacienda Teya
(via Rte. 180) ■■➤

C. 60
C. 65

B

C. 21
C. 27
C. 15
C. 25
C. 60

Del Depotista

C. 27

■ La Tradición

C. 29

Avenida Cupules

C. 31

C. 62

C. 21

Presidente □
InterContinental

C. 33-B

C. 35

Casa Azul

C. 62
C. 60
C. 58

Rescoldos ■

C. 56

Parque
Santa Ana

Hotel Marionetas □

Café Lucia ■

C. 62

Casa del Balam □

Pancho's ■■ ■ Amaro

Gran Hotel □
Piedra de Agua □

Zócalo 🚻

PLAZA ◆
GRANDE

C. 61

C. 63

◆ CATHEDRAL
DE MÉDRIA

C

Kuuk ■
Ristorante Bologna ■
Trotter's ■
La Tratto ■

C. 68-A *C. 25-A*

C. 27

C. 27-A

C. 29

Paseo del Montejo

Fiesta
Americana
Mérida
□

Hyatt Regency
Mérida □

Holiday Inn
Mérida □

C. 54

C. 35

C. 37

Paseo del Montejo

C. 39

Rosas & Xocolate □
Rosas & Xocolate Restaurant ■

C. 41

PALACIO ◆
CANTÓN

C. 56

C. 43

C. 45

Casa
Lecanda
□

C. 47

Hotel Casa □
San Angel

C. 49

C. 51 Hotel del
Peregrino
□ □ Villa Tievoli

Hotel Julamis □
C. 56 *C. 53* *C. 52*
C. 54

C. 55

C. 57

Los Almendros ■

C. 59

C. 52

Hacienda
San José □➤

Hotel Dolores
Alba Mérida □

D

C. 17

C. 19

Dante's ■

C. 21

C. 56
C. 52

Av. Pérez Ponce

C. 33-A

C. 33

C. 50

C. 39

10 de Mayo

C. 46

C. 50
C. 48

C. 44

KEY

□ *Hotels*
■ *Restaurants*
⬍ *following reviews
indicates a map-grid
coordinate*

24 hours in advance; small windows in "Adrian" room; no children under 12; pool is more of a showpiece than a place to swim. [$] *Rooms from: $220* ✉ *Calle 47, No. 471, between calles 54 and 56, Col. Centro* ☎ *999/928–0112* 🌐 *www.casalecanda.com* 🛏 *7 rooms* 🍴 *Breakfast* ✣ *C4.*

$$ B&B/INN 🏨 **Casa Mexilio.** Built in the late 1800s, this Venetian-inspired townhouse is now an intimate hotel with antique furniture and colorful tile floors just four blocks from Plaza Grande. **Pros:** pleasant courtyard; easy walk downtown; free international calls. **Cons:** small bathrooms; no elevator; no children under 16; off-site parking. [$] *Rooms from: $95* ✉ *Calle 68, No. 495, between calles 57 and 59, Col. Centro* ☎ *999/928–2505, 888/819–0024* 🌐 *www.casamexilio.com* 🛏 *6 rooms* 🍴 *Breakfast* ✣ *A5.*

$$ HOTEL FAMILY 🏨 **Fiesta Americana Mérida.** This posh hotel, a branch of a dependable Mexican chain, echoes the grandeur of the mansions on Paseo Montejo, and its spacious lobby is filled with colonial accents, plush armchairs, and gleaming marble. **Pros:** comfortable beds; tasty breakfast buffet; shopping downstairs; free kids club. **Cons:** a taxi ride from downtown; some amenities cost extra. [$] *Rooms from: $161* ✉ *Paseo Montejo 451, at Av. Colón, Paseo Montejo* ☎ *999/942–1111, 877/927–7666* 🌐 *www.fiestaamericana.com* 🛏 *323 rooms, 27 suites* 🍴 *Multiple meal plans* ✣ *C2.*

$ HOTEL 🏨 **Gran Hotel.** Cozily situated on Parque Hidalgo, this legendary 1901 hotel has extremely high ceilings, wrought-iron balcony and stair rails, and ornately patterned tile floors. **Pros:** beautiful antique decorations; great rates; in the middle of downtown shops and services. **Cons:** downtown noise; no elevator makes upstairs rooms a hike; parking is sometimes unavailable (check ahead if you are driving). [$] *Rooms from: $72* ✉ *Calle 60, No. 496, at Parque Hidalgo, Col. Centro* ☎ *999/923–6963* 🌐 *www.granhoteldemerida.com* 🛏 *21 rooms, 7 suites* 🍴 *No meals* ✣ *B6.*

$$$$ HOTEL 🏨 **Hacienda San José.** One of five haciendas in the Starwood Luxury Collection, this former cattle ranch has fully restored guest rooms throughout its 25 lush acres. **Pros:** authentic hacienda experience; rooms have jungle Jacuzzis; guests receive complimentary 10-min massage. **Cons:** jungle setting too remote for some; difficult to find; 45 mins from Mérida; spotty Wi-Fi. [$] *Rooms from: $400* ✉ *Carr. Tixkobob-Tekanto, Km 30, Tixkokob* ☎ *999/924–1333* 🌐 *www.thehaciendas.com* 🛏 *15 rooms* 🍴 *Multiple meal plans* ✣ *C6.*

$$$ HOTEL Fodor's Choice ★ 🏨 **Hacienda Xcanatún.** Although this stunningly restored 18th-century henequen hacienda is only 13 km (8 miles) from Mérida, it feels a world away. **Pros:** outstanding restaurant; stellar service; expansive gardens; two wheelchair-accessible rooms. **Cons:** a drive from the city; pricey; not suitable for children. [$] *Rooms from: $265* ✉ *Carretera 261, Km 12, 13 km (8 miles) north of Mérida* ☎ *999/930–2140, 888/883–3633* 🌐 *www.xcanatun.com* 🛏 *5 rooms, 13 suites* 🍴 *No meals* ✣ *B1.*

$ HOTEL 🏨 **Holiday Inn Mérida.** Possibly the most light-filled hotel in Mérida, the Holiday Inn has an open center courtyard and floor-to-ceiling windows throughout the colorful lobby and tiled dining room. **Pros:** spacious rooms; nice breakfast buffet; pleasant courtyard. **Cons:** 1½ km (1 mile) from downtown; pool too small for serious swimming; gym not well equipped. $ *Rooms from: $90* ⊠ *Av. Colón 498, at Calle 60, Paseo Montejo* ☎ *999/942–8800, 877/834–3613* ⊕ *www.holidayinn.com.mx* ⊷ *198 rooms, 15 suites* ⊙| *No meals* ✛ *C3.*

$$
HOTEL
⊞ **Hotel Casa San Angel.** The comfortable lobby of this small hotel has an open-air central courtyard with a fountain surrounded by plants. **Pros:** unique setting; comfortable rooms with spacious bathrooms; fantastic service. **Cons:** small pool; no children under 15; those with allergies might have issues with two resident cats. $ *Rooms from: $180* ⊠ *Paseo Montejo 1, at Calle 49, Col. Centro* ☎ *999/928–1800* ⊕ *www. hotelcasasanangel.com* ⊷ *12 rooms, 3 suites* ⊙| *No meals* ✛ *C5.*

$
B&B/INN
⊞ **Hotel del Peregrino.** This restored colonial home with high ceilings and brightly painted walls mixes in modern furnishings to create a comfortable, inexpensive option near the center of Mérida. **Pros:** inexpensive; easy walk downtown; gracious staff can arrange tours and Spanish tutoring; communal computer. **Cons:** spacious but basic rooms; kitchen and lounge areas can get noisy; mediocre breakfast; off-site pool. $ *Rooms from: $72* ⊠ *Calle 51, No. 488, between calles 54 and 56, Col. Centro* ☎ *999/924–3007* ⊕ *www.hoteldelperegrino.com* ⊷ *17 rooms* ⊙| *Breakfast* ✛ *C5.*

$
HOTEL
⊞ **Hotel Dolores Alba Mérida.** If you can look beyond the plastic flowers, cement bed frames, and vending machines at reception, this cheerful hotel can be quite a bargain—especially the rooms in the newer wing that have powerful air-conditioning, comfy beds, and amenities like large TVs and balconies. **Pros:** great prices; nice pool; short walk to Plaza Grande. **Cons:** mediocre breakfast; Internet in common areas only; loud a/c; no bathroom amenities. $ *Rooms from: $60* ⊠ *Calle 63, No. 464, between calles 52 and 54, Col. Centro* ☎ *999/928–5650* ⊕ *www.doloresalba.com* ⊷ *80 rooms* ⊙| *Breakfast* ✛ *C6.*

$$
HOTEL
⊞ **Hotel Hacienda Mérida.** This urban oasis features a dramatic pool surrounded by pillared archways draped with white curtains. **Pros:** walking distance to city center; great service; one of the few luxury haciendas that allows children. **Cons:** slow Internet; no restaurant; building facade showing a bit of wear. $ *Rooms from: $129* ⊠ *Calle 62, No. 439, between calles 51 and 53, Col. Centro* ☎ *999/924–4363* ⊕ *www. hotelhaciendamerida.com* ⊷ *14 rooms* ⊙| *No meals* ✛ *B5.*

$
B&B/INN
Fodor's Choice
★
⊞ **Hotel Julamis.** With room rates just below the competition, this 200-year-old artist-owned hotel is a Mérida leader when it comes to value and service. **Pros:** remarkable rates; halfway between Paseo de Montejo and historic center; great views from rooftop bar. **Cons:** no children under 12; credit cards not accepted. $ *Rooms from: $69* ⊠ *Calle 53, No. 475B, at Calle 54, Col. Centro* ☎ *999/924–1818* ⊕ *www.hoteljulamis.com* ⊷ *6 rooms; 1 suite* ▭ *No credit cards* ⊙| *Breakfast* ✛ *C5.*

$$
B&B/INN
⊞ **Hotel Marionetas.** Attentive proprietors Daniel and Sofija Bosco have created this lovely B&B on a quiet street seven blocks from the main plaza. **Pros:** intimate feel; personal attention from proprietors and staff; calming courtyard and pool area. **Cons:** reservations needed well in advance; restaurant only serves breakfast; no bathtubs; no children under 12; off-site parking. $ *Rooms from: $95* ⊠ *Calle 49, No. 516, between calles 62 and 64, Col. Centro* ☎ *999/928–3377* ⊕ *www.*

hotelmarionetas.com 🛏 *8 rooms, 1 suite* 🍴 *Breakfast* ✥ *B5.*

$ B&B/INN 🏨 **Hotel Medio Mundo.** Painted in primary colors, this restored house in a residential part of downtown has Mediterranean accents, thick original walls, and well-preserved tile floors. **Pros:** great location; friendly staff; reasonable rates. **Cons:** some steep stairs; no children under 8; off-site parking; three rooms have fans instead of a/c. [$] *Rooms from: $76* ✉ *Calle 55, No. 533, between calles 64 and 66, Col. Centro* ☎ *999/924–5472* 🌐 *www.hotelmediomundo.com* 🛏 *10 rooms* 🍴 *Breakfast* ✥ *B5.*

MAKING YOURSELF AT HOME

There are a few online agencies that can help you rent a home if you plan on staying in the area for a while. At 🌐 *www.bestofyucatan.com*, for example, you can find some stunningly remodeled old Mérida homes and haciendas through an agency called Urbano Rentals.

$$ HOTEL 🏨 **Hyatt Regency Mérida.** The city's first deluxe hotel is still among its most elegant. **Pros:** attentive service; reasonably priced compared to neighboring hotels; popular bistro; nice fitness center. **Cons:** far from downtown; extra charge for Internet and in-room coffee. [$] *Rooms from: $110* ✉ *Av. Colón s/n, at Calle 60, Paseo Montejo* ☎ *999/942–1234, 800/233–1234* 🌐 *merida.regency.hyatt.com.mx* 🛏 *285 rooms, 4 suites* 🍴 *Multiple meal plans* ✥ *C2.*

$$ HOTEL 🏨 **La Misión de Fray Diego.** The elegant accommodations in this former 1900s convent still retain their colonial charm, and tasteful touches (like crucifixes and statues) ensure they look divine. **Pros:** courteous staff; great restaurant; charming property; centrally located. **Cons:** a bit of a climb to third-floor rooms; no children under 12; stairwell not well lighted at night. [$] *Rooms from: $135* ✉ *Calle 61, No. 524, between calles 64 and 66, Col. Centro* ☎ *999/924–1111, 866/639–2933* 🌐 *www.lamisiondefraydiego.com* 🛏 *20 rooms, 6 suites* 🍴 *Breakfast* ✥ *A6.*

$ HOTEL 🏨 **Piedra de Agua.** This converted 1842 mansion has been renovated for maximum comfort without compromising its historical charm. **Pros:** centrally located; communal computer. **Cons:** small bathrooms; some street noise; off-site parking. [$] *Rooms from: $88* ✉ *Calle 60, No. 498, between 59 and 61, Col. Centro* ☎ *999/924–2300* 🌐 *www.piedradeagua.com* 🛏 *20 rooms* 🍴 *No meals* ✥ *B6.*

$$ HOTEL 🏨 **Presidente InterContinental Villa Mercedes Mérida.** A salmon-color replica of a 19th-century French-colonial mansion, the Presidente is a bit of a hike from the main plaza but sits right next to the Santiago church and public square, where a live band attracts whirling couples on Tuesday evenings. **Pros:** spacious rooms; comfortable beds; helpful staff; good value. **Cons:** far from Plaza Grande; extra charge for Wi-Fi. [$] *Rooms from: $114* ✉ *Av. Colón 500, between calles 60 and 62, Col. Centro* ☎ *999/942–9000, 800/344–0548* 🌐 *www.grupopresidente.com.mx* 🛏 *127 rooms, 4 suites* 🍴 *Multiple meal plans* ✥ *B2.*

$$$ B&B/INN 🏨 **Rosas & Xocolate.** Designed with romance in mind, this boutique hotel has a roses and chocolate theme that carries from the pink exterior to the chocolate soaps in the bathrooms and the Belgian truffles in the gift shop. **Pros:** beautiful architecture; great breakfasts; remarkable

showers and mattresses; well-equipped gym. **Cons:** small pool in a very public area; no elevator; not suitable for children. [$] *Rooms from: $235* ✉ *Paseo Montejo 480, at Calle 41, Col. Centro* ☎ *999/924–2992* 🌐 *www.rosasandxocolate.com* 🛏 *14 rooms, 3 suites* 🍴 *Breakfast* ✥ *C4.*

$ B&B/INN Fodor's Choice ★ **Villa Tievoli.** The proprietors of this intimate B&B clearly have an eye for detail: for proof, consider the breakfast china—they keep 30 different patterns so that you won't have to see the same plates twice during your stay. **Pros:** gracious, knowledgeable owners; creative breakfasts; great rates. **Cons:** step down from bathroom to room; no parking; tiny sign makes it difficult to find. [$] *Rooms from: $84* ✉ *Calle 54, No. 455, between calles 51 and 53, Col. Centro* ☎ *1999/242–7474 (mobile), 407/369–8602 in the U.S.* 🌐 *www.thevillatievoli.com* 🛏 *3 rooms* 💳 *No credit cards* 🍴 *Breakfast* ✥ *C5.*

NIGHTLIFE

Mérida comes into its own once the sun begins to set and the heat of the afternoon gives way to the cool of the evening. The city has an active and diverse cultural life, which includes free government-sponsored music and dance performances many evenings, as well as sidewalk art shows in local parks. On Thursday at 9 pm Meridanos enjoy an evening of outdoor entertainment at the **Serenata Yucateca**, held in **Parque Santa Lucía** (Calles 60 and 55); you'll see trios, the local orchestra, and soloists performing compositions by Yucatecan composers. On Saturday evenings after 7 pm the **Noche Mexicana** (corner of Paseo Montejo and Calle 47) hosts different musical and cultural events. More free music, dance, comedy, and regional handicrafts can be found at the **Corazón de Mérida,** on Calle 60 between the main plaza and Calle 55. From 8 pm to 1 am, multiple bandstands throughout this area (which is closed to traffic) entertain locals and visitors with an ever-changing playbill, from grunge to classical.

On Sunday, six blocks around Plaza Grande are closed off to traffic, and you can see performances—often mariachi and marimba bands or folkloric dancers—at Plaza Santa Lucía, Parque Hidalgo, and the main plaza. For a schedule of current performances, consult the tourist offices, the local newspapers, or the posters at the Teatro Peón Contreras and Centro Cultural de Mérida Olimpo.

The city center and Paseo Montejo area are largely safe at night with throngs of people out enjoying themselves. (Standard precautions about watching your things apply, of course.) Restaurants and nightspots are happy to call you a taxi or have a guard hail one for you when you're ready to call it a night.

BARS AND DANCE CLUBS

Mérida has always been a great city to walk in by day and dance in by night. Meridanos love music, and they love to dance, but since they also have to work, many clubs are open only on weekend nights, or Thursday through Sunday. **TIP→ Be aware that it's becoming commonplace for discos and restaurants with live music and "comedy" acts (geared toward young people) to invite customers onstage for some rather shocking "audience participation" acts. Since these are otherwise fine** establishments, we can only suggest that you let your sense of outrage be your guide. Locals don't seem to mind.

Café Peón Contreras. The café-bar at Mérida's landmark 1908 theater is one of the most happening nightspots in town. Tables spill onto the street, where locals gather to hear balladeers singing romantic and politically inspired songs. The drinks are expensive and the food is nothing special, so only go if you want culture, live music, and an opportunity to splurge. ⊠ *Teatro Peón Contreras, Calle 60, between calles 57 and 59, facing Parque de la Madre, Col. Centro* ☎ *999/924–7003* ☉ *Daily 6–11 pm.*

El Nuevo Tucho. You can expect cheesy cabaret-style entertainment and comedy acts with no drink minimum and no cover at El Nuevo Tucho— but this isn't just a place for young people. Families come to dine here as well. There's music for dancing in the cavernous—sometimes full, sometimes empty—venue. Drinks come with free appetizers. Plan for midday entertainment since this place closes at 2 pm on weekdays and at 5 pm on Saturday. ⊠ *Calle 60, No. 482, between calles 55 and 57, Col. Centro* ☎ *999/924–2323* ⊕ *www.eltucho.inmerida.com* ☉ *Weekdays 8 am–2 pm, Sat. 8 am–5 pm.*

La Parrilla. "Location, location, location" is the allure of this loud and colorful drinking establishment. Right in the heart of Plaza Grande— but with branches around the city—the tourist magnet offers live music and drinks served in plastic yard glasses. It's one of the best spots to grab a beer and watch Mérida in action. ■ TIP→ Check the website for weekly promotions. ⊠ *Calle 60, No. 502, between calles 59 and 61, Col. Centro* ☎ *999/928–1691* ⊕ *www.laparrillamerida.com* ☉ *Daily 11 am–2 am.*

Mayan Pub. A pleasant atmosphere, flowing beer, and live music are what make this bar one of Mérida's best-kept secrets (you might want to pass on the food). Grab a spot in the beer garden where you can listen to live reggae, rock, or jazz. A rather worn billiard table and occasional entertainment—such as belly dancers and fire spinners— draw in a decent crowd. ⊠ *Calle 62, No. 473, between calles 55 and 57, Col. Centro* ☎ *999/968–7341* ⊕ *www.mayanpub.com* ☉ *Wed.–Sun. 7 pm–3 am.*

Parque de Santiago. If dancing to the likes of Los Panchos and other romantic trios of the 1940s is more your style, don't miss the Tuesday-night ritual at Parque de Santiago, where older folks and the occasional young lovers gather for dancing under the stars at 8:30 pm. Although it's just a few blocks west of the plaza, take a taxi to and from at night. ⊠ *Calles 59 and 72, Col. Centro.*

Slavia. Enormously popular and rightly so, the red-walled Slavia is an exotic Middle Eastern beauty. There are all sorts of nooks where you can be alone yet together with upscale meridanos. Ambient music in the background, low lighting, beaded curtains, embroidered tablecloths, mirrors, and sumptuous pillows and settees surrounding low tables produce a fabulous vibe that you won't find anywhere else in Mérida. ⊠ *Calle 29, No. 490, at Paseo Montejo* ☎ *999/926–6587* ☉ *Daily 5 pm–2 am.*

The plaza outside the Catedral de Mérida is a popular gathering spot.

FOLKLORIC SHOWS

Universidad Autónoma de Yucatán. Pop into the university's main building to check the bulletin boards just inside the entrance for upcoming cultural events. The **Ballet Folklórico de Yucatán** presents a combination of music, dance, and theater here most Fridays at 9 pm (think Mexico City's famous Ballet Folklórico de México, but on a slightly smaller scale); tickets are a bargain at MX$70. There are no shows from August 1 to September 22 or during the last two weeks of December. ⊠ *Calle 60 between calles 57 and 59, Col. Centro* ☎ *999/924–6729* ⊕ *www.uady.mx.*

SHOPPING

When it comes to shopping, Mérida has something for everyone from souvenir junkies to the most discriminating of market trollers. If you're looking for a more standard shopping experience, or need to grab some new tennis shoes or a pair of jeans, there are also a few shopping malls in town.

Crafts at reasonable prices can be found in the markets, parks, and plazas, and local art can be picked up at one of the many galleries, for the art scene here is burgeoning. Be aware that there have been reports of vendors increasing the prices of their art and crafts by the hundreds, claiming that the value of their wares is far greater than it really is. Most vendors are honest, so be sure to shop around to acquaint yourself with the kinds of crafts and the levels of quality that are available. Once you have an idea of what's out there, you'll be better able to spot fraud, and you may even have some fun bargaining.

MALLS

Gran Plaza. Mérida has several shopping malls, but the largest and nicest, Gran Plaza, has more than 200 shops and a multiplex theater. It's just outside town, on the highway to Progreso (called Carretera a Progreso beyond the Mérida city limits). ⊠ *Calle 50 Diagonal, No. 460, Fracc. Gonzalo Guerrero* ☎ *999/944–7658* ⊕ *www.granplaza.com.mx.*

Plaza Las Américas. This pleasant mall houses more than 114 stores and eateries (including Sears and McDonalds) plus the Cinépolis movie theater complex. ⊠ *Calle 21, No. 327, between calles 50 and 52, Col. Miguel Hidalgo* ☎ *999/987–3521.*

MARKETS

Bazar de Artes Populares. As its name implies, "popular art," or handicrafts, are sold here beginning at 9 am on Sunday. ⊠ *Parque Santa Lucía, at calles 60 and 55, Col. Centro* ☉ *Sun. 9–5.*

Mercado de Artesanías García Rejón. Although many deal in the same wares, the shops or stalls of the García Rejón Crafts Market sell some quality items, and the shopping experience here can be less of a hassle than at the municipal market. You'll find reasonable prices on palm-fiber hats, hammocks, leather sandals, jewelry, handmade guitars, and locally made liqueurs. Persistent but polite bargaining may get you even better deals. ⊠ *Calles 65 and 60, Col. Centro* ☉ *Weekdays 9–6, Sat. 9–4, Sun. 9–1.*

Mercado Lucas de Gálvez. Sellers of chiles, herbs, seafood, and fruit fill this pungent and labyrinthine municipal market. In the early morning the first floor is jammed with housewives and restaurateurs shopping for the freshest fish and produce. The stairs at calles 56 and 57 lead to the second-floor **Bazar de Artesanías Municipales**, where you'll find local pottery, embroidered clothes, guayabera shirts, hammocks, straw bags, sturdy leather huaraches, and piñatas in every imaginable shape and color. Note that most prices are inflated, and vendors expect you'll bargain—one way to begin is to politely request a discount. ⚠ **Be wary of pickpockets within the market.** ⊠ *Calles 56 and 67, Col. Centro* ☉ *Mon.–Sat. 8–6.*

RECOMMENDED STORES

BOOKS

Librería Dante. The Mérida-based bookstore chain Dante has the best selection of Spanish-language books around the peninsula. It is especially strong on books for kids and works dealing with Yucatecan nature. ⊠ *Calle 17, No. 138B, at Prolongación Paseo Montejo, Col. Itzimná* ☎ *999/927–7676* ⊕ *www.editorialdante.com* ☉ *Daily 8:30 am–10:30 pm.*

CLOTHING

Canul. You might not wear a guayabera to a business meeting as some men in Mexico do, but the shirts are cool, comfortable, and attractive. For a good selection, try Canul. Custom shirts take a week to tailor, in sizes 4 to 52. ⊠ *Calle 62, No. 484, between calles 57 and 59, Col. Centro* ☎ *999/923–0158* ⊕ *www.camiseriacanul.com.mx* ☉ *Mon.–Sat. 8:30–8, Sun. 10–1.*

CLOSE UP

Hamacas: A Primer

Yucatecan artisans are known for creating some of the finest *hamacas*, or hammocks, in the country. For the most part, the shops of Mérida are the best places in Yucatán to buy these beautiful, practical items—though if you travel to some of the outlying small towns, like Tixkokob, Izamal, and Ek Balam, you may find cheaper prices, and enjoy the experience as well.

One of the first decisions you'll have to make when buying a hamaca is whether to choose one made from cotton or nylon: nylon dries more quickly and is therefore well suited to humid climates, but cotton is softer and more comfortable (though its colors tend to fade faster). You'll also see that hamacas come in both double-thread and single-thread weaves; the double-thread ones are sturdiest because they're more densely woven.

Hamacas come in a variety of sizes, too. A *sencillo* (cen-*see*-yoh) hammock is meant for just one person (although most people find it's a rather tight fit), a *doble* (*doh*-blay), on the other hand, is very comfortable for one but crowded for two. *Matrimonial* or king-size hammocks accommodate two, and *familiares* or *matrimoniales especiales* can theoretically sleep an entire family. (Yucatecans tend to be smaller than Anglos are, and also lie diagonally in hammocks rather than end-to-end.)

For a good-quality king-size nylon or cotton hamaca, expect to pay about MX$450; sencillos go for about MX$300. Unless you're an expert, it's best to buy a hammock at a specialty shop, where you can climb in to try the size. The proprietors will also give you tips on washing, storing, and hanging your hammock. There are lots of hammock stores near Mérida's municipal market on Calle 58, between calles 69 and 73.

Guayaberas Jack. This spot has an excellent selection of guayaberas in 18 colors; they also sell typical women's cotton *filipinas* (house dresses), blouses, dresses, classy straw handbags, and lovely rayon *rebozos* (shawls) from San Luis Potosí. Guayaberas can be made to order, allegedly in less than a day, to fit anyone from a year-old baby to a 240-pound man, and anything in the shop can be altered or custom-made. Everything here is of fine quality, and is often quite different from the clothes sold in neighboring shops—the prices reflect this superior quality. You can make purchases on their website as well. ✉ *Calle 59, No. 507A, between calles 60 and 62, Col. Centro* ☎ *999/928–6002* ⊕ *www. guayaberasjack.com.mx* ⊙ *Mon.–Sat. 10–8, Sun. 10–2:30.*

Mexicanísimo. Sleek, clean-lined clothing made from natural fibers for both women and men are available at Mexicanísimo, a boutique inside the Gran Hotel. ✉ *Gran Hotel, Calle 60, No. 496, at Parque Hidalgo, Col. Centro* ☎ *999/923–8132* ⊕ *www.granhotelmerida.com* ⊙ *Weekdays 9–1 and 3–8, Sat. 9–2.*

JEWELRY

Joyería Colonial. Shop for malachite, turquoise, and other semiprecious stones set in silver at Joyería Colonial. ⊠ *Calle 60, No. 502-B, between calles 61 and 63, Col. Centro* ☎ *999/923–5838* ⊙ *Daily 9–9.*

LOCAL GOODS AND CRAFTS

Casa de Cera. This small shop sells signed collectible indigenous beeswax figurines. ⊠ *Calle 74A, No. 430E, between calles 41 and 43, Col. Centro* ☎ *999/920–0219* ⊙ *Mon.–Sat. 9–5.*

Casa de las Artesanías Ki-Huic. Visit the government-run Casa de las Artesanías Ki-Huic for folk art from throughout Yucatán. There's a showcase of hard-to-find traditional filigree jewelry in silver, gold, and gold-dipped versions. ⊠ *Calle 63, No. 503A, between calles 64 and 66, Col. Centro* ☎ *999/928–6676* ⊙ *Daily 9–5.*

El Mayab. For a multitude of hammocks, head to El Mayab. ⊠ *Calle 58, No. 553-A, at Calle 71, Col. Centro* ☎ *999/924–0853* ⊙ *Mon.–Sat. 9 am–10 pm.*

El Xiric. You can buy hammocks made to order—choose from standard nylon and cotton, super-soft processed sisal, Brazilian-style (six-stringed), or crocheted. You can also purchase xtabentún, as well as jewelry, black pottery, woven goods from Oaxaca, T-shirts, and souvenirs. ⊠ *Calle 57A, No. 15, Pasaje Congreso, Col. Centro* ☎ *999/924–9906* ⊙ *Daily 8 am–10 pm.*

Hamacas El Aguacate. A great place to purchase hammocks is Hamacas El Aguacate, a family-run outfit with many sizes and designs. ⊠ *Calle 58, No. 604, at Calle 73, Col. Centro* ☎ *999/289–5789, 999/928–6265* ⊕ *www.hamacaselaguacate.com.mx* ⊙ *Weekdays 9 am–10 pm, Sat. 9–5.*

La Casa de las Artesanías. This government-run craft store offers all kinds of local items at fair prices. There's a smaller branch in front of the Palacio Cantón on the Paseo de Montejo, but this main branch offers the best selection. ⊠ *Calle 63,, No. 513, between calles 64 and 66, Col. Centro* ☎ *999/928–6676* ⊙ *Mon.–Sat. 9–8, Sun 9–1.*

Miniaturas. A delightful and diverse assortment of crafts is sold here, but the store specializes in miniatures. ⊠ *Calle 59, No. 507A, between calles 60 and 62, Col. Centro* ☎ *999/928–6503* ⊙ *Mon.–Sat. 9–8.*

SPORTS AND THE OUTDOORS

BASEBALL

Estadio Kukulcán. Baseball is played with enthusiasm between February and July at Estadio Kukulcán. There are also tennis courts, soccer courts, and an Olympic pool here. It's most common to buy your tickets at the on-site booth the day of the game. ■**TIP➜ If you're interested in Pok ta Pok, the ritual Mayan ball game, the city tourist office sponsors a free exhibition each Friday night in front of the cathedral.** ⊠ *Circuito Colonias, Calle 6, No. 315, across street from Pemex gas station and next to Santa Clara Brewery, Col. Unidad Morelos* ☎ *999/940–4261* ◪ *Tickets MX$30–MX$230.*

GOLF

FAMILY **Club de Golf de Yucatán.** If you want to be able to boast that you golfed on the site of an ancient Mayan city, here's your chance. The state's first course encompasses a portion of the grounds of nearby Dzibilchaltún, although no Mayan structures were disturbed in the facility's construction. This 18-hole championship course is open for public play seven days a week; carts are available, and clubs can be rented. The property also includes tennis courts, a swimming pool, restaurant, gym, and miniature golf course. ⊠ *Carretera Mérida–Progreso, Km 14.5, Xcantún* ☏ *999/922–0071* ⊕ *www.golfyucatan.com* ✉ *MX$1410 for 18 holes* 🏌 *18 holes. 6590 yards. Par 72.* ☉ *Pro shop closed Mon.*

SIDE TRIP TO IZAMAL

68 km (42 miles) east of Mérida.

You won't find too many sights in beautiful Izamal, but you'll almost certainly be taken by its carefully cared-for architecture. The downtown area shines with remodeled buildings, new roads, and a signature paint color that strikingly contrasts with the blue sky. One of the best examples of a Spanish colonial community in the Yucatán, Izamal is nicknamed "Ciudad Amarilla" (Yellow City), because its most important edifices are a golden ocher. It's also sometimes called "the City of Three Cultures," because of its combined pre-Hispanic, colonial, and contemporary influences. Although unsophisticated, Izamal is a charming and neighborly alternative to the sometimes frenetic tourism of Mérida. Hotels are humble, and the few restaurants here offer basic fare. For those who enjoy a quieter, slower-pace vacation, it's worth considering as a base.

GETTING HERE AND AROUND

The drive east from Mérida takes less than an hour on Carretera 180. *Calesas* (horse-drawn carriages) are stationed at the town's large main square, fronting the lovely cathedral, day and night. Drivers—their English capabilities vary widely—charge about MX$70 an hour for sightseeing, and many will also take you on a shopping tour for whichever items you're interested in buying (for instance, hammocks or jewelry). Pick up a brochure at the visitor center for details.

VISITOR INFORMATION

Oficina de Turismo ⊠ *Calle 30, No. 323, between calles 31 and 31A, Centro* ☏ *988/954–1096* ⊕ *Daily 9–7.*

EXPLORING

Centro Cultural y Artesanal Izamal. Banamex has set up this small, well-organized art museum right on the main plaza. There are all kinds of high-quality crafts on display, from textiles and ceramics to papier-mâché and woodwork. The center also has little on-site café and gift shop. ⊠ *Calle 31, No. 201, Centro* ☏ *988/954–1012* ⊕ *www. centroculturalizamal.org.mx* ✉ *MX$28* ☉ *Tues.–Sat. 10–8, Sun. 10–5.*

Ex-Convento e Iglesia de San Antonio de Padua. Facing the main plaza, the enormous 16th-century former monastery and church of St. Anthony of Padua is perched on—and built from—the remains of a Mayan pyramid

San Antonio de Padua was built from the remains of a Mayan pyramid.

devoted to Itzámná, god of the heavens. The monastery's ocher-painted church, where Pope John Paul II led prayers in 1993, has a gigantic atrium (supposedly second in size only to the Vatican's) facing a colonnaded facade and rows of 75 white-trimmed arches. The Virgin of the Immaculate Conception, to whom the church is dedicated, is the patron saint of the Yucatán. A statue of Nuestra Señora de Izamal, or Our Lady of Izamal, was brought here from Guatemala in 1562 by Bishop Diego de Landa. Miracles are ascribed to her, and a yearly pilgrimage takes place in her honor. Frescoes of saints at the front of the church, once plastered over, were rediscovered and refurbished in 1996.

The monastery and church are now illuminated in a light-and-sound show of the type usually shown at archaeological sites. You can catch a Spanish-only narration and the play of lights on the nearly 500-year-old structure at 8:30 pm Tuesday, Thursday, Friday, and Saturday—buy tickets (MX$63) on-site at 8. ■TIP→ Diagonally across from the cathedral, the small municipal market is worth a wander. It's the kind of place where if you stop to watch how the merchants prepare food, they may let you in on their cooking secrets. ⊠ *Bounded by calles 31, 28, 33, and 30.*

Kinich Kakmó (*Kinich Kak Moo*). The Kinich Kakmó pyramid is the largest pre-Hispanic building in the Yucatán, and it's all that remains of the royal Mayan city that flourished here between AD 250 and 600. Dedicated to Zamná, Mayan god of the dew, the massive structure is more remarkable for its size than for any remaining decoration; however, it's nonetheless an impressive monument. You can scale it from the stairs on the south face for a view of the cathedral and surrounding countryside. ✉ *Calle 39 at Calle 40* 🎟 *Free; video camera fee $2* ⏲ *Daily 8–5.*

WHERE TO EAT

$ MEXICAN 🍴 **Los Mestizos.** This humble restaurant has brightly painted walls; even the ceiling fans are painted a vivid orange. The "Combinado los Mestizos" on the dinner menu offers a taste of several regional specialties including *salbutes* and *panuchos*—both typical appetizers of fried cornmeal, the latter stuffed with beans—as well as chicken and turkey dishes. A far less common dish called *dzotobichay* is a tamale made with chaya leaves. There's a bit of a view of the church beyond the marketplace from the rooftop terrace. Los Mestizos is a great place to get an early start to or wind down from a long day of sightseeing. [$] *Average main: 98 MP* ✉ *Calle 33, No. 301, behind the market, Centro* ☎ *988/954–0289* 💳 *No credit cards.*

$ MEXICAN 🍴 **Restaurante Kinich.** At the entrance to the town's most comfortable eatery, a small shop sells a carefully selected and cleverly displayed collection of local folk art. Beyond this, you enter a dining area with white tablecloths under a wide palapa, which is surrounded by plants and a burbling fountain; in a small hut in the back, women make tortillas the old-fashioned way—by hand. Menu highlights include locally made *longaniza* (a tasty grilled pork sausage) and excellent sopa de lima. The restaurant is open evenings until 8, but keeps later hours when there's a sound-and-light show downtown. [$] *Average main: 127 MP* ✉ *Calle 27, No. 299, between calles 28 and 30* ☎ *988/954–0489.*

6

WHERE TO STAY

$$$ B&B/INN 🏨 **Hacienda Sacnicte.** Three miles north of town, this hacienda (whose name refers to a local white flower) dates from 1811, but it's been restored to strike a perfect balance between the old and new with beautifully appointed suites and spacious bathrooms. **Pros:** rate includes delicious breakfast; thoughtful design; wonderful staff. **Cons:** owners rarely on site; pricey; not centrally located. [$] *Rooms from: $275* ✉ *Carretera a Tekal de Venegas, Km. 5* ☎ *1988/967–4668 (mobile)* 🌐 *www.haciendasacnicte.com* 🛏 *10 suites* 🍽 *Breakfast.*

$ B&B/INN Fodor's Choice ★ 🏨 **Hacienda Santo Domingo.** Built on a 44-acre property, this hotel has freestanding rooms separated by carefully tended gardens full of exotic plants and fruit trees. **Pros:** freestanding rooms; owners offer transportation to Chichén Itzá; close to town center; cooking lessons available. **Cons:** Wi-Fi in common areas only; not everyone loves animals. [$] *Rooms from: $65* ✉ *Calle 18, between calles 33 and 35* ☎ *1988/967–6136 (mobile)* 🌐 *www.izamalhotel.com* 🛏 *10 rooms* 💳 *No credit cards* 🍽 *Breakfast.*

$ B&B/INN 🏨 **Hotel Macan Ché.** Each artsy bungalow here has its own themed décor: the Asian room has a Chinese checkers board and origami decorations, while the Safari room has artifacts from Mexico and Africa. **Pros:** full breakfast included; great price; private yoga classes available; huge bathtubs. **Cons:** several blocks from central plaza. [$] *Rooms from: $70* ✉ *Calle 22, No. 305, between calles 33 and 35* ☎ *988/954–0287* 🌐 *www.macanche.com* 🛏 *15 rooms* 💳 *No credit cards* 🍽 *Breakfast.*

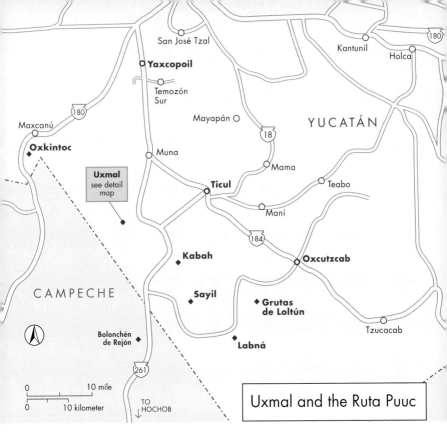

Uxmal and the Ruta Puuc

Uxmal
see detail
map

SHOPPING

Hecho a Mano. Just off the main square, Hecho a Mano is the only place in town to buy folk art from all over Mexico. You'll find something to suit any budget, including a growing collection of textiles. ⊠ *Calle 31A, No. 308, Centro* ☎ *988/954–0344.*

UXMAL AND THE RUTA PUUC

The Ruta Puuc, or hilly route, is a highlight of any visit to Yucatán. The series of secondary roads that wind through one of the state's least populated areas not only lead you from one fantastic Mayan ruin to another, but to an impressive cave system, various restored haciendas, and numerous villages where you can stop for a bite to eat and feel the unique rhythm of the Yucatecan countryside.

Uxmal, meaning thrice-built city, is the largest site along the Ruta Puuc. Several smaller satellite sites—including Kabah, Sayil, and Labná—are all well worth a visit. Another memorable Ruta Puuc attraction is the Grutas de Loltún, Yucatán's most extensive cave system. Here you can still see evidence of ancient Mayan rituals. If you plan on exploring the cave, take along sturdy shoes and a flashlight. If you want to use

Uxmal is an example of the Puuc architectural style.

your video camera at any of the sites, expect to pay a MX$25–MX$35 charge.

TIMING

It's possible to visit the sites on the Ruta Puuc in one long day or over the course of two days. Almost every Mérida-based tour operator does the former, but the latter is recommended if you have the time and your own transportation; roads are well marked and easy to navigate, since the archaeological attractions line up one right after another. Most of the sites are open from 8 to 5 only, so to devote any less time means either skipping deserving locales or rushing through them. To do Uxmal justice, you'll want to spend anywhere from 3 to 5 hours exploring; smaller ruins can easily be seen in 20 to 30 minutes. Plan on spending a couple of hours at the Grutas de Loltún; be aware that guided tours through the cave are mandatory. If you plan on spending the night in Uxmal, you may want to start your trip off at the Grutas de Loltún and work your way toward Uxmal. To reach the caves from Mérida, take Carretera 261 to Muná and turn left on Carretera 184. From there, it's about 65 km (40 miles) to Oxkutzcab. Once in Oxkutzcab, simply follow the signs to the Grutas de Loltún. ■ TIP→ It's important to fill up on fuel and cash before entering the area, because both gas stations and ATMs are hard to come by.

UXMAL

78 km (48 miles) south of Mérida on Carretera 261.

If Chichén Itzá is the most expansive Mayan ruin in Yucatán, Uxmal is arguably the most elegant. The architecture here reflects the late classical renaissance of the 7th to 9th centuries, and is contemporary with that of Palenque and Tikal, among other great Mayan cities of the southern highlands. Uxmal is considered the finest and most extensively excavated example of Puuc architecture, which embraces such details as ornate stone mosaics and friezes on the upper walls, intricate cornices, rows of columns, and soaring vaulted arches.

You could easily spend a couple of days exploring the ruins—just keep in mind that the only entertainment offered outside them is provided by hotels and the odd restaurant. The upside is that, unlike some other remote ruin sites, you can buy food, drinks, and souvenirs at the entrance.

GETTING HERE AND AROUND

If you plan to drive, take Carretera 180 south out of Mérida, and then get on Carretera 261 in Umán. This will take you south all the way to Uxmal.

EXPLORING

Choco-Story México. Located on a cocoa plantation near the Uxmal ruins, this museum highlights the history of cocoa and its relationship with the Mayan culture. Tours take place in traditional homes where you can learn about the cultivation of cocoa and the process of making chocolate. At the end, you'll be treated to a traditional Mayan drink, prepared with organic cocoa and local spices. ⊠ *Carretera 261, Km 78, near Hacienda Uxmal* ☎ *1999/289–9914 cell* ⊕ *www.choco-storymexico. com* ⊠ *MX$127* ⊙ *Daily 9–7:30.*

Fodor'sChoice
★

Uxmal. Although much of Uxmal has yet to be excavated and restored, the following buildings in particular merit attention:

At 125 feet high, the **Pirámide del Adivino** is the tallest and most prominent structure at the site. Unlike most other Mayan pyramids, which are stepped and angular, this "Pyramid of the Magician" has a softer, more-refined round-corner design. This structure was rebuilt five times over hundreds of years, each time on the same foundation, so artifacts found here represent several different kingdoms. The pyramid has a stairway on its western side that leads through a giant open-mouthed mask to two temples at the summit. During restoration work in 2002 the grave of a high-ranking Maya official, a ceramic mask, and a jade necklace were discovered within the pyramid. Ongoing excavations continue to reveal exciting new finds, still under study. Climbing is prohibited.

West of the pyramid lies the **Cuadrángulo de las Monjas**, often considered to be the finest part of Uxmal. It reminded the conquistadors of typical convent buildings in Old Spain (Monjas means nuns). You may enter the four buildings, each comprised of a series of low, gracefully repetitive chambers that look onto a central patio. Elaborate symbolic decorations—masks, geometric patterns, coiling snakes, and some phallic figures—blanket the upper facades.

Heading south, you'll pass a small ball court before reaching the **Palacio del Gobernador**. Covering five acres and rising over an immense acropolis, the palace lies at the heart of what may have been Uxmal's administrative center. It faces east while the rest of Uxmal faces west, and archaeologists suggest this allowed the structure to serve as an observatory for the planet Venus.

The **Cuadrángalo de los Pájaros** (Quadrangle of the Birds), takes its name from the repeating pattern of doves, which decorates the upper part of the building's frieze. The building is composed of a series of small chambers. In one of these, archaeologists discovered a statue of the ruler Chac (not to be confused with Chaac, the rain god), who was thought to have dwelled there.

A nightly sound-and-light show recounts Mayan legends. The colored light brings out details of carvings and mosaics that are easy to miss when the sun is shining. The show is narrated in Spanish, but earphones (MX$40) provide an English translation. **■ TIP→ In the summer months, tarantulas are a common sight on the grounds at Uxmal.** ✉ *78 km (48 mi) south of Mérida on Carretera 261* 🌐 *www.inah.gob.mx* 🎟 *Site, museum, and sound-and-light show MX$188; use of video camera MX$60* ⏲ *Daily 10–5; sound-and-light show, Apr.–Oct., daily at 8 pm, Nov.–Mar., daily at 7 pm.*

6

WHERE TO EAT

$ MEXICAN 🍴 **Cana Nah.** Although this large roadside spot mainly caters to the groups visiting Uxmal, locals recommend it as the most formally established eatery in the area, and the friendly owners are happy to serve small parties (they'll squeeze you in among the tour groups). The basic menu includes local dishes like sopa de lima and pollo pibil, and such universals as fried chicken and vegetable soup. Approach the salsa on the table with a bit of caution: it's made almost purely of habanero chiles. A small on-site shop sells pieces of popular art including figurines of *los aluxes,* the mischievous "lords of the jungle" that Mayan legend says protect farmers' fields. [$] *Average main: 127 MP* ✉ *Carretera Muna–Uxmal, 4 km (2½ miles) north of Uxmal* ☎ *1999/109–7513 cell* 💳 *No credit cards* ⏲ *No dinner.*

WHERE TO STAY

$ B&B/INN 🏨 **Flycatcher Inn.** Although branding itself as a boutique hotel, the Flycatcher Inn actually comprises seven freestanding casitas, each brightly decorated with yellow walls and Mayan art. **Pros:** great base to explore ruins; clean rooms; delicious breakfasts. **Cons:** no closets or drawers; no children under 6; no restaurant. [$] *Rooms from: $60* ✉ *Corner of Carretera 261 and Calle 20, Santa Elena* ☎ *997/978–5350* 🌐 *www.flycatcherinn.com* 🛏 *7 rooms* 🍽 *Breakfast.*

$$ HOTEL 🏨 **Hacienda Uxmal.** Uxmal's original lodging offers rooms that are simply but elegantly decorated; fronted by wide, furnished verandas, each has comfortable beds and an ample bathroom with a bathtub (some also have a hot tub). **Pros:** good service; good restaurant; pretty gardens; interesting on-site activities. **Cons:** Wi-Fi in common areas only; lacks true hacienda charm; tourists arrive by the busload. [$] *Rooms*

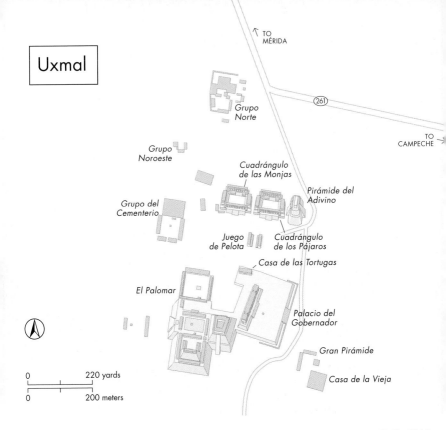

Uxmal

TO
MÉRIDA

261

TO
CAMPECHE

Grupo
Norte

Grupo
Noroeste

Cuadrángulo
de las Monjas

Pirámide del
Adivino

Grupo del
Cementerio

Juego
de Pelota

Cuadrángulo
de los Pájaros

Casa de las Tortugas

El Palomar

Palacio del
Gobernador

Gran Pirámide

Casa de la Vieja

0   220 yards

0   200 meters

from: $108 ✉ Carretera 261, Km 78 ☎ 998/887–2495, 877/240–5864 ⊕ www.mayaland.com ⤳ 54 rooms, 8 suites ⎮◎⎮ No meals.

$$ **The Lodge at Uxmal.** The outwardly rustic, thatch-roof buildings here
HOTEL   have red-tile floors, hand carved doors and rocking chairs, stained
glass windows, and local weavings. **Pros:** directly across from Uxmal
entrance; simple yet beautiful rooms; big pools; gracious staff. **Cons:**
expensive for rustic rooms. $ *Rooms from: $175 ✉ Carretera Uxmal,
Km 78 ☎ 998/887–2495, 877/240–5864 ⊕ www.mayaland.com ⤳ 30
rooms, 10 suites ⎮◎⎮ No meals.*

$ **The Pickled Onion B&B.** Owner Valerie Pickles has carved out a lovely
B&B/INN   little paradise with six bungalows and a wonderful restaurant on the
outskirts of Santa Elena. **Pros:** food at restaurant is made from scratch;
communal computer; amazing rates; wonderful owner. **Cons:** no Wi-Fi
in rooms; no a/c; rustic setting is not for everyone. $ *Rooms from: $45
✉ Carretera 261, Santa Elena(just after Centro), between Uxmal and
Kabah ☎ 1997/111–7922 (mobile) ⊕ www.thepickledonionyucatan.
com ⤳ 8 rooms ⎮◎⎮ Breakfast.*

KABAH

23 km (14 miles) south of Uxmal.

Kabah. The most important buildings at Kabah (meaning "lord of the powerful hand" in Mayan) were built between AD 600 and 900, during the later part of the classic era. A ceremonial center of almost Grecian beauty, it was once linked to Uxmal by a *sacbé*, or raised paved road, at the end of which looms a great independent arch—now across the highway from the main ruins. The 151-foot-long **Palacio de los Mascarones** (Palace of the Masks) boasts a three-dimensional mosaic of 250 masks of inlaid stones. On the central plaza, you can see ground-level wells called *chultunes*, which were used to store precious rainwater. ■TIP→ The site officially opens at 8 am, but the staff doesn't usually show up until 9. ☒ *Carretera 261, 23 km (14 miles) south of Uxmal* MX$42 ☉ *Daily 8–5.*

SAYIL

9 km (5½ miles) south of Kabah.

Sayil. Experts believe that Sayil, or "place of the red ants," flourished between AD 800 and 1000. It's renowned primarily for its majestic **Gran Palacio.** Built on a hill, the three-story structure is adorned with decorations of animals and other figures, and contains more than 80 rooms. The structure recalls Palenque in its use of multiple planes, columned porticoes, and sober cornices. Also on the grounds is a stela in the shape of a phallus—an obvious symbol of fertility. ☒ *Carretera 31E, 9 km (5½ miles) south of Kabah* MX$42 ☉ *Daily 8–5.*

LABNÁ

9 km (5½ miles) south of Sayil.

Labná. The striking monumental structure at Labná (which means "old house" or "abandoned house") is a fanciful corbelled arch with elaborate latticework and a small chamber on each side; it served as the starting point for the road to Uxmal. The site was used mainly by royalty and the military elite. ☒ *Carretera 31E, 9 km (5½ miles) south of Sayil* MX$42 ☉ *Daily 8–5.*

GRUTAS DE LOLTÚN

19 km (12 miles) northeast of Labná.

FAMILY **Grutas de Loltún.** The Loltún ("stone flower" in Mayan) is one of the largest, most fascinating cave systems on the Yucatán Peninsula. Long ago, Mayan ceremonies were routinely held inside these mysterious caverns, and artifacts unearthed in them date as far back as 800 BC. The topography itself is intriguing: there are stalactites, stalagmites, and limestone formations known by such names as Ear of Corn and Cathedral. Illuminated pathways meander a little over a kilometer through the caves, most of which are quite spacious and well ventilated (claustrophobics needn't worry). Nine different openings allow air and some (but not much) light to filter in. Moisture can make these paths

The Grutas de Loltún is an extensive cave system.

somewhat slippery so be sure to wear shoes that grip. ■ **TIP→** You can enter only with a guide. Although they earn a very small salary, guides mostly survive on tips—so be generous. ⊠ *Carretera 31E, 19 km (12 miles) northeast of Labná ⊹ Down an unmarked rd. toward Oxkutzcab* 📧 *MX$140; parking MX$28* ⊙ *Daily 8–5. Scheduled tours at 9:30, 12:30, 3, and 4 (Spanish); 11 and 2 (English).*

TICUL

27 km (17½ miles) northwest of Grutas de Loltún, 28 km (17 miles) east of Uxmal, 100 km (62 miles) south of Mérida.

One of the larger communities in the Yucatán, Ticul (with a population of around 21,000) is a good base for exploring the Puuc region—provided you don't mind rudimentary hotels and a limited choice of simple restaurants. Many descendants of the Xiu Dynasty, which ruled Uxmal until the conquest, still live here. Industries include the fabrication of shoes and *huipiles* (the traditional white embroidered dresses worn by indigenous women) as well as much of the pottery you see around the Yucatán. Ticul also has a handsome 17th-century church.

GETTING HERE AND AROUND

Ticul is an easy drive south of Mérida, along the Ruta Puuc. Follow Carretera 180 to Umán, where you'll get on the Carretera 261 to Muná; from Muná, simply follow the signs to Ticul by way of Carretera 184.

EXPLORING

Arte Maya. This ceramics workshop produces museum-quality replicas of archaeological pieces found throughout Mexico. It also creates souvenir-quality pieces that are more affordable and more easily transported. ⊠ *Calle 23, No. 301, at very entrance to town, next to the cemetery* ☎ *997/972–0901* ⊕ *www.artemaya.com.mx.*

Iglesia de San Antonio de Padua. This evocatively faded red church is typical of the Yucatán's colonial sanctuaries. It has been ransacked on more than one occasion, but the Black Christ altarpiece is original. The best view might be from the outside, where you can take in the facade and savor the slow pace of the town as families ride by in carts attached to bicycles and locals mill around in traditional Mayan dress. ⊠ *Town square, Centro.*

OFF THE BEATEN PATH

Mayapán. Those who are enamored with Mayan ruins may want to make a 42-km (26-mile) detour north from Ticul (or 43 km [27 miles] south from Mérida) to Mayapán, the last of the major city-states on the peninsula that flourished during the postclassic era. It was demolished in 1450, presumably by war. It's thought that the city, with an architectural style reminiscent of Uxmal, was as big as Chichén Itzá, and there are more than 4,000 mounds, which might lend truth to this. At its height, the population could have been well more than 12,000. A half dozen mounds have been excavated, including the palaces of Mayan royalty and the temple of the benign god Kukulcán, where stucco sculptures and murals in vivid reds and oranges have been uncovered. ■TIP➜ Be sure you head toward the Mayapán ruins (just south of Telchaquillo) and not the town of Mayapán, since they are far apart. ⊠ *Off road to left before Telchaquillo (follow signs)* 🖼 *MX$42* ☉ *Daily 8–5.*

WHERE TO EAT

$
MEXICAN

✕ **El Príncipe Tutul-Xiu.** About 15 km (9 miles) east of Ticul in the little town of Maní, this open restaurant under a giant palapa roof is an inviting spot for lunch or an early dinner (it closes at 7 pm). Though you'll find the same Yucatecan dishes here as elsewhere—pollo pibil, sopa de lima—the preparation is excellent and portions are generous. Best of all is the poc chuc—little bites of pork marinated in sour orange, garlic, and chiles and grilled over charcoal. $ *Average main: 113 MP* ⊠ *Calle 26, No. 208, between calles 25 and 27, Mani* ☎ *997/978–4257* ⊕ *www.restaurantestutulxiu.com.*

$
PIZZA

✕ **Pizzería La Góndola.** The wonderful smells of fresh-baked bread and pizza waft from this small corner establishment between the market and the main square. Scenes of Old Italy and the Yucatán adorn bright yellow walls, and patrons pull padded folding chairs up to yellow-tile tables, or take their orders to go. Pizza is the name of the game here, but tortas and pastas are also served. ■TIP➜ Note that the restaurant, although open daily, closes from 1 to 5 pm. $ *Average main: 127 MP* ⊠ *Calle 23, No. 208, at Calle 26A* ☎ *997/972–0112* ▭ *No credit cards* ☉ *No lunch.*

6

WHERE TO STAY

$$$$ HOTEL Fodor's Choice ★ **Hacienda Temozón.** With its mahogany furnishings, carved wooden doors, intricate mosaic floors, and air of genteel sophistication, this converted henequen estate exudes luxury. **Pros:** part of Starwood's Luxury Collection; beautiful grounds and rooms; massages can be arranged in private cenote. **Cons:** expensive meals; must drive to nearby ruins; 45 mins from Mérida. [$] *Rooms from: $330* ✉ *Carretera 261, Km 182, Temozón Sur, turn off 4 km (2½ miles) south of Yaxcopoil* ☎ *999/923–8089, 888/625–5144* 🌐 *www.thehaciendas.com* 🛏 *28 rooms, 1 suite* 🍴 *No meals.*

$ HOTEL **Hotel Plaza.** While they get no points for creativity as far as their name is concerned, this hotel does have a convenient location about a block from the main plaza. **Pros:** downtown location; clean rooms. **Cons:** no frills; street noise and church bells might keep you up late or wake you early; 6% surcharge for paying with credit card. [$] *Rooms from: $38* ✉ *Calle 23, No. 202, between calles 26 and 26A* ☎ *997/972–0484* 🌐 *www.hotelplazayucatan.com* 🛏 *30 rooms* 🍴 *No meals.*

CHICHÉN ITZÁ AND THE MAYAN INTERIOR

Although hordes of buses arrive daily at Chichén Itzá, dropping off groups of tourists only to whisk them away a few hours later, visiting this way is almost criminal. The area around the celebrated ruins is dotted with stunning cenotes, numerous smaller archaeological sites, and sleepy little communities, which may make you feel like you've stepped back in time. The pint-size town of Pisté is barely more than an outpost, where visitors to Chichén Itzá can rest at small hotels. But picturesque Valladolid, the second-largest city in the state, is notable for its cenotes and beautiful 16th-century church. Here, perhaps while enjoying a traditional ice cream in the central plaza, you notice that things seem to move at a slower pace.

CHICHÉN ITZÁ

120 km (74 miles) east of Mérida. 48 km (30 miles) west of Valladolid.

In 2007, this sublime Mayan city was named one of the "New 7 Wonders of the World"—a distinction that puts Chichén Itzá on par with Peru's Machu Picchu and the Great Wall of China; now more than a million people per year come from all over the world to admire it. Those who are devoting more than a day to the magnificent and mysterious ruins often stay 2 km (1½ miles) west in Pisté, a tiny town that feels more like a base camp. Hotels, restaurants, and shops there tend to be less expensive than those just outside the ruins in the Zona Hotelera (Hotel Zone).

GETTING HERE AND AROUND

Aeropuerto Internacional Chichén Itzá (CZA) serves only private and charter planes, so virtually everyone comes by road. From Mérida, you can reach Chichén Itzá along the Carretera 180D or Carretera 180 in two or three hours respectively. For a more scenic and interesting alternative, head east on Carretera 281 to Tixkokob (a Maya

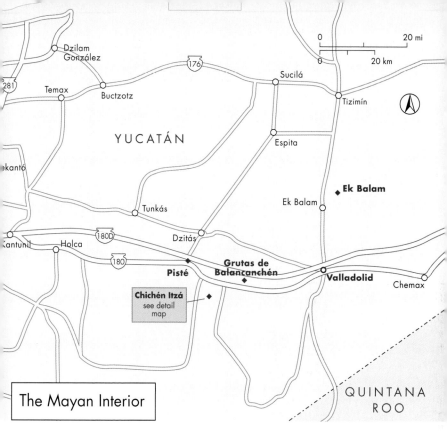

The Mayan Interior

community famous for its hammock weavers) and carry on through Citilcúm and Izamal. From there, drive through the small, untouristy towns of Dzudzal and Xanaba en route to Kantunil, where you can hop on the toll road or continue on the free road that parallels it through Holca and Libre Unión (both of which have very swimmable cenotes). The trip will take four to five hours.

EXPLORING

Fodor'sChoice **Chichén Itzá.** One of the most dramatically beautiful ancient Mayan
★ cities, Chichén Itzá (chee-*chen* eet-*zah*) draws over one million visitors annually. Since the remains of this once-thriving kingdom were rediscovered by Europeans in the mid-1800s, many of the travelers making the pilgrimage here have been archaeologists and scholars, who study the structures and glyphs and try to piece together the mysteries surrounding them. While the artifacts here give fascinating insight into Mayan civilization, they also raise many unanswered questions.

The name of this ancient city, which means "the mouth of the well of the Itzá," is a mystery in and of itself. Although it likely refers to the valuable water sources at the site (there are several cenotes here), experts have little information about who might have actually founded the city—some structures, likely built in the 5th century, predate the

Continued on page 302

The towering **El Castillo** pyramid, nearly 80 feet high, is the most striking structure at Chichén Itzá. Each side of the pyramid has 91 steps, which, with the addition of the topmost platform, equal 365, one for each day of the calendar year. At the vernal and autumnal equinoxes, thousands of people gather to watch as the shadow of the serpent god Kukulcán seems to slither down the side of the pyramid.

CHICHÉN ITZÁ

One of the most beautiful of the ancient Maya cities, Chichén Itzá draws some 3,000 visitors a day from all over the world. Since the remains of this once-thriving kingdom were discovered by Europeans in the mid 1800s, many of the travelers who make the pilgrimage here have been archaeologists and scholars who study the structures and glyphs and try to piece together the mysteries surrounding them. While the artifacts here give fascinating insight into the Maya civilization, they also raise many, many unanswered questions.

The name of this ancient city, which means "the mouth of the well of the Itzás," is a mystery in and of itself. Although it likely refers to the valuable water sources at the site (there are several sinkholes here), experts have little information about who might have actually founded the city—some structures, likely built in the 5th century, pre-date the arrival of the Itzás who occupied the city starting around the late 8th and early 9th centuries. The rea-

son why the Itzás abandoned the city, around 1224, is also unknown.

Scholars and archaeologists aside, most of the visitors that converge on Chichén Itzá come to marvel at its beauty, not ponder its significance. This ancient metropolis, which encompasses 6 square km (2½ square mi), is known around the world as one of the most stunning and well-preserved Maya sites in existence.

(opposite) The main pyramid El Castillo is also called Temple of Kukulcán, (top) Carvings of ball players adorn the walls of the *juego de pelota*, (bottom) Maya statue.

MAJOR SITES AND ATTRACTIONS

Rows of freestanding columns where the roof has long since disintegrated

The sight of the immense ❶ **El Castillo** pyramid, rising imposingly yet gracefully from the surrounding plain, has been known to produce goose pimples on sight. El Castillo (The Castle) dominates the site both in size and in the symmetry of its perfect proportions. Open-jawed serpent statues adorn the corners of each of the pyramid's four stairways, honoring the legendary priest-king Kukulcán (also known as Quetzalcóatl), an incarnation of the feathered serpent god. More serpents appear at the top of the building as sculpted columns. At the spring and fall equinoxes, the afternoon light strikes the trapezoidal structure so that the shadow of the snake-god appears to undulate down the side of the pyramid to bless the fertile earth. Thousands of people travel to the site each year to see this phenomenon.

At the base of the temple on the north side, an interior staircase leads to two marvelous statues deep within: a stone jaguar, and the intermediate god Chacmool. As usual, Chacmool is in a reclining position, with a flat spot on the belly for receiving sacrifices. On the ❷ **Anexo del Templo de los Jaguares** (Annex to the Temple of the Jaguars), just west of El Castillo, bas-relief carvings represent more important deities. On the bottom of the columns is the rain god Tlaloc. It's no surprise that his tears represent rain—but why is the Toltec god Tlaloc honored here, instead of the Maya rain god, Chaac?

That's one of many questions that archaeologists and epigraphers have been trying to answer, ever since John Lloyd Stephens and Frederick Catherwood, the first English-speaking explorers to discover the site, first hacked their way through the surrounding forest in 1840. Scholars once thought that the symbols of foreign gods and differing architectural styles at Chichén Itzá proved it was conquered by the Toltecs of central Mexico. (As well as representations of Tlaloc, the site also has a tzompantli—a stone platform decorated with row upon row of sculpted human skulls, which is a distinctively Toltec-style structure.) Most experts now agree, however, that Chichén Itzá was only influenced—not conquered—by Toltec trading partners from the north.

The flat part of a reclining Chacmool statue is where sacrificial offerings were laid.

It's believed that Mayan ball players had to pass some sort of ball through high stone loops.

Games may have ended with beheadings.

Just west of the Anexo del Templo de los Jaguares is another puzzle: the auditory marvel of Chichén Itzá's main ball court. At 490 feet, this **3 Juego de Pelota** is the largest in Mesoamerica. Yet if you stand at one end of the playing field and whisper something to a friend at the other end, incredibly, you will be heard. The game played on this ball court was apparently something like soccer (no hands were used), but it likely had some sort of ritualistic significance. Carvings on the low walls surrounding the field show a decapitation, blood spurting from the victim's neck to fertilize the earth. Whether this is a historical depiction (perhaps the losers or winners of the game were sacrificed?) or a symbolic scene, we can only guess.

On the other side of El Castillo, just before a small temple dedicated to the planet Venus, a ruined sacbé, or white road leads to the **4 Cenote Sagrado** (Holy Well, or Sinkhole), which was also probably used for ritualistic purposes. Jacques Cousteau and his companions recovered about 80 skeletons from this deep, straight-sided, subsurface pond, as well as thousands of pieces of jewelry and figures of jade, obsidian, wood, bone, and turquoise. In direct alignment with this cloudy green cenote, on the other side of El Castillo, the **5 Xtaloc sinkhole** was kept pristine, undoubtedly for bathing and drinking. Adjacent to this water source is a steam

TIPS

To get more in-depth information about the ruins, hire a multilingual guide at the ticket booth. Guides charge about MXP 750 for a group of up to 7 people. Tours generally last about two hours. 🎫 MXP 64 🕒 Ruins daily 8–5.

TO
MÉRIDA

If you stand at one end of the juego de pelota and whisper something to a friend at the opposite end, incredibly, you will be heard.

Juego de Pelota **3**

Anexo del Templo **2**
de los Jaguares

Parking

**Tourist
Module**

Templo del
Osario
6

0   1/8 mi
0   1/8 km

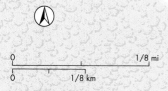

The spiral staircased El Caracol was used as an astronomical observatory.

Casa Roja **7**

8
Casa del
Venado

Structures at the Grupo de las Monjas have some of the site's most exquisite carvings and masks.

El Caracol **9**

Templo de los
Panales
Cuadrados **13**

Akab
Dzib **12**

Anexo de las Monjas **11**
10
Grupo de
las Monjas

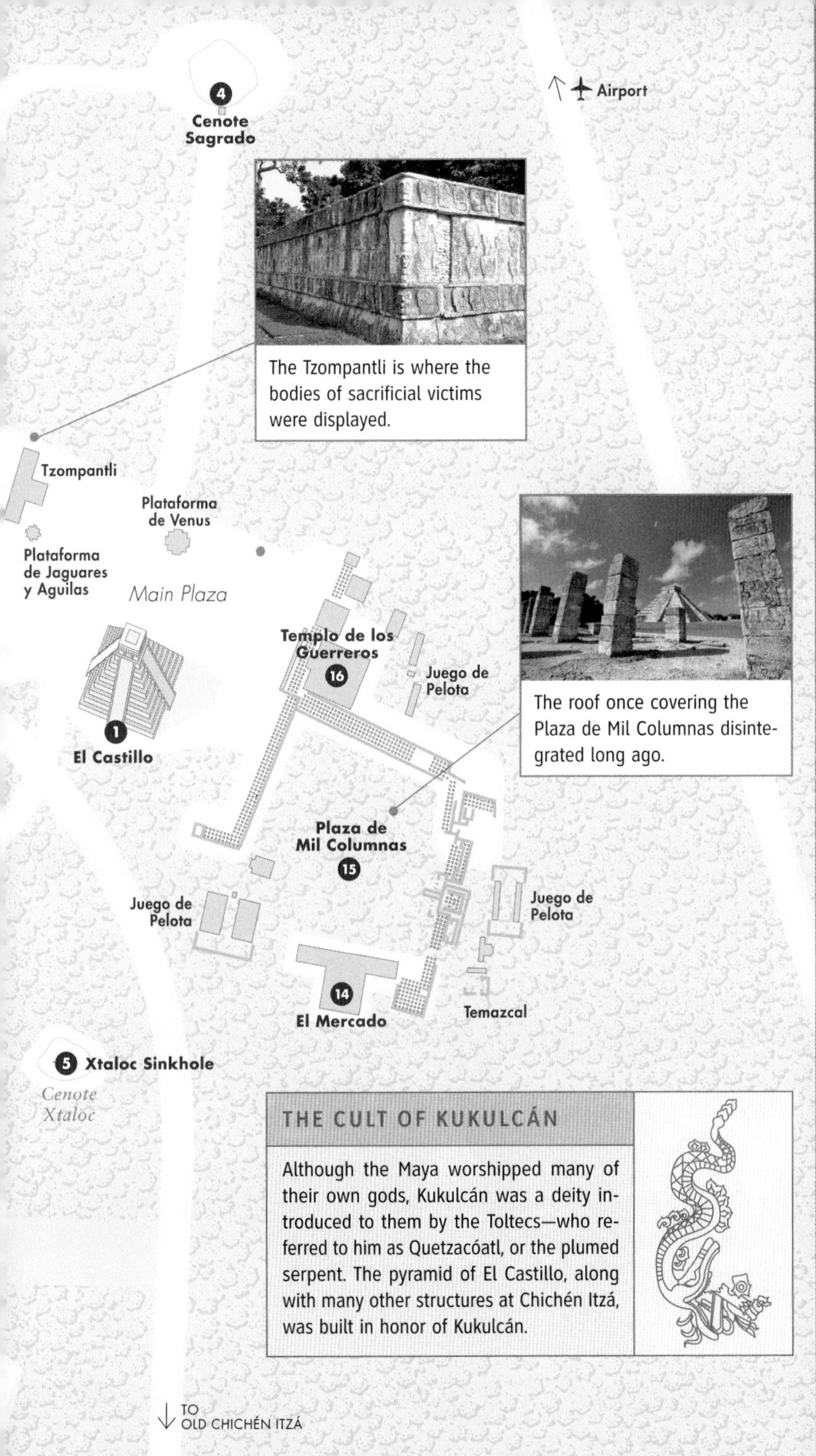
Airport
4 Cenote Sagrado
Tzompantli
Plataforma de Venus
Plataforma de Jaguares y Aguilas
Main Plaza
Templo de los Guerreros 16
Juego de Pelota
1 El Castillo
Plaza de Mil Columnas 15
Juego de Pelota
Juego de Pelota
14 El Mercado
Temazcal
5 Xtaloc Sinkhole
Cenote Xtaloc
TO OLD CHICHÉN ITZÁ

The Tzompantli is where the bodies of sacrificial victims were displayed.

The roof once covering the Plaza de Mil Columnas disintegrated long ago.

THE CULT OF KUKULCÁN

Although the Maya worshipped many of their own gods, Kukulcán was a deity introduced to them by the Toltecs—who referred to him as Quetzacóatl, or the plumed serpent. The pyramid of El Castillo, along with many other structures at Chichén Itzá, was built in honor of Kukulcán.

bath, its interior lined with benches along the wall like those you'd see in any steam room today. Outside, a tiny pool was used for cooling down during the ritual.

The older Mayan structures at Chichén Itzá are south and west of Cenote Xtaloc. Archaeologists have been restoring several buildings in this area, including the ❻ **Templo del Osario** (Ossuary Temple), which, as its name implies, concealed several tombs with skeletons and offerings. Behind the smaller ❼ **Casa Roja** (Red House) and ❽ **Casa del Venado** (House of the Deer) are the site's oldest structures, including ❾ **El Caracol** (The Snail), one of the few round buildings built by the Maya, with a spiral staircase within. Clearly built as a celestial observatory, it has eight tiny windows precisely aligned with the points of the compass rose. Scholars now know that Maya priests studied the planets and the stars; in fact, they were able to accurately predict the orbits of Venus and the moon, and the appearance of comets and eclipses. To modern astronomers, this is nothing short of amazing.

The Maya of Chichén Itzá were not just scholars, however. They were skilled artisans and architects as well. South of El Caracol, the ❿ **Grupo de las Monjas** (The Nunnery complex) has some of the site's most exquisite façades. A combination of Puuc and Chenes styles dominates here, with playful latticework, masks, and gargoyle-like serpents. On the east side of the ⓫ **Anexo de las Monjas** (Nunnery Annex), the Chenes facade celebrates the rain god Chaac. In typical style, the doorway represents an entrance into the underworld; figures of Chaac decorate the ornate façade above.

South of the Nunnery Complex is an area where field archaeologists are still excavating (fewer than a quarter of the structures at Chichén Itzá have been fully restored). If you have more than a superficial interest in the site—and can convince the authorities ahead of time of your importance, or at least your interest in archaeology—you can explore this area, which is generally not open to the public. Otherwise, head back toward El Castillo past the ruins of a housing compound called ⓬ **Akab Dzib**

The doorway of the Anexo de las Monjas represents an entrance to the underworld.

The Templo de los Guerreros shows the influence of Toltec architecture.

and the ⓭ **Templo de los Panales Cuadrados** (Temple of the Square Panels). The latter of these buildings shows more evidence of Toltec influence: instead of weight-bearing Mayan arches—or "false arches"—that traditionally supported stone roofs, this structure has stone columns but no roof. This means that the building was once roofed, Toltec-style, with perishable materials (most likely palm thatch or wood) that have long since disintegrated.

Beyond El Caracol, Casa Roja, and El Osario, the right-hand path follows an ancient sacbé, now collapsed. A mud-and-straw hut, which the Maya called a na, has been reproduced here to show the simple implements used before and after the Spanish conquest. On one side of the room are a typical pre-Hispanic table, seat, fire pit, and reed baskets; on the other, the Christian cross and colonial-style table of the post-conquest Maya.

Behind the tiny oval house, several unexcavated mounds still guard their secrets. The path meanders through a small grove of oak and slender bean trees to the building known today as ⓮ **El Mercado.** This market was likely one end of a huge outdoor market whose counterpart structure, on the other side of the grove, is the ⓯ **Plaza de Mil Columnas** (Plaza of the Thousand Columns). In typical Toltec-Maya style, the roof once covering the parallel rows of round stone columns in this long arcade has disappeared, giving the place a strangely Greek—and distinctly non-Maya—look. But the curvy-nosed Chaacs on the corners of the adjacent ⓰ **Templo de los Guerreros** are pure Maya. Why their noses are pointing down, like an upside-down "U," instead of up, as usual, is just another mystery to be solved.

Columns at Templo de los Guerreros.

arrival of the Itzá who occupied the city starting around the late 8th and early 9th centuries. Why the Itzá abandoned the city in the early 1200s is also unknown, as is its subsequent role.

Of course, most of the visitors that converge on Chichén Itzá come to marvel at its beauty, not ponder its significance. Even among laypeople, this ancient metropolis, which encompasses 6-square km (2.25-square miles), is known around the world as one of the most stunning and well-preserved Mayan sites in existence.

✉ *off Carretera 180, 2 km (1½ miles) east of Pisté* 🌐 *chichenitza.inah.gob.mx* 🎫 *MX$204* 🕒 *Daily 8–5.*

Parque Ik Kil. When you've exhausted your interest in archaeology—or are just plain exhausted—Parque Ik Kil (meaning "place of the winds") offers a refreshing change of pace. Located across from the Dolores Alba hotel in Pisté, it has a lovely cenote you can swim in. If you're going to eat in the adjacent restaurant, you don't need to pay the entrance fee. Lockers, changing facilities, showers, and life jackets are available. ✉ *Carretera 180, Km 122, Pisté* 🎫 *MX$85* 💳 *No credit cards* 🕒 *Daily 8–6.*

WHERE TO STAY

$ HOTEL 🏨 **Dolores Alba Chichén.** A longtime favorite of international travelers, this family-run spot with a small motel feel is the best budget choice near the ruins. **Pros:** close to ruins; transport to ruins is included (return transport is not). **Cons:** restaurant leaves much to be desired; small rooms; furniture and linens look a little past their prime, weak Wi-Fi signal. [$] *Rooms from: $67* ✉ *Carretera 180, Km 122, Pisté, 3 km (2 miles) east of Chichén Itzá* ☎ *985/851–0117* 🌐 *www.doloresalba.com* 🛏 *32 rooms* 🍴 *Breakfast.*

$$ HOTEL Fodor's Choice ★ 🏨 **Hacienda Chichén Resort.** This refurbished hacienda with a butter-yellow exterior has beautiful gardens and an inviting pool surrounded by palms. **Pros:** designated cottages (gated) for travelers with pets; short walk from ruins; beautiful gardens; amazing spa; on-site organic farm; provides community outreach. **Cons:** pricey; restaurant food just OK. [$] *Rooms from: $169* ✉ *Carretera 180, Km 120, Pisté* ☎ *999/924–4222, 877/631–4005* 🌐 *www.haciendachichen.com* 🛏 *28 rooms* 🍴 *No meals.*

$ HOTEL 🏨 **Hotel Chichén Itzá.** Just over 1½ km (1 mile) from the ruins in the town of Pisté, this two-story hotel surrounding a pool feels like a motel in a very unlikely setting: a large grassy area edged with banana and other tropical trees and flowers. **Pros:** minutes from ruins; big pool; kind staff. **Cons:** mediocre food; room amenities vary (check out a few if possible). [$] *Rooms from: $74* ✉ *Calle 15, No. 45, Pisté* ☎ *985/851–0022, 877/631–4005* 🌐 *www.mayaland.com* 🛏 *44 rooms* 🍴 *Multiple meal plans.*

GRUTAS DE BALANCANCHÉN

6 km (4 miles) east of Chichén Itzá, 38 km (24 miles) west of Valladolid.

FAMILY **Grutas de Balankanché.** How often do you get the chance to wander below the earth? These caves—the Mayan name of which translates as either "throne of the jaguar caves" or "caves of the hidden throne"—are dank and sometimes slippery slopes into an amazing rocky underworld. They are lighted to best show off their lumpy limestone stalactites and nichelike side caves. It's a privilege also to view in situ vases, jars, and incense burners once used in sacred rituals. These were discovered in the 1950s, and left right as they were. An arrangement of tiny *metates* (stone mortars for grinding corn) is particularly moving. At the end of the line is the underground cenote where Maya priests worshipped Chaac, the rain god. A sound-and-light show recounts Mayan history. From Chichén Itzá, you can catch a bus or taxi or arrange a tour at the Mayaland hotel. Although there's a six-person minimum, the ticket vendor will often allow even a pair of visitors to take the tour. ⚠ **Wear comfortable, nonslip walking shoes, and be brutally honest with yourself about your capabilities before venturing in. Do not attempt if you're claustrophobic or have heart or respiratory problems—the climb is steep, and the caves are hot and humid.** ⊠ *6 km (4 miles) east of Chichén Itzá* ☏ *MX$113, including tour and sound-and-light show* ⊗ *Daily 9–5. Tours at 9:30, 11, 12:30, 2, 3, and 4 (English); 9, noon, 2, and 4 (Spanish); and 10 (French).*

VALLADOLID

Fodor'sChoice ★ *161 km (97 miles) east of Mérida, 44 km (27 miles) east of Chichén Itzá, 146 km (88 miles) west of Cancún.*

The second-largest city in Yucatán State, picturesque Valladolid (pronounced vye-ah-do-*leed*) is seeing a big boom in popularity among travelers en route to or from Chichén Itzá. (It's a far closer base for exploring the ruins than either Mérida or Cancún.) Francisco de Montejo founded Valladolid in 1543 on the site of the Mayan town of Sisal. The city suffered during the Caste War of the Yucatán—when the Maya in revolt killed nearly all Spanish residents—and again during the Mexican Revolution.

Despite its turbulent history, Valladolid's downtown contains many colonial and 19th-century structures. For a taste of local life, check out the Sunday morning demonstrations of Yucatecan folk dancing in the main square; you can return at 8 pm, when the city's orchestra plays elegant, stylized *danzón*—waltzlike music to which expressionless couples swirl (think tango: no smiling allowed).

If you need help getting oriented, Valladolid's phenomenal municipal tourist office is open daily on the southeast corner of the square. You can also look for the bilingual tourist police dressed in spiffy white polo shirts and navy-blue baseball caps and trousers.

GETTING HERE AND AROUND

The drive from Mérida to Valladolid via the toll road takes about two hours; budget about 2½ hours if driving from Cancún. The tolls will be about MX$152 and MX$180 respectively. The free road cuts through several small towns where speed bumps, street repairs, and traffic increases travel time significantly. ADO (⊕ *www.ado.com.mx*) has direct buses from Mérida to Valladolid, and other Mexican cities.

VISITOR INFORMATION

Oficina de Turismo ⊠ *Palacio Municipal, Calle 40 at Calle 41* ☎ *985/856–2551* ⊕ *www.valladolid.travel* ⊙ *Weekdays 8 am–9 pm, weekends 9–7.*

EXPLORING

Fodor's Choice **Casa de los Venados.** A vintage mansion just south of Valladolid's central
★ square contains Mexico's largest private collection of folk art. Rooms
around the gracious courtyard contain some 3,000 pieces, with Día de
los Muertos (Day of the Dead) figures being a specialty. The assemblage
is impressive; even without it, though, the house would be worth touring. This hacienda-style building dates from the early 17th century,
and restoration was engineered by the same architect who designed
Mérida's ultramodern Gran Museo del Mundo Maya (don't worry—the
results here preserved its colonial elegance). The Casa de los Venados
opens to the public each morning for a 90-minute bilingual tour. Just
show up, no reservations needed. Admission is a bargain, and all proceeds help fund local health-care projects. ⊠ *Calle 40, No. 204, Centro*
☎ *985/856–2289* ⊕ *www.casadelosvenados.com* 🖃 *MX$70* ⊙ *Tours
daily at 10 am.*

Cenote Samulá. Perhaps the most photographed cenote in the Yucatán,
this sinkhole is located across the road from Cenote X-Keken, about
5 km (3 miles) west of the main square. A narrow stairway leads to
crystal-clear water where tree vines dangle overhead and hundreds of
birds nest between the stalactites. Don't be alarmed by the tiny *Garra
rufa* fish that nibble at your feet—they are actually eating away the
dead skin cells. Guides offer tours for tips. ⊠ *On old hwy. to Chichén
Itzá* ☎ *MX$70* ⊙ *Daily 9–4.*

FAMILY **Cenote X-Keken.** Five kilometers (3 miles) west of the main square, you
can swim with the catfish in lovely, mysterious Cenote X-Keken, which
is in a cave illuminated by a small natural skylight. There are toilets
and changing facilities but no lockers. Directly across the street is the
equally stunning Cenote Samulá. Guides offer tours for tips. ⊠ *On old
hwy. to Chichén Itzá* 🖃 *MX$70* ⊙ *Daily 9–4.*

Cenote Zací. A large, round, and beautiful sinkhole right in town, Cenote
Zací is sometimes crowded with tourists and local boys clowning it up;
at other times, it's deserted. Leaves from the tall old trees surrounding
the sinkhole float on the surface, but the water itself is quite clean. If
you're not up for a dip, visit the adjacent handicraft shop or have a bite
at the popular, thatch-roof restaurant overlooking the water. ⊠ *Calles
36 and 37* ☎ *985/856–0721* 🖃 *MX$20.*

Ex-Convento y Iglesia San Bernadino. Five long blocks away from the main
plaza is the 16th-century, terra-cotta Ex-Convento y Iglesia San Bernadino, a Franciscan church and former monastery. The church was actually built over Cenote Sis-Há, which served as a clean water source for
the monks. You can view the cenote through a grate in the well-house
where much of the original stone still remains. ■**TIP➜ If the priest
is around, ask him to show you the 16th-century frescoes, protected
behind curtains near the altarpiece. The lack of proportion in the human
figures shows the initial clumsiness of indigenous artists in reproducing
the Christian saints.** ⊠ *Calle 41A, Centro* ☎ *985/856–2160.*

CLOSE UP

Sacred Cenotes

To the ancient (and tradition-bound modern) Maya, holes in the ground—be they sinkholes, cenotes, or caves—are considered conduits to the world of the spirits. As sources of water in a land of no surface rivers, sinkholes are of special importance. Cenotes like Balancanchén, near Chichén Itzá, were used as prayer sites and shrines. Sacred objects and sacrificial victims were thrown in the sacred cenote at Chichén Itzá, and in others near large ceremonial centers in ancient times.

There are at least 2,800 known cenotes in the Yucatán. Rainwater sinks through the peninsula's thin soil and porous limestone to create underground rivers, while leaving the dry surface river-free.

Some pondlike sinkholes are found near ground level; most require a bit more effort to access, however. Near downtown Valladolid, Cenote Zací is named for the Mayan town conquered by the Spanish. It's a relatively simple saunter down a series of cement steps to reach the cool green water.

Lesser-known sinkholes are yours to discover, especially in the area labeled "zona de cenotes." To explore this area southeast of Mérida, you can hire a guide through the Yucatán State tourism office or, if you're already in Valladolid, through its city tourism office. Another option is to head directly for the ex-hacienda of Chunkanan, 3 km (2 miles) from the town of Cuzama, about 30 minutes southeast of Mérida. Here former henequen workers will hitch their horses to tiny open railway carts to take you along the unused train tracks. The reward for this bumpy, sometimes dusty ride is a swim in several incredible cenotes.

Almost every local has a "secret" cenote; ask around, and perhaps you'll find a favorite of your own.

Iglesia de San Servacio. On the south side of the city's main plaza stands the large Iglesia de San Servacio, sometimes spelled "San Gervasio." Although many refer to it as a *catedral*, it is not the seat of the diocese—that's in Mérida. Its limestone exterior is impressive, but the interior is rather plain. The church makes a stunning anchor for the plaza when illuminated at night. ⊠ *Calle 41, between calles 40 and 42* ⊗ *Daily 8–8*.

WHERE TO EAT

$$ ✕ **Casa Italia.** If there was a "Best Pizza in Mexico" contest, this restored

ITALIAN colonial gem a couple of blocks north of the main square would be nominated. Lots of reds and yellows brighten the interior, and the outdoor patio overlooking Parque de la Candelaria becomes prime real estate on beautiful evenings. With 30 years in the restaurant business, most of them spent back in Italy, the owners here know pizza. They whip up 11 varieties, as well as sweet and salted focaccia and enormous calzones. A selection of Italian wines rounds out the offerings. ■**TIP**➡ Casa Italia opens at 7—come early if you want to snag a patio table. $ *Average main: 155 MP* ⊠ *Calle 35, No. 202J, between calles 42 and 44, Centro* ☎ *985/856–5539* ⊕ *www.casaitaliamexico.com* ⊗ *Closed Sun. and Mon. No lunch.*

$$ ✕ **El Atrio.** Valladolid's newest entry
MEXICAN in the restaurant sweepstakes occupies an elegant colonial house on the south side of the main square and specializes in hearty Yucatecan cuisine. *Pollo X'catik* (chicken baked in butter cream) and the city's eponymous dish, *lomitos de Valladolid* (cubed pork loin in a tomato-chile sauce), are menu highlights. If you're not feeling quite so adventurous, you can opt for an entry on the *mar y tierra* page (loosely translated as "surf and

> **DID YOU KNOW?**
>
> Valladolid is renowned for its *longaniza en escabeche*—a sausage dish made with pork, beef, or venison, served in many of the restaurants facing the square. While you're here, also be sure to sample *xtabentún* (pronounced eesh-tah-ben-toon), a liqueur that combines anise, honey, and rum.

turf"). The small front dining room is stylish, but try snagging a table in the leafy back courtyard—it's perfect for lunch on a hot afternoon. El Atrio keeps long hours, opening at 7 am and going strong until 1 am. $ *Average main: 170 MP* ⊠ *Calle 41, No. 204A, between calles 40 and 42, Centro* ☎ *985/856–2394.*

$ ✕ **La Cantina.** This colorful cantina, right on the main square, has
MEXICAN brightly painted tables and chairs with sombreros that act as lampshades. The festive vibe is matched with a menu of lime soup, chicken fajitas, tacos, enchiladas, and cochinita pibil served with warm tortillas. Since it's open late, many locals drop by for a cocktail or Mayan-chocolate drink. For a meal with a view, choose an outside table and watch Valladolid in action. $ *Average main: 113 MP* ⊠ *Calle 41, No. 202, Centro* ☎ *985/856–0999.*

$$$ ✕ **Taberna de los Frailes.** The "Tavern of the Monks" sits above Cenote
MEXICAN FUSION Sis Ha and overlooks the ancient stonework of the Ex-Convento y
Fodor's Choice Iglesia San Bernadino. Despite its historic location, the restaurant is
★ equally known for its extraordinary Mayan cuisine and Yucatecan dishes like *pescado tikin xic* (fish marinated with adobo de achiote and sour oranges), *pavo en relleno negro* (turkey medallions stuffed with pork and hard-boiled egg in Mayan pepper sauce), and *pechuga en pipian* (roasted chicken in pumpkin-seed sauce). For something light, try the grilled watermelon salad or *sikil pak,* a dip made from roasted pumpkin seeds, tomatoes, and Mayan spices. The three separate dining areas—garden lounge, stone cocktail bar, and palapa dining room—give the place an elegant, modern feel while still adhering to traditional Mayan architecture. $ *Average main: $16* ⊠ *Calle 49,, No. 235* ☎ *985/856–0689* ⊕ *www.tabernadelosfrailes.com.*

WHERE TO STAY

$$ ⌂ **Casa Hamaca.** A pleasant escape from the heat and hubbub of the city,
B&B/INN comfortable Casa Hamaca is named for the inviting hammocks hanging in its guest quarters. **Pros:** lush, cool greenery; knowledgeable owner; powerful Wi-Fi. **Cons:** 15-min walk to city center; exterior makes a disappointing first impression. $ *Rooms from: $110* ⊠ *Calle 49, No. 202, at Calle 40, Centro* ☎ *985/856–5287, 201/984–1900 in the U.S.* ⊕ *www.casahamaca.com* ⇄ *8 rooms* ⦿l *Breakfast.*

You can swim in Cenote X-Keken (for a price).

$ B&B/INN **Casa Marlene.** The good folks at Casa Tia Micha have opened a second colonial-style lodging just down the street, and it's another winner. **Pros:** gracious hosts; huge breakfasts. **Cons:** small pool; staff are eager to please, but there may be some language issues if you don't speak Spanish. [$] *Rooms from: $96* ✉ *Calle 39, No. 193, between calles 38 and 40, Centro* ☎ *985/856–0499* 🌐 *www.casadelatiamicha.com* 🛏 *4 rooms, 2 suites* 🍴 *Breakfast.*

$$ B&B/INN Fodor's Choice ★ **Casa Tía Micha.** More than a century old, this colonial home has been beautifully transformed into a five-bedroom hotel that is owned and operated by "Micha's" grandchildren. **Pros:** homemade breakfast; friendly staff; clean rooms; secure parking. **Cons:** some street noise; weak Wi-Fi signal. [$] *Rooms from: $112* ✉ *Calle 39, No. 197, between calles 38 and 40, Centro* ☎ *985/856–0499* 🌐 *www.casadelatiamicha.com* 🛏 *1 room, 2 suites* 🍴 *Breakfast.*

$$ HOTEL **Ecotel Quinta Regia.** Mixing the colonial with modern Mexican, Ecotel Quinta Regia's whitewashed rooms are accented with a brightly colored wall, wrought-iron ceiling and wall fixtures, and hand-carved furniture; the nicest standard rooms have orchard-view terraces, while junior suites have balconies (overlooking the parking area), small kitchens, a living-dining area, and spa baths. **Pros:** recently remodeled; Wi-Fi throughout. **Cons:** 15-min walk to central plaza; bland restaurant. [$] *Rooms from: $116* ✉ *Calle 40, No. 160A, at Calle 27* ☎ *985/856–3472* 🌐 *www.ecotelquintaregia.com.mx* 🛏 *99 rooms, 11 suites* 🍴 *No meals.*

$$ HOTEL **El Mesón del Marqués.** On the north side of the main square, this well-preserved, old hacienda house was built around a lovely, open patio and has comfortable rooms with air-conditioning, Wi–Fi, and

safes. **Pros:** great downtown location; nice outdoor areas; 24-hour room service; free parking. **Cons:** food could be better; rooms lack charm of public areas; mostly shaded pool. [$] *Rooms from: $88* ✉ *Calle 39, No. 203, between calles 40 and 42, Centro* ☎ *985/856–2073* 🌐 *www.mesondelmarques.com* 🛏 *80 rooms, 10 suites* 🍴 *No meals.*

SHOPPING

Yalat Arte Mexicano. Located on the main square, this small shop sells clothing, crafts, jewelry, pottery, and masks from southeast Mexico. ✉ *Calle 41, No. 204, between calles 40 and 42, Centro* ☎ *985/856–1969* 🕘 *Daily 9–8.*

EK BALAM

30 km (18 miles) north of Valladolid.

The large Ek Balam ("black jaguar") site was known to 19th-century archaeologists; however, excavation and mapping didn't really get underway until the 1990s, making this one of the "newest" rediscovered Mayan complexes.

GETTING HERE AND AROUND

If you don't have your own vehicle, *colectivos* (shared taxis) to Ek Balam leave from Calle 44 between calles 35 and 37 in Valladolid throughout the day; the fare is MX$50 per person. You'll pay a private taxi driver MX$300 to MX$350 for the round trip and an hour's wait.

EXPLORING

Ek Balam. The ruins at Ek Balam are best known for the amazingly well-preserved stucco panels on the Templo de los Frisos. A giant mask crowns its summit, and its friezes contain wonderful carvings of figures often referred to as "angels" (because they have wings)—but which more likely represented nobles in ceremonial dress.

As is common with ancient Mayan structures, this temple, styled like those in the lowland region of Chenes, is superimposed upon earlier ones. The temple was a mausoleum for ruler Ukin Kan Lek Tok, who was buried with priceless funerary objects, including perforated seashells, jade, mother-of-pearl pendants, and small bone masks with movable jaws. At the bases at either end of the temple, the leader's name is inscribed on the forked tongue of a carved serpent. (Mayan culture ascribed no negative connotation to the snake.) A contemporary of Uxmal and Cobá, the city may have been a satellite city to Chichén Itzá, which rose to power as Ek Balam waned.

This site is also notable for its two concentric walls—a rare configuration in the Mayan world—that surround the 45 structures in the main sector. They may have provided defense or, perhaps, symbolized the ruling elite that lived within. In addition, Ek Balam has a ball court and many freestanding *stelae* (stone pillars carved with commemorative glyphs or images). New Age groups occasionally converge here for prayers and seminars, but the site is usually quite sparsely visited, which adds to the mystery and allure.

■TIP→ This is one of the few Mayan sites where visitors are permitted to climb the structures. Be aware, though, that the trend in the

Yucatán is to prohibit such activity, so the situation could change at any time. Some visitors report a dizzying sensation on descent here; for safety's sake, climbing is not recommended. ✉ *Off Carretera 295, 30 km (18 miles) north of Valladolid* 🌐 *www.inah.gob.mx* 🎟 *MX$122* 🕓 *Daily 8–5.*

WHERE TO STAY

$ HOTEL 🏨 **Genesis Eco-Oasis.** Close to the Ek Balam ruins, this simple retreat is modeled on local dwellings; cabins of stucco, wood, and thatch surround a casually maintained open area with a ritual sweat lodge, meditation room, and bio-filtered swimming pool. **Pros:** intimate and eco-friendly; cultural programs; near Ek Balam. **Cons:** early-morning crowing roosters; sometimes difficult to make phone reservations pitted road to hotel; best suited to dog lovers. [$] *Rooms from: $65* ✉ *2 km (1 mile) northwest of Ek Balam* ✥ *Turn left on last road before entrance to Ek Balam ruins. Continue 2 km (1 mile) northwest toward Ek Balam village and follow signs to Genesis.* ☎ *1985/101–0277 (mobile)* 🌐 *www.genesisretreat.com* 🛏 *9 cabins* 💳 *No credit cards* 🍴 *No meals.*

PROGRESO AND THE NORTH COAST

Various routes lead from Mérida to towns along the coast, which are spread across a distance of 380 km (236 miles). Separate roads connect the state capital with the laid-back village of Celestún, which serves as the entrance to an ecological marine reserve that extends south to just beyond the Campeche border. Carretera 261 leads due north from Mérida to the relatively modern but humble port of Progreso, where meridanos spend their holidays. To get to some of the small beach towns east of Progreso, head east on Carretera 176 out of Mérida, and then cut north on one of the many access roads. Not as picturesque as the Rivera Maya coastline, beaches here are wide and generally shadeless.

The terrain in this part of the peninsula is absolutely flat. Tall trees are scarce because the region was almost entirely cleared for coconut palms in the early 19th century and again for henequen in the early 20th century. Locals still tend some of the old fields of henequen, even though there's little profit to be made now from the rope fiber it produces. Other former plantation fields are wildly overgrown with scrub, and are identifiable only by the low, white stone walls that used to mark their boundaries. Many bird species make their home in this area, and butterflies swarm in profusion throughout the dry season.

CELESTÚN

90 km (56 miles) west of Mérida.

When someone says "Celestún," think pink. The estuaries of this biosphere reserve are home to an amazing flock of flamingos. The gateway to it, a tranquil fishing village of the same name, sits at the end of a spit of land separating the Celestún estuary from the Gulf of Mexico.

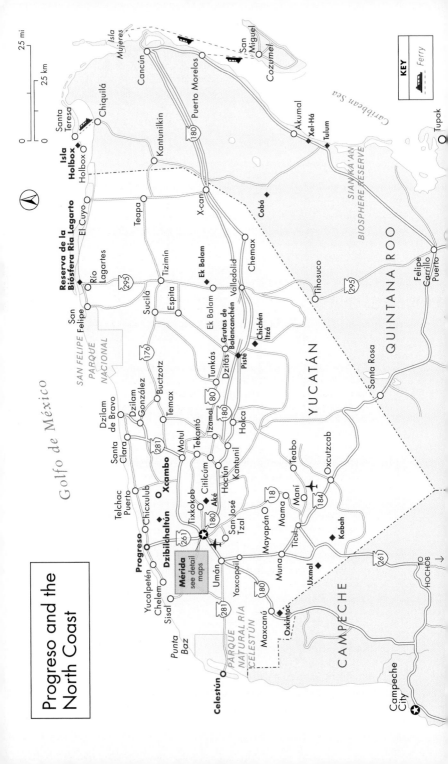

GETTING HERE AND AROUND

Every Mérida tour operator offers Celestún excursions several times per week. If you'd rather come independently, you can drive or take a second-class bus from Mérida's Noroeste Terminal (Calle 67 at Calle 50); multiple depart each day, and the round-trip fare is about MX$80. Within Celestún, moto-taxis are your best bet; they charge about MX$10 around town and MX$15 to go out to the boats from the central plaza. Make sure you establish the fare before you get on, as sometimes drivers will try to charge foreign tourists significantly higher rates.

EXPLORING

Reserva de la Biósfera Ría Celestún. Celestún is the point of entry to the Reserva de la Biósfera Ría Celestún, a 146,000-acre wildlife reserve with extensive mangrove forests and one of the largest colonies of flamingos in North America. Clouds of the pink birds soar above the estuary all year, but the best months for seeing them in abundance are November through March. This is also the fourth-largest wintering ground for ducks of the Gulf-coast region, and more than 365 other species of birds, plus a large sea-turtle population, make their home here. Mexican and American conservation programs protect the birds, as well as the endangered hawksbill and loggerhead marine tortoises, and species such as the blue crab and crocodile. Other endangered species that inhabit the area are the ocelot, the jaguar, and the spider monkey.

The park is set among rocks, islets, and white-sand beaches. There's good fishing here, too, and several cenotes that are wonderful for swimming. Most Mérida travel agencies run boat tours of the *ría* (estuary) in the early morning or late afternoon, but it's not usually necessary to make a reservation in advance.

▓TIP➡ To see the birds, hire a fishing boat at the entrance to town (they hang out under the bridge leading into Celestún). A 75-minute tour for up to six people costs about MX$920; a 2-hour tour costs around MX$1,770. Although more expensive (MX$990 per person), local tour expert "Alex" specializes in ecotours and donates a portion of the proceeds to the Celestún Conservation Program (call Hotel Eco Paraíso to book). Popular with Mexican vacationers, the park's sandy beach is pleasant during the morning but tends to get windy in the afternoon. And, unfortunately, mosquitoes gather in great numbers on the beach at dawn and dusk, particularly during winter months, making a walk on the beach uncomfortable. Most hotels offer mosquito netting around the beds, but bring along a good cream or spray to keep the bugs away. ✉ *90 km (56 miles) west of Mérida* ☎ *998/916–2100 Tours booked through Hotel Eco Paraíso.*

BEACHES

Celestún Beach. This village may not have the classic beaches of the Caribbean, but it does have several kilometers of lovely coastline, perfect for long walks and seashell collecting. There are no crowds, even at the main beach in town, and the water is a pretty green-emerald color. The nicest stretch is at Hotel Eco Paraíso, home to 5 km (3 miles) of white sandy beaches, where turtles nest from April through July and bottlenose dolphins can be seen swimming. The waters are usually tranquil until late afternoon; when winds pick up, this isn't the best place for a dip—but it's perfect for relaxing or kayaking (rentals are available at the hotel). There are no lifeguards on duty, so ask hotel staff about rip currents and incoming swells. **Amenities:** food and drink; water sports (through the hotel). **Best For:** walking. ✉ *Hotel Eco Paraíso.*

WHERE TO STAY

$ B&B/INN **Casa de Celeste Vida.** Owned by Canadian expats, this three-bedroom guest house is directly on the beach, making it one of the best values in town. **Pros:** isolated beach; less than a mile from town; gated property with secure parking; **Cons:** two-night minimum stay; mosquitoes can be a problem; no a/c; credit cards not accepted; non-animal lovers might have an issue with rescued dogs on the property. [$] *Rooms from: $90* ✉ *49E Calle, No. 12* ☎ *988/916–2536* 🌐 *www.hotelcelestevida.com* 🛏 *3 rooms* 💳 *No credit cards* 🍴 *No meals.*

$$$ HOTEL Fodor's Choice ★ **Hotel Eco Paraíso.** On an old coconut plantation outside town, this hotel offers classy comfort in thatch-roof bungalows along a shell-strewn beach. **Pros:** on the beach; garden showers; good service; breakfast basket delivered to your door. **Cons:** a drive from main plaza; no a/c; bland menu; Wi-Fi in common areas only. [$] *Rooms from: $280* ✉ *Camino Viejo a Sisal, Km 10* ☎ *988/916–2100, 800/400–3333* 🌐 *www.ecoparaiso.com* 🛏 *24 cabanas, 8 suites* 🍴 *Multiple meal plans.*

DZIBILCHALTÚN

16 km (10 miles) north of Mérida.

FAMILY **Dzibilchaltún.** Meaning "the place with writing on flat stones," Dzibilchaltún (dzi-bil-chal-*toon*) isn't a place you'd travel miles out of your way to see. But since it's not far off the road, about halfway between Progreso and Mérida, it's convenient and, in its own way, interesting. More than 16 square km (6 square miles) of land here is cluttered with mounds, platforms, piles of rubble, plazas, and stelae. Although only a few buildings have been excavated to date, scientists find Dzibilchaltún fascinating because of the sculpture and ceramics from all periods of Mayan civilization that have been unearthed. The area may have been settled as early as 500 BC and was inhabited until the time of the conquest. At its height, there were around 40,000 people living here.

The site's most notable structure is the tiny **Templo de las Siete Muñecas** ("Temple of the Seven Dolls"). It's a long stroll down a flat dirt track lined with flowering bushes and trees to get to the low, trapezoidal temple exemplifying the late preclassic style. During the spring and fall equinoxes, sunbeams fall at the exact center of two windows opposite each other inside one of the temple rooms. Studies have found that a similar phenomenon occurs at the full moon between March 20 and April 20.

Another attraction is the ruined open chapel built by the Spaniards for the indigenous people. Actually, to be accurate, the Spanish forced indigenous laborers to build it as a place of worship for themselves: a sort of pre-Hispanic "separate but equal" scenario. One of the best reasons to visit Dzibilchaltún, though, is **Xlacah Cenote**. The site's sinkhole, with crystalline water the color of smoked green glass, is ideal for a cooling swim after walking around the ruins. Before leaving, visit the small but impressive **Museo Pueblo Maya,** which contains the seven crude dolls that gave the Temple of the Seven Dolls its name. It also traces the area's Hispanic history, and highlights contemporary crafts from the region.

To reach Dzibilchaltún from Mérida, drive north on Carretera Mérida-Progreso; after 10 km (6 miles), turn right at the sign for the ruins and continue another 3 km (2 miles) until you reach a village. Just after you pass the village, take your first right toward the archaeological site. If you don't have a car, you can come by cab from Mérida (about MX$350 one way) or Progreso (about MX$1130, including round-trip transport and two hours at the ruins): alternatively, you can catch a *colectivo* (shared van) from Mérida's Parque San Juan or Progreso's main dock. 🖾 *MX$122, including museum; parking MX$28; video fee MX$56* ☺ *Daily 8–5. Museum closed Mon.; cenote closes at 4 pm.*

PROGRESO

16 km (10 miles) north of Dzibilchaltún, 32 km (20 miles) north of Mérida.

The waterfront town closest to Mérida, Progreso is not particularly historic. It's not terribly picturesque either; nevertheless, it provokes a certain sentimental fondness for those who know it well. On weekdays during most of the year the beaches are deserted, but over Easter and in summer they're packed with families from Mérida. Progreso has also started attracting cruise ships, and twice-weekly arrivals bring in tourist traffic. The town's charm—or lack thereof—seems to hinge on the weather. When the sun is shining, the water appears a translucent green and feels bathtub-warm, and the fine sand makes for lovely long walks. When the wind blows during one of Yucatán's winter *nortes,* gray water churns with whitecaps and sand blows in your face. Whether the weather is good or bad, however, everyone ends up eventually at one of the restaurants lining the main street, Calle 19, across from the oceanfront *malecón.* These all serve cold beer, seafood cocktails, and freshly grilled fish. There's also a small downtown area, between Calle 80 and Calle 31, with eateries that dish out simpler fare (like tortas and tacos), plus shops, banks, and supermarkets.

Although Progreso is close enough to Mérida to make it an easy day trip, several smaller hotels that have cropped up over the past few years make it a decent alternative base for those wanting to explore more of the untouristy coast. Just west of Progreso, the fishing villages of Chelem and Chuburna are beginning to offer walking, kayaking, and cycling tours ending with a boat trip through the mangroves for about MX$400. This is ecotourism in its infancy, and excursions are best set up ahead of time through the Progreso tourism office. Experienced divers can explore sunken ships at the Alacranes Reef, about 120 km (74 miles) offshore, although infrastructure is limited. Pérez Island, part of the reef, supports a large population of sea turtles and seabirds. Arrangements for the boat trip can be made through individuals at the private marina at neighboring Yucaltepén, which is 6 km (4 miles) from Progreso.

GETTING HERE AND AROUND

To drive from Mérida, head out of town via Paseo de Montejo and keep going north. It's a straight shot to the beach. Buses bound for Progreso leave Mérida from Calle 62, No. 524, between calles 65 and 67.

Visitor Information Oficina de Turismo ⊠ *Casa de la Cultura, Calles 80 between calles 31 and 33, Centro* ☎ *969/935–0104* ⊕ *www.ayuntamiento de progreso.gob.mx* ⊙ *Daily 9–7.*

BEACHES

Progreso Beach. If you're looking for a pristine, Caribbean-style strand, you'd better look elsewhere. The primary draw of Progreso's main beach is its proximity to Mérida, which often leaves the sand packed with tourists and locals alike during summer weekends and holidays. Water shoes are recommended since sharp, slippery rocks lurk below the surface, making this a poor spot for diving or snorkeling. The beach is void of shade, so your best bet is to find refuge in one of the eateries lining the long malecón (boardwalk) that runs along the shore. Several restaurant owners rent beach chairs by the hour, but beware: Progreso's peddlers are relentless and leave only once they receive a small tip. Despite its drawbacks, the water here offers a refreshing escape from the bustling city. ■TIP➜ **Cruise ships dock in Progreso about twice a week—to avoid the crowds, walk toward the lighthouse. Amenities:** food and drink; toilets (for restaurant patrons). **Best for:** partiers; walking. ⊠ *Av. Malecón at Calle 28.*

WHERE TO EAT

$ ✕ **Eladio's.** An outpost of lively Eladio's in Mérida, this bar and restau-
MEXICAN rant is extremely popular with cruise-ship passengers who disembark in Progreso. You can sample typical Yucatecan dishes like longaniza asada and pollo pibil while seated beneath a tall palapa on the beach; as you'd expect, fresh seafood dishes are also on the menu. Tasty appetizers are free with your drinks, and there are plenty to choose from. Live music every afternoon except Tuesday adds to the party atmosphere. $ *Average main: 113 MP* ⊠ *Av. Malecón s/n, at Calle 80, Centro* ☎ *969/935–5670* ⊕ *www.eladios.com.mx.*

$$ ✕ **Flamingos.** This restaurant facing Progreso's long cement promenade
SEAFOOD is a cut above its neighbors. Service is professional and attentive, and soon after arriving you'll get at least one free appetizer—maybe black beans with corn tortillas or a plate of shredded shark meat stewed with tomatoes. The creamy cilantro soup is a little too cheesy (literally, not figuratively), but the large fish fillets are perfectly breaded and lightly fried. Breakfast is served after 7 am. There's a full bar, and although there's no air-conditioning, large, glassless windows let in the ocean breeze. $ *Average main: 170 MP* ⊠ *Calle 19, No. 144D, at Calle 72* ☎ *969/935–2122.*

WHERE TO STAY

$ **Playa Linda Hotel.** Located directly across from the beach, the Playa
HOTEL Linda has clean rooms, incredible rates, and the best view in Progreso.
Pros: great value; across from the beach. **Cons:** no restaurant; staff
doesn't speak English; no amenities. $ *Rooms from: $55 ⊠ Calle 76,
between calles 19 and 21 ☎ 985/858–0519, 999/220–8318 ⊕ www.
playalindayucatan.com ⟳ 7 rooms* ¶○¶ *No meals.*

$ **Progreso Beach Hotel.** This small hotel is across from the water and
HOTEL close to all the restaurants along the malecón. **Pros:** inexpensive; swimming pool. **Cons:** sparse rooms; Wi-Fi in common areas only; uncomfortable beds. $ *Rooms from: $50 ⊠ Calle 21, No. 150, between calles
66 and 68 ☎ 969/935–5079 ⊕ www.progreso-beach.com ⟳ 51 rooms*
¶○¶ *No meals.*

XCAMBO

32 km (20 miles) west of Progreso.

Xcambo. Surrounded by a plantation where disease-resistant coconut
trees are being developed, the Xcambo (*ish*-cam-bo) site is a couple of
miles inland following the turnoff for Xtampu. Salt, a much-sought-
after commodity in the ancient world, was produced in this area and
made it prosperous. Indeed, the bones of 600 former residents discovered in burial plots showed they had been healthier than the average
Maya. Two plazas have been restored so far, surrounded by rather plain
structures. The tallest temple is the Xcambo, also known as the Pyramid of the Cross. On a clear day you can see the coast from the summit. Ceramics found at the site indicate that the city traded with other
Mayan groups as far afield as Guatemala, Teotihuácan, and Belize.
The Catholic church here was built by dismantling some of the ancient
structures, and, until recently, locals hauled off the cut stones to build
fences and foundations. ⊠ *32 km (20 miles) west of Progreso ✛ Located between Progreso and Telchac Puerto, 3 km (2 miles) south of the
coastal road; turn off Carretera Progreso–Dzilam de Bravo at Xtampu*
🎟 *Donation ⊗ Daily 8–5.*

RESERVA DE LA BIÓSFERA RÍA LAGARTOS

105 km (65 miles) north of Valladolid.

The mangroves of the Ría Lagartos Biosphere Reserve make up one of
southern Mexico's most important wildlife sanctuaries. Birds are the
big draw here, and with 300-plus resident and migratory species, there's
plenty for avian enthusiasts to see.

GETTING HERE AND AROUND

You can make the journey from Valladolid (1½ hours by car, two hours
by bus) as a day trip; add one hour if you're coming from Mérida, and
three hours from Cancún. Buses leave Mérida and Valladolid regularly
from the second-class terminals bound for either Río Lagartos (note that
the town is called Río Lagartos, the park Ría Lagartos) or San Felipe,
which is 10 km (6 miles) west of the park.

EXPLORING

FAMILY   **Reserva de la Biósfera Ría Lagartos.** This national park, which encompasses a long estuary, was developed with ecotourism in mind—although most of the alligators for which it and the village were named have long since been hunted into extinction. The real spectacle these days is the birds. More than 380 species nest and feed in the area, including flocks of flamingos, snowy and red egrets, white ibis, great white herons, cormorants, pelicans, and peregrine falcons. Fishing is good, too, and the protected leatherback, hawksbill, and green turtles lay their eggs on the beach at night.

Booking an excursion through Restaurante Ría Maya is the easiest way to visit the 149,000-acre park. Call ahead to reserve an English-speaking guide with their tour company, **Río Lagartos Adventures** (☎ 986/862–0452 ⊕ *www.riolagartosadventures.com*). Boat trips will take you through mangrove forests to flamingo feeding grounds (where, as an added bonus, you can paint your body with supposedly therapeutic white clay). A 2½-hour tour, accommodating five or six people, costs MX$1065; a 3½-hour bird-watching tour is MX$1275 (both per boat, not per person). Shorter sunset trips and four-hour photography safaris are offered for MX$710 and $1700 respectively. The night tour in search of crocs takes 2½ hours (one to four passengers, MX$1275). Boats can also be hired to transport you to an area beach and pick you up at a designated time (1–10 passengers, MX$285). ■ **TIP→** Mosquitoes are known to gather at dusk in unpleasantly large swarms in May, June, and July. Bring repellent to fend them off. ⊠ *Río Lagartos, 115 km (71 miles) north of Valladolid* ⊕ *www.riolagartosadventures.com* ⌨*MX$35.*

WHERE TO EAT

$ ✕ **Restaurante Ría Maya.** Grab a seat in this palapa restaurant directly SEAFOOD   across from the water, and watch the day's catch come straight from the docks. With a seashell-strewn floor and plastic tables, it's far from fancy, but you're sure to leave satisfied. The menu features all the local specialties like ceviche, seafood soup, fish fillet stuffed with shrimp, and breaded seafood rolled into a ball and deep fried. In season (July–December) you can order lobster and octopus cooked several different ways. Owner Diego Núñez and his family also operate Río Lagartos Adventures and can fix you up with area tours. $ *Average main: 127 MP* ⊠ *Calle 19, No. 134, on the waterfront, 50 meters from the lighthouse, Río Lagartos* ☎ *986/862–0452* ⊕ *www.riolagartos restaurante.com.*

WHERE TO STAY

$ ⌂ **Hotel Punta Ponto.** The main draw here is the friendly, personal atten-HOTEL   tion the owners lavish on guests. **Pros:** waterfront location; friendly staff. **Cons:** spartan accommodations; some street noise; rooms could use a makeover. $ *Rooms from: $55* ⊠ *Calle 9 Diagonal, No. 140, Río Lagartos* ☎ *986/862–0509* ⊕ *www.hotelpuntaponto.com* ⌨*9 rooms, 1 suite* ⊟ *No credit cards* ⏐⊙⏐ *Breakfast.*

$ ⌂ **Hotel Tabasco Río.** Right on the plaza, this hotel has a bright center HOTEL   courtyard covered with skylights that allow light to shine on the tables where breakfast is served. **Pros:** well-appointed rooms; hotel package can include meals and tours. **Cons:** not on water; Wi-Fi in common areas only. $ *Rooms from: $48* ⊠ *Calle 12, No. 115, Río Lagartos* ☎ *986/862–0016* ⊕ *www.tabascoriohotel.com* ⤳ *19 rooms* ⦿ *No meals.*

$ ⛳ **Hotel Villa de Pescadores.** The nicest choice in Río Lagartos has 12
HOTEL rooms with TVs, private balconies, water views, and colorful décor; stone walls and tile floors keep rooms rather cool, but there are fans and air-conditioning for those who need an extra breeze. **Pros:** great views; gracious owner; clean rooms; best location in town; private parking lot. **Cons:** restaurant closed for dinner in low season; four floors but no elevator; Wi-Fi in common areas only. $ *Rooms from: $68* ⊠ *Calle 14 and Av. Malecon, Río Lagartos* ☎ *986/862–0020* ⊕ *www. hotelriolagartos.com.mx* ⤳ *12* ⦿ *No meals.*

ISLA HOLBOX

Fodor'sChoice *141 km (87 miles) northeast of Valladolid.*
★
Only 25 km (16 miles) long, tiny Isla Holbox sits at the eastern end of the Ría Lagartos estuary and is just across the Quintana Roo state line. Fishing fans come for the ample supply of pampano, bass, and barracuda, while birders appreciate the many avian species that fill the mangrove estuaries on the island's leeward side. Beach bums love the sandy strands strewn with seashells; although the water is often murky—the Gulf of Mexico and the Caribbean come together here—it's shallow and warm, and there are some nice places to swim. Sandy streets lead to simple seafood restaurants where conch, octopus, and other delicacies are always fresh. Lodgings here range from bare-bones to beach-luxe, and hotel owners can help set up fishing and bird-watching excursions, as well as expeditions to see the whale sharks that cruise offshore June through August.

Isla's population numbers some 2,000 lucky souls, and in summer it seems there are as many biting bugs per person. Bring plenty of mosquito repellent. Many locals use baby oil as a natural protection against no-seeums, also known as biting midges.

GETTING HERE AND AROUND

From Río Lagartos, take Carretera 176 to Kantunilkin, and then head north on the unnumbered road for 44 km (27 miles) to the port town of Chiquilá (road signs direct you simply to "Holbox"). From Cancún, take the 180 free road toward Mérida and pass through the small town of Leona Vicario; follow the signs to Kantunilkin and continue 40 km (25 miles) until you reach Chiquilá. The drive from Cancún to Chiquilá takes about three hours depending on road conditions. The road is long and pitted with potholes, so avoid driving at night. You can park at 5 Hermanos, which has covered stalls across from the port for MX$56 a day, and continue by boat to the island.

Ferry schedules vary, but there are normally crossings on the hour from around 6 am to 7 pm. The fare is MX$50, and the trip takes about 35 minutes. Speed boats will take you over for double the price in half the time. A car ferry makes the trip at 6 am daily, returning at 1 pm, but it's

Most visitors access Isla Holbox by ferry.

recommended to leave your car in Chiquilá. If you're feeling flush, Isla Holbox has a rustic airport with a shell-bordered runway that receives small airplanes. You can charter a five-passenger Cesna through Aero-Saab; round-trip airfare from Cancún, Cozumel, or Playa del Carmen will cost your group MX$14400 to MX$17300.

Little golf-cart taxis ply the island for about MX$200 an hour; you can rent your own for MX$120 an hour (you may be able to negotiate a better price if you're renting for several hours or traveling in low season). Some hotels also offer complimentary bikes for guests.

Airline Contacts AeroSaab ☎ *998/873–0501 in Playa del Carmen* ⊕ *www. aerosaab.com.*

WHERE TO EAT

$$$ ✕ **Casa Nostra.** You can't get much closer to dining on the beach than
ITALIAN this: at Casa Nostra, a little palapa restaurant, water laps just below the tables on the sandy shore. A creative menu created by its Sicilian chef, Giuseppe Genovese (commonly known as "Beppe"), blends Italian, Mediterranean, and Caribbean cuisine. Locals gather for seafood pasta, grilled lobster, octopus salad, and fresh ceviche, all bathed in garlic and olive oil. Breads, sausages, and pizzas are made from scratch in the small kitchen where Beppe works his magic. The pizza topped with smoked ham, mozzarella, and arugula makes a perfect starter for two. ■TIP➔ **This is the only spot on the island where you'll find authentic espresso, sorbet, and tiramisù.** Ⓢ *Average main: 226 MP* ⊠ *Hotel La Palapa, Av. Morelos 231, Isla Holbox* ☎ *984/875–2121* ⊕ *www. xperiencehotelsrestorts.com.*

$$ SUSHI **El Sushi Holbox.** This tiny restaurant fills a void in island cuisine with the day's catch transformed into the sushi roll of your choice. Local favorites include the Holbox Rainbow made with shrimp, salmon, tuna, and sea bass. Nearly every roll is stuffed with cream cheese, an ingredient that makes the sushi far from authentic yet memorably tasty. Placing a sweet spin on the menu is the Banana Roll with shrimp, avocado, and cream cheese topped with fried banana and eel sauce. The restaurant also serves Thai dishes and has a full cocktail menu—the ginger margarita packs a punch. *Average main: 170 MP* ✉ *Plaza El Pueblito, Av. Tiburón Ballena, top floor, Isla Holbox* ☎ *1984/132–9507* *Closed Mon. No lunch.*

$$$ ECLECTIC **Mandarina.** On the ground floor of Casa Las Tortugas, Mandarina has indoor and outdoor seating just feet from the sand. Chef Jorge Melul, a master baker, has become known on the island for his homemade breads, cakes, and pastas. Nearly every item on the menu is organic, with most ingredients coming from Mandarina's garden or farms in neighboring Solferino. The daily catch is purchased directly from the fishermen who dock on the shores. For a memorable meal, start with shrimp tempura dipped in chipotle cream or homemade pesto. The fish, cooked in white wine and topped with spinach and pears, is light and satisfying. If it's just ambience you're after, head to the rooftop bar for a reasonably priced basil mojito or ginger margarita. *Average main: 212 MP* ✉ *Casa Las Tortugas, Calle Igualdad s/n, Isla Holbox* ☎ *984/875–2129* *www.holboxcasalastortugas.com.*

6

$$ SEAFOOD **Zarabanda Restaurante.** Near the main square, this unpretentious family-run restaurant is one of the oldest (and most affordable) eateries on the island, and it's considered one of the best places to try island-style food. There are quite a few tasty seafood dishes, including a huge *mariscada* for two that includes a fish fillet, a whole fish, a lobster, and octopus on a bed of shredded lettuce. The delicious seafood soup includes the freshest seasonal seafood and is an island classic. People come here for the food and not the ambience, so grab a seat at a plastic table, listen to the Mexican music, and take your pick from the extensive menu. *Average main: 170 MP* ✉ *Calle Palomino s/n, Isla Holbox* ☎ *984/875–2094* *No credit cards.*

TIP→ Luckily, the island has several ATMs—some smaller businesses accept cash only.

WHERE TO STAY

$$ HOTEL Fodor's Choice ★ **Casa Las Tortugas.** This romantic "bohemian-chic" spot has a prime location and one of the only spas on Holbox. **Pros:** on-site kitesurfing school; excellent location; organic restaurant. **Cons:** not all rooms have ocean views; usually booked far in advance. *Rooms from: $170* ✉ *Calle Igualdad s/n, Isla Holbox* ☎ *984/875–2129* *www.holboxcasalastortugas.com* *14 rooms, 7 suites* *Breakfast.*

$$$ HOTEL **Casa Sandra.** Rustic meets five-star at this boutique hotel, elegantly landscaped with winding pathways leading to two-story casitas draped in bougainvillea. **Pros:** Ayurveda treatments; 500-thread-count Egyptian cotton sheets; good restaurant. **Cons:** some rooms get kitchen noise; expensive restaurant; not all rooms have ocean views. *Rooms from:*

$249 ⊠ Calle de la Igualdad s/n, Isla Holbox ☎ 984/875–2171 ⊕ www. casasandra.com ⌁ 15 rooms, 5 suites ⦿ Breakfast.

$$$ ⬚ **Hotel Las Nubes.** Remotely located on the northeast side of the island,
HOTEL   this quiet waterfront retreat is the most luxurious (and expensive) Hol-
Fodor'sChoice   box hotel. **Pros:** unobstructed views; peaceful location; bikes for explor-
★   ing. **Cons:** expensive; small beach; far from town. Ⓢ *Rooms from: $270
⊠ Paseo Kuka s/n, Esq. Calle Camarón, Isla Holbox ☎ 984/875–2300
⊕ www.lasnubesdeholbox.com ⌁ 19 rooms, 5 suites ⦿ Breakfast.*

$$ ⬚ **Hotel Mawimbi.** Known for its Mexican hospitality, this small hotel is
HOTEL   made up of brightly painted beachside bungalows. **Pros:** inexpensive;
suspended beach beds are great for relaxing. **Cons:** entryway rooms
lack privacy. Ⓢ *Rooms from: $130 ⊠ Calle Igualdad s/n, Isla Holbox
☎ 984/875–2003 ⊕ www.mawimbi.net ⌁ 11 rooms ⦿ Breakfast.*

$$$ ⬚ **Hotel Villas Flamingos.** If you are looking for simplicity, tranquility,
HOTEL   and an eco-friendly atmosphere, this is your place. **Pros:** eco-friendly
property; nice pool; only beach house on the island. **Cons:** far from
town; rustic design is not for everyone; rooms could use some upgrades.
Ⓢ *Rooms from: $225 ⊠ Calle paseo Kuka s/n, Isla Holbox ☎ 1984/875–
2167 ⊕ www.villasflamingos.com ⌁ 30 rooms ⦿ Breakfast.*

$$ ⬚ **Villas Delfines.** This fishermen's lodge consists of 20 pleasant, palapa-
HOTEL   topped cabins by the beach. **Pros:** eco-friendly property; nice Saturday
grill (high season only). **Cons:** 15-minute walk to village's main square;
Wi-Fi in common areas only; slightly dated rooms. Ⓢ *Rooms from:
$148 ⊠ Calle Paso Kuka s/n, Isla Holbox ☎ 984/875–2196 ⊕ www.
villasdelfines.com ⌁ 20 cabins ⦿ Multiple meal plans.*

$$ ⬚ **Villas HM Paraíso del Mar.** Despite the thatched roofs and rustic ambi-
RESORT   ence, rooms at the island's largest property—HM is a Spanish hotel
chain—are loaded with everything you could want to be comfortable.
Pros: nice breakfast buffet; island's only all-inclusive property. **Cons:**
some rooms lack ocean views; seaweed on shore; Wi-Fi in common
areas only. Ⓢ *Rooms from: $157 ⊠ Av. Plutarco Elias s/n, Isla Holbox
☎ 984/875–2062 ⊕ www.hmhotels.net ⌁ 52 rooms, 6 suites ⦿ Mul-
tiple meal plans.*

SPORTS AND OUTDOORS

Sailing Isla Holbox. Two-hour sunset cruises can be arranged through
Hotel Puerto Holbox. The 26-foot sailboat holds up to four passen-
gers and is available for fishing trips or sunset excursions. Drinks
and appetizers are included in the rate. ⊠ *Hotel Puerto Holbox, Av.
Pedro Joaquín Coldwell s/n, Isla Holbox ☎ 984/875–2157 ⊕ www.
hotelpuertoholbox.com ☉ From MX$1680.*

SHOPPING

Artesanías Las Chicas. Sandra Thomson, a New York native who has lived
on the island for years, runs Artesanías Las Chicas, a small shop with
a delightful collection of arts and crafts. She carries everything from
rings and mirrors to sophisticated hammocks and purses from all over
Mexico. ⊠ *Calle Igualdad s/n, Isla Holbox ☎ 984/875–2430.*

CAMPECHE

"*¡Quiero estar ahí!*" proclaim the colorful license plates in the state of Campeche. "I want to be there!" After one visit, you'll likely say the same. Campeche City, the state capital, is one of the best-kept secrets in the Yucatán. Its beautifully preserved colonial district is brimming with historic sites, museums, cafés, and restaurants—all within easy walking distance of each other. Yet the city is far smaller and more easygoing than its Yucatecan cousin, Mérida. Its unique history (it was once a favorite target of seafaring pirates) has left a mark. Many of the protective walls that were built to safeguard inhabitants are still standing, and the colorful colonial buildings were constructed with safety in mind; they're markedly less ornate than their counterparts elsewhere on the peninsula, with well-barred windows and impressively heavy-looking doors. The 18th-century fort at the south end of town lets you imagine Campeche's dangerous past, and is home to a fascinating collection of Mayan artifacts taken from area archaeological sites.

Although the city is the state's most accessible spot and a good hub for exploring, there's much more to Campeche than its capital. Beyond the city lie the famous ruins of Edzná, a short detour south of Carreteras 180 and 188. The southern reaches of the state turn a bit wilder with the remnants of 10 Mayan cities strung out through the rain forest on or near Carretera 186. Just be advised that dining and accommodation options get more basic when you venture this far from the city; you'll encounter fewer English speakers off the beaten path, too, so pack a Spanish-English dictionary if you don't have at least rudimentary Spanish. ■ TIP→ Anglophones use "Campeche City" to distinguish the capital from the rest of the state. Spanish speakers call both simply "Campeche," so let context be your guide.

CAMPECHE CITY

174 km (108 miles) southwest of Mérida.

In picturesque Campeche, block upon block of restored buildings with lovely facades, all painted in bright colors, meet the sea. Tiny balconies overlook clean, geometrically paved streets, and charming old street lamps illuminate the scene at night. While the heart of the city, a UNESCO World Heritage Site, looks as if it has been constructed purely for touristic purposes, you'll find just as many workaday businesses here as you will trendy restaurants and boutique hotels.

In colonial days the city center was completely enclosed within a 10-foot-thick wall. Two stone archways (originally there were four)—one facing the sea, the other the land—provided the only access. The defensive walls also served as a de facto class demarcation. Within them lived the ruling elite. Outside were the barrios, with slaves from Cuba, and everyone else.

On strategic corners, seven *baluartes,* or bastions, gave militiamen a platform from which to fight off pirates and the other ruffians that continually plagued this beautiful city on the bay. But it wasn't until

1771, when the Fuerte de San Miguel was built on a hilltop outside town, that pirates finally stopped attacking the city.

■TIP→ Campeche's historic center is easily navigable—walking is always your best bet. Narrow streets and lack of parking spaces can make driving a bit frustrating, although motorists here are polite and mellow. Streets running roughly north–south are even-numbered, and those running east–west are odd-numbered. The historic center has a perimeter stretching 2½ km (1½ miles).

GETTING HERE AND AROUND

Aeroméxico and Interjet fly several times daily from Mexico City to Aeropuerto Internacional Alberto Acuña Ongay in Campeche City. The airport is just north of downtown; taxis—the only means of transportation to and from the facility—charge about MX$120 for the 16-km (10-mile) trip.

Buses operated by ADO (⊕ *www.ado.com.mx*) connect Campeche City to points all over the Yucatán Peninsula. If you're driving, Campeche City is about 2 to 2½ hours from Mérida when you choose the 180-km (99-mile) *via corta* (short way) on Carretera 180. The alternative route, the 250-km (155-mile) *via ruinas* (ruins route) on Carretera 261, takes three to four hours, but passes some major Mayan sites.

Within Campeche City, the route of interest to most visitors is along Avenida Ruíz Cortínez. A ride on a bus costs the equivalent of about 30¢. You can hail taxis on the street, plus there are stands by the bus stations, the municipal market, and Parque Principal. The minimum fare is MX$25; after 11 pm, prices may be slightly higher. There's a small fee (less than MX$6) to call for a cab through Radio Taxi.

Taxi Contacts **Radio Taxi** ☎ *981/815–8888*.

VISITOR INFORMATION

You'll see numerous Información Turística signs around town, but most are storefront tour outfits hoping to sell you excursions rather than unbiased sources of information. The city and state of Campeche each operates official tourist-information offices staffed by phenomenal people who can answer your questions.

Contacts **Oficina de Turismo de Campeche** (*Municipal Tourist Office*). ✉ *Parque Principal, Calle 55, between calles 8 and 10, Centro* ☎ *981/811–3989* ☾ *Weekdays 9–9, weekends 9–5.* **Oficina de Turismo de Campeche** ✉ *Plaza Moch Couoh, Av. Ruíz Cortínez s/n, Centro* ☎ *981/127–3300* ⊕ *www.campeche. travel.*

EXPLORING

TOP ATTRACTIONS

Baluarte de la Soledad. The largest of the bastions was originally built to protect the **Puerta de Mar,** a sea gate that served as one of four original entrances to the city. Because it uses no supporting walls, it resembles a Roman triumphal arch. Baluarte de la Soledad has comparatively complete parapets and embrasures that offer views of the cathedral, municipal buildings, and old houses along Calle 8. The museum inside—**Museo de Arquitectura Maya,** dedicated to Mayan architecture—is closed for

A STREETCAR NAMED EL GUAPO

Guided trolley tours of historic Campeche City generally leave from Calle 10 on Parque Principal on the hour from 9 to 9. Be prepared for delayed departures, though, since trolleys take off only when at least eight tickets have been sold. You can buy yours ahead of time at the adjacent kiosk or wait until you're onboard. The one-hour tour costs MX$100 (MX$60 for kids under 12),

and, if asked, guides will do their best to speak English. The "Guapo" ("handsome") trolley makes trips around the historic center and Malecón; the "Superguapo" takes in the city center, the Reducto de San José, and Fuerte San Miguel. Note that trips run less frequently in the off-season, so it's always best to double-check schedules at the kiosk.

renovations at this writing. ⊠ *Calle 8, between calles 55 and 57, Centro* ☎ *981/816–9136* ⊕ *www.inah.gob.mx.*

Baluarte de San Carlos. This bastion, where Calle 8 curves around and becomes Circuito Baluartes, houses the **Museo de la Ciudad.** The museum contains a small collection of historical artifacts, including several Spanish suits of armor and a beautifully inscribed silver scepter. Captured pirates were once jailed in the stifling basement dungeon. ■ **TIP→ The unshaded rooftop provides an ocean view that's lovely at sunset.** ⊠ *Calle 8, between calles 65 and 63, Circuito Baluartes, Centro* 🖼 *MX$42* ⊗ *Daily 9–8.*

Calle 59. Some of Campeche's finest homes were built on this street between calles 8 and 18. Most of the two-story structures were originally dual-purpose, with warehouses on the ground floor and living quarters above; these days, behind the delicate grillwork and lace curtains, you can glimpse genteel scenes of local life. The best-preserved houses are between calles 14 and 18 (many of those closer to the sea have been remodeled or destroyed by fire). Campeche's INAH (Instituto Nacional de Antropología e Historia) office, between calles 14 and 16, is a prime example; each month it displays a different archaeological artifact in its courtyard. At the end of Calle 59 is Puerta de Mar, a main entrance to the historic city. ■ **TIP→ Look for the names of the apostles carved into the lintels of houses between calles 16 and 18.**

Casa Seis. One of the city's earliest colonial homes now serves as a cultural center. Fully restored, its rooms are furnished with period antiques and a few well-chosen reproductions; original frescoes at the tops of the walls remain, and you can see patches of the painted "wallpaper" that once covered the walls, serving to simulate European trends in an environment where real wallpaper wouldn't adhere due to the humidity. There is a small coffee shop on-site, plus a gift shop selling products from Campeche. The Moorish courtyard is occasionally used as a space for exhibits and lectures. Activities occur here several evenings a week. *Vivo Recuerdo,* a musical/theater interpretation of Campeche's history, is presented Thursday through Sunday; *Con Sabor a Chocolate,* a chocolate-making demonstration, takes place on Friday and

CLOSE UP

Campeche's History

Campeche City's gulf location played a pivotal role in its history. Ah-Kim-Pech (Mayan for "lord of the serpent tick," from which the name Campeche is derived) was the capital of an indigenous settlement here, long before the Spaniards arrived in 1517. In 1540 the conquerors—led by Francisco de Montejo and later by his son and nephew—established a real foothold at Campeche (originally called San Francisco de Campeche), using it as a base for the conquest of the peninsula.

At the time, Campeche City was the Gulf's only port and shipyard. So Spanish ships, loaded with cargoes of treasure plundered from Mayan, Aztec, and other indigenous civilizations, dropped anchor here en route from Veracruz to Cuba, New Orleans, and Spain. As news of the riches spread, Campeche's shores were soon overrun with pirates. From the mid-1500s to the early 1700s, such notorious corsairs as Diego the Mulatto, Lorenzillo, Peg Leg, Henry Morgan, and Barbillas swooped in repeatedly from Tris—or Isla de Términos, as Isla del Carmen was then known—pillaging and burning the city and massacring its people.

Finally, after years of appeals to the Spanish crown, Campeche received funds to build a protective wall, with four gates and eight bastions, around the town center. For a while afterward, the city thrived on its exports, especially *palo de tinte*—a valuable dyewood more precious than gold due to the nascent European textile industry's demand for it—but also hardwoods, chicle, salt, and henequen. However, when the port of Sisal opened on the northern Yucatán coast in 1811, Campeche's monopoly on gulf traffic ended, and its economy quickly declined. During the 19th and 20th centuries, Campeche, like most of the Yucatán Peninsula, had little to do with the rest of Mexico. Left to their own devices, *campechanos* lived in relative isolation until the petroleum boom of the 1970s brought businessmen from Mexico City, Europe, and the United States to its provincial doorstep.

Campeche City's history still shapes the community today. Remnants of its gates and bastions split the city into two main districts: the historical center (where relatively few people live) and the newer residential areas. Because the city was long preoccupied with defense, the colonial architecture is less flamboyant here than elsewhere in Mexico. The narrow flagstone streets reflect the confines of the city's walls, and homes here emphasize the practical over the decorative. Still, government decrees have helped keep the colonial structures in good condition despite the damaging effects of humidity and salt air. An air of antiquity remains.

6

Saturday. ⊠ *Parque Principal, Calle 57, between calles 10 and 8, Centro* ☎ *981/816–1782* 📧 *House MX$28; Vivo Recurrdo MX$113; Con Sabor a Chocolate MX$85* ⊙ *Daily 9–9; Vivo Recuerdo, Thurs.–Sun. at 9:30 pm; Con Sabor a Chocolate, Fri. and Sat. at 6:30 pm.*

Catedral de la Inmaculada Concepción. It took two centuries (from 1650 to 1850) to finish the Cathedral of the Immaculate Conception, and, as a result, it incorporates both neoclassical and Renaissance elements. On

Campeche City

the simple limestone exterior, sculptures of saints in niches are covered in black netting to discourage pigeons from unintentional desecration. The church's neoclassical interior is also somewhat plain and sparse. The high point of its collection, now housed in the side chapel museum, is a magnificent Holy Sepulchre carved from ebony and decorated with stamped silver angels, flowers, and decorative curlicues. Each angel holds a symbol of the Stations of the Cross. ⊠ *Parque Principal, Calle 55, between calles 8 and 10, Centro* 🕿 *981/816–2524* 🎫 *Free* 🕙 *Daily 9–8.*

FAMILY **Fuerte de San Miguel.** Near the city's southwest end, Avenida Ruíz Cortínez winds its way to this hilltop fort with a breathtaking view of the Bay of Campeche. Built between 1779 and 1801 and dedicated to the archangel Michael, the fort was positioned to blast enemy ships with its long-range cannons. As soon as it was completed, pirates stopped attacking the city. In fact, the cannons were fired only once, in 1842, when General Santa Anna used Fuerte de San Miguel to put down a revolt by Yucatecan separatists seeking independence from Mexico.

The fort houses the 10-room **Museo de la Arqueología Maya.** Exhibits include the skeletons of long-ago Maya royals, complete with jewelry and pottery, which are arranged just as they were found in Calakmul tombs. Other archaeological treasures are funeral vessels, wonderfully expressive figurines and whistles from Isla de Jaina, stelae and stucco masks from the Mayan ruins, and an excellent pottery collection. Most information is in Spanish only, but many of the pieces speak for themselves. ■TIP→ **The gift shop sells replicas of artifacts.** ✉ *Av. Francisco Morazán s/n, Cerro de Buenavista* ☎ *981/816–9111* ⊕ *www.inah.gob. mx* ✆ *MX$42* ⊙ *Tues.–Sun. 8:30–5.*

Malecón. A broad sidewalk, more than 4 km (2½ miles) long, runs the length of Campeche's waterfront boulevard, from northeast of the Debliz hotel to the Justo Sierra Méndez monument at the southwest edge of downtown. With its landscaping, sculptures, rest areas, and fountains lighted up at night in neon colors, the promenade attracts walkers, joggers, and cyclists. (Note the separate paths for each.) On weekend nights, students turn the malecón into a party zone, and families with young children fill the parks on both sides of the promenade after 7 or 8 pm, staying out surprisingly late to enjoy the cooler evening temperatures. ✉ *Av. Rodolfo Ruiz Cortínez.*

Parque Principal (*Plaza de la Independencia*). Also known as the Plaza de la Independencia, this central park is small by Mexican standards, though picturesque with a beautiful view of Catedral de la Inmaculada Concepción. In its center is an old-fashioned kiosk. One half of it contains the municipal tourist office; the other houses a pleasant café-bar, where you can sit and watch residents out for an evening stroll and listen to the itinerant musicians who often show up to play traditional ballads in the evenings. ✉ *Bounded by calles 8, 10, 55, and 57, Centro.*

FAMILY **Puerta de Tierra.** The Land Gate, where Old Campeche ends, is the only one of the four city gates with its basic structure intact. The stone arch interrupts a stretch of the partially crenellated wall, 26-feet high and 10-feet thick, that once encircled the city. Walk the wall's full length to the **Baluarte San Juan** for excellent views of both the old and new cities. The staircase leads down to an old well, underground storage area, and dungeon. Thursday through Sunday evening, there's a one-hour light show accompanied by music and dance at Puerta de Tierra. ✉ *Calles 18 and 59, Centro* ✆ *Sound-and-light show MX$57* ⊙ *Sound-and-light show, Thurs.–Sun. at 8 pm.*

WORTH NOTING

Baluarte de San Pedro. Built in 1686 to protect the city from pirate attacks, this bastion flanked by watchtowers now houses one of the city's few worthwhile handicraft shops. The collection is small but of high quality, and prices are reasonable. On the roof are well-preserved corner watchtowers. You can also check out (but not use) the original 17th-century toilet. ✉ *Calles 18 and 51, Circuito Baluartes, Centro* ✆ *Free* ⊙ *Daily 9–5.*

Baluarte de Santiago. The last of the bastions to be built has been transformed into the **X'much Haltún Botanical Gardens.** It contains more than 200 plant species, including the enormous ceiba tree, which had spiritual importance to the Maya, symbolizing a link between heaven, earth, and the underworld. The original bastion, erected in 1704, was demolished at the turn of the 20th century, then rebuilt in the 1950s. ✉ *Calles 8 and 49, Circuito Baluartes, Centro* ✆ *MX$14, includes* *admission to Baluarte San Juan and Bastión de San Francisco* ⊙ *Mon.–Sat. 9–8, Sun. 9–4.*

Ex-Templo de San José. The Jesuits built this fine baroque church in honor of Saint Joseph just before they were booted out of the New World in 1767. Its block-long facade and portal are covered with blue-and-yellow Talavera tiles and crowned with seven narrow stone finials—resembling both the roof combs on many Mayan temples and the combs Spanish women once wore in their elaborate hairdos. You can ask the guard (who should be somewhere on the grounds) to let you in. From the outside you can admire Campeche's first lighthouse, built in 1864, and perched atop the right-hand tower. ⊠ *Calles 10 and 63, Centro* ☏ *981/816–2292.*

Iglesia de San Francisco. With its flat, boldly painted facade and bells ensconced under small arches instead of in bell towers, the Church of Saint Francis looks more like a Mexican city hall than a Catholic church. Outside the city center in a residential neighborhood, the beautifully restored temple is Campeche's oldest. It marks the spot where some say the first Mass on the North American continent was held in 1517—though the same claim has been made for Veracruz and Cozumel. One of conquistador Hernán Cortés's grandsons was baptized here, and the baptismal font still stands. ⊠ *Avs. Miguel Alemán and Mariano Escobedo, San Francisco* ☏ *981/816–2925* 🎫 *Free* ⊙ *Daily 10–7.*

Iglesia de San Román. Like most Franciscan churches, this one is sober and plain, and its single bell tower is the only ornamentation. The equally sparse interior is brightened a bit by some colorful stained-glass windows, and the carved and inlaid altarpiece serves as a beautiful backdrop for an ebony image of Jesus, the "Black Christ," brought from Italy in about 1575. Although understandably skeptical of Christianity, the indigenous people, whom the Spaniards forced into perpetual servitude, eventually came to associate this black Christ figure with miracles. As legend has it, a ship that refused to carry the holy statue was lost at sea, while the ship that accepted it reached Campeche in record time. To this day, the Feast of San Román—when worshippers carry a black-wood Christ and silver filigree cross through the streets—remains a solemn but colorful affair. ⊠ *Calles 10 and Bravo, San Román* ☏ *981/816–3303* 🎫 *Free* ⊙ *Daily 7–1 and 3–7.*

Iglesia y Ex-Convento de San Roque. The elaborately carved main altarpiece and matching side altars here were restored inch by inch, and this long, narrow house of worship now adds more than ever to historic Calle 59's old-fashioned beauty. Built in 1565, it was originally called Iglesia de San Francisco for Saint Francis. In addition to a statue of Francis, humbler-looking saints peer out from smaller niches. ⊠ *Calles 12 and 59, Centro* ☏ *981/816–3144* 🎫 *Free* ⊙ *Daily 8:30–noon and 5–7.*

Mansión Carvajal. Built in the early 20th century by one of the Yucatán's wealthiest plantation owners, Fernando Carvajal Estrada, this eclectic mansion is a reminder of the city's heyday, when Campeche was the peninsula's only port. Local legend insists that the art-nouveau staircase with Carrara marble steps and iron balustrade, built and delivered in one piece from Italy, was too big and had to be shipped back and

Campeche's historic center is easy to explore on foot.

redone. These days the mansion is filled with government offices—you'll have to stretch your imagination a bit to picture how it once was. ✉ *Calle 10, No. 584, between calles 51 and 53, Centro* ☎ *981/816–7419* ✉ *Free* ⊘ *Weekdays 9–2:30.*

FAMILY **Reducto de San José el Alto.** This lofty redoubt, or stronghold, at the northwest end of town, is home to the **Museo de Armas y Barcos.** Displays in former soldiers' and watchmen's rooms focus on 18th-century weapons of siege and defense. You'll also see manuscripts, religious art, and ships in bottles. The view is terrific from the top of the ramparts, which were once used to spot invading ships. The Superguapo sightseeing trolley stops here on its rounds for about 10 minutes. ✉ *Av. Escénica s/n, Cerro de Bellavista* ☎ *981/816–2460* ⊕ *www.inah.gob.mx* ✉ *MX$42* ⊘ *Tues.–Sun. 8–5.*

WHERE TO EAT

$$ ✗ **Casa Vieja de los Arcos.** Whether you're having a meal or an evening
MEXICAN cocktail, try to snag a table on this eatery's outdoor balcony for a fabulous view over Campeche's main plaza. You wouldn't know it from the tiny entrance, but the interior is large and inviting, and the brightly painted walls are crammed with eclectic art. The menu displays a rich sampling of Mexican dishes including coconut shrimp, chicken fajitas, cochinita pibil, and *pan de cazón* (shredded shark with black beans and tortillas). In addition to pastas, salads, and regional food, you'll find a good selection of aperitifs and digestifs. The view (not the service) is the main draw. To get here, look for the narrow stairway on Parque Principal's southeast side. $ *Average main: 184 MP* ✉ *Parque Principal, Calle*

10, No. 319 Altos, between calles 57 and 55, Centro ☎ *981/811–8016* ⊕ *casaviejacampeche.blogspot.com* ▱ *No credit cards* ⊗ *No lunch.*

$ ✕ **Cenaduría Portales.** Campechano families come here to enjoy a light

MEXICAN supper, perhaps a delicious sandwich *claveteado* of honey-and-clove-spiked ham, along with a typical drink like *agua de chaya*, a mixture of pineapple water and chaya (a leafy vegetable similar to spinach). Cenaduría Portales opens at 6 pm, but most people arrive between 8 and midnight. The dining area is a wide colonial veranda with marble flooring and tables decked out in plastic tablecloths. No alcohol is served, and you simply mark your choices on the paper menu: for tacos, "m" means *maíz*, or corn; for tortillas, "h" stands for *harina*, or flour. ■TIP➔ On weekends, try the tamal torteado, a tamale with beans, tomato sauce, turkey, and pork wrapped in banana leaves—although not listed on the menu, it's available on request. Ⓢ *Average main: 113 MP* ⊠ *Calle 10, No. 86, at Portales San Francisco, 8 blocks northeast of Parque Principal, San Francisco* ☎ *981/811–1491* ⊗ *No lunch.*

$ ✕ **Chocol Ha.** Follow your nose to this chocolate café, where the aro-

BAKERY mas of French pastries and rich cocoa waft into Campeche's narrow streets. Tucked inside a stone-walled colonial building are small wooden tables and a collection of antiques, like a vintage cash register still used for ringing up transactions. Drink recipes originated from the owner's research into Mayan traditions and her time spent with local families; prepared with the purest form of organic cocoa, they're infused with mint, chile, and more. Non–chocolate lovers can enjoy all-natural fruit juices made with jicama and piña. Crêpes and cookies make nice accompaniments. A small gift shop sells locally made products and blocks of dark chocolate. Ⓢ *Average main: 88 MP* ⊠ *Calle 59, No. 30, between calles 12 and 14, Centro* ☎ *981/811–7893* ⊗ *Closed Sun.*

$$ ✕ **La Pigua.** This is hands-down the town's favorite lunch spot. The

SEAFOOD seafood is delicious, and the setting is unusual: glass walls replicate

Fodor'sChoice an oblong Mayan house, incorporating the profusion of plants out-

★ side as a design element. As the sun goes down, candles adorn the white-linen tablecloths, and soft blue lighting illuminates the outside atrium. A truly ambitious meal might start with a plate of calamari, stone-crab claws, or *camarones al coco* (coconut-encrusted shrimp). Memorable mains include pan de cazón (a shark meat casserole that's one of Campeche's most distinctive dishes) and fresh robalo fish topped with puréed cilantro, parsley, orange, and olive oil. For dessert, the classic choice is *ate,* slabs of super-condensed mango, sweet potato, or other fruit or vegetable jelly served with tangy Gouda cheese. Ⓢ *Average main: 170 MP* ⊠ *Av. Miguel Alemán 179A, between calles 49A and 49B, Col. San Martin* ☎ *981/811–3365* ⊕ *www.lapigua.com.mx* ⊗ *No dinner Sun.–Tues.*

$ ✕ **Luz de Luna.** Inside a colonial-era building, this small family-run res-

MEXICAN taurant is decorated with Mexican crafts. Since most customers are tourists, you'll find familiar favorites like burritos, pasta, sandwiches, and fajitas on the enormous menu. Grilled fish and steak are served with rice and shredded lettuce, as are the rolled tacos and enchiladas topped with red or green chile sauce. There are only five tables, but somehow this place can seem overwhelmingly busy on a packed night. Early risers might want to stop by for French toast or one of their breakfast crêpes. Take note, Luz de Luna does not serve alcohol. $ *Average main: 113 MP* ✉ *Calle 59, No. 6, between calles 10 and 12, Centro Historico* ☎ *981/134–7158* ⊘ *Closed Sun.*

$$ × **Marganzo.** Traditional Yucatecan dishes—like *panuchos* (fried masa
MEXICAN cakes stuffed with beans and piled high with shredded meat, lettuce, sour onions, and other toppings) or *chile mestizo* (poblano pepper stuffed with shredded meat)—are the specialty at Marganzo. If you aren't sure what to order, ask to see the album containing photos of top dishes with multilingual captions; waitresses, dressed in colorful skirts from the region, will also offer helpful explanations. The lunch and dinner menus are finished off with a complimentary tamarind margarita, and a guitar trio performs some evenings. But this is also a great place for breakfast if you want to get an early start on sightseeing. ■ TIP→ **You can try plain agua de chaya here—in other restaurants the chaya-flavored water is often sweetened with pineapple.** $ *Average main: 170 MP* ✉ *Calle 8, No. 267, between calles 57 and 59, Col. Centro* ☎ *981/811–3898* ⊕ *www.marganzo.com.*

WHERE TO STAY

$$$ ⬚ **Casa Don Gustavo.** This antique-filled 18th-century mansion is one
HOTEL of Campeche's historic masterpieces—the roof even retains its original
Fodor'sChoice tiles from Marbella, Spain. **Pros:** lovely restaurant; impeccable rooms;
★ colonial touches; surprisingly quiet despite central location. **Cons:** no children under 8 years old; small pool. $ *Rooms from: $200* ✉ *Calle 59, No. 4, between calles 10 and 8, Centro* ☎ *981/816–8090* ⊕ *www. casadongustavo.com* ⤳ *10 suites* ⦿| *No meals.*

$$$$ ⬚ **Hacienda Puerta Campeche.** Just across from the Puerta de Tierra, 17th-
HOTEL century mansions that span nearly an entire city block were reconfigured to create this lovely Starwood hotel. **Pros:** stunning surroundings; calm atmosphere; excellent restaurant. **Cons:** expensive; not really a hacienda; shaded pool. $ *Rooms from: $256* ✉ *Calle 59, No. 71, between calles 16 and 18, Centro* ☎ *981/816–7508, 888/625–5144* ⊕ *www.thehaciendas.com* ⤳ *10 rooms, 5 suites* ⦿| *No meals.*

$$ ⬚ **Hotel Castelmar.** This renovated hotel in the heart of downtown is an
HOTEL elegant and comfortable place to relax. **Pros:** great downtown location; pretty building and rooms. **Cons:** street noise at night can be a problem; rooms vary; small bathrooms. $ *Rooms from: $100* ✉ *Calle 61, No. 2, between calles 8 and 10, Centro* ☎ *981/811–1204* ⊕ *www. castelmarhotel.com* ⤳ *23 rooms, 3 suites* ⦿| *No meals.*

$ ⬚ **Hotel Francis Drake.** This small, yellow hotel in the center of town
HOTEL is one of the more affordable options if you can deal with such issues as street noise, tiny bathrooms, cold-water showers, and weak Wi-Fi signals. **Pros:** helpful staff; good location; black-out curtains; breakfast included. **Cons:** windows in some rooms open above garage and exhaust enters; small bathrooms; traffic noise can be irritating at night. $ *Rooms from: $90* ✉ *Calle 12, No. 207, between calles 63 and 65, Centro* ☎ *981/811–5626, 981/811–5627* ⊕ *www.hotelfrancisdrake. com* ⤳ *12 rooms, 12 suites* ⦿| *Breakfast.*

$$ ⬚ **Hotel Plaza Campeche.** Across from Plaza St. Martín, this ochre
HOTEL hotel is one of the largest and grandest in Campeche. **Pros:** designated

parking area; spacious rooms; good location. **Cons:** small pool; no children under 13; street noise; must cross a very busy street if walking. [$] *Rooms from: $150* ✉ *Calle 10 and Circuito Baluartes, between calles 49-B and 49-C, Centro* ☎ *981/811–9900* 🌐 *www.hotelplazacampeche.com* 🛏 *67 rooms, 16 suites* 🍴 *No meals.*

$$ B&B/INN ⭐ **Hotel Socaire.** Layering the new on top of the old can be fraught with risks, but this hotel in a restored colonial building with accents of contemporary art strikes just the right balance. **Pros:** attentive service; good rates; great combination of old and new. **Cons:** spotty Wi-Fi in rooms; staff is eager to please but speak mainly Spanish. [$] *Rooms from: $100* ✉ *Calle 55, No. 22, between calles 12 and 14, Centro* ☎ *981/811–2130* 🌐 *www.hotelsocaire.com.mx* 🛏 *7 rooms* 🍴 *Breakfast.*

NIGHTLIFE

The monthly minimagazine Cartelera Cultural lists events on Campeche City's active cultural calendar. Pick it up at any hotel. Listings are in Spanish, but they're easily deciphered. In December, concerts and other cultural events take place as part of the Festival del Centro Histórico. Year-round, a few restaurant bars are open along the malecón. Locals like to show up around 10 pm to enjoy the cool evening air.

SHOPPING

Bazar Artesanal. This government-run bazaar offers a wide range of local crafts, including some that are hard to come by—like bull horns carved into necklaces and earrings using an old technique that only a small number of families in Campeche State still know about. All prices are fixed, so there's no need to bargain. ✉ *Plaza Ah Kim Pech, Col. Centro* 🕒 *Mon.–Sat. 9–5.*

Mercado Prinicipal. The city's commercial heart is its main market, where locals shop for seafood, produce, and housewares in a newly refurbished setting. You'll find little of tourist interest here, but the clothing section has some nice, inexpensive embroidered and beaded pieces among the jeans and T-shirts. Next to the market is a small yellow bridge aptly named **Puente de los Perros**—where four white plaster dogs guard the area. ✉ *Av. Baluartes Este and Calle 53, Centro* 🕒 *Daily dawn–dusk.*

SPORTS AND THE OUTDOORS

Campeche Tarpon. Alejandro, and other local fishermen from Campeche Tarpon, can arrange fly-fishing excursions to nearby mangroves, flats, creeks, and lagoons. ☎ *1981/120–4708 (mobile), 888/777–5060* 🌐 *www.campechetarpon.com.*

Tarpon Town. This company offers the city's only fully licensed fishing tours, and they're experts in tailoring fishing trips to individual needs. ✉ *Marina Bahía Azul s/n* ☎ *1981/133–2135 (mobile)* 🌐 *www.tarpontown.com.*

EDZNÁ

61 km (37 miles) southeast of Campeche City.

With its smorgasbord of Mayan architectural styles, Edzná is considered by archaeologists to be one of the peninsula's most important ruin complexes; and although it's less than an hour's drive southeast of Campeche

City, the site sees few tour groups. The scarcity of camera-carrying visitors intensifies the feeling of communion with nature, and with the Maya who built this once-flourishing commercial and ceremonial city.

GETTING HERE AND AROUND

From Campeche, take Carretera 261 heading east toward Holpechén. The turnoff for Edzná is clearly marked about 55 km (34 miles) southeast of Campeche.

EXPLORING

Fodor's Choice ★ **Edzná.** A major metropolis in its day, Edzná was situated at a crossroads between cities in modern-day Guatemala and the states of Chiapas and Yucatán. This "out-of-state" influence can be appreciated in its mélange of architectural elements. Roof combs and corbeled arches evoke those at Yaxchilán and Palenque, in Chiapas; giant stone masks resemble the Petén-style architecture of southern Campeche and northern Guatemala.

Edzná began as a humble agricultural settlement around 300 BC, reaching its pinnacle in the late classic period, between AD 600 and 900, then gradually waning in importance until being all but abandoned in the early 15th century. Today soft breezes blow through groves of slender trees where brilliant orange and black birds spring from branch to branch. Clouds scuttle across a blue backdrop, perfectly framing the mossy remains of once-great structures.

The best place to survey the site is from the 102-foot tall **Pirámide de los Cinco Pisos**, built on the raised platform of the **Gran Acrópolis** (Great Acropolis). This five-story pyramid culminates in a tiny temple crowned by a roof comb. Hieroglyphs were carved into the vertical faces of the 15 steps between each level, and some were re-cemented in place by archaeologists, although not necessarily in the correct order. On these stones, as well as on stelae throughout the site, you can see faint depictions of the opulent attire once worn by the Maya ruling class—quetzal feathers, jade pectorals, and jaguar-skin skirts.

The Pirámide de los Cinco Pisos was constructed so that on certain dates the setting sun would illuminate the mask of the creator-god, Itzamna, inside one of the pyramid's rooms. This happens annually on May 1, 2, and 3, the beginning of the planting season for the Maya—then and now. It also occurs on August 7, 8, and 9, the days of harvesting and giving thanks. On the pyramid's top level sit the ruins of three temples and a ritual steam bath.

West of the Great Acropolis, the Puuc-style **Plataforma de los Cuchillos** (Platform of the Knives) was so named by the archaeological team that found a number of flint knives inside. To the south, four buildings surround a smaller structure called the **Pequeña Acrópolis**. Twin sun-god masks with huge protruding eyes, sharply filed teeth, and oversize tongues flank the **Templo de los Mascarones** (Temple of the Masks, or Building 414), adjacent to the Small Acropolis. The mask at bottom left (east) represents the rising sun; the right mask represents the setting sun.

If you're not driving, consider taking one of the inexpensive day trips offered by tour operators in Campeche. Convenience aside, a guide can point out features often missed by the untrained eye, such as the

remains of arrow-straight sacbés. These raised roads in their day connected one important ceremonial building within the city to the next, and also linked Edzná to trading partners throughout the peninsula. ⊠ *Carretera 188, 61 km (37 miles) southeast of Campeche City* ⊕ *www. inah.gob.mx* ⊠ *$M48* ⊙ *Daily 8–5. Sound-and-light show Nov.–Mar., daily at 7 pm; Apr.–Oct., daily at 8 pm.*

WHERE TO STAY

$$$$
HOTEL
Fodor'sChoice
★

🏛 **Hacienda Uayamón.** Once a hacienda, this luxury hotel pays homage to the building's history by carefully preserving its original architecture and décor: the library has exposed-beam ceilings, cane chairs, sisal carpets, and wooden bookshelves at least 12 feet high. **Pros:** stunning grounds; beautiful, spacious rooms; elegant restaurant; bikes and bird-watching tours available. **Cons:** expensive; difficult to find; weak Wi-Fi signal. $ *Rooms from: $400* ⊠ *Carretera Campeche-ZA Edzná, 20 km (12½ miles) northwest of Edzná* ☎ *981/813–0530, 888/625–5144* ⊕ *www.thehaciendas.com* ⤴ *10 suites, 2 deluxe suites* 🍽 *No meals.*

SANTA ROSA XTAMPAK

107 km (64 miles) east of Campeche City.

Santa Rosa Xtampak. A fabulous example of the zoomorphic architectural element of Chenes architecture, Xtampak's **Casa de la Boca del Serpiente** (House of the Serpent's Mouth) has a perfectly preserved and integrated zoomorphic entrance. Here the mouth of the creator-god Itzámná stretches wide to reveal a perfectly proportioned inner chamber. The importance of this city during the classic period is shown by the large number of public buildings and ceremonial plazas here. Archaeologists believe there are around 100 structures, although only 12 have been cleared. The most exciting find was the colossal **Palacio** in the western plaza. Inside, two inner staircases run the length of the structure, leading to different levels and ending in subterranean chambers. Such a combination was extremely rare in Mayan temples. ⊠ *Off Carretera 261, Km 79, Xtampak, 30 km (18 miles) down signed side road* ⊠ *MX$35* ⊙ *Daily 8–5.*

HOCHOB

109 km (67 miles) southeast of Campeche City.

Hochob. This small Mayan site is an excellent example of the Chenes architectural style, which flourished from about AD 100 to 1000. Most ruins in this area were built on the highest possible elevation to prevent flooding during the rainy season, and Hochob is no exception. It rests high on a hill overlooking the surrounding valleys. Another indication that these are Chenes ruins is the number of *chultunes*, or cisterns, in the area.

Since work began at Hochob in the early 1980s, four temples and palaces have been excavated, including two that have been fully restored. Intricate and perfectly preserved geometric designs cover the temple known as **Estructura II**, which are typical of the Chenes style. The doorway represents the open mouth of Itzámná, the creator god, and above it the eyes bulge and fangs are bared on either side of the base.

It takes a bit of imagination to see the structure as a mask, as color no doubt originally enhanced the effect. Squinting helps a bit: the figure's "eyes" are said to be squinting as well. But anyone can appreciate the intense geometric relief carvings decorating the facades, including long cascades of Chaac masks along the sides. Evidence of roof combs can be seen at the top of the building. Ask the guard to show you the series of natural and man-made chultunes that extend into the forest.

If you're driving from Campeche, take Carretera 180 toward Holpechén and continue until you reach Carretera 261. Follow the road approximately 40 km (25 miles) toward Dzibalchen, then take the dirt road toward the town of Chencoh until you reach Hochob, 15 km (9 miles) ahead. ⊠ *Dzibalchén–Chencho Rd., 15 km (9 miles) west of Dzibilnocac* 🌐 *MX$42* 🕐 *Daily 8–5.*

CARRETERA 186 INTO CAMPECHE

Xpujil, Chicanná, Calakmul . . . exotic, far-flung-sounding names dot the map along this stretch of jungle territory. These are places where the creatures of the forest outnumber the tourists: in Calakmul, four- and five-story ceiba trees sway as families of spider monkeys swing through the canopy; in Xpujil, brilliant blue motmots fly from tree to tree in long, swoopy arcs.

The vestiges of at least 10 little-known Mayan cities lie hidden off Carretera 186 between Escárcega and Chetumal. You can see Xpujil, Becán, Hormiguero, and Chicanná in one rather rushed day by starting out early from Chetumal and spending the night in Xpujil. If you plan to visit Calakmul, spend the first night at Xpujil, arriving at Calakmul as soon as the site opens the next day. That provides the best chance to see armadillos, wild turkeys, families of howler and spider monkeys, and other wildlife.

TOURS

Río Bec Dreams. Rick Bertram and Diane Lalonde (owners of the Río Bec Dreams hotel) join forces with knowledgeable archaeologist Dan Griffin to lead comprehensive tours around ancient local sites. All three are native English speakers and enthusiastic guides. Expect to pay between MX$430 and MX$2,150, depending on the site. Be sure to book ahead, in person or by email. ⊠ *Carretera 186, Km 142, Xpujil* ✉ *info@riobecdreams.com* ⊕ *www.riobecdreams.com* 🌐 *From MX$430.*

Servidores Turísticos Calakmul. There aren't many good tour guides in the region. Some of the most reliable are part of a community organization called Servidores Turísticos Calakmul. They offer bicycle tours, horseback tours, and tours where spotting plants and animals is the main focus. All can be customized to meet your interests, including trips that span across several days with overnight stays in the jungle. ■ TIP➔ If your Spanish is shaky, ask for Leticia, who speaks basic English and has years of guiding experience. ⊠ *Av. Calakmul between Okolwitz and Payan, Xpujil* ☎ *983/871–6064* ⊕ *www.ecoturismocalakmul.com* 🌐 *From MX$715.*

XPUJIL

300 km (186 miles) southeast of Campeche City, 125 km (78 miles) west of Chetumal.

The highway briefly widens to four lanes around the town of Xpujil, which acts as the service center for Carretera 186. This is the place to stock up on food and sundries; more importantly, from the history lover's perspective, the town is the gateway to a string of Mayan ruins, including those that share its name.

GETTING HERE AND AROUND

From Chetumal, on the coast of Quintana Roo, it's about 125 km (78 miles) to Xpujil. Carretera 186 is in good condition, although it's not well lighted, so avoid driving at night. The ruins are just west of the town. **■TIP→ Most hotels in the Xpujil area close around 11 pm. So, regardless of whether you have a reservation, you may find yourself locked out of all but the seediest lodgings if you show up late.**

EXPLORING

Xpujil. Meaning "cat's tail," Xpujil (pronounced ish-poo-*hil)* takes its name from the reedy plant that grows in the area. Elaborately carved facades and doorways in the shape of monsters' mouths reflect the Chenes style, while adjacent pyramid towers connected by a long platform show the influence of Río Bec architects.

6

Some of the buildings have lost a lot of their stones, making them resemble "day after" sand castles. In **Edificio I,** three towers—believed to have been used by priests and royalty—were once crowned by false temples, and at the front of each are the remains of four vaulted rooms, each oriented toward one of the compass points. On the back side of the central tower is a huge mask of the rain god Chaac. Quite a few other building groups amid the forests of gum trees and *palo mulato* (so called for its bark with both dark and light patches) have yet to be excavated. ✉ *Off Carretera 186, Km 150, west of the town of Xpujil* 🎟 *MX$42* 🕒 *Daily 8–5.*

WHERE TO STAY

$$ HOTEL 🏨 **Chicanná Ecovillage Resort.** Surrounded by lush gardens and tropical plants, the ample rooms here are located in two-story stucco duplexes that are topped with thatch roofs; each has tile floors, an overhead fan, screened windows, a wide porch or balcony, and one king or two double beds. **Pros:** convenient to several ruins in the Río Bec region; spacious rooms; pleasant balconies; eco-friendly design. **Cons:** restaurant is just OK; Wi-Fi in reception area only; no a/c. [$] *Rooms from: $100* ✉ *Carretera 186, Km 144, 9 km (5½ miles) west of Xpujil* ☎ *981/811–9193* 🌐 *www.chicannaecovillageresort.com* 🛏 *46 rooms* 🍴 *Breakfast.*

$ B&B/INN 🏨 **Río Bec Dreams.** The moment you arrive at this hotel in the middle of the jungle, you'll be invited to pull up a chair at the bar, flip through literature about the area, and swap stories with the owners and other guests. **Pros:** laundry service; wonderful restaurant; owners are attentive and excellent guides. **Cons:** some rooms lack private bathrooms; no a/c; reservations by email only. [$] *Rooms from: $70* ✉ *Carretera 186, Km 142, Xpujil* 🌐 *www.riobecdreams.com* 🛏 *4 bungalows, 3 cabanas* 💳 *No credit cards* 🍴 *No meals.*

CHICANNÁ

264 km (164 miles) southeast of Campeche City, 10 km (6½ miles) west of Xpujil.

Thought to have been a satellite community of the larger, more commercial city of Becán, a couple of miles farther west, Chicanná ("house of the serpent's mouth") was also in its prime during the late classic period.

Chicanná. Of the four buildings surrounding the main plaza, Estructura II, on the east side, is the most impressive. On its intricate facade are well-preserved sculpted reliefs and faces with long twisted noses—symbols of Chaac. In typical Chenes style, the doorway represents the mouth of the creator-god Itzámná. Surrounding the opening are large crossed eyes, fierce fangs, and earrings to complete the stone mask, which still bears traces of blue and red pigments. ⊠ *Off Carretera 186, Km. 141, 10 km (6½ miles) west of Xpujil* 🖾 MX$42 ⊙ *Daily 8–5.*

BECÁN

266 km (165 miles) southeast of Campeche City, 8 km (5 miles) west of Xpujil.

Becán (usually translated as "canyon of water," referring to the moat) is thought to have been an important city within the Río Bec group, which encompassed Xpujil, Chicanná, and Río Bec.

Becán. An interesting feature here is the defensive moat—unusual among ancient Mayan cities—though barely evident today. Seven ruined gateways, once the only entrances to the guarded city, may have clued archaeologists to its presence. Most of the site's many buildings date from between about AD 600 and 1000, but since there are no traditionally inscribed stelae listing details of royal births, deaths, battles, and ascendancies to the throne, archaeologists have had to do a lot of guessing about what transpired here.

You can climb several of the structures to get a view of the area, and even spot some of Xpuhil's towers above the treetops. Duck into **Estructura VIII,** where underground passages lead to small subterranean rooms and to a concealed staircase that reaches the top of the temple. One of several buildings surrounding a central plaza, Estructura VIII has lateral towers and a giant zoomorphic mask on its central facade. It was used for religious rituals, including bloodletting rites during which the elite pierced earlobes and genitals, among other sensitive body parts, in order to present their blood to the gods. ⊠ *Off Carretera 186, Km 145, 8 km (5 miles) west of Xpujil* 🖾 MX$56 ⊙ *Daily 8–5.*

HORMIGUERO

272 km (169 miles) southeast of Campeche City, 30 km (18 miles) southwest of Xpujil.

Bumping down the badly potholed, 8-km (5-mile) road leading to this site may give you an appreciation for the explorers who first found and excavated it in 1933. Hidden throughout the forest are at least five magnificent temples, two of which have been excavated to reveal ornate facades covered with zoomorphic figures whose mouths are the doorways.

Hormiguero. The buildings here were constructed roughly between 400 BC and AD 1100 in the Río Bec style, with rounded lateral towers and ornamental stairways, the latter built to give an illusion of height, which they do wonderfully. The facade of **Estructura II,** the largest structure on the site, is intricately carved and well preserved. **Estructura V** has some admirable Chaac masks arranged in a cascade atop a pyramid. Nearby is a perfectly round *chultun* (cistern), and seemingly emerging from the earth, the eerily etched designs of a still-unexcavated structure.

Hormiguero is Spanish for "anthill," referring both to the looters' tunnels that honeycombed the ruins when archaeologists discovered them and to the number of enormous anthills in the area. Among the other fauna sharing the jungle here are several species of poisonous snake. △ Although the snakes mainly come out at night, you should always be careful of where you walk and, when climbing, where you put your hands. ⊠ *30 km (18 miles) southwest of Xpujil* ⧉ *Free* ⊙ *Daily 8–5.*

RESERVA DE LA BIÓSFERA CALAKMUL

365 km (227 miles) southeast of Campeche City, 107 km (66 miles) southwest of Xpujil.

Vast, lovely, green, and mysterious Calakmul may not stay a secret for much longer. You won't see any tour buses in the parking lot, and on an average day, site employees and laborers still outnumber the visitors traipsing along the moss-tinged dirt paths that snake through the jungle. But things are changing. The nearest town, Xpujil, already has Internet service and a handful of restaurants and hotels. So if you're looking for untrammeled Mexican wilderness, don't put off a trip here any longer.

GETTING HERE AND AROUND

If you don't have your own vehicle, private drivers in Xpujil charge about MX$1500 for round-trip transportation to the reserve. But the easiest option is to arrange a guided excursion with Río Bec Dreams or Servidores Turísticos Calakmul.

EXPLORING

Fodor'sChoice ★ **Reserva de la Biósfera Calakmul.** Encompassing some 1.8 million acres of land along the Guatemalan border, Calakmul was declared a protected biosphere reserve in 1989 and is the largest reserve of its kind in Mexico (Sian Ka'an in Quintana Roo is second with 1.3 million acres). All kinds of flora and fauna thrive here, including wildcats, spider and howler monkeys, hundreds of exotic birds, orchid varieties, butterflies, and reptiles. (There's no shortage of insects, either, so don't forget the bug repellent.)

The centerpiece of the reserve, however, is the ruined Mayan city that shares the name Calakmul (which translates as "two adjacent towers"). Although Carretera 186 runs right through the reserve, you'll need to drive about 1½ hours from the highway along a 60-km (37-mile) authorized entry road to get to the site. Structures here are still being excavated, but fortunately the dense surrounding jungle is being left in its natural state: as you walk among the ruined palaces and tumbled stelae, you'll hear the guttural calls of howler monkeys, and see massive strangler figs enveloping equally massive trees.

This magnificent city, now in ruins, wasn't always so lonely. Anthropologists estimate that in its heyday (between AD 542 and 695) the region was inhabited by more than 50,000 Maya. Archaeologists have mapped more than 6,800 structures and found 180 stelae. Perhaps the most monumental discovery thus far has been the remains of royal ruler Gran Garra de Jaguar (Great Jaguar Claw). His body was wrapped (but not embalmed) in a shroud of palm leaf, lime, and fine cloth, and locked away in a royal tomb in about AD 700. In an adjacent crypt, a young woman wearing fine jewelry and an elaborately painted wood-and-stucco headdress was entombed together with a child. Their identity remains a mystery. The artifacts and skeletal remains have been moved to the Museo de la Arqueología Maya in Campeche City.

Unlike those at Chichén Itzá (which also peaked in importance during the classic era) the pyramids and palaces throughout Calakmul can be climbed to achieve soaring vistas. You can choose to explore the site along a short, medium, or long path, but all three eventually lead to magnificent **Templo II** and **Templo VII**—twin pyramids separated by an immense plaza. Templo II, at 175 feet, is the peninsula's tallest Mayan building. Scientists are studying a huge, intact stucco frieze deep within this structure, so it's not currently open to visitors.

Arrangements for an English-speaking tour guide should be made beforehand with Servidores Turísticos Calakmul, Río Bec Dreams, or through Chicanná Ecovillage near Xpujil. Camping is permitted at Km 6 with the Servidores Turistícos Calakmul after paying caretakers at the entrance gate. You can set up camp near the second checkpoint. Even if day-tripping, though, you'll need to bring your own food and water, as the only place to buy a snack is near the second entrance inside the museum. ■TIP→ You effectively pay three entrance fees; MX$42 per person and MX$70 per vehicle to the owners of the first 20 km (12½ miles) which is private land, MX$70 per person to enter the reserve at the second gate located at the museum, and another MX$70 per person at the entrance to the ruins. ⊠ *Off Carretera 186, Km 65, 107 km (66 miles) southwest of Xpujil* ✛ *Drive 98 km (60 miles) east of Escárcega to turnoff at Cohuás, then 60 km (37 miles) south to Calakmul* ⌑ *$M70 per car (more for larger vehicles), plus MX$182 per person* ☉ *Daily 8–5; museum daily 7–3.*

WHERE TO STAY

$$ 🏨 **Hotel Puerta Calakmul.** Just outside the entrance to Reserva de la Biós-
HOTEL fera Calakmul, this ecological retreat has gravel pathways that wind through the jungle to 15 private cabanas, each rustic in design with palapas, tree stump nightstands, and parchment paper lampshades inlaid with leaves and bits of bark. **Pros:** closest lodgings to Biósfera Calakmul; peaceful setting; guided tours available. **Cons:** Wi-Fi in restaurant only; pricey for what you get; back cabanas experience some highway noise. Ⓢ *Rooms from: $160* ⊠ *Carretera 186, Km 98, Calakmul* ☎ *998/892–2624* ⊕ *www.puertacalakmul.mx* ⤳ *15 cabanas* ▭ *No credit cards* ⦿❘ *No meals.*

SPANISH VOCABULARY

	ENGLISH	SPANISH	PRONUNCIATION

BASICS

	ENGLISH	SPANISH	PRONUNCIATION
	Yes/no	Sí/no	see/no
	Please	Por favor	pore fah-**vore**
	May I?	¿Me permite?	may pair-**mee**-tay
	Thank you (very much)	(Muchas) gracias	(**moo**-chas) **grah**-see-as
	You're welcome	De nada	day **nah**-dah
	Excuse me	Con permiso	con pair-**mee**-so
	Pardon me	¿Perdón?	pair-**dohn**
	Could you tell me?	¿Podría decirme?	po-dree-ah deh-**seer**-meh
	I'm sorry	Lo siento	lo see-**en**-toh
	Good morning!	¡Buenos días!	**bway**-nohs **dee**-ahs
	Good afternoon!	¡Buenas tardes!	**bway**-nahs **tar**-dess
	Good evening!	¡Buenas noches!	**bway**-nahs **no**-chess
	Good-bye!	¡Adiós!/¡Hasta luego!	ah-dee-**ohss/ah** -stah **lwe**-go
	Mr./Mrs.	Señor/Señora	sen-**yor**/sen-**yohr**-ah
	Miss	Señorita	sen-yo-**ree**-tah
	Pleased to meet you	Mucho gusto	**moo**-cho **goose**-toh
	How are you?	¿Cómo está usted?	**ko**-mo es-**tah** oo-**sted**
	Very well, thank you.	Muy bien, gracias.	**moo**-ee bee-**en**, **grah**-see-as
	And you?	¿Y usted?	ee oos-**ted**
	Hello (on the telephone)	Diga	**dee**-gah

NUMBERS

	1	un, uno	oon, **oo**-no
	2	dos	dos
	3	tres	tress
	4	cuatro	**kwah**-tro
	5	cinco	**sink**-oh

ENGLISH	SPANISH	PRONUNCIATION
6	seis	saice
7	siete	see-**et**-eh
8	ocho	**o**-cho
9	nueve	new-**eh**-vey
10	diez	dee-**es**
11	once	**ohn**-seh
12	doce	**doh**-seh
13	trece	**treh**-seh
14	catorce	ka-**tohr**-seh
15	quince	**keen**-seh
16	dieciséis	dee-**es**-ee-**saice**
17	diecisiete	dee-**es**-ee-see-**et**-eh
18	dieciocho	dee-**es**-ee-**o**-cho
19	diecinueve	**dee**-**es**-ee-new-**ev**-eh
20	veinte	**vain**-teh
21	veinte y uno/veintiuno	**vain**-te-oo-**noh**
30	treinta	**train**-tah
32	treinta y dos	train-tay-**dohs**
40	cuarenta	kwah-**ren**-tah
43	cuarenta y tres	kwah-**ren**-tay-**tress**
50	cincuenta	seen-**kwen**-tah
54	cincuenta y cuatro	seen-**kwen**-tay **kwah**-tro
60	sesenta	sess-**en**-tah
65	sesenta y cinco	sess-**en**-tay **seen**-ko
70	setenta	set-**en**-tah
76	setenta y seis	set-**en**-tay **saice**
80	ochenta	oh-**chen**-tah
87	ochenta y siete	oh-**chen**-tay see-**yet**-eh
90	noventa	no-**ven**-tah
98	noventa y ocho	no-**ven**-tah-**o**-choh

ENGLISH	SPANISH	PRONUNCIATION
100	cien	see-**en**
101	ciento uno	see-**en**-toh **oo**-noh
200	doscientos	doh-see-**en**-tohss
500	quinientos	keen-**yen**-tohss
700	setecientos	set-eh-see-**en**-tohss
900	novecientos	no-veh-see-**en**-tohss
1,000	mil	meel
2,000	dos mil	dohs meel
1,000,000	un millón	oon meel-**yohn**

COLORS

black	negro	**neh**-groh
blue	azul	ah-**sool**
brown	café	kah-**feh**
green	verde	**ver**-deh
pink	rosa	**ro**-sah
purple	morado	mo-**rah**-doh
orange	naranja	na-**rahn**-hah
red	rojo	**roh**-hoh
white	blanco	**blahn**-koh
yellow	amarillo	ah-mah-**ree**-yoh

DAYS OF THE WEEK

Sunday	domingo	doe-**meen**-goh
Monday	lunes	**loo**-ness
Tuesday	martes	**mahr**-tess
Wednesday	miércoles	me-**air**-koh-less
Thursday	jueves	hoo-**ev**-ess
Friday	viernes	vee-**air**-ness
Saturday	sábado	**sah**-bah-doh

ENGLISH	SPANISH	PRONUNCIATION

MONTHS

ENGLISH	SPANISH	PRONUNCIATION
January	enero	eh-**neh**-roh
February	febrero	feh-**breh**-roh
March	marzo	**mahr**-soh
April	abril	ah-**breel**
May	mayo	**my**-oh
June	junio	**hoo**-nee-oh
July	julio	**hoo**-lee-yoh
August	agosto	ah-**ghost**-toh
September	septiembre	sep-tee-**em**-breh
October	octubre	oak-**too**-breh
November	noviembre	no-vee-**em**-breh
December	diciembre	dee-see-**em**-breh

USEFUL PHRASES

ENGLISH	SPANISH	PRONUNCIATION
Do you speak English?	¿Habla usted inglés?	**ah**-blah oos-**ted** in-**glehs**
I don't speak Spanish	No hablo español	no **ah**-bloh es-pahn-**yol**
I don't understand (you)	No entiendo	no en-tee-**en**-doh
I understand (you)	Entiendo	en-tee-**en**-doh
I don't know	No sé	no seh
I am American/ British	Soy americano (americana)/inglés(a)	soy ah-meh-ree-**kah**-no (ah-meh-ree-**kah**-nah)/in-**glehs(ah)**
What's your name?	¿Cómo se llama usted?	koh-mo seh **yah**-mah oos-**ted**
My name is . . .	Me llamo . . .	may **yah**-moh
What time is it?	¿Qué hora es?	keh **o**-rah es
It is one, two, three . . . o'clock.	Es la una/Son las dos, tres . . .	es la **oo**-nah/sohnahs dohs, tress
Yes, please/No, thank you	Sí, por favor/No, gracias	**see** pohr fah-**vor**/no **grah**-see-us
How?	¿Cómo?	**koh**-mo

ENGLISH	SPANISH	PRONUNCIATION
When?	¿Cuándo?	**kwahn**-doh
This/Next week	Esta semana/ la semana que entra	es-teh seh-**mah**-nah/ lah seh-**mah**-nah keh **en**-trah
This/Next month	Este mes/el próximo mes	es-teh mehs/el **proke**-see-mo mehs
This/Next year	Este año/el año que viene	es-teh **ahn**-yo/el **ahn**-yo keh vee-**yen**-ay
Yesterday/today/ tomorrow	Ayer/hoy/mañana	ah-**yehr**/oy/ mahn-**yah**-nah
This morning/ afternoon	Esta mañana/ tarde	es-tah mahn-**yah**-nah/ **tar**-deh
Tonight	Esta noche	es-tah **no**-cheh
What?	¿Qué?	keh
What is it?	¿Qué es esto?	keh es **es**-toh
Why?	¿Por qué?	pore **keh**
Who?	¿Quién?	kee-**yen**
Where is . . . ?	¿Dónde está . . . ?	**dohn**-deh es-**tah**
the train station?	la estación del tren?	la es-tah-see-on del trehn
the subway station?	la estación del tren subterráneo?	la es-ta-see-**on** del trehn la es-ta-see-**on** soob-teh-**rrahn**-eh-oh
the bus stop?	la parada del autobus?	la pah-**rah**-dah del ow-toh-**boos**
the post office?	la oficina de correos?	la oh-fee-**see**-nah deh koh-**rreh**-os
the bank?	el banco?	el **bahn**-koh
the hotel?	el hotel?	el oh-**tel**
the store?	la tienda?	la tee-**en**-dah
the cashier?	la caja?	la **kah**-hah
the museum?	el museo?	el moo-**seh**-oh
the hospital?	el hospital?	el ohss-pee-**tal**
the elevator?	el ascensor?	el ah-**sen**-sohr
the bathroom?	el baño?	el **bahn**-yoh

ENGLISH	SPANISH	PRONUNCIATION
Here/there	Aquí/allá	ah-**key**/ah-**yah**
Open/closed	Abierto/cerrado	ah-bee-**er**-toh/ ser-**ah**-doh
Left/right	Izquierda/derecha	iss-key-**er**-dah/ dare-**eh**-chah
Straight ahead	Derecho	dare-**eh**-choh
Is it near/far?	¿Está cerca/lejos?	es-**tah sehr**-kah/ **leh**-hoss
I'd like . . .	Quisiera . . .	kee-see-ehr-ah
a room	un cuarto/una habitación	oon **kwahr**-toh/ **oo**-nah ah-bee- tah-see-**on**
the key	la llave	lah **yah**-veh
a newspaper	un periódico	oon pehr-ee-**oh**-dee-koh
a stamp	un sello de correo	oon **seh**-yo deh korr-ee-oh
I'd like to buy . . .	Quisiera comprar . . .	kee-see-**ehr**-ah kohm-**prahr**
cigarettes	cigarrillos	ce-ga-**ree**-yohs
matches	cerillos	ser-**ee**-ohs
a dictionary	un diccionario	oon deek-see-oh-**nah**-ree-oh
soap	jabón	hah-**bohn**
sunglasses	gafas de sol	**ga**-fahs deh sohl
suntan lotion	Loción bronceadora	loh-see-**ohn** brohn-seh-ah-**do**-rah
a map	un mapa	oon **mah**-pah
a magazine	una revista	**oon**-ah reh-**veess**-tah
paper	papel	pah-**pel**
envelopes	sobres	**so**-brehs
a postcard	una tarjeta postal	**oon**-ah tar-**het**-ah post-**ahl**
How much is it?	¿Cuánto cuesta?	**kwahn**-toh **kwes**-tah
It's expensive/ cheap	Está caro/barato	es-**tah kah**-roh/ bah-**rah**-toh

ENGLISH	SPANISH	PRONUNCIATION
A little/a lot	Un poquito/ mucho	oon poh-**kee**-toh/ **moo**-choh
More/less	Más/menos	mahss/**men**-ohss
Enough/too much/too little	Suficiente/ demasiado/ muy poco	soo-fee-see-**en**-teh/ deh-mah-see-**ah**-doh/ **moo**-ee poh-koh
Telephone	Teléfono	tel-**ef**-oh-no
Telegram	Telegrama	teh-leh-**grah**-mah
I am ill	Estoy enfermo(a)	es-**toy** en-**fehr**-moh(mah)
Please call a doctor	Por favor llame a un medico	pohr fah-**vor ya**-meh ah oon **med**-ee-koh

ON THE ROAD

Avenue	Avenida	ah-ven-**ee**-dah
Broad, tree-lined boulevard	Bulevar	boo-leh-**var**
Fertile plain	Vega	**veh**-gah
Highway	Carretera	car-reh-**ter**-ah
Mountain pass	Puerto	poo-**ehr**-toh
Street	Calle	**cah**-yeh
Waterfront promenade	Rambla	**rahm**-blah
Wharf	Embarcadero	em-bar-cah-**deh**-ro

IN TOWN

Cathedral	Catedral	cah-teh-**dral**
Church	Templo/Iglesia	**tem**-plo/ee-**glehs**-see-ah
City hall	Casa de gobierno	kah-sah deh go-bee-**ehr**-no
Door, gate	Puerta portón	poo-**ehr**-tah por-**ton**
Entrance/exit	Entrada/salida	en-**trah**-dah/ sah-**lee**-dah
Inn, rustic bar, or restaurant	Taverna	tah-**vehr**-nah
Main square	Plaza principal	plah-thah prin-see-**pahl**

ENGLISH	SPANISH	PRONUNCIATION

DINING OUT

Can you recommend a good restaurant?	¿Puede recomendarme un buen restaurante?	**pweh**-deh rreh-koh-mehn-**dahr**-me oon bwehn rrehs-tow-**rahn**-teh?
Where is it located?	¿Dónde está situado?	**dohn**-deh ehs-**tah** see-**twah**-doh?
Do I need reservations?	¿Se necesita una reservación?	seh neh-seh-**see**-tah **oo**-nah rreh-sehr- bah-**syohn**?
I'd like to reserve a table . . .	Quisiera reservar una mesa . . .	kee-**syeh**-rah rreh-sehr-**bahr oo**-nah **meh**-sah . . .
for two people.	para dos personas.	**pah**-rah dohs pehr-**soh**-nahs
for this evening.	para esta noche.	**pah**-rah **ehs**-tah **noh**-cheh
for 8 PM	para las ocho de la noche.	**pah**-rah lahs **oh**-choh deh lah **noh**-cheh
A bottle of . . .	Una botella de . . .	**oo**-nah bo-**teh**-yah deh
A cup of . . .	Una taza de . . .	**oo**-nah **tah**-thah deh
A glass of . . .	Un vaso de . . .	oon **vah**-so deh
Ashtray	Un cenicero	oon sen-ee-**seh**-roh
Bill/check	La cuenta	lah **kwen**-tah
Bread	El pan	el pahn
Breakfast	El desayuno	el deh-sah-**yoon**-oh
Butter	La mantequilla	lah man-teh-**key**-yah
Cheers!	¡Salud!	sah-**lood**
Cocktail	Un aperitivo	oon ah-pehr-ee-**tee**-voh
Dinner	La cena	lah **seh**-nah
Dish	Un plato	oon **plah**-toh
Menu of the day	Menú del día	meh-**noo** del **dee**-ah
Enjoy!	¡Buen provecho!	bwehn pro-**veh**-cho
Fixed-price menu	Menú fijo o turistico	meh-**noo fee**-hoh oh too-**ree**-stee-coh

ENGLISH	SPANISH	PRONUNCIATION
Fork	El tenedor	el ten-eh-**dor**
Is the tip included?	¿Está incluida la propina?	es-**tah** in-cloo-**ee**-dah lah pro-**pee**-nah
Knife	El cuchillo	el koo-**chee**-yo
Large portion of savory snacks	Raciónes	rah-see-**oh**-nehs
Lunch	La comida	lah koh-**mee**-dah
Menu	La carta, el menú	lah **cart**-ah, el meh-**noo**
Napkin	La servilleta	lah sehr-vee-**yet**-ah
Pepper	La pimienta	lah pee-me-**en**-tah
Please give me	Por favor déme	pore fah-**vor deh**-meh
Salt	La sal	lah sahl
Savory snacks	Tapas	**tah**-pahs
Spoon	Una cuchara	**oo**-nah koo-**chah**-rah
Sugar	El azúcar	el ah-**thu**-kar
Waiter!/Waitress!	¡Por favor Señor/ Señorita!	pohr fah-**vor** sen-**yor**/ sen-yor-**ee**-tah

TRAVEL SMART
CANCÚN AND THE
RIVIERA MAYA

GETTING HERE AND AROUND

▌AIR TRAVEL

Cancún is 4½ hours from New York and Chicago, 4 hours from Los Angeles, 3 hours from Dallas, and 2½ hours from Miami. Flights to Cozumel and Mérida are comparable in length. There are direct flights to Cancún from hub airports such as New York, Boston, Washington, D.C., Houston, Dallas, Miami, Chicago, Los Angeles, Orlando, Ft. Lauderdale, Charlotte, and Atlanta. You can reach it from other locales on connecting flights; some arrive via Mexico City, where you must pass through customs before transferring to a domestic flight to Cancún.

Charter flights, especially those leaving from Cancún, are notorious for last-minute changes. Be sure to ask for an updated telephone number from your charter company before you leave, so you can verify departures times. Most recommend that you call within 48 hours of departure. This check-in also applies to commercial airlines, although their departure times are more dependable, and changes are usually due to weather conditions rather than to seat sales.

Airline-Security Issues Transportation Security Administration. The Transportation Security Administration has answers for almost every question that might arise. ☎ 866/289–9673 in the U.S. and Canada ⊕ www.tsa.gov.

AIRPORTS

Cancún Aeropuerto Internacional (CUN) is the area's major gateway, though some people now choose to fly directly to Cozumel (CZM). The inland Aeropuerto Internacional Manuel Crescencio Rejón (MID), in Mérida, is smaller but closer to the major Mayan ruins. Campeche (CPE) and Chetumal (CTM) have even smaller airports served primarily by domestic carriers. Some locales have airstrips for small planes; there's also an airport at Chichén (CZA), handling chartered flights, but

most people fly into Cancún and travel onward by bus or car.

In peak season, passenger waiting lines can be long and slow-moving; plan accordingly.

It's 20 to 30 minutes from the Zona Hotelera to the Cancún airport or from downtown Mérida or Campeche to theirs. Allow 1½ hours from Playa del Carmen to the Cancún airport. The Cozumel airport is less than 10 minutes from downtown Cozumel.

Contacts Aeropuerto Internacional Alberto Acuña Ongay (Campeche Aeropuerto Internacional). ⊠ Av. Lopez Portillo s/n, Campeche ☎ 981/823–4059 ⊕ www.asa.gob.mx. **Aeropuerto Internacional Manuel Crescencio Rejón** (Mérida Aeropuerto Internacional). ⊠ Av. Itzáes, Km 14.5, Mérida ☎ 999/940–6090 ⊕ www.asur.com.mx. **Cancún Aeropuerto Internacional** ⊠ Carretera Cancun-Chetumal, Km 22, Cancún ☎ 998/848–7200 ⊕ www.cancun-airport.com. **Chetumal Aeropuerto Internacional** ⊠ Prolong Av. Efrain Aguila, Chetumal. **Cozumel Aeropuerto Internacional** ⊠ Av. 65 and Blvd. Aeropuerto, Cozumel ☎ 987/872–2081 ⊕ www.asur.com.mx.

GROUND TRANSPORTATION

As you exit the Cancún airport, transportation operators can be overwhelming as they eagerly wave signs and yell names to arriving passengers. If you're taking the bus, walk past the bar and toward the right where tickets are available from a small booth. There is a bus leaving every hour from the airport to downtown Cancún.

It's not uncommon to be told that you just missed the last bus, taxi, or van to your destination. This is actually a ploy to get you to use the transportation company that is "assisting" you. Ask around if you're not entirely sure. Always arrive with small bills for taxi or bus fare, otherwise you're liable to get ripped off. Check the identification of transportation operators and don't allow anyone to "help" you with your luggage. Many people perform this task on commission for specific transportation companies. Worse yet, they might end up disappearing into the crowd with your baggage.

Some of the major hotels send shuttles to pick up arriving guests; it's worth checking before you arrive at the airport. Private taxis from the airport charge reasonable rates within Cancún. Airport shuttle vans, which charge set rates based on your destination, are another option; however, they sometimes take forever before filling up and getting under way. There are taxi and shuttle desks in the baggage-claim area, just before you exit the terminal. Go to the ones with posted prices, but keep in mind that rates are much higher for last-minute bookings as opposed to pre-arranged ground transportation reserved online. For round-trip transportation from the airport to the Riviera Maya, it's worth looking for a shuttle service, as a private taxi can be prohibitively expensive. Some can be arranged beforehand by phone or online. Cancún Valet rents per van, rather than per person, for up to 10 passengers, making it a good value for couples, families, and groups. Prices from the airport to the Hotel Zone, Playa del Carmen, and Tulum, as well as intermittent points are reasonable: MX$540 to Cancún (MX$946 round-trip) or MX$1013 to Playa del Carmen (MX$1825 round-trip), for example. Cancún Airport Transportation charges MX$473 per couple or individual, one-way, to the Hotel Zone (MX$743 round-trip) or MX$811 to Playa del Carmen (MX$1487 round-trip).

Contacts Cancún Airport Transportation ☎ 998/210–3317 ⊕ www.cancuntransfers. com. **Cancún Valet** ☎ 888/479–9095 in the U.S. and Canada, 998/848–3634 ⊕ www. cancunvalet.com.

FLIGHTS

International, national, and regional carriers serve the Yucatán Peninsula. The most convenient flight from the United States is nonstop on either a domestic or Mexican airline. Flying within the Yucatán is neither cost-effective nor time-efficient. Given the additional time needed for check-in, you might as well drive or take a bus to your destination, unless you're continuing on by plane.

Since all the major airlines listed here fly to Cancún—and often have the cheapest and most frequent flights there—it's worthwhile to consider it as a jumping-off point even if you don't plan on visiting the city. At this writing, more than 450 flights land daily in Cancún. Airlines that serve it include Aeroméxico, Air Canada, American, Delta, Frontier, Interjet, JetBlue, Southwest, Spirit, United, US Airways, Virgin, and Volaris. American, Delta, Frontier, Interjet, and United also fly to Cozumel. Aeroméxico, Interjet, United, and Volaris fly to Mérida. Mayair offers domestic flights from Cancún to Cozumel and Mérida. ■TIP→ **When you arrive at the airport, hang onto your FMM (Forma Migratoria Multiple para Extranjeros, or "tourist permit") because you'll need it again on departure.**

Airline Contacts Aeroméxico ☎ 800/237– 6639 in the U.S. and Canada, 01800/021–4000 toll-free in Mexico, 55/513–4000 ⊕ www. aeromexico.com. **Air Canada** ☎ 888/247– 2262 in the U.S. and Canada, 01800/719– 2827 toll-free in Mexico, 514/393–3333 ⊕ www.aircanada.com. **American Airlines** ☎ 800/433–7300 in the U.S. and Canada, 01800/904-6000 toll-free in Mexico ⊕ www. aa.com. **Delta Airlines** ☎ 800/221–1212 for U.S. reservations, 800/241–4141 for international reservations ⊕ www.delta. com. **Frontier** ☎ 800/432–1359 in the U.S. and Canada, 01800/432–1359 toll-free in Mexico ⊕ www.frontierairlines.com. **Interjet** ☎ 866/285–9525 in the U.S., 01800/011–2345 toll-free in Mexico ⊕ www.interjet.com.mx. **JetBlue** ☎ 800/538–2583 in the U.S. and Canada, 001800/861–3372 toll-free in Mexico

⊕ *www.jetblue.com*. **Mayair** ☏ *998/881–9413 in Cancun, 987/872–3609 in Cozumel* ⊕ *www.mayair.com.mx*. **Southwest Airlines** ☏ *800/435–9792 in the U.S. and Canada, 214/932–0333* ⊕ *www.southwest.com*. **Spirit Airlines** ☏ *800/772–7117 in the U.S. and Canada, 855/822–0464* ⊕ *www.spirit.com*. **United Airlines** ☏ *800/864–8331 in the U.S. and Canada, 01800/900–5000 toll-free in Mexico* ⊕ *www.united.com*. **US Airways** ☏ *800/428–4322 in the U.S. and Canada, 01800/428–4322 toll-free in Mexico* ⊕ *www.usairways.com*. **Virgin America** ☏ *877/359–8474 in the U.S. and Canada, 01877/359–8474 toll-free in Mexico* ⊕ *www.virginamerica.com*. **Volaris** ☏ *866/988–3527 in the U.S. and Canada, 01800/122–8000 toll-free in Mexico* ⊕ *www.volaris.com*.

▮ BOAT AND FERRY TRAVEL

The Yucatán is served by a number of ferries and boats. Most popular are the efficient speedboats that run between Playa del Carmen and Cozumel or from Puerto Juárez, Punta Sam, and Isla Mujeres. Vessels also run from Chiquila to Isla Holbox. Most carriers follow set schedules, with the exception of those going to the smaller, less visited islands. But departure times can vary with the weather and with the number of passengers. Visitcancun.com, travelyucatan.com, and granpuerto.com.mx have information on water taxis and ferries, though you should always confirm the details before heading down to the docks.

▮ BUS TRAVEL

The extensive Mexican bus network is a great means of getting around. Service is frequent, and tickets can be purchased on the spot (except during holidays and on long weekends, when advance purchase is crucial). Bring something to eat on long trips in case you don't like the restaurant or market where the bus stops. Bring toilet tissue and wear a sweater, as the air-conditioning is often set on high. Most buses play videos or television until midnight, so bring earplugs if you're bothered by noise. Smoking is prohibited on Mexican buses.

Bus companies here offer several classes of service: first-class (*primera clase*), deluxe or executive class (*de lujo* or *ejecutivo*), and second class (*segunda*). First-class and executive-class buses are generally punctual and have comfortable air-conditioned coaches with bathrooms, movies, reclining seats with seat belts, and refreshments. They take the fastest route (usually on safer, well-paved toll roads) and make few stops between points. Less desirable, second-class vehicles connect smaller, secondary routes; they also run along some long-distance routes, often taking slower, local roads. They're tolerable, but are usually cramped and make many stops. The class of travel will be listed on your printed ticket—if you see "*económico*" printed next to "*servicio*," you've been booked on a second-class bus. At many bus stations, one counter will represent several lines and classes of service, and mistakes do happen. ADO is the Yucatán's principal first-class bus company, and Mayab (operated by ADO) is the second-class line. Most bus tickets, including first-class (or executive) and second-class, can be reserved ahead of time in person at ticket offices. ADO also allows you to reserve tickets online 48 hours in advance.

If you're staying in the Riviera Maya, *colectivos* (minibuses) run along Carretera 307 from Cancún to Tulum. Although affordable, traveling by bus means you'll have to either walk or organize additional transportation from the bus stop.

Bus travel in the Yucatán, as throughout Mexico, is inexpensive by U.S. standards, with rates averaging MX$80 per hour depending on the level of luxury (or lack of it). Schedules are posted at bus stations; the bus leaves more or less around the listed time. Often, if all the seats have been sold, the bus will leave early.

Typical times and fares on first-class buses are: Cancún to Mérida, 4 hours,

MX$400; Cancún to Campeche, 7 hours, MX$600; Mérida to Campeche, 2½ hours, MX$200; and Cancún to Mexico City, 25 hours, MX$1,818.

Bus Contacts ADO ☎ 01800/900–0105 toll-free in Mexico, 55/5133–2424 ⊕ www.ado. com.mx.

▌CAR TRAVEL

Renting a car is generally expensive in and around Cancún; if you're not traveling far afield, don't bother to rent, as you'll be able to arrange taxi service to nearby sights through your hotel.

However, taxis for longer trips—to Playa del Carmen, for instance—can be pricey, so renting a car for a day or two of exploring may be more economical. As a rule, local agencies might have better rates than major companies, but if you're looking for a reliable car, it's best to stick with a brand you recognize. You can get the same kind of midsize and luxury cars in Mexico that you can rent in the United States. Economy usually refers to a small car barely fitting four passengers, which may or may not come with air-conditioning. Pancake-flat Yucatán makes for fairly easy driving, although side roads may have inadequate (or no) signposting; four-wheel-drive vehicles aren't necessary unless you plan on traveling to sites far off the beaten path in rainy season. If you'll require a child's car seat, request one when booking.

You won't need a car on Isla Mujeres or Isla Holbox, which are too small to make driving practical, nor in Playa del Carmen, because the downtown area is quite compact and the main street is blocked off to vehicles. Cars can actually feel like a burden in Mérida and Campeche City, because of the narrow cobbled streets and the lack of parking spaces. You'll need a car in Cozumel only if you wish to explore the eastern side of the island.

Car-rental agencies in Mexico require you to purchase a CDW or Collision Damage Waiver (starting at $30 per day), and Mexico Liability Auto Insurance (starting at $13 per day). Regardless of any coverage afforded by your credit-card company, you must purchase liability insurance. If you are caught without coverage, fines start at $200. Keep in mind that although you might have reserved a rental car for only $8 per day, full coverage insurance will cost you about $45 per day. Additional theft protection and personal injury policies are optional. Since most U.S. insurance policies are not recognized in Mexico (including those purchased online at time of booking), it is best to buy insurance directly at the counter with the rental car provider.

Be sure that you've been provided with proof of such insurance; if you drive without it, you're not only liable for damages, but you're also breaking the law. If you're in a car accident and you don't have insurance, you may be placed in jail until you're proven innocent. If anyone is injured you'll remain in jail until you make retribution to all injured parties and their families—which will likely cost you thousands of dollars. Mexican laws seem to favor nationals.

Even if you're absolutely certain you're fully covered by your credit-card company, we recommend you purchase full coverage insurance in Mexico. Getting into a car accident in Mexico would be harrowing enough without having to navigate the bureaucracy of your credit-card company to clear things up with Mexican authorities. Make sure that your insurance covers the cost for an attorney and claims adjusters who will come to the scene of an accident. Buying insurance makes renting a car in Mexico one of the most expensive parts of the trip, but in this case it's better to be safe than frugal.

Before setting out on any car trip, check your vehicle's fuel, oil, fluids, tires, windshield wipers, and lights. It's even a good idea to check the stereo if you are planning a long road trip. Don't forget to pack an adapter for your phone or iPod if you want to listen to your own music. Gas stations and mechanics can be hard to find, especially in more remote areas. Consult a map and have your route in mind as you drive.

Be aware that Mexican drivers often think nothing of tailgating, speeding, and weaving in and out of traffic. Drive defensively and keep your cool. When stopping for traffic or at a red light, always leave sufficient room between your car and the one ahead so you can maneuver to safety if necessary. On the highway, a left-turn signal in Mexico means the driver is signaling those behind that it's safe to pass. Blinking hazard lights means that traffic is stopped up ahead and to slow down. Always aim to be at your destination by sunset because roads may be pitted with potholes and void of streetlights and signs. In Mexico the minimum driving age is 18, but most rental-car agencies have a minimum age requirement between 21 and 25; some have a surcharge for drivers under 25. Your own driver's license is acceptable; there's no reason to get an international driver's license.

Regional Car Rental Contacts Adocar Rental ☎ 998/849–4233 ⊕ www.adocarrental. com. **Rentadora ISIS** ☎ 984/879–3111 in Playa Del Carmen, 987/872–3367 in Cozumel ⊕ www.rentadoraisis.com.mx. **U-Save Car Rental** ☎ 1998/246–0756 (mobile), 998/886–0393 (office) ⊕ www.usave.com. **Ventura** ☎ 800/717–0443 in the U.S., 01800/821–8854 toll-free in Mexico ⊕ www.venturacarrental. com.

Major Car Rental Contacts Alamo ☎ 855/533–1196 ⊕ www.alamo.com. **Avis** ☎ 800/331–1212 in the U.S. and Canada, 01800/288–8888 toll-free in Mexico ⊕ www. avis.com. **Budget** ☎ 800/527–0700 in the U.S. and Canada, 800/472–3325 outside the U.S. and Canada ⊕ www.budget.com. **Hertz** ☎ 800/654–3001 in the U.S. and Canada ⊕ www.hertz.com. **National Car Rental** ☎ 800/227–7368 in the U.S. and Canada ⊕ www.nationalcar.com.

GASOLINE

Pemex, Mexico's government-owned petroleum monopoly, franchises all gas stations, so prices throughout the Yucatán—and the country—are the same. Overall, prices run slightly higher (around 15% more) than in the United States. Gas is always sold in liters. Premium unleaded (called *premium*), the red pump, and regular unleaded (*magna*), the green pump, are available nationwide. Fuel quality is generally lower than that in the United States and Europe, but it has improved enough so that your car will run acceptably.

Some stations accept credit cards and a few have ATMs, but don't count on it—make sure you have pesos handy. When paying by credit card, don't be surprised if the gas attendant makes a photocopy of your passport since this is a normal practice. It is best to pay in cash since attendants often run your credit card twice, claiming it didn't work the first time, thus leaving you with two charges on your statement. Ask for a *recibo* (receipt) just in case you need to present it to your credit card company for evidence.

There are no self-service stations in Mexico. Ask the attendant to fill your tank ("*lleno* (YAY-noh), *por favor*") or ask for a specific amount in pesos to avoid being overcharged. Check to make sure that the attendant has set the meter back to zero and that the price is shown. Watch the attendant check the oil as well—to make sure you actually need it—and watch while he pours it into your car. Never pay before the gas is pumped, even if the attendant asks you to. Always tip your attendant a few pesos. Finally, keep your gas tank full, because gas stations are not plentiful in this area. If you run out of gas in a small village and there's no gas station for miles, ask if there's a store that sells gas from containers.

PARKING

A circle with a diagonal line superimposed on the letter *E* (for *estacionamiento*) means "no parking." A red curb means parking is restricted at all times, and a white curb is designated for loading and unloading only. A blue curb is for handicap parking, a green curb allows parking during specific hours, and a yellow curb means that the parking space is private. ■**TIP**➡ **If you're ticketed, your license plate will be taken to a nearby police station and will only be returned upon payment of the infraction. Never park overnight on the street, and never leave anything of value in an unattended car.** When in doubt, choose a parking lot; it will probably be safer anyway. Lots are plentiful, though not always clearly marked, and fees are reasonable—as little as MX$60 for a half day. Sometimes you park your own car; more often, though, you hand the keys over to an attendant. Tip him and ask that he look after your vehicle.

ROAD CONDITIONS

The road system in the Yucatán Peninsula is extensive and generally in good repair. Carretera 307 parallels most of the Caribbean Coast from Punta Sam, north of Cancún, to Tulum; here it turns inward for a stretch before returning to the coast at Chetumal and the Belize border. Carretera 180 runs west from Cancún to Valladolid, Chichén Itzá, and Mérida, then turns southwest to Campeche, Ciudad del Carmen, and on to Villahermosa. From Mérida, the winding, more scenic Carretera 261 also leads to some of the more off-the-beaten-track archaeological sites on the way south to Campeche and Escárcega, where it joins Carretera 186 going east to Chetumal. These highways are two-lane roads. Carretera 295 (from the north coast to Valladolid and Felipe Carrillo Puerto) is also a good two-lane road.

The *autopista,* or *carretera de cuota,* is a four-lane toll highway between Cancún and Mérida. Designated as the 180D, it runs roughly parallel to Carretera 180 and cuts driving time between the two cities to about 4½ hours. Tolls between Mérida and Cancún total about MX$415 (you must pay in pesos), and the stretches between highway exits are long, sometimes as much as 75 miles. Be careful when driving on this road, as it retains the heat from the sun and can make your tires blow if they have low pressure or worn threads.

Many secondary roads are in bad condition—unpaved, unmarked, and full of potholes. If you must take one of these roads, the best course is to allow plenty of daylight hours and never travel at night. Slow down when approaching towns and villages—which you're forced to do by the *topes* (speed bumps)—and because of the added presence of people and animals. Locals selling oranges, candy, or other food will almost certainly approach your car.

MEXICAN DRIVERS

Mexicans are generally skilled drivers, but they do drive quite fast, even on twisting or extraordinarily dark roads. That said, Mexicans motorists are in some ways more courteous than U.S. ones—it's customary, for example, for drivers to put on their hazard lights to warn the cars behind them of poor road conditions, slow-downs, or upcoming speed bumps; oncoming cars may flash their lights at you for the same reasons.

ROADSIDE EMERGENCIES

The Mexican Tourism Ministry operates a fleet of some 1,800 pickup trucks, known as Angeles Verdes, or the Green Angels, an organization in existence since the early 1960s that assists motorists on major highways. Dial 078 from any cell phone or Telmex phone booth and your call will be routed to the Green Angels' dispatch office. The bilingual drivers provide mechanical help, first aid, radio-telephone communication, basic supplies and small parts, towing, and tourist information. Services are free, and spare parts, fuel, and lubricants are provided at cost. Tips are always appreciated, and are sometimes openly solicited.

The Green Angels patrol fixed sections of the major highways twice daily 8 am to dusk, later on holiday weekends. If your car breaks down, pull as far as possible off the road, lift the hood, hail a passing vehicle, and ask the driver to notify the patrol. Most bus and truck drivers will be quite helpful. Don't accept rides from strangers. If you witness an accident, don't stop to help since witnesses are often detained for questioning for long periods of time. Instead find the nearest official.

Emergency Service Contacts Angeles Verdes ☎ *078 nationwide for Angeles Verdes and tourist emergency line, 91/5250-0123 for Ministry of Tourism hotline.*

RULES OF THE ROAD

There are two absolutely essential points to remember about driving in Mexico. First and foremost is to carry Mexican auto insurance. If you injure anyone in an accident, you could well be jailed—whether it was your fault or not—unless you have insurance. Second, if you enter Mexico with a car, you must leave with it. In recent years the high rate of U.S. vehicles being sold illegally in Mexico has caused the Mexican government to enact stringent regulations for bringing a car into the country. You must be in your foreign vehicle at all times when it's driven. You cannot lend it to another person. Do not, under any circumstances, let a national drive your car. It's illegal for Mexicans to drive foreign-owned cars; if a national is caught driving your car, the car will be impounded by customs and you will receive a stiff fine. Newer models of vans, SUVs, and pickup trucks can be impossible to get back once impounded.

You must cross the border with the following documents: title or registration for your vehicle, a valid passport, proof of insurance, a credit card (MasterCard or Visa only), and a valid driver's license with a photo. You'll also need a temporary car-importation permit and an FMM (tourist permit). The title-holder, driver, and credit-card owner must be one and the same—that is, if your spouse's name is on the title of the car and yours isn't,

you cannot be the one to bring the car into the country. For financed, leased, rental, or company cars, you must bring a notarized letter of permission from the bank, lien holder, rental agency, or company. When you submit your paperwork at the border and pay the approximate US$50 charge on your credit card, you'll receive a car permit and a sticker to put on your vehicle. The permit is valid for the same amount of time as your tourist visa, which is up to 180 days. You may go back and forth across the border during this six-month period, as long as you check with immigration and bring all your permit paperwork with you. If you're planning to stay and keep your car in Mexico for longer than six months, however, you'll have to get a new permit before the original one expires. In addition to the permit fee, your credit card will be charged a deposit based on the age of your car. This fee is to guarantee return of the vehicle to U.S. territory. If your car is older than 2000, you'll pay $200; cars between 2001 and 2006 will be charged $300; and anything newer than 2007 will cost $400. This amount is refunded in full 24 hours after you cancel your permit, unless you have passed the expiration date or left your car in Mexico. Upon your departure from Mexico, the permit for temporary importation must be cancelled at Customs or you will not receive your refunded deposit.

One way to minimize hassle when you cross the border with a car is to have your paperwork done in advance at a branch of Sanborn's Mexico Auto Insurance; you'll find an office in almost every town on the U.S.–Mexico border. Average daily insurance rates start around $45. The fact that you drove in with a car is stamped on your tourist card, which you must give to immigration authorities at departure. If an emergency arises and you must fly home, there are complicated customs procedures to face.

When you sign up for Mexican car insurance, you should receive a booklet on Mexican rules of the road. It really is a good idea to read it to avoid breaking laws that differ from those of your country. If an oncoming vehicle flicks its lights at you in the daytime, slow down: it could mean trouble ahead. When approaching a narrow bridge, the first vehicle to flash its lights has right of way. One-way streets are common. One-way traffic is indicated by an arrow; two-way, by a double-pointed arrow. Other road signs follow the widespread system of international symbols.

Mileage and speed limits are given in kilometers: 100 kph and 80 kph (62 mph and 50 mph, respectively) are the most common maximums. A few of the toll roads allow 110 kph (68 mph). In cities and small towns, observe the posted speed limits, which can be as low as 20 kph (12 mph). Seat belts are required by law throughout Mexico.

Drunk-driving laws are fairly harsh in Mexico, and if you're caught you'll go to jail immediately. It's hard to know what the country's blood-alcohol limit really is. Everyone seems to have a different idea about it; this means it's probably being handled in a discretionary way, which is nerve-racking, to say the least. The best way to avoid any problems is simply not to drink and drive. Right turns on red are not allowed, and texting while driving is not permitted. Foreigners must pay speeding penalties on the spot, which can be steep. Some minor traffic violations can be dismissed until you return your rental car by simply showing your "Tourist Traffic Card" available from several car-rental agencies.

If you encounter a police checkpoint, stay calm. These are simply routine checks for weapons and drugs; customarily they'll check out the car's registration, look in the back seat, the trunk, and at the undercarriage with a mirror. Basic Spanish does help during these stops, though a smile and polite demeanor will go a long way.

Contact Sanborn's Mexico Auto Insurance ☎ *800/222–0158 in the U.S. and Canada* ⊕ *www.sanbornsinsurance.com.*

SAFETY ON THE ROAD

Never drive at night in remote and rural areas. Although there are few *banditos* on the roads here, more common problems are large potholes, free-roaming animals, cars with no working lights, and road-hogging trucks. Getting assistance is difficult. If you must travel at night, use the toll roads whenever possible; although costly, they're much safer.

Some of the biggest hassles on the road might be from police who pull you over for supposedly breaking the law, or for being a good prospect for a scam. Remember to be polite—displays of anger will only make matters worse—and be aware that a police officer might be pulling you over for something you didn't do. Although efforts are being made to fight corruption, it's still a fact of life in Mexico. The MX$100 (and up) it costs to get your license back is definitely supplementary income for the officer who pulled you over with no intention of taking you down to police headquarters.

▌ CRUISE SHIP TRAVEL

Cozumel and Playa del Carmen (ships dock in Calica, south of town) have become increasingly popular ports for Caribbean cruises, as have Mahahual (commonly known as Puerto Costa Maya) and Progreso (near Mérida). Due to heavy traffic, Cozumel and Playa del Carmen have limited the number of ships coming into their ports. Vessels usually dock in Mahahual two to four times a week and in Progreso twice weekly.

▌ TAXI TRAVEL

Taxis are ubiquitous in both cities and larger towns. The standard taxi is a mid-size, four-door sedan. Drivers generally speak English, either enough to negotiate

360 < **Travel Smart Cancún and the Riviera Maya**

the fare or, in some cases, enough for a lively discussion of national politics.

In addition to private taxis, many cities have bargain-price collective taxi services using minibuses and sedans. The service is called *colectivo* or *pesero*. Such vehicles run along fixed routes, and you hail them on the street and tell the driver where you're headed. He charges you based on how far you're going on that route. Note that drivers often run out of change, so being able to pay the exact amount can help make your ride smoother.

AIRPORT TAXIS

For safety, you should only take the authorized taxi service from most airports. A metered taxi has a *taximetro,* and if a cab has one, ask the driver what the rates are. Most taxis, particularly those in resort areas, are unmetered. Always confirm the fare before setting out. Major hotels post rate sheets, or you can ask a concierge or front-desk person what the rates should be. Note that even the posted rates are inflated, so always try to negotiate a slightly better price. Clearly, if any cabbie asks for more than the posted fare you're being grossly overcharged.

A surcharge of 20% to 40% may be added at night, usually after 11 pm.

If a driver doesn't know the address you give him, he'll radio either a dispatcher or other cabbie to get the info, or drive to the neighborhood and ask around. When you've negotiated the fare before starting, you needn't pay extra if the cabbie has to drive around a bit to find the address.

Tipping isn't customary, unless the driver helps you with your bags.

ESSENTIALS

■ ACCOMMODATIONS

The price and quality of accommodations in the Yucatán Peninsula vary from luxury resorts and coastal villas to seedy hostels and eco-friendly cabanas. Near Mérida and Campeche, many historic haciendas have been converted into luxury accommodations. You may find bargains while you're on the road, but if your comfort threshold is high, look for an English-speaking staff, guaranteed dollar rates, and toll-free reservation numbers. Mexico doesn't have an official star-rating system, but the usual number of stars (five being the ultimate) denotes the most luxury and amenities, while a two-star hotel might have a ceiling fan and TV with local channels only. "Gran turismo" is a special category of hotel that may or may not have all the accoutrements of a five-star hotel (such as minibars) but is nonetheless at the top of the heap, both in price and level of service and sophistication. All-inclusive hotels are a good option for families since the price of the room usually includes children's activities and meals.

APARTMENT AND HOUSE RENTALS

Local agencies that specialize in renting out apartments, condos, villas, and private homes can be found in many tourist locales. International agencies are another option, and rental websites such ⊕ *www.airbnb.com* or ⊕ *www.homeaway.com* are increasingly popular.

Contacts Akumal Villas ☎ *866/535-1324 in the U.S. and Canada, 984/875-9088* ⊕ *www.akumal-villas.com*. **Caribbean Realty** ☎ *910/543-0019, 984/873-5218* ⊕ *www.puertoaventurasrentals.com*. **Cozumel Villas** ☎ *866/564-4427 in the U.S. and Canada, 406/686-9169* ⊕ *www.cozumelvillas.com*. **Lost Oasis Island Rentals** ☎ *998/887-0951, 831/331-6424* ⊕ *www.lostoasis.net*. **Real Estate Yucatán** ☎ *999/944-1315* ⊕ *www.realestateyucatan.com*. **Turquoise Water**

Rentals ☎ *877/254-9791 in the U.S. and Canada, 586/207-5920* ⊕ *www.turquoisewater.com*. **Villas & Apartments Abroad** ☎ *212/213-6435* ⊕ *www.vaanyc.com*. **Villas International** ☎ *415/499-9490, 800/221-2260 in the U.S.* ⊕ *www.villasintl.com*. **Villas of Distinction** ☎ *800/289-0900 in the U.S. and Canada* ⊕ *www.villasofdistinction.com*.

HOTELS

Hotel rates are subject to the 16% value-added tax, in addition to a 2% to 3% hotel tax. Service charges and meals generally aren't included in the quoted rates. Make sure to ask if tax is included and take this into account when comparing properties.

High- and low-season rates can vary significantly. In the off-season, Cancún hotels can cost one-third to one-half what they cost during peak periods. Keep in mind, however, that this is also the time that many hotels undergo necessary repairs or renovations.

Hotels in this guide have private bathrooms with showers, unless stated otherwise; bathtubs aren't common in inexpensive hotels and properties in smaller towns.

Reservations are easy to make online. If you choose this route, be sure to book at least two days in advance of your stay, and always print out your confirmation. Although major resorts are generally efficient at keeping up with online bookings, there's often a lag, and the reservation desks that handle such things may be closed on weekends. If you prefer to make phone reservations, hotels in the larger urban areas will have someone on staff who speaks English. In smaller destinations, you'll have to make your reservations in Spanish. In more remote areas (like Xcalak), you'll have to make reservations by email since most properties don't have telephones.

It's essential to reserve in advance if you're traveling to the resort areas in high season (late November through Easter), and it's recommended, though not always necessary, to do so elsewhere during high season. Resorts popular with college students tend to fill up in the summer months and during Spring Break (generally March through April). Overbooking is a common practice in some parts, especially in Cancún. To protect yourself, get a written confirmation via email.

▌ COMMUNICATIONS

INTERNET

If you're traveling with a laptop, lock it in your hotel safe when you go out. If your computer cable is three-prong, you might want to bring a two-prong adapter, as some wall outlets in hotels are compatible for two-prong devices only. Although uncommon, you might also consider investing in a Mexican surge protector (available at most electronics stores for about $20) that can handle the brownouts and fluctuations in voltage at "off grid" locations.

In Cancún, free Wi-Fi is available in most large hotels, at least in public areas. Cost for an in-room connection starts at a whopping MX$338 per day. The cost for public Internet is as much as MX$10 per minute.

PHONES

A few of Cancún's all-inclusive resorts are now offering free calls to the U.S. and Canada, but be sure to ask in advance. Otherwise, minimize costs by purchasing a Ladatel card and relying on pay phones, or using your international calling card. If you want to call a restaurant or local business, you can save money by simply walking to the concierge and asking the representative to make the call on your behalf.

The country code for Mexico is 52. When calling a Mexico number from abroad, dial the country code and then all of the numbers listed for the entry.

CALLING WITHIN MEXICO

Towns and cities throughout Mexico now have standardized three-digit area codes (LADAs) and seven-digit phone numbers. (In Mexico City, Monterrey, and Guadalajara the area code is two digits followed by an eight-digit local number.) While increasingly rare, numbers in brochures and other literature—even business cards—are sometimes written in the old style, with five or six digits. To call national long-distance, dial 01, the area code, and the seven-digit number.

Directory assistance is 040 for telephone lines run by Telmex, the former government-owned telephone monopoly that still holds near-monopoly status in Mexico. While you can reach 040 from other phone lines, operators generally don't give you any information, except, perhaps, the directory assistance line for the provider you're using. For international assistance, dial 00 first for an international operator and most likely you'll get one who speaks English; tell the operator in what city, state, and country you require directory assistance, and he or she will connect you.

CALLING OUTSIDE MEXICO

To make an international call, dial 00 before the country code, area code, and number. The country code for the United States and Canada is 1; for the United Kingdom it's 44.

An affordable method for making local or long-distance calls is to buy a prepaid phone card and dial direct (⇨ *see Calling Cards*). Another option is to find a *caseta de larga distancia*, a telephone service usually operated out of a store such as a *papelería* (stationery store), pharmacy, restaurant, or other small business; look for the phone symbol on the door. These, however, are few and far between, and most only allow collect calls. To make a direct long-distance call, tell the person on duty the number you'd like to phone; she or he will charge a connecting fee and, most likely, an additional charge per minute (you must pay in pesos). Rates seem to vary widely.

It's usually better to call *por cobrar* (collect) from a pay phone—but be sure to avoid phones near tourist areas that advertise, in English, "Call the U.S. or Canada here!" These charge an outrageous fee per minute. When in doubt, dial the operator and ask for rates.

Access Code Contacts AT&T Direct

☎ *800/225–5288 in the U.S and Canada, 01800/288–2872 toll-free in Mexico* ⊕ *www. att.com.* **Sprint International Access** ☎ *001877/294–9003 toll-free in Mexico, 888/226–7212 in the U.S. and Canada* ⊕ *www. sprint.com.*

CALLING CARDS

In most parts of the country, pay phones (predominantly operated by Telmex) accept only prepaid cards (*tarjetas Lada*), sold in 30-, 50-, 100-, or 200-peso denominations at newsstands, pharmacies, minimarkets, or grocery stores. There are pay phones all over the place—on street corners, in bus stations, and so on. They usually have two unmarked slots, one for a Ladatel card (a Spanish acronym for "long-distance direct dialing") and the other for a credit card. These are primarily for Mexican bank cards, but some accept Visa or MasterCard, though *not* U.S. phone credit cards.

To use a Ladatel card, simply insert it in the appropriate slot. To change instructions to English, push the ABC button on the left hand side of the dial pad. Dial 001 (for calls to the States) or 01 (for long-distance calls within Mexico) and the area code and number you're trying to reach. Local calls may also be placed with the card. Credit is deleted from the card as you use it, and your balance is displayed on a small screen on the phone.

MOBILE PHONES

If you have a multiband phone (some countries use frequencies different from those used in the United States) and your service provider uses the world-standard GSM network (as do T-Mobile and AT&T), you can probably use your cell phone abroad without issues. If your carrier is Sprint, Verizon, or U.S Cellular, then you are on the CDMA system, which means you're better off renting a local phone or having your provider add an international plan. Otherwise, you'll be subject to global roaming fees: these can be steep ($2 a minute is considered reasonable), and you normally pay the toll charges for incoming calls. It's almost always cheaper to send a text message (usually 25¢ or less). If you have a laptop or smartphone, the most affordable way to call is through Skype. If the person you are calling also has a Skype account, you can make international calls for free through the Internet.

If you just want to make local calls, consider buying a new SIM card (your provider may have to unlock your phone for you to use it) plus a prepaid service plan in the destination. You'll then have a local number and can make local calls at local rates. If your trip is extensive, you could also simply buy a new pay-as-you-go cell phone in your destination, as the initial cost will be offset over time.

Mobile Phone Contacts Cancún Valet.

Cell phones can be rented through Cancún Valet: expect to pay at 69¢ per minute to/from the United States, Canada, and Europe. ☎ *888/479–9095 in the U.S. and Canada, 01800/226–2868 toll-free in Mexico* ⊕ *www. cancunvalet.com.*

TOLL-FREE NUMBERS

Toll-free numbers in Mexico start with an 800 or 877 prefix. To reach them, you need to dial 01 before the number. Some toll-free numbers use 95 or 001 instead of 01 to connect. In this guide, Mexico-only toll-free numbers are noted as such. Unless otherwise specified, numbers with toll-free prefixes generally work north of the border only. Those that do work to access a U.S. company from Mexico may or may not be free; those that aren't should give you the chance to hang up before being charged. Directory assistance is 040. **Some hotels charge for**

800 numbers made from guest rooms, so double check before dialing.

CUSTOMS AND DUTIES

Upon entering Mexico, you'll be given a baggage-declaration form—you can fill out one per family. You'll also be given an FMM (tourist card), to be stamped at immigration. Keep this card for the duration of your trip, since you'll need to present it upon departure. Otherwise you'll need to visit an immigration office and pay a fine before leaving the country. Minors traveling without an adult must carry notarized written permission from a parent or guardian. Most airports have a random bag-inspection scheme in place. When you pick up your bags you'll approach something that looks like a stoplight. Present your form to the attendant, press the button, and if you get a green light you (and the rest of your family) may proceed. If you get a red light, you may be subject to further questioning or inspection. You're allowed to bring in 3 liters of spirits or 6 liters of wine for personal use; 200 cigarettes, 25 cigars, or 200 grams of tobacco. You aren't allowed to bring in firearms or ammunition, meat, vegetables, plants, fruit, or flowers. Mexico also allows you to bring one cat, one dog, or up to four canaries into the country if you have these two things: (1) a pet health certificate signed by a registered veterinarian in the United States and issued not more than 72 hours before the animal enters Mexico; and (2) a pet-vaccination certificate showing that the animal has been treated for rabies, hepatitis, pip, and leptospirosis.

For more information or details on bringing other animals or more than one type of animal, contact a Mexican consulate. Aduana Mexico (Mexican Customs) has an informative website. You can also get customs information from a Mexican consulate; many major American cities as well as border towns have them. To find the consulate nearest you, check the Ministry of Foreign Affairs website, select Consular Services from the menu on the left, and scroll down.

Consulate Contacts Aduana Mexico
☎ 877/448–8728 in the U.S., 01800/463 –6728 toll-free in Mexico ⊕ www.aduanas.gob. mx. **Ministry of Foreign Affairs** ☎ 202/728– 1600, 53/686–5581 in Mexico ⊕ www.sre.gob. mx/en. **U.S. Customs and Border Protection** ☎ 877/227–5511 in the U.S., 202/325–8000 outside the U.S. ⊕ www.cbp.gov.

EATING OUT

The restaurants we list are the cream of the crop in each price category.
⇨ *For information on food-related health issues, see Health.*

MEALS AND MEALTIMES

Desayuno can be either a breakfast sweet roll and coffee or milk or a full breakfast of an egg dish such as *huevos a la mexicana* (scrambled eggs with chopped tomato, onion, and chiles), *huevos rancheros* (fried eggs on a tortilla covered with salsa), or *huevos con jamón* (scrambled eggs with ham), plus juice and toast or tortillas. Some cafés don't open until 8 or 8:30, in which case hotel restaurants are the best bets for early risers. *Panaderías* (bakeries) open early and provide the cheapest breakfast you'll find—a bag of assorted rolls and pastries will likely cost less than MX$20.

Traditionally, lunch is called *comida* or *almuerzo* and is the biggest meal of the day. Most restaurants start serving lunch no earlier than 1 pm and traditional businesses close between 2 pm and 4 pm for this meal. It usually includes soup, a main dish, and dessert. Regional specialties include *pan de cazón* (baby shark shredded and layered with tortillas, black beans, and tomato sauce) in Campeche; *pollo pibil* (chicken baked in banana leaves) in Mérida; and *tikin xic* (fish in a sour-orange sauce) on the coast. Restaurants in tourist areas also serve American-style food such as hamburgers, pizza, and pasta. The evening meal is called *cena*, which is sometimes replaced by *merienda*, a lighter meal between lunch and dinner. Most restaurants are open daily for lunch and dinner during high season (late November through April), but hours may be reduced during the rest of the year. It's always a good idea to phone ahead.

Unless otherwise noted, the restaurants listed in this guide are open daily for lunch and dinner.

PAYING

Most small restaurants do not take credit cards. Larger restaurants and those catering to tourists typically accept Master-Card and Visa.

⇨ *For tipping guidelines, see Tipping.*

RESERVATIONS AND DRESS

During high season, it's a good idea to make a reservation if you can. In Cancún, for example, they're expected at the nicer restaurants. Some restaurants accept online reservations, although it's always wise to confirm by phone. We mention them specifically only when reservations are essential (there's no other way you'll ever get a table) or when they're not accepted. Large parties should always call ahead to check the reservations policy. We mention dress only when men are required to wear a jacket.

WINES, BEER, AND SPIRITS

Almost all restaurants in the region serve beer and some Mexican spirits. Larger restaurants have beer, wine, and spirits. Some of the more expensive all-inclusive resorts offer top-shelf international liquor brands but will serve them only if you specifically request the brands by name (otherwise, expect a hangover). The Mexican wine industry is relatively small, but notable producers include L.A. Cetto, Bodegas de Santo Tomás, Pedro Domecq, and Monte Xanic. As well as offering Mexican vintages, restaurants may offer Chilean, Spanish, Italian, and French wines at reasonable prices. You pay more for imported liquor such as vodka, brandy, and whiskey; some brands of tequila and

rum are less expensive. Take the opportunity to try some of the higher-end, small-batch tequila—it's a completely different experience from what you might be used to. Some small lunch places called *loncherías* don't sell alcohol. Almost all corner stores sell beer, brandy, cheap wine, and tequila. Grocery stores carry all brands of beer, wine, and spirits. Liquor stores are rare and usually carry specialty items. You must be 18 to buy liquor, but this rule is often overlooked.

▌ELECTRICITY

Electrical converters are not necessary because Mexico operates on the 60-cycle, 120-volt system. However, outlets at some of the older hotels have not been updated to accommodate three-prong and polarized plugs (those with one larger prong), so it's a good idea to bring an adapter.

▌EMERGENCIES

It's helpful, albeit daunting, to know ahead of time that you're not protected by the laws of your native land once you're on Mexican soil. However, if you get into a scrape with the law, you can call the Citizens' Emergency Center in the United States. In Mexico, you can also call INFOTUR, the 24-hour English-speaking hotline of the Mexico Ministry of Tourism (Sectur). The hotline can provide immediate assistance as well as general, nonemergency guidance. In Cancún, an emergency 911 call center is available. In Mérida and environs, you can contact the tourist police (☎ 999/930–3200 ext. 40031), although getting an English speaker is hit or miss. In an emergency, call ☎ 060 from any phone.

Consulates and Embassies U.S. Consulate ⊠ Calle 60, No. 338, Col. Alcala Martin, Centro, Mérida ☎ 999/942–5700 ⊕ merida.usconsulate.gov. **U.S. Consular Agency Cancún** ⊠ Blvd. Kukulcán, Km 13, Zona Hotelera, Cancún ☎ 998/883–0272 ⊙ Weekdays 8 am–1 pm (by appointment only). **U.S. Embassy** ⊠ Paseo de la Reforma 305, Col. Cuauhtémoc, Mexico City ☎ 55/5080–2000 ext. 0 ⊕ mexico.usembassy.gov.

General Emergency Contacts Air Ambulance Network ☎ 800/880–9451 in the U.S. and Canada, 01800/010–0027 toll-free in Mexico ⊕ www.airambulancenetwork.com. **Angeles Verdes** (Emergency roadside assistance in Mexico). ☎ 078. **Citizens' Emergency Center** ☎ 888/407–4747 in the U.S., 202/501–4444 outside the U.S. ⊕ www.travel.state.gov. **Global Life Flight** ☎ 01800/305–9400 toll-free in Mexico, 01800/361–1600 toll-free in Mexico, 800/831–9307 in the U.S. and Canada ⊕ www.globallifeflight.com. **INFOTUR** ☎ 01800/903–9200 toll-free in Mexico ⊕ www.sectur.gob.mx.

▌ HEALTH

According to the U.S. government's National Centers for Disease Control and Prevention (CDC) there's a limited risk of malaria in certain rural areas of the Yucatán Peninsula, especially the states of Campeche and Quintana Roo. Dengue fever is also a limited risk along the Caribbean Coast. Travelers in mostly urban areas need not worry, nor do travelers who rarely leave artificial resort environs.

To safeguard yourself against mosquito-borne diseases like malaria and dengue, use mosquito nets (provided at most beach and jungle properties), wear clothing that covers the body, apply repellent containing DEET, and use spray for flying insects in living and sleeping areas. If you consider taking anti-malarial pills, remember that the side effects of some medications can be quite strong, and the current strain of Mexican malaria can be cured with the right medication. There's no vaccine to combat dengue.

Health Warnings National Centers for Disease Control & Prevention (CDC). ☎ 800/232–4636 for international travelers' health line ⊕ www.cdc.gov/travel.

FOOD AND DRINK

In Mexico the biggest health risk is traveler's diarrhea caused by consuming contaminated fruit, vegetables, water (ice included), and unpasteurized milk or milk products.

Drink only bottled water or water that has been boiled for at least 10 minutes, even when you're brushing your teeth. At restaurants off the beaten path, be sure to ask for *agua mineral* (mineral water) or *agua purificada* (purified water). When ordering cold drinks at questionable establishments, skip the ice: *sin hielo*. (You can usually identify ice made commercially from purified water by its uniform barrel shape and the hole in the center.) Hotels with water-purification systems will post signs to that effect in the rooms; even then, be wary. Although salads in tourist-oriented areas have usually been hygienically prepared, when in doubt don't eat any raw vegetables or fruits that haven't been, or can't be, peeled (e.g., lettuce and tomatoes). In coastal towns like Celestún, the shrimp may be fresh, but it has been known to cause Montezuma's Revenge for travelers with sensitive stomachs.

REMEDIES

Mild cases of diarrhea may respond to Imodium (known generically as loperamide or lomotil) or Pepto-Bismol (not as strong), both of which you can buy over the counter. Keep in mind, though, that these drugs can complicate more serious illnesses. Drink plenty of bottled water or tea. Chamomile tea (*té de manzanilla*) is a good remedy, and it's readily available in restaurants throughout Mexico.

In severe cases, hydrate with Gatorade or a salt-sugar solution (½ teaspoon salt and 4 tablespoons sugar per quart of water). You can also balance out your pH levels by drinking a glass of water with a tablespoon of baking soda, which acts as a natural antacid. If your fever and diarrhea last more than three days, see a doctor—you may have picked up a parasite that requires prescription medication.

PESTS

It's best to be cautious and go indoors at dusk (called the "mosquito hour" by locals). An excellent brand of *repelente de insectos* (insect repellent) called Autan is readily available; don't use it on children under age two. If you want to bring a mosquito repellent from home, make sure it has at least 20% DEET or it won't be effective. If you're hiking in the jungle or near standing water, wear repellent and/or long pants and sleeves; if you're camping in the jungle, use a mosquito net and invest in a package of mosquito coils (sold in most stores). Isla Holbox is often riddled with tiny mosquitoes and "no-seeums" after the rains. Island locals use baby oil as a natural repellent. If you plan on visiting one of the many *cenotes* (subterranean water bodies) throughout the Yucatán, be sure to bring waterproof insect repellent.

Another local flying pest is the *tabaño*, a type of deer fly, which resembles a common household fly with yellow stripes. Some people swell up after being bitten, but taking an antihistamine can help. Watch out for the small red ants, as their bites can be quite irritating.

Scorpions also live in the region; their sting is similar to a bee sting. They're rarely fatal, but can cause strong reactions in small children and the elderly. Clean all cuts carefully (especially those produced by coral), as the rate of infection is much higher here.

The Yucatán has many poisonous snakes. The coral snake, easily identified by its black and red markings, should be avoided at all costs since its bite is fatal. If you're planning any jungle hikes, be sure to wear hard-sole shoes and stay on the path. For more remote areas, hire a guide and make sure there's an anti-venom kit accompanying you on the trip.

SUNBURN

More common hazards to travelers in the Yucatán are sunburn and heat exhaustion. The sun is strong here; it takes fewer than 20 minutes to get a serious burn. When practical, avoid the sun between 11 am and 3 pm. Wear a hat and use sunscreen, preferably something with zinc oxide. You should drink more fluids than you do at home—Mexico is probably hotter than what you're used to and you'll perspire more. Rest in the afternoon and stay out of the sun to avoid heat exhaustion. The first signs of dehydration and heat exhaustion are dizziness, extreme irritability, and fatigue.

TRIP INSURANCE

If you aren't interested in purchasing comprehensive trip coverage, consider buying medical-only travel insurance. Neither Medicare nor some private insurers cover medical expenses anywhere outside the United States. Medical-only policies typically reimburse you for medical care (excluding that related to preexisting conditions), hospitalization abroad, and provide for evacuation. You still have to pay the bills and await reimbursement from the insurer, though.

Another option is to sign up with a medical-evacuation assistance company. A membership in one of these companies gets you doctor referrals, emergency evacuation or repatriation, 24-hour hotlines for medical consultation, and other assistance. International SOS and AirMed International provide evacuation services and medical referrals. MedjetAssist offers medical evacuation.

Medical Assistance Companies AirMed International ☎ 205/443–4840, 800/356–2161 in the U.S. and Canada ⊕ www.airmed.com. International SOS ☎ 215/942–8226 ⊕ www.internationalsos.com. MedjetAssist ☎ 800/527–7478 in the U.S. and Canada, 205/595–6626 ⊕ www.medjetassist.com.

Medical-Only Insurers International Medical Group (IMG). ☎ 800/628–4664 in the U.S. and Canada, 317/655–4500 ⊕ www.imglobal.com. Wallach & Company ☎ 800/237–6615 in the U.S. and Canada, 540/687–3166 ⊕ www.wallach.com.

▌ HOURS OF OPERATION

In well-traveled places such as Cancún, Isla Mujeres, Playa del Carmen, Mérida, and Cozumel, businesses generally are open during posted hours. In more off-the-beaten-path areas, neighbors can tell you when the owner will return.

Most banks are open weekdays from 9 to 5 but might exchange money only until noon. Many are open Saturday until noon or 1 pm. Most businesses are open weekdays 9 to 2 and 4 to 7.

Some gas stations are open 24 hours, although those off main highways usually close from midnight (or even earlier) until 6 am.

Most museums throughout Mexico are closed on Monday and open 8 to 5 the rest of the week. But it's best to call ahead or ask at your hotel. Hours of sights and attractions in this book are denoted by a clock icon (🕒).

The larger pharmacies are usually open daily 8 am to 10 pm; smaller ones are often closed on Sunday. Cancún, Campeche, and Mérida all have at least one 24-hour pharmacy.

Tourist-oriented stores in Cancún, Mérida, Playa del Carmen, and Cozumel are usually open 10 to 9 Monday through Saturday and on Sunday afternoon. Shops in more traditional areas may close weekdays between 1 pm and 4 pm, opening again in the evening. They're generally closed Sunday.

▌ MAIL

Mail can be sent from your hotel or the *oficina de correos* (post office). Be fore-warned, however, that mail service to, within, and from Mexico is notoriously slow and can take anywhere from 10 days to, well, never. Don't send anything of value to or from Mexico via mail, including cash, checks, or credit-card numbers.

SHIPPING PACKAGES

Hotel concierges can recommend international carriers, such as DHL, Estafeta, or Federal Express, which give your package a tracking number and ensure its arrival back home.

▌ MONEY

Because the value of the currency fluctuates, and since most hotels quote rates in U.S. dollars, we've listed hotel prices in this book in dollars; all other prices are listed in Mexican pesos.

U.S. dollar bills (but not coins) are widely accepted in many parts of the Yucatán, particularly in Cancún and Cozumel; however, you may get your change back in pesos. Many restaurants, tourist shops and market vendors, as well as virtually all hotel service personnel, also accept dollars. Wherever you are, though, watch out for bad exchange rates—you'll generally do better paying in pesos. Note that many smaller businesses and most highway toll booths accept only pesos.

ATMS AND BANKS

In 2010, Mexican authorities passed a law stating that foreign travelers may not exchange more than US$1500 (cash) per person, per month into Mexican pesos. Mexican travelers are also limited to US$1500 cash per person, per month, with the added restriction of no more than US$300 cash per day. Other methods of payment including credit cards, traveler's checks, and non-American foreign currencies are not affected by this law.

When exchanging foreign currency at banks and hotels in Mexico, you must show your passport. ATMs (*cajeros automáticos*) are commonplace in key tourist areas. All airports and many gas stations have them, but many bus stations do not. Rural locales also often lack ATMs (truly remote ones, like Xcalak near Belize, don't have ATMs or banks, and businesses there don't accept credit cards). Unless you're in a major city or resort area, treat ATMs as you would gas stations—don't assume you'll be able to find one in a pinch. In smaller towns, even when they're present, machines are often out of order or out of cash.

Cirrus and Plus are the most frequently found networks. Your own bank will probably charge a transaction fee for withdrawing money in Mexico (up to $8 a pop); the foreign bank you use may also charge a fee. Before you leave home, ask your bank if they have an agreement with a Mexican counterpart to waive or charge reduced fees for cash withdrawals. For example, Bank of America account holders can withdraw money from Santander-Serfin ATMs free of charge. Regardless of the fee, you'll usually get a better rate of exchange at an ATM than you will at a currency-exchange office or even when changing money in a bank.

■TIP→ **PINs with more than four digits are not recognized at ATMs in Mexico. If your PIN has five or more numbers, remember to change it before you leave.**

CREDIT CARDS

Throughout this guide, it's safe to assume that businesses accept major credit cards unless the service information reads ▬ *No credit cards.*

It's a good idea to inform your credit-card company before you travel to Mexico, especially if you don't travel internationally very often. Otherwise, the credit-card company might put a hold on your card owing to unusual activity—not a good thing halfway through your trip. Record all your credit-card numbers—as well as the phone numbers to call if your cards are lost or stolen—in a safe place, so you're prepared should something go wrong.

Note that some credit-card companies *and* the banks that issue them add substantial percentages to all foreign transactions. Check on these fees before leaving home, so there won't be any surprises when you get the bill.

Credit cards are accepted in most tourist areas. Smaller, less expensive restaurants and shops, however, tend to take only cash. In general, credit cards aren't accepted in small towns and villages. The most widely accepted cards are MasterCard and Visa; American Express is not widely accepted in Mexico except at large international chain hotels and resorts. When shopping, you can usually get better prices if you pay with cash.

In Mexico the decision to pay cash or use a credit card might depend on whether the establishment in which you're making a purchase finds bargaining for prices acceptable. To avoid fraud, it's wise to make sure that "pesos" or the initials M.N. (*moneda nacional,* or national currency) is clearly marked on all credit-card receipts, unless the charge was made in U.S. dollars.

CURRENCY AND EXCHANGE

Check with your bank, the financial pages of your local newspaper, or ⊕ *www. xe.com* for current exchange rates.

Mexican currency comes in denominations of 10-, 20-, 50-, 100-, 200-, 500-, and 1000-peso bills. The latter are not very common, and many establishments refuse to accept them due to a lack of change. Coins come in denominations of 1, 2, 5, 10, 20, and 100 pesos. Many of the coins are very similar, so check carefully. Of the older coins you may occasionally see a 10 or 20 or more often a 50 *centavo* (cent) piece.

Most banks change money only on weekdays until noon (though they stay open until 5), whereas *casas de cambio* (private exchange offices) generally stay open until 6 or 9 and often operate on weekends. Bring your passport when you exchange money. Bank rates are regulated by the federal government but vary slightly from bank to bank, while casas de cambio have slightly more variable rates.

■TIP→ Many shop and restaurant owners are unable to make change for large bills. Enough of these encounters may compel you to request billetes chicos (small bills) when you exchange money.

Contacts XE.com ⊕ *www.xe.com.*

■ PACKING

Pack lightly, because you may want to save space in your suitcase for purchases. The Yucatán is filled with bargains on clothing, leather goods, jewelry, and other crafts. If you purchase pottery or ceramics, make sure they're carefully wrapped in your check-in luggage since TSA regulations prohibit these items from being in your carry-on.

Bring lightweight clothes, bathing suits, sun hats, and cover-ups for the Caribbean beach towns, but also pack a light jacket or sweater to wear in chilly, air-conditioned restaurants, or to tide you over during a rainstorm or an unusual cool spell. For trips to rural areas or Mérida, where dress is typically more conservative and shorts are considered inappropriate, make sure you have at least one pair of slacks. Comfortable walking shoes with rubber soles are a good idea, both for exploring ruins and for walking around cities. Lightweight rain gear and an umbrella are a good idea during the rainy season. Cancún is the dressiest spot on the peninsula; however, even fancy restaurants there don't usually require men to wear jackets, opting instead for a "resort elegant" dress code.

Pack sunscreen and sunglasses for the Yucatán's strong sun. Other handy items—especially if you're using budget hotels and restaurants or going off the beaten path—include toilet paper, hand sanitizer, facial tissues, a plastic water bottle, and a flashlight (for occasional power outages). Snorkelers should consider bringing their own equipment unless traveling light is a priority; reef shoes with rubber soles for rocky underwater surfaces are also advised. To avoid problems at customs, bring your prescription drugs in the original pill bottle or with a current prescription. Don't count on purchasing necessary OTC or prescription meds (such as sleeping pills); the same brands are not always available in Mexico.

■ PASSPORTS AND VISAS

A tourist visa (FMM) and valid passport are required for all visitors to Mexico traveling by air. If you're arriving by plane, the standard tourist visa forms will be given to you while you're onboard. They're also available through travel agents and Mexican consulates and at the border if you're entering by land. In addition to having your visa form, you must prove your citizenship.

■TIP→ You're given a portion of the FMM upon entering Mexico. Keep track of this document throughout your trip: you will need it when you depart. You'll be asked to submit it, along with your ticket and passport, to airline representatives at the gate when boarding for departure. If you lose your tourist card, plan to spend some time (and about US$80) sorting it out with Mexican officials at the immigration office before your flight home.

Contacts **U.S. Department of State**
☎ *877/487–2778 in the U.S.* ⊕ *www.state.gov.*

■ RESTROOMS

Expect to find reasonably clean flushing toilets and running water at public restrooms in the major tourist destinations and at tourist attractions. Toilet tissue and soap are usually, but not always, on hand. Although many markets, gas stations, bus and train stations, and the like have public facilities, you usually have to pay about MX$5 for the privilege of using them. Some smaller hotels in Xcalak, Mahahual, and Isla Holbox have eco-friendly toilets, which utilize low water or sawdust for composting. Remember that unless otherwise indicated you should put your used toilet paper in the wastebasket next to the toilet. Many plumbing systems in Mexico still can't handle accumulations of toilet paper.

▌SAFETY

Unfortunately, Mexico as a whole has seen a dramatic increase in violence over the past few years, but most of this has been concentrated along border zones and in less touristy areas. In 2013, six murders took place on the outskirts of Cancún— all of which were drug-related. Nevertheless, the Yucatán Peninsula remains one of the safest parts of the country.

With that said, you should always use common sense. Take advantage of hotel safes when available, and carry your own baggage whenever possible unless you're checking into a hotel. Leave expensive jewelry at home, since it often entices thieves and will mark you as a *turista* who can afford to be robbed.

When traveling with all your money, be sure to keep an eye on your belongings at all times and distribute your cash and any valuables between different bags and items of clothing. Do not reach for your money stash in public. If you carry a purse, choose one with a zipper and a thick strap that you can drape across your body; adjust the length so that the purse sits in front of you at or above hip level.

There have been reports of travelers being victimized after imbibing drinks that have been drugged in Cancún nightclubs. Never drink alone with strangers, watch your drink being poured, and keep your eye on it at all times. Avoid driving on desolate streets, don't travel at night, and never pick up hitchhikers or hitchhike yourself.

Use ATMs during the day and in big commercial areas. Avoid the glass-enclosed street variety where you may be more vulnerable to thieves who force you to withdraw money for them.

Cancún's Zona Hotelera (Hotel Zone) is a high-trafficked tourist area, making it extremely safe for those who want to relax at the beach or explore the string of shops and restaurants that line Boulevard Kukulcán. Security has increased on this main strip, which means you'll most likely see armed tourist police driving up and down the boulevard. There is also a security checkpoint that marks the entrance to the Zona Hotelera on Boulevard Kukulcán in front of Playa Delfines. Tourists are rarely stopped here. Less visited by tourists, El Centro (downtown Cancún) should be avoided late at night. An act of violence in 2010 resulted in the C4 Surveillance and Rescue Center installing video cameras in strategic points throughout the city. Additionally, an emergency 911 Call Center is now in place.

Bear in mind that reporting a crime to the police is often a frustrating experience unless you speak excellent Spanish and have a great deal of patience. If you're victimized, contact your local consular agent or the consular section of your country's embassy in Mexico City.

A woman traveling alone will be the subject of much curiosity, since traditional Mexican women do not generally choose to travel unaccompanied. Don't walk on deserted beaches alone, and make sure your hotel room is securely locked when you retire.

Part of the machismo culture is being flirtatious and showing off in front of *compadres,* and lone women are likely to be subjected to catcalls, although this is less true in the Yucatán than in other parts of Mexico. Although annoying, it's essentially harmless. The best way to get rid of unwanted attention is to simply ignore the advances. It's best not to enter into a discussion with harassers, even if you speak Spanish. When the suitor is persistent say "no" to whatever is said, walk briskly, and leave immediately for a safe place, such as a nearby store. Dressing conservatively may help—clothing such as halter tops, miniskirts, or shorts may be inappropriate in more conservative rural areas. Never go topless on the beach. Mexico does have laws against topless sunbathing on public beaches (although they are not enforced); moreover, Mexicans, in general, don't engage in the practice, and men may misinterpret your doing so as an invitation.

■TIP➜ Distribute your cash, credit cards, IDs, and other valuables between a deep front pocket, an inside jacket or vest pocket, and a hidden money pouch. Don't reach for the money pouch once you're in public.

BEACHES

Empty coastlines can be susceptible to car break-ins and theft. Most resorts notify beachgoers of coastal conditions by displayed colored flags. ■TIP➜ Don't swim when the black danger flag flies; a red or yellow flag indicates that you should proceed with caution, and a green flag means the waters are safe. You will seldom see the green flag—even when the water is tranquil—so swim cautiously. Beware: the calmest-looking waters can still have currents and riptides. Ignoring these warning flags has resulted in at least one tourist drowning each season.

If visiting isolated beaches, bring sunscreen and drinking water to avoid overexposure and dehydration. Take note that waves are most powerful during December, and that hurricane season lasts from June through November.

■ TAXES

An air-departure tax of around US$50 is almost always included as part of your ticket price (check with your airline if you're unsure); if for some reason it's not included or only partially included, you must pay the remainder in cash at the airport.

Mexico has a value-added tax (V.A.T.), or IVA (*impuesto de valor agregado*), of 16% (10% along the Cancún–Chetumal corridor). Many establishments already include the IVA in their quoted price. When comparing rates, it's important to know whether yours does. Occasionally (and illegally) it may be waived for cash purchases; this is nothing for you to worry about. Hotel taxes also apply. The amount is the V.A.T. plus 3% in Quintana Roo, plus 2% in the states of Yucatán and Campeche.

Those who arrive in Mexico by air or cruise ship are eligible to be reimbursed for the value-added tax they were charged on items bought in Mexican stores. There are, of course, some restrictions. You must have paid by credit card (from outside of Mexico) or cash, and your purchases must have totaled MX$1200. While making purchases, you must show your passport and get a receipt and refund form. On departure, you can visit a kiosk at the Cancún airport to receive half of your refund in the form of a credit (in pesos, to a max of MX$10000) that can be applied to more shopping but not meals or hotel stays; the remainder will be credited to your credit card or bank account.

■ TIME

Mexico has three time zones. Baja California (*norte*) is on Pacific Standard Time. Baja California Sur and the northwest states are on Mountain Time. The rest of the country is on Central Standard Time, which is two hours ahead of Pacific Time. Cancún and all of the areas covered in this book are on Central Standard Time.

TIPPING

When tipping in Mexico, remember that the minimum wage is only about $5 a day and that many in the tourism industry don't earn much more. There are also Mexicans who think in dollars and know, for example, that in the United States porters are tipped $1 to $2 a bag. Many of them expect the peso equivalent from foreigners. Though dollars are widely accepted in Cancún and Cozumel, you should always tip using local currency whenever possible, so that service personnel aren't stuck going to the bank to exchange dollars for pesos.

What follows are some guidelines. Naturally, larger tips are always welcome: porters and bellhops, MX$10 per bag at airports and moderate and inexpensive hotels and MX$20 per person per bag at expensive hotels; maids, MX$20 per night (all hotels); waiters, 15% to 20% of the bill, depending on service, and less in simpler restaurants (anywhere you are, make sure a service charge hasn't already been added, a practice that's particularly common in resorts); bartenders, 15% to 20% of the bill, depending on service (and, perhaps, on how many drinks you've had); taxi drivers, MX$10 only if the driver helps you with your bags. Tipping cabbies isn't usual, and they often overcharge tourists when possible. Tip tour guides MX$50 per half day, MX$100 for a full day; drivers about half as much. Gas-station attendants expect MX$3 to MX$5 unless they check the oil, tires, and so on, in which case tip more; parking attendants, MX$10 to MX$20, even if it's for valet parking at a theater or restaurant that charges for the service.

TOURS

With offices in Cancún and Mérida, Gray Line offers wide geographic coverage plus a broad range of packages for both day trips and overnight junkets, so it can deliver most experiences on the typical tourist wish list. Mérida-based Ecoturismo Yucatán leads guided tours that hit the region's archaeological and cultural highlights; other options focus on nature, cuisine, and active pursuits. Alltournative is recommended for sustainable adventure tours on the coast; it specializes in archaeological and eco-oriented excursions. Eco Colors runs single- and multiday trips to the wildlife reserves at Isla Holbox and Sian Ka'an, and to remote Mayan ruin sites; bird-watching and biking excursions are also available. California Native includes guide service, accommodations, breakfast, and most lunches in its seven-day trip with stops at Mérida, Izamal, Chichén Itzá, Ek Balam, Uxmal, and Edzná.

Recommended Companies Alltournative ✉ *Carretera Chetumal-Puerto Juarez, Km 287, in front of the Playacar development (after Centro Maya and Hong Kong Restaurant), Playa del Carmen* ☎ *984/803–9999, 877/437–4990 in the U.S. and Canada* ⊕ *www.alltournative. com.* **California Native** ☎ *800/926–1140 in the U.S. and Canada, 310/642–1140* ⊕ *www. calnative.com.* **EcoColors** ✉ *Calle Camaron 32, Sm 27, El Centro, Cancún* ☎ *998/884–9580 in Mexico, 866/376–5056 in the U.S.* ⊕ *www. ecotravelmexico.com.* **Ecoturismo Yucatán** ✉ *Calle 3, No. 235, between 32A and 34, Col. Pensiones, Mérida* ☎ *999/920–2772, 999/920–2742* ⊕ *www.ecoyuc.com.mx.* **Gray Line Cancún** ☎ *998/887–2495, 01800/719–5465 toll-free in Mexico, 877/240–5864 in the U.S. and Canada* ⊕ *www.graylinecancun.com.* **Gray Line Yucatán** ☎ *998/887–2495, 01800/719–5465 toll-free in Mexico, 877/240–5864 in the U.S. and Canada* ⊕ *www.graylineyucatan.com.*

SPECIAL-INTEREST TOURS
ADVENTURE
Contacts Green Tortoise Adventure Travel ☎ *800/867–8647 in the U.S. and Canada, 415/956–7500* ⊕ *www.greentortoise.com.* **TrekAmerica** ☎ *800/873–5872 in the U.S.* ⊕ *www.trekamerica.com.*

ART AND ARCHAEOLOGY
Contacts Far Horizons Archaeological & Cultural Trips ☎ *800/552–4575 in the U.S. and Canada, 415/482–8400* ⊕ *www.*

farhorizons.com. **The Mayan Traveler** ☎ *888/843–6292 in the U.S., 281/367–3386* ⊕ *www.themayantraveler.com.*

BIKING

Contacts Backroads ☎ *800/462–2848 in the U.S. and Canada, 510/527–1555* ⊕ *www. backroads.com.*

DIVING

Contacts Scuba Travel Ventures ☎ *800/298–9009 in the U.S. and Canada, 619/303–4878* ⊕ *www.scubatravelventures. com.*

FISHING

Contacts Fishing International ☎ *800/950– 4242 in the U.S. and Canada, 530/743–4242* ⊕ *www.fishinginternational.com.*

LANGUAGE PROGRAMS

Contacts Institute of Modern Spanish ✉ *Calle 15, No. 500B, between 16A and 18, Col. Maya, Mérida* ☎ *877/463–7432 in the U.S. and Canada, 999/911–0790 in Mexico* ⊕ *www. modernspanish.org.*

▌ VISITOR INFORMATION

ONLINE TRAVEL TOOLS

The official website for Mexico tourism has information on tourist attractions and activities, plus an overview of Mexican history and culture. Yucatán Today (⊕ *www. yucatantoday.com*) and Loco Gringo (⊕ *www.locogringo.com*) have comprehensive information on nightlife, hotel listings, archaeological sites, area history, maps, and more. Other helpful sites for travelers include ⊕ *www.cancun.travel,* ⊕ *www.cancun.bz,* ⊕ *www.cozumelmy cozumel.com,* ⊕ *www.islamujeres.info,* and ⊕ *www.travelyucatan.com.*

Contacts Mexico Tourism Board ☎ *800/446–3942 in the U.S. and Canada* ⊕ *www.visitmexico.com.*

INDEX

PHOTO CREDITS

Front cover: Getty Images/Tetra images RF [Description: Beach with ancient Mayan ruins]. 1, Kreder Katja/age fotostock. 2, Stuart Pearce/age fotostock. 5, cancuncd.com. Chapter 1: Experience Cancun: 8-9, ESCUDERO Patrick / age fotostock. 10, Mike Liu/Shutterstock. 11(left), Lipbomb/Flickr. 11 (right), GUILLERMO ALDANA/Mexico Tourism Board. 14, Cancun CVB. 15 (left), cancuncd.com. 15 (right), BRUCE HERMAN/Mexico Tourism Board. 16 (left), Curtis Kautzer/Shutterstock. 16 (top center), urosr/Shutterstock.16 (top right), Agnes Csondor/iStockphoto. 16 (bottom right), SEUX Paule / age fotostock. 17 (top left), Drimi/Shutterstock. 17 (bottom left), Alicia Navarrete Alonso/wikipedia.org. 17 (topcenter), travelpixpro/iStockphoto. 17 (right), Scott Prokop/Shutterstock. 18 and 19 (left), Cancun CVB. 19 (right), BRUCE HERMAN/Mexico Tourism Board. 21 (left), idreamphoto/Shutterstock. 21 (right), Alfredo Schaufelberger/Shutterstock. 22, aceshot1/Shutterstock. 23, Yarek Gora/iStockphoto. 24, Byron W.Moore/Shutterstock. 26, Chris Cheadle / age fotostock. Chapter 2: Cancun: 27, Victor Elias / age fotostock. 28 (top), Keith Pomakis/wikipedia.org. 28 (bottom), Joao Virissimo/Shutterstock. 29, David Davis/Shutterstock. 30, Cancun CVB. 31 (top), Thelmadatter/wikipedia.org. 31 (bottom), malias/Flickr. 32, aceshot1/Shutterstock. 41, JTB Photo / age fotostock. 63, Marriott International. 64, Courtesy of NIZUC Resort & Spa. 71, csp/Shutterstock. 72 (top left), Alfredo Schaufelberger/Shutterstock. 72 (bottom left), wikipedia.org. 72 (right), Casa Herradura/Brown-Forman. 73 (top left), csp/Shutterstock. 73 (bottom left), Alfredo Schaufelberger/Shutterstock. 73 (top center), Jesus Cervantes/Shutterstock. 73 (bottom center), Blaine Harrington / age fotostock. 73 (top right), Jesus Cervantes/Shutterstock. 73 (bottom right), Jesus Cervantes/Shutterstock. 73 (bottom), Smithsonian Institution Archives. 74 (top left), Eduard Stelmakh/Shutterstock. 74 (center left), svry/Shutterstock. 74 (bottom left), National Archives and Records Administration. 74 (top right), Andrew Penner/iStockphoto. 74 (bottom right), BlueOrange Studio/Shutterstock. 75 (top right), Patricia Hofmeester/Shutterstock. 75, (top left), Sony Ho / Shutterstock. 75 (bottom left), csp/Shutterstock. 76 (left), The Patrón Spirits Company. 76 (right), rick/Flickr. 77 (top left), Casa Herradura/Brown-Forman. 77 (bottom left), shrk/Flickr. 77 (right), Neil Setchfield / Alamy. 87, Cancun CVB. Chapter 3: Isla Mujeres: 89, Cancun CVB. 90, Bruce Herman/Mexico Tourism Board. 91, Chie Ushio. 92, rj lerich/Shutterstock. 102, Eddy Galeotti / Shutterstock. 116, Chris Cheadle / age fotostock. Chapter 4: The Riviera Maya: 119, Stuart Pearce / age fotostock. 120 (left), Bruce Herman/Mexico Tourism Board. 120 (right), Philip Coblentz/Brand X Pictures. 122, Markus Sevcik/Shutterstock. 128, amResorts. 138, Rosewood Hotels & Resorts. 142-43, Ken Welsh / age fotostock. 152, Corbis. 159, SEUX Paule / age fotostock. 161, Doug Plummer/age fotostock. 162, Jose Enrique Molino/age fotostock. 163 (left), Ales Liska/Shutterstock. 163 (right), Stefano Paterna/age fotostock. 164 (top), Ken Welsh/age fotostock. 164 (bottom) Qing Ding/Shutterstock. 165, Philip Coblentz/Brand X Pictures. 171, Cancun CVB. 179, Matty Symons/Shutterstock. 187, Nataliya Hora/iStockphoto. 193, urosr/Shutterstock. 198, Almaplena Eco Resort & Beach Club. 202, Linda Vermeulen/ http://www.mermaidskissgallery.com. Chapter 5: Cozumel: 205, B&Y Photography Inc. / age fotostock. 206 (top), Bruce Herman/Mexico Tourism Board. 206 (bottom), George Kirkaldie/Flickr. 207, eschipul/Flickr. 208, cancuncd.com. 214, Ron Buskirk / age fotostock. 216, Mark Newman / age fotostock. 221, SuperStock/age fotostock. 226, Alvaro Leiva / age fotostock. 231, The Leading Hotels of the World. 235, SuperStock/age fotostock. 239, cancuncd.com. 240 (top left), tslane888/Flickr. 240 (bottom left), pato_garza/Flickr. 240 (top right), tslane888/Flickr. 240 (bottom right), Mike Bauer/Shutterstock. 242 (top), sethbienek/Flickr. 242 (bottom), tubuceo/Shutterstock. 243 (bottom), Julie de Leseleuc/iStockphoto. 244, Jerry McElroy/iStockphoto. Chapter 6: Yucatán and Campeche States: 247, SEUX Paule / age fotostock. 248, GUILLERMO ALDANA/Mexico Tourism Board. 250, JTB Photo Communications, Inc. / Alamy. 251 (top), gonzalovalenzuela/Flickr. 251 (bottom), Hippietrail/wikipedia.org. 252, redsquarephoto/Shutterstock. 262, MAISANT Ludovic / age fotostock. 273, Stuart Pearce / age fotostock. 277, Jose Peral / age fotostock. 282, Jo Ann Snover/iStockphoto. 285, Dmitry Rukhlenko/iStockphoto. 290, Stefano Paterna / age fotostock. 294, David Davis/Shutterstock. 295 (top), Corbis. 295 (bottom), Fedor Selivanov/Shutterstock. 296 (top), Bernard Gagnon/wikipedia.org. 296 (bottom), Richard Gillard/iStockphoto. 297 (top), Jos. A. Granados/Cancun CVB. 297 (top inset), Luis Casta.eda/age fotostock. 297 (bottom), Jo Ann Snover/iStockphoto. 298 (top), Sylvain Lapensée-Ricard/iStockphoto. 298 (bottom), Fcb981/wikipedia.org. 299 (top), Philip Baird/anthroarcheart.org. 299 (bottom), Mexico Tourism Board. 300, Jo Ann Snover/iStockphoto. 301 (top), Markus Sevcik/iStockphoto. 301 (bottom), Deanna Bean/iStockphoto. 307, Alex James Bramwell/Shutterstock. 318, Adalberto Ríos Szalay / age fotostock. 323, Strigl Egmont / age fotostock. 329, Targa / age fotostock. 334, Wojtek Buss / age fotostock. Back cover (from left to right): Zbiq/Shutterstock; cancuncd.com; The Leading Hotels of the World. Spine: Worachat Sodsri/Shutterstock.

About Our Writers: All photos are courtesy of the writers except for the following: Marlise Kast-Myers, courtesy of Benjamin Myers; Mark S. Lindsey, courtesy of Denise Lindsey.

NOTES

NOTES

ABOUT OUR WRITERS

As a freelance journalist and author, Marlise Kast-Myers has contributed to more than 50 publications, including *Forbes, Surfer, San Diego Magazine,* and the *New York Post.* Her passion for traveling has taken her to 80 countries and led her to establish short-term residency in Switzerland, the Dominican Republic, Spain, and Costa Rica. Following the release of her memoir, *Tabloid Prodigy,* Marlise co-authored Fodor's Guides to Mexico, San Diego, Panama, Puerto Rico, Vietnam, Los Cabos, and Peru. She served as a photojournalist for *Surf Guide to Costa Rica* and has written *Day & Overnight Hikes on California's Pacific Crest Trail.* Now based in San Diego, she is currently working on her next full-length manuscript. Marlise updated Cancún, Isla Mujeres, and Riviera Maya for this edition.

After years of traveling around the Caribbean and North America, Mark S. Lindsey and his wife, Denise, took the plunge and bought a home in Cozumel. He now splits his time between Mexico and Virginia, where he still practices architecture. A former open-wheel race car champion, he designs sportscar road courses and NASCAR racetrack facilities in the U.S. and Canada. While in Mexico, he stays busy scuba diving, kiteboarding, and spearfishing and is always on the hunt for the next great margarita and a hole in the wall with the best tacos. Mark updated Cozumel for this edition.

San José, Costa Rica–based freelance writer and pharmacist Jeffrey Van Fleet has spent the better part of the last two decades enjoying Latin America's rainy seasons and Wisconsin's winters. (Most people would try to do it the other way around.) He never passes up the chance to visit Mexico and, in particular, the less-explored paths of the Yucatán peninsula. Jeff is a regular contributor to Costa Rica's English-language newspaper, the *Tico Times,* and has covered Central America for United Airlines' inflight magazine *Hemispheres.* He has contributed to Fodor's guides to Mexico, Los Cabos & Baja, Costa Rica, Panama, Guatemala, Honduras, Peru, Chile, Argentina, and Central and South America. Jeff updated the Yucatán and Campeche States for this edition.